NCLEX-RN TEST PLAN STUDY GUIDE

NEXT GENERATION

2025-2026

✓ A Complete Review of the NCLEX
✓ Detailing All Content Categories and Structure of The Test Plan
✓ Success Strategies
✓ 10 Full Length Next Generation Exam Questions with Answers/Rationales
Cheat Sheets on:
  ✓ Normal Lab Values
  ✓ Fluid and Electrolyte Imbalances
  ✓ ABG Analysis
  ✓ EKG Interpretation
  ✓ Medication Classifications & Nursing Implications
  ✓ Common Disorders

A BLUEPRINT TO SUCCESS

GAYLE SMITH MEBANE, MSN Ed, RN

Published by: Rise2Write Publishing LLC
ISBN: 979-8-9928622-5-6
www.rise2write.com

Disclaimer
Medicine and nursing are continuously changing practices. The author and publisher have reviewed all information in this book with resources believed to be reliable and accurate and have made every effort to provide information that is up to date with best practices at the time of publication. Despite our best efforts we cannot disregard the possibility of human error and continual change in best practices, the author, publisher, and any other party involved in the production of this work cannot warrant that the information contained herein is complete or fully accurate. This book is intended for informational and educational purposes only. The content within is not a substitute for professional medical advice, diagnosis, or treatment. Readers are advised to consult a licensed healthcare provider or expert for specific concerns, questions, or medical conditions. The author, publisher, and all other parties involved in this work disclaim all responsibility from any errors contained with this work and from the results from the use of this information. The author and publisher disclaim any liability for any direct or indirect loss or damage arising from reliance upon the information contained herein. By reading this manuscript, the reader acknowledges and agrees to these terms and conditions.

NCLEX-RN®, NCLEX®NCLEX, are registered trademarks of the National Council of State Boards of Nursing, INC. and hold no affiliation or support of this product. The NCLEX Test Plan is protected by copyright and is the property of the National Council of State Boards of Nursing, Inc. All rights reserved.

DEDICATION

I am thankful and eternally grateful to my Lord and Savior Jesus for all that I am and could ever hope to be.

This book is dedicated to my family. My husband, Lawrence, my closest friend, a confidant, and a rock that I can count on through thick and thin. My son, Lymuel, whose positive attitude, loving spirit, and relentless faith keeps me encouraged. My granddaughter, Dejah, a trailblazer and change agent with a giving heart. My granddaughter, Gabrielle, who I am very proud of for challenging herself to reach higher goals and seeking new opportunities with confidence. My grandson, Ameer, who I am proud of for his excellent character and high achievements in academics and sports. Azariah, my youngest grand, who has a keen eye for details, who is a very smart and engaged learner. To my mother, Ruth, and father, Thomas, for the memories I have of you that will forever make my heart smile. To my siblings, Ehue, Bruce, Alan, Brenda, Tommy, Mark, and Deborah, for all your love and support that is a solid foundation that inspires us and keeps us grounded. Family, I love each of you dearly.

MODULE 4: PSYCHOSOCIAL INTEGRITY NURSING TASK --------------------169

MODULE 5: BASIC CARE AND COMFORT NURSING TASK--------------------223

MODULE 8: PHYSIOLOGICAL ADAPTATION

INTRODUCTION

Dear Nursing Students

Congratulations to all of you who have completed the nursing program and all the hard work you have done to reach this stage on your journey to become nurses. The momentum must continue as you prepare to take and pass the National Council Licensure Examination (NCLEX), the national examination for the licensing of nurses in the United States. The NCLEX is the standardized exam that nursing graduates like you must pass to become licensed as registered nurses in the U.S. and Canada. It's not just a test of knowledge, it's designed to assess your ability to apply clinical judgment and make safe, effective decisions in real-world nursing scenarios. The exam uses a format called Computerized Adaptive Testing (CAT), which adjusts the difficulty of questions based on your performance. It includes a mix of question types like multiple choice, "select all that apply," drag-and-drop, and case studies that reflect real patient care situations.

The NCLEX-RN Test Plan

The Test Plan for the NCLEX-RN was developed by the National Council of State Boards of Nursing, Inc. (NCSBN). The purpose of the Test Plan is to provide detailed information about the content areas tested in the NCLEX-RN Examination. NCSBN encourages candidates to review the NCLEX Test Plan before their exam appointment. The Test Plan is your official blueprint for what to expect on the examination. The content in the Test Plan is organized into four major **Client Needs** categories. Two of the four categories are divided into subcategories. The Client needs Categories was chosen by NCSBN because it provides a universal structure for defining nursing actions and competencies expected across all healthcare settings. This approach ensures that the exam evaluates not just what nurses know, but how they apply that knowledge. The Test Plan helps students (like you!) tailor your preparation efficiently by showing what to focus on. Candidates who take the exam are not just guessing what might appear on test day, the NCLEX-RN Test Plan is like the GPS for your NCLEX journey.

The NCLEX Test Plan Study Guide

This Test Plan Study Guide is systematically organized into Modules corresponding to the Nursing Tasks listed in the NCLEX Test Plan under the **Client Needs** categories. Each Module covers Nursing Tasks by describing in detail what the real-world actions and decisions entry-level nurses are expected to perform safely and effectively. These Nursing Task are your blueprint for what to expect on the NCLEX and essential competencies that entry-level nurses must know. The following table is a list of the client needs categories with the proportion of test items on the NCLEX-RN, followed by a description of Client Needs by category. The NCLEX-RN Test Plan Study Guide also provides a comprehensive overview of the NGN NCLEX-RN and full length NGN NCLEX style test with answers and rationales.

Client Needs Category	Subcategory	Distribution of Content	Percentage of Test Items
Safe and Effective Care Environment	Management of Care	Coordinating client care and interdisciplinary collaboration	17-23%
Safe and Effective Care Environment	Safety and Infection Control	Preventing harm and controlling infection	9-15%
Health Promotion and Maintenance		Promoting wellness and early detection	6-12%
Psychosocial Integrity		Providing emotional support and coping mechanisms	6-12%
Physiological Integrity	Basic Care and Comfort	Providing support with activities of daily living	6-12%
Physiological Integrity	Pharmacological and Parenteral Therapies	Administering medication and IV therapy	12-18%
Physiological Integrity	Reduction of Risk Potential	Minimizing complications	9-15%
Physiological Integrity	Physiological Adaptation	Managing chronic and acute health conditions	11-17%

Description Of Client Needs

The Client Needs categories are presented in the NCLEX-RN Test Plan, followed by a list of Task Statements. The Task Statements with each Client Needs category are also listed in this study guide to emphasize clinical judgment, nursing skills, communication, cultural competence, and teaching/learning principles. These are essential competencies that entry-level registered nurses must demonstrate to ensure safe and effective care.

Client Needs Categories as listed in the NCLEX-RN Test Plan

Management of Care
The Registered Nurse creates a safe and supportive environment for clients and healthcare personnel by actively promoting a culture of safety and implementing measures to prevent errors, reduce risks, and ensure optimal outcomes. This involves maintaining a clean and organized care setting, utilizing evidence-based practices, and fostering open communication channels among the healthcare team

Safety and Infection Control
Registered nurses (RNs) play an essential role in ensuring safety and infection control within healthcare settings. Their expertise and vigilance are pivotal in preventing the spread of infections and safeguarding both clients and healthcare personnel from environmental and health hazards.

Health Promotion and Maintenance
The Registered Nurses play a pivotal role in health promotion and maintenance, facilitating wellness across different stages of life. Their expertise serves as a cornerstone for patient education, preventive care, and the management of health risks, ensuring that individuals and communities achieve optimal health outcomes.

Psychosocial Integrity
This aspect of care requires Registered Nurses to look beyond the physical symptoms and address the broader emotional and psychological challenges

patients may face during their healthcare journey. Psychosocial integrity is integral to holistic nursing, ensuring that patients are treated not only as individuals with illnesses but as multidimensional beings with diverse needs.

Basic Care and Comfort

The Registered Nurse provides care aimed at improving a patient's overall condition, alleviating discomfort, and promoting healing. This aspect of nursing is particularly significant for individuals undergoing treatment, recovering from surgeries, or managing chronic illnesses.

Pharmacological & Parenteral Therapies

The Registered nurses (RNs) responsibilities in administering pharmacological and parenteral therapies are guided by clinical expertise, patient-centered care principles, and adherence to safety standards. Pharmacological and parenteral therapies involve the administration of medications to treat or prevent diseases. RNs have specific responsibilities to ensure the safe and effective use of these therapies in clinical practice.

Reduction of Risk Potential

The reduction of risk potential is a critical component of a Registered Nurse's role, focusing on identifying and mitigating factors that could compromise a patient's safety or recovery. This involves monitoring for signs of complications, ensuring proper usage of medical equipment, and adhering to infection control protocols. RNs are vigilant in assessing changes in a patient's condition, implementing preventative measures, and educating patients and their families about strategies to manage risks effectively.

Physiological Adaptation

Physiological adaptation refers to the ability of the body to adjust to internal or external stressors, such as illness, injury, or surgery. Registered Nurses role in this process is monitoring vital signs, administering treatments, and providing interventions that support the body's natural healing mechanisms. They assess and respond to changes in the patient's physiological status, advocate for timely medical interventions, and educate patients on strategies to enhance their recovery. Through a combination of clinical skills and compassionate care, RNs ensure that patients achieve optimal adaptation to their health challenges.

How To Use The NCLEX Test Plan Study Guide

1. Read the comprehensive overview of the Next Generation NCLEX-RN

2. Read all of the NCLEX Success Strategies.

3. To maximize your preparation, review each Module thoroughly while identifying your weaker areas. Begin by focusing your studying on these weaknesses to ensure a stronger understanding before revisiting more familiar content. This targeted approach will help build confidence and improve overall performance.

4. Review the Cheat Sheets on Normal Labs, Fluid and Electrolyte Imbalances, ABG analysis, EKG interpretation, Common Disorders, Medication Classifications and Nursing Implications.

5. Complete the NGN NCLEX questions with answers and rationale at the end of the book as an assessment. This will reinforce your review of the content and enhance your test taking skills.

Final Thoughts
The NCLEX is a challenging yet achievable milestone in your nursing journey. By following these strategies, staying disciplined, and maintaining confidence in your abilities, you can successfully pass the exam and step into your new career as a licensed nurse. Remember, preparation is key, and persistence pays off!

Anxiety
Anxiety is a common concern when preparing to take your unit exams, the HESI, and ultimately the NCLEX. A certain level of anxiety is normal because it enhances awareness and keeps us alert. Examine what works to manage your anxiety and maintain a level that keeps you aware. A long walk, some music you enjoy, a cup of chamomile tea, or physical exercise can help decrease anxiety. What works for one person doesn't always work for another, so make sure you find what works for you.

Attitude

Demonstrating a positive attitude is a major key in this process. Decisions determine our destiny. Hence, make the decision to face this challenge with the right attitude and expect to get back what you put in. The work is challenging, but the reward is worth it for you, your family, and those you serve as a member of this profession. You can and will meet this challenge successfully!

THE NEXT GENERATION NCLEX
A Comprehensive Overview

The Next Generation National Council Licensure Examination (NCLEX) represents a significant advancement in the way nursing proficiency is assessed, ensuring that candidates possess the critical thinking and clinical judgment required for today's complex healthcare environments. With its updated format and innovative assessment methods, the exam addresses the ever-evolving demands of patient care and safety.

What Is the NCLEX?
The NCLEX is a standardized exam designed to evaluate whether a candidate is ready to begin practicing as an entry-level nurse. Administered by the National Council of State Boards of Nursing (NCSBN), the exam is a vital step for licensure as a registered nurse (RN) or licensed practical/vocational nurse (LPN/VN) in the United States and Canada.

Shift to Next Generation NCLEX
In response to the rapidly changing healthcare landscape, the NCSBN introduced the Next Generation NCLEX (NGN) in 2023. This version builds upon the prior exam structure but includes enhanced features designed to better measure clinical judgment and decision-making skills. The goal is to ensure nurses are equipped to handle complex scenarios and provide safe and effective care.

Key Features of the Next Generation NCLEX
The NGN incorporates several innovative elements that distinguish it from the previous version:

1. Case-Based Approach
One of the hallmark features of the NGN is its focus on case-based questions. These questions present candidates with realistic patient scenarios, requiring them to analyze information, prioritize actions, and make appropriate decisions.

This format simulates actual clinical situations, offering a more practical assessment of a candidate's readiness.

2. Clinical Judgment Measurement Model

The NGN utilizes the NCSBN Clinical Judgment Measurement Model (NCJMM), which structures questions around six cognitive steps:

- Recognizing cues
- Analyzing cues
- Prioritizing hypotheses
- Generating solutions
- Taking Action
- Evaluating outcomes

This model ensures that candidates are tested on their ability to think critically and make sound judgments, particularly in high-stakes situations.

3. New Question Formats

The NGN introduces a variety of question formats to better evaluate a candidate's skills:

- Drop-down menus: Questions with multiple-choice answers presented in a drop-down format.
- Drag-and-drop: Tasks where candidates must organize or arrange items based on clinical priorities.
- Matrix grids: Questions where candidates select multiple answers across rows and columns.
- Extended multiple response: A broader range of answer options, allowing for multiple correct choices.
- Case Study (Electronic Health Record): Measures understanding of complex clinical scenarios.
- Bow-tie: Requires critical thinking and decision-making.

The NGN exam uses a polytomous scoring model, providing partial credit for questions with multiple inputs. This scoring method differs from the current NCLEX format, which awards either full credit or no credit.

- Zero/One Scoring: Earns a point for each correct answer and zero points for incorrect answers, which are added for a total score.
- Plus/Minus Scoring: Earns a point for a correct answer but loses a point for an incorrect answer.
- Rationale Scoring: Points are earned only when the selected response reflects a proper understanding of the question's rationale.

The NGN exam includes a minimum of 70 and a maximum of 135 questions. The exam uses Computerized Adaptive Testing (CAT) to adjust the difficulty level based on previous answers.

- The test continues until it is 95% confident in the pass or fail result, or until time runs out or the maximum number of questions is reached.
- Test takers have five hours to complete the exam.

Preparation Strategies for the NGN Exam
- Focus on understanding nursing concepts to think critically and make informed clinical decisions.
- Understand the material rather than memorizing facts.
- Start studying early and prioritize weak areas.
- Practice NCLEX-style questions daily.
- Review missed questions, focusing on the pathophysiology of diseases and the mechanisms of action of medications.

The Next Generation NCLEX exam, is designed to assess critical thinking skills in nursing graduates. It moves beyond rote memorization, focusing instead on how well you can apply nursing concepts to real-world patient scenarios.

Why the NGN Matters
The NGN addresses several critical needs in nursing education and practice:

- Improved readiness: By focusing on clinical judgment, the exam ensures nurses are better prepared to handle complex patient scenarios upon entering the workforce.
- Enhanced patient safety: Strong clinical judgment is directly tied to safer patient care, reducing the risk of errors and adverse events.
- Alignment with modern healthcare: The NGN reflects the realities of today's healthcare systems, which prioritize interdisciplinary teamwork and adaptive problem-solving.

How to Prepare for the NGN

Success on the NGN requires thorough preparation and familiarity with its unique format. Here are some strategies for candidates:

Understand the NCSBN Clinical Judgment Measurement Model (NCJMM)
The NCJMM is broadly defined as the process by which healthcare professionals gather and interpret patient data, weigh evidence, apply knowledge, and make decisions about patient care. It integrates critical thinking, problem-solving, and ethical reasoning to ensure the best outcomes for patients. A Clinical Judgment Measurement Model is designed to assess, analyze, and refine the ability of healthcare professionals to make sound judgments in complex and often high-pressure environments. Learning the six steps of the NCJMM is essential for mastering the NGN. Candidates should practice applying these steps to various clinical scenarios.

1. Recognizing Cues
The first step involves identifying relevant information from the clinical scenario. This could include patient symptoms, medical history, or laboratory results. Recognizing cues is critical in understanding the current situation and setting the stage for effective decision-making.

2. Analyzing Cues
Once cues have been identified, it is essential to analyze their meaning and significance. This step involves interpreting the data to determine what it reveals about the patient's condition, enabling candidates to prioritize and focus on the most critical aspects of care.

3. Prioritizing Hypotheses

In this step, candidates generate potential explanations or hypotheses for the patient's condition based on the analyzed cues. These hypotheses are then ranked or prioritized based on their likelihood and urgency, ensuring that the focus remains on the most probable and severe issues.

4. Generating Solutions

After prioritizing hypotheses, candidates develop a list of potential interventions or actions to address the patient's needs. This step requires critical thinking and creativity to ensure that the solutions are both effective and evidence based.

5. Taking Action

This step involves implementing the chosen interventions. It is the practical application of the generated solutions, requiring candidates to act decisively and efficiently while considering patient safety and ethical standards.

6. Evaluating Outcomes

The final step focuses on assessing the effectiveness of the interventions. Candidates must evaluate whether the actions taken have resolved the patient's issues or if further adjustments are needed, completing the clinical judgment cycle.

Practice Case-Based Questions

Engage with study materials and practice exams that include case-based questions. These resources help candidates build confidence in analyzing patient data and making decisions.

Familiarize Yourself with New Formats

Become comfortable with the NGN's innovative question types, such as matrix grids and drag-and-drop tasks. Many test prep platforms now offer simulations of these formats.

Focus on Critical Thinking

Since the NGN emphasizes clinical judgment, candidates should hone their critical thinking and problem-solving skills. This can be achieved through case studies, group discussions, and reflective exercises.

The Next Generation NCLEX represents a transformative step in assessing nursing competence, ensuring that candidates are equipped to meet the challenges of modern healthcare. Its focus on clinical judgment, realistic scenarios, and innovative formats makes it a robust and adaptive tool for evaluating the next generation of nurses. By embracing this evolution, nursing professionals and educators can contribute to a safer and more effective healthcare system.

NCLEX SUCCESS STRATEGIES

Develop a Study Plan

- Effective preparation begins with a structured study plan:
- Set realistic goals: Dedicate sufficient time daily or weekly for study, tailored to your schedule.
- Identify weak areas: Focus on topics where you feel less confident, such as pharmacology, pediatrics, or mental health nursing.
- Use a study calendar: Break your preparation into manageable chunks, assigning specific content areas to each week.

Practice with Questions Regularly

The key to mastering the NCLEX is consistent practice:

- Simulate the exam environment: Set aside time to complete full-length practice tests under timed conditions.
- Analyze your mistakes: Review incorrect answers to understand why you missed them and how to approach similar questions in the future.
- Emphasize priority-setting: Many NCLEX questions require you to identify the most critical nursing intervention.

Brush Up on Key Content Areas

- The NCLEX covers a wide range of nursing topics. Ensure you are well-versed in the following areas:
- Pharmacology: Memorize high-yield drug classes and their side effects.
- Safety and Infection Control: Understand protocols for protecting patients and healthcare workers.
- Health Promotion: Study developmental milestones, nutrition, and preventative care.
- Psychosocial Integrity: Review mental health conditions and therapeutic communication techniques.

Take Care of Yourself

- Your physical and mental well-being are critical to exam success:
- Get enough sleep: Aim for 7-8 hours of rest each night to maintain focus.
- Exercise and eat healthily: Physical activity and a balanced diet can boost concentration and energy levels.
- Manage stress: Practice mindfulness, meditation, or yoga to keep anxiety in check.

Master Test-Taking Strategies

- Effective test-taking techniques can give you an edge on exam day:
- Read questions carefully: Understand what is being asked before jumping to conclusions.
- Use the process of elimination: Narrow down answer choices to improve your odds of selecting the correct one.
- Stay calm under pressure: If a question is challenging, take a deep breath and focus on what you know.

Look out for Positive and Negative Event Questions

- A positive event question uses strategic words that ask you to select an option that is correct; for example, the question may read: "Which statement by a client indicates an understanding of the side effects of the prescribed medication?"
- A negative event question uses strategic words that ask you to select an option that is incorrect; for example, the question may read: "Which statement by a client indicates a need for further teaching about the side effects of the prescribed medication?"

Eliminating Comparable or Alike Options

- Look for options that are comparable or alike; these options will include a similar concept or nursing action.

- Comparable or alike options can often be eliminated as possible answers.

- The client needs to avoid taking any over-the-counter medications or other medications such as herbal preparations unless approved by the healthcare provider.
- The client needs to avoid consuming alcohol.
- Medications are never administered if the prescription is difficult to read, unclear, or identifies a medication dose that is not normal.

Questions that Require Prioritizing

Questions in the examination may require the skill of prioritizing nursing actions. Look for strategic words (e.g., first, highest priority, immediate, most important) in the question that indicate the need to prioritize and remember that when a question requires prioritization, all options may be correct.

Strategies Useful in Prioritizing Include
- The ABCs
- Maslow's Hierarchy of Needs theory
- The five steps of the nursing process
- Triage the level of care

Use the ABC strategy to prioritize the option to assess or treat the airway and breathing when treating patients in acute emergencies.
- Airway
- Breathing
- Circulation

Maslow's hierarchy of needs outlines five levels of human needs. Use this strategy to prioritize patient care. Identifying physiological needs and safety needs is crucial when determining the order of importance.

- Physiology: Need for food, shelter, water, sleep, oxygen, and sexual expression.
- Safety: Preventing harm, ensuring security and order, and maintaining physical safety.
- Love and Belonging: Giving and receiving affection and companionship, identification with a group, respect for others, self-esteem, and success in work.
- Self-Actualization: Fulfillment of potential.

Use The five steps of the nursing process as a strategy that serves as a framework for identifying initial nursing actions and interventions, thereby eliminating choices that do not prioritize patient care.

- Assessment
- Diagnosis
- Outcome/Planning
- Implementation
- Evaluation

Utilize Triage the level of care as a method to eliminate or narrow down the choices to the top two options. This strategy will help prioritize choices based on the needs of the patient, with the most critical needs first.

Red: Critical client. Stop and treat immediately.

Yellow: Could be seriously ill. Exercise caution in assessment. Treat within 30 to 60 minutes.

Green: Go ahead and move to the next client.

Black: Dead or dying.

MODULE 1

SAFE AND EFFECTIVE CARE ENVIRONMENT MANAGEMENT OF CARE NURSING TASK

Provide education to clients and staff about client rights and responsibilities

Educating clients and staff about rights and responsibilities is a critical step in creating a transparent and supportive environment. By respecting and upholding these principles, institutions can build trust and ensure the well-being and empowerment of their clients.

Client Rights

Clients have specific rights that must be respected and always upheld. These rights are fundamental to maintaining their dignity, autonomy, and well-being during their care or interaction with any institution. Key rights include:

- Right not to be subjected to unnecessary restraints: Clients have the right to be free from physical or psychological restraints that are not medically or legally justified.
- Right to habeas corpus: Clients may request a hearing at any time to seek release from a hospital or institution if they believe their confinement is unwarranted.
- Right to information about diagnosis, prognosis, and treatment: Clients are entitled to clear, thorough, and timely communication regarding their health status and the care being provided.
- Right to information on the charges of service: Transparency in billing and charges ensure clients understand the costs associated with their care.
- Right to communicate with people outside the hospital: Clients can maintain connections with others through writing, telephone calls, and personal visits.

- Right to keep clothing and personal effects: Clients have the right to retain their personal belongings unless specifically restricted for safety or medical reasons.
- Right to be employed: Employment rights remain intact unless legally restricted, allowing clients to work if they choose to do so.
- Right to religious freedom: Clients can practice their religion freely without interference, subject to safety and institutional considerations.
- Right to execute wills: Clients retain the legal capacity to draft, modify, or execute wills during their care.
- Right to retain licenses, privileges, or permits: Legal licenses, such as driver's or professional licenses, are not to be revoked unless mandated by law.

Client Responsibilities

While clients have rights, they also bear responsibilities to ensure a harmonious and efficient relationship with staff and the institution. These include:

- Honesty: Clients should provide accurate information about their medical history, symptoms, and other relevant details.
- Respect for staff and others: Clients are expected to treat staff, other clients, and visitors with kindness and respect.
- Adherence to policies: Clients must follow institutional policies, including safety and procedural guidelines.
- Participation in care: Clients should actively engage in their care process and make informed decisions about their treatment.
- Financial obligations: Clients are responsible for addressing any financial charges as agreed upon with the institution.

Educational Strategies

To ensure clients and staff understand these rights and responsibilities, the following educational methods can be implemented:

For Clients:
- Orientation sessions: Provide introductory sessions upon admission to explain rights and responsibilities.
- Accessible documentation: Distribute easy-to-read brochures or digital materials outlining key points.
- Workshops: Organize interactive workshops that allow clients to ask questions and discuss their rights and responsibilities.

For Staff:
- Training programs: Conduct regular training sessions to ensure staff are fully aware of client rights and how to support them.
- Role-playing exercises: Use role-playing scenarios to help staff practice handling sensitive situations involving client rights.
- Policy reviews: Encourage regular reviews of institutional policies to align with legal and ethical standards.

 Advocate for client rights and needs

Advocate for client rights and needs

Ensure the ethical treatment of individuals who receive medical or other professional health care services. Without exception, all persons in all settings are entitled to receive ethical treatment.
- Recognize the client's right to refuse treatment/procedures.
- Discuss treatment options/decisions with the client.
- Provide education to clients and staff about client rights and responsibilities.
- Evaluate client/staff understanding of client rights.

Patient Bill of Rights
- Right to accessible health care.
- Right to coordination and continuity of health care.
- Right to courteous and individualized health care.

- Right to information about the qualifications, names, and titles of personnel delivering care.
- Right to refuse observation by individuals not directly involved in care.
- Right to privacy and confidentiality.
- Right to informed consent.
- Right to treatment and to refuse treatment.
- Right to treatment in the least restrictive setting.
- Right not to be subjected to unnecessary restraints.
- Right to habeas corpus; may request a hearing at any time to be released from the hospital.
- Right to information about diagnosis, prognosis, and treatment.
- Right to information on the charges of service.
- Right to communicate with people outside the hospital through writing, telephone, and personal visits.
- Right to keep clothing and personal effects.
- Right to be employed.
- Right to religious freedom.
- Right to execute wills.
- Right to retain licenses, privileges, or permits established by the law, such as a driver's or professional license.

Collaborate with multi-disciplinary team member

Registered nurses collaborate with multi-disciplinary team members in several impactful ways to ensure high-quality patient care:

Participation in Interdisciplinary Team Conferences

Registered nurses actively participate in interdisciplinary team conferences, where professionals from diverse disciplines come together to discuss and resolve complex patient care challenges. These conferences allow nurses to advocate for clients, foster commitment to client care, and employ group skills such as negotiation, conflict resolution, and consensus-building.

Nurses utilize creative problem-solving and decision-making skills to achieve optimal patient outcomes.

Coordination and Communication

As primary clinical professionals with direct patient contact, registered nurses are central to the coordination between doctors, nurses, pharmacists, social workers, therapists, and other caregivers. This coordination ensures that all team members are effectively aligned in their efforts to provide comprehensive care.

Conflict Management

In situations where conflict arises among team members, clients, or families, nurses engage in managing and resolving disputes. They may employ assertive communication techniques and conflict resolution strategies. If necessary, nurses can seek guidance from organizational ethics committees to mediate unresolved conflicts.

Effective Communication

Daily communication among health care professionals is vital for the smooth operation of multi-disciplinary teams. Registered nurses support communication that is accurate, timely, and coherent to avoid disruptions and ensure clarity in patient care. They promote psychological safety in the workplace by mitigating issues related to power dynamics and fostering respectful interaction.

Manage conflict among clients and health care staff

Nurses employ several key strategies in managing conflicts among clients, health care staff and families:

Assertive Communication and Conflict Resolution

Nurses employ assertive communication techniques and conflict resolution strategies to address disputes effectively. This includes fostering respectful dialogue and negotiation among the parties involved. By addressing issues promptly and with clarity, they help de-escalate tensions and maintain a collaborative atmosphere.

Ethics Committees

When conflicts cannot be resolved through direct communication or team efforts, nurses can consult organizational ethics committees. These committees mediate unresolved issues by guiding discussions and facilitating fair solutions. While committees do not make clinical decisions, they play a crucial role as neutral mediators in complex disputes.

Promoting Psychological Safety

Nurses contribute to a healthy workplace environment by ensuring that communication is accurate, timely, and coherent. They address power dynamics and foster an environment of mutual respect. This psychological safety reduces incivility and fear within the team, which are often sources of conflict.

Through these methods, registered nurses ensure that conflicts are managed constructively, leading to better outcomes for both patients and the healthcare team.

Maintain client confidentiality and privacy

Nurses maintain client confidentiality and privacy by adhering to ethical principles, institutional policies, and legal standards such as the Health Insurance Portability and Accountability Act (HIPAA). They secure personal health information (PHI), which includes identifiable details about a client's health, treatment, and payments, ensuring it is used appropriately and accessible only to authorized individuals.

Nurses educate clients about their privacy rights and legal protections, while ensuring compliance with protocols to prevent unauthorized disclosure of confidential information. Violations of confidentiality can expose nurses to legal liability, emphasizing the importance of these practices. Clients also have the right to file complaints if their privacy rights are breached.

Confidentiality

Patients have a right to privacy in the health care system.

Nurses are bound to protect clients' confidentiality by ethical principles and standards, and by institutional and agency policies and procedures.

Disclosure of confidential information exposes the nurse to liability for invasion of the patient's privacy.

Health Insurance Portability and Accountability Act (HIPAA)

- The Health Insurance Portability and Accountability Act outlines how personal health information (PHI) can be used and how the client can access the information.
- PHI includes individually identifiable information that relates to the client's past, present, or future health, treatment, and payment for health care services.
- The act requires healthcare agencies to keep PHI private, provides information to the client about the legal responsibilities regarding privacy, and explains the client's rights concerning PHI.
- The client may file a complaint if the client believes that privacy rights have been violated.

Provide/Receive hand-off of care (report) on assigned clients

The hand-off of care, also known as a handover report, is a critical process in the healthcare system where patient information is transferred from one nurse or healthcare provider to another. It ensures continuity of care and enhances patient safety by providing an accurate and comprehensive summary of the patient's condition, treatment, and care needs.

Key Elements of a Hand-Off Report

To ensure an effective hand-off, the report should include the following essential elements:

- Patient's Identifying Information: Name, age, medical record number, and any other relevant demographics.

- Reason for Admission: A brief description of why the patient is receiving care, including diagnoses, and presenting symptoms.
- Summary of Current Condition: The patient's vital signs, physical assessment findings, and any recent changes in their condition.
- Ongoing Treatments and Interventions: Medications, therapies, and other care being provided, including the timing and effectiveness of these interventions.
- Pending Tests or Procedures: Any diagnostic tests, lab results, or treatments that are scheduled or awaiting completion.
- Special Considerations: Allergies, dietary restrictions, mobility limitations, or any other important patient-specific needs.
- Plan of Care: Short- and long-term goals, as well as any anticipated changes in treatment.

Strategies to Enhance Quality of Hand-of Report

- Be Structured: Use a standardized format such as SBAR (Situation, Background, Assessment, Recommendation) to organize the information clearly and concisely.
- Be Clear and Concise: Avoid unnecessary details while focusing on critical information that impacts patient care.
- Ensure Accuracy: Double-check the information to ensure it is up-to-date and accurate.
- Engage in Active Listening: When receiving a report, listen carefully, take notes, and ask questions if clarification is needed.
- Minimize Interruptions: Conduct the hand-off in an environment free from distractions to maintain focus and ensure all critical information is conveyed.

Benefits of an Effective Hand-Off

- Enhancing Patient Safety: Reducing the risk of errors and omissions in care delivery.
- Improving Continuity of Care: Ensuring that incoming nurses have the information they need to provide seamless and informed care.

- Building Trust Among Care Teams: Fostering collaboration and mutual understanding between outgoing and incoming staff.

Use approved terminology when documenting care

One of the nurses' essential duties is documenting patient care accurately and comprehensively. Utilizing approved terminology when documenting care is vital for maintaining clarity, ensuring consistency, and safeguarding patient records. This practice upholds professional standards and facilitates effective communication across interdisciplinary teams.

The Importance of Approved Terminology

Consistency Across Records
Using standardized language ensures that patient records are comprehensible to all who access them. Approved terminology eliminates ambiguity, enabling other healthcare providers to understand the patient's history, treatment plans, and progress without confusion.

Compliance with Legal and Ethical Standards
Approved terminology allows nurses to comply with legal and ethical guidelines in healthcare documentation. Records may be reviewed for audits, insurance claims, or in legal cases, making it critical that they are accurate, impartial, and professional.

Enhancing Patient Safety
Errors in documentation can lead to miscommunication, which in turn may jeopardize patient safety. Standardized terminology helps prevent misunderstandings and ensures that care instructions and observations are conveyed effectively.

Key Practices for Using Approved Terminology

<u>Understanding Standardized Terminology Systems</u>
Nurses often use standardized systems such as the International Classification for Nursing Practice (ICNP), the North American Nursing Diagnosis Association (NANDA), and the Systematized Nomenclature of Medicine (SNOMED). Familiarity with these systems allows nurses to align their documentation practices with global standards.

<u>Avoiding Abbreviations Unless Widely Accepted</u>
While abbreviations can save time, not all are universally understood. Nurses are encouraged to use abbreviations approved by their healthcare facility or by standard organizations such as the Joint Commission, avoiding unofficial or ambiguous shorthand.

<u>Accurately Describing Observations and Actions</u>
Approved terminology enables nurses to describe patient assessments, interventions, and outcomes accurately. For example, instead of using subjective phrases like "doing better," nurses might specify measurable details such as "temperature reduced to 37°C, respiratory rate normal at 16 breaths per minute."

<u>Using Electronic Health Records (EHR) Effectively</u>
Many healthcare facilities use EHR systems, which often incorporate approved terminology libraries. Nurses should leverage these resources to document care efficiently and accurately, ensuring adherence to institutional and regulatory standards.

Using approved terminology when documenting care is an integral part of nursing practice. It ensures clarity, professionalism, and accuracy while promoting patient safety and facilitating communication among healthcare providers. Although challenges such as time constraints and unfamiliarity with systems exist, strategies like training, guidelines, and leveraging technology can help overcome these obstacles. By mastering the use of standardized language, nurses uphold the integrity of healthcare documentation and contribute to the broader goal of delivering high-quality patient care.

Safely admit, transfer and/or discharge a client

Procedures for nurses to safely admit, transfer, and discharge clients require meticulous attention to detail, effective communication, and adherence to clinical protocols to guarantee patient safety and continuity of care.

Admission Procedures

The admission process involves welcoming a client into the healthcare facility, assessing their needs, and ensuring they are comfortably settled. The steps include:

Preparation
- Ensure the client's room is clean, well-prepared, and equipped with necessary medical supplies.
- Review the client's medical history, referral documents, and any pre-admission instructions.

Patient Orientation
- Greet the client warmly and introduce yourself as part of the healthcare team.
- Provide a tour of the facility and explain available services, emergency procedures, and visiting hours.

Documentation and Assessment
- Complete the admission forms, including personal and medical information.
- Perform a comprehensive nursing assessment, including vital signs, physical examination, and psychosocial evaluation.
- Document all findings in the patient's medical record.

Communication

- Inform the client about their care plan and address any questions or concerns.
- Collaborate with the multidisciplinary team to create a personalized care plan.

Transfer Procedures

Client transfers, whether within the same facility or to another institution, require careful planning and coordination to prevent disruptions in care. The steps include:

Assessment and Preparation

- Evaluate the client's medical condition to ensure they are stable for transfer.
- Prepare all necessary transfer documentation, such as a summary of care, medication list, and discharge instructions.

Communication

- Notify the receiving department or facility in advance, providing all relevant information about the client's condition.
- Ensure the client and their family are informed about the reason for the transfer and what to expect.

Safe Transport

- Arrange appropriate transportation, whether by wheelchair, stretcher, or ambulance, depending on the client's condition.
- Accompany the client if necessary, ensuring their comfort and safety throughout the journey.

Handoff

- Provide a detailed report to the receiving nurse or healthcare provider, ensuring continuity of care.
- Document the transfer in the client's medical record.

Discharge Procedures

The discharge process marks the transition of a client from the healthcare setting to their home or another facility. This step is critical in preventing readmissions and ensuring the client's well-being.

Assessment and Preparation
- Determine the client's readiness for discharge based on their medical and functional status.
- Prepare discharge instructions, including medication regimens, follow-up appointments, and home care recommendations.

Client Education
- Clearly explain discharge instructions to the client and their family, ensuring they understand their care plan.
- Provide written materials and contact information for questions or emergencies.

Coordination of Care
- Arrange for any needed home health services, equipment, or community resources.
- Communicate with the client's primary care provider to ensure a smooth transition.

Final Checks
- Verify that all belongings, documents, and medications are returned to the client.
- Document the discharge process in the client's medical record.

The admission, transfer, and discharge of clients are fundamental nursing responsibilities that demand precision, thoroughness, and compassion. By adhering to these standardized procedures, nurses ensure not only the safety and comfort of their clients but also the seamless delivery of care across all transitions.

👤 Prioritize the delivery of client care based on acuity

In the dynamic and high-pressure environment of healthcare, nurses are often tasked with the pivotal responsibility of prioritizing client care. This prioritization is not arbitrary but is anchored in the concept of acuity — the severity of a patient's condition. Acuity levels help nurses make informed decisions about who requires immediate attention, who can wait, and how to allocate limited resources efficiently. Below is an exploration of how nurses utilize acuity to guide care delivery, ensuring optimal outcomes for patients.

Understanding Acuity in Nursing

Acuity refers to the degree of severity of a patient's illness or injury and the corresponding need for medical attention and intervention. It is a critical metric used in healthcare settings to determine the level of care a patient requires. High-acuity patients often have life-threatening conditions that necessitate immediate and intensive care, while low-acuity patients may have routine or non-urgent needs.

Nurses assess acuity through a combination of clinical judgment, standardized tools, and institutional protocols. Factors such as vital signs, lab results, pain levels, and the patient's ability to perform daily activities can all contribute to an acuity score. This score serves as a guide, allowing nurses to rank patients based on their immediate needs.

Key Principles of Care Prioritization
The ABC Framework
One of the most well-known tools in nursing prioritization is the ABC framework. Airway, Breathing, and Circulation. This approach is rooted in the basic principles of life support and focuses on addressing the most critical physiological needs first:

- Airway: Ensuring the patient has a clear and unobstructed airway.

- Breathing: Evaluating and supporting adequate respiratory function.
- Circulation: Assessing and managing blood flow and perfusion.

Patients with compromised airways or respiratory difficulties automatically take precedence over those with less urgent needs. The ABC framework serves as a foundational guideline, particularly in emergency care settings.

Maslow's Hierarchy of Needs

Another critical framework nurses use is Maslow's hierarchy of needs. This model prioritizes care based on human needs, starting with physiological necessities such as breathing, hydration, and nutrition, followed by safety, psychological well-being, and self-actualization. For example, a patient experiencing severe dehydration will be prioritized over a patient seeking emotional support for anxiety, as the former addresses a basic physiological requirement.

Triage Protocols

Triage is an essential component in prioritizing care, especially in emergency departments and disaster situations. The process involves quickly categorizing patients based on the severity of their conditions. Many hospitals adopt color-coded triage systems:

- Red: Immediate care needed for life-threatening conditions.
- Yellow: Urgent care for conditions that are serious but not immediately life-threatening.
- Green: Non-urgent care for minor injuries or illnesses.
- Black: Expectant care for patients with little to no chance of survival.

Triage ensures that patients with the highest acuity are attended to first, thereby optimizing resource utilization and outcomes.

Steps in Acuity-Based Prioritization

Initial Assessment

The first step in prioritization is conducting a comprehensive initial assessment. Nurses use a combination of observation, patient interviews, and diagnostic tools to determine the acuity level. For example, a patient presenting severe chest pain and shortness of breath would be flagged as high acuity due to the potential for a cardiac event.

Continuous Monitoring

Patient conditions can change rapidly, making continuous monitoring essential. Nurses must remain vigilant, reassessing acuity levels as new information becomes available. For instance, a patient initially admitted for a routine procedure may develop complications that elevate their acuity level, necessitating a shift in care priorities.

Collaboration

Effective prioritization often requires collaboration among healthcare team members. Nurses work closely with physicians, specialists, and other support staff to ensure that high-acuity patients receive timely interventions. Interdisciplinary communication is key to aligning priorities and delivering cohesive care.

Acuity-based prioritization is a cornerstone of nursing practice, enabling healthcare providers to deliver care efficiently and effectively. By leveraging tools such as the ABC framework, Maslow's hierarchy, and triage protocols, nurses can navigate the complexities of patient care with confidence. While challenges such as resource constraints and ethical dilemmas persist, advancements in technology and ongoing education provide valuable support. Ultimately, the ability to prioritize care based on acuity reflects a nurse's expertise, compassion, and dedication to improving patient outcomes.

Recognize and report ethical dilemmas

Nurses play a vital role in the healthcare system, not only as caregivers but also as advocates for patients' well-being and rights. Their professional responsibilities often place them at the intersection of complex situations that require ethical judgment. Recognizing and reporting ethical dilemmas is an integral part of their practice, ensuring that patient care aligns with moral, legal, and professional standards.

Understanding Ethical Dilemmas in Nursing

An ethical dilemma arises when a nurse faces two or more conflicting moral principles or situations where the right course of action is unclear. These dilemmas often involve issues related to patient autonomy, confidentiality, informed consent, resource allocation, and end-of-life care. For example, a nurse might struggle with whether to respect a patient's refusal of treatment or intervene to save their life, creating a tension between autonomy and beneficence.

Steps to Recognize Ethical Dilemmas

Identifying Ethical Principles

To recognize an ethical dilemma, nurses must have a solid foundation in the ethical principles that guide their profession. These include:

- Autonomy: Respecting the patient's right to make their own decisions.
- Beneficence: Acting in the best interest of the patient.
- Nonmaleficence: Avoiding harm to the patient.
- Justice: Ensuring fairness in care and resource allocation.

When these principles come into conflict, the situation may signal the presence of an ethical dilemma.

Observing Signs of Ethical Distress

Ethical dilemmas often manifest as feelings of discomfort, uncertainty, or moral distress. Nurses may notice these emotions when they are unable to reconcile their professional responsibilities with the situation at hand. For instance, a nurse might feel uneasy about withholding information from a patient as instructed by family members, knowing it conflicts with the principle of patient autonomy.

Reviewing Clinical and Contextual Factors

Nurses must evaluate the clinical and contextual factors surrounding the dilemma. This includes gathering all relevant information about the patient's condition, preferences, and cultural values, as well as understanding the policies, legal requirements, and institutional guidelines influencing the situation.

Consulting with Colleagues

Ethical dilemmas are rarely solved in isolation. Nurses should collaborate with colleagues, including physicians, social workers, and other healthcare professionals, to gain diverse perspectives on the situation. This team-based approach can help clarify whether the issue constitutes an ethical dilemma or a misunderstanding of clinical practices.

Approaches to Reporting Ethical Dilemmas

Once an ethical dilemma is identified, nurses must take steps to report it appropriately. This ensures accountability and facilitates resolution while maintaining the highest standards of patient care.

Documenting the Dilemma

Thorough documentation is the first step in reporting an ethical dilemma. Nurses should record the details of the situation, including:

- The nature of the ethical conflict.
- Actions taken and their outcomes.
- Discussions with patients, families, and colleagues.
- Relevant medical and legal information.

Accurate documentation provides a clear record for review and supports ethical decision-making.

Utilizing Ethical Frameworks

Nurses can use ethical frameworks to structure their reports. One commonly used model is the Four-Component Model, which examines:

- Moral sensitivity: Recognizing the ethical dimensions of the situation.
- Moral judgment: Deciding the most ethical course of action.
- Moral motivation: Prioritizing ethical values over self-interest.
- Moral character: Demonstrating perseverance and integrity in action.

Applying such frameworks ensures that the report is comprehensive and reflects ethical reasoning.

Escalating to Supervisors and Ethics Committees

If the dilemma cannot be resolved at the individual level, nurses should escalate the issue to their supervisors or institutional ethics committees. These bodies often have the expertise to mediate complex ethical conflicts and provide recommendations based on policy and ethics codes.

Adhering to Legal and Professional Guidelines

Reporting should align with legal and professional standards, such as those outlined by nursing boards and healthcare institutions. Nurses must ensure that their actions comply with confidentiality laws, informed consent requirements, and reporting protocols.

Recognizing and reporting ethical dilemmas is a critical aspect of nursing practice that safeguards patient rights and upholds professional integrity. By understanding ethical principles, observing signs of distress, consulting with colleagues, and following structured reporting protocols, nurses can navigate these challenges effectively. Institutions play a vital role in supporting nurses by fostering a culture of ethics, providing resources, and prioritizing education. Ultimately, the ability to address ethical dilemmas empowers nurses to deliver compassionate, equitable, and morally sound care.

Practice in a manner consistent with the nurses' code of ethics

The nurses' code of ethics serves as a fundamental framework guiding nursing professionals in delivering compassionate, safe, and ethical care. Adhering to this code requires a deep understanding of its principles and their consistent application throughout all aspects of nursing practice. Below are ways in which nurses align their practice with the ethics outlined in their professional code.

Respect for the Dignity and Rights of Patients

Nurses prioritize the inherent dignity and rights of every patient. This involves:

- Advocacy: Standing up for patients' rights, especially in situations where they are vulnerable or unable to express their needs.
- Confidentiality: Protecting patient information and maintaining strict privacy in accordance with legal and ethical standards.
- Cultural Competence: Delivering care that respects the diverse cultural, spiritual, and personal values of patients.

Commitment to Patient Care

Ethical nursing practice centers on unwavering commitment to patient well-being. Nurses embody this by:

- Providing Safe and Competent Care: Ensuring that all interventions are evidence-based and aligned with contemporary nursing standards.
- Prioritizing Needs: Placing patient needs above personal interests during care delivery.
- Empathy and Compassion: Approaching each patient with kindness, understanding, and sensitivity.

Collaboration and Professional Integrity

Nurses thrive in collaborative environments, striving for professional integrity in their interactions with colleagues, patients, and the broader healthcare system.

- Interprofessional Collaboration: Engaging with other healthcare professionals to ensure comprehensive and coordinated care.
- Honesty and Transparency: Communicating openly and truthfully in all professional matters, including managing errors and misunderstandings.
- Accountability: Taking responsibility for their actions and decisions while seeking continuous improvement and learning.

Ensuring Justice and Equity in Care

Nurses practice with a commitment to justice, ensuring equitable access to healthcare services and advocating for social change. Specific actions include:

- Addressing Disparities: Working to eliminate barriers to care, especially for marginalized or underserved populations.
- Allocating Resources Fairly: Making ethical decisions regarding the use and distribution of healthcare resources.

Lifelong Learning and Ethical Development

To maintain ethical excellence, nurses engage in continuous education and self-reflection. This involves:

- Staying Informed: Keeping up to date with advancements in healthcare, ethics, and policies.
- Reflective Practice: Regularly evaluating their own actions and decisions to identify areas for improvement.

Advocating for the Nursing Profession

Beyond patient care, nurses support the integrity and advancement of their profession by:

- Promoting Ethical Standards: Encouraging adherence to ethical practices among peers and new nurses.
- Participating in Policy Development: Contributing to policy-making processes that shape ethical healthcare practices.

Practicing in alignment with the nurses' code of ethics is a dynamic process that requires dedication, empathy, and a commitment to excellence. By upholding these principles, nurses not only enhance patient care but also contribute to a culture of trust, respect, and ethical integrity within the healthcare system.

Verify the client receives education and consents for care/procedures

The process of verifying that a client receives education and gives informed consent for care and procedures is a critical responsibility of nurses. It ensures ethical compliance, protects patient autonomy, and fosters a trusting relationship between healthcare providers and clients. This document outlines the standard practices and strategies nurses employ to verify client education and informed consent.

Client Education

Providing Comprehensive Information

Nurses play a central role in ensuring clients are fully educated about their medical conditions, care plans, and proposed procedures. This involves:

- Explaining the procedure or treatment in clear, non-technical language.
- Discussing the purpose, benefits, and risks associated with the procedure.
- Addressing potential alternatives and their implications.
- Offering visual aids, pamphlets, or videos for better understanding.

Assessing Understanding

To confirm that clients comprehend the information provided, nurses often:

- Ask clients to repeat the information in their own words (the "teach-back" method).

- Pose questions related to the procedure or care plan to gauge understanding.
- Observe non-verbal cues indicating confusion or hesitation.
- Encourage clients to ask questions and express concerns freely.

Cultural and Language Sensitivity

Nurses ensure that education is tailored to meet the cultural and linguistic needs of the client by:

- Using interpreters or translation services when language barriers exist.
- Respecting cultural practices and preferences related to healthcare.
- Adjusting communication styles to align with the client's comfort level.

Informed Consent

Definition and Importance

Informed consent is the process by which clients are made aware of and agree to care and procedures after understanding all relevant information. It is a legal and ethical safeguard that upholds the principles of autonomy and self-determination.

Steps in Verifying Informed Consent

Nurses perform several actions to ensure informed consent is properly obtained:

- Confirming that the client has received all necessary information regarding the care or procedure.
- Ensuring the client has had sufficient time to review the information and make a decision.
- Verifying that the client understands the information through methods such as teach-back or questioning.
- Documenting the client's consent accurately in their medical record.
- Ensuring the consent form is signed and witnessed, if required.

Special Considerations

Certain situations require additional measures to validate consent:

- Clients with diminished capacity: Nurses must ensure that guardians or legal representatives provide consent on behalf of clients unable to make decisions independently.
- Emergency situations: In cases where consent cannot be obtained due to urgency, nurses document the rationale for proceeding without formal consent.
- Children and adolescents: Parental or legal guardian consent is required, and nurses ensure both the child and guardian understand the procedure.

Ongoing Validation

Informed consent is not a one-time event. Nurses continuously ensure that clients remain informed throughout their care journey by:

- Providing updates if the care plan or procedure changes.
- Re-confirming consent for new or additional treatments.
- Addressing new concerns or questions raised by the client.

Documentation

Accurate and thorough documentation is essential in verifying client education and informed consent. Nurses ensure:

- Records reflect the information provided to the client.
- Notes indicate the client's level of understanding and any questions they asked.
- Consent forms are signed and stored appropriately.

By verifying the receipt of education and informed consent, nurses uphold ethical standards, protect patient rights, and foster better health outcomes. The process involves clear communication, ongoing assessment, and meticulous documentation, ensuring that clients are empowered to make informed decisions about their care.

Receive, verify, and implement health care provider orders

The process of receiving, verifying, and implementing health care provider orders is a critical responsibility in ensuring safe and effective patient care. Each step must be meticulously executed to prevent errors, uphold standards of care, and maintain patient safety.

Receiving Health Care Provider Orders

Health care providers, such as physicians, nurse practitioners, or physician assistants, issue orders to guide the treatment and care of patients. Orders may be written (in paper charts or electronic health records), verbal, or telephone orders.

To receive these orders effectively:
- Listen attentively or read the written order carefully to ensure comprehension.
- Confirm the patient's identity by using at least two unique identifiers, such as name and date of birth, to avoid errors.
- Check the clarity of the order; it should be specific, unambiguous, and complete. For instance, medication orders should include drug name, dosage, route, and frequency.
- Document the order accurately in the patient's medical record, including the date, time, and the name of the provider who gave the order.

Verifying Health Care Provider Orders

Verification is essential to ensure that the order aligns with the patient's condition and care plan. It is a safeguard against potentially harmful mistakes.

Steps to verify orders include:
- Cross-checking the order with the patient's medical history, allergy list, and current medications.
- Clarifying ambiguous or incomplete orders with the provider. Never assume; always confirm to resolve uncertainties.
- Assessing the appropriateness of the order for the patient's current condition, including checking for contraindications or potential interactions.
- Ensuring compliance with institutional policies, legal regulations, and professional standards.

In some cases, health care staff may utilize "readback" techniques for verbal or telephone orders. This involves repeating the order back to the provider to confirm its accuracy.

Implementing Health Care Provider Orders

Once verified, orders must be promptly and accurately implemented to deliver the intended care.

Key steps include:
- Preparing the necessary materials, medications, or equipment as per the order.
- Communicating with the patient about the planned procedures or medications, including their purpose and what to expect.
- Executing the order, whether it involves administering medication, conducting a procedure, or applying a treatment. Follow established protocols to ensure precision and safety.

- Monitoring the patient for expected outcomes and potential adverse effects, documenting observations as appropriate.
- Updating the health care team about the care provided and any relevant patient responses to maintain continuity.

Challenges may arise in this process, such as unclear orders, discrepancies in patient information, or resource constraints. Effective communication, critical thinking, and teamwork are essential to address these issues. In all cases, patient safety and quality of care should be the guiding priorities.

Receiving, verifying, and implementing health care provider orders are interconnected steps that form the backbone of patient care delivery. By adhering to systematic approaches, health care professionals can minimize errors, foster trust, and enhance health outcomes. This process underscores the collaborative nature of medical practice, where every action contributes to the well-being of the patient.

Utilize resources to promote quality client care

Nurses are stewards of healthcare excellence, their ability to utilize available resources effectively is crucial in promoting quality client care. Nurses leverage resources to enhance outcomes, maintain patient safety, and ensure comprehensive care delivery.

Understanding Quality Client Care

Quality client care refers to the delivery of healthcare services that are safe, effective, patient-centered, timely, efficient, and equitable. Nurses are integral to achieving these objectives, as they are often the first point of contact for patients. Their actions and decisions significantly influence patient experiences and outcomes.

Key Resources Nurses Utilize

Human Resources
One of the most valuable resources nurses rely on is their colleagues and interdisciplinary teams. Collaboration with physicians, therapists, social workers, and administrative staff ensures a holistic approach to patient care. Nurses often act as coordinators, ensuring that communication between team members is clear and that all aspects of a patient's needs are addressed.

Educational Resources
Nurses utilize educational tools and materials to keep themselves informed about the latest practices, procedures, and treatments. Continuing education programs, professional workshops, and access to medical journals help nurses stay updated and improve their skills.

Technological Resources
The integration of technology into healthcare has revolutionized nursing practices. Nurses use electronic health records (EHRs) to access patient histories, monitor vital signs, and document care plans. Telehealth platforms allow nurses to provide consultations and follow-up care remotely, extending their reach to underserved populations.

Pharmacological and Diagnostic Resources
Effective use of pharmacological resources ensures that patients receive the correct medications in the appropriate dosages. Nurses also rely on diagnostic tools, such as laboratory tests and imaging equipment, to assess patient conditions accurately and provide timely interventions.

Community Resources
Community-based resources, including support groups, home care services, and educational programs, are vital for promoting patient well-being outside clinical settings. Nurses often act as a bridge between patients and these resources, ensuring continuity of care.

Strategies for Resource Utilization

<u>Prioritization and Organization</u>
Nurses must prioritize tasks and organize resources efficiently to ensure that patients receive timely and appropriate care. This includes scheduling treatments, coordinating with other healthcare providers, and managing workloads to avoid burnout.

<u>Advocacy and Referral</u>
Nurses advocate for patients by identifying their needs and referring them to appropriate services. For instance, a nurse may refer a patient to a nutritionist for dietary concerns or to a social worker for assistance with housing.

<u>Patient Education</u>
Educating patients about their conditions, medications, and self-care practices empower them to take an active role in their health management. Nurses utilize pamphlets, videos, and one-on-one counseling to ensure that patients understand their care plans.

<u>Research and Evidence-Based Practice</u>
Nurses contribute to quality care by incorporating evidence-based practices into their routines. They rely on clinical guidelines, research studies, and best practices to make informed decisions that enhance patient outcomes.

<u>Resource Optimization</u>
Resource optimization involves making the most of available tools and supplies while minimizing waste. For example, nurses may develop strategies to conserve materials like gloves and syringes during shortages without compromising patient care.

Nurses are indispensable to the healthcare system, not only as caregivers but also as resource managers. Their ability to utilize human, technological, educational, and community resources effectively ensures that patients receive high-quality care. By embracing strategies like prioritization, advocacy, and evidence-based practice, nurses uphold the principles of safe, efficient, and patient-centered care. Despite challenges, their commitment to resource utilization continues to have a profound impact on healthcare delivery and patient well-being.

Recognize limitations of self and others and utilize resources

Nursing is an intricate profession that requires a balance of clinical expertise, emotional intelligence, and adaptability. Recognizing one's limitations, as well as those of colleagues, is a critical aspect of delivering safe, effective, and ethical care. Equally important is the ability to utilize available resources to address these limitations. Below, we explore strategies that nurses employ to achieve this.

Recognizing Personal Limitations

Self-Reflection and Assessment
Nurses often engage in self-reflection to identify areas where their knowledge, skills, or emotional resilience may be insufficient. This includes evaluating their familiarity with medical procedures, understanding of specific diseases, or ability to manage stress and fatigue. Journaling, peer feedback, and professional evaluations can help nurses gain a clear perspective of their strengths and areas for improvement.

Continuing Education and Training
The healthcare field is constantly evolving, and nurses must stay updated on the latest developments. Recognizing knowledge gaps may prompt enrollment in courses, certifications, or workshops to enhance their expertise. This proactive approach ensures that nurses are adequately prepared to tackle emerging challenges.

Seeking Support
Acknowledging limitations is not a sign of weakness but a mark of professionalism. Nurses often seek guidance from supervisors, physicians, or

more experienced colleagues when faced with uncertainties. Open communication fosters an environment of trust and safety, ensuring that patient care is not compromised.

Recognizing the Limitations of Others

Team Collaboration and Observation

Effective teamwork requires recognizing when colleagues may be struggling or when their expertise does not align with a particular task. By observing behaviors, listening to concerns, and maintaining open dialogues, nurses can identify when a team member needs assistance or additional resources.

Delegation and Role Assignment

In collaborative settings, nurses often delegate tasks based on the strengths and limitations of their peers. Understanding each team member's competencies ensures that responsibilities are assigned appropriately, optimizing patient outcomes.

Promoting Accountability

Recognizing limitations also involves fostering accountability within the team. Nurses encourage their colleagues to speak up about challenges they face and create an environment where asking for help is normalized and respected.

Utilizing Available Resources

Institutional Resources

Healthcare institutions provide a wealth of resources, including access to specialists, advanced medical equipment, and training programs. Nurses utilize these resources to bridge gaps in care and knowledge, ensuring comprehensive patient treatment.

Using Technology

Modern nursing practice is enriched by technological advancements such as electronic health records (EHRs), decision-support systems, and online medical databases. Nurses rely on these tools to enhance their clinical judgment and address limitations in information processing or recall.

Building Peer Networks

Developing strong relationships within the professional community allows nurses to share insights, seek advice, and tap into collective expertise. Peer networks often serve as valuable resources in solving complex problems or navigating novel situations.

Engaging Patients and Families

In many cases, patients and their families possess unique insights into their conditions and preferences. Nurses recognize this and actively involve them in decision-making processes, utilizing their input as a vital resource for personalized care.

Recognizing limitations, whether personal or in others, is a fundamental aspect of nursing that underscores the commitment to compassionate and competent care. By utilizing resources effectively, nurses not only address these limitations but also strengthen the collaborative and adaptive nature of healthcare delivery. This dynamic approach ensures that patient safety and well-being remain central to nursing practice.

Report on client conditions as required by law

Nurses play an essential role in safeguarding public health and ensuring the well-being of their clients. As part of their professional responsibilities, nurses are required by law to report specific client conditions to relevant authorities. These legal mandates are designed to ensure prompt intervention, protect vulnerable populations, and prevent the spread of communicable diseases. This document explores how nurses fulfill these obligations, the conditions they report, and the procedures involved.

Legal Foundations for Reporting

The obligation for nurses to report client conditions stems from multiple legal sources, including federal, state, and local regulations. These laws are typically guided by public health frameworks and aim to strike a balance between individual privacy and societal well-being. Two common areas of legal reporting include the following:

- Communicable Diseases: Nurses must report cases of specific infectious conditions, such as tuberculosis, HIV/AIDS, or COVID-19, to public health authorities.
- Abuse and Neglect: Nurses are mandated to report suspected cases of child abuse, elder abuse, or domestic violence to child protective services or other designated agencies.

Conditions That Require Reporting

The conditions that nurses must report vary based on jurisdiction but typically include:

- Notifiable Diseases: A list of diseases designated by public health agencies that require immediate reporting, such as measles, hepatitis, and certain sexually transmitted infections.
- Injuries Related to Criminal Activity: Cases such as gunshot wounds or stab wounds are usually subject to mandatory reporting.
- Substance Abuse During Pregnancy: In some areas, nurses must report substance use that may harm the fetus.
- Mental Health Threats: Situations where a client poses an imminent risk to themselves or others may require reporting under mental health laws.

Reporting Process

The process of reporting client conditions involves several key steps:

1. Recognizing the Condition

Nurses must be vigilant in assessing client symptoms and behaviors to determine if they fall under mandatory reporting requirements. Training and professional guidelines often assist in this recognition.

2. Documenting Findings

Detailed and accurate documentation is crucial. Nurses need to record symptoms, observations, and any other relevant information that supports their decision to report.

3. Informing Supervisors

In many cases, nurses must first inform their supervisors or facility management before proceeding with an official report.

4. Filing the Report

Reports are usually filed with designated authorities such as local health departments, social services, or law enforcement. The method of reporting—whether via phone, electronic submission, or official forms—depends on local regulations.

5. Ensuring Confidentiality

While reporting is mandatory, nurses must adhere to confidentiality laws such as HIPAA in the United States, ensuring that client information is disclosed only to authorized parties.

Legal Protections for Nurses

To encourage reporting, many jurisdictions provide legal protections for nurses who fulfill their mandatory reporting duties. These protections often include:

- Immunity: Nurses who report in good faith are typically protected from civil or criminal liability.

- Confidentiality: The identity of the reporting nurse is often kept confidential to protect them from retaliation.

Ethical Considerations

Reporting client conditions involves navigating ethical dilemmas, especially when client trust may be affected. Nurses must balance their duty to report with their commitment to provide compassionate care. Open communication with clients about legal requirements can help mitigate misunderstandings and foster trust.

The legal obligation for nurses to report client conditions is a vital component of public health and social welfare systems. By adhering to mandated reporting laws, nurses not only fulfill their professional duties but also contribute to broader societal goals of health, safety, and justice. Staying informed about reporting requirements in their jurisdiction and seeking ongoing education ensures that nurses can carry out these responsibilities effectively and ethically.

 Provide care within the legal scope of practice

Scope of practice

Scope of practice refers to the services a trained health professional is qualified to perform and allowed to undertake based on their professional nursing license. For nursing students and future nurses, it is essential to determine whether they can perform the requested task according to their legal scope of practice.

Why this is important
Patient health and safety may be compromised when health care professionals, such as registered nurses, licensed practical nurses, practitioners, or physician assistants, perform services that exceed their education and clinical training.

Nurses are required to comply with the regulations set by the Nurse Practice Act (NPA) in the state where they work. The NPA, enacted by the state's legislature, defines the scope of practice for nurses and establishes regulations for nursing practice.

If nurses do not adhere to the standards and scope of practice outlined by the NPA, the state Board of Nursing can revoke their nursing license.

Registered Nurses Legal Scope of Practice

Registered nurses (RNs) must operate strictly within the boundaries defined by their legal scope of practice to ensure patient safety and uphold professional standards. This scope is determined by the Nurse Practice Act (NPA) in the state where they are licensed, and includes duties such as patient assessments, developing care plans, administering medications, and educating patients on their health conditions. It is imperative for RNs to regularly familiarize themselves with any updates or changes to their NPA, as state laws and regulations may evolve over time.

Understanding and adhering to the scope of practice has far-reaching implications. It not only safeguards the nurse's license but also protects patients from potential harm caused by inadequately trained individuals performing advanced procedures. For example, while RNs may have the authority to administer certain medications, prescribing drugs or performing complex surgical interventions typically falls outside their scope and requires advanced certification or licensure. When nurses exceed their scope, they risk facing legal consequences, including license suspension or revocation, and jeopardize the trust placed in the nursing profession.

To mitigate risks, RNs should seek additional certifications or advanced training if they wish to expand their qualifications. Collaboration with colleagues and comprehensive communication ensures tasks are delegated appropriately, respecting the expertise each professional brings to the healthcare team. Ultimately, staying within the legal scope of practice not only strengthens the integrity of nursing but also enhances patient care outcomes.

Participate in performance improvement

Quality improvement (QI) in health care refers to systematic efforts to enhance the effectiveness, efficiency, and safety of care provided to patients. Rooted in evidence-based practices and collaborative efforts, QI seeks to identify areas for improvement by analyzing data, understanding gaps, and implementing solutions tailored to specific challenges. The goal is not only to meet established standards but to exceed them, ensuring that every aspect of patient care, whether clinical procedures or administrative processes, contributes to better outcomes and overall client satisfaction. QI activities focus on reducing errors, optimizing resources, and fostering a culture of continuous learning and adaptation within health care settings.

How Nurses Can Participate in Quality Improvement

Nurses play a crucial role in quality improvement (QI) in healthcare by actively engaging in systematic efforts to enhance care outcomes and ensure patient safety. Their participation in QI activities includes the following steps:

Steps for Participation in Quality Improvement

- Identifying Opportunities: Nurses should identify areas where care quality or patient safety can be improved, focusing on recurring issues or trends.
- Team Collaboration: Collaborate with multidisciplinary teams to develop and execute QI initiatives.
- Data Collection and Analysis: Gather and analyze data on care processes, outcomes, and existing gaps using evidence-based practices, healthcare standards, and research studies.
- Process Review: Conduct thorough and collaborative reviews of the processes under examination to pinpoint inefficiencies or barriers to quality care.
- Addressing Gaps: Develop and implement solutions to address gaps in care that affect patient outcomes and satisfaction.
-

Focus Areas

The most effective QI activities prioritize:

- High-risk areas.
- Costly areas (human or monetary).
- High-volume processes.
- Problem-prone processes.

By adhering to these steps and applying evidence-based practices, nurses contribute to fostering a culture of continuous improvement, ensuring that healthcare systems not only meet but exceed established standards for patient care.

Assess the need for referrals and obtain necessary orders

Nurses play a pivotal role in ensuring that patients receive comprehensive and coordinated care. Assessing the need for referrals and obtaining necessary orders are critical components of this process, requiring clinical judgment, communication skills, and a thorough understanding of healthcare protocols. Below is a detailed exploration of how nurses accomplish these tasks effectively.

Assessing the Need for Referrals

<u>Understanding the Patient's Condition</u>
The first step in assessing the need for referrals is to conduct a thorough evaluation of the patient's health status. This includes:

- Reviewing the patient's medical history and current symptoms.
- Identifying abnormalities or conditions requiring specialized care.
- Utilizing diagnostic tools such as physical exams, lab tests, and imaging reports.

Recognizing Specialized Care Requirements

Nurses must be vigilant in recognizing when patient needs go beyond the scope of general care. Typical scenarios for referrals include:

- Chronic illnesses requiring specialist management, such as cardiology or endocrinology.
- Acute conditions needing emergency or surgical intervention.
- Mental health concerns necessitating psychiatric or psychological support.
- Social determinants of health requiring assistance from social services or community programs.

Effective Communication with Patients

Engaging patients is essential to understanding their needs and preferences. Nurses should:

- Discuss the potential benefits and necessity of a referral.
- Answer any questions to ensure the patient is informed and comfortable with the decision.

Collaborating with the Healthcare Team

Consulting Physicians and Specialists

After identifying the need for a referral, the nurse communicates with the patient's primary care provider or relevant specialists. This involves:

- Presenting findings and concerns to justify the referral.
- Discussing possible options for specialized care.

Advocating for the Patient

Nurses often act as advocates to ensure timely and appropriate referrals. They may need to:

- Highlight the urgency of the patient's condition.

- Clarify doubts or provide additional information to the provider.

Obtaining Necessary Orders

Formalizing the Referral Process

Once the decision to refer is made, nurses assist in obtaining the necessary orders. This typically includes:

- Requesting written or electronic orders from the physician for the referral.
- Ensuring that the orders align with the patient's medical needs and insurance requirements.

Documentation and Record Keeping

Accurate documentation is critical for continuity of care. Nurses ensure:

- All referral-related orders are correctly recorded in the patient's medical chart.
- Referral notes include details about the reason, type of specialist, and expected outcomes.

Coordinating Next Steps

Nurses may also facilitate the referral process by:

- Booking appointments with the specialist or service.
- Providing patients with instructions for the upcoming referral visit.
- Ensuring the referring provider has all necessary patient information to deliver care effectively.

Following Up on Referrals

Monitoring Patient Progress

At post-referral, nurses continue to play a role by:

- Following up with patients to check their progress and satisfaction with the referred care.

- Communicating with the specialist to obtain updates and recommendations.

Closing the Loop

To maintain seamless care coordination, nurses integrate feedback from the referral into the patient's overall treatment plan, ensuring all healthcare providers involved are informed.

Assessing the need for referrals and obtaining necessary orders are fundamental nursing responsibilities that ensure patients receive the right care at the right time. Through careful evaluation, effective communication, collaboration with healthcare teams, and diligent follow-up, nurses optimize outcomes and enhance patient satisfaction. This process reflects their indispensable role in healthcare systems worldwide.

MODULE 2

SAFE AND EFFECTIVE CARE ENVIRONMEN
SAFETY AND INFECTION CONTROL
NURSING TASK

 Assess client for allergies and intervene as needed

Allergy assessment and intervention are crucial aspects of nursing care to ensure patient safety and well-being. Allergies can range from mild irritations to severe anaphylactic reactions, and nurses play a vital role in identifying, managing, and preventing complications. This document outlines the methods nurses use to assess clients for allergies and the interventions they employ as needed.

What Are Allergies?

An allergy is an immune system response to a substance (allergen) that is typically harmless to most people. Common allergens include:

- Food (e.g., peanuts, shellfish, or dairy)
- Medications (e.g., antibiotics like penicillin)
- Environmental factors (e.g., pollen, dust mites, or animal dander)
- Insect stings
- Latex

Allergic reactions can manifest skin irritations, respiratory issues, gastrointestinal disturbances, or anaphylaxis, a life-threatening condition requiring immediate medical care.

Assessing Clients for Allergies

Initial Assessment
Nurses begin by gathering detailed information during the client's admission or initial interaction. This includes:

- Medical history: Asking about known allergies, previous allergic reactions, and family history of allergies.
- Current symptoms: Identifying any signs of allergic reactions such as rash, swelling, itching, shortness of breath, or gastrointestinal upset.
- Medication history: Reviewing prescribed and over-the-counter medications to identify potential allergens.

Clinical Observation
Nurses should remain vigilant for symptoms that may indicate an allergic reaction. These include:

- Skin changes like hives or redness
- Respiratory difficulties such as wheezing or nasal congestion
- Swelling of the face, lips, tongue, or throat
- Gastrointestinal issues like vomiting or diarrhea

Diagnostic Tests
If allergies are suspected but not confirmed, nurses may coordinate diagnostic tests such as:

- Skin prick tests: Introducing small amounts of allergens into the skin to observe reactions.
- Blood tests: Measuring levels of immunoglobulin E (IgE) antibodies specific to allergens.
- Elimination diets: Identifying food allergies by removing suspected allergens from the diet.

While nurses may not perform these tests directly, they support their execution by preparing clients and monitoring post-test responses.

Intervening as Needed

Preventive Measures

Once allergies are identified, nurses can implement strategies to reduce exposure to allergens:

- Documenting allergies prominently in medical records.
- Communicating known allergies to all members of the healthcare team.
- Educating clients and caregivers on avoiding allergens in daily life.
- Ensuring that hospital environments are free from allergens such as latex.

Managing Mild to Moderate Reactions

For mild allergic reactions, nurses may provide:

Antihistamines: Medications like diphenhydramine (Benadryl) to reduce symptoms such as itching or swelling.

- Topical treatments: Creams or ointments to soothe skin irritations.
- Monitoring: Observing symptoms to ensure they do not progress to severe reactions.

Addressing Severe Reactions: Anaphylaxis

Anaphylaxis requires immediate intervention. Nurses should:

- Administer epinephrine: The first-line treatment delivered via an auto-injector (EpiPen).
- Position the client: Laying them flat with their legs elevated to improve blood flow.
- Provide oxygen: Using a mask or nasal cannula to support breathing.
- Call for emergency assistance: Activating the emergency response system to ensure rapid transport and advanced care.

Continuous monitoring of vital signs is essential during and after anaphylaxis management.

Education and Advocacy

Nurses also play an important role in empowering clients to manage their allergies effectively. This includes:

- Teaching clients how to use epinephrine auto-injectors.
- Providing guidance on reading food and medication labels.
- Encouraging clients to wear medical alert bracelets.
- Advocating for allergy-safe policies in schools, workplaces, and public settings.

Allergy assessment and intervention are integral components of nursing care. By identifying allergens, preventing exposure, and managing reactions promptly, nurses safeguard their clients' health and enhance their quality of life. Through vigilance, education, and advocacy, nurses ensure that clients with allergies receive the comprehensive care they need.

Assess client care environment

Assessing the client care environment involves identifying potential hazards that could compromise safety or well-being. This includes ensuring cleanliness, monitoring temperature and ventilation, and removing any allergens or irritants that could trigger reactions. Evaluate the availability and functionality of medical equipment, and confirm that emergency supplies, such as epinephrine and other allergy treatments, are accessible. Regularly review and reinforce protocols for infection prevention and ensure that staff are trained to maintain a safe and supportive environment for clients.

The patient care environment plays a critical role in ensuring safety, preventing complications, and fostering recovery. Whether in a hospital or at home, assessing and maintaining an environment that supports a patient's health requires a comprehensive approach. This document outlines key considerations for evaluating patient care environments in both hospitals and homes, focusing on safety, functionality, and comfort.

Assessing the Patient Care Environment in Hospitals

Identifying Potential Hazards

In hospitals, priority must be given to identifying hazards that could compromise patient safety. This includes:

- Ensuring cleanliness to prevent infections
- Monitoring temperature, lighting, and ventilation to maintain comfort
- Removing potential allergens or irritants, such as dust, strong odors, or certain cleaning products

Availability and Functionality of Equipment

A comprehensive assessment requires evaluating the availability and proper functioning of medical equipment. Key actions include:

- Confirming that essential devices, such as monitors, oxygen tanks, and infusion pumps, are operational
- Checking the stock of emergency supplies, including epinephrine, antihistamines, and other medications for allergic reactions
- Ensuring that infection prevention supplies, such as gloves, masks, and hand sanitizers, are readily accessible

Protocols and Staff Training

Staff must be prepared to handle medical and environmental emergencies. Ensure:

- Regular review of infection prevention protocols
- Training staff to recognize allergic reactions and administer emergency treatments, such as epinephrine
- Routine drills to reinforce responses to life-threatening situations

Assessing the Patient Care Environment at Home

Minimizing Environmental Risks

In home settings, the focus shifts to creating a safe and comfortable living environment by:

- Eliminating potential allergens, such as pet dander, mold, and dust
- Using air purifiers to improve ventilation and air quality
- Ensuring proper storage of medications, with easy access to emergency treatments

Adapting Space for Patient Needs

Homes may require modifications to accommodate a patient's specific needs. Consider:

- Installing grab bars and ramps for mobility support
- Organizing the living space to reduce fall risks, such as loose rugs or clutter
- Maintaining a calm and quiet atmosphere to reduce stress

Educating Caregivers

Family members or other caregivers at home should be empowered with knowledge and skills to ensure patient safety:

- Providing training on recognizing and managing allergic reactions
- Teaching how to use medical equipment correctly
- Establishing clear protocols for emergencies, including when to call for professional medical help

Whether in a hospital or at home, a well-assessed and maintained patient care environment is fundamental to promoting health and safety. By identifying hazards, ensuring the availability of necessary tools, and educating caregivers or staff, healthcare providers can create a supportive space that addresses the unique needs of each patient. Regular evaluations and updates to care environments will help uphold the highest standards of patient well-being.

Promote staff safety

Registered nurses play a significant role in promoting staff safety within healthcare settings. Their expertise enables them to act as advocates for best practices while fostering a culture of vigilance. By observing workplace conditions, nurses can identify potential hazards and suggest improvements to enhance safety protocols. They also serve as mentors, guiding junior staff through safe handling techniques for patients and equipment. In addition, their involvement in training sessions on infection control and emergency preparedness further solidifies a secure working environment. Through collaboration, education, and active participation in safety initiatives, registered nurses ensure both their colleagues and patients benefit from a protected and harmonious healthcare space.

A robust approach to staff safety enhances the overall healthcare environment and boosts morale, productivity, and quality of service. Key measures include:

Comprehensive Training
Equip healthcare staff with regular training on workplace safety, infection control, and handling hazardous materials. Training sessions should address ergonomic practices to prevent injuries from lifting or repetitive motions.

Ensuring Proper Equipment and Infrastructure
Supply staff with personal protective equipment (PPE) that meets high standards and ensures its accessibility. Maintain medical machinery and tools to reduce risks of malfunction or accidents. Additionally, establish designated areas for rest and recuperation to support mental health.

Promoting Mental Health and Well-being

Implement programs focusing on stress management, counseling services, and work-life balance initiatives. Encourage open communication to prevent burnout and provide avenues for staff to report safety concerns without fear of reprisal.

Establishing a Culture of Safety

Foster a workplace culture that prioritizes safety through clear policies and protocols. Regularly evaluate staff feedback to identify vulnerabilities and continuously improve practices. Conduct drills for emergencies to always ensure preparedness.

 Protect client from injury

Nurses safeguard clients from potential injuries by implementing rigorous safety protocols, providing vigilant care, and fostering an environment that prioritizes patient well-being. Their responsibilities are multidimensional, encompassing both proactive and reactive measures to minimize risks in healthcare settings.

Identifying Risk Factors

Nurses begin the process of injury prevention by assessing individual client needs. This involves:

- Conducting thorough risk assessments upon client admission to identify vulnerabilities such as fall risks, allergies, or medication interactions.
- Monitoring clients for changes in their condition, which could increase their susceptibility to injury.
- Reviewing medical histories to detect patterns or conditions that require specific precautions.

Implementing Safety Measures

Nurses employ a variety of strategies to protect clients from harm:

- Fall Prevention: Ensuring that clients have easy access to call buttons, installing bed rails when appropriate, and providing non-slip socks or footwear.
- Medication Safety: Double-checking prescriptions, administering medications accurately, and educating clients about their correct usage.
- Infection Control: Observing strict hygiene protocols, including handwashing, sterilizing equipment, and isolating patients with contagious conditions.
- Safe Mobility Assistance: Helping clients move safely using assistive devices, ensuring clear pathways, and offering guidance during transfers.

Promoting Client Education

Educating clients is an integral part of injury prevention. Nurses provide information tailored to individual needs, such as:

- Advising clients on lifestyle modifications to reduce risks, like dietary recommendations or exercise routines.
- Explaining the safe use of medical equipment or assistive devices.
- Teaching techniques for managing chronic conditions effectively, such as diabetes or hypertension.

Collaborating with a Multidisciplinary Team

Nurses work closely with other healthcare professionals to ensure a holistic approach to client safety. This collaboration includes:

- Sharing observations and concerns with doctors, therapists, or social workers.
- Participating in care plan meetings to discuss preventive strategies.
- Advocating for interventions or resources required to reduce injury risks.

Monitoring and Responding to Emergencies

Apart from preventive measures, nurses remain alert to address emergencies that might lead to injuries. They are trained to:

- Provide immediate care during accidents or adverse events.
- Recognize early signs of complications, such as strokes or cardiac issues, and act swiftly to mitigate harm.
- Document incidents accurately and participate in reviews to improve future safety protocols.

Utilizing Technology for Safety

Modern healthcare systems incorporate technology to assist in injury prevention. Nurses leverage tools such as:

- Electronic health records (EHRs) to track patient histories and flag potential hazards.
- Monitoring systems that alert staff to changes in vital signs or bed alarms.
- Training simulations to practice handling emergency situations effectively.

Creating a Supportive Environment

Nurses also focus on fostering a safe and welcoming atmosphere for clients, which reduces stress and prevents injuries. This includes:

- Ensuring that rooms are organized, clean, and free from hazards.
- Cultivating trust through clear communication and compassionate care.
- Encouraging clients to share concerns or fears about their safety.

The role of nurses in protecting clients from injury is both profound and dynamic. Their commitment to comprehensive care, coupled with their vigilance and expertise, ensures that clients remain safe and secure during their time in healthcare facilities. By continually evolving their practices to incorporate new knowledge and technologies, nurses uphold the highest standards of patient safety.

🧑‍⚕️ Properly identify client when providing care

Proper identification of clients is a critical component of nursing care to ensure safety, prevent errors, and establish trust. Accurate identification minimizes risks such as medication errors, incorrect treatments, and miscommunication between healthcare teams. It is a fundamental practice guided by ethical standards and regulatory requirements.

Steps for Proper Client Identification

Use of Two Identifiers

One of the most reliable practices is using at least two identifiers to confirm the client's identity. Common identifiers include:

- Full Name: The client's legal name as recorded in healthcare documents.
- Date of Birth: A unique and personal identifier typically used alongside the name.
- Medical Record Number: A hospital-specific identification number unique to each client.
- Government ID: If applicable, an official document such as a driver's license or health card.

Verification Process

The nurse should verify these identifiers directly with the client or their documentation:

- Ask the client to state their name and date of birth rather than confirming information provided by the nurse.
- Match this information against medical records, wristbands, or other identification tools.
- Ensure that the identifiers are consistently used across all forms of communication and documentation.

Utilizing Identification Tools

Hospitals and clinics often provide physical identification tools, such as:

- Wristbands: Wristbands containing the client's identifiers are typically used in inpatient settings.
- Bedside Charts: For clients in a healthcare facility, charts near their bed can help confirm identity.

Communication with the Client

Clear communication is vital to avoid confusion:

- Introduce yourself and explain the importance of verification to the client.
- Be respectful and sensitive, especially if the client feels anxious or uncomfortable.
- Ensure that language barriers are addressed, using interpreters where necessary.

Key Considerations

Special Circumstances

In some situations, identifying a client might require additional measures:

- Unconscious Clients: Use medical records, wristbands, or family members for confirmation.
- Children: Verify identity with their guardians or accompanying adults.
- Clients with Cognitive Impairments: Collaborate with caregivers or family members for accurate identification.

Privacy and Confidentiality

When verifying identity, nurses must ensure that client information remains confidential:

- Avoid discussing identifiers in public areas.
- Secure any documentation or tools used for verification.

Compliance with Protocols

Adhering to healthcare facility policies and legal regulations is essential:

- Follow organizational guidelines for identification practices.
- Ensure compliance with standards set by governing bodies, such as HIPAA in the United States.

Proper client identification is a cornerstone of safe and effective nursing care. Following standardized practices, using appropriate tools, and maintaining clear communication ensure a secure environment for clients. By prioritizing accuracy and upholding confidentiality, nurses can contribute significantly to the overall quality of healthcare services.

Verify appropriateness and accuracy of a treatment order

Nurses play a critical role in ensuring patient safety and effective care delivery. One of their key responsibilities involves verifying the appropriateness and accuracy of treatment orders. This process is vital to identifying potential errors, ensuring adherence to evidence-based practices, and ultimately safeguarding patients from harm. This document outlines the steps, techniques, and principles that nurses employ to verify treatment orders effectively.

Understanding Treatment Orders

Treatment orders are specific instructions provided by authorized healthcare providers, such as physicians or advanced practice nurses, regarding the medications, therapies, or interventions required for a patient's care. These orders can include prescription medications, diagnostic tests, therapeutic procedures, or dietary instructions. Nurses act as intermediaries, ensuring that these orders are accurate, appropriate for the patient, and implemented correctly.

Steps to Verify Appropriateness and Accuracy

<u>Thorough Review of the Order</u>

The first step in verifying a treatment order is comprehensively reviewing its details. This includes:

- Assessing the patient's name and identification to ensure the order corresponds to the correct individual.
- Examining the specifics of the order, such as the medication name, dose, route, frequency, and duration for medications, or the precise details of a procedure.
- Cross-checking the date and time of the order to confirm its timeliness and relevance to the patient's condition.

<u>Ensuring Legibility and Clarity</u>

Treatment orders must be clear and legible. Nurses verify:

- That the handwriting (if handwritten) or electronic format is easy to understand, leaving no room for ambiguity.
- That the order uses standard abbreviations and avoids potentially confusing terminology.
- Any unclear instructions are clarified directly with the issuing healthcare provider.

<u>Cross-Referencing Patient Information</u>

To ensure the treatment order aligns with the patient's medical history and current condition, nurses:

- Review the patient's medical record, including allergies, past reactions, and chronic conditions.
- Compare the treatment order against laboratory test results, diagnostic imaging, and ongoing treatments.

For example, if a medication order is issued, the nurse must confirm that the patient does not have an allergy to that medication, or a contraindication based on their health status.

Checking for Appropriateness

The appropriateness of a treatment order is determined by evaluating its alignment with:

- The patient's diagnosis or presenting condition.
- Current evidence-based guidelines and protocols.
- Standard practices within the healthcare facility.

If discrepancies are identified—such as an incorrect dosage or an order that contradicts established protocols—nurses must escalate the issue for further review.

Confirming Dosage and Calculations

For medication orders, verifying the accuracy of dosages is particularly critical. Nurses:

- Double-check calculations, especially for pediatric, elderly, or critically ill patients who may require weight-based dosages or special considerations.
- Use available resources, such as drug reference guides or institutional software, to confirm proper dosages.

Collaborative Confirmation

When necessary, nurses engage in collaborative discussions with the prescribing provider, pharmacists, or other members of the healthcare team to:

- Clarify ambiguities in order.
- Resolve potential conflicts or concerns regarding the appropriateness of the intervention.
- Gain additional insights or recommendations to ensure optimal patient care.

Utilizing Technology

Modern healthcare facilities leverage technology to enhance the verification process. Nurses often use:

Electronic Health Records (EHRs) with integrated decision-support tools that flag potential medication interactions or contraindications.

- Barcoding systems for medications, which allow nurses to scan and match the medication to the order and the patient's wristband, reducing errors significantly.

Common Challenges and Solutions

Ambiguous Orders

Challenge: Orders that lack clarity or specificity can lead to errors.

Solution: Nurses should never hesitate to contact the prescribing provider for clarification.

High Workload

Challenge: In busy clinical settings, verifying orders thoroughly may seem challenging.

Solution: Utilizing checklists, technology, and prioritization techniques can enhance efficiency without compromising safety.

Resistance to Questions

Challenge: Some providers may view questions about their orders as a challenge to their authority.

Solution: Nurses should frame their concerns collaboratively, emphasizing patient safety as the primary goal.

Verifying the appropriateness and accuracy of treatment orders is a cornerstone of nursing practice. By adhering to systematic processes, leveraging technology, and fostering collaborative communication, nurses ensure that their patients receive safe, effective, and individualized care. This diligent approach not only minimizes the risk of medical errors but also reinforces the integrity and trust that underpin the healthcare profession.

Participate in emergency planning and response

Registered nurses (RNs) participation spans from preparation to recovery, demonstrating their dedication to public health and their ability to operate effectively under pressure.

Emergency Preparedness and Planning

Registered nurses actively contribute to the development of emergency plans that address the potential health impacts of disasters. Their responsibilities include:

Hazard Identification and Risk Assessment
RNs collaborate with public health officials and emergency management teams to identify potential hazards, such as natural disasters, pandemics, or chemical spills. They assess the risks to vulnerable populations, such as children, older adults, and individuals with chronic illnesses, and recommend measures to mitigate these risks.

Development of Emergency Response Protocols
Nurses provide input on protocols that ensure efficient and effective responses to emergencies. These protocols may include triage procedures, evacuation plans, and the allocation of medical resources. Their clinical expertise is critical in designing systems that prioritize patient care during high-stress situations.

Community Education and Training
Registered nurses often lead community outreach programs aimed at educating the public about disaster preparedness. They conduct workshops and training sessions on topics such as first aid, infection control, and evacuation procedures.

By empowering individuals and families, RNs help build resilient communities capable of responding to emergencies effectively.

Drills and Simulations

Participating in emergency drills and simulations allows nurses to test and refine response plans. Their involvement ensures that plans are practical and that medical teams are prepared for real-world scenarios. Through these exercises, RNs gain valuable experience in coordinating with other emergency responders, such as paramedics, firefighters, and law enforcement.

Response During Emergencies

When disaster strikes, registered nurses are on the front lines, providing immediate care and ensuring the efficient functioning of medical systems. Their roles during emergency response include:

Rapid Triage and Patient Assessment

RNs are skilled in triage—a critical process that involves assessing the severity of patients' conditions and prioritizing care accordingly. Their ability to make quick, informed decisions helps allocate limited resources effectively and save lives.

Direct Patient Care

Nurses deliver essential medical care to individuals affected by emergencies, ranging from administering medications and dressing wounds to providing emotional support. Their compassionate approach helps stabilize patients both physically and emotionally during traumatic events.

Coordination and Communication

Registered nurses act as liaisons between medical teams, patients, and emergency responders. Their clear communication is vital in ensuring that everyone involved understands their roles and responsibilities. They also use their organizational skills to manage patient flow and resource distribution in chaotic environments.

Infection Control Measures

In situations such as pandemics or disease outbreaks, RNs implement infection control measures to prevent the spread of illness. They educate both patients and responders on hygiene practices and monitor for signs of infection among affected populations.

Psychosocial Support

Disasters can have profound psychological impacts on individuals and communities. Nurses provide counseling and support to help patients cope with fear, anxiety, and loss. Their empathetic care contributes to the overall recovery process.

Recovery and Aftermath

The role of registered nurses extends beyond the immediate response phase. In the aftermath of emergencies, they are involved in recovery efforts that aim to restore health services and promote long-term healing.

Post-Disaster Health Assessments

Nurses conduct health assessments to identify lingering effects of the disaster, such as injuries, infections, or mental health issues. They ensure that affected individuals receive the necessary follow-up care and support.

Rebuilding Medical Infrastructure

RNs assist in restoring healthcare facilities and services disrupted by emergencies. This may involve reorganizing clinics, restocking supplies, and training staff on updated protocols.

Community Support Programs

Registered nurses often participate in programs designed to help communities recover from disasters. They may organize health fairs, provide vaccinations, or facilitate support groups to address the emotional and physical needs of affected populations.

Evaluation and Improvement of Emergency Plans

After an emergency, nurses review the effectiveness of response plans and suggest improvements based on their experiences. This continual evaluation process ensures that future plans are more robust and better equipped to handle similar situations.

Registered nurses are integral to emergency planning and response, providing expertise, care, and leadership throughout all phases of disaster management. Their ability to adapt to rapidly changing circumstances and prioritize patient welfare ensures they remain a cornerstone of public health during crises. By addressing challenges and fostering collaboration, RNs continue to strengthen their role in safeguarding communities against emergencies.

Use ergonomic principles when providing care

To ensure optimal safety and efficiency, nurses should adopt ergonomic principles when providing patient care. This includes maintaining proper body mechanics, such as bending at the knees rather than the waist when lifting, keeping heavy loads close to the body, and avoiding repetitive strain movements. Using assistive devices like lift equipment or slide sheets can reduce physical stress and minimize the risk of injury. Adjustable workstations and adequate lighting further ensure a comfortable environment that promotes both nurse wellbeing and patient safety.'

Safe client handling techniques include
- Do not lift patients by yourself.
- Know that injuries aren't always from a single event.
- Body mechanics are not enough.
- Injuries are not "part of the job".
- Take time and space to do it right.
- Report injuries as soon as possible.
- Implement assistive devices in your facility.

Ergonomics

Ergonomics is also referred to as human factors or human factors engineering (HFE), involves the application of psychological and physiological principles to the design and engineering of products, processes, and systems. The primary objectives of human factors engineering are to minimize human error, enhance productivity and system efficiency, and improve safety, health, and comfort, with a particular emphasis on the interaction between humans and equipment.

Ergonomics Principles of Body Mechanics for Healthcare workers

- Keep the back, neck and pelvis, and feet aligned.
- Avoid twisting.
- Flex knees and keep feet wide apart.
- Position self-close to the client (or object being lifted).
- Use arms and legs (not back).
- Slide client toward yourself, using a pull sheet.
- When transferring a client onto a stretcher, a slide board is more appropriate.
- Set (tighten) abdominal and gluteal muscles in preparation for the move.
- Person with the heaviest load coordinates efforts of the team involved by counting to three.

Follow procedures for handling biohazardous and hazardous materials

Biohazardous and Hazardous Materials

Hazardous materials are defined as those things that are not biological but remain hazardous to human beings including patients and staff. Examples of hazardous materials are chemicals and radiation.

- The US Occupational Safety and Health Administration mandates that information about all hazardous materials is readily accessible to workers including those who work in the health care environment. Information about hazardous materials is found on Material Safety Data Sheets which are published and distributed to the users of their products to fulfill the mandates of OSHA and to protect workers.

- Material Safety Data Sheets (MSDS) include the name of the product, information about the product's risks, measures, such as washing the skin, which must be taken when a person has been exposed to some risk relating to the product and information about the procedures for using, handling, disposing of and storing the product.

- Biohazardous waste is defined as biological waste that can be hazardous to humans. Sharp items and bed linens that are contaminated with blood or other bodily fluids, such as feces, are considered biohazardous medical waste. It is essential that the nurse maintain standard precautions when collecting urine and stool specimens. These precautions include washing hands before and after collecting, wearing gloves during the procedure, and storing the specimen in a biohazardous material container or plastic bag during transport to the laboratory. The careful handling and disposal of all hazardous materials protects staff, clients, and visitors from harm.

Proper disposal methods must be strictly followed to ensure safety. Sharps, such as needles, should be placed immediately into puncture-proof sharps containers, while other hazardous waste must be segregated and labeled correctly for disposal. Nurses must also ensure that personal protective equipment (PPE) is always worn when handling such materials to prevent contamination or accidental exposure. Regular training and adherence to protocols are essential to maintain a safe environment for both healthcare workers and patients.

Educate client on safety issues

Ensuring patient safety is a fundamental aspect of healthcare, and nurses play a critical role in educating patients on various safety concerns. Effective education not only minimizes risks but also empowers patients to actively participate in their own care. Below are the keyways nurses educate patients on safety issues:

Understanding Patient Needs

Nurses begin by assessing the individual needs, circumstances, and educational levels of their patients. Tailoring information ensures that safety measures are comprehensible and practical for each patient. For example, a nurse may use simple language and visual aids for patients with limited health literacy.

Medication Safety

One common area of patient education is medication safety. Nurses guide patients on:

- Proper dosing schedules and methods (e.g., whether to take medication with food).
- Recognizing potential side effects and knowing when to report them.
- The importance of adhering to prescribed medications and avoiding self-medication.

By providing clear instructions, written guides, and demonstrating techniques (such as using injection devices), nurses reduce the risk of medication errors.

Fall Prevention

For patients at risk of falls, particularly the elderly or those recovering from surgery, nurses educate them on:

- Keeping their environment clutter-free and well-lit.
- Using assistive devices like walkers or canes appropriately.
- Wearing non-slip footwear and avoiding loose clothing.

Additionally, nurses may provide instructions on how to get up safely after a fall or when to seek immediate help.

Infection Control

Preventing infections is another crucial aspect of patient safety education. Nurses inform patients about:

- Proper hand hygiene techniques, such as washing hands for at least 20 seconds.
- Wound care procedures to prevent infections.
- Recognizing symptoms of infections like fever, swelling, or redness.

They may also educate patients about maintaining cleanliness at home and the importance of vaccinations.

Equipment and Device Safety

Patients who require medical devices—such as oxygen tanks or insulin pumps—receive education from nurses on proper usage, maintenance, and troubleshooting. Visual demonstrations and written instructions help patients feel confident in handling such equipment safely.

Emergency Preparedness

Nurses guide patients on how to respond in emergencies, such as allergic reactions, asthma attacks, or cardiac issues. They provide:

- Information on recognizing early warning signs.
- Steps to take before professional help arrives.
- Emergency contact numbers and instructions on using medical alert devices.

Health Lifestyle and Daily Safety Tips

Beyond clinical concerns, nurses offer advice on general health and safety, including:

- Maintaining a balanced diet to support recovery and overall health.
- Staying hydrated and avoiding unnecessary physical exertion.
- Practicing safe mobility techniques and ergonomic postures.

Interactive Education Techniques

Effective patient education often involves interactive strategies:

- Demonstrations: Nurses show patients how to perform daily tasks safely, such as dressing a wound or administering medication.
- Use of Visual Aids: Charts, videos, and pamphlets make complex information easier to understand.
- Teach-Back Method: Patients explain back what they've learned, ensuring comprehension.

Follow-Up and Reinforcement

Education is not a one-time event. Nurses regularly check in to reinforce safety measures, answer questions, and adapt instructions based on the patient's progress. These follow-ups ensure that patients continue practicing safe habits over time.

Collaborative Approach

Nurses often collaborate with families, caregivers, and other healthcare professionals to ensure safety education is holistic and consistent. Family members are encouraged to engage and assist patients in adhering to safety protocols.

Acknowledge and document practice errors and near misses

Nursing is a vital profession that operates at the forefront of patient care. However, due to the complexity and high stakes of healthcare environments, errors and near misses sometimes occur. Acknowledging and documenting these incidents transparently is essential for improving safety, learning from mistakes, and fostering a culture of accountability.

Acknowledging Practice Errors and Near Misses

<u>Recognizing the Importance of Honesty</u>

Acknowledging practice errors and near misses begins with a commitment to honesty and transparency. Nurses are often the first to detect such issues, and their willingness to report them serves as a cornerstone of patient safety initiatives.

<u>Creating a Non-Punitive Culture</u>

A key factor in encouraging nurses to acknowledge errors is fostering a non-punitive culture. Healthcare organizations must emphasize learning from mistakes rather than punishing individuals, ensuring that nurses feel safe to report incidents without fear of retribution.

<u>Collaboration and Communication</u>

When errors or near misses occur, nurses should immediately communicate with their team members, supervisors, or healthcare leaders. This ensures that corrective actions can be implemented promptly and effectively. Regular team debriefings and open channels of communication help identify underlying causes and prevent recurrence.

Documenting Practice Errors and Near Misses

<u>Incident Reporting Systems</u>

Most healthcare facilities use standardized incident reporting systems to document practice errors and near misses. These systems collect detailed information, including:

- Description of the error or near miss
- The date, time, and location of the event
- Details of those involved (while maintaining patient confidentiality)
- An analysis of contributing factors
- Actions taken to address the event

The goal of these reports is to identify trends and improve overall safety protocols.

Adhering to Documentation Guidelines

Correct documentation is critical for creating an accurate record of events. Nurses must ensure that reports are:

- Factual and objective, avoiding subjective language
- Completed promptly to ensure accuracy
- Compliant with legal and institutional policies

Documenting practice errors and near misses is not only an ethical obligation but also a legal requirement in many cases.

Utilizing Root Cause Analysis

In addition to incident reporting, root cause analysis (RCA) is a systematic approach used to investigate errors and near misses. Nurses often participate in RCA processes, helping to identify the underlying issues that contributed to the incident. This method ensures that solutions address systemic problems rather than isolated mistakes.

Learning and Improvement

Feedback Mechanisms

After documentation, providing feedback to nurses is essential for fostering growth. Constructive feedback helps professionals understand how to prevent similar incidents in the future.

Role of Continuing Education

Nurses are encouraged to participate in training sessions and workshops that focus on error prevention, communication strategies, and best practices. Many healthcare organizations incorporate lessons from documented errors into training programs, ensuring that the workforce remains vigilant and informed.

Report, intervene, and/or escalate unsafe practice of health care personnel

Nurses play a critical role in safeguarding the well-being of patients by identifying, addressing, and escalating unsafe practices in healthcare settings.

Their vigilance and proactive actions can prevent harm, promote professional accountability, and ensure compliance with ethical standards. Below is an exploration of how nurses report, intervene, and escalate unsafe practices in the healthcare environment.

Recognizing Unsafe Practices

The first step in addressing unsafe practices is recognizing them. Unsafe behaviors can range from improper hand hygiene and medication errors to neglect of patient care and breaches of protocol. Nurses are often the first to observe such practices due to their close interaction with patients and other healthcare personnel. Signs of unsafe practices may include:

- Failure to follow established protocols or guidelines.
- Lack of proper documentation or reporting.
- Unprofessional behavior, such as impaired judgment due to substance use.
- Use of outdated or incorrect techniques in patient care.
- Neglect or abuse of patients.

Reporting Unsafe Practices

Reporting unsafe practices is a crucial step in ensuring that these issues are addressed effectively. Nurses are guided by their professional code of ethics to report any behavior that jeopardizes patient safety. The process generally involves:

Internal Reporting
Nurses are encouraged to report incidents to their immediate supervisors or managers. Many healthcare institutions have established incident reporting systems, such as online platforms or written forms, which allow staff to document and submit details of unsafe practices.

Confidentiality and Anonymity
In many cases, reporting systems are designed to ensure confidentiality or allow anonymous reporting to protect the whistleblower from potential retaliation.

Documentation
Thorough documentation is key to supporting the report. Nurses should record the date, time, location, individuals involved, and a detailed account of the unsafe practice.

Intervening in Unsafe Practices

When nurses encounter an immediate threat to patient safety, intervention may be necessary to prevent harm. This can include:

- Speaking up to alert the individual engaging in unsafe practice.
- Providing immediate education or guidance to correct behavior.
- Taking over a procedure or task that is being performed incorrectly, if within the nurse's scope of practice.
- Notifying supervisory personnel to intervene directly.

Interventions must be handled professionally and respectfully to maintain a collaborative work environment while emphasizing the importance of patient safety.

Escalating Unsafe Practices

If reporting and intervention do not result in corrective action, or if the unsafe practice persists, escalation becomes necessary. This involves:

Notifying Higher Management
Reports may be escalated to department heads, hospital administrators, or risk management teams.

Involving External Authorities

In cases where internal escalation is ineffective, nurses may report unsafe practices to regulatory bodies, such as state boards of nursing, accreditation organizations, or professional associations.

Legal Action

As a last resort, whistleblowing to external agencies or legal entities may be necessary. Nurses are protected under whistleblower laws, which shield them from retaliation for reporting serious ethical or legal violations.

Support and Resources for Nurses

Addressing unsafe practices can be challenging, and nurses may face resistance or fear retaliation. To support them, institutions can:

- Provide training on recognizing and reporting unsafe practices.
- Establish a culture of safety where reporting is encouraged and valued.
- Offer counseling or peer support for those involved in reporting incidents.
- Implement clear policies and procedures for handling reports and escalating concerns.

Nurses serve as the backbone of patient safety and are pivotal in identifying, addressing, and escalating unsafe practices in healthcare. By adhering to ethical guidelines, leveraging institutional resources, and advocating for a culture of safety, nurses ensure that healthcare environments remain dedicated to high standards of care and professional accountability. Their commitment not only protects patients but also fosters trust and integrity within the healthcare system.

Facilitate appropriate and safe use of equipment

Nurses play a pivotal role in the healthcare system, ensuring the appropriate and safe use of medical equipment. This responsibility encompasses patient care, staff education, and adherence to protocols in dynamic and often high-pressure environments. Their vigilance and expertise are crucial to fostering a culture of safety and efficiency in healthcare organizations. Below, we explore the ways in which nurses contribute to facilitating the proper and safe use of equipment.

The Importance of Safe Equipment Use

Medical equipment is integral to diagnosing, treating, and monitoring patients. However, improper use or failure to maintain this equipment can lead to adverse outcomes, jeopardizing patient health and safety. Nurses are often frontline operators and overseers of medical devices, making their role indispensable in preventing equipment-related incidents.

Nurses as Educators

Training and Knowledge Dissemination
Nurses frequently educate staff and patients about the correct use of medical devices. They provide hands-on training sessions, demonstrations, and guidance to ensure everyone understands the functionality and limitations of the equipment. These educational initiatives minimize risks associated with misuse, such as incorrect readings from monitors or injuries from improperly handled tools.

Patient Instruction
In cases where patients are discharged with devices such as oxygen tanks, mobility aids, or insulin pumps, nurses take the time to explain their safe operation. Clear communication, including step-by-step instructions, helps patients and caregivers feel confident using the equipment, reducing the likelihood of errors or accidents.

Maintaining Equipment Standards

Inspection and Maintenance

Nurses routinely check equipment for signs of wear, malfunction, or contamination. They report issues to appropriate departments for repair or replacement and ensure that maintenance schedules are adhered to. Regular inspections are essential to maintaining the reliability of life-saving devices like ventilators, infusion pumps, and defibrillators.

Adherence to Protocols

Nurses follow established guidelines and protocols to verify that equipment is functioning optimally before use. For example, surgical nurses meticulously assess tools for sterility and proper calibration prior to procedures. Such vigilance prevents complications arising from substandard equipment.

Nurses and Risk Mitigation

Incident Reporting

When equipment-related issues arise, nurses are often the first to identify and report them. Their detailed documentation of incidents facilitates timely corrective measures and informs future improvements in equipment design or protocols.

Advocacy for Safety

Nurses advocate for the acquisition of user-friendly, advanced equipment that enhances safety. Their feedback influences administrative decisions and procurement strategies, ensuring the organization invests in devices that meet high safety standards.

Promoting Team Collaboration

Effective use of medical equipment requires collaborative effort. Nurses coordinate with other healthcare professionals, including technicians and physicians, to ensure equipment use aligns with the specific needs of patients. Their communication skills enable seamless integration of technology into patient care.

Keeping Up with Advancements

Continuing Education

To stay current in an era of rapidly evolving medical technology, nurses participate in continuing education programs. These include workshops, online courses, and certification programs focusing on new devices and techniques. Knowledge updates empower nurses to use equipment effectively and introduce innovations into their practice.

Adaptability

Nurses demonstrate adaptability by swiftly learning and mastering new technologies introduced to the healthcare setting. Their ability to adapt ensures that patients benefit from the latest advancements without delay.

Nurses are the cornerstone of safe and effective equipment use in healthcare. Through education, maintenance, risk mitigation, and adaptability, they uphold standards that protect patients and enhance the quality of care. Their commitment to safety serves as a foundation for trust in medical technology, ensuring its potential is fully realized. As medical equipment continues to evolve, nurses will remain pivotal in bridging the gap between innovation and patient care.

 Follow security plan and procedures

By adhering to established security plans and procedures, nurses help protect patients, staff, and sensitive information while ensuring smooth operations. Nurses effectively follow these plans and procedures in various aspects of their responsibilities.

Training and Orientation

Nurses begin their adherence to security protocols with comprehensive training during onboarding. Hospitals and healthcare facilities provide detailed instructions on policies such as data protection, emergency response, and physical security. Routine refreshers help nurses stay updated on any procedural changes.

Patient Identification Protocols

One of the essential security practices for nurses is ensuring proper patient identification. Nurses regularly verify patient identities through wristbands, ID numbers, and other methods before administering medications or treatments. This prevents errors and ensures the right care is delivered to the right individual.

Data Protection and Confidentiality

Nurses handle a vast amount of sensitive patient information. They follow strict procedures for maintaining confidentiality, such as:

- Accessing electronic medical records only when authorized and necessary.
- Avoiding sharing passwords or leaving documents unsecured.
- Adhering to HIPAA or similar regulations to protect patient data privacy.

Emergency Preparedness

During emergencies, whether involving natural disasters, fires, or violent incidents, nurses follow well-defined security plans. This includes:

- Evacuating patients safely according to designated routes.
- Collaborating with security teams to manage threats.
- Communicating effectively with colleagues and first responders.

Workplace Violence Prevention

Given the vulnerabilities in healthcare settings, nurses are trained in recognizing and de-escalating potentially violent situations. Following security plans may involve:

- Reporting suspicious activity to the appropriate authorities.
- Using personal alarms or other safety tools provided by the facility.
- Participating in drills for active shooter or violent scenarios.

Infection Control Measures

Security in healthcare also extends to infection control. Nurses follow procedures to minimize the spread of disease, such as:

- Wearing appropriate personal protective equipment (PPE).
- Adhering to strict hand hygiene protocols.
- Isolating infectious patients according to facility guidelines.

Controlled Access to Facilities

Nurses often work in areas requiring controlled access, such as operating rooms or pediatric wards. They ensure these areas remain secure by:

- Using ID badges to enter restricted zones.
- Monitoring who enters and exits sensitive areas.
- Reporting any breaches or anomalies in access control.

Medication and Equipment Security

To prevent theft or misuse, nurses follow protocols for safeguarding medications and medical equipment:

- Storing medications in secure, locked cabinets.
- Documenting the dispensing and administration of controlled substances.
- Conducting regular inventory checks on supplies and equipment.

Collaboration with Security Teams

Nurses work closely with hospital security teams to uphold these standards. Regular meetings, incident reporting, and joint drills ensure that everyone is prepared to handle potential threats.

Compliance Monitoring and Reporting

Finally, nurses are responsible for reporting any breaches or irregularities in security protocols. Facilities often have systems in place allowing staff to anonymously report concerns, ensuring accountability and continuous improvement.

By diligently following security plans and procedures, nurses ensure a safe and secure environment for all. Their vigilance, training, and teamwork are vital to the overall success of healthcare operations and the protection of patients and colleagues alike.

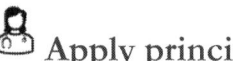 Apply principles of infection prevention

In health care settings, infection prevention is a critical component of patient safety and public health. Nurses, being frontline caregivers, play a pivotal role in implementing and upholding these principles. Their rigorous application of infection prevention measures not only protects patients but also health care workers and the broader community from the spread of diseases. Here, we delve into the various strategies and methods nurses use to ensure optimal infection prevention.

Understanding Infection Prevention in Nursing

Infection prevention encompasses a set of practices designed to prevent the transmission of infectious agents. These measures are guided by principles such as hand hygiene, the use of personal protective equipment (PPE), sterilization of equipment, and adherence to protocols for managing infectious diseases. Nurses are trained to employ these measures consistently and effectively within their scope of practice.

Core Principles of Infection Prevention

Hand Hygiene

Hand hygiene is regarded as the most effective way to prevent the spread of infections. Nurses are trained to follow the "Five Moments for Hand Hygiene" as recommended by the World Health Organization (WHO):

- Before touching a patient
- Before clean/aseptic procedures
- After body fluid exposure risk
- After touching a patient
- After touching patient surroundings

Nurses utilize alcohol-based hand rubs or antimicrobial soaps and water, depending on the situation, and ensure thorough cleaning of all hand surfaces.

Use of Personal Protective Equipment (PPE)

PPE, such as gloves, masks, gowns, and eye protection, acts as a barrier to infectious agents. Nurses are adept at selecting the appropriate PPE based on the level of exposure risk and type of procedure. For example:

- Gloves are used for contact with blood, bodily fluids, or contaminated surfaces.
- Masks and respirators are worn during procedures that generate aerosols or when dealing with airborne infections like tuberculosis.
- Gowns and aprons provide full-body protection during surgeries or when dealing with large fluid spills.

Aseptic Technique

Nurses follow strict aseptic techniques during medical procedures to prevent infections in sterile areas of the body. This includes:

- Proper cleaning and disinfection of the skin before inserting catheters or needles
- Using sterilized instruments and equipment
- Maintaining a sterile field during procedures

These practices are crucial in surgeries, wound care, and intravenous line insertions to minimize the risk of infections like sepsis.

Environmental Cleaning and Disinfection

The cleanliness of the health care environment is essential for infection control. Nurses ensure that patient rooms, operating theaters, and equipment are thoroughly cleaned and disinfected according to established protocols. High-touch surfaces such as bed rails, doorknobs, and medical devices are given special attention to reduce microbial contamination.

Safe Handling and Disposal of Waste

Medical waste, including used sharps, contaminated dressings, and bodily fluids, poses a significant risk if not handled properly. Nurses adhere to strict guidelines for waste segregation, using color-coded bins to separate infectious and non-infectious waste. Sharps are disposed of in puncture-proof containers to prevent needle-stick injuries.

Vaccination and Immunization

Nurses play an active role in promoting vaccinations for both patients and health care staff. Vaccines protect against diseases such as influenza, hepatitis B, and COVID-19, reducing the risk of outbreaks in health care settings. Nurses also ensure that their own vaccinations are up to date to protect themselves and their patients.

Education and Training

Infection prevention requires continuous education and vigilance. Nurses are trained in the latest guidelines and technologies for infection control. They conduct patient education sessions to promote hygienic practices, such as proper handwashing and respiratory etiquette, which help reduce community transmission of infections.

Antimicrobial Stewardship

To combat the growing threat of antimicrobial resistance, nurses advocate for the judicious use of antibiotics. They collaborate with physicians to ensure that antibiotics are prescribed only when necessary and educate patients about completing their prescribed courses.

Specialized Infection Prevention Practices

In certain medical settings, nurses employ additional measures tailored to specific risks:

Isolation Precautions

Patients with highly contagious diseases are placed in isolation to prevent the spread of pathogens. Nurses manage isolation rooms by wearing appropriate PPE, limiting visitor access, and ensuring that waste and linens are handled with care.

Care for Immunocompromised Patients

Patients undergoing chemotherapy, organ transplantation, or living with HIV/AIDS are more vulnerable to infections. Nurses take extra precautions, such as using HEPA filters, ensuring strict asepsis, and administering prophylactic medications to protect these patients.

Outbreak Management

During disease outbreaks, such as those caused by norovirus or COVID-19, nurses are at the forefront of containment efforts. They identify symptomatic patients, implement quarantine measures, and assist in mass testing and vaccinations.

Challenges in Infection Prevention

While nurses are committed to infection prevention, they face challenges such as:

- Shortages of PPE during pandemics
- High patient-to-nurse ratios, which can compromise adherence to protocols
- Emerging pathogens that require rapid updates to practices
- Resistance from patients or families to comply with prevention measures

Overcoming these challenges requires institutional support, continuous education, and the development of resilient health care systems.

The Impact of Nurses in Infection Prevention

The dedication of nurses to infection prevention has far-reaching effects:

- Reducing hospital-acquired infections, such as MRSA and C. difficile
- Enhancing patient outcomes and recovery rates
- Promoting public trust in the health care system
- Limiting the spread of epidemics and pandemics

By combining scientific knowledge with compassionate care, nurses serve as the backbone of infection prevention in health care.

Infection prevention is a cornerstone of quality health care, and nurses are its vigilant guardians. Through meticulous adherence to protocols, education, and innovation, they protect lives and uphold the integrity of the health care system. As the world continues to face evolving infectious threats, the role of nurses in infection control remains indispensable, ensuring a safer and healthier future for all.

Educate client and staff regarding infection prevention measures

Registered nurses (RNs) educate both clients and staff about infection prevention measures. This responsibility is essential for maintaining public health, reducing the spread of infectious diseases, and ensuring the safety of healthcare environments. Through a combination of direct client interaction, professional training sessions, and adherence to evidence-based practices, RNs serve as the frontline resource in infection control education. Below, we explore the ways in which registered nurses educate their clients and colleagues on this vital topic.

Educating Clients: Empowering Individuals

One of the primary responsibilities of an RN is to educate clients about infection prevention strategies tailored to their individual health needs. This educational process involves clear communication, practical demonstrations, and consistent follow-up to ensure the information is understood and implemented effectively.

Understanding the Client's Needs
To provide effective education, RNs start by assessing the client's knowledge level, cultural beliefs, and specific health concerns. This allows the nurse to customize their approach, ensuring that the client is receptive to learning. For example, some clients may require detailed explanations about hand hygiene and respiratory etiquette, while others may need guidance on managing chronic conditions to reduce susceptibility to infections.

Teaching Basic Infection Prevention Practices
RNs educate clients on fundamental practices such as:

- Hand hygiene: Demonstrating proper handwashing techniques with soap and water or the use of alcohol-based hand sanitizers.
- Respiratory hygiene: Advising clients to cover their mouth and nose with a tissue or elbow when coughing or sneezing.

- Personal protective equipment (PPE): Explaining the use of masks and gloves in situations where extra protection is needed.
- Proper cleaning techniques: Teaching clients how to disinfect surfaces and manage laundry to minimize pathogen spread.

Addressing Specific Scenarios

For clients with specific medical conditions, RNs provide tailored infection prevention advice. Examples include:

- Post-surgical patients: Instructions on wound care to prevent infections.
- Immunocompromised individuals: Guidance on avoiding crowded places and maintaining a clean-living environment.
- Families with infectious illnesses: Educating on quarantine measures and symptom management.

Utilizing Educational Materials

Nurses often provide brochures, videos, and posters that reinforce the infection prevention strategies discussed during consultations. These materials allow clients to revisit the information at their convenience and share it with others in their household.

Encouraging Questions and Feedback

A key aspect of client education is making the process interactive. RNs encourage clients to ask questions and clarify doubts, ensuring that they feel confident in their ability to implement the measures. Regular check-ins during follow-up visits help reinforce the practices and address any challenges the client may face.

Educating Staff: Building a Culture of Safety

In addition to client education, RNs are integral to training healthcare staff. They ensure that infection prevention protocols are understood, respected, and consistently followed.

Providing Comprehensive Training Programs

RNs conduct training sessions for healthcare staff, covering topics such as:

- Standard precautions: Ensuring staff understand and adhere to guidelines for hand hygiene, PPE use, and safe injection practices.
- Transmission-based precautions: Educating staff on airborne, droplet, and contact precautions for specific pathogens.
- Sterilization and disinfection: Training staff in cleaning medical equipment and disinfecting surfaces to prevent cross-contamination.
- Waste management: Teaching the safe disposal of biomedical waste and sharps.

Leading by Example

RNs serve as role models for infection prevention practices. By consistently following protocols and demonstrating best practices, they inspire staff to do the same. Their behaviors reinforce the importance of maintaining high standards in hygiene and safety.

Conducting Audits and Feedback Sessions

RNs often participate in auditing infection control processes within healthcare facilities. They review staff compliance with hand hygiene, PPE use, and cleaning protocols. After audits, they provide constructive feedback and solutions for improvement.

Promoting Collaboration

Registered nurses foster communication among healthcare teams to ensure a unified approach to infection prevention. They encourage staff to share observations and suggestions, creating an environment where everyone feels responsible for maintaining safety.

<u>Staying Updated on Current Guidelines</u>

In the ever-evolving field of healthcare, RNs stay informed about the latest infection control guidelines from organizations like the CDC and WHO. They integrate these updates into training programs, ensuring that staff are equipped with the most current knowledge.

Challenges in Infection Prevention Education

Despite their efforts, RNs may face challenges in educating clients and staff. Some of these include:

- Resistance to change: Clients or staff may be hesitant to adopt new habits or protocols.
- Language barriers: Effective communication may require translators or bilingual materials.
- Resource limitations: Lack of access to PPE or sanitation supplies can hinder efforts.
- Misinformation: Addressing false beliefs or myths about infection prevention requires patience and clarity.

RNs employ creative problem-solving and persistence to overcome these obstacles.

The Impact of Nurse-Led Education

Effective education by registered nurses leads to significant benefits, including:

- Reduced infection rates in healthcare settings and communities.
- Empowered clients who take an active role in their own health.
- Enhanced staff compliance with infection prevention protocols.

- Improved overall public health outcomes.

By promoting awareness and knowledge, RNs contribute to a safer and healthier environment for everyone. Registered nurses are vital educators in the realm of infection prevention. Their ability to communicate, train, and inspire change ensures that both clients and staff are well-equipped to combat the spread of infectious diseases. Through their dedication and expertise, RNs build a foundation of safety, resilience, and trust in healthcare practices, ultimately safeguarding communities and saving lives.

Follow requirements when using restraints

The use of restraints in healthcare settings is a serious decision that requires registered nurses (RNs) to adhere to strict guidelines, regulations, and ethical principles. Restraints should always be used as a last resort, ensuring the safety of the patient and others while preserving the dignity and rights of the individual. The following outlines how registered nurses follow requirements when using restraints.

Understanding Restraints

Restraints are tools or methods used to prevent a patient from harming themselves or others. They can be physical, chemical, or environmental. Examples include:

- Physical restraints, such as wrist or ankle straps.
- Chemical restraints, such as sedative medications administered specifically to manage behavior.
- Environmental restraints, such as locked doors or seclusion rooms.

Registered nurses must recognize that the use of restraints carries significant ethical, legal, and medical implications. They are obliged to ensure that the use of restraints complies with both institutional policies and regulatory standards.

Principles Guiding the Use of Restraints

1. Patient-Centered Care

RNs must prioritize the patient's well-being and dignity, using restraints only when necessary and in the least restrictive manner. Communication with the patient and their family members is essential to explain the rationale for restraint use and to address any concerns.

2. Legal and Ethical Considerations

Nurses must ensure that the use of restraints complies with state, federal, and institutional regulations. In many jurisdictions, the use of restraints is governed by laws that require:
- Proper documentation and justification for their use.
- Time limits on the duration of restraint use.
- Regular reassessment of the patient's condition.

Ethically, the principles of autonomy, beneficence, non-maleficence, and justice must guide the decision-making process.

Steps for Registered Nurses to Follow Requirements

Assessment and Documentation

Before applying restraints, nurses must conduct a thorough assessment of the patient's physical and mental state. This includes identifying:
- Underlying causes of agitation or aggression, such as pain, confusion, or medication side effects.
- Possible alternatives to restraints, such as verbal de-escalation techniques or environmental modifications.

Comprehensive documentation is critical. This includes:
- The reason for restraint use.
- The type of restraint applied.
- The outcome of the intervention.

Obtaining Authorization

Restraints should only be used under the order of a licensed healthcare provider, such as a physician. In emergency situations, RNs may initiate restraint use, but they must notify the appropriate provider and obtain authorization as soon as possible.

3. Implementing the Least Restrictive Option

Registered nurses are required to choose the least restrictive form of restraint that meets the patient's needs. For example:

- Using verbal de-escalation or distraction techniques before resorting to physical restraints.
- Opting for a lap belt instead of full wrist and ankle restraints, if appropriate.

Monitoring and Reassessment

Continuous monitoring of the patient's physical and psychological condition is essential while restraints are in use. Nurses must:

- Check circulation, skin integrity, and comfort at regular intervals.
- Reassess the need for restraints frequently and remove them as soon as it is safe to do so.

Monitoring also includes assessing the patient's response to the restraints and any changes in their behavior or medical condition.

Education and Communication

Educating patients, families, and caregivers about the reasons for restraint use is crucial. Nurses should communicate clearly and compassionately, ensuring that everyone involved understands the situation and the steps being taken to ensure safety.

Alternative Strategies for Restraints

Before resorting to restraints, RNs should explore alternative strategies, such as:

- Providing a calm and quiet environment.
- Offering activities or items to redirect attention.
- Addressing unmet physiological needs, such as hunger or pain.
- Ensuring the presence of a family member or caregiver to provide comfort.

Training and Competency

Registered nurses must undergo regular training on the proper use of restraints. This includes:

- Learning about de-escalation techniques and alternative interventions.
- Understanding the legal and ethical implications of restraint use.
- Practicing the safe application and removal of restraints.

Competency assessments ensure that nurses remain up to date with best practices and institutional policies. The use of restraints is a complex and sensitive aspect of nursing care that requires careful consideration, adherence to regulations, and a commitment to patient-centered care. Registered nurses play a critical role in ensuring that restraints are used safely, ethically, and only when necessary. By following established guidelines and seeking to minimize restraint use, nurses uphold the principles of patient dignity and safety while providing high-quality care.

MODULE 3

HEALTH PROMOTION & MAINTENANCE NURSING TASK

Provide care & education for the newborns/infants/toddlers birth to 2yrs

Nurses play a crucial role in providing care and education to newborns, infants, and toddlers during their first two years of life. This period is marked by rapid growth and development, requiring specialized attention to ensure the health and well-being of the child. Below is a detailed guide on how nurses support these young clients and their families.

Care for Newborns (Birth to 1 Month)

Initial Assessment and Support
From the moment of birth, nurses assess the newborn's health through Apgar scoring, which evaluates heart rate, respiration, muscle tone, reflex response, and skin color. This assessment helps determine whether immediate medical intervention is needed.

Nurses also monitor vital signs, ensure proper thermoregulation, and assess feeding abilities, either through breastfeeding or formula feeding. They provide guidance on initiating breastfeeding and managing common challenges such as latch issues or milk supply.

Promoting Bonding and Comfort
Encouraging skin-to-skin contact between the newborn and parents is essential for bonding and emotional security. Nurses educate parents on soothing techniques such as swaddling, gentle rocking, and responding to the baby's cues.

Health and Hygiene
Newborns have delicate skin that requires proper care. Nurses educate parents on safe bathing practices, umbilical cord care, and diapering to prevent infections and rashes. Immunizations, such as the hepatitis B vaccine, are administered according to the recommended schedule.

Parental Education
Parents often have many questions during the newborn phase. Nurses provide resources and guidance on recognizing signs of illness, safe sleep practices to prevent sudden infant death syndrome (SIDS) and creating a nurturing environment.

Care for Infants (1 Month to 12 Months)
Monitoring Growth and Development
During the infant stage, nurses track milestones such as weight gain, height, and head circumference growth. Developmental milestones—like rolling over, sitting up, and babbling—are closely monitored to ensure the child is on track.

Nutritional Guidance
As the infant grows, feeding transitions from exclusive breastfeeding or formula to the introduction of solid foods around six months. Nurses educate parents on selecting appropriate foods, avoiding choking hazards, and ensuring adequate intake of essential nutrients such as iron and vitamin D.

Immunizations and Preventive Care
Nurses administer vaccines following the standard immunization schedule, which includes shots for polio, rotavirus, DTaP (diphtheria, tetanus, and pertussis), and others. They emphasize the importance of these vaccines in preventing serious illnesses.

Safety Education
In this exploration phase, infants are prone to accidents. Nurses educate parents on childproofing their homes, selecting safe toys, and preventing falls or injuries.

Topics like car seat safety and ensuring safe sleeping environments are also covered.

Parental Support and Resources

Infant care can be overwhelming for new parents. Nurses provide resources for stress management, parenting classes, and support groups. They also educate parents on recognizing signs of postpartum depression and seeking help when needed.

Care for Toddlers (12 Months to 2 Years)

Facilitating Independence

Toddlers are increasingly mobile and curious, making this phase both exciting and challenging for caregivers. Nurses guide parents on encouraging autonomy while setting limits for safety.

Nutrition and Feeding Practices

Nurses educate parents on transitioning to family meals while maintaining balanced nutrition. Tips on managing picky eating and ensuring proper hydration are provided.

Milestone Monitoring

Nurses assess developmental milestones like walking, speaking first words, and engaging in simple play. Delays or concerns are addressed promptly through referrals to specialists if necessary.

Behavioral Guidance

Toddlers often exhibit tantrums and testing boundaries. Nurses help parents develop strategies for positive discipline, managing behavior, and fostering emotional regulation.

Health and Hygiene

Maintaining hygiene becomes more interactive with toddlers. Nurses teach parents about dental care, including the importance of first visits to a pediatric dentist and establishing brushing routines.

Safety Education

With increased mobility comes higher risks for accidents. Nurses work with parents to ensure a safe home environment, teach water safety, and continue emphasizing car seat usage.

Educational Role of Nurses

Beyond direct care, nurses act as educators to empower parents and caregivers. They provide evidence-based information tailored to each developmental stage and address any concerns or questions with compassion.

Building Trust

Establishing rapport with families is essential. Nurses listen actively, provide reassurance, and respect cultural and individual preferences in caregiving.

Encouraging Preventive Care

Nurses emphasize regular check-ups, developmental screenings, and adherence to vaccination schedules. These measures are vital for detecting potential issues early.

Promoting Family Involvement

A holistic approach includes the entire family in caregiving. Nurses encourage siblings and extended family members to play a supportive role in the child's development.

The first two years of a child's life are foundational for lifelong health and development. Nurses play an integral part in guiding families through this critical period, offering compassionate care and education to ensure both the child and caregivers thrive. Their expertise and dedication provide a strong foundation upon which families can build healthy, fulfilling lives.

Provide care and education for preschool/school age/adolescent ages 3-17

Nurses play a crucial role in the development, health, and well-being of children and adolescents, tailoring their care and education to meet the developmental and psychological needs of each age group. For clients aged 3 through 17 years, nursing practices encompass preventive care, acute and chronic illness management, health education, and emotional support. This document explores how nurses effectively provide care and education for preschool, school-age, and adolescent clients.

Care and Education for Preschool Clients (Ages 3-5)

Preschool-aged children are in a critical period of growth and learning, requiring care that supports their physical, emotional, and cognitive development. Nurses working with this age group focus on creating a safe and engaging environment that encourages trust and curiosity.

Health Assessments and Preventive Care
- Nurses conduct regular growth and developmental screenings to ensure the child is meeting milestones.
- Immunizations are administered according to established schedules, and parents are educated on their importance.
- Preventive measures such as hygiene education (e.g., handwashing) and accident prevention are emphasized.

Psychosocial Care

- Building rapport with young children involves using play and familiar objects to alleviate anxiety during medical visits.
- Nurses provide emotional reassurance through gentle communication and positive reinforcement.
- They collaborate with parents to address behavioral concerns, such as temper tantrums or separation anxiety.

Health Education

- Nurses educate parents on nutrition, reinforcing the importance of balanced diets that include fruits, vegetables, and essential nutrients.
- They provide tips on establishing healthy sleep routines and managing common illnesses, such as colds or ear infections.
- Safety education focuses on child-proofing the home and practicing outdoor safety, like wearing helmets and using car seats.

Care and Education for School-Age Clients (Ages 6-12)

School-age children are developing independence and cognitive skills, making it an ideal time to instill lifelong health habits. Nurses cater to this age group with appropriate age communication and active involvement in their care.

Health Assessments and Interventions

- Regular check-ups include vision, hearing, and dental screenings, as well as monitoring conditions like scoliosis or obesity.
- Nurses manage acute illnesses (e.g., strep throat) and chronic conditions (e.g., asthma or diabetes), teaching children and parents about proper management.

Psychosocial Support

- School-age children often face social and academic pressures; nurses address these by promoting self-esteem and teaching coping mechanisms.
- They encourage open communication with caregivers and teachers to identify and manage stressors, such as bullying.

Health Education

- Nurses educate children about the importance of personal hygiene, including brushing teeth, bathing, and wearing clean clothes.
- They teach basic health skills, such as recognizing symptoms of illness and knowing when to seek help.
- Discussions on nutrition focus on healthy eating habits and the risks of consuming excessive sugar or fast food.
- Safety lessons include road safety, internet safety, and first-aid basics.

Care and Education for Adolescent Clients (Ages 13-17)

Adolescents undergo significant physical, emotional, and social changes, requiring specialized care that respects their growing autonomy while addressing their unique health concerns.

Comprehensive Health Screenings

- Nurses monitor puberty-related changes and provide guidance on managing physical and emotional transitions.
- Screenings include mental health evaluations for issues like anxiety, depression, or eating disorders.
- Sexual health assessments and education are provided in a confidential and respectful manner.

Psychosocial and Emotional Support

- Nurses create a safe space for adolescents to discuss concerns about identity, relationships, or academic pressures.
- They educate adolescents on managing stress and building resilience, equipping them with tools to handle challenges.
- For those struggling with mental health challenges, nurses provide referrals to specialists while offering continuous support.

Health Education

- Sexual health education is a key focus, covering topics like contraception, sexually transmitted infections (STIs), and consent.

- Nurses educate adolescents on the dangers of substance abuse, including drugs, alcohol, and vaping.
- They emphasize the importance of balanced nutrition, regular physical activity, and adequate sleep for overall well-being.
- Safety lessons address topics such as safe driving practices, recognizing abusive relationships, and understanding the risks of social media.

Family-Centered Care Across All Age Groups

Nurses recognize the essential role families play in supporting the health and development of children and adolescents. They engage parents and caregivers in care plans to align education and interventions with family values.

Parent and Caregiver Education

- Nurses educate families on how to recognize developmental milestones and potential delays.
- They teach parents how to manage common childhood illnesses at home and when to seek medical attention.
- For chronic conditions, nurses provide training on medication administration, lifestyle adjustments, and emergency preparedness.

Promoting Communication
- Nurses encourage open and honest communication between children, adolescents, and their families.
- They offer advice on addressing sensitive subjects, such as mental or sexual health, with consideration of the appropriate age.

Nurses play an indispensable role in the holistic care of clients aged 3 through 17 years. By tailoring their approach to the developmental needs of preschool, school-age, and adolescent clients, they promote physical health, emotional well-being, and lifelong healthy habits. Through education, preventive care, and compassionate support, nurses empower young clients and their families to navigate each stage of growth with confidence and resilience.

Provide care and education for the adult client ages 18 through 64 years

As a registered nurse, providing care and education for adult clients aged 18 to 64 years involves addressing a wide range of health needs and promoting wellness across different life stages. This includes conducting thorough health assessments, discussing preventive measures, and offering guidance on lifestyle choices that enhance physical, mental, and emotional well-being.

- For younger adults, topics such as stress management, reproductive health, and nutrition are often central to care plans.
- Middle-aged adults may require a focus on chronic disease prevention, screenings, and strategies for maintaining mobility and independence.

Effective communication is essential, encouraging adults to actively participate in their health decisions. Nurses should remain culturally sensitive and mindful of diverse backgrounds to ensure care is personalized and inclusive. By fostering a supportive environment, registered nurses empower adults to take control of their health, navigate challenges, and thrive during this important span of life.

Young Adults

For younger adults, topics such as stress management, reproductive health, and nutrition are often central to care plans. It is important to educate patients that most adults require at least 30 minutes of moderate physical activity, such as brisk walking or cycling, at least five days per week. Some young adults engage in risky sexual behaviors that can lead to negative health outcomes. These behaviors, although they may indicate a certain freedom from commitment, can increase the risk of sexually transmitted diseases (STDs) in both males and females. Additionally, domestic violence should be assessed in both men and women. Half of all mental health disorders in adulthood start at age 18, but most cases are undetected and untreated.

Health promotion for young adults should include

- Provide age-appropriate comprehensive sexuality related education
- Encourage opportunities to develop life skills
- Educate on services that are acceptable, equitable, appropriate, and effective
- Foster a safe and supportive environment when providing care
- Inform on the importance of preventive health care such as well-visits, immunizations, and mental health
- Teach the importance of advocating for themselves as they transition to adulthood

Health Screenings for Young Adults

Screening	Details	Recommended Age	Frequency
Cervical Cancer	Pap test to check for cancerous or precancerous cells	21-29	Every three years
Cervical Cancer	Pap tests or HPV tests	30+	Pap tests every three years or HPV tests every five years
Cholesterol	Measures LDL and HDL levels	Men: 35, Women: 45	Not specified
Diabetes	Blood test checks glucose levels	35	Not specified

Middle Adulthood

Middle-aged adults may require a focus on chronic disease prevention, screenings, and strategies for maintaining mobility and independence. Health assessments conducted during middle adulthood should address the physiological and psychological issues commonly experienced during this stage of life, including heart disease, diabetes, obesity, hypertension, arthritis, chronic obstructive pulmonary disease (COPD), migraines, anxiety, and depression. The information collected should be used to guide patient care and education.

Health promotion activities for individuals in middle adulthood should emphasize adequate rest, leisurely activities, regular exercise, balanced nutrition, satisfactory sexual function, and the reduction and cessation of tobacco and alcohol use. Adults should be encouraged to undergo regular health screenings such as blood pressure checks, colonoscopies, prostate examinations for men, and mammograms and Pap smears for women. Domestic violence should be assessed in both men and women.

Provide Education on Prevention of Common Health Risks in Middle Adulthood

Heart Disease

- Consume a healthy diet and engage in regular exercise.
- Cease smoking.
- Reduce intake of foods high in cholesterol.
- Identify and treat high blood pressure.
- Maintain an ideal weight.
- Take low-dose aspirin under physician guidance.

Cancer and cancer-related deaths

- Be aware of cancer symptoms.
- Perform self-examinations.
- Get regular check-ups, screenings, and immunizations.
- Avoid tobacco, sun exposure, pollutants, and x-ray exposure.
- Eat a healthy diet, exercise daily and maintain an appropriate weight.
- Consume alcohol only in moderation.

Health screening for Middle Adulthood

Type of Cancer	Screening Recommendation	Screening Age	Screening Tool	Additional Information
Breast cancer	All women	40	Mammogram	Every one to two years
Colorectal cancer	Both men and women	45	Colonoscopy	Other tests: FIT, gFOBT
Lung cancer	Both Men and women with 20 pack-year smoking history	50	LDCT scans	Pack-years: packs/day x years smoked

Prostate cancer	Some men	50	PSA blood test, digital rectal exam	

👤 Provide care and education for the adult client ages 65 years and over

Registered nurses play a crucial role in providing comprehensive care and education to adults aged 65 years and older. They focus on promoting healthy aging, managing chronic conditions, and preventing illness through regular health assessments and screenings. Education includes guidance on medication management, proper nutrition, physical activity, fall prevention, and mental health support. Nurses also collaborate with families and caregivers to ensure a supportive environment that enhances the quality of life for older adults.

- Many older adults live active and healthy lives, but as aging occurs, bodies and minds change. To stay healthy, adults should eat a balanced diet, keep active both mentally and physically, refrain from smoking, practice safety habits, and get regular health care check-ups.

- Screening tests needed depend on the person's age, gender, family history, and risk factors for certain diseases. For example, being overweight may increase the risk of developing diabetes and exacerbate many other comorbid conditions. Screening should be a primary focus of health promotion because of the potential for early detection of cancers such as breast and colorectal cancer.

- Patient education on cancer prevention, vaccinations that protect against influenza and pneumococcal disease, screenings for the early detection of diabetes, lipid disorders, osteoporosis, and hypertension, risk assessment, elder abuse, and smoking cessation counseling, being sensitive to cultural, language, and other differences among older adults when providing health-promotion information.

- Assessment of abuse in older adults, especially those who are experiencing cognitive changes and those who rely on others for their care.

- Limitations in activities because of chronic conditions increase with age, older adults with chronic disabilities receive either informal care from family or friends or formal care from services.

Home Care of Older Adults

- Collaboration among health care agencies and providers is needed to provide care for older adults in the home.
- Home health care should be considered for older adults being discharged from the hospital.
- Services include skilled nursing care; physical, occupational, and speech-language therapies; medical social services; and home health aide care.
- Home health agencies conduct assessments in the patient's environment and determine the patient's ability to perform ADLs independently.
- Patient and family education is provided so that proper care continues even when the agency is not present.
-

Health Screenings or Older Adults

All women over 65 and men at high risk should get a bone density screening to check for signs of osteoporosis, a progressive disease that causes bones to become very brittle and break easily. Doctors use a low-dose X-ray called a DEXA scan to measure the thickness and strength of your bones.

Screening such as blood pressure checks, cholesterol tests and diabetes screenings are important to continue as you get older. But you may stop other screenings, depending on your risk factors and previous test results. Your doctor may recommend stopping:

Cancer Type	Screening Age
Cervical cancer	after age 65
Prostate cancer	after age 70
Breast cancer	after age 75
Colorectal cancer	after age 75
Lung cancer	after age 80

Provide prenatal care and education

Prenatal care and education are vital components of ensuring a healthy pregnancy and preparing expectant parents for the arrival of their child.

Registered nurses' contributions are multifaceted, encompassing clinical assessments, health promotion, risk management, and psychological guidance. Prenatal care refers to the medical and educational services provided during pregnancy to monitor the health of both the mother and the developing fetus. It includes regular check-ups, screenings, and interventions aimed at preventing complications and fostering a healthy pregnancy. Registered nurses, often working in collaboration with obstetricians, midwives, and other healthcare professionals, are integral to delivering care that is both comprehensive and individualized.

Importance of Prenatal Education

Education is a cornerstone of prenatal care, enabling expectant parents to understand the changes happening in their bodies, the needs of their developing child, and how to prepare for childbirth and parenthood. Registered nurses focus on delivering evidence-based information tailored to the unique circumstances and concerns of each family, ensuring that parents feel confident and well-equipped.

The Role of Registered Nurses

Registered nurses serve as key facilitators in prenatal care and education through their specialized knowledge, compassionate approach, and ability to build trusting relationships with patients. Their responsibilities span clinical, educational, and emotional domains.

Clinical Responsibilities
- Health Assessments: Nurses conduct regular assessments to track vital signs, weight gain, fetal development, and overall maternal health.
- Screening and Monitoring: They oversee screenings for conditions such as gestational diabetes, preeclampsia, and fetal anomalies, ensuring early detection and timely intervention.

- Administering Tests: Registered nurses may assist with ultrasounds, blood tests, and other diagnostic procedures to ensure the pregnancy is progressing normally.
- Managing Health Conditions: For mothers with preexisting conditions, nurses collaborate with specialists to adapt care plans to reduce risks during pregnancy.

Educational Responsibilities

One of the most impactful roles of registered nurses is educating expectant parents about their pregnancy journey and beyond. Key topics covered include:

- Nutrition and Wellness: Nurses provide advice on maintaining a balanced diet, staying hydrated, and managing pregnancy-related symptoms such as nausea and fatigue.
- Infant Development: Understanding fetal milestones helps parents connect with their baby and recognize the importance of their own health in supporting development.
- Labor and Delivery Preparation: Nurses educate parents about the stages of labor, pain management options, and what to expect during delivery.
- Postnatal Care: Guidance on breastfeeding, infant hygiene, and maternal recovery ensures parents are prepared for the postpartum period.

Emotional and Psychological Support

Pregnancy can be an emotional rollercoaster, and registered nurses provide critical support to help parents navigate this experience. They offer:

- Empathy and Counseling: Nurses listen to concerns and provide reassurance, creating a safe space for parents to express their fears and joys.
- Stress Management Techniques: Teaching relaxation exercises, mindfulness practices, and coping strategies to reduce anxiety during pregnancy.
- Support Networks: Nurses often connect parents to community resources, support groups, and educational workshops for additional assistance.

Challenges in Prenatal Care

Registered nurses face several challenges in their roles, including:

- Access to Care: Disparities in healthcare access can make it difficult for some families to receive adequate prenatal services.
- Cultural Sensitivity: Nurses must adapt their educational strategies to respect diverse cultural beliefs and practices surrounding pregnancy.
- High-Risk Pregnancies: Managing complex cases requires specialized knowledge and coordination among multiple healthcare providers.

Registered nurses are indispensable in the realm of prenatal care and education, acting as both caregivers and educators to prepare families for the challenges and joys of parenthood. Their holistic approach ensures not only the physical health of mother and baby but also the emotional and psychological well-being of the entire family. Through their dedication, expertise, and compassion, registered nurses empower parents to embrace their pregnancy journey with confidence and resilience, setting the foundation for a healthy and happy future.

Pregnancy Assessment

History of pregnancies and births for the antepartum client
TPAL is a system used to describe obstetrical history
- T=term births (38-40 weeks)
- P=preterm births (20-37 weeks)
- A=abortions (< 20 weeks)
- L=living children

Example: a woman who has 2 living children born as preterm twins in her first pregnancy would be designated as: TPAL 0-1-0-2 - 0 term births, 1 delivery prior to 37 weeks gestation (preterm), 0 pregnancies ending in spontaneous or induced abortions, and 2 living children.

GPA terminology is sometimes combined with TPAL terminology

- G gravida (number of pregnancies)
- P para (number of births of viable offspring)
- A (abortions)
- L= Living

Example: Mom is 38 weeks pregnant. She had 2 kids that were born full term. One preterm was twins. She had 2 abortions.
Gravid - 6
Parity - 3

Present pregnancy is included in the gravida. Gravida is the number of times that mom has been pregnant (pregnant 5 times plus the present pregnancy now). Parity would be 3 deliveries for the mother, because the twins are one delivery. A pregnancy that is less than 38 weeks, but more than 20 weeks is premature, 20-37 weeks is preterm.

Terminology
- EDB – Estimated date of birth. (Baby due)
- EDD – Estimated date of delivery
-

Methods to determine EDB
Nagels Rule
- 1st day of {LMP (last menstrual period) – 3months} + 7 days.
- Example: August 14, 2004, is LMP count – 3 months starting with the month of July.
- The month is May. Next, you add 7 to 14 and that equals 21. The estimated date of delivery is May 21, 2004.

Fundal Height Measurement
- The fundal height should be the same or close to the gestational weeks
- A tape measure is used to measure (cm) the top of the symphysis pubis to the top of the fundus.
- When the fetus develops up to 20 weeks, the fundus can be felt at the umbilical; from that time on it goes up one cm/week. Ex: if the woman is 26

weeks, the top of the symphysis pubis to the top of the fundus should measure 26 cm.

- If it measures 30 cm and she is in her 20th week, then we must think about what is going on. She could have a huge baby. She may have multiple gestations or too much amniotic fluid. In any case, they may refer her to do and ultrasound to determine what is going on and to make sure everything is ok.
  - If she is 26 weeks and she is measuring 22cm, that is another reason to be concerned. Baby could have (IUGR) Intrauterine Growth Retardation – baby does not develop the way he/she should.

Signs of Pregnancy

Presumptive / Subjective

"I missed a period." Presuming that they are pregnant.
Amenorrhea: missing one or more periods.
Nausea and vomiting (weakest sign of pregnancy).
Fatigue.
Breast changes.
Quickening:1st fetal movements that a female feels. Possible to just be gas too.

Probable / Objective (not positive)

Hegar's sign: Softening and thinning of lower uterine segment at about sixth week of gestation.
Goodell's sign: Softening of cervix, beginning at second month of gestation.
Chadwick's sign: Bluish coloration of mucous membranes of cervix, vagina, vulva at about sixth week of gestation.
Ballottement: Rebounding of fetus against examiner's fingers on palpation.

Positive signs (diagnostic).

Fetal heart rate.
Active fetal movement.
Outline of fetus on x-ray.

Positive / Diagnostic

Fetal heart tones: audible with a stethoscope at 18-20 weeks, using a Doppler audible at 10 to 12 weeks.

Ultrasound per vagina gestational sac seen at 6 weeks.
Fetal movement: felt by examiner at 20 to 24 weeks, felt by mother at 16- 20 weeks.
Quickening can be felt differently during primigravida (1st pregnancy) and multigravida (many pregnancies).
Primigravida quickening can be felt at 20 weeks gestation.
Multigravida quickening can be felt at 16 weeks gestation. Mom can feel it earlier because she knows what she is feeling. Recognizes what she is feeling due to previous pregnancies.

Physiological and Psychological changes

Weight Gain
Normal weight gain based on BMI is 25-35 lbs: 2-5lbs 1st trimester, then 1 lb per week
If triplets or more, the weight gain is more.
Pregnant women do not have to eat for two.
Distribution of pounds
Fetus, placenta, amniotic fluid: 11 lbs.
Uterus: 2 lbs. (2oz-2.2lbs)
Blood Volume: 4 lbs.
Breast:3 lbs.
Maternal stores: 10lbs.
Skin
Increased pigmentation.
Appearance of Linea nigra.
Chloasma may appear.
Striae may appear.
Vascular spider nevi may appear.
Cardiovascular
Pulse may increase 10 beats/min.
Respiratory
Oxygen consumption increases by 15% to 20%.
Blood pressure may decrease in the second trimester.
Gastrointestinal
Nausea and vomiting may occur from first through third months.
Constipation may occur.
Hemorrhoids may develop.
Renal
Frequency of urination increases in first and third trimesters.
Endocrine
Basal metabolic rate rises.

Musculoskeletal
Center of gravity changes.
Lumbosacral curve increases.
Relaxing and increased mobility of pelvic joints.
Reproductive
Uterus enlarges with an increase in number and size of blood vessels.
Cervix becomes shorter, more elastic, and larger in diameter.
Maturation of new follicles is blocked.
Increases in vaginal secretions.
Breast size increases.
Colostrum may appear from breasts.
Psychological
Ambivalence.
Acceptance.
Emotional lability.
Body image changes.
Relationship with fetus.

Patient Education regarding discomforts

- If mom complains of nausea, this is a suitable time to advise on methods to relieve nausea. Ex: Nausea – eat some crackers.

- If mom complains of feeling lightheaded, Ex: Lightheaded - sit on side of bed and dangle legs, then stand up.

- If mom has an unhealthy attitude. Attitude towards the pregnancy is important because, if the person is in denial, they are not going to take care of themselves as they would if they were happy about the pregnancy. Ex: Denial - Talk to women to find out how things are going… if they are happy about the pregnancy. Get a feeling to see how she feels about the pregnancy. Teens can be scared.

Pregnancy Related Diagnostic Test

Blood type and Rh factor
Having a Rh-negative blood type is not an illness and usually does not affect a person's health, however, it can affect pregnancy.
If a woman is Rh-negative and her baby is Rh-positive, then the woman's body will approach the Rh-positive protein as a foreign object, if her immune system is exposed to it.

Rhogam is an injection designed to help prevent immune-system problems related to a Rh-negative mother whose baby is Rh-positive.
For a first pregnancy, RhoGAM is typically injected at about 28 weeks and then again within 72 hours post-delivery.
For any subsequent pregnancies, RhoGAM is administered regularly during the second half of the pregnancy.
Rubella Titer
A client with a negative Titer (<1:8) has a risk of contracting rubella, which can be transmitted to the fetus and cause birth anomalies. Therefore, it is recommended to assess the Titer before conception.
If negative titer, client must be using effective birth control at time of immunization, must be counseled not be become pregnant for 3 months following immunization.
Tuberculin skin test
Positive test indicates need for chest x-ray to rule out active disease.
In pregnant client, x-ray cannot be performed until after 20th week of gestation.
Hepatitis B surface antigens
Recommended for all women because of prevalence of disease in general population.
Urinalysis and urine culture
Levels of 2+ to 4+ protein in urine may indicate infection or preeclampsia.
Ultrasonography
Identify fetal and maternal structures .
Assists in confirming gestational age and estimated date of confinement.
Biophysical profile
Fetal breathing movements, fetal movements, fetal tine, amniotic fluid index, and fetal heart rate patterns via noninvasive assessment.
Doppler blood flow analysis
Studies blood flow in fetus and placenta.
Percutaneous umbilical blood sampling
If fetal blood sampling is necessary, insert needle in fetal umbilical vessel under ultrasound guidance.
Amniocentesis
Aspiration of amniotic fluid may be done from 13th to 14th week of gestation.
Used to determine genetic disorders, metabolic defects, fetal lung maturity.
Risks include maternal hemorrhage, infection, abruptio placentae, premature rupture of membranes.
Fern test
Microscopic slide test to determine presence of amniotic fluid leakage.
Nonstress test
Performed to assess placental function and oxygenation.
Assesses fetal well-being.

Fibronectin test
Sampling of cervical secretions.
Positive results indicate onset of labor in 1 to 3 weeks.
Contraction stress test
Performed to assess placental oxygenation and function.
Assesses fetal ability to tolerate labor, fetal well-being.
Measles, Mumps and Rubella (MMR)
If a person is not immune, they cannot receive the Rubella injection during pregnancy. They will have to get it after the pregnancy.

Other Testing

Kick counts (fetal movement counting).

Hemoglobin and hematocrit levels.

Papanicolaou smear.

Sexually transmitted infections.

Provide care and education to an antepartum client or a client in labor

To provide care to an antepartum client or a client in labor, registered nurses begin by conducting thorough assessments to monitor maternal and fetal health. This process includes checking vital signs, tracking fetal development, and identifying any signs of complications. Nurses also prioritize effective communication, ensuring that clients understand their health status, labor progression, and any medical interventions that may be necessary.

- In labor, their role expands to encompass pain management strategies such as breathing techniques, position changes, or administering medications when needed. They act as advocates, liaising between the client and other members of the healthcare team to ensure a seamless experience. Emotional support is equally critical, as nurses offer words of encouragement and reassurance during the intense moments of labor and delivery.

- For antepartum care, education is a cornerstone of their approach. Nurses empower clients with knowledge about pregnancy stages, nutritional guidelines, and warning signs to watch for. They also foster a proactive attitude by guiding clients toward creating birth plans, preparing for postpartum recovery, and understanding newborn care essentials.

- Through these multifaceted efforts, registered nurses remain steadfast in their mission to nurture both the physical and emotional well-being of their clients, setting the stage for a positive and memorable childbirth experience.

Monitoring a client in Labor

Process of Labor and Delivery

Process: Coordinated sequence of involuntary uterine contractions to move fetus through birth canal, to delivery, actual birth of newborn. Four major factors interact during normal childbirth; four Ps of labor depend on each other for safe delivery.
Powers: Uterine contractions.
Passageway: Mother's rigid bony pelvis, soft tissues of cervix, pelvic floor, vagina, introitus.
Passenger: Fetus, membranes, placenta.
Psyche: Woman's emotional system.
Attitude: Relationship of fetal body parts to one another.
Lie: Relationship of spine of fetus to spine of mother.

Presentation

Portion of fetus that enters pelvic inlet first.
Presenting part: Specific fetal structure lying nearest cervix.
Position: Relationship of assigned area of presenting part to maternal pelvis.
Station: Measurement of progress of descent in centimeters above or below midplane, from presenting part to ischial spine.

Mechanisms of Labor

Assessment
Lightening, in which the fetus descends into pelvis about 2 weeks before delivery
Braxton-Hick's contractions increase
Vaginal show present, vaginal mucosa congested, vaginal mucus increases.
Cervical mucus plug is passed.
Cervix ripens, becoming soft, partly effaced, may begin to dilate.
Mother has sudden burst of energy, often known as "nesting."
Loss of 1 to 3 lb from water loss as fluid shifts secondary to hormonal changes before labor.
Spontaneous rupture of membranes occurs.
True labor
Contractions increase in duration and intensity
Cervical dilation, effacement are progressive
False labor

Exaggeration of normal contractions
Labor does not produce dilation, effacement, or descent
Contractions are irregular, without progression
Walking has no effect on contractions; often relieves false labor
Breathing Techniques
Provide focus during contractions.
Promote relaxation and oxygenation.
Begin with simple breathing patterns to more complex.

Fetal Monitoring

Normal FHR 110 to 160 beats/min

External fetal monitoring
Noninvasive, performed using Doppler ultrasonic transducer, transducer, fastened with belt, should be placed on side of mother where fetal back is located (Leopold's maneuvers)
Internal fetal monitoring
Invasive, requires rupturing of membranes, attachment of electrode to presenting part of fetus, mother must be dilated 2 to 3 cm to perform this procedure.
Periodic patterns in FHR
If change occurs, turn mother to left side, administer oxygen as prescribed.
Accelerations may occur with fetal movement or contractions.
Early decelerations occur during contractions when fetal head is pressed against woman's pelvis require no intervention.
Late decelerations usually associated with impaired placental exchange or uteroplacental insufficiency require interventions to improve placental blood flow and fetal oxygenation, including immediate delivery of fetus.
Variable decelerations usually caused by umbilical cord compression, require change in maternal positioning.
Hypertonic uterine activity
Non reassuring FHR patterns.
Leopold's Maneuvers
To determine presentation and position of fetus
If head is in fundus, hard, round movable object felt, if buttocks in fundus, then soft, irregular shape, more difficult to move.
Back of fetus should be felt on one side of abdomen.
Irregular knobs and lumps, hands, feet, elbows, and knees felt on opposite side of abdomen.
Interventions (throughout the labor process)
Monitor maternal vital signs.

Monitor FHR via ultrasound Doppler, fetoscope, or electronic fetal monitor.
Assess FHR before, during, and after a contraction, noting that the normal FHR is 110 to 160 beats/minute.
Monitor uterine contractions by palpation or tocodynamometer, determining frequency, duration, and intensity.
Assess status of cervical dilation and effacement.
Assess fetal station presentation and position by Leopold's maneuvers.
Assist with pelvic examination and prepare for a fern test.
If the membranes have ruptured, assess the fetal heart rate because of the risk of collapsed umbilical cord, and assess the color of the amniotic fluid because meconium-stained fluid can indicate fetal distress.

Provide post-partum care and education

Registered nurses play a crucial role in providing post-partum care and education to new mothers. Their focus includes:

Education
- Teaching breastfeeding techniques to ensure successful nursing.
- Helping mothers recognize signs of infection and monitor lochia (post-partum bleeding).
- Guiding new mothers on proper nutrition and hydration to support their recovery.
- Promoting emotional well-being and providing resources for mental health support.

Encouragement and Resources
- Encouraging open communication about concerns or unusual symptoms.
- Offering access to lactation consultants and mental health care professionals.
- Ensuring the mother feels supported during the transition into parenthood.

Care and Support
- Assisting with perineal care to promote healing.
- Managing pain and discomfort effectively.
- Encouraging rest and recovery during the post-partum period.

Postpartum Assessment

Vital signs

Hyperthermia common in first 24 hours.
Bradycardia common in first week.
Involution
Rapid decrease in size of uterus as it returns to prepregnant state. Fundal height decreases one fingerbreadth (1 cm) per day.
Lochia
Discharge from uterus, consists of blood from vessels of placental site and debris.
Rubra (red) occurs from delivery to day 3.
Serosa (brownish pink) occurs from days 4 to 10.
Alba (white) occurs from days 10 to 14.
Breasts
Continue to secrete colostrum.
Become distended with milk on third day.
Engorgement occurs in 48 to 72 hours in non–breast-feeding mothers.
Breast-feeding will relieve engorgement.
Cervix
Involution occurs, after 1 week, muscle begins to regenerate.
Vagina
Distention decreases, although muscle tone is never completely restored to pre gravida state.
Ovarian function and menstruation
Menstrual flow resumes within 8 weeks in non–breast-feeding mothers, usually within 3 to 4 months in breast-feeding mothers.
Urinary Tract
May have initial urinary retention. diuresis begins in first 12 hours after delivery.
Gastrointestinal Tract
Mother is usually hungry after delivery.
Constipation, hemorrhoids common.

Postpartum Interventions

Administer Rho(D) immune globulin (RhoGAM) as prescribed within 72 hours postpartum to Rh-negative mother who has given birth to Rh-positive baby.
Monitor maternal vital signs, lochia, fundal height, perineal edema and discoloration, presence of signs of hemorrhage, breasts for engorgement, bowel status, intake, and output.
Facilitate bonding with newborn.
Client teaching.
Demonstrate newborn care skills as appropriate.
Demonstrate breast-feeding or formula-feeding techniques.

Assess/educate family/population/ community about health risks

Registered nurses (RNs) are integral members of the healthcare system, serving at the forefront of patient care and health promotion. Their role extends beyond bedside care to encompass the assessment and education of clients about health risks, with a particular focus on family, population, and community dynamics. This multifaceted approach enables RNs to address health issues holistically and promote well-being across diverse populations.

Assessment of Health Risks

Family-Centered Risk Assessment
Health risks often run in families, influenced by genetic, behavioral, and environmental factors. Registered nurses are trained to assess these risks by:

- Evaluating family health histories to identify hereditary conditions such as diabetes, heart disease, or cancer.
- Exploring lifestyle habits, such as diet, physical activity, and substance use, which may impact family members collectively.
- Identifying environmental risks, such as exposure to pollutants, that disproportionately affect certain families.

By gathering this information, nurses can provide tailored guidance to families, empowering them to mitigate risks and adopt healthier practices.

Population-Wide Risk Analysis
At the population level, health risks may emerge from common socio-economic, cultural, or environmental factors. Registered nurses utilize epidemiological data and community health assessments to:

- Identify trends in chronic diseases, such as the prevalence of hypertension in specific demographics.
- Monitor outbreaks of infectious diseases and their impact on populations.
- Assess disparities in access to healthcare services among underserved groups.

This population-focused approach enables nurses to recommend interventions that address widespread health challenges and promote equity in care delivery.

Community-Based Risk Evaluation

Communities play a vital role in shaping individual and collective health. Registered nurses assess community-specific health risks by:

- Conducting surveys and focus groups to understand local health concerns.
- Analyzing geographic factors, such as the prevalence of food deserts or high crime rates, which contribute to health disparities.
- Collaborating with local organizations and stakeholders to identify resources and gaps in healthcare infrastructure.

These insights allow nurses to design and implement community-specific health promotion programs, ensuring interventions are relevant and impactful.

Education on Health Risks

Empowering Families Through Knowledge

Education is a cornerstone of nursing practice, and RNs play a pivotal role in equipping families with the knowledge they need to make informed decisions. This includes:

- Teaching families about the implications of genetic predispositions and the importance of regular screenings.
- Providing guidance on nutrition, exercise, and stress management tailored to family structures and routines.
- Addressing misconceptions or cultural beliefs that may hinder the adoption of healthy behaviors.

By fostering open communication, nurses help families build resilience and self-efficacy in managing their health.

Population Health Education

Nurses also serve as educators at the population level, leveraging public health campaigns and community outreach to disseminate critical information. Their efforts may include:

- Hosting workshops on disease prevention, such as vaccination drives or anti-smoking initiatives.
- Developing educational materials, including pamphlets, videos, and digital content, to reach diverse audiences.
- Partnering with schools, workplaces, and religious institutions to promote health literacy.

These initiatives aim to raise awareness, reduce stigma, and encourage proactive health behaviors across populations.

Fostering Community Health Awareness

To address community-specific risks, registered nurses engage in targeted educational efforts that resonate with local populations. Examples include:

- Organizing health fairs that offer free screenings and consultations.
- Training community health workers to act as liaisons between healthcare providers and residents.
- Advocating policies that address systemic issues, such as housing quality or food security, that influence community health.

Through these actions, nurses help bridge gaps in knowledge and resources, contributing to sustainable improvements in community well-being.

The Impact of RNs on Health Risk Management

The dual role of assessment and education positions registered nurses as crucial agents of change in health risk management. Their efforts lead to:

- Early detection of health issues, reducing the burden of preventable diseases.
- Enhanced understanding of health risks among families, populations, and communities.
- Empowered individuals and groups capable of making healthier choices.

Moreover, the holistic approach adopted by RNs fosters a culture of prevention and equity, addressing not only immediate health concerns but also the social determinants of health.

Registered nurses are at the heart of efforts to assess and educate clients about health risks, with a focus on family, population, and community contexts. Their work not only improves individual and collective health outcomes but also lays the foundation for a more equitable and resilient healthcare system. By addressing challenges and embracing opportunities, RNs will continue to play a transformative role in shaping the future of health and well-being.

Assess clients' readiness to learn, learning preferences & barriers

Nurses play a pivotal role in client education, empowering individuals to manage their health and make informed decisions. However, effective teaching begins with understanding the client's readiness to learn, their preferred learning styles, and any barriers that may impede the process. This comprehensive assessment helps nurses tailor their approach to ensure optimal engagement and knowledge retention.

Assessing Readiness to Learn

Readiness to learn refers to the client's willingness and ability to receive, process, and apply new knowledge. Assessing readiness involves evaluating emotional, cognitive, and physical states, alongside situational factors that influence their openness to learning.

Emotional Readiness
Emotional readiness is often influenced by the client's psychological state. Nurses can:

- Observe the client's mood and demeanor to detect signs of anxiety, stress, or depression.

- Engage in open-ended conversations to gauge emotional stability and interest in learning.
- Ask direct questions about their feelings toward the topic, such as, "Do you feel comfortable discussing this?"

Cognitive Readiness

The capacity to understand and process information is critical to learning. Nurses should:

- Evaluate cognitive function through simple exercises, such as asking the client to summarize previous discussions.
- Consider any neurological conditions or medications that may impair comprehension.
- Assess language proficiency to ensure materials are presented in a way the client can understand.

Physical Readiness

Health issues and physical discomfort can influence the client's ability to focus. Nurses can:

- Check for signs of fatigue, pain, or other conditions that may interfere with attention.
- Ask if the client feels physically prepared to engage in learning activities.
- Plan educational sessions at times when the client is most alert and comfortable.

Understanding Learning Preferences

Acknowledging individual learning preferences enhances the efficiency of educational efforts. These preferences can be categorized into three primary styles: visual, auditory, and kinesthetic.

Visual Learners

Visual learners benefit from materials that engage their sight. Nurses can:

- Use charts, diagrams, and videos to illustrate concepts.
- Provide written instructions and pamphlets for independent review.
- Encourage notetaking during discussions.

Auditory Learners

Auditory learners absorb information best through listening and speaking. Nurses should:

- Explain concepts verbally and engage in discussions.
- Provide access to podcasts or audio recordings relevant to the topic.
- Encourage clients to repeat information aloud to reinforce learning.

Kinesthetic Learners

Kinesthetic learners prefer hands-on experiences and active participation. Nurses can:

- Incorporate demonstrations and practice sessions into educational activities.
- Use models or equipment for interactive learning.
- Encourage role-playing or simulations when discussing complex topics.

Identifying Barriers to Learning

Barriers to learning can hinder the client's ability to comprehend and apply information. Nurses must identify these challenges to adapt their teaching strategies effectively.

Physical Barriers

Physical obstacles such as illness, fatigue, or sensory impairments may impede learning. Strategies include:

- Addressing pain and discomfort before beginning education sessions.

- Providing adaptive tools, such as magnifiers or hearing aids, when necessary.
- Scheduling sessions when the client feels most physically capable.

Emotional Barriers

Fear, anxiety, or lack of motivation can negatively affect learning. Nurses should:

- Foster a supportive and nonjudgmental atmosphere to encourage openness.
- Break down complex topics into manageable segments to reduce overwhelm.
- Incorporate motivational techniques, such as setting attainable goals.

Cultural and Language Barriers

Clients from diverse backgrounds may face challenges related to language proficiency or cultural differences. Nurses can:

- Utilize interpreters or bilingual materials when necessary.
- Respect cultural beliefs and practices by aligning education with the client's values.
- Avoid medical jargon and simplify language to ensure clarity.

Environmental Barriers

Distractions in the learning environment can hinder focus. Nurses should:

- Choose quiet, well-lit spaces for education sessions.
- Minimize interruptions by setting clear boundaries during learning activities.
- Provide materials for review in case the client is unable to concentrate fully.

Strategies for Comprehensive Assessment

To effectively assess readiness, preferences, and barriers, nurses can employ the following strategies:

- Conduct structured interviews with open-ended questions to explore the client's perspective.
- Use standardized tools and questionnaires to evaluate cognitive and emotional states.
- Observe non-verbal cues such as body language and facial expressions during interactions.
- Collaborate with family members or caregivers to gain deeper insight into the client's needs.
- Document findings to ensure continuity of care and facilitate tailored teaching approaches.

Assessing clients' readiness to learn, understanding their learning preferences, and identifying barriers are essential steps in nursing practice. By addressing these aspects comprehensively, nurses can empower clients with the knowledge and skills necessary to manage their health effectively. This personalized approach not only enhances the quality of education but also fosters trust and collaboration between nurses and clients, leading to better health outcomes.

Plan and/or participate in community health education

Community health education is a cornerstone of public health, aimed at improving the overall well-being of populations by addressing their healthcare needs and promoting healthier lifestyles. Nurses play a critical role in planning and participating in such educational initiatives. Their unique position as healthcare providers and trusted community figures places them at the forefront of efforts to educate, engage, and empower communities.

Understanding the Role of Nurses in Community Health Education

Nurses serve as educators, advocates, and facilitators in community health education. Their responsibilities often involve identifying health concerns, tailoring interventions to meet community needs, and bridging gaps between healthcare systems and populations.

<u>Key Activities in Health Education</u>
- Identifying Community Needs: Nurses conduct assessments to pinpoint prevalent health issues within a community, such as chronic diseases, communicable illnesses, or lifestyle-related concerns.
- Developing Educational Content: Based on the identified needs, nurses create tailored health education materials that address specific concerns, ensuring clarity and accessibility for diverse audiences.
- Delivering Health Education: They conduct workshops, seminars, and health fairs, using interactive and engaging methods to deliver information effectively.
- Collaborating with Stakeholders: Nurses often work alongside other public health professionals, local organizations, schools, and policymakers to expand the reach and impact of their educational efforts.

Planning Community Health Education

The planning process is a collaborative effort requiring careful research, strategic thinking, and resource allocation. Nurses contribute by:

<u>Needs Assessments</u>
Conducting community surveys, focus groups, and health screenings helps nurses gather data about health disparities, risk factors, and priority areas. In communities with high rates of diabetes, nurses often provide education on nutrition, exercise, and blood sugar management.

<u>Setting Goals and Objectives</u>
After identifying needs, nurses establish clear, measurable objectives. For example, if the goal is to reduce smoking rates in a community, an objective might be to increase awareness about the health risks of smoking by hosting monthly educational events.

Program Design

Nurses design programs that integrate evidence-based practices and culturally sensitive approaches. These programs may include interactive sessions, visual aids, and multilingual resources to cater to diverse audiences.

Resource Allocation

Ensuring access to necessary resources—such as educational materials, funding, and venues—is crucial. Nurses often advocate for these resources and seek support from local health departments or nonprofit organizations.

Monitoring and Evaluation

Nurses measure the effectiveness of their programs by collecting feedback, analyzing outcomes, and adjusting improve future efforts. For instance, they might track attendance rates, knowledge retention, or changes in health behaviors.

Participating in Community Health Education

Beyond planning, nurses actively engage in the delivery and promotion of health education initiatives. Their participation often includes:

Building Trust and Relationships

Nurses leverage their trusted position in the community to establish rapport and encourage participation. Their empathetic communication style makes them approachable and relatable to diverse populations.

Facilitating Workshops and Seminars

Nurses lead interactive sessions on topics such as preventive care, disease management, mental health, and family planning. These workshops provide a platform for community members to ask questions and share their concerns.

Providing One-on-One Counseling

In addition to group education, nurses offer personalized guidance to individuals who need specific advice or support. For example, they might counsel patients on managing chronic conditions or adopting healthier habits.

Advocating for Health Equity

Nurses act as advocates by addressing social determinants of health and promoting equity in healthcare access. They use education as a tool to empower marginalized groups and reduce disparities.

Collaborating for Greater Impact

Participation often involves partnerships with schools, workplaces, religious organizations, and community centers. Nurses work collaboratively to expand the scope and impact of their educational endeavors.

Challenges and Solutions

Despite their critical role, nurses face challenges in community health education, such as limited funding, cultural barriers, and resistance to change. Addressing these issues requires innovation and collaboration.

Overcoming Cultural Barriers

By fostering cultural competency and inclusiveness, nurses ensure their programs resonate with diverse populations. This might involve incorporating community traditions, beliefs, and values into educational content.

Securing Funding and Resources

Seeking financial support and collaborating with local organizations can provide nurses with the resources needed to maintain educational initiatives.

Encouraging Behavioral Change

Implementing motivational interviewing techniques and providing ongoing support can help nurses inspire individuals to adopt healthier habits.

The Role of Nurses in Community Health Education

The efforts of nurses in planning and participating in community health education yield tangible benefits. They empower individuals with the knowledge and skills to make informed decisions about their health, foster community resilience, and contribute to the reduction of healthcare disparities.

Improved Public Health Outcomes
Educational initiatives led by nurses often result in increased vaccination rates, reduced prevalence of chronic diseases, and improved overall health literacy.

Strengthened Community Relationships
Through their direct involvement, nurses build trust and foster lasting relationships that enhance collaboration between communities and healthcare systems.

Promotion of Preventive Care
Nurses' focus on education equips people to adopt preventive measures, reducing the burden on healthcare facilities and improving quality of life.

Nurses play an indispensable role in community health education, blending their clinical expertise with compassionate engagement to address the needs of diverse populations. By planning and participating in educational initiatives, they not only improve health outcomes but also inspire communities to take charge of their well-being. Their work exemplifies the power of knowledge as a tool for empowerment and transformation.

Educate client about preventative care and health maintenance

Methods of Education

Registered nurses employ a variety of strategies to effectively educate clients about preventative care and health maintenance:

Individualized Consultations

RNs often provide personalized education during one-on-one consultations. These sessions allow nurses to assess clients' unique needs, health risks, and lifestyle factors. By tailoring recommendations to everyone, nurses ensure that the advice is relevant and actionable.

Group Health Education Sessions

In settings such as clinics or community centers, RNs conduct group sessions on topics like nutrition, exercise, stress management, and disease prevention. These forums encourage peer interaction and foster a supportive learning environment.

Use of Visual and Written Materials

To make health information accessible, RNs utilize brochures, infographics, videos, and pamphlets. These materials simplify complex medical concepts and serve as reference tools that clients can revisit after consultations.

Technology-Based Education

With the rise of telehealth and digital resources, RNs leverage technology to educate clients remotely. Online webinars, apps, and virtual consultations enable nurses to reach a broader audience and provide continuous support.

Demonstrations and Practical Guidance

For topics such as proper hygiene, administering medications, or self-check techniques, RNs often use demonstrations to ensure clients understand and can reliably implement recommendations.

Key Topics Covered

Registered nurses focus on several key areas when educating clients about preventative care and health maintenance:

Importance of Regular Screenings and Check-Ups

RNs emphasize the significance of regular health screenings, such as blood pressure monitoring, cancer screenings, and cholesterol checks. Early detection can lead to timely interventions and improved outcomes.

Vaccination Education

Nurses educate clients about the benefits of vaccines, including seasonal flu shots, childhood immunizations, and vaccines for conditions like COVID-19 or HPV. They address concerns and ensure clients understand the role vaccinations play in preventing disease.

Healthy Lifestyle Choices

Registered nurses advocate for balanced diets, regular physical activity, proper sleep patterns, and stress management techniques. These foundational habits contribute to long-term health maintenance.

Chronic Disease Prevention

RNs provide actionable advice on preventing chronic illnesses such as diabetes, heart disease, and obesity. This includes tips on nutrition, exercise, and avoiding tobacco and excessive alcohol consumption.

Mental Health Awareness

Recognizing the importance of mental well-being, nurses educate clients on strategies to manage stress, seek counseling, and maintain emotional balance.

Communication Techniques

Effective communication is essential for registered nurses when conveying health information. They employ the following techniques to ensure clarity and engagement:

- Active Listening: Nurses listen attentively to clients' questions and concerns, creating a safe space for open dialogue.

- Empathy: By showing understanding and compassion, RNs build trust and encourage clients to share their experiences.
- Simplified Language: Nurses avoid medical jargon, using straightforward language to ensure clients grasp the key points.
- Interactive Approach: RNs promote a two-way conversation, encouraging questions and feedback to tailor their guidance effectively.

Challenges and Solutions

Registered nurses may encounter challenges in educating clients, such as resistance to change, cultural barriers, or misinformation. Strategies to overcome these barriers include:

- Cultural Sensitivity: Understanding and respecting cultural norms and beliefs to ensure recommendations align with clients' values.
- Addressing Misinformation: Providing evidence-based information to counter myths and misconceptions about health practices.
- Motivational Techniques: Using positive reinforcement and goal setting to inspire clients to adopt healthier behaviors.

The Impact of RN-Led Education

Registered nurses' educational efforts result in numerous benefits, including:

- Improved patient knowledge and confidence in managing their health.
- Reduced incidence of preventable diseases and hospitalizations.
- Enhanced doctor-patient collaboration, as educated clients are more likely to engage in their care plans.
- A healthier community, contributing to overall public health improvements.

Registered nurses are instrumental in guiding clients toward preventative care and health maintenance. Through personalized education, effective communication, and evidence-based recommendations, they empower individuals to make informed decisions about their health. Their dedication not only improves individual well-being but also strengthens the collective health of communities.

Provide resources to minimize communication barriers

Communication is a cornerstone of effective healthcare delivery. Nurses, as primary caregivers, play an essential role in fostering collaboration, understanding, and trust among patients, families, and healthcare teams. Effective communication is vital, yet barriers such as language differences, cultural misunderstandings, or cognitive impairments can hinder the exchange of information. To address these challenges, nurses utilize a range of strategies and resources to minimize communication barriers.

Understanding Communication Barriers

Communication barriers in healthcare can stem from diverse sources, including:

- Language Differences: Patients who speak different languages or have limited proficiency in the primary language of healthcare providers may struggle to convey their needs or understand medical advice.
- Cultural Factors: Diverse cultural norms, values, and expectations can shape the way individuals communicate and interpret information.
- Physical or Sensory Impairments: Hearing loss, visual impairments, or speech difficulties may impede patients' ability to understand or articulate their concerns.
- Cognitive Challenges: Conditions such as dementia, stroke, or developmental disorders can affect a patient's ability to comprehend or express their thoughts.
- Emotional Barriers: Anxiety, stress, or fear may cause patients to avoid or misinterpret communication with healthcare providers.

Nurses as Facilitators of Effective Communication

To ensure every patient receives appropriate care, nurses employ a variety of strategies and resources to overcome communication barriers.

Providing Language Support

Language differences are among the most common communication barriers. Nurses address this by:

- Using Professional Interpreters: Collaborating with interpreters ensures accurate translation of medical information and patient concerns.
- Accessing Translation Tools: Leveraging technology such as translation apps or software to facilitate real-time communication.
- Offering Multilingual Educational Materials: Providing pamphlets, brochures, or videos in multiple languages tailored to patients' needs.
- Learning Basic Phrases: Acquiring foundational knowledge of common phrases in frequently spoken languages to establish rapport and ease communication.

Adopting Culturally Competent Practices

Cultural awareness enhances the nurse-patient relationship and minimizes misunderstandings. Strategies include:

- Cultural Sensitivity Training: Participating in training programs to understand diverse cultural beliefs and practices.
- Respecting Cultural Preferences: Adapting communication styles to align with patients' cultural norms, such as making eye contact or the choice of formal versus informal language.
- Utilizing Cultural Brokers: Working with individuals who understand both healthcare systems and specific cultural contexts to bridge gaps.

Supporting Patients with Physical or Sensory Impairments

Nurses tailor communication strategies to patients with physical challenges, such as:

- Encouraging Non-Verbal Communication: Utilizing gestures, visual aids, or written notes for patients with speech or hearing impairments.
- Providing Assistive Devices: Offering hearing aids, text-to-speech software, or Braille materials to support patients' needs.
- Ensuring Accessible Environments: Creating spaces where patients can comfortably engage in communication, free from excessive noise or distractions.

Managing Cognitive and Emotional Barriers

Patients with cognitive challenges or heightened emotions require empathetic and clear communication. Nurses employ:

- Simplifying Information: Breaking down complex medical concepts into manageable pieces with plain language.
- Using Visual Narratives: Explaining procedures or treatments through diagrams, pictures, or videos.
- Practicing Active Listening: Paying close attention to patients' concerns and responding thoughtfully to ensure they feel heard and understood.
- Building Trust: Establishing a compassionate environment where patients feel comfortable expressing their fears or uncertainties.

Collaborative Efforts in Healthcare Teams

Effective communication extends beyond the individual nurse. Healthcare teams work collaboratively with:

- Standardize Communication Protocols: Developing consistent practices such as the use of SBAR (Situation, Background, Assessment, Recommendation) to relay information.
- Incorporate Patient Advocates: Engaging advocates who specialize in navigating healthcare systems and providing personalized support.
- Conduct Regular Evaluations: Assessing the effectiveness of communication strategies and adapting them based on patient feedback.

The Role of Education and Continuous Improvement

Healthcare systems thrive on continuous development. Nurses contribute by:

- Participating in Continuing Education: Gaining knowledge about emerging communication tools and strategies.
- Promoting Patient Education: Empowering patients with the knowledge to independently advocate for their needs.
- Sharing Best Practices: Collaborating with peers to exchange successful communication techniques.

Nurses are indispensable in breaking down communication barriers in healthcare. Through their expertise, empathy, and resourcefulness, they ensure that every patient, regardless of language, culture, or physical ability, receives the care and understanding they deserve. By fostering an environment of inclusivity and collaboration, nurses not only enhance patient outcomes but also contribute to a healthcare system rooted in equity and compassion.

Perform targeted screening assessments

Targeted screening assessments play an essential role in clinical care, enabling nurses to identify specific health risks and conditions efficiently and effectively. These focused evaluations ensure that patients receive timely interventions tailored to their needs. This document explores the methods, procedures, and considerations involved when nurses perform targeted screening assessments.

The Purpose of Targeted Screening Assessments

Screening assessments aim to identify health issues in specific populations or individuals based on their medical history, risk factors, or presenting symptoms. Unlike comprehensive assessments, targeted screenings focus on areas, such as cardiovascular health, diabetes risk, mental health, or infectious diseases.

The purpose includes:

- Early Detection: Identifying conditions in their early stages to prevent complications.
- Risk Assessment: Evaluating potential health risks based on demographics or lifestyle factors.
- Guiding Treatment: Providing actionable insights for healthcare interventions.

Key Steps in Performing Targeted Screening Assessments

Nurses follow systematic steps to ensure these evaluations are accurate and meaningful.

Pre-Assessment Preparation

Before conducting a screening, nurses gather relevant information to understand the context of the assessment:

- Review the patient's medical history, including family history and previous screenings.
- Understand the patient's lifestyle factors, such as diet, exercise, and habits like smoking or alcohol use.
- Identify population-specific risks (e.g., age-related concerns, occupational hazards).
- Educate the patient about the purpose and importance of the screening to ease any apprehension.

Conducting the Screening

The actual screening process involves targeted questioning, examinations, and tests:

- History Taking: Nurses ask focused questions based on the target area, such as symptoms, behaviors, or environmental exposures.
- Physical Examination: Observations or measurements relevant to the screening, such as blood pressure, weight, or skin checks.
- Diagnostic Tests: Administer specific tests such as glucose levels for diabetes or cholesterol panels for heart disease.

Utilizing Screening Tools

Nurses use specialized tools and guidelines to enhance accuracy:

- Standardized Questionnaires: Tools like PHQ-9 for depression or CAGE for substance abuse.
- Electronic Health Records (EHR): Technology helps streamline data collection, tracking, and analysis.
- Clinical Guidelines: Protocols and recommendations from organizations like the CDC or WHO.

Interpreting Results

After collecting data, results are analyzed to determine the presence or likelihood of conditions. Nurses:

- Compare findings with established norms or thresholds.
- Identify red flags requiring further investigation or immediate intervention.

Communicating Findings

Once results are interpreted, nurses discuss them with patients, providing clarity and guidance:

- Ensure that patients understand their health status.

- Offer recommendations for lifestyle adjustments or follow-up actions.

Challenges Faced During Targeted Screening

While targeted screening is invaluable, nurses may encounter challenges:

- Patient Reluctance: Some individuals may be hesitant to participate due to fear of results or invasive procedures.
- Resource Limitations: Access to advanced tools or tests may be restricted in certain settings.
- Time Constraints: Busy clinical environments can limit the depth of assessments.

Specialized Areas of Screening

Targeted screening can focus on a wide range of health issues:

Cardiovascular Screenings

Nurses assess risks for heart disease through blood pressure checks, cholesterol testing, and lifestyle evaluations.

Diabetes Screenings

Blood glucose levels, BMI, and family history are examined to identify individuals at risk.

Mental Health Assessments

Tools like PHQ-9 or GAD-7 help nurses evaluate depression, anxiety, or other psychological conditions.

Infectious Disease Screening

Screening for STIs, tuberculosis, or COVID-19 involves focused tests and contact tracing.

The Role of Education and Advocacy

Nurses play a crucial role in educating patients about the importance of screenings. Advocacy efforts focus on:

- Promoting awareness of health risks and benefits of early detection.
- Encouraging underserved populations to seek screenings.
- Reducing stigma surrounding certain conditions like mental health or STIs.

Targeted screening assessments are a cornerstone of modern nursing practice, allowing for effective risk identification and early intervention. Through preparation, precise tools, and compassionate communication, nurses help empower patients to take charge of their health. Despite challenges, advancements in technology and increased awareness continue to improve the efficacy of these critical evaluations.

Educate client about prevention & treatment of high-risk health behaviors

High-risk health behaviors, such as smoking, excessive alcohol consumption, drug abuse, unhealthy eating habits, and physical inactivity, pose significant threats to individuals' well-being and can lead to chronic illnesses, mental health challenges, and reduced quality of life. Educating clients on the prevention and treatment of these behaviors is critical in fostering healthier communities. This guide explores strategies to engage clients in understanding, preventing, and addressing high-risk health behaviors.

Understanding High-Risk Health Behaviors
Defining High-Risk Behaviors
High-risk health behaviors refer to actions or habits that increase the likelihood of negative health outcomes. These behaviors can range from substance abuse and unprotected sexual activity to neglecting mental health and avoiding

preventive medical care. Understanding these behaviors is the first step in addressing them.

The Impact of High-Risk Behaviors

The consequences of high-risk behaviors often extend beyond the individual. Families, communities, and health systems bear the burden of these behaviors through increased healthcare costs, emotional distress, and lost productivity. For instance:

- Smoking is a leading cause of preventable diseases like lung cancer, heart disease, and stroke.
- Excessive alcohol consumption contributes to liver diseases, accidents, and violence.
- Drug abuse can lead to addiction, mental health disorders, and social instability.

Providing clients with knowledge about these impacts empowers them to make informed decisions about their health.

Prevention Strategies

Building Awareness

Creating awareness about the risks associated with certain behaviors is foundational. Educational efforts should focus on:

- Sharing evidence-based information about the short- and long-term consequences of high-risk behaviors.
- Using relatable case studies and real-life examples to make the information personal and impactful.
- Tailoring messages to the age, cultural background, and educational level of the client.

Encouraging Healthy Lifestyle Choices

Encouraging clients to adopt healthier habits can significantly reduce the likelihood of engaging in high-risk behaviors. Focus on:

- Promoting balanced diets, adequate hydration, and regular physical activity.
- Highlighting the importance of sleep and stress management techniques.
- Encouraging participation in community support groups or wellness programs.

Empowering Through Education

Education is a powerful tool for prevention. Host workshops, webinars, or one-on-one sessions to educate clients about:

- Recognizing triggers and risk factors associated with high-risk behaviors.
- Developing coping mechanisms to deal with stress, peer pressure, and emotional challenges.
- Understanding health screenings and the importance of early intervention.

Strengthening Protective Factors

Protective factors can shield individuals from engaging in harmful behaviors. Enhance these by:

- Promoting strong family and social connections.
- Encouraging participation in structured activities, such as sports or volunteer work.
- Building skills in decision-making, communication, and problem-solving.

Treatment Approaches

Open Communication

Creating an environment of trust and openness is essential for addressing high-risk behaviors. Effective communication involves:

- Listening without judgment to understand the client's perspective.
- Providing a safe space for clients to express their concerns and challenges.

- Using motivational interviewing techniques to inspire change.

<u>Access to Professional Support</u>

Clients often need professional guidance to overcome high-risk behaviors. Recommend resources such as:

- Therapists or counselors specializing in addiction, mental health, or behavioral health.
- Medical professionals for screenings, treatments, and medication management.
- Support groups like Alcoholics Anonymous or Narcotics Anonymous.

<u>Behavioral Therapy and Counseling</u>

Behavioral interventions can help clients identify and modify their actions. Popular methods include:

- Cognitive Behavioral Therapy (CBT) to address underlying thoughts and emotional patterns.
- Dialectical Behavior Therapy (DBT) for emotional regulation and interpersonal effectiveness.
- Family therapy to address relational dynamics and support systems.

<u>Creating a Personalized Action Plan</u>

Every client is unique, and their treatment should reflect their individual needs. Develop an action plan that includes:

- Setting achievable goals and milestones.
- Identifying potential barriers and strategies to overcome them.
- Tracking progress and celebrating successes, no matter how small.

Leveraging Technology and Media

<u>Digital Tools</u>

Technology can assist in educating and supporting clients. Encourage the use of:

- Mobile apps for tracking health habits and goals.
- Online counseling sessions for convenient access to support.
- Social media campaigns to spread awareness and share success stories.

Multimedia Resources
Visual and audio materials can enhance the learning experience. Use:

- Infographics and videos, to explain complex concepts simply.
- Podcasts and webinars featuring experts in health and wellness.
- Interactive tools like quizzes and surveys to engage clients.

Overcoming Barriers

Cultural Sensitivity
Clients may come from diverse backgrounds with unique beliefs and values. Tailor your approach by:

- Respecting cultural traditions and practices.
- Using language and examples that resonate with the client's experiences.
- Involving community leaders or influencers to foster trust.

Addressing Stigma
Shame and stigma often prevent individuals from seeking help. Combat this by:

- Normalizing discussions around mental health and addiction.
- Highlighting success stories of individuals who overcame high-risk behaviors.
- Creating anonymous channels for clients to seek information or assistance.

Ensuring Accessibility
Clients should have easy access to resources and support. Achieve this by:

- Offering services at convenient locations or online.
- Providing materials in multiple languages and formats.
- Ensuring affordability through sliding scale fees or free programs.

Educating clients about the prevention and treatment of high-risk health behaviors is not just about providing information; it is about fostering trust, empowerment, and collaboration. By taking a holistic and client-centered approach, health professionals can guide individuals toward healthier choices and create ripple effects that benefit families, communities, and society at large. Together, we can build a future where everyone has the tools and support needed to lead fulfilling and healthy lives.

Assess client ability to manage care in-home and plan care accordingly

Registered nurses (RNs) expertise enables them to conduct thorough assessments and develop tailored care plans that address the unique needs of each client to manage their care in the home environment. Here's an overview of the process:

Assessing Client Ability to Manage Care in a Home Environment

Initial Evaluation
Registered nurses begin by conducting an initial evaluation. This includes:

- Health status assessment: Reviewing medical history, current diagnoses, medications, and physical limitations.
- Cognitive and psychological evaluation: Determining the client's mental capacity to understand and follow care instructions, as well as their emotional readiness for self-management.
- Functional abilities: Observing the client's mobility, dexterity, and ability to perform daily activities such as bathing, eating, and taking medications.

Home Environment Assessment

RNs examine the client's home setting to identify potential barriers or facilitators to effective care. This involves:

- Safety assessment: Checking for fall hazards, accessibility of necessary spaces (like bathrooms and kitchens), and the presence of supportive equipment such as handrails.
- Support system evaluation: Assessing the availability of caregivers or family members who can assist with daily tasks.
- Availability of resources: Ensuring access to medical supplies, medications, and transportation for follow-up care or emergencies.

Client Perspective and Preferences

Registered nurses incorporate the client's preferences by:

- Discussing their goals, concerns, and expectations regarding home care.
- Considering cultural, linguistic, and lifestyle factors that may impact care decisions.

Planning Care Accordingly

Developing a Personalized Care Plan

Based on the assessment, RNs craft a care plan that aligns with the client's abilities and needs. Key components include:

- Setting achievable goals: Outlining short-term and long-term objectives for the client's health and well-being.
- Intervention strategies: Recommending specific actions such as medication schedules, physical therapy routines, or dietary changes.
- Resource allocation: Securing necessary equipment, services, and referrals to specialists or community programs.

Education and Skill Building

RNs empower clients and caregivers by providing education and training. This may include:

- Teaching clients how to administer medications safely.
- Demonstrating techniques for wound care, mobility exercises, or equipment use.
- Providing written guidelines or videos for reference.

Collaboration and Follow-Up

Collaboration is essential for effective care. Registered nurses:

- Work closely with physicians, therapists, and social workers to ensure cohesive care delivery.
- Schedule regular follow-up visits to monitor progress, address concerns, and adjust the care plan, as necessary.
- Encourage open communication with clients and their families to identify challenges early.

Assessing a client's ability to manage care in a home environment requires a holistic approach that considers physical, cognitive, emotional, and logistical factors. By developing a personalized care plan and fostering collaboration, registered nurses help clients achieve independence and improve their quality of life while ensuring their safety and well-being

Perform comprehensive health assessments

One of their key responsibilities of the registered nurse is to perform comprehensive health assessments. These assessments enable them to gather pertinent information about a patient's physical, psychological, and social health, laying the groundwork for diagnosing conditions, planning care, and ensuring effective patient outcomes.

Steps in a Comprehensive Health Assessment

A comprehensive health assessment is a systematic and thorough process that involves multiple steps:

<u>Preparing for the Assessment</u>
Before performing the assessment, RNs ensure they have all the necessary tools and information:

- Review the patient's medical history, including past illnesses, surgeries, family history, and current medications.
- Prepare the environment to ensure privacy, comfort, and proper lighting.
- Establish rapport with the patient to foster trust and open communication.

<u>Conducting the Patient Interview</u>
The interview includes collecting subjective data directly from the patient:

- Chief Complaint: The primary reason for the patient's visit.
- History of Present Illness (HPI): Details about the onset, duration, severity, and nature of current symptoms.
- Medical and Family History: Information on past health issues, genetic predispositions, and family illnesses.
- Lifestyle and Social History: Factors such as diet, exercise, substance use, occupation, and living arrangements.

Active listening and empathetic communication are essential during this stage.

Performing the Physical Examination

The physical examination provides objective data and involves a head-to-toe approach:

- Inspection: Observing the patient's appearance, posture, skin condition, and overall demeanor.
- Auscultation: Using a stethoscope to listen to heart, lung, and bowel sounds.
- Palpation: Feeling for abnormalities such as lumps, swelling, or tenderness.
- Percussion: Tapping on body areas to detect differences in sound that may indicate underlying issues.
- Vital Signs: Measuring blood pressure, heart rate, respiratory rate, temperature, and oxygen saturation.

Assessing Psychosocial and Emotional Health

Comprehensive health assessments also consider the patient's mental health and emotional well-being:

- Screening for symptoms of anxiety, depression, or other psychological conditions.
- Evaluating coping mechanisms, support systems, and stress levels.

This step is especially important for understanding how a patient's mental health may impact their physical health.

Documenting and Analyzing Findings

Once the assessment is complete, RNs document their findings accurately and comprehensively:

- Record both subjective and objective data.
- Summarize key findings and identify potential health issues.

- Collaborate with other healthcare professionals if further evaluation or interventions are needed.

Proper documentation ensures continuity of care and serves as a vital reference for the healthcare team.

The Importance of Comprehensive Health Assessments

Comprehensive health assessments are invaluable for several reasons:

- They provide a holistic view of the patient's health, considering physical, mental, and social factors.
- They help identify underlying conditions that may not be immediately apparent.
- They allow for early detection of potential health risks, enabling timely interventions.
- They enhance patient-centered care by addressing individual needs and preferences.

The ability of registered nurses to perform comprehensive health assessments is a cornerstone of quality healthcare. By systematically gathering and analyzing information about their patients, RNs ensure that care plans are tailored, effective, and responsive to everyone's unique circumstances. This not only improves health outcomes but also fosters trust and collaboration between patients and healthcare providers.

MODULE 4

PSYCHOSOCIAL INTEGRITY NURSING TASK

Assess client for abuse or neglect and report, intervene, and/or escalate

Registered nurses play a crucial role in identifying and addressing abuse or neglect. As front-line healthcare providers, they are often among the first to recognize the signs of maltreatment in vulnerable populations. Their responsibilities include assessing clients for abuse or neglect, reporting suspicions to appropriate authorities, intervening to ensure the safety of the client, and escalating the matter when necessary.

Assessment of Clients for Abuse or Neglect

The assessment process is a delicate, systematic approach that involves observation, communication, and documentation. Registered nurses rely on their clinical expertise, compassion, and established guidelines to identify signs of abuse or neglect.

Key Steps in Assessment
- Observation: Nurses observe physical signs such as bruises, burns, fractures, malnutrition, poor hygiene, or untreated medical conditions. Behavioral indicators, including withdrawal, fearfulness, depression, or anxiety, are also assessed.
- Effective Communication: Nurses establish a rapport with the client to encourage them to speak openly. They ask non-judgmental and open-ended questions in a private setting to explore concerns.
- Review of History: A thorough medical and social history is reviewed to identify inconsistencies or patterns indicative of abuse or neglect.
- Use of Screening Tools: When available, standardized abuse screening tools are employed to guide the assessment process.

Reporting Suspected Abuse or Neglect

Registered nurses are mandated reporters in many jurisdictions, meaning they are legally obligated to report any reasonable suspicion of abuse or neglect.

Steps for Reporting
- Documentation: Detailed and accurate records of the client's condition, statements, and the nurse's observations are maintained.
- Following Institutional Protocols: Nurses adhere to their workplace policies and procedures for reporting abuse or neglect.
- Notifying Authorities: Reports are made to child protective services, adult protective services, or law enforcement agencies, depending on the situation and legal requirements.

Intervention

Intervention focuses on ensuring the immediate safety and well-being of the client. Nurses take appropriate actions based on their assessment findings.

Key Interventions
- Ensuring Safety: If the client is in immediate danger, nurses take steps to remove them from the unsafe environment, if possible, or notify authorities.
- Providing Emotional Support: Nurses offer reassurance, empathy, and a non-judgmental attitude to help the client feel secure and supported.
- Coordinating Care: Nurses collaborate with social workers, counselors, and other interdisciplinary team members to provide comprehensive care to the client.

Escalation

When abuse or neglect is suspected but not adequately addressed, escalation becomes necessary. This ensures that the matter receives appropriate attention and action.

Escalation Process

- Notifying Supervisors: Nurses inform their immediate supervisors or managers to seek guidance and support.
- Involving Senior Management: If needed, the issue is brought to the attention of senior leaders within the organization.
- Engaging External Authorities: When internal escalation does not resolve the situation, external agencies or regulatory bodies are contacted.

The assessment and management of abuse or neglect are essential components of a registered nurse's duty to protect their clients. Through meticulous assessment, prompt reporting, compassionate intervention, and appropriate escalation, nurses uphold their commitment to client safety and advocacy. By adhering to established protocols and leveraging interdisciplinary teamwork, they play a pivotal role in addressing abuse and neglect effectively.

Incorporate behavioral management techniques when caring for a client

Registered nurses play a critical role in applying behavioral management techniques to provide holistic and compassionate care for their clients. These techniques are essential for addressing emotional, psychological, and behavioral challenges, ensuring improved outcomes, and fostering a supportive environment.

Understanding Behavioral Management

Behavioral management involves strategies designed to influence and guide a client's actions and responses in a positive way. The goal is to promote healthier behaviors while reducing harmful or disruptive patterns. For registered nurses, integrating these techniques requires sensitivity, consistency, and a deep understanding of the client's unique needs.

Key Behavioral Management Techniques

1. Building Trust and Rapport

Nurses establish a foundation of trust by fostering open communication, showing empathy, and creating a safe environment. Trust allows clients to feel valued and supported, which is essential for effective behavioral management.

2. Positive Reinforcement

By acknowledging and rewarding desired behaviors, nurses encourage clients to repeat those actions. This can include verbal praise, recognition, or tangible incentives, all tailored to the client's preferences and needs.

3. Setting Clear Expectations

Nurses help clients by clearly defining acceptable behaviors and establishing realistic goals. Communicating these boundaries ensures that clients understand what is required of them, reducing confusion and conflict.

4. Utilizing De-escalation Techniques

In situations where a client displays distress or agitation, de-escalation techniques are crucial. Nurses use calming language, maintain a composed demeanor, and employ non-threatening body language to reduce tension and prevent escalation.

5. Teaching Coping Strategies

Nurses empower clients by teaching techniques to manage stress, anxiety, and other emotional challenges. These strategies may include mindfulness exercises, breathing techniques, or structured problem-solving approaches.

6. Monitoring Behavioral Triggers

Nurses identify and document specific triggers that may lead to negative behaviors. This awareness allows for proactive intervention and the development of personalized care plans that minimize exposure to these triggers.

7. Encouraging Self-Reflection

Through guided conversations and therapeutic activities, nurses encourage clients to reflect on their actions and emotions. This self-awareness helps clients recognize patterns and take ownership of their behavior.

Integrating Behavioral Management into Care Plans

Behavioral management techniques are most effective when integrated into a client's broader care plan. Nurses collaborate with interdisciplinary teams, including psychologists, counselors, and social workers, to create comprehensive strategies tailored to the client's needs. Documentation of progress and regular evaluation ensure that these interventions remain relevant and effective.

Challenges in Behavioral Management

While behavioral management techniques can be transformative, they also present challenges. Nurses must navigate resistance from clients, maintain consistency despite workload pressures, and adapt approaches to diverse cultural and individual backgrounds. Continuous training and reflective practice are essential to overcoming these obstacles.

Incorporating behavioral management techniques is a vital aspect of nursing care, enabling registered nurses to address the complex emotional and behavioral needs of their clients. By applying strategies such as positive reinforcement, de-escalation, and coping skills training, nurses help foster resilience, improve outcomes, and uphold their commitment to compassionate and effective care.

Assess client for substance abuse and/or toxicities and intervene as needed

Substance abuse and toxicities represent significant challenges in healthcare, requiring precise assessment and timely intervention. Registered nurses play a pivotal role in addressing these issues by employing clinical acumen, therapeutic communication, and evidence-based practices. This document outlines the steps nurses take to assess clients for substance abuse and toxicities and provides an overview of intervention strategies tailored to individual needs.

Assessment of Substance Abuse and Toxicities

<u>Initial Client Interaction</u>
During initial encounters, registered nurses create a safe and nonjudgmental environment to encourage open communication. This begins with a detailed history, including inquiries about substance use patterns, frequency, duration, and the type of substances involved. Nurses also assess psychosocial factors such as stressors, family dynamics, and lifestyle influences that may contribute to substance dependency.

<u>Clinical Signs and Symptoms</u>
Registered nurses are trained to identify physical and behavioral indicators of substance abuse and toxicities. Key signs include:

- Disorientation, confusion, or altered mental status
- Physical symptoms like tremors, dilated or constricted pupils, respiratory distress
- Behavioral changes such as heightened aggression, anxiety, or withdrawal
- Presence of drug paraphernalia or self-reported substance use

<u>Screening Tools</u>
To aid in assessment, nurses utilize validated screening tools such as:

- CAGE Questionnaire for alcohol dependency
- SBIRT (Screening, Brief Intervention, and Referral to Treatment) for various substances
- Clinical laboratory tests, including blood toxicology screens, urine tests, and liver function panels

These tools provide critical insights into the severity of substance abuse and guide further interventions.

Recognizing Withdrawal Symptoms

Nurses are trained to detect withdrawal symptoms associated with specific substances. Common withdrawal presentations include:

- Alcohol withdrawal: tremors, sweating, nausea, seizures
- Opioid withdrawal: agitation, muscle pain, insomnia, gastrointestinal distress
- Stimulant withdrawal: fatigue, depression, vivid dreams

Early recognition is vital to prevent complications such as delirium tremens or overdoses.

Intervention Strategies

Immediate Stabilization

For clients facing acute toxicities or withdrawal symptoms, nurses prioritize stabilization through:

- Monitoring vital signs and ensuring airway patency
- Administering prescribed medications, such as benzodiazepines for alcohol withdrawal or naloxone for opioid overdose
- Providing hydration and electrolyte balance

Therapeutic Communication

Registered nurses use empathetic and motivational interviewing techniques to build rapport. This approach encourages clients to discuss their substance use openly and explore their readiness for change. Nurses emphasize the importance of seeking help without fear of judgment.

Collaborative Care

Effective intervention requires collaboration with interdisciplinary teams, including physicians, addiction specialists, and mental health counselors. Nurses coordinate care plans, ensuring that clients receive comprehensive support tailored to their physical and emotional needs.

Referral and Follow-Up

Beyond immediate care, nurses connect clients with outpatient programs, inpatient rehabilitation facilities, or support groups like Alcoholics Anonymous and Narcotics Anonymous. Follow-up visits are scheduled to monitor progress, adjust care plans, and provide encouragement.

Education and Coping Skills

Nurses educate clients and their families about the risks of continued substance use and the benefits of recovery. They teach coping mechanisms to manage cravings and stress, such as mindfulness, exercise, and structured routines.

Registered nurses are frontline caregivers in the battle against substance abuse and toxicities. Their expertise in assessment, intervention, and education empowers clients to navigate the complexities of recovery. By fostering trust, implementing evidence-based strategies, and collaborating with interdisciplinary teams, nurses uphold their commitment to compassionate and effective care that transforms lives.

Assess client's ability to cope with life changes and provide support

The nurses' role in assessing a client's ability to cope with life changes and providing appropriate support. whether they are related to health, career, family, or emotional well-being can significantly impact a person's physical and psychological state. It is essential for RNs to evaluate these impacts and ensure a holistic approach to care that addresses both immediate and long-term needs.

This document explores the methods RNs use to assess coping abilities and the strategies they employ to provide support.

Assessing the Client's Ability to Cope

<u>Building Trust and Establishing Rapport</u>
The first step in assessing a client's coping ability is to establish a trusting relationship. This involves active listening, empathy, and creating a safe, non-judgmental space where clients feel comfortable discussing their concerns. By fostering open communication, the RN gains deeper insights into the client's emotional state and personal experiences.

<u>Conducting a Comprehensive Patient History</u>
RNs collect detailed information about a client's personal, medical, and psychosocial background. Questions may include:

- Have you experienced similar changes or stressors in the past? How did you cope?
- What support systems do you rely on (e.g., family, friends, community resources)?
- Are there specific fears or concerns you have about this life change?

This history provides context and a framework for understanding the client's current challenges.

<u>Observing Behavioral and Emotional Responses</u>
RNs closely observe the client's verbal and non-verbal cues during interactions. Indicators such as withdrawal, irritability, tearfulness, or reluctance to engage may signal difficulties in coping. Behavioral patterns like changes in sleep, appetite, or personal hygiene are also important clues.

<u>Utilizing Assessment Tools</u>
Standardized tools can assist in evaluating a client's coping mechanisms. Examples include:

- Stress and Coping Self-Assessment Scales: These measure perceived stress levels, and the methods clients use to cope.
- Depression and Anxiety Inventories: Tools like the Beck Depression Inventory can identify underlying emotional challenges that may hinder coping.
- Quality-of-Life Questionnaires: These assess how life change is affecting the client's overall well-being.

Identifying Risk Factors

RNs assess risk factors that might exacerbate a client's difficulty in coping, such as:

- History of mental health disorders
- Limited social support network
- Chronic health conditions
- Financial or housing instability

Early identification of these risks can guide the RN in tailoring interventions.

Providing Support for the Client

Developing a Care Plan

Based on the assessment, the RN collaborates with the client to create a personalized care plan. This plan prioritizes the client's goals and incorporates strategies to manage the stress associated with change.

Emotional Support and Counseling

RNs provide emotional support by validating the client's feelings and offering reassurance. They use therapeutic communication techniques, such as reflective listening and paraphrasing, to help clients process their emotions. If needed, RNs may refer clients to professional counselors or therapists.

Connecting Clients to Resources

RNs facilitate access to support systems such as:

- Support groups for people undergoing similar life changes
- Community resources, including housing or financial assistance
- Healthcare services, including mental health specialists

Linking clients to these resources ensures they have a network of support beyond the clinical setting.

Teaching Coping Strategies

RNs educate clients on effective coping mechanisms, such as:

- Stress-Management Techniques: Deep breathing, mindfulness, and relaxation exercises.
- Time Management: Breaking tasks into smaller, achievable steps to reduce overwhelm.
- Healthy Lifestyle Habits: Encouraging balanced nutrition, regular exercise, and adequate sleep.

These strategies empower clients to take control of their well-being.

Monitoring and Follow-Up

Coping is a dynamic process that evolves over time. RNs schedule regular follow-ups with clients to reassess their progress and address any new challenges. Changes to the care plan are implemented as necessary to maintain ongoing support.

Case Example

Consider a client who has recently been diagnosed with a chronic illness. The RN begins by discussing the client's understanding of the diagnosis and their immediate concerns. Through open dialogue, the RN learns that the client feels isolated and overwhelmed. After identifying these challenges, the RN connects the client to a chronic illness support group and teaches techniques for stress management. Regular check-ins ensure the client feels supported throughout their journey.

Registered nurses play an essential role in assessing and supporting clients through life changes. By combining clinical expertise with compassionate care, they help individuals navigate challenges, build resilience, and achieve a greater sense of well-being. Through effective assessment and tailored interventions, RNs make a meaningful impact on their clients' lives.

 Assess the potential for violence and use safety precautions

Registered nurses have the ability to assess the potential for violence and implement safety precautions essential in reducing risks to patients, staff, and the public. Violence in healthcare settings may arise from patients, visitors, or even staff members, and nurses must be equipped with the skills and knowledge to address these threats effectively.

Understanding the Potential for Violence

RNs assess the potential for violence by identifying key risk factors and warning signs. This process involves both direct observation and a comprehensive understanding of the patient's history and current situation.

Key Risk Factors
- History of Violence: Patients or individuals with a history of aggressive behavior may be more likely to exhibit violence.
- Substance Abuse: Alcohol or drug intoxication can impair judgment and exacerbate aggression.

- Mental Health Conditions: Certain psychiatric conditions, such as schizophrenia or personality disorders, may increase the risk of violent outbursts.
- Stressors: Environmental or situational stress, including pain, frustration, or fear, may provoke aggression.
- Demographic Factors: Age, gender, or cultural background can occasionally play a role in behavioral patterns.

Warning Signs

During interactions with patients, RNs observe behaviors that may signal impending violence:

- Raised voice or shouting
- Physical agitation, such as pacing or clenched fists
- Threatening statements or gestures
- Hostile demeanor or refusal to follow instructions
- Sudden changes in behavior, such as withdrawal followed by agitation

Assessment Techniques

Registered nurses utilize specific techniques to evaluate the risk of violence. These include:

Behavioral Observation

Behavioral observation focuses on identifying immediate risks based on the individual's actions, tone, and interaction with others. RNs are trained to recognize subtle cues that may indicate escalating aggression.

Communication and Interviews

Effective communication allows nurses to explore underlying causes of distress and potential triggers for violence. Open-ended questions and empathic listening can de-escalate tension and provide insight into the individual's mindset.

Collaborative Assessments

Nurses often work in interdisciplinary teams to assess risks, incorporating input from social workers, psychologists, and physicians to form a comprehensive understanding of the situation.

Safety Precautions

Safety precautions are crucial in preventing and mitigating violent incidents. RNs implement measures tailored to the specific risks identified during the assessment process.

Environmental Modifications
- Secure Layouts: Ensure that patient rooms and public spaces are free from potential weapons or objects that could be used to cause harm.
- Accessible Exits: Position furniture and equipment to allow quick access to exits in case evacuation is necessary.
- Surveillance Systems: Use video monitoring for high-risk areas to detect and respond promptly to incidents.

De-escalation Strategies
- Calm Communication: Speak in a soft, non-threatening tone to defuse tension.
- Empathy: Demonstrate understanding and concern for the individual's feelings to build trust.
- Setting Boundaries: Clearly outline acceptable behavior and consequences for aggression.

Personal Safety Measures

RNs must prioritize their own safety while addressing threats:

- Maintain a safe distance from individuals who appear agitated.
- Position yourself near an exit when interacting with potentially violent individuals.
- Avoid turning your back on agitated individuals.
- Carry personal alarms or communication devices for emergency situations.

Training and Education

Education is key to equipping RNs with the necessary skills for violence prevention. Many institutions offer specialized training programs, such as:

- Crisis Prevention Training: Techniques for managing aggression and preventing escalation.
- Conflict Resolution: Strategies for resolving disputes effectively.
- Self-defense: Physical techniques for protecting oneself in extreme situations.

Post-Incident Management

When violent incidents occur, RNs must manage the aftermath carefully to ensure the safety and recovery of all parties involved.

Documentation and Reporting

Accurate documentation of the incident, including descriptions of behaviors and responses, is critical for understanding patterns and preventing future occurrences. Reports are often shared with risk management teams and law enforcement, if necessary.

Support for Victims

RNs provide emotional and physical support to victims of violence, addressing immediate needs and referring them to counseling or other resources.

<u>Debriefing and Reflection</u>
Debriefing sessions allow healthcare teams to analyze the incident, identify areas for improvement, and refine safety protocols.

Registered nurses are at the forefront of violence prevention in healthcare settings. Through diligent assessment, proactive safety measures, and comprehensive training, they create safer environments for everyone. Their ability to identify risks, intervene effectively, and adapt to challenging situations underscores their critical role in enhancing patient and staff well-being.

Incorporating client cultural practices/beliefs

Recognizing and integrating clients' cultural practices and beliefs into care plans not only enhances the quality of care but also fosters trust, respect, and positive health outcomes. This process, known as culturally competent care, requires sensitivity, awareness, and a commitment to understanding diverse cultural perspectives. Here, we explore the strategies, benefits, and challenges that registered nurses encounter when incorporating cultural practices and beliefs into their care.

Understanding Cultural Competence

Cultural competence in healthcare refers to the ability of professionals to effectively deliver services that meet the social, cultural, and linguistic needs of patients. For registered nurses, this means understanding and respecting the values, traditions, and belief systems of individuals from a variety of backgrounds. It also involves being mindful of how these cultural factors influence health behaviors, attitudes towards medical interventions, and expectations around care.

The Importance of Cultural Sensitivity

Cultural sensitivity is the foundation of culturally competent care. It allows nurses to:

- Build trust and rapport with clients.
- Reduce misunderstandings and miscommunication.
- Enhance patient satisfaction and adherence to treatment plans.
- Improve health outcomes by addressing specific cultural health practices and needs.

Without cultural sensitivity, patients may feel misunderstood or marginalized, which can lead to diminished trust in healthcare providers and poorer health outcomes.

Strategies for Incorporating Client Cultural Practices and Beliefs

To effectively integrate cultural practices and beliefs into care planning, registered nurses must employ a variety of strategies. These approaches ensure that care is both respectful and relevant to the patient's individual and cultural context.

Conducting a Cultural Assessment
A cultural assessment involves gathering information about a client's cultural background, beliefs, and practices. Nurses can ask respectful, open-ended questions to learn more about:

- Preferred language for communication.
- Dietary practices and restrictions.
- Spiritual or religious beliefs and rituals.
- Health beliefs, including views on illness, treatment, and healing.
- Family dynamics and decision-making roles.

For instance, some cultures prioritize the involvement of extended family in health decisions, while others may focus on individual autonomy. Understanding these dynamics helps ensure that care aligns with the client's expectations and preferences.

Utilizing Interpreters and Translation Services

Language barriers are one of the most common challenges in providing culturally competent care. Registered nurses can use professional interpreters or translation services to ensure clear communication. It is essential to avoid relying on family members for interpretation, as this can compromise confidentiality and accuracy.

Adapting Care Plans to Cultural Needs

Once a cultural assessment is complete, nurses can tailor care plans to incorporate specific practices and beliefs. Examples include:

- Accommodating dietary restrictions, such as halal, kosher, or vegetarian diets.
- Respecting religious practices, such as prayer times or the use of particular garments.
- Integrating traditional healing practices, such as herbal remedies or acupuncture, when safe and appropriate.
- Allowing rituals or ceremonies that hold spiritual significance for the patient and their family.

Flexibility and creativity are key in finding ways to honor these practices while maintaining medical safety and efficacy.

Building Cultural Knowledge

Nurses can continuously expand their cultural knowledge by:

- Participating in cultural competence training and workshops.
- Engaging with diverse communities to learn firsthand about their traditions and values.
- Staying informed about research and guidelines related to culturally competent care.

A proactive approach to learning helps nurses remain adaptable in their practice and better equipped to meet the needs of their patients.

Collaborating with Multidisciplinary Teams

Registered nurses often work within multidisciplinary teams that include social workers, chaplains, dietitians, and cultural liaisons. These professionals can provide valuable insights and resources to address specific cultural considerations. For instance, a chaplain may help facilitate religious rituals, or a dietitian may suggest culturally appropriate meal plans.

Advocating for Patients

Advocacy is a powerful tool for ensuring that patients' cultural practices and beliefs are respected within the healthcare system. Nurses can advocate by:

- Educating colleagues about the importance of cultural competence.
- Addressing discriminatory or insensitive practices.
- Promoting policies that support diversity and inclusion in healthcare settings.

Advocating for patients helps create an environment where cultural differences are celebrated rather than overlooked.

Challenges in Incorporating Cultural Practices

While the benefits of culturally competent care are clear, nurses may encounter challenges in their efforts to integrate cultural practices and beliefs into care plans. These challenges include:

Time Constraints

The fast-paced nature of healthcare can make it difficult for nurses to conduct thorough cultural assessments or engage in meaningful dialogue with patients.

Limited Resources

Some healthcare settings may lack the resources needed to support cultural competence, such as interpreters or training programs.

Conflicting Beliefs

There may be instances where a patient's cultural practices or beliefs conflict with evidence-based medical practices. In such cases, nurses must navigate these situations with sensitivity, seeking compromises that prioritize patient safety while respecting cultural values.

Implicit Bias

Unconscious biases can influence how healthcare providers perceive and interact with patients from different cultural backgrounds. Nurses must engage in self-reflection and seek to recognize and address their own biases.

The Impact of Cultural Competence

When registered nurses successfully incorporate cultural practices and beliefs into care, the impact can be profound. Patients feel seen, heard, and respected, which can lead to:

- Higher levels of trust in healthcare providers.
- Improved adherence to treatment plans.
- Better communication and understanding between patients and providers.
- Enhanced overall health outcomes.

Incorporating client cultural practices and beliefs into nursing care is not just a professional responsibility, it is a moral imperative that upholds the principles of respect, dignity, and equity. By embracing cultural competence, registered nurses can provide holistic and personalized care that honors the unique identities of their patients. As the world becomes increasingly diverse, the ability to integrate cultural considerations into healthcare will remain an essential skill for nurses and other healthcare professionals. Through education, empathy, and collaboration, the nursing profession can continue to lead the way in delivering compassionate, culturally sensitive care for all.

Provide end-of-life care and education to clients

Registered nurses (RNs) combine clinical expertise with emotional support to ensure that individuals experience dignity, comfort, and understanding during their final days.

Providing Compassionate Care

At the heart of end-of-life care lies compassion. Registered nurses strive to create a calming and respectful environment for clients and their families. They offer:

- Pain and Symptom Management: RNs assess and address physical discomfort, such as pain, shortness of breath, or nausea, through medication management and comfort measures.
- Emotional Support: Nurses provide a compassionate presence, listening to fears, concerns, and wishes while validating emotions of both the client and their loved ones.
- Personalized Care: Each client receives individualized care tailored to their preferences, cultural beliefs, and spiritual needs.

Educating Clients and Families

Education is a cornerstone of end-of-life care, empowering clients, and families to make informed decisions. Registered nurses provide:

- Information About the Dying Process: Nurses explain physical and emotional changes clients may experience, demystifying the process to ease fear and uncertainty.
- Guidance on Decision-Making: RNs help families understand advanced directives, palliative care options, and hospice services, enabling them to honor the client's wishes.
- Practical Tips: Nurses educate caregivers on how to manage medications, adjust positioning for comfort, and recognize signs of distress or approaching death.

Collaborating With Interdisciplinary Teams

Registered nurses work alongside physicians, social workers, spiritual counselors, and other professionals to provide holistic care. This teamwork includes:

- Coordinating Care: RNs act as liaisons, ensuring seamless communication between clients, families, and healthcare providers.
- Advocating for Clients: Nurses advocate for treatments and interventions that align with the client's values and goals.

Supporting Grief and Bereavement

Even after a client passes, the role of the registered nurse continues. Support for grieving families includes:

- Providing Resources: Nurses connect families with grief counseling, support groups, and community resources.
- Follow-Up: A call or visit from the nurse can provide comfort and closure during the initial stages of bereavement.

Embracing Cultural and Spiritual Sensitivity

End-of-life care is deeply personal and often influenced by cultural and spiritual beliefs. Registered nurses respect and incorporate these elements by:

- Listening to and honoring cultural practices and rituals.
- Facilitating access to spiritual care providers, such as chaplains or faith leaders.

Registered nurses are essential to ensuring quality end-of-life care. Through their expertise, compassion, and commitment to education, they help clients and families navigate one of life's most challenging journeys with dignity and peace. Their work not only alleviates physical suffering but also provides a sense of comfort and understanding that remains invaluable during the final chapter of life.

Assessing client support system to aid in plan of care

Registered nurses evaluate a client's support system to create an effective and personalized plan of care. A support system consists of the people, resources, and structures that a client can rely on for physical, emotional, and practical assistance during their healthcare journey.

The Importance of Understanding Support Systems

Support systems profoundly impact a client's ability to manage their health conditions, follow treatment plans, and cope with challenges. Research has shown that strong social support leads to better health outcomes, improved adherence to medical regimens, and reduced levels of stress and anxiety. Conversely, a lack of support can exacerbate health issues and impede recovery.

For RNs, assessing support systems means understanding the client's social dynamics, emotional resilience, and available resources. This knowledge enables nurses to tailor interventions, address gaps, and advocate for additional support when necessary.

Methods for Assessing Support Systems

RNs employ a variety of tools and techniques to assess a client's support system. These include direct communication, structured assessments, observational skills, and collaboration with other healthcare professionals.

Conducting Interviews

Interviews are a primary method for gathering information about a client's support system. During these conversations, RNs ask open-ended questions to learn about family relationships, friendships, caregiving arrangements, and community ties. Questions may include:

- Who do you turn to for emotional support?
- Do you have someone to assist with daily activities if needed?
- Are there individuals who help you manage your healthcare appointments or medications?
- Do you feel supported by your family or social circle?

These discussions also allow nurses to evaluate the quality of these relationships and identify any conflicts or stressors that might hinder effective support.

Using Standardized Assessment Tools

Many healthcare settings provide standardized tools to assess support systems. Examples include:

- Social Support Questionnaires: These evaluate the availability, frequency, and satisfaction of social support.
- Caregiver Strain Index (CSI): Useful for understanding the burden on family members or caregivers helping the client.
- Functional Independence Measures: These assess the level of independence versus reliance on support systems.

These tools provide measurable data that can be crucial for identifying needs and crafting effective interventions.

Observing Interactions

Observational skills are essential when evaluating support systems. RNs may observe how clients interact with family members or caregivers during hospital visits, appointments, or home visits (if applicable). Clues about the strength of a support system can emerge from body language, tone of communication, and willingness to cooperate.

Collaborating with Multidisciplinary Teams

Healthcare is a collaborative effort, and RNs often consult social workers, case managers, or therapists to obtain a fuller picture of the client's support system. These professionals may have insights into family dynamics, financial constraints, or housing conditions that impact support.

Key Elements of a Support System

When assessing a client's support system, RNs focus on several core elements:

- Family and Friends: Identifying individuals who provide emotional and practical support.
- Caregivers: Evaluating caregiving arrangements, including hired professionals or family members.
- Community Resources: Exploring available resources such as support groups, faith-based organizations, and local programs.
- Financial Stability: Assessing whether financial constraints limit access to supportive services or medical care.
- Housing and Environment: Determining if a client's living conditions are conducive to recovery and overall well-being.

Integrating Findings into a Plan of Care

Once a support system has been assessed, RNs incorporate their findings into the care plan, ensuring that the client's unique circumstances are addressed comprehensively.

Strengthening Existing Support

If the assessment reveals a robust support system, RNs can focus on leveraging these strengths. They may involve family members or caregivers in educational sessions to ensure that they understand the client's needs and can provide effective assistance. Encouraging open communication within the network can also enhance collaboration and mutual support.

Addressing Gaps

When gaps are identified, RNs actively work to fill them. This may include:

- Referring clients to social services for financial or housing aid.
- Connecting clients with community organizations or support groups.
- Arranging for home healthcare services or other professional caregiving options.

RNs also advocate on behalf of clients, ensuring they receive the resources necessary to minimize vulnerabilities.

Educating and Empowering Clients

Education is an essential aspect of building a sustainable support system. RNs teach clients about available resources, coping strategies, and self-advocacy. Empowering clients to seek and maintain support can foster independence and resilience.

Monitoring and Reevaluating

Support systems are dynamic and may change over time due to personal, social, or health-related factors. RNs continuously monitor the effectiveness of the support system and reevaluate it during follow-up visits or care transitions. This ensures that the clients' needs are consistently met throughout their healthcare journey.

Assessing a client's support system is a cornerstone of nursing practice that allows registered nurses to deliver comprehensive, client-centered care. By understanding the nuances of the client's support network, RNs can craft plans that enhance recovery, foster independence, and improve overall health outcomes. Combining compassionate communication, structured tools, and interdisciplinary collaboration, nurses ensure that no aspect of care is overlooked, ultimately empowering clients to thrive in their healthcare journey.

Provide care for a client experiencing grief or loss

Registered nurses provide holistic care to clients experiencing grief or loss. This care requires not only medical expertise but also empathy, active listening, and a compassionate approach to addressing emotional and psychological needs. Outlined below are essential methods through which nurses can provide support to clients during challenging periods.

Assessment and Understanding

The first step for a registered nurse is understanding the unique grief experience of the client. Grief manifests differently in individuals, depending on factors such as culture, personal beliefs, past experiences, and the nature of the loss.

- Active Listening: RNs should create a safe space where clients feel comfortable expressing their emotions and thoughts without fear of judgment.
- Observation: Identifying physical, emotional, and behavioral symptoms of grief, such as crying, withdrawal, loss of appetite, or difficulty sleeping, is essential.
- Open Communication: Asking open-ended questions can help clients articulate their feelings and share their needs.
- Cultural Sensitivity: Understanding cultural practices and traditions related to grief is important in providing respectful and appropriate care.

Providing Emotional Support

RNs should provide emotional support that helps clients navigate their grief in a healthy way.

- Empathy: Expressing genuine care and understanding can help clients feel less isolated in their grief journey.
- Validation: Acknowledging the client's feelings as normal and valid is vital in helping them process their loss.
- Encouraging Expression: RNs can encourage clients to talk, write, or express their emotions through other outlets like art or music therapy.

Educating Clients and Families

Knowledge empowers clients and their families to better understand grief and cope with its implications.

- Grief Process: RNs can explain the stages of grief (denial, anger, bargaining, depression, and acceptance) while emphasizing that grief is not linear and varies for everyone.
- Self-Care Tips: Encouraging practices such as proper nutrition, hydration, rest, and physical activity to support overall well-being during grief.
- Available Resources: Informing clients about counseling services, bereavement support groups, or community resources can provide additional help.

Collaborating with Multidisciplinary Teams

Grief often requires a team effort involving healthcare professionals from different specializations.

- Referral to Counselors or Therapists: For clients who need specialized mental health support, RNs can assist in connecting them with licensed counselors or therapists.
- Spiritual Care: If appropriate, RNs can liaise with chaplains or spiritual advisors who align with the client's beliefs.
- Social Work Involvement: Social workers can provide practical assistance, such as navigating financial or legal challenges related to the loss.

Addressing Physical Needs

Grief can manifest physically, and RNs must monitor and address these symptoms.

- Managing Health Symptoms: RNs should assess for stress-related conditions such as high blood pressure, headaches, or gastrointestinal issues and provide appropriate interventions.
- Medication Management: If prescribed, nurses can educate clients about medications for anxiety, depression, or sleep disturbances, ensuring safe usage.

Supporting Family and Caregivers

The ripple effects of grief often extend to a client's family and caregivers. Nurses can play a key role in supporting these individuals by:

- Providing Guidance: Educating families on how to support the grieving individual effectively without feeling overwhelmed themselves.
- Encouraging Respite: Reminding caregivers to take breaks and focus on their own well-being to offer sustainable support.

Recognizing Complicated Grief

In some cases, grief may become prolonged or complicated, requiring heightened intervention.

- Monitoring for Red Flags: Signs such as persistent depression, inability to function in daily life, or substance abuse indicate the need for specialized care.
- Facilitating Intervention: RNs can advocate for timely mental health referrals to ensure the client receives the support they need.

Providing care for clients experiencing grief or loss is a multifaceted responsibility that calls for both technical skill and deep compassion. By adopting a client-centered approach, registered nurses can guide individuals through their grief, ensuring they feel supported, understood, and empowered to find healing in their own time.

Provide care & education for acute and chronic psychosocial health issues

Nurses are at the forefront of addressing a wide range of mental and behavioral health conditions, including addictions, anxiety, depression, post-traumatic stress disorder (PTSD), phobias, obsessive-compulsive disorder (OCD), mood disorders, bipolar disorder, schizophrenia, dementia, and eating disorders. Through their clinical expertise and patient-centered approach, registered nurses ensure that individuals receive comprehensive care that promotes recovery, resilience, and well-being.

Assessment and Diagnosis

One of the first steps in addressing psychosocial health challenges is a thorough assessment of a patient's mental, emotional, and physical health. Registered nurses are trained to:

- Conduct detailed patient interviews to gather information about symptoms, medical history, and social circumstances.
- Utilize validated screening tools to identify specific mental health issues such as anxiety, depression, or substance use disorders.
- Observe and document changes in behavior, mood, and cognitive functioning.

Accurate assessment is essential for developing an individualized care plan and coordinating with other professionals, such as psychiatrists, psychologists, and social workers.

Providing Direct Care

Registered nurses are instrumental in delivering direct care for individuals with psychosocial health issues. This includes:

Medication Management

RNs ensure that patients adhere to prescribed medications, monitor their effectiveness, and educate them about potential side effects. For instance, they may administer antipsychotics for schizophrenia or mood stabilizers for bipolar disorder. They also advocate for patients by communicating concerns about medication efficacy to prescribing physicians.

Crisis Intervention

For patients experiencing acute episodes, such as panic attacks, suicidal thoughts, or psychotic breaks, RNs provide immediate care to stabilize their condition. In these high-stakes situations, nurses employ de-escalation techniques and ensure the patient's safety.

Therapeutic Communication

Nurses establish trusting relationships with patients through active listening and empathetic dialogue. This therapeutic communication helps patients feel understood and supported, which is vital for their emotional well-being.

Health Monitoring

For individuals with chronic conditions like dementia or eating disorders, RNs monitor physical health indicators such as weight, vital signs, and nutritional intake. This holistic approach ensures that physical complications do not exacerbate mental health problems.

Education and Advocacy

Education is a cornerstone of nursing care in mental health. RNs empower patients and their families by providing knowledge about their condition, treatment options, and coping strategies. Here's how nurses excel in this area:

- Explaining the nature of mental health conditions, such as how PTSD affects the brain or how stress contributes to anxiety.
- Teaching patients' practical skills like mindfulness, relaxation techniques, and problem-solving strategies to manage symptoms effectively.
- Guiding families on how to support loved ones, understand triggers, and promote a positive environment for recovery.

Additionally, registered nurses often act as advocates for their patients by helping them navigate healthcare systems, access community resources, and combat stigma associated with mental health challenges.

Coordination of Multidisciplinary Care

Psychosocial health issues often require input from various healthcare professionals, and RNs are pivotal in coordinating this multidisciplinary approach. For instance:

- They collaborate with therapists to ensure that a patient's psychotherapy aligns with their medication regimen.
- They communicate with social workers to address economic or housing challenges that may impact mental health.
- They participate in case management meetings to discuss progress and adjust care plans as needed.

This collaboration ensures that care is cohesive, comprehensive, and tailored to the individual's unique needs.

Long-Term Support for Chronic Conditions

Many psychosocial health issues, such as dementia or chronic mood disorders, require ongoing care. Registered nurses provide long-term support by:

Encouraging Adherence to Treatment Plans

Patients with chronic conditions may struggle with adherence to treatment over time. RNs provide encouragement, reminders, and resources to help patients stay on track.

Promoting Self-Management

Through education and support, nurses help patients develop self-management skills, enabling them to take an active role in their care. For example, individuals with OCD may learn how to identify and challenge intrusive thoughts, while those with bipolar disorder may learn to recognize early signs of mood changes.

Building Resilience

RNs engage patients in discussions about resilience and coping. They emphasize the importance of social connections, physical activity, and healthy routines in maintaining mental health.

Community Outreach and Preventive Care

Beyond hospital and clinical settings, registered nurses often engage in community outreach to educate the public about mental health and prevent the escalation of psychosocial health issues. These efforts include:

- Hosting workshops on stress management and substance abuse prevention.
- Screening for mental health conditions at community health events.
- Partnering with schools, workplaces, and organizations to promote mental well-being.

By addressing psychosocial health at the community level, RNs contribute to a broader culture of awareness and support.

The role of nurses in providing care and education for acute and chronic psychosocial health issues is vast and multifaceted. Through their expertise, compassion, and advocacy, they help individuals navigate the complexities of mental health challenges while promoting recovery and resilience. Whether through direct patient care, education, or community outreach, RNs remain at the heart of efforts to improve psychosocial well-being for individuals and communities alike.

Assess psychosocial factors influencing care and plan interventions

Nurses address not only the physical but also the psychosocial aspects of a patient's well-being. Psychosocial factors significantly influence health outcomes and the effectiveness of care plans. These factors include occupational, spiritual, environmental, and financial considerations, among others. Here's how RNs assess these factors and plan interventions tailored to individual needs.

Assessing Psychosocial Factors

Occupational Factors

RNs assess the patient's occupation and work environment to understand its impact on their health and treatment. This includes evaluating:

- Physical demands of the job that may exacerbate health conditions.
- Exposure to occupational hazards, such as chemicals or repetitive strain.
- Workplace stress and its effect on mental health.
- Availability of health benefits, sick leave, and job security.

To gather this information, RNs may conduct interviews, use questionnaires, or collaborate with occupational therapists.

Spiritual Factors

Spirituality can be a source of strength and coping for many patients. RNs assess:

- The patient's spiritual beliefs and practices.
- How these beliefs influence health decisions, such as diet, medication, or end-of-life care.
- Access to spiritual support, such as clergy or faith communities.

Assessment often involves sensitive, open-ended questions like, "Do your spiritual beliefs provide comfort during illness?" or "How can we support your spiritual needs?"

Environmental Factors

The patient's living conditions and surroundings are crucial to understanding potential barriers to recovery. RNs assess:

- Housing stability and safety.
- Access to essentials like clean water, nutritious food, and transportation.
- Proximity to healthcare facilities.

Home visits, patient interviews, and collaboration with social workers can provide insights into environmental challenges.

Financial Factors

Financial constraints often affect treatment adherence and access to resources. RNs evaluate:

- The patient's ability to afford medications, treatments, and transportation.
- Insurance coverage and out-of-pocket costs.
- Availability of community resources or financial aid programs.

This assessment may involve coordinating with case managers or financial counselors.

Planning Interventions

Once psychosocial factors have been assessed, RNs collaborate with the patient, their family, and the healthcare team to create a care plan. Interventions may include:

Addressing Occupational Issues
- Referring the patient to vocational rehabilitation services.
- Providing ergonomic recommendations to prevent injury.
- Educating employers about necessary accommodations for health conditions.

Supporting Spiritual Needs
- Facilitating access to chaplains or faith-based support groups.
- Incorporating the patient's spiritual practices into the care plan, such as prayer or meditation time.
- Respecting dietary or cultural practices linked to spirituality.

Improving the Environment
- Referring the patient to housing assistance programs if needed.
- Ensuring access to transportation for medical appointments.
- Providing health education on maintaining a safe and hygienic living space.

Alleviating Financial Strain
- Connecting patients with social services or non-profits that offer financial aid.
- Helping patients apply for insurance or medication assistance programs.
- Exploring telehealth options to reduce travel costs.

By thoroughly assessing psychosocial factors and implementing tailored interventions, registered nurses ensure that care plans address the full spectrum of a patient's needs. This holistic approach fosters better health outcomes, enhances patient satisfaction, and empowers individuals to overcome barriers in their healing journey. RNs, as advocates and problem-solvers, continue to play an indispensable role in integrating psychosocial considerations into comprehensive healthcare.

Provide care for clients with visual/auditory/cognitive alterations

Understanding Visual Impairment

Visual impairment encompasses a spectrum of vision difficulties, ranging from partial vision loss to complete blindness. This condition may arise from various causes, such as age-related macular degeneration, glaucoma, diabetic retinopathy, congenital issues, or trauma. Understanding the type and extent of visual impairment is integral to planning appropriate care.

Assessment and Evaluation
Registered nurses begin the care process with a comprehensive assessment of the client's visual capabilities, daily challenges, and emotional well-being. This entails:

- Medical history: Reviewing the client's medical, surgical, and familial history to identify underlying causes of visual impairment.
- Functional assessment: Evaluating how visual impairment affects daily activities like reading, mobility, cooking, and self-care.
- Psychosocial evaluation: Assessing the emotional impact of vision loss, including feelings of isolation, depression, or anxiety.
- Collaboration: Working with ophthalmologists, optometrists, and other specialists to ensure a holistic approach to treatment.

Developing an Individualized Care Plan
Registered nurses tailor care plans to suit the unique needs of each client, focusing on strategies to maximize residual vision, adapt environments, and improve coping mechanisms.

Promoting Safety

Maintaining safety is paramount for clients with visual impairment. Nurses implement precautions to prevent falls, injuries, or accidents:

- Ensuring that walking paths are clear of obstacles and furniture.
- Advising the use of bright and contrasting colors to highlight important objects and areas.
- Encouraging the installation of grab bars, non-slip mats, and railings in bathrooms and along staircases.
- Providing orientation to the environment, including clear labeling of items like medications, food containers, and appliances.

Enhancing Communication

Effective communication techniques are essential to ensure the nurse-client relationship remains strong and supportive:

- Speaking clearly and addressing the client by name to maintain attention.
- Providing detailed verbal descriptions instead of relying on visual cues.
- Encouraging the use of tactile communication tools, such as Braille, raised symbols, or audio devices.

Encouraging Independence

Registered nurses empower clients by teaching skills that foster independence:

- Providing training on assistive technologies like screen readers, magnifiers, and voice-activated tools.
- Encouraging the use of orientation and mobility aids, such as canes or guide dogs.
- Collaborating with occupational therapists to adapt routines and environments for better accessibility.

<u>Emotional and Psychological Support</u>

Visual impairment can lead to profound emotional challenges. Registered nurses offer psychological care through:

- Active listening: Creating a safe space for clients to share their fears, frustrations, and hopes.
- Counseling: Connecting clients with support groups or professional counselors to help them navigate the emotional impact of vision loss.
- Building resilience: Encouraging positive coping strategies, such as mindfulness, relaxation techniques, and social engagement.

<u>Education and Advocacy</u>

Registered nurses educate clients and their families about visual impairment, available resources, and practical strategies to improve daily life. Key educational efforts include:

- Providing information on low-vision services, rehabilitation programs, and community resources.
- Teaching family members effective ways to assist the client without fostering dependency.
- Advocating for accessibility and inclusivity in public spaces, workplaces, and social settings.

<u>Monitoring and Follow-up</u>

Ongoing care is vital to ensure the client's needs are continuously met. Nurses perform regular evaluations to:

- Track changes in vision or health status.
- Adjust care plans based on new challenges or goals.
- Provide continued emotional and educational support.

Understanding Auditory Alterations

Auditory alterations, such as hearing loss or other conditions affecting the ear, can profoundly impact an individual's quality of life, communication abilities, and social interactions. Registered nurses play a critical role in providing care and fostering resilience for clients experiencing auditory challenges. Through a combination of medical expertise, patient education, advocacy, and emotional support, nurses help these clients navigate their difficulties and lead fulfilling lives.

Assessment and Identification

Identifying auditory alterations is the first step in providing effective care. Registered nurses perform comprehensive assessments to understand the client's auditory challenges. This process includes:

- History Taking: Gathering information about the onset, progression, and impact of hearing difficulties.
- Observation: Monitoring communication patterns, behaviors, and any signs of frustration or isolation caused by auditory issues.
- Screening: Utilizing basic hearing tests or referring clients to audiologists for advanced evaluations.
- Environmental Assessment: Identifying factors in the client's surroundings that may exacerbate auditory challenges, such as excessive noise or lack of accessibility.

Creating Individualized Care Plans

Once auditory alterations are identified, registered nurses collaborate with clients to create tailored care plans. These plans focus on addressing specific needs and enhancing the client's overall well-being. Key components of such plans include:

- Assistive Devices: Helping clients access and use hearing aids, cochlear implants, or other auditory aids effectively.
- Communication Strategies: Teaching techniques such as lip reading, sign language, or using written communication to ensure the client can express themselves and understand others.

- Environmental Modifications: Advising on ways to reduce background noise, improve lighting for visual cues, and ensure sound alerts are accessible.
- Referrals: Connecting clients with audiologists, speech therapists, or other specialists for further support and treatment.

Education and Advocacy

Registered nurses empower clients through education and advocacy. They provide practical knowledge on managing auditory alterations and ensure clients have access to resources. This includes:

- Teaching Coping Mechanisms: Helping clients adapt psychologically to hearing loss and develop strategies for maintaining independence.
- Family Support: Training family members to communicate effectively with the client and create a supportive environment.
- Public Advocacy: Advocating for auditory accessibility in public spaces, workplaces, and social settings to ensure inclusivity.
- Resource Sharing: Guiding clients to local or national organizations focused on auditory health and support.

Monitoring and Continuous Care

Ongoing care is essential to address changes in auditory health and ensure long-term support. Nurses conduct regular follow-ups to:

- Assess changes in hearing abilities or health status.
- Update care plans based on evolving needs or challenges.
- Provide emotional encouragement and educational updates on emerging technologies or therapies.

Continuous engagement with clients helps prevent feelings of isolation and ensures they can maintain their social connections and autonomy.

Psychosocial Support

Auditory alterations can lead to frustration, anxiety, or depression, stemming from difficulties in communication and social integration. Registered nurses address these emotional challenges through:

- Counseling: Offering emotional support to help clients navigate the impact of auditory changes.

- Community Integration: Encouraging participation in support groups or social activities tailored for individuals with hearing difficulties.

Auditory alterations are profound conditions, but with the skilled and empathetic care of registered nurses, clients can live fulfilling and empowered lives. Their holistic approach creates an environment of safety, inclusivity, and adaptability, enabling individuals to overcome challenges and embrace life with resilience and dignity.

Understanding Cognitive Alterations

Clients experiencing cognitive alterations require specialized care that encompasses their physical, emotional, and social needs. Registered nurses play a vital role in delivering this care through their expertise, empathy, and holistic approach. Below are the key strategies nurses employ to support individuals with cognitive challenges:

Assessment and Individualized Care Planning

Registered nurses begin by conducting thorough assessments to understand the client's specific cognitive needs, strengths, and limitations. This includes:

- Evaluating memory, attention, problem-solving abilities, and other cognitive functions.
- Identifying potential triggers or contributing factors to cognitive decline, such as medical conditions, medications, or environmental stressors.
- Collaborating with clients, caregivers, and interdisciplinary teams to create individualized care plans that prioritize the client's well-being and autonomy.

Promoting Safe and Supportive Environments

Creating a safe and structured environment is crucial for clients with cognitive alterations. Registered nurses provide care by:

- Minimizing environmental distractions to promote focus and reduce confusion.
- Ensuring adequate lighting and clear signage to support navigation and orientation.

- Implementing safety measures to prevent falls or injuries, such as removing hazards and ensuring accessibility.

Encouraging Cognitive Stimulation

Nurses recognize the importance of maintaining and improving cognitive function through engaging activities. They promote stimulation by:

- Encouraging participation in activities that challenge cognitive skills, such as puzzles, memory games, and creative exercises.
- Facilitating meaningful social interactions to reduce isolation and enhance emotional well-being.
- Incorporating reminiscence therapy to connect clients with their past experiences and foster a sense of identity.

Supporting Emotional and Psychological Well-Being

The emotional impact of cognitive alterations can be profound. Registered nurses provide support by:

- Offering counseling and reassurance to reduce anxiety, fear, and frustration.
- Promoting optimism and resilience by helping clients view cognitive challenges as manageable aspects of their lives.
- Encouraging self-expression and communication to ensure clients feel heard and understood.

Family and Caregiver Involvement

Registered nurses understand the significance of family and caregiver roles in cognitive care. They:

- Educate families and caregivers about cognitive alterations and their impact on daily living.
- Provide training on effective communication techniques and strategies to support the client's independence.
- Offer guidance on coping mechanisms and stress management to maintain caregiver well-being.

Adaptability and Empowerment

Registered nurses help clients adapt to cognitive changes while fostering empowerment. Their approach includes:

- Introducing tools and techniques to support memory and organization, such as calendars or reminders.
- Encouraging clients to participate actively in decision-making about their care and lifestyle.
- Reinforcing a sense of dignity by respecting the client's preferences and strengths.

Cognitive alterations may present unique challenges, but with the holistic and compassionate care of registered nurses, clients can adapt, thrive, and live fulfilling lives. Their dedication creates environments of safety, inclusiveness, and empowerment, enabling individuals to embrace life with resilience and dignity.

Recognizing non-verbal cues to physical and psychological stressors

Understanding Non-Verbal Cues

Non-verbal cues can encompass a wide range of behaviors and physical signs. These cues often manifest in the patient's body language, facial expressions, vocal tones, and physiological responses. Registered nurses are trained to interpret these signals in the context of the patient's overall condition and environment.

Physical Stress Indicators
Patients experiencing physical stress often exhibit specific non-verbal behaviors, including:

- Facial Expressions: Furrowed brows, grimacing, or wincing may suggest pain or discomfort.

- Body Posture: Guarding a particular area of the body or adopting rigid, tense postures can indicate physical distress.
- Changes in Movement: Restlessness, fidgeting, or an inability to remain still might be signs of physical pain or discomfort.
- Altered Breathing Patterns: Shallow, rapid breathing or labored respiration may indicate pain or a medical condition affecting respiratory function.
- Skin Changes: Pallor, sweating, or flushed skin may signal stress, fever, or underlying conditions.

Psychological Stress Indicators

Recognizing psychological stress requires close attention to subtler non-verbal cues, including:

- Eye Contact: Avoiding eye contact or staring into space may indicate anxiety, depression, or a sense of detachment.
- Vocal Tone: A soft, trembling, or cracked voice may suggest emotional distress or fear.
- Behavioral Changes: Withdrawal, irritability, or excessive nervous habits like nail-biting or pacing can point to psychological strain.
- Tearfulness: Visible tears, even if suppressed, are a clear indication of emotional upset.
- Appearance: Neglected personal hygiene or disheveled appearance can be a sign of psychological stress or depression.

Techniques for Identifying Non-Verbal Cues

Registered nurses employ various techniques to recognize and interpret non-verbal cues effectively:

- Active Observation: Paying close attention to subtle changes in a patient's appearance, behavior, and interaction patterns.

- Establishing Rapport: Building trust so that patients feel comfortable expressing themselves, both verbally and non-verbally.
- Contextual Evaluation: Considering the patient's medical history, cultural background, and situational factors to better understand their cues.
- Empathy and Intuition: Using emotional intelligence to sense distress that may not be immediately visible.
- Collaboration: Consulting with other healthcare professionals and family members to gain a holistic view of the patient's condition.

Responding to Non-Verbal Cues

Once non-verbal stress indicators are recognized, the nurse's response is crucial in addressing the underlying issues:

- Assessment: Conducting a thorough evaluation to identify the source of the stressor, whether physical or psychological.
- Comfort Measures: Providing immediate relief through pain management, repositioning, or creating a calming environment.
- Communication: Encouraging the patient to verbalize their concerns, offering reassurance, and providing emotional support.
- Intervention: Implementing medical or psychological interventions in collaboration with a multidisciplinary team.
- Follow-Up: Monitoring the patient's response to interventions and adjusting care plans as needed.

The Importance of Cultural Sensitivity

Cultural factors significantly influence how patients express pain and distress. For instance, some cultures may encourage the suppression of visible emotional responses, while others may be more expressive. Registered nurses must be culturally competent to avoid misinterpreting non-verbal cues.

The ability to recognize non-verbal cues to physical and psychological stressors is foundational to the role of a registered nurse. By honing their observational skills, maintaining empathetic communication, and adopting a patient-centered approach, nurses can ensure that their patients receive the comprehensive care they need. Ultimately, this skill not only improves clinical outcomes but also fosters a deeper sense of trust and comfort between patients and caregivers.

Use therapeutic communication techniques

Effective communication is the cornerstone of nursing practice, and therapeutic communication techniques play a pivotal role in creating meaningful interactions between registered nurses (RNs) and their patients. These techniques are tailored to establish trust, alleviate anxiety, and promote healing by fostering an environment where patients feel heard, understood, and supported. Below, we delve into how registered nurses use therapeutic communication to enhance patient care and create positive healthcare experiences.

Understanding Therapeutic Communication

Therapeutic communication is a specialized form of interaction centered on improving the mental, emotional, and physical well-being of patients. Unlike casual conversations, therapeutic interactions are intentional, purposeful, and guided by empathy and active listening. RNs use these techniques to build rapport, ensure clear understanding of medical processes, and empower patients to express concerns.

Key Techniques in Therapeutic Communication

Registered nurses employ various methods to engage patients effectively. These techniques are designed to address the diverse needs of individuals in different healthcare scenarios.

Active Listening

One of the foundational techniques in therapeutic communication is active listening. RNs focus entirely on what the patient is saying, both verbally and nonverbally. This involves maintaining eye contact, nodding to show understanding, and refraining from interrupting. Active listening demonstrates respect and validates the patient's feelings, helping them feel valued and understood.

Empathy

Empathy allows nurses to connect deeply with patients by understanding their emotions and perspectives. By putting themselves in the patient's shoes, RNs can respond compassionately and create an atmosphere of trust. Simple phrases like "I understand this must be difficult for you" help convey empathy.

Open-Ended Questions

To encourage patients to speak freely, RNs use open-ended questions. These questions, such as "Can you tell me more about how you're feeling?" or "What concerns do you have about your treatment?" invite detailed responses and facilitate a better understanding of the patient's needs.

Nonverbal Communication

Nonverbal cues, such as facial expressions, posture, and gestures, play a crucial role in therapeutic communication. A warm smile or a reassuring touch can often convey support and comfort more effectively than words. RNs are attuned to patients' nonverbal signals, using them to gauge emotions and adapt their approach.

Clarification and Summarization

To ensure mutual understanding, RNs often clarify and summarize what patients communicate. For example, a nurse might say, "Just to make sure I understand, you're saying that the pain is worse in the evenings?" This technique eliminates confusion and reassures patients that their concerns are being accurately addressed.

Validation

Validation involves affirming the patient's feelings and experiences. Statements like "It's normal to feel anxious before surgery" help patients feel accepted and reduce feelings of isolation.

Silence

Silence can be a powerful tool in therapeutic communication. Allowing pauses gives patients time to collect their thoughts and express themselves without feeling rushed. It conveys patience and respect for their need to process emotions.

Providing Information

Registered nurses use therapeutic communication to educate patients about their conditions, treatments, and recovery processes. By framing information in an understandable and supportive manner, RNs empower patients to make informed decisions about their care.

Applying Therapeutic Communication in Practice

The use of therapeutic communication techniques extends across various aspects of nursing practice, from initial assessments to ongoing patient care.

During Patient Assessment

At the start of patient interactions, RNs use therapeutic communication to gather information about medical history, symptoms, and emotional concerns. By creating a safe environment for conversation, nurses can elicit accurate and comprehensive responses.

In Crisis Situations

During emergencies or heightened emotional states, therapeutic communication becomes critical. Nurses use calming tones, reassuring gestures, and concise explanations to reduce patient anxiety and foster cooperation.

Supporting Mental Health

In mental health settings, therapeutic communication is vital in helping patients navigate feelings of distress, depression, or anxiety. Nurses use empathy and validation to encourage patients to share their thoughts and accept support.

End-of-Life Care

In palliative or hospice care, therapeutic communication helps patients and families cope with grief and uncertainty. RNs provide comfort, answer difficult questions, and create space for emotional expression, ensuring dignity and respect during challenging times.

Benefits of Therapeutic Communication

The use of therapeutic communication techniques by registered nurses leads to numerous positive outcomes in patient care:

- Enhanced Trust: Patients feel confident in their care providers, which fosters a stronger therapeutic alliance.
- Improved Emotional Well-being: Patients experience reduced stress and anxiety, promoting better recovery.
- Greater Patient Satisfaction: Effective communication increases satisfaction with care and treatment plans.
- Better Compliance: Patients are more likely to follow prescribed treatments when they feel understood and respected.
- Stronger Rapport: Communication lays the foundation for a lasting nurse-patient relationship based on mutual understanding.

Therapeutic communication is an indispensable skill for registered nurses, empowering them to connect with patients on a deeper level. By employing empathy, active listening, and other techniques, nurses create an environment of trust and healing that enhances the overall quality of care. As healthcare evolves, RNs must continue developing their communication skills to meet the diverse needs of their patients and uphold the values of compassionate care.

Promoting a therapeutic environment

Nurse promotes a therapeutic environment that fosters healing, comfort, and emotional well-being for patients. Their ability to create this space is rooted in a blend of clinical expertise, compassionate communication, and commitment to holistic care. Below, we explore the ways in which RNs cultivate and maintain such an environment.

Understanding Therapeutic Environment

A therapeutic environment refers to a setting that supports physical, emotional, and psychological well-being. It is designed to reduce stress, promote recovery, and enhance the overall experience of care. For registered nurses, creating this environment is not limited to physical spaces but extends to interpersonal interactions, cultural sensitivity, and the implementation of evidence-based practices.

Effective Communication

Active Listening

Registered nurses promote a therapeutic environment by actively listening to their patients. This involves giving undivided attention, acknowledging concerns, and validating their feelings. Active listening helps establish trust and encourages patients to share openly, which is critical for accurate assessments and personalized care plans.

Clear and Compassionate Communication

RNs use clear, jargon-free language to explain procedures, treatments, and care plans. By ensuring patients understand what is happening, nurses reduce anxiety and empower patients to participate in their own care. Compassionate communication also helps patients feel valued and understood, fostering a sense of security.

Maintaining Physical Comfort and Safety

Pain Management

Addressing pain is a cornerstone of creating a therapeutic environment. Registered nurses regularly assess pain levels and collaborate with patients to manage discomfort, whether through medication, relaxation techniques, or alternative therapies.

Clean and Organized Spaces

The physical surroundings of a healthcare facility significantly impact patient comfort. RNs ensure that patient areas are clean, quiet, and orderly, minimizing disruptions and promoting rest.

Ensuring Patient Safety

Safety is a fundamental aspect of the therapeutic environment. Nurses conduct regular safety checks, mitigate risks such as falls, and educate patients about safety protocols. This creates a sense of stability and trust.

Emotional Support and Advocacy

Building Trusting Relationships

Establishing rapport is central to a therapeutic environment. RNs develop trusting relationships by being approachable, empathetic, and nonjudgmental, thereby creating an atmosphere where patients feel comfortable sharing concerns and fears.

Cultural Competence

Understanding and respecting cultural differences is vital for emotional support. Registered nurses tailor care to align patients' cultural values and practices, ensuring inclusivity and respect.

Advocacy

RNs act as advocates for their patients, ensuring their voices are heard in clinical settings. They help bridge gaps between patients and other healthcare providers, facilitate access to resources, and address any barriers to effective care.

Holistic Care Practices

Mind-Body Connection

Nurses recognize the interplay between physical health and emotional well-being. They incorporate holistic approaches such as mindfulness, meditation, and breathing exercises to support the mind-body connection.

Spiritual Care

For patients who find comfort in spirituality, RNs provide support by facilitating access to chaplain services, creating opportunities for prayer or meditation, and respecting spiritual preferences.

Promoting Patient Autonomy

Registered nurses encourage patients to actively participate in their care decisions, thereby fostering empowerment. They educate patients about their conditions, treatment options, and possible outcomes, allowing them to make informed choices.

Interdisciplinary Collaboration

RNs work closely with physicians, therapists, social workers, and other healthcare professionals to ensure cohesive and comprehensive care. This collaboration contributes to a well-rounded therapeutic environment, addressing all aspects of patient needs.

Continuous Improvement and Education

Professional Development

Registered nurses stay informed about the latest research and advancements in therapeutic care, continuously improving their skills and knowledge to provide high-quality care.

Feedback and Adaptation

RNs actively seek feedback from patients and families to assess the effectiveness of the therapeutic environment and implement changes as needed.

Registered nurses are integral to the creation and maintenance of a therapeutic environment. Through effective communication, emotional support, physical safety, holistic care, patient advocacy, and ongoing education, they ensure that healthcare settings are places of healing and comfort. Their dedication not only enhances patient outcomes but also elevates the overall experience of care, making them indispensable in any clinical setting.

MODULE 5

PHYSIOLOGICAL INTEGRITY: BASIC CARE AND COMFORT NURSING TASK

Assist clients to compensate for physical or sensory Impairments

Nurses play an essential role in helping clients with physical or sensory impairments navigate their daily lives with dignity and independence. They use clinical expertise and empathy to create personalized strategies, promoting empowerment and adaptability.

Understanding Physical and Sensory Impairments

Physical impairments refer to limitations in a person's ability to move, coordinate, or control their body. Examples include conditions such as paralysis, amputation, or musculoskeletal disorders. Sensory impairments, on the other hand, involve deficits in sight, hearing, touch, taste, or smell, with common examples being blindness, deafness, and neuropathy.

Both types of impairments significantly impact daily living, requiring tailored interventions to ensure individuals can maintain quality of life, independence, and safety. Nurses are at the forefront of facilitating this adaptation process, advocating for each client's needs within medical, social, and personal contexts.

Assessment and Individualized Planning

Nurses begin by conducting comprehensive assessments to understand the scope and impact of a client's impairment. This includes evaluating their physical limitations, sensory deficits, emotional state, and social circumstances. Tools such as functional assessments, sensory testing, and consultations with interdisciplinary teams provide a detailed picture, enabling nurses to identify specific challenges.

Based on these insights, nurses collaborate with clients and their families to develop individualized care plans. These plans outline strategies and goals, which may range from enhancing mobility to fostering better communication. The emphasis is always on person-centered care, ensuring the client's preferences and aspirations are respected.

Facilitating Mobility and Independence

Physical impairments often limit mobility, but nurses employ several methods to help clients overcome these challenges:

Physical Therapy and Exercise
Nurses work with physical therapists to design exercise regimens that strengthen muscles, improve coordination, and enhance endurance. For clients with paralysis or limited mobility, passive range-of-motion exercises help prevent stiffness and maintain joint flexibility.

Assistive Devices
Nurses educate clients on using mobility aids such as wheelchairs, walkers, canes, and prosthetics. They provide training on proper techniques to prevent injuries and maximize the effectiveness of these tools. For instance, a nurse might teach an amputee how to balance crutches or navigate stairs with a prosthetic limb.

Environmental Modifications
Ensuring a client's environment is accessible is another critical role of nurses. They may recommend adjustments such as grab bars in bathrooms, ramps for wheelchair access, or rearranging furniture to create safe pathways. These modifications reduce fall risks and promote greater independence.

Enhancing Communication for Sensory Impairments

Clients with sensory impairments often face challenges in communication, which can hinder their interaction with others and their environment. Nurses play an instrumental role in bridging these gaps:

Supporting Clients with Visual Impairment

For clients with blindness or low vision, nurses provide tools such as magnifiers, screen readers, or braille resources. They also teach techniques like tactile navigation—using touch to identify items or spaces—and provide training to use white canes for mobility.

Assisting Clients with Hearing Impairment

For clients who are deaf or hard of hearing, nurses facilitate access to hearing aids, cochlear implants, or other assistive devices. They might also coordinate with sign language interpreters or teach basic sign language to clients and their families. Ensuring clear written communication is another important strategy, particularly in medical settings where instructions are critical.

Promoting Emotional and Psychological Well-being

Living with an impairment can affect a person's mental health, leading to feelings of frustration, isolation, or depression. Nurses provide emotional support that is integral to holistic care:

Fostering Resilience

Nurses encourage clients to focus on their strengths and celebrate small achievements. This positive reinforcement builds confidence and resilience, helping clients adapt to their new circumstances.

Counseling and Support Groups

Nurses may provide counseling themselves or connect clients to professional therapists and peer support groups. Sharing experiences with others facing similar challenges can be immensely empowering for individuals coping with impairments.

Advocating for Clients

Nurses often act as advocates, ensuring that clients have access to community resources, financial assistance, and legal protections. They may liaise with organizations specializing in disability support to secure services such as vocational training or accessible housing.

Education and Training

Empowering clients and their families through education is a cornerstone of nursing care. Nurses teach practical skills tailored to each impairment:

Self-care Techniques
Clients with physical impairments may learn how to safely transfer from a wheelchair to a bed, while those with sensory impairments might practice adaptive cooking techniques. Nurses demonstrate these activities, ensuring clients feel confident in performing them independently.

Caregiver Training
Family members and caregivers are often included in the education process. Nurses provide tips on assisting with daily tasks, managing medical equipment, and recognizing complications. This collaborative approach fosters a supportive care network.

Using Technology

Advances in technology offer innovative solutions to address physical and sensory impairments. Nurses familiarize clients with these tools:

Assistive Technologies
From voice-activated devices to smart home systems, technology can make daily tasks more manageable. Nurses guide clients in using tools such as screen readers, speech-to-text applications, and GPS systems for the visually impaired.

Telehealth

For clients with mobility challenges, telehealth services provide a convenient way to access medical consultations, therapy sessions, and support groups. Nurses play a pivotal role in facilitating these virtual interactions.

Emphasizing Holistic Care

Above all, nurses adopt a holistic approach that addresses the physical, emotional, and social dimensions of living with an impairment. By building trusting relationships, they inspire clients to see beyond their limitations and embrace the possibilities ahead.

Nurses are essential partners in helping clients compensate for physical and sensory impairments. Through personalized care, adaptive strategies, and unwavering support, they empower individuals to lead fulfilling lives. Their dedication not only enhances the well-being of their clients but also underscores the profound impact of compassionate nursing care on society.

Assess & managing clients with alterations in bowel/bladder elimination

Nurses assess and managing clients who experience alterations in bowel and bladder elimination. These conditions can significantly affect a client's quality of life, and appropriate interventions are essential for improving comfort, function, and overall health. Below is an overview of the steps RNs take to assess and manage these issues.

Assessment of Bowel and Bladder Elimination Alterations

Effective care begins with a thorough and systematic assessment of the client's elimination patterns. Key elements of this process include:

Collecting a Comprehensive Health History

RNs should gather detailed information about the clients:

- Frequency, consistency, color, and odor of bowel movements or urine output
- Presence of pain, discomfort, or difficulty during elimination
- Dietary habits, fluid intake, and activity level
- Use of medications, including laxatives, diuretics, or anticholinergics
- History of chronic conditions such as irritable bowel syndrome, urinary tract infections, or diabetes

Physical Examination

The nurse conducts a focused physical examination, which may include:

- Inspection of the abdomen for distension or abnormal masses
- Auscultation of bowel sounds to assess gastrointestinal activity
- Palpation to detect tenderness or signs of constipation
- Inspection of the perineal area for signs of infection, irritation, or incontinence

Diagnostic Testing

RNs may facilitate and interpret the results of diagnostic tests, such as:

- Urinalysis and urine culture to identify infections
- Stool tests to detect blood, infection, or parasites
- Bladder scans to assess residual urine volume
- Imaging studies, such as X-rays or ultrasounds, if ordered by a physician

Management of Alterations in Elimination

Once the assessment is complete, the RN develops and implements a care plan tailored to the client's needs. Management strategies include:

Addressing Underlying Causes

Collaborating with the healthcare team to treat underlying medical conditions—such as infections, obstructions, or neurological disorders—is essential for resolving elimination issues.

Promoting Healthy Habits

RNs educate clients on lifestyle modifications to improve elimination patterns, such as:

- Increasing dietary fiber intake to ease constipation
- Encouraging adequate hydration to prevent urinary retention and dehydration
- Incorporating regular physical activity to promote bowel motility

Administering Medications

RNs may administer or recommend medications as prescribed, including:

- Laxatives or stool softeners for constipation
- Antidiarrheal agents for diarrhea
- Antibiotics for urinary tract infections
- Bladder relaxants for overactive bladder

Utilizing Medical Devices

In some cases, medical devices may be necessary, such as:

- Catheters for clients experiencing urinary retention
- Ostomy care for clients with surgically created elimination outlets

Behavioral and Cognitive Interventions

RNs can implement techniques to support clients with elimination issues due to cognitive or behavioral factors, including:

- Bladder training programs to manage incontinence
- Toileting schedules to establish regular elimination patterns

Monitoring and Evaluation

Management does not end with intervention; RNs must continually evaluate the client's response to the care plan. This includes:

- Tracking changes in elimination patterns
- Assessing the effectiveness of medications or interventions
- Communicating with the client and their family to ensure satisfaction and adherence

Collaborative Care

RNs often work as part of a multidisciplinary team, collaborating with physicians, nutritionists, physical therapists, and other healthcare professionals to optimize outcomes for clients experiencing elimination alterations.

Through comprehensive assessment, tailored interventions, and ongoing evaluation, registered nurses play a pivotal role in managing alterations in bowel and bladder elimination. By addressing both the physiological and emotional aspects of these conditions, RNs help clients regain comfort, dignity, and quality of life.

Perform Irrigations

Irrigation is a common medical procedure conducted by registered nurses (RNs) to cleanse organs or body parts, remove debris, or deliver medication. The technique varies depending on the area being treated, such as the bladder, ear, or eye. Below is an explanation of how RNs generally perform these procedures, following proper aseptic and professional standards.

Bladder Irrigation

Bladder irrigation is typically performed to clear blood clots, administer medication, or prevent catheter blockage.

Procedure:
- Preparation: The RN ensures the patient is comfortable and explains the procedure to reduce anxiety. Supplies, including sterile saline or prescribed solution, a syringe, gloves, and a catheter, are prepared.
- Maintaining Aseptic Technique: The RN uses hand hygiene and dons sterile gloves before handling any equipment to prevent infection.
- Accessing the Catheter: If the patient has an indwelling catheter, the RN clamps the drainage tubing and connects the syringe with irrigation solution to the catheter's access port.
- Gentle Irrigation: The solution is introduced slowly and steadily to avoid causing discomfort or trauma to the bladder.
- Assessment: The RN observes the outflow for clarity, presence of clots, or debris and monitors the patient for adverse reactions, such as pain or discomfort.
- Documentation: After the irrigation, the RN records the procedure, including the type and volume of solution used, any findings, and the patient's response.

Ear Irrigation

Ear irrigation is performed to remove wax buildup, foreign objects, or debris that may impair hearing or cause discomfort.

Procedure:
- Preparation: The RN ensures the patient is seated upright with a towel draped over their shoulder. A kidney-shaped basin is provided to catch fluid.
- Solution Temperature: The irrigation solution, typically warm water, or saline, is brought to body temperature to prevent dizziness or discomfort.

- Introduction of Solution: Using a bulb syringe or an irrigation kit, the RN gently directs the solution into the ear canal, avoiding forceful pressure.
- Observation: The RN monitors the outflow for wax, debris, or other material and ensures the patient's comfort throughout the procedure.
- Aftercare: The ear is dried using a clean towel or tissue. The RN advises the patient to avoid inserting objects into the ear canal in the future.

Eye Irrigation

Eye irrigation is used to flush out foreign bodies, chemicals, or irritants from the eye.

Procedure:

- Preparation: The RN positions the patient in a comfortable, reclined position with the affected eye facing upward. A sterile irrigation solution, such as saline or an eyewash, is prepared.
- Protection: Protective gear, like gloves and goggles, is worn to ensure safety during the procedure.
- Flushing the Eye: The RN uses a sterile syringe or a specialized irrigation device to gently flush the solution from the inner corner of the eye outward. This prevents contaminants from flowing into the unaffected eye.
- Monitoring: The RN observes the eye for signs of persistent irritation or injury and assesses the patient's comfort level.
- Follow-Up: If necessary, the RN applies prescribed eye drops or ointment and provides aftercare instructions.

General Considerations

Nurses ensure that all irrigation procedures are performed with precision, care, and adherence to medical protocols. They assess the patient's condition before and after the procedure and address any complications promptly. Communication with the patient or caregiver is essential to ensure understanding and cooperation.

By maintaining a patient-centered approach and following these guidelines, RNs can perform irrigations effectively to promote healing and comfort.

Performing skin assessment & implement measures to maintain skin

Skin assessment and the implementation of measures to maintain skin integrity are critical responsibilities for registered nurses. The skin, as the body's largest organ, serves as a barrier against pathogens, regulates temperature, and provides sensory feedback. Effective management of skin health is vital, especially for patients who are at risk of skin breakdown, infections, or pressure injuries.

Performing a Skin Assessment

Registered nurses follow a systematic approach to assess the skin, ensuring that all areas are thoroughly examined. The process involves both observation and palpation to evaluate skin condition, color, texture, and integrity.

Steps in Skin Assessment
- Visual Inspection: Observe the skin for signs of redness, discoloration, wounds, rashes, dryness, or swelling. Pay close attention to areas prone to pressure injuries, such as bony prominences.
- Palpation: Use gentle touch to assess skin temperature, moisture levels, and texture. This can also identify areas of tenderness or induration.
- Documentation: Record findings accurately, including descriptions of any abnormalities, the size and location of wounds, and the presence of bruising or lesions.
- Risk Assessment: Utilize tools like the Braden Scale to evaluate the patient's risk for pressure ulcers. This helps prioritize preventive measures.

Common Indicators to Note
Registered nurses should be vigilant for the following signs:

- Skin discoloration, such as cyanosis, jaundice, or erythema
- Presence of wounds, ulcers, or pressure injuries
- Dry, cracked, or peeling skin
- Edema or abnormal swelling
- Unusual textures, such as leathery or overly thin skin

Maintaining Skin Integrity

Once the assessment is complete, registered nurses take proactive measures to maintain skin integrity and prevent skin breakdown. These interventions are tailored to the patient's individual needs and risk factors.

Preventive Measures
- Regular Positioning: For patients with limited mobility, reposition them every two hours to reduce pressure on vulnerable areas.
- Pressure-relieving Devices: Use specialized mattresses, cushions, or heel protectors to alleviate pressure.
- Skin Hygiene: Ensure the skin is kept clean and dry. Use gentle, pH-balanced cleansers and avoid harsh chemicals that can strip away natural oils.
- Hydration: Encourage patients to drink adequate fluids to maintain skin elasticity and hydration.
- Nutritional Support: Provide a diet rich in proteins, vitamins, and minerals to promote skin repair and resilience.

Care for Specific Skin Conditions
Registered nurses employ specialized care strategies depending on the skin's condition:

- Wound Care: Clean wounds using sterile techniques, apply suitable dressings, and monitor for signs of infection.
- Managing Dry Skin: Apply moisturizers to prevent cracking and reduce the risk of secondary infections.

- Treating Pressure Injuries: Use advanced wound care techniques, such as hydrocolloid dressings or foam dressings, to promote healing.

Patient Education

Educating patients on how to care for their skin is essential:

- Teach proper hygiene practices
- Advice on wearing loose and breathable clothing
- Encourage self-inspection for early detection of skin abnormalities

Through diligent skin assessments and the implementation of tailored preventive measures, registered nurses play a key role in safeguarding skin integrity. Their efforts not only improve the patient's quality of life but also prevent serious complications such as pressure ulcers and infections. By combining clinical expertise with compassionate care, nurses ensure the skin remains healthy and resilient across diverse patient scenarios.

Apply, Maintenance, and Remove orthopedic devices

Orthopedic devices play a crucial role in supporting, stabilizing, or protecting bones, joints, and muscles during recovery from injury or surgery. Registered nurses (RNs) are often tasked with applying, maintaining, or removing these devices, ensuring proper functionality and patient comfort. Below is an overview of the key responsibilities and techniques involved.

Applying Orthopedic Devices

The application of orthopedic devices requires precision and adherence to standardized procedures to ensure patient safety and device effectiveness. Common devices include braces, splints, casts, and traction systems.

Steps for Application:

- Assessment: Evaluate the affected area for swelling, skin integrity, or circulation issues before starting the application process. Obtain the necessary orders from a physician or advanced practitioner.
- Preparation: Gather all required materials, including the device, padding, and tools (e.g., bandages or scissors). Explain the procedure to the patient to alleviate anxiety and gain cooperation.
- Positioning: Properly position the patient to ensure comfort and accessibility to the area being treated. Maintain alignment of the affected limb or joint as instructed.
- Application: Secure the device as per manufacturer guidelines or physician instructions. Ensure that it fits snugly without causing discomfort or restricting blood flow.
- Verification: Check alignment, fitness, and stability of the device. Verify that the device does not cause undue pressure or impede circulation.

Maintaining Orthopedic Devices

Maintaining orthopedic devices ensures they remain functional and effective throughout the recovery process. Proper care also helps prevent complications such as skin breakdown or infections.

Key Steps for Maintenance:

- Regular Assessment: Check the device daily for signs of wear, damage, or improper alignment. Inspect the patient's skin for redness, irritation, or pressure sores.
- Cleaning: Follow manufacturer recommendations for cleaning the device. For removable braces or splints, clean frequently to maintain hygiene.
- Patient Education: Teach patients how to care for the device, including when to notify healthcare professionals about potential issues such as swelling or discomfort.
- Adjustments: Make necessary adjustments to ensure continued proper fit, especially in cases of swelling reduction or post-operative changes.

Removing Orthopedic Devices

Removal of orthopedic devices is typically required once the prescribed period has elapsed or if complications necessitate it. This process should be carried out with care to avoid injury or discomfort.

Steps for Removal:
- Assessment: Confirm the physician's order for device removal and evaluate the patient's condition to ensure readiness.
- Preparation: Inform the patient about the procedure and what sensations they may experience, such as slight discomfort or pressure.
- Removal Process:
- For casts: Use a cast cutter with care to avoid injuring the skin beneath. Cut along the designated lines and gently remove the cast in sections.
- For braces or splints: Unfasten straps or Velcro closures, ensuring minimal movement of the affected limb.
- For traction systems: Follow specific protocols for releasing tension and dismantling the setup.

Post-removal Care: Examine the area for any signs of skin irritation, muscle atrophy, or joint stiffness. Provide instructions for physical therapy or continued care if necessary.

Safety and Documentation

Throughout the application, maintenance, and removal of orthopedic devices, proper safety measures are paramount. RNs should:

- Monitor for signs of neurovascular compromise, such as numbness, tingling, or discoloration.
- Document all procedures, including patient assessments, interventions, and outcomes.
- Communicate with the healthcare team regarding any changes in the patient's condition or device-related concerns.

Registered nurses play an essential role in ensuring the effective use of orthopedic devices. By following best practices for application, maintenance, and removal, they contribute significantly to patient recovery and overall well-being. Their expertise and attention to detail are critical in preventing complications and promoting optimal outcomes.

Implementing measures to promote circulation

Effective circulation support minimizes the likelihood of blood clots, pressure injuries, and other complications while improving oxygen delivery and metabolic waste removal throughout the body.

Active and Passive Range of Motion Exercises

Active Range of Motion (AROM)

Active range of motion exercises involve the patient moving their joints and muscles independently under the guidance of an RN. These exercises are particularly useful for patients who have partial mobility and can engage in physical movement. Benefits include improved circulation, enhanced muscle strength, and better joint flexibility. Examples include:

- Stretching arms and legs
- Performing gentle rotations of the neck and shoulders
- Flexing and extending joints like elbows and knees

Passive Range of Motion (PROM)

For patients unable to move independently, the RN performs passive range of motion exercises. These exercises involve the nurse manually moving the patient's limbs to improve blood flow and prevent joint stiffness or muscle atrophy. Techniques may include:

- Lifting and lowering the arms or legs

- Rotating ankles or wrists
- Gently stretching fingers and toes

These exercises are especially beneficial in post-operative care or for individuals with neurological impairments.

Positioning

Correct positioning is crucial for optimal circulation and pressure relief. RNs use positioning techniques to ensure that patients are comfortable, and blood flow isn't restricted. Key measures include:

- Elevating legs slightly to reduce swelling and improve venous return
- Ensuring proper spinal alignment to prevent undue pressure on blood vessels
- Using specialized cushions or mattresses to avoid pressure injuries
- Shifting patient positions regularly, as often as every 2 hours, to promote circulation and prevent skin breakdown

Mobilization

Encouraging and assisting patients with mobilization is one of the most effective strategies to enhance circulation. RNs implement mobilization techniques based on the patient's condition:

Early Ambulation

Getting patients out of bed and walking as soon as possible post-surgery or injury improves venous and arterial circulation, boosts respiratory function, and reduces risks of deep vein thrombosis (DVT). Nurses may:

- Assist with walking aids such as walkers or canes
- Supervise short walks around the hospital room or hallway

Bedside Movement

For patients who cannot walk, bedside exercises such as sitting up, dangling legs off the bed, or rotating hips can stimulate circulation.

Use of Mechanical Devices

In cases where physical movement is severely limited, RNs may employ mechanical aids including:

- Sequential compression devices (SCDs)
- Pneumatic compression stockings
- Standard compression garments

These devices mimic the effects of movement by applying controlled pressure to promote blood flow.

Additional Measures

Beyond physical interventions, registered nurses also optimize circulation through:

- Hydration: Encouraging fluid intake to maintain blood volume and viscosity
- Nutrition: Advising on a balanced diet rich in nutrients that support vascular health
- Skin care: Regularly inspecting and caring for the skin to prevent circulatory complications

Promoting circulation is a critical aspect of patient care that requires the dedicated efforts of registered nurses. Through active and passive range of motion exercises, careful positioning, mobilization, and supplementary measures, RNs can significantly enhance a patient's recovery, prevent complications, and improve overall well-being. Their expertise ensures that circulatory health remains an integral part of holistic patient care.

Assess client for pain and intervene as appropriate

Pain management is one of the most fundamental responsibilities of nursing care. Effective assessment and intervention are critical for improving patient outcomes and ensuring comfort. This guide outlines the process by which nurses assess clients for pain and intervene appropriately.

Assessing Pain

Pain assessment is a multifaceted process that involves gathering comprehensive information about the client's pain experience. Nurses utilize various tools and techniques to evaluate pain accurately.

Communication with the Client

Understanding a patient's pain begins with effective communication. Nurses ask open-ended questions such as:

- "Can you describe the pain you are feeling?"
- "When did the pain begin?"
- "What makes the pain better or worse?"

Pain Scales

Nurses commonly use standardized pain scales to quantify the intensity of pain:

- Numeric Pain Scale: Clients rate their pain on a scale of 0 (no pain) to 10 (worst possible pain).
- Visual Analog Scale (VAS): Clients point to a position on a line that represents their current pain level.
- Faces Pain Scale: Particularly useful for children or non-verbal patients, this scale uses facial expressions to indicate levels of discomfort.

Observation
In cases where clients are unable to verbalize their pain, nurses observe for non-verbal indicators such as:

- Facial grimacing
- Guarding or restricted movement
- Changes in vital signs, such as increased heart rate or blood pressure
- Restlessness or agitation

Comprehensive Pain Assessment
In addition to intensity, nurses assess other dimensions of the pain:

- Location: The exact area where pain is felt.
- Quality: The type of pain (e.g., sharp, dull, burning, throbbing).
- Duration: Whether the pain is acute or chronic.
- Impact: How the pain affects daily activities, sleep, and emotional well-being.

Intervening Appropriately

Once pain has been assessed, nurses implement interventions tailored to the client's needs. These may include pharmacological, non-pharmacological, and collaborative approaches.

Pharmacological Interventions
Medications are often prescribed to manage pain. Nurses ensure the proper administration and monitoring of these drugs:

- Non-opioids: Includes acetaminophen and NSAIDs for mild to moderate pain.
- Opioids: Used for severe pain, with careful monitoring for side effects like respiratory depression.

- Adjuvants: Medications like antidepressants or anticonvulsants for neuropathic pain.

Non-Pharmacological Interventions

Nurses utilize various techniques to complement or replace pharmacological treatments:

- Physical Therapy: Recommending exercises, heat, or cold therapy to alleviate pain.
- Relaxation Techniques: Encouraging deep breathing, meditation, or guided imagery.
- Distraction: Engaging patients in activities like listening to music or watching a movie.
- Massages: Gentle massage to relieve muscle tension and improve circulation.

Patient Education

Clients benefit from understanding their pain and how to manage it. Nurses educate patients on:

- The importance of adhering to prescribed medications
- Recognizing signs of worsening pain
- Lifestyle modifications, such as proper posture and adequate rest

Collaborative Care

Nurses often work with interdisciplinary teams to address complex pain cases. They consult with:

- Physicians for medication adjustments
- Physical therapists for rehabilitation
- Counselors for emotional and psychological support

Monitoring and Reevaluating

Effective pain management is an ongoing process. Nurses regularly monitor the client's response to interventions, reassess pain levels, and modify care plans as needed. Documentation of pain assessments and interventions ensures clear communication among healthcare providers.

Assessing and managing pain requires a holistic and patient-centered approach. By combining clinical skills, communication, and compassion, nurses play a vital role in alleviating suffering and enhancing the quality of life for their clients.

Recognize complementary therapies and identify potential benefits/contraindications

Complementary therapies, such as aromatherapy, acupressure, and dietary supplements, have gained widespread popularity in enhancing well-being and providing support alongside conventional medical treatments. Nurses play a crucial role in recognizing, evaluating, and integrating these therapies into patient care when appropriate. This guide explores how nurses identify the potential benefits and contraindications of complementary therapies and ensure their safe and effective use.

Understanding Complementary Therapies

Complementary therapies encompass a broad spectrum of practices that aim to support physical, emotional, and mental health. While not intended to replace conventional medical treatments, these therapies can augment patient care by addressing holistic needs. Common complementary therapies include:

- Aromatherapy: The use of essential oils to promote relaxation, reduce stress, and alleviate symptoms such as pain or nausea.
- Acupressure: A technique based on traditional Chinese medicine involving the application of pressure to specific points on the body to relieve tension, improve circulation, and promote healing.

- Dietary Supplements: Vitamins, minerals, and herbal products that may support health and immune function.

How Nurses Recognize Complementary Therapies

Patient Communication

Nurses often begin by engaging in open and respectful conversations with patients to understand their interest in and use complementary therapies. By building trust and rapport, nurses can uncover details about patients' preferences and experiences, allowing for a comprehensive assessment.

Education and Training

Many nursing curricula include education on complementary therapies, providing foundational knowledge about their uses and mechanisms. Nurses may also pursue additional certifications or training to deepen their expertise in specific therapies such as aromatherapy or acupressure.

Evidence-Based Practice

Recognizing complementary therapies means staying updated on the latest research and evidence regarding their efficacy and safety. Nurses often consult peer-reviewed journals, clinical trials, and guidelines from reputable organizations to determine which therapies are appropriate for integration into care.

Identifying Potential Benefits

Holistic Patient Assessment

Nurses assess patients holistically to identify areas where complementary therapies may offer benefits. For example, they evaluate physical symptoms, psychological distress, and lifestyle factors to determine how therapies can address these needs.

Personalized Care Plans

Nurses consider each patient's unique situation to recommend therapies tailored to their health goals. For instance:

- For Pain Management: Acupressure may be suggested to relieve chronic pain or tension headaches.
- For Stress Relief: Aromatherapy using lavender or chamomile oils can promote relaxation and improve sleep quality.
- For Nutritional Deficiencies: Supplements such as vitamin D or iron may address deficiencies identified through lab tests.

Improved Patient Outcomes

Complementary therapies can enhance patient outcomes by improving overall well-being, reducing reliance on pharmaceutical interventions, and empowering patients to take an active role in their health.

Recognizing Contraindications

Patient History and Medical Conditions

Nurses carefully review patients' medical histories and chronic conditions to identify contraindications. For example:

- Aromatherapy may trigger allergies or asthma in sensitive individuals.
- Acupressure may be inappropriate for patients with bleeding disorders or recent surgery.
- Certain supplements, like St. John's Wort, may interact with medications such as antidepressants or blood thinners.

Medication Interactions

Nurses assess potential drug interactions with complementary therapies to ensure patient safety. They consult pharmacological databases and collaborate with pharmacists to identify risks associated with combining therapies with prescribed medications.

Pregnancy and Special Populations

Certain complementary therapies may be unsuitable for pregnant individuals, children, or older adults. Nurses consider these factors when recommending or integrating therapies, prioritizing safe and evidence-based choices.

Integrating Complementary Therapies into Nursing Practice

Collaborative Care

Nurses work closely with other healthcare providers, such as physicians, dietitians, and physical therapists, to ensure complementary therapies align with the overall treatment plan. Communication within interdisciplinary teams is vital for safe and effective integration.

Patient Education

Nurses educate patients about the benefits, risks, and proper use of complementary therapies. For example, they may offer guidance on how to safely use essential oils or recommend reputable brands for dietary supplements.

Monitoring and Evaluation

After implementing complementary therapies, nurses monitor patients for effectiveness and adverse effects. Regular follow-ups allow nurses to adjust care plans as needed, ensuring therapies continue to support patient goals.

Complementary therapies offer valuable opportunities to enhance patient care and promote holistic well-being. By recognizing their potential benefits and identifying contraindications, nurses ensure these therapies are used safely and effectively. Through education, collaboration, and patient-centered practice, nurses empower individuals to explore integrative approaches to health while maintaining the highest standards of care.

Provide non-pharmacological comfort measures

Nurses ensure the comfort and well-being of their patients beyond administering medication. They employ a range of non-pharmacological comfort measures that address physical, emotional, and psychological needs. These approaches are particularly valuable for patients who may not tolerate certain medications, prefer holistic remedies, or require supplementary care to enhance their overall experience. Below, we delve into the methods nurses use to provide this essential care.

Physical Comfort Measures

Positioning and Mobility

Proper positioning and mobility adjustments are beneficial for reducing discomfort and preventing complications such as pressure ulcers. Nurses often reposition patients who are bedridden every two hours, ensuring even weight distribution and improved circulation. For mobile patients, encouraging light movement or physical therapy can enhance comfort and reduce muscle stiffness.

Application of Heat and Cold

Heat and cold therapy can provide significant relief for conditions such as muscle pain, swelling, or inflammation. Nurses may apply a warm compress to relax tense muscles or use cold packs to reduce swelling and numb localized pain. These measures are carefully monitored to avoid burns or frostbite.

Massage Therapy

Massaging tense or sore areas can help alleviate pain and improve blood circulation. Nurses often use gentle techniques to reduce stress and promote relaxation. This simple yet effective intervention is especially valuable for patients experiencing chronic pain or anxiety.

Emotional and Psychological Support

Active Listening

One of the simplest yet most impactful comfort measures is listening to the patient. By providing undivided attention, nurses help patients feel valued and understood. This empathetic interaction can significantly reduce feelings of isolation or anxiety.

Guided Imagery and Relaxation Techniques

Guided imagery involves encouraging patients to visualize calming scenarios, such as a serene beach or a lush forest. This mental exercise, often combined with deep breathing techniques, helps reduce stress and promote relaxation. Nurses may guide these sessions or provide resources to practice independently.

Emotional Reassurance

Patients often experience fear or uncertainty, particularly when facing major diagnoses or treatments. Nurses provide emotional reassurance by explaining procedures clearly, offering words of encouragement, or simply being present during difficult moments.

Environmental Adjustments

Optimizing Room Conditions

Adjusting the patient's environment plays a significant role in their comfort. Nurses ensure that the room is adequately lit, free of excessive noise, and maintained at a comfortable temperature. These seemingly small changes can make a substantial difference in the patient's experience.

Providing Personal Items

Personal belongings, such as a favorite blanket, photographs, or a cherished book, can provide immense comfort to patients. Nurses often encourage family members to bring items that promote a sense of familiarity and security.

Cognitive and Recreational Activities

Engaging in Hobbies or Pastimes

For patients who are able, participating in hobbies or pastimes can be a therapeutic distraction from pain or discomfort. Nurses may arrange for activities such as reading, art therapy, or music therapy, tailored to the patient's interests and abilities.

Pet Therapy

Interactions with therapy animals have been widely recognized for their ability to reduce stress and enhance emotional well-being. Nurses may coordinate visits from therapy dogs or cats to provide companionship and comfort.

Patient and Family Education

Teaching Coping Strategies
Nurses educate patients and their families about coping techniques to manage stress and discomfort. This might include breathing exercises, mindfulness practices, or simple stretches that can be performed independently.

Informing About Available Resources
Providing information about support groups, counseling services, or additional resources equips patients and families to better navigate their challenges. Nurses act as a bridge to these services, ensuring holistic care extends beyond the hospital setting.

Spiritual Support
Encouraging Reflection and Spiritual Practices
For many patients, spirituality is a source of strength and comfort. Nurses support patients by encouraging prayer, meditation, or reflection, respecting their

individual beliefs and practices. Hospital chaplaincy services may also be involved in offering added spiritual guidance.

The Importance of Non-Pharmacological Interventions

These comfort measures are not only effective but also demonstrate the nurse's commitment to treating the patient rather than merely addressing symptoms. By incorporating non-pharmacological techniques, nurses enhance the overall patient experience, reduce reliance on medication, and foster a sense of dignity and well-being.

Non-pharmacological comfort measures are a cornerstone of nursing care. Through physical adjustments, emotional support, environmental changes, and spiritual guidance, nurses create a holistic approach to comfort and healing. These interventions underscore the art of nursing, reminding us that care is as much about compassion as it is about clinical precision. By embracing these techniques, nurses continue to make a profound impact on the lives of their patients.

 Evaluate the client's nutritional status and Intervene as needed

Nutrition is a cornerstone of health and recovery, and understanding a client's dietary requirements enables nurses to provide effective care and promote overall well-being.

Evaluating Nutritional Status

The evaluation of a client's nutritional status is a systematic process involving multiple steps. Nurses use both subjective and objective methods to assess dietary habits, physical health, and metabolic needs. Key components include:

Gathering Health History
Nurses begin by collecting a detailed health history, which encompasses:

- Existing medical conditions such as diabetes, hypertension, or gastrointestinal disorders.
- Allergies or intolerances to certain foods.
- Medications that may affect appetite, digestion, or nutrient absorption.
- Lifestyle factors, including alcohol consumption, smoking, and physical activity levels.

Conducting Nutritional Screenings

Nutritional screenings involve:

- Evaluating dietary patterns through food diaries or 24-hour dietary recalls.
- Using standardized tools such as the Mini Nutritional Assessment (MNA) or Malnutrition Screening Tool (MST).

These screenings help nurses identify risk factors such as inadequate caloric intake, vitamin deficiencies, or excessive consumption of unhealthy foods.

Physical Assessment

A physical assessment includes:

- Measuring body weight and height to calculate Body Mass Index (BMI).
- Observing signs of malnutrition, such as brittle hair, dry skin, or muscle wasting.
- Assessing hydration levels through skin turgor and mucous membrane checks.

Laboratory Tests

When necessary, nurses collaborate with healthcare providers to order laboratory tests that provide deeper insights into nutritional health. These may include:

- Blood tests to measure levels of vitamins, minerals, glucose, and cholesterol.
- Urinalysis to detect signs of dehydration or kidney function impairments.

Intervening as Needed

Once the evaluation is complete, nurses devise and implement tailored interventions to address the client's nutritional needs. These interventions aim to optimize health outcomes and support recovery.

Education and Counseling
Nurses provide education on:

- Balanced diets that meet the client's caloric and nutrient needs.
- Reading food labels to avoid allergens or excess sugar and sodium.
- Meal planning techniques to ensure variety and nutritional adequacy.

Counseling sessions are personalized to address specific dietary habits and challenges.

Collaboration with Dietitians
For clients with complex nutritional needs, nurses often coordinate care with registered dietitians. Together, they develop detailed meal plans and strategies tailored to medical conditions such as renal failure or malabsorption syndromes.

Monitoring and Adjustments
Nurses continuously monitor the client's progress and adjust interventions, as necessary. This includes:

- Regularly tracking weight changes and BMI fluctuations.
- Reassessing lab results to measure improvements in nutrient levels.
- Identifying and addressing barriers to compliance, such as financial constraints or cultural preferences.

Administering Nutritional Support
In cases where clients are unable to meet their needs through oral intake, nurses may administer:

- Enteral nutrition via feeding tubes.
- Parenteral nutrition through intravenous methods.

These approaches ensure essential nutrients are delivered effectively during recovery periods.

Provide client nutrition through tube feedings

Tube feeding, also known as enteral nutrition, is a method of delivering nutrients directly into the gastrointestinal tract when a client is unable to consume food orally. This essential intervention requires a nurse's expertise to ensure that the client receives adequate nutrition safely and effectively.

Types of Tube Feeding

Nurses may administer nutrition through different types of feeding tubes, depending on the client's medical condition and nutritional needs:

- Nasogastric Tube (NG Tube): Inserted through the nose and extending into the stomach, this is commonly used for short-term feeding.
- Naso-intestinal Tube: Similar to an NG tube, but extends into the small intestine, used for individuals with gastric motility issues.
- Gastrostomy Tube (G-Tube): Surgically placed directly into the stomach for long-term feeding needs.
- Jejunostomy Tube (J-Tube): Surgically placed into the jejunum for long-term feeding, often used when the stomach cannot tolerate feedings.

The Nurse's Responsibilities

Assessment and Care Planning

The nurse begins by assessing the client's medical history, nutritional needs, and ability to tolerate enteral feeding. Factors such as caloric requirements, fluid needs, and potential complications like aspiration or tube blockage are considered. A feeding plan is then developed in collaboration with the healthcare team.

Tube Placement Verification

Before starting any feeding, it is critical to confirm that the feeding tube is in the correct position. Nurses use several techniques for verification:

- Auscultation: Injecting air into the tube and listening for a gurgling sound in the stomach.
- Aspiration: Drawing gastric contents and checking pH levels.
- Radiological Confirmation: An X-ray may be used for precise placement verification.

Preparation of the Feeding Solution

The nurse ensures that the prescribed formula matches the client's dietary needs, whether it is a standard formula or one tailored for specific conditions like diabetes or renal insufficiency. The solution is checked for expiration and brought to room temperature before administration.

Administering the Feeding

Tube feedings can be delivered in several ways, and the nurse ensures appropriate methods are followed:

- Bolus Feeding: Administered in larger volumes at set intervals, mimicking a regular mealtime.
- Continuous Feeding: Delivered slowly over several hours using a pump.
- Cyclic Feeding: Administered intermittently, often overnight, to allow for normal daytime activities.

The feeding tube is flushed with water before and after the feeding to maintain tube patency.

Monitoring and Managing Complications

Throughout the feeding process, the nurse monitors for complications such as:

- Aspiration: Ensuring that the client's head is elevated during and after feedings reduces the risk of inhaling the feeding solution.
- Tube Blockage: Nurses flush the tube regularly and use protocols for clearing obstructions.
- Gastrointestinal Issues: Symptoms like bloating, diarrhea, or constipation are managed through adjustments to the feeding rate or formula.

The nurse also observes signs of infection at the insertion site for gastrostomy or jejunostomy tubes.

Documentation and Communication

Accurate documentation is crucial. The nurse records the type and amount of feeding solution administered, the client's tolerance, and any complications encountered. This information is shared with the healthcare team to make necessary adjustments.

Education and Support

The nurse plays a key role in educating clients and caregivers about tube feeding at home. This includes instructions on:

- Proper cleaning and maintenance of the feeding tube.
- Techniques for preparing and administering feedings.
- Recognizing signs of complications and knowing when to seek medical help.

Ongoing support ensures that clients and caregivers feel confident in managing tube feedings independently.

Providing nutrition through tube feeding is a vital aspect of nursing care for clients who cannot eat orally. By ensuring accurate placement, proper administration, and diligent monitoring, nurses play a critical role in achieving optimal nutritional outcomes while preventing complications. This comprehensive approach not only sustains the client's physical health but also enhances their overall quality of life.

Evaluating client Intake and Output and intervene as needed

Monitoring client intake and output is a fundamental responsibility of nurses as part of ensuring optimal health and fluid balance. The process involves measuring all fluids consumed and excreted by the client, providing essential data to evaluate hydration status, kidney function, and overall health. This guide explores how nurses systematically evaluate intake/output and intervene when necessary.

Understanding Intake and Output

What Constitutes Intake?

Intake refers to all fluids a client consumes or receives, which may include:

- Oral fluids, such as water, juice, and soup
- Intravenous fluids administered for hydration or medication
- Enteral feedings delivered through feeding tubes
- Medications in liquid form

What Constitutes Output?

Output encompasses all fluids the body eliminates, including:

- Urine
- Feces, especially if liquid or diarrhea is present
- Vomitus
- Drainage from wounds or surgical sites
- Perspiration in excessive amounts

Evaluation of Client Intake and Output

Monitoring Techniques

Nurses employ various techniques to accurately assess intake and output:

- Use of intake and output sheets to record fluid volumes
- Measurement of urine output with collection devices such as graduated cylinders
- Observation and documentation of unusual excretions, such as excessive vomiting or sweating
- Regular communication with clients or caregivers to capture dietary and fluid consumption

Assessment Criteria
When evaluating intake and output, nurses focus on:

- Fluid balance: Comparing intake and output to identify deficits or excesses
- Patterns and trends over time: Monitoring changes in fluid intake or output that may indicate an underlying condition
- Color, odor, and consistency of output: Assessing signs of infection or other health concerns

Interventions Based on Evaluations

Upon identifying imbalances, nurses take targeted actions to address issues:

Dehydration
For insufficient fluid intake or excessive output, nurses may:

- Encourage clients to drink water or other hydrating fluids
- Administer intravenous fluids to restore hydration
- Educate clients on the importance of maintaining adequate fluid levels

Fluid Overload
In cases of excessive fluid intake or inadequate output, interventions include:

- Restricting fluid intake temporarily

- Administering diuretics to promote fluid elimination
- Monitoring symptoms such as edema or difficulty breathing

Abnormal Output

If output suggests health issues, nurses may:

- Collect samples for laboratory analysis to diagnose infections or kidney dysfunction
- Coordinate with physicians to adjust medication or treatment plans
- Manage nausea, vomiting, or diarrhea with appropriate medications

Documentation and Communication

Effective documentation of intake and output ensures accurate tracking and facilitates communication among healthcare providers. Nurses must:

- Record all measurements promptly and accurately
- Note anomalies or sudden changes in fluid balance
- Share findings during team discussions or rounds to inform decision-making

By closely monitoring and evaluating client intake and output, nurses play a crucial role in maintaining fluid balance and preventing complications. Through timely interventions and effective communication, they ensure clients receive appropriate care tailored to their individual needs.

Assessing client activities of daily living and assist when needed

Activities of daily living (ADLs) are fundamental tasks that individuals perform to maintain their personal care and functioning, such as eating, bathing, dressing, toileting, and mobility. Assessing a client's ability to perform these tasks is a critical role for nurses, as it helps ensure the client's independence, safety, and overall quality of life. Nurses utilize systematic approaches to evaluate performance and intervene when assistance is required.

Assessment of Activities of Daily Living

Initial Evaluation

The assessment of ADLs begins with an initial evaluation, often conducted through interviews, observations, and standardized tools such as the Katz Index of Independence in ADLs or the Barthel Index. Nurses may ask specific questions about the client's daily routine, challenges they face, and any assistive devices they use. Observing the client as they perform tasks also provides valuable insight into their physical, cognitive, and emotional capabilities.

Clinical Observations

Nurses assess the client's ability in areas such as:

- Physical strength and mobility: Observing gait, coordination, and motor skills to identify limitations.
- Cognitive function: Evaluating memory, decision-making, and attention span as they relate to task performance.
- Emotional well-being: Understanding how psychological factors, such as anxiety or depression, impact ADLs.

These observations are crucial for creating a complete picture of the client's capabilities and needs.

Incorporating Family and Caregiver Insights

Family members and caregivers often provide valuable input, especially for clients who may struggle to articulate their challenges. Nurses engage with these individuals to obtain a holistic understanding of the client's abilities and daily habits.

Assisting Clients with Activities of Daily Living

Tailored Interventions

Once a nurse identifies areas where assistance is needed, they implement tailored interventions. These may include:

- Physical support: Helping clients with mobility, such as transferring from bed to chair or assisting with walking.
- Guidance and education: Teaching clients' strategies for completing ADLs more efficiently or safely, such as using adaptive tools or techniques.
- Emotional encouragement: Providing motivation and reassurance to clients who feel overwhelmed or discouraged.

Utilization of Assistive Devices

Nurses recommend and demonstrate the use of assistive devices, such as walkers, shower chairs, and specialized utensils, to enhance the client's independence. They also ensure that these tools are appropriately adjusted and safe to use.

Collaboration with Multidisciplinary Teams

In complex cases, nurses work closely with occupational therapists, physical therapists, and social workers to optimize support for the client. Together, they create comprehensive care plans that address both immediate needs and long-term goals.

Monitoring Progress and Adjusting Care Plans

Nurses continuously monitor the client's progress with ADLs, noting improvements or declines. Regular reassessments allow for adjustments to care plans, ensuring that interventions remain effective and relevant.

Assessing and assisting clients with activities of daily living is an essential component of nursing care. By adopting a systematic, individualized approach, nurses help clients maintain their independence, enhance their quality of life, and navigate challenges with dignity and confidence. Through thoughtful evaluation, tailored support, and collaboration with other professionals, nurses play a pivotal role in promoting health and well-being in daily living.

🧑‍⚕️ Perform postmortem Care

Post-mortem care is a sensitive and essential responsibility carried out by registered nurses to ensure the dignity and respect of the deceased, as well as to provide support to grieving families. This process involves both physical and emotional elements, and it must be performed with the utmost professionalism and compassion.

Steps Involved in Post-Mortem Care

Steps	Description
Confirming Death	Confirmation of death by a physician or authorized healthcare provider. Nurses ensure that this confirmation is recorded in the patient's medical records.
Preparing the Environment	Creating a calm and respectful environment. Curtains or screens may be used to maintain privacy, and any medical equipment that is no longer needed is removed or tidied.
Ensuring Proper Identification	The deceased must be accurately identified using wristbands or other identification methods to avoid any errors during the subsequent processes. Documentation is critical.
Preparing the Body	Handling the body to preserve dignity and appearance. Steps include closing the eyes, cleaning the body, and positioning it in a natural and peaceful posture.
Respecting Cultural and Religious Practices	Remaining sensitive to the cultural and religious preferences of the deceased and their family, involving specific rituals, prayers, or handling of the body.
Supporting the Family	Providing emotional support to the grieving family by listening, offering comforting words, and answering questions. Guiding them through next steps, such as contacting a funeral home.
Completing Documentation	Accurate and thorough documentation, including recording the time of death, personal belongings, and any special instructions or observations.

Coordinating with Relevant Services	Coordinating with relevant services for further processes.

Finally, the nurse ensures a smooth transition of the deceased to the designated mortuary or funeral home, coordinating with transport services and ensuring all required paperwork is completed.

Through these steps, registered nurses ensure that post-mortem care is carried out with dignity, compassion, and respect, honoring the life of the individual and supporting their loved ones during a difficult time.

Assess client sleep/rest patterns and intervene as needed

Sleep and rest are vital components of health and well-being, impacting physical, mental, and emotional states. Nurses play a crucial role in assessing and addressing sleep/rest patterns to promote optimal health outcomes for clients. This document explores the methods of assessment and interventions used in nursing practice.

Assessing Client Sleep/Rest Patterns

Proper assessment of a client's sleep/rest patterns is essential for identifying disturbances and planning effective interventions. Nurses use a combination of subjective and objective methods to gather information about the client's sleep habits and quality.

Subjective Assessment
Sleep History: Nurses begin by obtaining a detailed sleep history from the client. This includes questions about:

- Typical bedtime and wake-up time
- Total hours of sleep
- Sleep latency (time taken to fall asleep)

- Frequency of waking during the night
- Presence of naps during the day
- Perceived sleep quality
- Factors impacting sleep (e.g., stress, environment, pain)

Sleep Diary: Clients may be asked to maintain a sleep diary for several days, documenting their sleep and wake patterns, activities before bed, and any disturbances experienced during the night.

Self-Reported Questionnaires: Tools such as the Pittsburgh Sleep Quality Index (PSQI) or Epworth Sleepiness Scale can help quantify sleep quality and daytime sleepiness.

Objective Assessment

Observation: Nurses assess the client's physical appearance and behavior, such as signs of fatigue, irritability, or difficulty concentrating, which may indicate sleep deprivation.

Monitoring Devices: In some cases, wearable devices or polysomnography may be used to measure sleep stages, breathing patterns, and other metrics.

Assessment of Environment: Evaluating external factors such as the client's sleep environment (e.g., room temperature, lighting, noise levels, and bedding comfort) provides insights into possible contributors to sleep disturbances.

Intervening as Needed

Once sleep/rest disturbances are identified, nurses implement interventions tailored to the client's needs. Interventions often fall into behavioral, environmental, and medical categories.

Behavioral Interventions

Sleep Hygiene Education: Nurses educate clients on practices that promote healthy sleep, including:

- Maintaining a consistent sleep schedule
- Creating a relaxing bedtime routine
- Avoiding stimulants (e.g., caffeine, nicotine) in the evening
- Limiting screen time before bed
- Engaging in regular physical activity during the day

Relaxation Techniques: Teaching clients relaxation methods such as deep breathing, progressive muscle relaxation, or meditation can help reduce anxiety and promote sleep.

Cognitive Behavioral Therapy for Insomnia (CBT-I): In collaboration with mental health professionals, nurses may recommend CBT-I to modify thought patterns and behaviors affecting sleep.

Environmental Interventions

Optimizing the Sleep Environment: Nurses provide recommendations to enhance the client's sleep setting, including:

- Ensuring the bedroom is dark, cool, and quiet
- Using blackout curtains or white noise machines
- Investing in comfortable bedding

Minimizing Disruptions: For hospitalized clients, nurses minimize disturbances by clustering care activities to avoid waking the client frequently during the night.

Medical Interventions

Pain Management: Addressing pain through medication or non-pharmacological measures can improve sleep for clients experiencing discomfort.

- *Medication:* Nurses may collaborate with healthcare providers to prescribe sleep aids or other medications for specific sleep disorders, such as insomnia or sleep apnea.
- *Referral to Specialists:* Clients with persistent sleep issues may be referred to a sleep specialist for further evaluation and treatment.

- Assessing and intervening in client sleep/rest patterns is a multidisciplinary and personalized process that requires both empathy and expertise. By addressing sleep disturbances effectively, nurses contribute significantly to the client's overall health and quality of life. Regular follow-ups and adjustments to interventions ensure that clients achieve sustainable improvements in their sleep/rest patterns.

MODULE 6
PHYSIOLOGICAL INTEGRITY: PHARMACOLOGICAL & PARENTERAL THERAPIES NURSING TASK

Administering Blood Products and Evaluate Client Response

Administering blood products is a critical and complex procedure in nursing that requires precision, vigilance, and adherence to protocol to ensure patient safety. Equally important is the evaluation of the client's response to the transfusion to promptly address any adverse reactions.

Steps for Administering Blood Products

Step	Details
Verify the Physician's Order	Ensure the order specifies the type of blood product, volume, and rate of infusion. Confirm that the order aligns with the client's clinical condition and lab results.
Obtain Informed Consent	Verify that the client or their legal representative has provided informed consent for the transfusion. Provide the client with detailed information about the procedure, its purpose, and potential risks.
Perform Pre-Transfusion Assessments	Obtain baseline vital signs (temperature, blood pressure, heart rate, and respiratory rate). Review the client's medical history, particularly for previous transfusion reactions or allergies. Conduct a physical assessment to identify any pre-existing signs or symptoms that could be confused with transfusion reactions.
Prepare the Equipment	Gather necessary supplies, including an IV set with a blood filter, infusion pump (if required), and emergency medications. Ensure that a patent intravenous (IV) line is established and that it is suitable for the transfusion.
Verify and Crossmatch	Crossmatch the blood product with the client's blood type and Rh factor. Double-check the blood product label against the client's identification band with another nurse to ensure accuracy. Inspect the blood product for clots, discoloration, or signs of contamination.
Administer the Blood Product	Begin the transfusion slowly, typically at a rate of 2 mL/min for the first 15 minutes. Stay with the client for the initial 15 minutes to

	monitor for any immediate adverse reactions. Gradually increase the infusion rate as prescribed, provided there are no signs of a reaction.
Monitor During Transfusion	Regularly assess the client's vital signs and overall condition. Watch for signs of transfusion reactions, such as fever, chills, rash, dyspnea, tachycardia, or hypotension. Document the time the transfusion started, the rate of infusion, and any observations.

Steps to Evaluating Client Response

Step	Actions
Immediate Assessment	Observe the client closely for the first 15–30 minutes, stop the transfusion immediately and notify the healthcare provider if any adverse reactions are observed
Mid-Transfusion Evaluation	Reassess vital signs and compare them to baseline values, confirm that the client is tolerating the transfusion without signs of distress
Post-Transfusion Monitoring	Obtain vital signs and conduct a physical assessment once the transfusion is complete, check for delayed reactions, such as fever or jaundice
Laboratory Follow-Up	Send post-transfusion blood samples to the lab for hemoglobin and hematocrit levels, monitor other indicators such as electrolyte levels, renal function, and coagulation profiles
Documentation	Record the type and volume of blood product administered, the duration of the transfusion, and the client's response, document any adverse reactions and the actions taken to manage them

Administering blood products and evaluating client responses are vital responsibilities that demand attention to detail and adherence to established protocols. By following these guidelines, nurses can enhance client safety, address complications promptly, and contribute to successful transfusion outcomes.

 Access and maintain central venous access devices

Central venous access devices (CVADs) are essential in modern healthcare for administering medications, fluids, blood products, and nutritional support, as well as for monitoring central venous pressure. These devices require meticulous care and maintenance to ensure their functionality and to minimize complications, such as infections or blockages.

Types of Central Venous Access Devices

CVADs come in various forms, each suited to specific clinical needs:

- Peripherally Inserted Central Catheters (PICCs): Inserted into a peripheral vein, typically in the arm, and advanced to the superior vena cava.
- Tunneled Catheters: Surgically implanted under the skin, often used for long-term therapy.
- Non-Tunneled Catheters: Typically placed directly into a central vein for short-term use.
- Implanted Ports: Devices placed under the skin for intermittent access.

Accessing Central Venous Access Devices

Accessing CVADs requires adherence to strict aseptic techniques to prevent infections. The following steps outline the process:

Steps	Details
Preparation	Verify the physician's order and ensure the correct medication or solution is prepared. Perform hand hygiene thoroughly and don gloves. Gather all necessary supplies, including sterile dressing kits, syringes, and antiseptics.
Assessing the Device	Inspect the site for signs of redness, swelling, or discharge, which may indicate infection. Check for patency by flushing the catheter with saline if prescribed.
Connection	Scrub the hub or injection cap with an alcohol pad for 15-30 seconds. Attach the syringe or IV tubing securely, ensuring a proper seal.
Administration	Administer medications or fluids slowly and monitor any adverse reactions. Flush the catheter with saline or heparin (if prescribed) following administration.

Maintaining Central Venous Access Devices

Protocol	Details
Daily Monitoring	Inspect the insertion site for signs of infection or complications. Ensure the dressing and security device are intact.
Flushing Protocol	Flush regularly using a push-pause technique to prevent blockage. Follow institutional guidelines regarding saline or heparin flushes.
Dressing Changes	Change sterile dressings based on institutional policy. Use transparent dressings for ease of inspection or gauze dressings for high-risk infections.
Preventing Infections	Maintain aseptic techniques during all handling and procedures. Educate patients on how to avoid contaminating the device.

Emergency Responses	Occlusion: Attempt to flush gently; if unsuccessful, notify the physician. Infection: Remove the device if necessary and administer antibiotics. Dislodgement: Secure the catheter and inform the healthcare team.
Patient Education	Teach patients the importance of hygiene and avoiding unnecessary handling of the device. Instruct them to report unusual symptoms, such as fever, pain, or swelling at the site.

Central venous access devices are indispensable in delivering critical care, and nurses play a pivotal role in ensuring their safe use and maintenance. By following rigorous protocols for accessing, monitoring, and maintaining CVADs, healthcare professionals can minimize complications and enhance patient outcomes.

How Nurses Perform Calculations for Medication Administration

When it comes to medication administration, accurate calculations are a cornerstone of nursing practice. A nurse's ability to perform these calculations correctly can mean the difference between effective treatment and potential harm.

Understanding the Basics

Before any calculation is performed, nurses must understand key pieces of information:

- Doctor's Orders: The prescribed dosage, route, and frequency of medication.
- Medication Information: The concentration, form (tablet, liquid, injection), and packaging details provided by the manufacturer.
- Patient-Specific Factors: Weight, age, kidney or liver function, and any known allergies.

Common Calculation Methods

Several standardized formulas and techniques are used to calculate medication dosages. These methods ensure consistency and accuracy.

The Formula Method
This is one of the most used approaches in nursing. The formula is:
(Desired Dose ÷ Available Dose) × Quantity = Amount to Administer
For example:
- A doctor orders 250 mg of medication.
- The medication is available in 500 mg tablets.
- Calculation: (250 ÷ 500) × 1 tablet = 0.5 tablet.

Dimensional Analysis
This method helps nurses convert units and ensure correct dosage by setting up a single equation. The focus is on canceling out units to arrive at the desired outcome.
For example:
- Order: 1.25 mg of medication.
- Supply: 2.5 mg per 1 mL.
- Calculation: (1.25 mg ÷ 2.5 mg) × 1 mL = 0.5 mL.
Ratio and Proportion
Nurses can use ratios to solve dosage problems:
(Available Dose : Quantity) = (Desired Dose : X)
For example:
- Supply: 10 mg per 2 mL.
- Order: 5 mg.
- Proportion: (10 mg : 2 mL) = (5 mg : X).
- Cross-multiply: 10 × X = 2 × 5.
- Solve for X: X = 1 mL.

Special Considerations for Pediatric and Geriatric Patients

For pediatric and elderly patients, calculations often require more precision due to differences in metabolic rates and drug sensitivities. This may involve:

- Weight-Based Dosage: Dosages are calculated per kilogram of body weight (e.g., mg/kg).

- Body Surface Area (BSA): Some medications are done based on the patient's BSA, which is calculated using their height and weight.

Technology-Assisted Calculations

Modern nursing practice often incorporates technology to reduce errors:

- Electronic Medical Records (EMRs): Many systems have built-in dosage calculators.
- Smart Infusion Pumps: These devices allow nurses to program dosages and infusion rates, minimizing human error.
- Mobile Apps: Dosage calculation apps help nurses quickly and accurately perform complex calculations.

Double-Checking and Verification

To ensure patient safety, calculations are always verified. This may involve:

- Independent double-checks with a colleague, especially for high-risk medications such as insulin or chemotherapy agents.
- Cross-referencing calculations with protocols and guidelines provided by the healthcare facility.

Common Errors and Avoidance

Mistakes in medication calculations can have serious consequences. Nurses avoid errors by:

- Ensuring they understand the order and the medication being administered.
- Using standard measurement units and avoiding assumptions.
- Taking their time to perform calculations and avoiding distractions.

- Seeking clarification from a pharmacist or physician if there is any uncertainty.

Performing calculations for medication administration is a critical skill for nurses. Through a combination of foundational knowledge, systematic methods, and verification processes, nurses ensure that patients receive the correct dosage safely and effectively. This meticulous attention to detail underscores the role of nurses as vital contributors to patient care and safety.

Evaluating Client Response to Medication Nursing

Nurses play a critical role in observing and assessing how clients respond to medications. This evaluation is essential for ensuring effective treatment, preventing adverse effects, and promoting overall health. The process involves continuous monitoring, communication, and analysis based on evidence-based practices.

Understanding Medication

Before administering medication, nurses must have a thorough understanding of its purpose, expected effects, dosage, and potential side effects. Familiarity with the pharmacological action of the drug allows nurses to anticipate how the client might respond and identify any deviations from normal outcomes. This includes reviewing the client's medical history, allergies, and possible contraindications.

Monitoring Physiological Responses

After the medication is administered, nurses closely monitor the client's physiological responses. This involves observing changes in vital signs, laboratory results, and physical symptoms. Key metrics include:

- Heart rate and blood pressure for cardiovascular medications
- Respiratory rate for medications affecting the lungs
- Blood glucose levels for diabetes management

- Pain levels for analgesics

Any abnormal findings, such as unexpected side effects or signs of toxicity, are promptly reported to a physician.

Assessing Behavioral and Psychological Responses

Medications can also impact mental health and behavior. Nurses evaluate the client's mood, cognitive function, and overall psychological well-being, particularly when administering medications for conditions like depression, anxiety, or schizophrenia. Behavioral changes, such as agitation or lethargy, may serve as indicators of medication effectiveness or adverse reactions.

Engaging in Client Communication

Open communication with the client is vital. Nurses encourage clients to share how they feel after taking medication, including any discomfort, relief, or unusual sensations. This dialogue provides insight into subjective responses that might not be evident through physical assessment alone. It also helps build trust and ensures clients understand their treatment.

Recording Observations

Documentation is a cornerstone of nursing practice. Nurses record all observations, including the time of administration, client reactions, and any interventions taken. This information becomes part of the medical record and supports continuity of care among healthcare providers.

Evaluating Long-Term Outcomes

Effective medication evaluation extends beyond immediate reactions. Nurses assess whether the client's condition is improving over time and whether treatment goals are being met. This includes tracking progress in chronic disease management, recovery rates, and quality of life indicators.

Collaborating with the Healthcare Team

Nurses often work as part of a multidisciplinary team, sharing their findings with physicians, pharmacists, and other healthcare professionals. Collaborative discussions enable adjustments to medication plans, dosing, or alternative treatments if necessary.

Educating the Client

Another essential aspect is client education. Nurses explain potential side effects, proper medication use, and the importance of adherence to prescribed regimens. Educating clients empowers them to recognize and report unusual responses to medication.

Evaluating client response to medication is a complex and dynamic process that requires vigilance and expertise. By integrating physiological monitoring, psychological assessment, effective communication, and thorough documentation, nurses ensure that medications achieve their intended outcomes safely and effectively. Their role is indispensable in promoting client health and wellbeing within the broader framework of healthcare.

Educate clients about medications

Medication education is a critical component of nursing care. By educating clients about the medications they are prescribed, nurses enable them to take an active role in their treatment, enhance medication adherence, reduce the risk of adverse effects, and improve overall health outcomes. Nurses act as advocates, educators, and communicators, bridging the gap between complex medical information and the patients who need to understand it.

The Role of Nurses in Medication Education

Nurses are often the primary point of contact for patients in healthcare settings, making them uniquely positioned to provide medication education. Their role involves:

- Assessing the Client's Knowledge: Understanding the patient's baseline knowledge, beliefs, and misconceptions about their medications.
- Explaining Medication Details: Discussing the purpose, dosage, timing, and potential side effects of the prescribed drugs.
- Ensuring Understanding: Using techniques such as teach-back methods to confirm the client comprehends the information.
- Addressing Barriers: Identifying and overcoming challenges like language barriers, literacy issues, or fears related to medication use.

Strategies for Effective Medication Education

Establishing a Rapport with the Client

Building trust is essential for effective communication. Nurses should take the time to understand the client's concerns and create a non-judgmental, supportive environment. Patients are more likely to ask questions and engage in discussions when they feel comfortable.

Providing Clear and Accurate Information

Nurses must ensure the information they provide is accurate, evidence-based, and tailored to the individual client's needs. Key points to cover include:

- Name of the Medication: Both generic and brand names.
- Purpose of the Medication: What condition it is intended to treat.
- Dosage and Administration: How and when the medication should be taken.
- Potential Side Effects: Common and rare side effects, and what to do if they occur.

- Interactions: Possible interactions with other drugs, food, or alcohol.

Using Visual Aids and Tools

Visual aids, such as charts, diagrams, pamphlets, or videos, can help enhance understanding. For example:

- A chart showing the times and dosages can simplify complex medication schedules.
- Illustrations of potential side effects may help clients recognize symptoms if they appear.

Employing the Teach-Back Method

The teach-back method involves asking clients to repeat the information in their own words. This technique ensures they understand the instructions and allows nurses to identify areas that need clarification. For example, a nurse might say, "Can you tell me how you'll take this medication at home?"

Addressing Health Literacy

Health literacy levels vary widely among patients. Nurses should use simple, non-technical language and avoid medical jargon. For clients who struggle with reading, visual or verbal explanations may be more effective than written instructions.

Encouraging Questions

Clients should feel comfortable asking questions about their medications. Nurses can prompt this by saying, "What questions do you have about this medication?" rather than "Do you have any questions?" This subtle shift invites dialogue and reduces the risk of patients withholding doubts.

Incorporating Cultural Sensitivity

Cultural factors can influence a client's understanding and beliefs about medications. Nurses should be aware of these factors and provide education that respects the client's cultural background. For instance, some patients might prefer herbal remedies over pharmaceuticals, and this preference should be acknowledged and addressed.

Providing Written Instructions

Supplementing verbal education with written materials reinforces understanding. These materials should be clear, concise, and available in the client's preferred language. Including bullet points, charts, or infographics can enhance readability.

Special Considerations

Pediatric Clients and Caregivers

When educating pediatric clients, nurses often involve caregivers in the process. It is important to tailor the information to the child's age and developmental level while ensuring caregivers clearly understand the medication regimen.

Elderly Clients

Elderly patients may have unique challenges, such as polypharmacy, memory issues, or physical impairments. Nurses should provide simplified instructions, involve family members when appropriate, and recommend tools like pill organizers to aid adherence.

Clients with Chronic Conditions

For clients managing chronic conditions, ongoing education is crucial. Nurses should provide periodic updates on medication adjustments, address new concerns, and help clients integrate the medication regimen into their daily routines.

Overcoming Challenges

Medication education is not without its challenges. Nurses may encounter:

- Time Constraints: Limited time to provide comprehensive education during a busy shift.

- Resistance or Non-Adherence: Some clients may be reluctant to take medications as prescribed due to personal beliefs or side effect fears.
- Complex Medication Regimens: Multi-drug schedules can be overwhelming for clients.

To overcome these challenges, nurses can collaborate with pharmacists, utilize digital tools like medication reminder apps, and prioritize follow-up care.

Effective medication education is a cornerstone of quality nursing care. By empowering clients with knowledge, nurses not only enhance compliance but also foster a sense of autonomy and confidence in managing their health. Through clear communication, cultural sensitivity, and innovative teaching strategies, nurses ensure that clients are well-equipped to use their medications safely and effectively. The goal is to create a partnership where the client feels supported and informed, leading to better health outcomes and a higher quality of life.

Prepare and give medications using rights of medication administration

Nurses play a critical role in ensuring patient safety by adhering to structured principles when preparing and administering medications. One of the most important frameworks for this process is the "Rights of Medication Administration," a set of guidelines designed to minimize errors and enhance the quality of care.

The Rights of Medication Administration

The "Rights of Medication Administration" provides a systematic approach to preparing and delivering medications safely and effectively. These rights include:

- Right Patient: Confirm the identity of the patient using at least two identifiers (e.g., name and date of birth).
- Right Medication: Verify that the medication matches the prescription or order, including the name, dosage, and form.

- Right Dose: Ensure the correct dosage is prepared, accounting for factors like patient weight or age if indicated.
- Right Route: Confirm the proper route of administration (e.g., oral, intravenous, subcutaneous).
- Right Time: Administer the medication at the correct time, adhering to prescribed schedules or intervals.
- Right Documentation: Record the administration of the medication accurately and immediately after it is given.
- Right Reason: Understand the purpose of the medication, ensuring it aligns with the patient's diagnosis and condition.
- Right Response: Monitor and evaluate the patient's reaction to the medication, including any side effects or therapeutic outcomes.

Steps to Prepare and Administer Medications

Preparation

The preparation phase requires attention to detail and a thorough understanding of the medication:

- Review the prescription: Read the doctor's order carefully and check for completeness, including the medication name, dosage, route, and timing.
- Gather supplies: Collect all necessary equipment, such as syringes, vials, medication trays, or infusion sets.
- Perform calculations: Double-check dosage calculations, especially for pediatric or high-risk medications.
- Check expiration dates: Ensure the medication has not expired and that the packaging is intact.
- Verify allergies: Confirm the patient has no known allergies to the medication being administered.

Verification

During this step, the nurse ensures compliance with the "Rights of Medication Administration":

- Cross-check labels: Compare the medication label with the prescription at least three times—when retrieving it, before preparing it, and before administering it.
- Double-check with a colleague: For high-risk medications, such as insulin or anticoagulants, have another nurse verify all aspects of the preparation.

Administration

The actual administration of the medication involves patient communication and precision:

- Identify the patient: Use two identifiers to confirm the patient's identity. Avoid using room numbers as identifiers.
- Explain the medication: Inform the patient about the drug being administered, its purpose, and any potential side effects.
- Follow proper technique: Use aseptic techniques to prepare and administer the medication, ensuring cleanliness and sterility.
- Monitor the patient: Observe for any immediate adverse reactions following the administration.

Documentation

Proper documentation is essential for continuity of care:

- Record details: Document the medication name, dose, route, time, and any observations or reactions.
- Report issues: If an error occurs or the patient experiences an adverse reaction, follow institutional protocols for reporting and managing the incident.

Additional Safety Measures

Nurses should also practice the following safety measures to reduce risks:

- Patient education: Provide the patient with information about their medications, including instructions for self-administration if applicable.
- Environment management: Minimize distractions in the workspace to maintain focus during preparation and administration.
- Continuous learning: Stay updated on new medications, protocols, and evidence-based practices.

By adhering to the "Rights of Medication Administration" and incorporating meticulous preparation, verification, and documentation practices, nurses ensure patient safety and effective treatment outcomes. This structured approach not only minimizes errors but also fosters a culture of trust and professionalism in healthcare settings.

Reviewing pertinent data prior to medication administration

Medication administration is a critical aspect of nursing practice, requiring precision, thoroughness, and vigilance. Reviewing pertinent patient data prior to administering medication is essential to ensure safety and efficacy.

Importance of Reviewing Pertinent Data

Administering medications without a comprehensive evaluation of the patient's clinical data can result in adverse outcomes, including allergic reactions, contraindications, or harmful drug interactions. By reviewing the patient's information meticulously, nurses can prevent errors and enhance the therapeutic effectiveness of medications.

Steps to Review Pertinent Data

Verifying Medical History

Nurses begin by consulting the patient's medical history, which provides an overview of chronic conditions, previous illnesses, surgeries, and any ongoing treatments. This step helps in identifying potential contraindications with the prescribed medication. For instance, a medication may be unsuitable for a patient with renal insufficiency or liver disease.

Checking Lab Results

Laboratory test results play a pivotal role in medication administration, as they provide insights into the patient's current physiological and biochemical state. Key lab results to review include:

- Renal Function: Medications metabolized or excreted by the kidneys require scrutiny of creatinine levels and glomerular filtration rates.
- Liver Enzymes: Elevated liver enzymes may indicate impaired liver function, affecting drug metabolism.
- Electrolyte Levels: Imbalances in sodium, potassium, or calcium levels can influence medication effectiveness and safety.
- Coagulation Profiles: For medications affecting blood clotting, such as anticoagulants, reviewing INR or PT levels is crucial.

Assessing Allergies

A thorough allergy check is essential. Nurses must confirm any known drug allergies, such as penicillin or sulfonamides, as well as non-drug allergies that may influence administration (e.g., latex allergies for syringes or bandages). It is best practice to ask patients about allergies directly, even if they are documented.

Reviewing Current Medications

Patients often take multiple medications simultaneously, which increases the risk of drug-drug interactions. Nurses should:

- Compare new prescriptions with the patient's current medication list.
- Identify potential interactions, such as those between anticoagulants and NSAIDs or antibiotics and oral contraceptives.
- Assess the timing of doses to prevent overlap or missed administration.

Confirming Contraindications

Contraindications are conditions or factors that make a particular medication harmful. Nurses should verify whether the prescribed drug is appropriate given the patient's health status. For example:

- A patient with asthma may be contraindicated for certain beta-blockers.
- A pregnant patient may need alternatives to medications with teratogenic potential.

Reviewing Potential Side Effects

Understanding the anticipated side effects of a medication allows nurses to monitor the patient's post-administration. This step includes:

- Checking whether the patient was previously affected by side effects of similar drugs.
- Educating the patient about expected symptoms and signs requiring immediate attention.

Utilizing Decision Support Tools

Many healthcare settings provide electronic medical records (EMRs) and clinical decision support tools. These systems offer alerts for allergies, interactions, or contraindications and allow nurses to double-check prescriptions efficiently.

Documentation and Communication

Accurate Documentation

Recording findings from the data review process is vital. Nurses document:

- Any allergies or contraindications identified.
- Lab results influencing the decision-making process.
- Administration details—time, dose, and route.

Collaborating with the Healthcare Team

When uncertainties arise regarding a medication, nurses consult prescribers, pharmacists, or other healthcare professionals. Open communication ensures clarity and prevents errors.

Patient Involvement

A critical part of medication safety is involving the patient:

- Educating the patient about the medication's purpose and potential side effects.
- Encouraging the patient to disclose any past experiences with similar drugs.
- Answering questions to alleviate concerns and build trust.

Reviewing pertinent patient data prior to medication administration is a cornerstone of nursing care. It safeguards patient health and minimizes risks associated with medication errors. Nurses combine clinical knowledge, critical thinking, and collaboration to ensure that every medication administered contributes positively to the patient's treatment plan. By adhering to these practices, nurses uphold the highest standards of patient safety and care.

Participate in medication reconciliation process

Medication reconciliation is a critical component of patient safety in healthcare. It involves a structured process of creating an accurate and comprehensive list of a patient's current medications, including dosages and frequencies, and comparing it with the physician's orders. Nurses play a pivotal role in this process to ensure that medication errors are identified and prevented during transitions of care.

What Is Medication Reconciliation?

Medication reconciliation is a systematic approach to reviewing and verifying all medications a patient takes to ensure consistency and safety. This process is especially important during hospital admissions, transfers, and discharges when the risk of medication discrepancies is higher.

The Nurse's Role in Medication Reconciliation

Gathering Accurate Medication Histories

Nurses are often the first point of contact for patients and play a significant role in collecting comprehensive medication histories. This involves:

- Asking patients or caregivers about all prescribed medications, over-the-counter drugs, supplements, and herbal remedies.
- Confirming details such as the name, dose, frequency, and route of each medication.
- Cross-referencing the patient's verbal account with existing medical records and pharmacy data.

Identifying Discrepancies

Nurses actively compare the patient's current medication list with the physician's orders to identify potential discrepancies. Common discrepancies include:

- Omissions of necessary medications.
- Incorrect dosages or frequencies.
- Addition of unnecessary medications.

Collaborating with the Healthcare Team

Nurses serve as a vital link between patients, physicians, and pharmacists. They collaborate closely with these stakeholders to resolve discrepancies by:

- Communicating findings to physicians and providing recommendations for adjustments.
- Clarifying unclear prescriptions with the pharmacy team.
- Ensuring that any changes are documented and explained to the patient.

Educating Patients

Education is a cornerstone of nursing practice. Nurses ensure that patients understand any changes made to their medication regimen by:

- Explaining the reasons for adjustments.
- Demonstrating how and when to take medications.
- Providing written instructions and answering any questions to enhance adherence.

Monitoring During Transitions of Care

Transitions, such as hospital discharge or transfer to another facility, are critical moments when medication errors can occur. Nurses take the following steps to ensure safety during these transitions:

- Double-checking the medication list against discharge orders.
- Ensuring the patient receives a reconciled list of medications to share with other healthcare providers.
- Following up with patients after discharge to address any concerns or issues with their medications.

The Importance of Nurses in Medication Reconciliation

Nurses' participation in medication reconciliation significantly reduces the risk of adverse drug events and improves overall patient care quality. Their attention to detail, patient-centered communication, and interdisciplinary collaboration ensure that medication regimens are accurate, safe, and effective.

The nurse's role in the medication reconciliation process is indispensable. Their involvement ensures a smooth, error-free transition of care, builds trust with patients, and upholds the standards of safe medication practices. As frontline caregivers, nurses contribute greatly to the success of this critical safety initiative.

Titrate dosage of medication based on assessment and ordered parameters

Titration of medication dosages is a critical responsibility for nurses, requiring careful assessment, adherence to ordered parameters, and an understanding of the patient's response to treatment. The process ensures optimal therapeutic effects while minimizing adverse reactions.

Definition of Titration

Titration in the medical context refers to the process of adjusting the dose of a medication to achieve the desired effect or therapeutic range. Nurses play a vital role in this dynamic process, particularly in settings such as intensive care units, pain management, or chronic disease treatment, where precise control of medication is essential.

Steps for Medication Titration

Understanding the Ordered Parameters

Before initiating titration, the nurse must thoroughly understand the physician's or prescriber's orders. These orders typically include:

- Starting or initial dose
- Maximum allowable dose
- Incremental adjustments (e.g., increase by 1 mg/hour)
- Frequency of adjustments (e.g., every 15 minutes, every 6 hours)
- Specific target outcomes (e.g., pain relief, blood pressure normalization, oxygen saturation improvement)

Conducting a Comprehensive Assessment

Assessment is a cornerstone of titration. The nurse evaluates the patient's condition to determine the need for dose adjustments. Key components of the assessment include:

- Vital signs: blood pressure, heart rate, respiratory rate, and oxygen saturation
- Laboratory results: blood glucose, plasma levels, electrolytes
- Physical manifestations: signs of pain, sedation level, or distress
- Subjective feedback: reports from the patient about symptom relief or side effects

Administering Medication Responsibly

The nurse administers the medication at the prescribed starting dose and monitors the patient's response. This step requires:

- Using appropriate administration routes (e.g., intravenous, oral, subcutaneous)
- Ensuring proper timing and intervals between doses

Adjusting Dosages Based on Response

Titration adjustments are made incrementally, guided by the ordered parameters and the patient's response. The nurse ensures:

- Increases are made if the therapeutic goal is not yet achieved and no adverse effects are noted
- Decreases are implemented if adverse effects occur or if the therapeutic goal is surpassed
- The patient is closely monitored after each adjustment

Documenting and Communicating Changes

The nurse meticulously documents all actions and observations during the titration process. This includes:

- Initial and adjusted doses
- Patient's response to each dose
- Any adverse effects or complications

Effective communication with the healthcare team is essential to ensure continuity of care and alignment on the patient's treatment plan.

Common Scenarios Requiring Titration

Pain Management

In cases of severe pain, opioids such as morphine or fentanyl are often titrated. The nurse adjusts the dose to balance pain relief with the risk of sedation or respiratory depression.

Blood Pressure Management

For hypertensive crises or hypotension, medications like nitroglycerin or norepinephrine are titrated to achieve target blood pressure levels while avoiding complications.

Insulin Therapy

In diabetic patients, insulin titration is guided by blood glucose levels, with adjustments made to avoid hypoglycemia or hyperglycemia.

Sedation in Critical Care

Sedatives such as propofol are titrated to maintain appropriate levels of sedation, often measured by sedation scales like the Richmond Agitation-Sedation Scale (RASS).

Considerations for Safe Titration

Safety is paramount in medication titration. Nurses must:

- Follow evidence-based protocols and institutional guidelines
- Be vigilant for signs of toxicity or overdose
- Educate patients and families about the titration process, when applicable

Titration of medication is a complex and dynamic process that requires the nurse to integrate clinical knowledge, assessment skills, and adherence to prescribed parameters. By carefully monitoring the patient's response and making informed adjustments, nurses ensure safe and effective delivery of care.

Dispose of medication safely

The safe disposal of medications is a critical practice in healthcare settings to ensure environmental protection, patient safety, and compliance with legal regulations. Nurses play a vital role in this process, as they are often the frontline professionals responsible for handling and disposing of medications.

The Importance of Safe Medication Disposal

Improper disposal of medications can lead to significant consequences, including:

- Environmental contamination, such as polluted waterways and soil degradation.
- Potential misuse or accidental ingestion of discarded drugs by humans or animals.
- Violation of legal and regulatory requirements, leading to penalties for healthcare facilities.
- Endangering public health by facilitating the circulation of expired or unused medications.

Given these risks, adhering to safe disposal protocols is essential in maintaining ethical and professional nursing standards.

Guidelines for Safe Disposal

Follow Facility Policies and Procedures

Nurses should start by understanding and adhering to the specific policies and procedures set by their healthcare facility. These protocols are often tailored to the regulations of the local or national jurisdiction, ensuring compliance with laws regarding medication disposal.

<u>Separate Medication Types</u>

Certain medications require special handling due to their chemical composition and potential risks. Nurses should segregate medications into categories, including:

- Controlled substances: These require tracking and documentation before disposal.
- Hazardous drugs: These may need to be disposed of in designated hazardous waste containers.
- Non-hazardous and expired medications: These can often be disposed of through standard protocols.
-

<u>Use Designated Disposal Containers</u>

Healthcare facilities typically provide specially designed containers for medication disposal. Examples include:

- Sharps containers: For disposing of needles and syringes.
- Pharmaceutical waste bins: For expired or unused medications.
- Hazardous waste containers: For drugs that require careful handling due to environmental or health risks.

<u>Partner with Authorized Disposal Services</u>

Nurses should ensure that unused or expired medications are handed off to authorized disposal or waste management services. These services are equipped to handle pharmaceutical waste in a manner compliant with environmental and safety regulations.

Specific Disposal Methods

<u>Return Programs and Take-Back Initiatives</u>

Many healthcare facilities and communities offer drug take-back programs, allowing nurses to return medications to designated locations for safe disposal. These programs are managed by regulatory agencies or pharmaceutical companies and are a secure option for disposing of controlled substances.

Incineration

Incineration is a common method for disposing of medications, especially controlled and hazardous substances. Nurses should ensure that earmarked medications for incineration are delivered to facilities equipped with appropriate incinerators.

Flushing Protocols

Although flushing medications down the sink or toilet was historically common, it is now discouraged due to its potential to contaminate water supplies. This method should only be used for specific medications approved by the Food and Drug Administration (FDA) or relevant authorities for safe flushing.

Chemical Neutralization

Certain hazardous drugs may undergo chemical neutralization processes before disposal. This ensures that harmful substances are rendered inert and safe for handling.

Best Practices for Nurses

Educate Patients

Nurses can help by educating patients on the importance of medication disposal and providing instructions or resources for safe practices at home, such as advising on community take-back programs.

Document Disposal Activities

Proper documentation ensures accountability and compliance. Nurses should record details of disposed medications, including type, quantity, method, and authorization.

Wear Appropriate Protective Equipment

When handling hazardous drugs, nurses should use personal protective equipment to minimize exposure and ensure safety.

Stay Updated on Regulations

Medication disposal regulations can evolve. Nurses must remain informed about changes to local, national, and international policies.

Challenges in Safe Disposal

While there are clear protocols, nurses may face challenges such as:

- Lack of resources, such as appropriate disposal containers.
- Limited access to authorized disposal services in certain regions.
- Confusion about regulatory compliance due to varying laws.

Addressing these challenges requires collaboration between healthcare leaders, policymakers, and professional organizations.

Safe disposal of medications is an essential aspect of healthcare practice, and nurses are at the forefront of this responsibility. By implementing proper disposal methods, adhering to regulations, and educating patients, nurses can protect both public health and the environment. A commitment to ongoing education, documentation, and ethical practices ensures that medication disposal remains a priority in healthcare settings worldwide.

Handle and maintain medication in a safe and controlled environment

Ensuring that medications are stored, prepared, and administered correctly is vital to patient safety and effective treatment.

Storage and Organization

Proper storage of medication is the first step to maintaining a controlled environment. Nurses ensure that:

- Medications are stored in designated areas: These areas are typically secure, temperature-controlled, and organized to ensure quick and accurate access.
- Controlled substances are locked: Narcotics and other high-risk drugs are stored in locked cabinets or automated dispensing units to prevent unauthorized access.
- Regular inventory is maintained: Nurses frequently conduct inventory checks to ensure that all medications are accounted for and to avoid stock shortages or overstocking.
- Expired medications are discarded: Expired or damaged drugs are promptly removed and disposed of according to established protocols to prevent accidental use.

Preparation and Verification

Before administering any medication, nurses adhere to strict procedures to ensure accuracy and safety:

- Reading and verifying orders: Medication orders from physicians are carefully read and re-verified to confirm the correct drug, dosage, route, and timing.
- Following the "Five Rights": Nurses always adhere to the Five Rights of medication administration:
- Right patient
- Right medication
- Right dose
- Right route
- Right time

Double-checking high-risk medications: For drugs with a narrow therapeutic index, such as insulin or anticoagulants, a second nurse often verifies the preparation to reduce errors.

Administration and Monitoring

During medication administration, nurses take steps to ensure patient safety:

- Patient identification: Nurses use two identifiers, such as the name and date of birth, to ensure the medication is being administered to the correct person.
- Patient education: Patients are informed about the medication they are receiving, including its purpose and potential side effects.
- Monitoring adverse reactions: Nurses closely observe patients for any signs of adverse effects or allergic reactions and report them immediately.

Documentation and Reporting

Accurate documentation is crucial for maintaining a controlled medication environment:

- Recording administered medications: Nurses document every medication given, including the time, dose, and route, in the patient's medical record.
- Incident reporting: If a medication error occurs, it is documented and reported following institutional protocols to ensure transparency and implement corrective measures.

Adherence to Legal and Ethical Standards

Nurses are guided by legal and ethical standards that uphold medication safety:

- Maintaining confidentiality: Patient information is handled with the utmost confidentiality in compliance with regulatory requirements, such as HIPAA in the United States.
- Continuing education: Nurses regularly update their knowledge on new drugs, protocols, and technologies to maintain competence in medication management.

Nurses are the cornerstone of medication safety in healthcare settings. Through meticulous organization, careful verification, vigilant monitoring, and adherence to ethical and legal standards, they create a safe and controlled environment for medication handling. Their diligence not only minimizes errors but also fosters trust and positive outcomes for patients.

Evaluate appropriateness and accuracy of medication order for client

Ensuring the appropriateness and accuracy of medication orders is one of the most critical responsibilities of nurses in healthcare settings. This meticulous process safeguards patients, prevents medication errors, and upholds professional standards. Nurses employ a combination of expertise, vigilance, and communication to evaluate medication orders.

Understanding Medication Orders

Medication orders are instructions provided by healthcare providers, typically physicians, detailing the type, dosage, and frequency of medication a patient should receive. These orders may also include specific instructions regarding the method of administration, such as oral, intravenous, or topical routes. Nurses act as intermediaries between physicians and patients, ensuring medication orders are administered correctly and assessing their appropriateness for the patient's condition.

Evaluating Appropriateness

Appropriateness refers to whether the medication order aligns with the patient's specific medical needs, health status, and treatment goals. Nurses employ several strategies to evaluate this:

Patient Assessment
Before considering the medication order, nurses perform a comprehensive assessment of the patient. This includes:

- Reviewing the patient's medical history to identify any pre-existing conditions, allergies, or contraindications.

- Evaluating current symptoms, diagnostic results, and clinical observations.
- Considering the patient's age, weight, and organ function, particularly liver and kidney performance, as these affect drug metabolism and excretion.

Compatibility with Diagnoses

Nurses cross-check the medication order with the patient's diagnosis to ensure the prescribed drug is appropriate. For example:

- An antibiotic prescription should correspond to a diagnosed infection.
- A pain management order must align with the level of pain documented.

If inconsistencies arise, nurses consult the prescribing physician for clarification or adjustments.

Considering Drug Interactions

Nurses review the patient's current medications to identify potential drug interactions. Some drugs can enhance, diminish, or alter the effects of other medications, leading to ineffective treatment or adverse reactions. Nurses frequently utilize electronic health records and drug interaction databases to verify compatibility.

Following Evidence-Based Guidelines

Nurses rely on evidence-based guidelines and protocols, such as those established by healthcare institutions or professional organizations, to determine if the medication aligns with best practices. For instance, certain drugs may be restricted for specific age groups or conditions.

Assessing Accuracy

Accuracy involves validating the precise details of the medication order, ensuring there are no errors in the prescription parameters.

Checking the "Five Rights"

Nurses adhere to the "Five Rights" of medication administration, which include:

- Right patient: Confirming the medication is intended for the correct individual by verifying identifiers such as name and date of birth.
- Right medication: Ensuring the prescribed drug matches the written order and is appropriate for the patient.
- Right dose: Verifying the dosage aligns with standard clinical guidelines and the patient's unique needs.
- Right route: Confirming the method of administration specified in the order.
- Right time: Ensuring timely administration as per the order to maintain therapeutic effectiveness.

Detecting Prescription Errors

Nurses scrutinize medication orders for common errors, such as:

- Illegible handwriting or ambiguous instructions.
- Incorrect dosage, especially with drugs requiring precise calculation, like pediatric or chemotherapy medications.
- Incomplete orders lacking essential details, such as the frequency of administration.

In cases of uncertainty, nurses promptly seek clarification from the prescribing physician.

Collaborating with Pharmacists

Pharmacists play an integral role in validating the accuracy of medication orders. Nurses consult pharmacists when specialized knowledge is needed, such as the effects of new or rare medications. Pharmacists often double-check the order and provide insights into dosing and administration techniques.

Preventing Medication Errors

Medication errors can have catastrophic consequences, ranging from mild side effects to severe health complications or fatalities. Nurses employ several preventative measures to avoid these errors:

Standardized Protocols
Healthcare institutions implement standardized protocols for prescribing, transcribing, and administering medications. Nurses follow these protocols to minimize inconsistencies.

Utilizing Technology
Electronic prescribing systems and barcoded medication administration (BCMA) tools are frequently used to reduce human error. Nurses scan barcodes on medication packaging and patient wristbands to confirm matches and ensure accuracy.

Encouraging Open Communication
Effective communication between nurses, physicians, pharmacists, and patients is crucial. Nurses educate patients about their medications, including potential side effects and the importance of adherence to the prescribed regimen.

Continued Education

Nurses actively engage in continuing education and training programs to stay informed about advancements in pharmacology, new drug releases, and updated protocols.

A Nurse's Ethical Responsibility

Nurses have an ethical duty to advocate for patient safety and well-being. When evaluating medication orders, they act as patient advocates, ensuring every step of the process prioritizes health outcomes and minimizes risks. If they encounter prescriptions that seem inappropriate or harmful, nurses are obligated to raise concerns and seek alternative solutions.

The evaluation of medication orders for appropriateness and accuracy exemplifies the critical role nurses play in modern healthcare. Their vigilance, expertise, and commitment to patient safety make them indispensable in preventing medication errors and ensuring effective treatments. By integrating clinical knowledge, technology, and ethical principles, nurses consistently uphold high standards of care while fostering trust and safety in the therapeutic journey of their patients.

Handle and administer high-risk medications safely

High-risk medications are those that bear a heightened risk of causing significant harm to patients if used improperly. Examples include anticoagulants, opioids, insulins, and chemotherapy agents. Nurses play a critical role in ensuring these medications are administered safely, as they are at the frontline of patient care.

Key Strategies for Safe Administration of high-risk

Understanding Medication
Knowledge is key to safety. Nurses must be thoroughly familiar with the high-risk medications they handle. This includes:

- Knowing their indications, dosages, routes of administration, and potential side effects.
- Understanding contraindications and special precautions associated with the medication.
- Staying updated on any changes to protocols or guidelines related to these drugs.

Double-Checking and Verification
Accuracy is non-negotiable. Nurses should always double-check high-risk medications to avoid errors. This involves:

- Performing independent double-checks with another qualified healthcare professional, especially for dosage calculations and infusion rates.
- Verifying the "Five Rights" of medication administration: the right patient, the right drug, the right dose, the right time, and the right route.

Clear Communication

Effective communication prevents errors. Nurses should maintain clear and accurate communication with colleagues and patients:

- Using standardized handoff tools to ensure critical information is passed on during shift changes.
- Educating patients about the purpose, potential side effects, and administration of their medications.

Safe Storage and Labeling

Proper storage reduces risks. High-risk medications should be stored securely to prevent unauthorized access. Best practices include:

- Clearly labeling medications to avoid confusion.
- Separating high-risk drugs from other medications to minimize the chance of mix-ups.

Utilizing Technology

Leveraging tools enhances safety. Technological advancements can assist nurses in mitigating risks:

- Using barcode scanning systems to ensure the correct medication is administered to the correct patient.
- Relying on smart infusion pumps for accurate delivery of intravenous medications.

Continuous Education and Training

Ongoing learning builds competence. Nurses should participate in regular training sessions to improve their skills and knowledge:

- Attending workshops and seminars focused on high-risk medication safety.
- Engaging in simulations to practice handling complex medication scenarios.

Monitoring and Reporting

Proactive oversight ensures prompt intervention. Nurses should closely monitor patients for adverse reactions and report any incidents immediately:

- Documenting all observations meticulously in the patient's medical record.
- Following institutional protocols for reporting medication errors or near misses.

Building a Culture of Safety

The safe administration of high-risk medications requires a collaborative effort and a culture of safety across the healthcare team. Nurses must feel empowered to ask questions, seek clarification when needed, and speak up about potential risks without fear of retribution. Institutions should support this culture by providing adequate resources and fostering teamwork.

Handling and administering high-risk medications are a significant responsibility for nurses. By adopting best practices such as thorough knowledge, verification processes, effective communication, and technology utilization, nurses can minimize errors and ensure patient safety. Continuous education and a strong culture of safety further enhance these efforts, making high-risk medication administration a carefully managed process. Through diligence and teamwork, nurses can uphold the highest standards of care when dealing with these critical medications.

Monitor intravenous infusion and maintain site

Intravenous (IV) therapy is a cornerstone of patient care, allowing for the administration of fluids, medications, and nutrients directly into the bloodstream. Effective monitoring and maintenance of IV infusion and the site are crucial for ensuring patient safety and therapeutic efficacy.

Monitoring Intravenous Infusion

Regular Assessment of Infusion

Nurses must routinely evaluate the infusion rate and ensure that it matches the prescribed rate. This includes:

- Checking the IV pump settings for accuracy.
- Observing the drip rate in manual IV setups.
- Monitoring for signs of infiltration, phlebitis, or blockage in the line.

Observing Patient Response

It is essential to assess the patient's response to the infusion:

- Monitor adverse reactions like swelling, redness, or discomfort around the site.
- Evaluate systemic responses such as fever, chills, or difficulty breathing, which may indicate an infection or allergic reaction.
- Ensure the patient is hydrated and comfortable during the infusion process.

Recording Data

Accurate documentation is crucial:

- Log the start time, type, and volume of IV fluids administered.
- Record changes in infusion rates or any issues encountered during monitoring.

- Document patient feedback and any interventions performed.

Maintaining the Intravenous Site

<u>Inspecting the Site</u>

The IV site should be inspected frequently for complications:

- Look for signs of infiltration, such as swelling or coolness around the site.
- Check for phlebitis, which appears as redness, warmth, or pain along the vein.
- Ensure the catheter is secure and free of leaks.

<u>Cleaning and Dressing the Site</u>

Proper hygiene and care are essential:

- Clean the IV site with an antiseptic solution as per hospital protocol.
- Replace dressings regularly to prevent infection.
- Ensure all connections are secure and sterile.

<u>Rotating the Site</u>

To minimize complications, the IV site may need to be rotated:

- Follow institutional guidelines on site rotation timing.
- Choose a new site that is easily accessible and suitable for IV therapy.
- Ensure patient comfort during the site change.

Educating the Patient

Patient involvement and education can greatly assist in maintaining the IV site:

- Inform the patient about signs of complications and instruct them to report any discomfort promptly.
- Discuss the importance of keeping the site clean and avoiding unnecessary movement.

- Reassure them about the process and answer any questions they may have. Monitoring IV infusion and maintaining the site require diligence, knowledge, and a patient-centered approach. By adhering to best practices, nurses can ensure the safe and effective delivery of intravenous therapy while minimizing risks and enhancing patient care.

Administration of medications for pain management

Pain management is a critical component of patient care, and nurses play an essential role in ensuring that medications for pain relief are administered safely and effectively. This process involves assessment, preparation, administration, and monitoring, all while adhering to medical protocols and patient needs.

Assessment of Pain

Before administering pain medication, nurses carefully assess the patient's level of pain. This is typically achieved through standardized scales such as the Numeric Pain Rating Scale (0-10), the Wong-Baker, FACES Pain Rating Scale, or other assessment tools suited to the patient's age, condition, and communication ability. Nurses consider factors such as the location, duration, and intensity of the pain, as well as any potential underlying causes.

Medication Preparation

Once pain is assessed, the nurse reviews the prescribed medication. This involves verifying the correct drug, dose, route, and timing according to the physician's orders. Nurses ensure that the medication corresponds to the patient's needs, considering allergies, potential drug interactions, and the patient's medical history. Common medications include non-opioids (such as acetaminophen and ibuprofen), opioids (like morphine and oxycodone), and adjuvant therapies such as antidepressants or anticonvulsants for neuropathic pain.

Double-Check Protocol
To ensure accuracy, nurses perform a "five rights" check:

- Right patient: Confirming the patient's identity.
- Right medication: Verifying the prescribed drug.
- Right dose: Ensuring the correct quantity.
- Right route: Confirming the method of administration (oral, intravenous, intramuscular, topical, etc.).
- Right time: Administering medication at the correct interval.

Administration Techniques

The administration method varies based on the type of medication and the patient's condition. Common routes include:

- Oral: Tablets, capsules, or liquid medications taken by mouth.
- Intravenous (IV): Direct delivery into the bloodstream for rapid relief.
- Intramuscular (IM): Injection into muscle tissue for prolonged effects.
- Topical: Creams, patches, or gels applied to the skin for localized pain relief.
- Subcutaneous: Injection under the skin for moderate, sustained pain relief.

Nurses follow strict protocols for aseptic techniques to minimize infection risks, particularly for injections and intravenous treatments.

Monitoring and Evaluation

After administering pain medication, nurses closely monitor the patient for effectiveness and side effects. This includes observing:

- Changes in pain levels: Assessing whether the medication has provided adequate relief.
- Adverse reactions: Watching for nausea, dizziness, sedation, respiratory depression, or allergic reactions.
- Vital signs: Checking blood pressure, heart rate, and respiratory function if the medication carries risks.

If the medication does not provide sufficient relief or causes adverse effects, the nurse communicates with the healthcare team to adjust the treatment plan.

Patient Education

Nurses also educate patients about their pain medication, explaining:

- The purpose of the medication and how it works.
- Proper usage, especially for oral medications or self-administered treatments.
- Potential side effects and when to report them.
- The importance of adhering to the prescribed schedule.

This ensures that patients are actively involved in their pain management and understand the treatments.

Documentation

Accurate documentation is a vital part of pain management. Nurses record the medication administered, including the name, dose, route, time, and patient response. This data becomes part of the patient's medical record and aids in continuity of care.

Nurses play a pivotal role in pain management by administering medications with precision and compassion. Their efforts ensure that patients receive appropriate relief while minimizing risks and side effects. Through careful assessment, education, and monitoring, nurses contribute significantly to improving the quality of life for those experiencing pain.

Handling and administering controlled substances

Nurses play a pivotal role in the safe handling and administration of controlled substances, which are regulated due to their potential for abuse and addiction. These responsibilities require strict adherence to legal and institutional guidelines, ensuring patient safety, ethical practice, and compliance with relevant laws.

Understanding Controlled Substances

Controlled substances are medications or drugs classified by governmental agencies, such as the Drug Enforcement Administration (DEA) in the United States, based on their potential for abuse, medical use, and dependence. These classifications, known as schedules, range from Schedule I (highest abuse potential and no accepted medical use) to Schedule V (lowest abuse potential).

Nurses must familiarize themselves with the classifications of drugs they administer, as this knowledge informs how these substances should be managed and the level of caution required.

Legal and Regulatory Guidelines

Knowledge of State and Federal Laws

Nurses must stay informed about both state and federal regulations governing controlled substances. For example, the Controlled Substances Act in the U.S. and similar legislation worldwide provide frameworks for safe handling.

Institutional Policies

Hospitals, clinics, and other healthcare institutions often have specific protocols for managing controlled substances. Nurses must follow these policies closely, as they often include steps for storage, documentation, administration, and disposal.

Licensure and Certification

Administering controlled substances typically requires appropriate licensure, such as a nursing license, and potentially additional certifications for advanced practice nurses. These credentials confirm that the nurse is qualified to handle these substances responsibly.

Storage and Security

Controlled substances must be stored securely to prevent unauthorized access and potential misuse. Key security measures include:

- Locked Cabinets or Safes: Controlled substances are often stored in designated, locked areas with restricted access.
- Inventory Management: Nurses should ensure accurate inventory records and report discrepancies immediately.

In some cases, automated dispensing systems add an extra layer of security, requiring individual login credentials and tracking all transactions.

Administration of Controlled Substances

Verification Process

One of the most important steps in administering controlled substances is ensuring the medication is correctly matched to the patient and prescription. Nurses typically follow the "five rights":

- Right patient
- Right medication
- Right dose
- Right route
- Right time

Additionally, verifying the legitimacy of prescriptions and identifying potential errors or red flags is essential.

Patient Assessment and Monitoring

Before administering controlled substances, nurses should conduct a thorough assessment of the patient, including their medical history, allergies, and current medications. Continuous monitoring after administration is equally important, especially for drugs with sedative or narcotic effects.

Documentation

Accurate and detailed documentation is critical when handling controlled substances. Nurses should record:

- Name, dosage, and route of the drug
- Time and date of administration
- Patient response and any side effects

Documentation not only ensures compliance but also provides a reliable record for future reference and audits.

Preventing Diversion and Misuse

Drug diversion, the unauthorized use of controlled substances, is a serious concern. Nurses must take proactive steps to prevent diversion, including:

- Strict adherence to security protocols
- Monitoring colleagues and ensuring team accountability
- Reporting suspicious activity to supervisors

Additionally, ethical awareness plays a key role in preventing misuse, as nurses are often the final checkpoint before a drug reaches the patient.

Disposal of Controlled Substances

Proper disposal methods are vital for preventing environmental contamination and misuse. Nurses should follow institutional guidelines and legal regulations for drug disposal, which may include:

- Returning unused medications to a pharmacy
- Using specially designated disposal containers

Documentation of disposal actions is often required to maintain compliance.

Continuing Education and Training

The medical field is continually evolving, and nurses must stay current on best practices for handling-controlled substances. Regular participation in training sessions, workshops, and certification programs can ensure that nurses remain competent in this critical area.

Ethical Considerations

Administering controlled substances comes with significant ethical responsibilities. Nurses must prioritize patient welfare and avoid situations that could lead to over prescription or unnecessary use of these drugs. Open communication with patients about potential risks and benefits is also essential.

Handling and administering controlled substances are a weighty responsibility that requires vigilance, professionalism, and adherence to regulatory guidelines. By understanding the legal framework, securing storage, verifying prescriptions, monitoring patients, documenting thoroughly, and preventing misuse, nurses can fulfill their role with integrity and contribute to patient safety. Continuous education and ethical commitment further reinforce their ability to manage these substances effectively, ensuring trust within the healthcare system.

Administer parenteral nutrition and evaluating client response

Parenteral nutrition (PN) is a method of providing nutrition intravenously to clients who are unable to meet their nutritional requirements via the gastrointestinal tract. For nurses, administering PN and evaluating the client's response is a critical responsibility that demands precision, attention to detail, and a thorough understanding of the client's condition.

Administering Parenteral Nutrition

<u>Preparing for Administration</u>
- Verify the prescription: Ensure the PN order matches the client's nutritional needs and is prepared according to prescribed formulations.
- Inspect the PN solution: Check for clarity, absence of particulate matter, and any signs of contamination such as discoloration or leaks.
- Follow aseptic techniques: Maintain sterile conditions when handling PN equipment to reduce the risk of infection.
- Install appropriate access: Confirm the presence of a central venous catheter (CVC) or peripherally inserted central catheter (PICC), depending

on whether total parenteral nutrition (TPN) or peripheral parenteral nutrition (PPN) is prescribed.

Administration Procedure

- Prime the tubing: Attach the PN bag to the infusion set, ensuring all air is removed from the tubing before connecting it to the client.
- Set the infusion rate: Program the infusion pump according to the prescribed rate, ensuring a gradual introduction of nutrients to avoid metabolic complications such as refeeding syndrome.
- Monitor for compatibility: Avoid mixing any medications with the PN solution unless explicitly directed by a physician, as it may lead to incompatibility reactions.
- Secure the infusion site: Ensure that the catheter and tubing are properly secured to prevent accidental dislodgement and to minimize the risk of infection.

Maintaining the Infusion

- Monitor infusion regularly: Check the infusion pump settings and ensure PN is being delivered accurately.
- Prevent complications: Regularly observe the catheter insertion site for signs of infection, phlebitis, or thrombosis. Monitor for systemic complications such as electrolyte imbalances or hyperglycemia.
- Replace equipment as required: Change PN bags and tubing according to institutional protocols, usually every 24 hours, to reduce the risk of contamination.

Evaluating Client Response

Monitoring Physical Indicators

- Daily weight measurements: Assess for appropriate weight gain or loss, indicating the nutritional adequacy of PN therapy.
- Fluid balance: Monitor input and output records to evaluate hydration and detect any fluid retention or imbalances.
- Signs of infection: Check for fever, chills, or redness and swelling at the catheter site, which may indicate an infection.

Laboratory Assessments

- Blood glucose levels: Regularly monitor for hyperglycemia or hypoglycemia, adjusting insulin coverage as needed.
- Electrolytes and organ function: Measure levels of potassium, magnesium, phosphate, liver enzymes, and renal function markers to detect any abnormalities.
- Serum albumin and prealbumin: Evaluate protein levels to confirm nutritional status and adequacy of PN.

Client Feedback and Observations

- Assess tolerance: Ask the client about any symptoms such as nausea, bloating, or fatigue that may indicate intolerance to PN.
- Review overall health improvement: Observe for signs of increased energy levels, improved wound healing, and better skin integrity as indicators of successful therapy.

Documentation

Maintain comprehensive records of PN administration and client response. Document infusion rates, any adjustments made, observed complications, laboratory results, and client feedback to ensure continuity of care.

Administering parenteral nutrition and evaluating its impact on the client requires a combination of technical skill and ongoing assessment. By adhering to best practices and maintaining vigilance, nurses can ensure that PN therapy is both safe and effective, contributing to the client's overall recovery and well-being.

MODULE 7

PHYSIOLOGICAL INTEGRITY: REDUCTION OF RISK POTENTIAL NURSING TASK

Assess and respond to changes and trends in client vital signs

Nurses monitor and respond to changes in client vital signs, which include temperature, pulse, respiration rate, blood pressure, and oxygen saturation. These parameters offer critical insights into a patient's health status and allow for timely interventions in cases of deterioration or anomalies.

Understanding Vital Signs

Vital signs are fundamental indicators of a person's physiological state. When monitored regularly, they reveal trends that can signal underlying conditions, acute changes, or improvements in health. Nurses are trained to interpret these signs holistically rather than in isolation, considering the patient's baseline measurements and the broader clinical picture.

Key Vital Signs

- Temperature: Reflects the body's ability to regulate heat and indicates conditions such as fever or hypothermia.
- Pulse: Measures heart rate and rhythm, offering insights into cardiovascular function.
- Respiration Rate: Indicates how effectively a patient is breathing and reflects respiratory health.
- Blood Pressure: Assesses the force of blood against the walls of arteries, crucial for detecting hypertension or hypotension.
- Oxygen Saturation: Measures the percentage of oxygen in the blood, essential for evaluating respiratory and circulatory systems.

Assessment of Vital Signs

Regular Monitoring

Nurses routinely measure vital signs using standardized equipment such as thermometers, sphygmomanometers, pulse oximeters, and respiratory monitors.

Frequency depends on the patient's condition, ranging from hourly checks in intensive care units to daily assessments in outpatient settings. These measurements are recorded meticulously to track trends over time.

Detecting Abnormal Trends

When assessing vital signs, nurses look for deviations from the normal range. For instance:

- A sudden spike in temperature could indicate infection.
- An irregular pulse might suggest arrhythmia or shock.
- Shallow or rapid breathing could lead to respiratory distress or metabolic imbalances.
- Elevated blood pressure may signal stress, medication side effects, or chronic conditions.
- Oxygen levels below 95% often suggest hypoxemia, requiring urgent attention.

To detect patterns, nurses compare current measurements with previous readings and consider factors such as age, medical history, and environmental influences.

Responding to Changes

Immediate Actions

When vital signs indicate acute changes, nurses are trained to act swiftly. Immediate interventions may include:

- Administering prescribed medications, such as antipyretics for fever or antihypertensives for high blood pressure.
- Initiating oxygen therapy for patients with low oxygen saturation.
- Positioning the patient to improve breathing or circulation.
- Contacting physicians or emergency responders if vital signs point to life-threatening conditions.

Documenting Trends

Accurate documentation is critical in nursing practice. Nurses maintain detailed records of vital signs to identify trends and guide treatment plans. These records serve as a communication tool among healthcare providers and are essential for legal and ethical considerations.

Patient Education

Nurses also educate patients and their caregivers about the importance of monitoring vital signs. They provide guidance on using home equipment, recognizing warning signs, and seeking medical attention when necessary. Empowering patients to track their health contributes to better outcomes.

Perform testing within scope of practice

Nurses conduct a variety of tests within their scope of practice. These tests, often performed at the bedside or in outpatient settings, provide vital information for diagnosis, monitoring, and treatment. The procedures, while straightforward in many cases, require adherence to professional standards, training, and protocol to ensure accuracy and patient safety.

Understanding the Scope of Practice

The scope of practice for nurses is defined by their licensing board, employer policies, and the healthcare setting in which they work. It includes tasks for which they are trained, certified, and authorized by local regulations. Performing diagnostic tests, such as ECGs and glucose monitoring, falls under this scope if the nurse has received adequate training and operates under established clinical guidelines.

Performing an Electrocardiogram (ECG)

An electrocardiogram is a non-invasive test that measures the electrical activity of the heart. Nurses often perform this test, particularly in emergency departments, medical-surgical units, and cardiac care settings.

Steps for Performing an ECG

Step	Details
Preparation	Confirm the physician's order, verify patient's identity, educate the patient, ensure comfortable position, clean and dry electrode area
Electrode Placement	Apply electrodes to specific locations on chest, arms, and legs, ensure proper adhesion and correct placement
Operating the ECG Machine	Attach leads from the machine to electrodes, input patient's information, ensure proper calibration
Monitoring and Completion	Monitor the machine, print or save results for physician review
Documentation	Record procedure in patient's medical chart, include observations or concerns

Performing Glucose Monitoring

Glucose monitoring is a common point-of-care test performed by nurses to measure blood sugar levels. This test is critical for patients with diabetes or those at risk of hyperglycemia or hypoglycemia.

Steps for Glucose Monitoring

Step	Details
Preparation	Gather supplies: glucometer, test strips, lancets, alcohol swabs. Confirm test order and verify patient's ID.
Patient Education	Inform the patient about the procedure and its purpose.
Performing the Test	Wash hands, wear gloves, clean fingertip, use lancet, place test strip, apply blood sample, wait for reading.
Interpreting Results	Compare results with normal range, notify physician if outside expected parameters.
Documentation and Follow-Up	

Monitor the results of diagnostic testing and intervene as needed

Nurses ensure patient safety and care by actively monitoring the results of diagnostic tests and intervening appropriately when results indicate abnormalities. Their responsibilities span from understanding the purpose of the diagnostic tests to taking timely action based on the results, ensuring optimal patient outcomes.

Monitoring Diagnostic Testing Results

<u>Understanding the Diagnostic Test</u>

Before monitoring begins, nurses must thoroughly understand the purpose and process of the diagnostic tests being conducted. This includes:

- Knowing the normal range of values for the test results.
- Recognizing the medical conditions or complications the test is meant to detect.
- Ensuring that the test is conducted under the correct circumstances (e.g., fasting requirements, correct specimen handling).

<u>Collecting and Verifying Results</u>

Nurses are typically responsible for ensuring that diagnostic test results are returned in a timely manner. This includes:

- Following up with the laboratory or diagnostic department if results are delayed.
- Verifying that the results correspond to the correct patient to avoid errors.

<u>Interpreting Results</u>

Although nurses do not diagnose, they must interpret results within the context of their knowledge of normal and abnormal values. By identifying red flags or critical results, they can determine when immediate intervention or escalation to a physician is necessary.

Intervening as Needed

<u>Communicating Critical Results</u>

When diagnostic test results indicate a potentially life-threatening condition, nurses must promptly communicate these findings to the appropriate healthcare providers. Effective communication includes:

- Providing a clear summary of the test results and their implications.

- Suggesting urgent actions, such as administering medications or preparing for emergency procedures.
-

Initiating Immediate Interventions

In some cases, nurses are required to act quickly before a physician is available. This may involve:

- Administering medications, such as insulin for critically high blood sugar levels or anticoagulants for abnormal coagulation profiles.
- Providing oxygen therapy or other supportive measures for patients in distress.

Documenting and Reassessing

After interventions are carried out, nurses meticulously document the actions taken, the patient's response, and any changes in condition. Continuous monitoring ensures that follow-up is conducted appropriately, and necessary modifications to the care plan are made.

Nurses serve as the frontline of healthcare, bridging the gap between diagnostic testing and effective patient care. By meticulously monitoring, interpreting, and acting upon diagnostic test results, they ensure that no critical details are overlooked, safeguarding the health and well-being of their patients. Their vigilance and expertise are invaluable in the dynamic environment of modern medicine.

Obtain blood specimens

Obtaining blood specimens is a fundamental skill in nursing practice, serving as a cornerstone for diagnostic and therapeutic purposes. Nurses follow a systematic process to ensure the procedure is safe, accurate, and comfortable for the patient. Below, the steps, techniques, and considerations involved in obtaining blood specimens are outlined.

Preparation

Before obtaining a blood specimen, nurses must prepare thoroughly to ensure the procedure runs smoothly and efficiently. This includes the following:

Preparation Steps	Details
Understanding the Patient's Medical History	Review medical history for conditions affecting blood draw
Gathering Equipment	Needles, Vacutainer tubes, Syringes, Tourniquet, Alcohol swabs, Gloves, Gauze, Adhesive bandages, Sharps container
Hand Hygiene	Wash hands thoroughly to minimize infection risk
Patient Communication	Explain procedure, address concerns to ease anxiety
Procedure Steps	Details
Positioning the Patient	Seated or lying down, arm extended and supported
Applying the Tourniquet	Applied above site to restrict venous flow
Choosing the Venipuncture Site	Median cubital vein, cephalic vein, basilic vein, hand veins
Cleaning the Skin	Clean site with alcohol swab or antiseptic solution
Performing the Venipuncture	Anchor vein, insert needle at 15-30 degrees, draw blood
Removing the Needle and Completing the Draw	Release tourniquet, remove needle, apply gauze, place adhesive bandage

Nurses ensure that the patient remains comfortable and monitor for any immediate adverse reactions, such as dizziness or swelling.

Post-Procedure

Procedure	Details
Labeling the Specimen	Each specimen is labeled accurately with the patient's information, date, and time of collection
Proper Disposal of Equipment	Used needles and other biohazardous materials are disposed of in a sharps container
Patient Aftercare	Nurses offer advice on post-procedure care, such as avoiding heavy lifting with the arm used for the draw
Documentation	Details of the blood draw, including the site, time, and any observations, are recorded in the patient's medical chart

Special Considerations

Nurses may encounter unique challenges during blood specimen collection, requiring adjustments to their approach. Examples include:

Pediatric Patients
Children may require shorter needles, extra reassurance, and distraction techniques to reduce anxiety.
Elderly Patients
Older adults often have fragile veins, requiring a gentle approach and careful site selection.
Patients with Difficult Venous Access
For patients with small or hard-to-locate veins, nurses may use alternative methods such as butterfly needles or ultrasound-guided venipuncture.
Urgent or Emergency Situations
In emergencies, blood specimens may need to be collected rapidly, prioritizing patient stability while maintaining accuracy.

Obtaining blood specimens is a critical nursing skill that requires precision, communication, and adherence to best practices. By following a systematic process, nurses ensure that specimens are collected safely and reliably, contributing to accurate diagnoses and effective treatment plans. Their expertise not only supports patient care but also underscores the importance of professionalism in healthcare.

Obtain specimens other than blood for diagnostic testing

Nurses collect specimens used to diagnose and monitor various medical conditions. While blood samples are commonly drawn, there are numerous other types of specimens that are essential for diagnostic testing.

Urine Specimens

Urine testing is one of the most common diagnostic methods, providing valuable insights into kidney function, infections, and metabolic disorders. Nurses obtain urine specimens in the following ways:

Clean-Catch Midstream Collection
Patients are instructed to begin urinating, stop midstream, and then collect urine in a sterile container. This method is often used to minimize contamination.
Catheterization
For patients unable to provide a sample via clean catch, nurses may use a catheter to collect urine directly from the bladder. This procedure ensures a sterile sample for testing.

24-Hour Urine Collection
Patients are asked to collect all urine over a 24-hour period. Nurses provide guidance on proper storage and ensure that the collection process is followed accurately.

Stool Specimens

Stool samples help diagnose gastrointestinal infections, parasitic conditions, and other digestive disorders. Nurses collect stool specimens by:

Providing Sterile Collection Kits

Patients are given containers, gloves, and instructions to collect stool samples at home or in a healthcare facility.

Assisting with Collection During Inpatient Care

For bedridden patients, nurses may assist in obtaining stool samples using bedpans or specimen collection devices.

Sputum Specimens

Sputum samples are vital for diagnosing respiratory infections and conditions such as tuberculosis. Nurses collect sputum specimens through:

Patient Expectoration

Patients are instructed to cough deeply and expel sputum into a sterile container, ensuring the sample comes from the lower respiratory tract.

Induced Sputum Collection

In cases where patients cannot produce sputum naturally, nurses may use saline nebulization to stimulate production.

Swabs for Specimen Collection

Swabs are used to collect samples from various parts of the body, including the throat, nasal passages, wounds, or skin. Nurses follow these methods:

Throat Swabs

Using a sterile swab, nurses collect samples from the patient's throat, often to test for infections like strep throat.

Nasal or Nasopharyngeal Swabs

These swabs are commonly used for respiratory virus testing, including influenza and COVID-19, by gently inserting a swab into the nasal cavity or nasopharynx.

<u>Wound Swabs</u>

For suspected wound infections, nurses use sterile swabs to collect pus or exudate from the affected area.

Other Specimen Types

In addition to the above, nurses may collect other types of diagnostic specimens:

<u>Skin Scraping or Biopsy</u>

For dermatological testing, nurses may assist in obtaining skin scrapings or small tissue biopsies under sterile conditions.

<u>Body Fluids</u>

Urine and blood aside, nurses may be involved in collecting cerebrospinal fluid (via lumbar puncture, typically performed by a physician), amniotic fluid, or synovial fluid, providing necessary assistance during the procedure.

Ensuring Safety and Accuracy

When obtaining specimens, nurses adhere to strict guidelines to ensure accuracy and safety. Key practices include:

- Using sterile equipment and techniques.
- Properly labeling specimens with patient identifiers.
- Maintaining chain of custody for transport to the laboratory.
- Educating patients on their role in the collection process.

Nurses are integral to the diagnostic process, employing a wide range of techniques to obtain specimens other than blood. Their expertise ensures that samples are collected safely and accurately, enabling timely and precise medical diagnoses.

Insert, maintain, or remove a nasal/oral gastrointestinal tube

Nasal and oral gastrointestinal tubes are vital medical tools used for various purposes, such as delivering nutrition, administering medication, draining stomach contents, and conducting diagnostic procedures. Nurses play a critical role in ensuring the safe insertion, maintenance, and removal of these tubes.

Purpose of Nasal/Oral Gastrointestinal Tubes

- Enteral feeding: Providing nutrition to patients unable to eat orally due to medical conditions.
- Medication administration: Delivering drugs directly into the gastrointestinal tract.
- Decompression: Removing gas or fluid build-up from the stomach or intestines.
- Sampling: Obtaining gastric contents for diagnostic analysis.

Insertion Process

Preparation

- Explain the procedure to the patient and address any concerns to ensure cooperation.
- Verify the physician's order and check for contraindications, such as nasal trauma or anatomical abnormalities.
- Gather necessary equipment, including the tube, lubricant, syringe, gloves, and tape.
- Wash your hands and don appropriate personal protective equipment (PPE).
- Position the patient in a high Fowler's position (sitting upright) to reduce aspiration risk.

Steps for Insertion

1. Measure the tube length from the tip of the nose to the earlobe and then to the xiphoid process to determine the insertion depth.
2. Lubricate the end of the tube with water-soluble lubricant for ease of insertion.
3. Insert the tube gently through the nostril or oral cavity, guiding it down the esophagus. Encourage the patient to swallow or sip water during insertion.
4. Confirm the placement by:
5. Auscultating air injection sounds using a syringe.

6. Aspirating gastric contents and checking their pH level.
7. Sending the patient for an X-ray, if needed, for definitive confirmation.
8. Secure the tube with adhesive tape to prevent displacement.

Maintenance

Routine Care

- Ensure the tube remains properly secured and positioned.
- Flush the tube regularly with water or saline to prevent clogging.
- Monitor for signs of infection, irritation, or pressure ulcers at the insertion site.
- Check the patency of the tube and its functionality during feeding or medication administration.
- Observe for abdominal discomfort, nausea, or vomiting, which may indicate improper placement or complications.

Patient Monitoring

- Assess the patient's hydration status and electrolyte balance, especially if the tube is used for decompression.
- Review daily intake and output records for any abnormalities.
- Provide oral and nasal hygiene to minimize discomfort and maintain cleanliness.

Removal Process

Preparation

- Explain the removal procedure to the patient and ensure their comfort.
- Wear gloves and gather necessary equipment, including a towel and syringe.
- Verify the physician's order for tube removal.

Steps for Removal

1. Flush the tube with water to ensure it is clear of residual contents.
2. Remove any securing tape or adhesive gently to avoid skin irritation.
3. Ask the patient to take a deep breath and hold it to reduce the risk of aspiration.
4. Withdraw the tube smoothly and steadily without excessive force.

5. Dispose of the tube according to hospital protocols and biohazard guidelines.

Proper insertion, maintenance, and removal of nasal/oral gastrointestinal tubes are crucial for patient safety and comfort. Nurses must follow standardized protocols while staying vigilant for complications and ensuring effective communication with the healthcare team. By upholding these practices, nurses contribute significantly to the patient's overall recovery and well-being.

Maintain percutaneous feeding tube

Percutaneous feeding tubes, such as percutaneous endoscopic gastrostomy (PEG) tubes, are essential medical devices that provide nutritional support for patients unable to consume food orally. Proper maintenance is crucial to prevent complications such as infections, blockages, or tube dislodgement.

Key Responsibilities in Maintaining a Percutaneous Feeding Tube

Assessment and Observation
Nurses should begin with a thorough assessment of the feeding tube site:

- Inspect the insertion site: Check for signs of redness, swelling, discharge, or tenderness, as these could indicate infection or irritation.
- Observe tube placement: Verify that the tube is securely positioned and has not shifted or dislodged.
- Monitor patient symptoms: Assess for any signs of discomfort, nausea, or vomiting, which may signal complications such as tube blockage or improper placement.

Hygiene and Infection Prevention
Maintaining cleanliness is vital to prevent infections at the insertion site:

- Daily cleaning: Use warm water and mild soap to gently clean the skin around the tube. Avoid harsh chemicals that may irritate the skin.

- Application of dressing: If prescribed, apply sterile dressing around the tube site, ensuring it is changed regularly to prevent moisture buildup.
- Hand hygiene: Perform hand hygiene before and after touching the feeding tube or the surrounding area.

<u>Tube Flushing</u>
Flushing the feeding tube is necessary to prevent blockages caused by formula residue or medication:

- Frequency: Flush the tube before and after each feeding or medication administration using sterile water or saline solution.
- Technique: Use a syringe to gently introduce the flushing solution, ensuring there is no excessive force that could damage the tube.
- Volume: Follow the healthcare provider's recommendations regarding the amount of flushing solution to use.

<u>Feeding Administration</u>

Proper feeding administration is essential for patient safety and tube functionality:

- Preparation: Ensure the feeding formula is at room temperature to prevent patient discomfort or irritation.
- Rate of administration: Use gravity or a feeding pump to deliver the formula at the prescribed flow rate.
- Bolus feeding vs. continuous feeding: Adjust the technique based on the patient's specific needs and medical orders.

Preventing Common Complications
<u>Infection</u>
Infections can occur at the insertion site or internally. Nurses should:

- Recognize symptoms: Redness, excessive discharge, fever, or pain at the site may indicate infection.
- Follow protocols: Adhere to strict aseptic techniques during care and consult the healthcare team if signs of infection appear.

Tube Blockage

Tube blockages are often caused by inadequate flushing or thick feeding formulas:

- Regular flushing: As mentioned earlier, flush before and after feedings and medication.
- Managing blockages: If a blockage occurs, try flushing with warm sterile water. Do not attempt to force the blockage as it can damage the tube.

Tube Dislodgement

Dislodgement can be caused by accidental pulling or improper securement:

- Securing the tube: Ensure the external fixation device is properly positioned and adjusted to prevent movement.
- Educating patients and caregivers: Provide guidance on minimizing movements and avoiding accidental pulling.

Patient and Caregiver Education

Nurses have an integral role in educating patients and their caregivers on feeding tube care:

- Daily care routines: Teach the importance of daily cleaning and flushing to prevent complications.
- Recognizing complications: Explain symptoms of infection, blockage, or dislodgement that require prompt medical attention.

- Safe feeding practices: Demonstrate proper techniques for administering feedings and medications.

Documentation and Communication

Effective documentation and communication ensure continuity of care:

- Record observations: Document tube maintenance activities, insertion site assessments, and patient responses.
- Report abnormalities: Communicate any complications or concerns to the healthcare team promptly.

Maintaining a percutaneous feeding tube requires meticulous attention to hygiene, proper technique, and patient education. Nurses are at the forefront of this care, ensuring that these vital devices function effectively while safeguarding patient health. Through diligent practices, complications can be minimized, and patients can benefit from consistent nutritional support during their recovery or ongoing care journey.

Apply and/or maintain devices used to promote venous return

Promoting venous return is a crucial aspect of patient care, particularly for individuals at risk of venous thromboembolism (VTE), deep vein thrombosis (DVT), or those with limited mobility. Devices such as anti-embolic stockings and sequential compression devices (SCDs) play a significant role in enhancing venous circulation and preventing complications. Nurses are vital in applying and maintaining these devices effectively, ensuring patient safety and comfort.

Anti-Embolic Stockings

Anti-embolic stockings, also known as compression stockings, are designed to apply graduated pressure to the legs, aiding venous return and reducing the risk of blood pooling.

Application

- Assessment: Before applying stockings, nurses should assess the patient's skin condition, circulation, and measure legs to determine the correct size.
- Preparing the Patient: Explain the purpose and benefits of the stockings to the patient. Ensure the legs are clean and dry before application.
- Proper Technique:
- Begin by rolling the stocking down to the heel.
- Place the foot into the stocking, ensuring the heel is positioned correctly.
- Gradually unroll the stocking over the leg without creating wrinkles or folds.
- Check that there is even pressure and no constriction at the top.

Maintenance

- Daily Inspection: Inspect the stockings daily for signs of wear, tear, or skin irritation underneath.
- Cleaning: Follow manufacturer guidelines for washing stockings to maintain their elasticity and hygiene.
- Periodic Replacement: Over time, stockings lose their effectiveness and should be replaced as recommended.

Sequential Compression Devices (SCDs)

SCDs use pneumatic compression to stimulate venous return by mimicking the natural muscle contractions of the legs.

Application

- Assessment: Evaluate the patient's skin integrity, circulation, and any contraindications such as wounds or infections.
- Preparing the Patient: Explain the procedure and ensure the patient is comfortable and positioned correctly, typically lying flat.
- Proper Technique:
- Wrap the compression sleeve around the patient's leg, ensuring a snug but not tight fit.
- Connect the sleeve to the pump, ensuring all tubing is secure.
- Turn on the device and adjust settings according to the physician's orders.

- Monitor for proper inflation and deflation cycles.

Maintenance

- Regular Monitoring: Check the device periodically to ensure it is functioning properly and that the patient's skin remains intact.
- Cleaning: Clean the sleeves as per manufacturer instructions to prevent skin infections.
- Storage: Store the device in a clean, dry area when not in use to avoid damage.

Best Practices

- Education: Educate patients and caregivers about the importance of these devices and their proper use.
- Documentation: Record the application and maintenance of devices in the patient's medical notes.
- Team Collaboration: Communicate with the healthcare team to address any issues or concerns regarding venous return devices.

Nurses play an essential role in ensuring the effective application and maintenance of devices that promote venous return. By adhering to best practices, they not only enhance patient outcomes but also prevent complications associated with impaired venous circulation. Proper technique, regular monitoring, and patient education are integral to the success of these interventions.

Use precautions to prevent injury and/or complications associated with a procedure or diagnosis

Nurses safeguard patients during medical procedures and in managing diagnoses. Their responsibilities include not only administering care but also taking precautionary measures to minimize risks and prevent injuries or complications. By adhering to a variety of evidence-based practices and protocols, nurses ensure optimal safety and outcomes for their patients.

The Importance of Precautions in Nursing

Medical procedures and diagnoses pose inherent risks to patients, whether from surgical interventions, medication administration, or diagnostic evaluations. Nurses act as the first line of defense in identifying, mitigating, and managing these risks. Precautionary measures are essential to prevent complications such as infections, bleeding, adverse drug reactions, and patient falls.

Key Precautionary Measures in Nursing

Adherence to Standard Precautions

One of the most fundamental practices nurses follow is adhering to standard precautions as outlined by health authorities such as the Centers for Disease Control and Prevention (CDC). These precautions include:

- Hand Hygiene: Thorough hand washing or the use of hand sanitizers before and after patient interactions.
- Use of Personal Protective Equipment (PPE): Gloves, masks, gowns, and eye protection to reduce exposure to pathogens.
- Aseptic Techniques: Ensuring sterile conditions during procedures like catheter insertion or wound dressing.

Risk Assessments and Patient Education

Nurses conduct detailed risk assessments before procedures or treatments, considering the patient's medical history, current health status, and potential vulnerabilities. For example:

- Screening for allergies before administering medications or using latex-based products.
- Assessing the risk of bleeding in patients on anticoagulants before invasive procedures.
- Providing patients and their families with clear instructions on post-procedure care and warning signs of complications.

Prevention of Infections

Healthcare-associated infections (HAIs) are a major concern in clinical settings. Nurses employ several strategies to prevent infections:

- Maintaining Sterile Fields: Ensuring that surgical instruments and dressing materials are properly sterilized.
- Monitoring for Symptoms: Watching for signs of infection such as redness, swelling, or fever in post-operative patients.
- Timely Catheter Care: Reducing the duration of catheter use and cleaning catheter insertion sites regularly.

Safe Medication Administration

Medication errors can lead to severe complications. Nurses follow the "Five Rights" of medication administration to ensure patient safety:

- Right Patient
- Right Medication
- Right Dose
- Right Route
- Right Time

Additionally, they double-check prescriptions, monitor for adverse drug reactions, and educate patients about potential side effects.

Fall Prevention Measures

Patients in healthcare settings are at an increased risk of falls, especially the elderly or those recovering from surgery. Nurses take the following precautions:

- Assessing patients for fall risks using standardized tools.
- Ensuring that beds are at appropriate heights and that call bells are within reach.
- Assisting patients during ambulation and providing non slip footwear.

Monitoring and Early Detection

A critical aspect of a nurse's role is continuous monitoring to detect early signs of complications. This includes:

- Regularly checking vital signs such as blood pressure, pulse, and oxygen saturation.
- Monitoring for changes in patient behavior or physical condition, such as confusion or sudden pain.
- Reacting promptly to warning signs like excessive bleeding or breathing difficulties.

Documentation and Communication

Accurate documentation and communication are vital to preventing errors and ensuring continuity of care. Nurses:

- Record every aspect of patient care, including medications administered, procedures performed, and observations made.
- Communicate effectively with other members of the healthcare team about patient needs and potential risks.
- Ensure that discharge instructions are clear and comprehensive.

Precautionary Measures in Specific Procedures

Surgical Procedures

In surgical settings, nurses focus on:

- Pre-operative assessments to identify risks such as clotting disorders or respiratory issues.
- Ensuring that surgical instruments and the operating room are sterile.
- Monitoring patients closely during anesthesia and post-operative recovery.

Diagnostic Procedures

For diagnostic procedures such as imaging or biopsies, nurses:

- Ensure that patients are properly positioned to avoid injury.
- Monitor for allergic reactions to contrast agents or sedatives.
- Provide reassurance and guidance to reduce patient anxiety.

Ongoing Education and Training

To maintain high standards of care, nurses undergo continuous education and training in precautionary measures. This includes:

- Participating in workshops and certifications on infection control, patient safety, and risk management.
- Staying updated on the latest clinical guidelines and research findings.
- Engaging in simulation training to practice handling emergencies and complications.

The role of nurses in preventing injuries and complications cannot be overstated. By implementing precautionary measures, conducting thorough assessments, and maintaining vigilant monitoring, nurses uphold the highest standards of patient safety. Their dedication, expertise, and proactive approach are instrumental in ensuring successful outcomes and enhancing the quality of healthcare delivery.

Evaluate client responses to procedures and treatments

Nurses assess and evaluate client responses to medical procedures and treatments. This process is essential to ensure the effectiveness of care and to identify any adverse reactions or necessary adjustments promptly.

Observation and Monitoring

Nurses begin by closely observing clients for physical, emotional, and behavioral responses. This includes:

- Vital signs: Regular monitoring of blood pressure, heart rate, respiratory rate, and temperature helps to detect any physiological changes.

- Physical appearance: Changes such as skin discoloration, swelling, or other visible symptoms are documented.
- Pain assessment: Nurses use pain scales to understand the intensity and nature of the client's pain and its progression.
- Behavioral cues: Non-verbal indicators such as facial expressions, posture, or restlessness may signal discomfort or distress.

Communication with Clients

Effective communication is fundamental to the evaluation process. Nurses engage with clients to gather subjective information, such as:

- Feedback: Asking clients about their feelings, symptoms, or overall experience with the treatment.
- Clarifications: Exploring any concerns or queries the client might have to ensure their understanding of the procedure.
- Emotional state: Assessing whether the procedure has impacted psychological well-being, such as anxiety or fear.

Utilization of Assessment Tools

Nurses employ standardized tools and techniques to evaluate responses objectively. Common tools include:

- Scales and charts: Pain scales, fluid balance charts, and mobility assessment tools to track progress.
- Diagnostic tests: Requesting laboratory or imaging tests when needed to verify clinical observations.
- Protocols: Following evidence-based guidelines for specific procedures, ensuring consistency in evaluation.

Documentation and Reporting

Evaluation involves meticulous documentation of observations and findings. Nurses ensure:

- Accuracy: Recording details such as time, treatment type, and response observed.
- Trends: Tracking changes over time to identify patterns or anomalies.
- Transparent communication: Sharing findings with other healthcare professionals for collaborative decision-making.

Intervention and Follow-Up

If clients exhibit adverse reactions or require further support, nurses take proactive steps:

- Immediate responses: Administering medication or applying first aid as per procedure protocols.
- Adjustments: Collaborating with physicians to modify treatment plans.
- Reassessment: Conducting ongoing evaluations after interventions to ensure stability and improvement.

Evaluating client responses is a dynamic and holistic process that combines clinical expertise, empathetic communication, and evidence-based practice. By meticulously observing, documenting, and intervening as needed, nurses ensure the highest quality of care and establish a foundation for the client's recovery and well-being.

Recognize trends and changes in client condition and intervene as needed

Nurses monitor and maintain the health and well-being of their clients. Recognizing trends and changes in a client's condition and intervening appropriately is a cornerstone of effective nursing care. This responsibility requires a combination of clinical knowledge, keen observation, critical thinking, and collaboration.

Continuous Assessment

One of the first steps in recognizing trends and changes is conducting continuous and thorough assessments. This process includes:

- Baseline data collection: Nurses begin by gathering baseline information about the client's vital signs, medical history, and current health status.
- Regular monitoring: Frequent assessments of vital signs, such as heart rate, blood pressure, respiratory rate, oxygen saturation, and temperature, help identify deviations from the baseline.
- Holistic observation: Paying attention to non-verbal cues like facial expressions, changes in behavior, or fatigue can offer insights into a client's condition.

Utilizing Technology and Tools

Advances in technology have equipped nurses with tools to identify changes more effectively:

- Electronic Health Records (EHR): EHR systems allow nurses to track and compare data trends over time, providing a comprehensive view of the client's health.
- Monitoring devices: Tools like continuous blood pressure monitors, telemetry, or pulse oximeters can provide real-time data on a client's physiological state.

Recognizing Early Warning Signs

Nurses are trained to recognize early signs of deterioration, such as:

- Unexplained changes in vital signs (e.g., tachycardia, hypotension)
- Alterations in mental status, such as confusion or lethargy
- Changes in skin color, temperature, or moisture
- Symptoms like shortness of breath, chest pain, or increased fatigue

Early recognition is critical, as it allows for timely interventions to prevent complications.

Critical Thinking and Decision-Making

Interpreting trends and changes requires critical thinking:

- Nurses must analyze data to identify patterns and assess their significance.
- They evaluate the client's response to treatments or medications to determine their effectiveness.
- They prioritize which changes require immediate attention versus those that can be monitored over time.

Communicating with the Healthcare Team

Nurses often collaborate with other healthcare professionals to ensure effective care:

- Reporting findings: Clear and concise communication of changes in a client's condition to physicians or specialists is crucial.
- Escalating care: If a client's condition worsens, nurses may activate rapid response teams or implement emergency protocols.

Timely Interventions

Once a trend or change is recognized, nurses take appropriate actions, including:

- Administering medications as prescribed
- Performing necessary procedures, such as wound care or oxygen therapy
- Educating and supporting the client and their family about changes in care plans

Documentation and Reflection

Nurses ensure that all observations, actions, and outcomes are accurately documented. This record-keeping is vital for continuity of care and legal purposes. Additionally, reflecting on their actions and outcomes helps nurses refine their practice and improve future interventions.

Recognizing trends and changes in a client's condition is an ongoing process that demands vigilance, expertise, and a proactive mindset. By combining technical skills, critical thinking, and effective communication, nurses can intervene promptly to safeguard their clients' health and contribute to positive outcomes in their care.

 Perform focused assessments

Focused assessments are a vital component of nursing practice, serving as targeted evaluations aimed at identifying specific issues in a patient's health status. These assessments allow nurses to concentrate on a particular area of concern, enabling timely interventions and improved patient outcomes. Unlike comprehensive assessments, which provide a holistic overview of a patient's health, focused assessments are narrower in scope but equally essential in clinical settings. Let us explore the methodology and significance of this practice in nursing care.

What is a Focused Assessment?

A focused assessment is a detailed, problem-oriented evaluation conducted when a patient presents with specific complaints or when an issue is identified during a routine check. For instance, if a patient reports chest pain, the nurse will perform a focused cardiac assessment rather than an all-encompassing examination. These assessments are dynamic and can be repeated as necessary to monitor changes in the patient's condition.

Steps in Performing a Focused Assessment

Preparation and Communication
Before conducting a focused assessment, the nurse must prepare thoroughly by reviewing the patient's medical history, current medications, and recent diagnostic results. Effective communication is crucial to establish trust and ensure patient cooperation. Nurses typically begin by explaining the purpose of the focused assessment and obtaining informed consent from the patient.

Subjective Data Collection

This step involves gathering information directly from the patient about their symptoms or complaints. Nurses use open-ended questions to encourage detailed responses. For example:

- "Can you describe the pain you're feeling?"
- "When did the symptoms start, and have they changed over time?"
- "What makes the symptoms better or worse?"

Subjective data provides the nurse with a clearer picture of the patient's experiences and concerns, forming the foundation for the next steps in the assessment.

Objective Data Collection

Objective data is gathered through physical examination and diagnostic tools. This step is highly specific and tailored to the area of concern. Below are examples of focused assessments for various bodily systems:

- Cardiovascular System: Assess heart rate, rhythm, blood pressure, and signs of edema or cyanosis.
- Respiratory System: Examine breathing rate, lung sounds, oxygen saturation, and the presence of wheezing or crackling sounds.
- Neurological System: Evaluate level of consciousness, reflexes, pupil response, and motor strength.
- Gastrointestinal System: Check for abdominal tenderness, bowel sounds, and signs of nausea or vomiting.

Documentation

Accurate and timely documentation is essential to ensure continuity of care. Nurses record both subjective and objective findings, noting any abnormalities, trends, or improvements. This information is shared with the healthcare team to facilitate collaboration and effective decision-making.

Follow-Up

Focused assessments are not one-time events. Nurses often need to reassess the patient to monitor progress or deterioration. For example, if a patient is being treated for localized pain, the nurse may conduct periodic assessments to evaluate the effectiveness of the treatment plan.

Key Principles of Focused Assessments

Clinical Reasoning

Nurses must use their clinical reasoning skills to prioritize which assessments to perform. The urgency and nature of the patient's complaint guide this process. For instance, in an emergency setting, a nurse may perform a rapid focused assessment to identify life-threatening conditions.

Patient-Centered Care

Every focused assessment should be tailored to the individual needs of the patient. Cultural sensitivity, emotional support, and respect for the patient's preferences are integral to delivering high-quality care.

Use of Technology

Advanced diagnostic tools such as portable ultrasound devices, blood glucose monitors, and telemetry systems can augment focused assessments. Technology enables nurses to obtain precise data quickly, improving the accuracy of their evaluations.

Examples of Focused Assessments in Practice

Focused Respiratory Assessment

In patients presenting with shortness of breath or a history of asthma, a focused respiratory assessment includes observing chest movements, measuring respiratory rate, and listening to lung sounds with a stethoscope. The nurse may also assess oxygen saturation using a pulse oximeter.

Focused Neurological Assessment

For patients with head injuries or symptoms of a stroke, the nurse performs a focused neurological assessment, which includes evaluating pupil size and response, assessing motor strength, and checking speech difficulties. Tools like the Glasgow Coma Scale may be used to quantify neurological function.

Focused Pain Assessment

Pain assessments are crucial for patients experiencing discomfort. Nurses use pain scales, such as the Numeric Rating Scale or Wong-Baker Faces Scale, to quantify the pain intensity. They also inquire about the location, nature, and duration of the pain to identify its cause and plan appropriate interventions.

The Importance of Focused Assessments

Focused assessments play an indispensable role in nursing by enabling timely identification and management of health issues. They are particularly valuable in:

- Emergency Situations: Rapid assessments can identify critical conditions like cardiac arrest or respiratory failure.
- Chronic Disease Management: Focused assessments help monitor conditions such as diabetes, hypertension, and chronic obstructive pulmonary disease (COPD).
- Surgical Recovery: Nurses perform specific assessments to detect complications like infections or blood clots in post-operative patients.

Focused assessments are a cornerstone of nursing practice, combining clinical expertise, patient-centered care, and technological innovation. By honing their skills in performing these targeted evaluations, nurses ensure that patients receive timely and effective interventions tailored to their specific needs. Whether in an emergency room, a long-term care facility, or a home care setting, the ability to conduct focused assessments remains a defining hallmark of professional nursing.

Educate client about treatments and procedures

Educating clients about treatments and procedures is a fundamental responsibility of nurses. This process ensures that patients are informed, engaged, and empowered to make decisions about their health. Effective education enhances patient outcomes, reduces anxiety, and fosters trust between the patient and healthcare provider.

Steps in Educating Clients

Assessing the Client's Needs

Before providing education, nurses assess the client's concerns, and readiness to learn. This involves:

- Understanding the client's current understanding of their condition and treatment.
- Identifying any barriers to learning, such as language, literacy, or cultural differences.
- Determining the client's preferred learning style, whether visual, auditory, or hands-on.

Using Simple and Clear Language

Nurses avoid medical jargon and communicate in a way that is easy to comprehend. Key strategies include:

- Breaking down complex procedures into manageable steps.
- Using analogies or metaphors to explain difficult concepts.
- Providing written materials or visual aids for reinforcement.

Providing Tailored Information

Education is personalized to suit the client's specific condition, treatment plan, and needs. Nurses ensure that information provided is:

- Relevant to the client's health goals and circumstances.

- Delivered at the right time in the care process to maximize understanding and retention.

Demonstrating Procedures

When teaching procedures, nurses often use demonstrations to increase clarity and confidence. Techniques include:

- Using models or medical equipment to simulate the procedure.
- Encouraging clients to practice under supervision.

This hands-on approach builds the client's confidence in self-care or procedural understanding.

Encouraging Questions and Discussions

Nurses create a safe and open environment where clients feel comfortable asking questions and discussing their concerns. Active listening and empathy are critical to ensuring clients feel heard and supported.

Providing Written and Digital Resources

To enhance retention, nurses supplement verbal education with written materials, videos, or reputable online resources. These tools allow clients to revisit the information at their own pace.

Verifying Understanding

Nurses assess whether the client has understood the information by asking them to explain it back or demonstrate what they have learned. This "teach-back" method helps identify and address any gaps in understanding.

Ensuring Continuous Education

Education is not a one-time event but an ongoing process. Nurses revisit and reinforce key points throughout the client's care journey, adapting to any changes in the client's condition or treatment.

Building Trust and Empathy

Effective education relies on a foundation of trust and empathy. Nurses take the time to build rapport with clients, showing genuine concern for their well-being. This emotional connection fosters a sense of safety and encourages clients to engage actively in their healthcare.

Benefits of Client Education

Educating clients about treatments and procedures offers numerous benefits, including:

- Improved adherence to treatment plans.
- Greater client satisfaction and reduced anxiety.
- Enhanced ability to make informed decisions about their care.
- Reduced risk of complications and readmissions.

Nurses educate clients about treatments and procedures, ensuring they are well-informed and confident in their care. By using clear communication, personalizing education, and fostering a supportive environment, nurses empower clients to take active roles in their health, ultimately contributing to better outcomes and experiences.

Provide preoperative and postoperative education

One of nurses most critical responsibilities is educating patients before and after surgical procedures. Providing clear, thorough, and empathetic preoperative and postoperative education ensures that patients and their families are well-prepared for surgery, recovery, and long-term health management.

Preoperative Education

Preoperative education aims to prepare patients mentally, emotionally, and physically for surgery. It also fosters trust and reduces anxiety, improving overall patient outcomes.

Building Rapport and Assessing Needs

Before diving into the educational process, nurses focus on building rapport with the patient. This involves:

- Introducing themselves and explaining their role in the care team.
- Creating a comfortable and supportive environment for open communication.
- Assessing the patient's knowledge of the upcoming procedure, their concerns, and any cultural or language barriers.

Understanding these factors allows nurses to tailor the education to the individual needs of the patient, addressing both medical and emotional aspects.

Providing Information About the Procedure

Nurses provide detailed information about the surgical process, including:

- The purpose and goals of the procedure.
- What the patient should expect on the day of the surgery, such as arrival times, check-in processes, and the sequence of events.
- Potential risks, complications, and benefits associated with the procedure.

By explaining these aspects in simple and accessible language, nurses help demystify the surgery and reduce patient apprehension.

Preoperative Instructions

Preoperative instructions are critical for ensuring the success of the surgery and minimizing risks. Nurses provide guidance on:

- Fasting Guidelines: Patients are often required to avoid food and liquids for a certain period before surgery. Nurses clearly explain these restrictions and their importance.
- Medication Management: Nurses review the patient's current medications and advise which should be taken or withheld before surgery, including anticoagulants, insulin, or dietary supplements.

- Hygiene Practices: Patients may need to follow specific hygiene protocols, such as using antibacterial soap or avoiding certain skincare products.
- Transportation Planning: Nurses remind patients to arrange for transportation to and from the healthcare facility, as they may not be able to drive post-surgery.

Addressing Emotional Concerns

Surgery can be a daunting experience, and patients often experience fear and anxiety about the unknown. Nurses provide emotional support by:

- Encouraging patients to ask questions and express their concerns.
- Reassuring them about the competence of the surgical team and the safety measures in place.
- Offering relaxation techniques, such as deep breathing exercises, to manage preoperative stress.

Educational Tools and Resources

To enhance understanding, nurses may use various educational tools, such as:

- Written materials or brochures summarizing key points.
- Visual aids, such as diagrams or videos, to explain surgical procedures.
- Online resources or apps that provide additional information and reminders.

These tools help patients retain critical information and feel more confident about the process.

Postoperative Education

Postoperative education is equally vital, as it equips patients with the knowledge and skills required for a smooth recovery and to prevent complications.

Immediate Postoperative Instructions

After the surgery, nurses take the time to explain immediate recovery expectations, including:

- Pain Management: Nurses educate patients about prescribed pain medications, their proper usage, and possible side effects. They may also introduce non-pharmacological pain relief methods such as ice packs or relaxation techniques.
- Dietary Recommendations: Depending on the procedure, patients may need to follow specific dietary guidelines, such as starting with clear liquids or avoiding certain foods.
- Activity Levels: Nurses inform patients about activity restrictions, such as avoiding heavy lifting, and provide guidance on safe mobility practices to prevent strain or injury.

Wound Care and Infection Prevention

Proper wound care is essential for healing and preventing infection. Nurses provide step-by-step instructions on:

- Cleaning and Dressing the Surgical Site
- Recognizing signs of infection, such as redness, swelling, or unusual discharge, and knowing when to seek medical attention.
- The importance of keeping the wound dry and following any specific care protocols recommended by the surgeon.

Monitoring and Follow-Up

Nurses emphasize the importance of follow-up appointments and provide details on:

- When and where the patient should attend post-surgery check-ups.
- What to expect during these appointments, such as suture removal or diagnostic tests.

- Encouraging patients to communicate any concerns or unexpected symptoms to their healthcare provider promptly.

Long-Term Recovery and Lifestyle Adjustments

For surgeries with prolonged recovery periods, nurses offer guidance on:

- Establishing realistic recovery timelines and goals.
- Adopting lifestyle changes, such as exercise or diet modifications, to support overall health and prevent recurrence of medical issues.
- Managing chronic conditions or rehabilitation programs, if applicable.

Family and Caregiver Education

In many cases, patients rely on family members or caregivers for support during recovery. Nurses extend their education efforts to these individuals by:

- Teaching them how to assist with wound care, medication administration, or mobility.
- Providing tips on creating a safe and supportive home environment for the patient.
- Encouraging them to look after their own well-being to avoid caregiver fatigue.

Challenges and Best Practices in Patient Education

While preoperative and postoperative education is critical, nurses often face challenges, such as time constraints, language barriers, or patient non-compliance. To overcome these hurdles, nurses employ best practices, including:

- Using plain and simple language to ensure clarity.
- Incorporating teach-back methods, where patients repeat the instructions to confirm understanding.

- Collaborating with interpreters or cultural liaisons to address language and cultural differences.
- Personalizing education to suit the individual needs and preferences of the patient.

Nurses are key educators who bridge the gap between complex medical procedures and patient understanding. Through effective preoperative and postoperative education, they empower patients to take an active role in their healthcare journey. This not only enhances patient outcomes but also fosters trust and strengthens the nurse-patient relationship. By combining clinical expertise with empathy and clear communication, nurses ensure that patients are well-prepared for every step of their surgical experience.

Provide preoperative care

Preoperative care is a critical component of surgical preparation, and nurses play an essential role in ensuring that patients are well-prepared physically, emotionally, and mentally. This care involves a combination of assessment, education, coordination, and emotional support tailored to individual patient needs.

Assessment and Patient Preparation

Nurses begin by conducting a thorough preoperative assessment. This includes:

- Medical history review: Gathering comprehensive information about the patient's health, medications, allergies, and previous surgeries.
- Physical examination: Checking vital signs, assessing physical health, and identifying any risk factors that could affect surgery or recovery.
- Diagnostic tests: Ensuring necessary tests such as blood work, X-rays, or ECGs are completed and reviewed.

Patients are also prepared physically for surgery:

- Ensuring fasting protocols are followed to prevent complications such as aspiration during anesthesia.
- Administering preoperative medications as prescribed, such as antibiotics or sedatives.
- Providing instructions about hygiene, such as washing with antiseptic soap or shaving the surgical site if required.

Patient Education

Nurses play a key role in educating patients about the surgical process to reduce anxiety and ensure compliance. They provide information about:

- The nature and purpose of the procedure.
- What to expect during surgery and recovery.
- Postoperative care, including pain management, mobility, and wound care.

Effective communication is vital, and nurses often use visual aids or written materials to reinforce understanding.

Coordination and Communication

Nurses act as liaisons between patients and the surgical team. They ensure that:

- All necessary documentation, including consent forms, is completed.
- Special instructions or concerns are communicated to the surgical team.
- Any additional consultations, such as those with anesthesiologists or specialists, are arranged.

Emotional Support

Preoperative care also includes addressing the emotional and psychological needs of patients. Nurses provide:

- Reassurance to alleviate fears and anxiety about the procedure.

- A listening ear to address patient concerns and answer questions.
- Encouragement to build confidence in the surgical team and the process.

Family members or caregivers may also be involved in creating a supportive environment for the patient.

Final Preoperative Checks

Before surgery, nurses ensure that all preparations are complete:

- Confirming the patient's identity and surgical site to prevent errors.
- Verifying adherence to fasting guidelines and medication instructions.
- Preparing the patient physically, such as positioning them appropriately or ensuring they are dressed in hospital attire.

These final checks are part of the broader surgical safety protocols designed to optimize outcomes.

Preoperative care provided by nurses is a multifaceted process aimed at ensuring patient readiness, minimizing risks, and fostering a sense of confidence and comfort. Through careful assessment, education, coordination, and emotional support, nurses play a vital role in the success of surgical procedures and the well-being of patients.

Manage client during a procedure with moderate sedation

Nurses ensure the safety, comfort, and effectiveness of medical procedures that involve moderate sedation. By combining clinical expertise, effective communication, and vigilance, nurses help to create a controlled and supportive environment for the client undergoing such procedures.

Understanding Moderate Sedation

Moderate sedation, also referred to as conscious sedation, is a medically induced state in which a client experiences reduced anxiety and discomfort while remaining responsive to verbal commands or light tactile stimulation. Unlike general anesthesia, moderate sedation does not involve complete unconsciousness, and respiratory and cardiovascular functions are typically maintained independently.

Key Goals of Moderate Sedation
- Reduction of anxiety and discomfort.
- Maintenance of client responsiveness.
- Preservation of vital functions (e.g., spontaneous breathing).
- Facilitation of the procedure while ensuring client safety.

Nursing Responsibilities Before the Procedure
Pre-procedure Assessment

A thorough pre-procedure assessment is essential to ensure the client is an appropriate candidate for moderate sedation. Nurses must:

- Review the client's medical history, including allergies, current medications, and any pre-existing conditions such as respiratory or cardiovascular issues.
- Conduct a physical examination, focusing on airway assessment and vital signs.
- Check laboratory results and ensure baseline data is recorded (e.g., oxygen saturation, blood pressure, and heart rate).
- Collaborate with the healthcare team to identify potential risks and contraindications.

Client Education and Consent
The nurse helps alleviate fears and prepares the client by:

- Providing clear explanations about the procedure and what to expect during sedation.
- Discussing the benefits and risks of moderate sedation.
- Ensuring informed consent is obtained and documented.
- Answering any questions or addressing concerns to build trust and confidence.

Preparation of Equipment

All necessary equipment and medications should be prepared and checked in advance. This includes:

- Monitoring devices for heart rate, blood pressure, oxygen saturation, and respiratory rate.
- Emergency equipment, such as a crash cart, suction apparatus, and airway management tools.
- Medications used for sedation, as well as reversal agents if needed.

Nursing Role During the Procedure

Monitoring and Observation

Continuous monitoring of the client's physiological status is a primary responsibility for the nurse. This involves:

- Tracking vital signs, including heart rate, respiratory rate, oxygen saturation, and blood pressure.
- Observing the client's level of sedation and responsiveness to verbal or tactile stimuli.
- Listening to signs of distress or complications, such as airway obstruction or hypoxia.
- Documenting all observations and changes in the client's status.

Communication and Reassurance

Effective communication is key during moderate sedation. Nurses should:

- Continuously interact with the client, offering reassurance and instructions as needed.
- Inform the client about each step of the procedure to provide a sense of control and security.
- Promptly address concerns or discomfort expressed by the client.

Intervention and Risk Management

Should complications arise, nurses must act swiftly to mitigate risks. This includes:

- Delivering supplemental oxygen if necessary.
- Adjusting the client's position to optimize airway patency.
- Administering reversal agents to counteract excessive sedation.
- Calling for additional medical assistance if the situation escalates.

Nursing Responsibilities After the Procedure

Post-procedure Monitoring

Once the procedure is complete, the nurse continues to monitor the client closely during recovery. Key tasks include:

- Evaluating vital signs and level of consciousness.
- Ensuring the client's airway remains unobstructed.
- Monitoring for adverse effects, such as nausea, dizziness, or delayed sedation reversal.

Providing Aftercare Instructions

It is important to educate the client about post-procedure care, including:

- Instructions regarding hydration, rest, and avoiding strenuous activities.
- Guidance on recognizing symptoms that require medical attention (e.g., persistent drowsiness, difficulty breathing).

- Informing the client about any follow-up appointments or tests.

Ensuring Safety and Comfort

Adhering to Protocols

Nurses must follow established protocols for sedation management, including:

- Using standardized sedation scales to assess the client's level of sedation.
- Complying with institutional guidelines for monitoring and documentation.

Advocating for the Client

Throughout the procedure, the nurse serves as the client's advocate, ensuring their well-being and dignity are upheld. This includes:

- Protecting the client's privacy and confidentiality.
- Collaborating with the healthcare team to prioritize the client's needs.

Managing clients during procedures with moderate sedation requires a combination of clinical expertise, vigilance, and compassion. Nurses are instrumental in preparing the client, monitoring their status, communicating effectively, and intervening when necessary to ensure a safe and successful outcome. By adhering to best practices and maintaining a client-centered approach, nurses help foster trust and deliver high-quality care in these critical settings.

Manage client following a procedure with moderate sedation

Following a procedure involving moderate sedation, the nurse plays a critical role in ensuring the client's safety, comfort, and recovery. Moderate sedation, also known as conscious sedation, allows the client to maintain airway reflexes and respond to verbal commands while reducing anxiety and discomfort. Proper post-procedure management is essential to minimize complications and promote optimal outcomes.

Immediate Post-Procedure Care

Monitoring Vital Signs

After the procedure, the nurse should closely monitor the client's vital signs, including:

- Respiratory rate and oxygen saturation to ensure adequate breathing
- Heart rate and blood pressure to detect any abnormalities
- Level of consciousness to assess alertness and responsiveness

Continuous monitoring should be maintained during the initial recovery phase, as sedation agents could still be active in the client's system.

Assessing Airway and Breathing

Ensuring the client's airway is clear and breathing is unlabored is vital. The nurse should:

- Observe for any signs of airway obstruction or respiratory distress
- Administer supplemental oxygen if needed
- Position the client appropriately, often in a semi-Fowler's position, to aid breathing

Post-Sedation Observation

Monitoring for Adverse Reactions

The nurse should be vigilant for any adverse reactions to sedation, such as:

- Nausea or vomiting
- Hypotension or hypertension
- Allergic reactions or signs of oversedation

Early identification and intervention are key to managing these issues effectively.

Pain Management

The client may experience discomfort or pain following the procedure. The nurse should:

- Assess the pain level using appropriate scales
- Administer analgesics as prescribed
- Offer non-pharmacological interventions, such as repositioning or using ice packs, if appropriate

Gradual Recovery and Discharge Preparation

<u>Encouraging Mobility</u>
Once the client is stable, the nurse should encourage gradual mobility to prevent complications such as blood clots. Assistance may be required initially, depending on the client's condition.

<u>Providing Instructions</u>
Before discharge, the nurse should educate the client and their caregivers regarding:

- Signs and symptoms to watch for, such as dizziness, excessive sleepiness, or difficulty breathing
- Medication administration and side effects
- Activity restrictions
- Follow-up appointments and when to seek medical attention

<u>Documentation</u>
Detailed documentation is crucial. The nurse should record:

- Vital signs and physical assessments
- Medications administered
- Any adverse reactions and interventions taken
- Client education provided

Proper nursing management following a procedure with moderate sedation ensures a smooth recovery and helps prevent complications. By prioritizing monitoring, communication, and education, nurses play an indispensable role in post-sedation care.

MODULE 8

PHYSIOLOGICAL INTEGRITY: PHYSIOLOGICAL ADAPTATION NURSING TASK

Assist with invasive procedures

Nurses ensure the success and safety of invasive procedures such as central line placement, thoracentesis, and bronchoscopy. Their responsibilities encompass a range of preparatory, intra-procedural, and post-procedural tasks that support the patient, the healthcare team, and the overall process.

Central Line Placement

Central line placement involves the insertion of a catheter into a large vein to administer medications, fluids, or obtain blood samples efficiently. Nurses assist in the following ways:

Pre-procedural Tasks:
- Verify the physician's order and confirm the patient's identity.
- Educate the patient about the procedure, addressing any concerns to reduce anxiety.
- Prepare the sterile field with necessary instruments, such as catheters, sterile gloves, and antiseptic solutions.
- Position the patient appropriately, often in a Trendelenburg position, to facilitate insertion.
- Ensure all equipment, such as ultrasound devices, is functioning correctly.

Intra-procedural Tasks:
- Maintain sterility by assisting the physician with tools and ensuring adherence to aseptic techniques.

- Monitor the patient's vital signs throughout the procedure to detect any complications.
- Provide reassurance to the patient during the procedure.

Post-procedural Tasks:
- Secure the central line and apply a sterile dressing.
- Document the procedure, including the type of catheter used, location of insertion, and patient response.
- Monitor the patient for immediate complications, such as bleeding or pneumothorax.

Thoracentesis

Thoracentesis involves the removal of fluid or air from the pleural space for diagnostic or therapeutic purposes. Nurses assist by performing the following:

Pre-procedural Tasks:
- Educate the patient about the procedure and obtain informed consent if required.
- Assist in positioning the patient, typically seated upright with arms resting on a table.
- Prepare the sterile field and required supplies, such as syringes, needles, and collection bottles.

Intra-procedural Tasks:
- Monitor patient vital signs and oxygen saturation.
- Hand instruments and supplies to the physician as needed.
- Provide emotional support and ensure the patient remains as still as possible.

Post-procedural Tasks:
- Apply sterile dressing to the puncture site.
- Monitor for complications, including pneumothorax or infection.
- Send collected fluid to the lab for analysis if required.

Bronchoscopy

Bronchoscopy is a diagnostic or therapeutic procedure involving the insertion of a bronchoscope to examine the airways. Nurses assist as follows:

Pre-procedural Tasks:
- Explain the procedure to the patient and ensure informed consent has been obtained.
- Prepare the bronchoscope and necessary accessories, ensuring sterility.
- Administer pre-procedural medications, such as sedatives, as ordered by the physician.

Intra-procedural Tasks:
- Monitor the patient's vital signs and oxygen levels continuously.
- Assist the physician by suctioning secretions, handling specimens, and ensuring smooth workflow.
- Provide reassurance to the patient and manage their comfort during the procedure.

Post-procedural Tasks:
- Observe the patient for complications, such as bleeding, hypoxia, or bronchospasm.
- Ensure specimens are labeled correctly and sent to the lab.
- Educate the patient on post-procedural care, including the importance of reporting any concerning symptoms.

The nurse's role in assisting with invasive procedures is critical to patient safety and the success of the intervention. By providing meticulous preparation, vigilant monitoring, and compassionate care, nurses ensure that these procedures are conducted efficiently and with minimal risk to the patient.

Implement and monitor phototherapy

Phototherapy is a widely employed treatment for conditions such as neonatal jaundice, psoriasis, eczema, and certain mood disorders like Seasonal Affective Disorder (SAD). Nurses play a crucial role in implementing and monitoring phototherapy to ensure its safety and effectiveness while minimizing potential risks.

Understanding Phototherapy

Phototherapy involves the use of light, natural or artificial, to treat medical conditions. The type of Phototherapy varies depending on the condition being treated. For example:

- Neonatal Jaundice: Blue or white light is used to break down excess bilirubin in newborns.
- Psoriasis and Eczema: UVB or UVA light is applied to reduce skin inflammation and cell proliferation.
- Seasonal Affective Disorder (SAD): Bright light therapy mimics sunlight to alleviate depressive symptoms.

Steps for Implementing Phototherapy

Assessing the Patient

Before initiating phototherapy, a thorough assessment of the patient's condition is essential. This includes:

- Reviewing medical history and contraindications (e.g., photosensitivity disorders, certain medications).
- Confirming the diagnosis and the specific need for phototherapy.
- Educating the patient or caregiver about the procedure, its purpose, and potential side effects.

Preparing the Equipment

Nurses must ensure that the equipment is appropriately set up and functioning. Key preparation steps include:

- Calibrating the light source to achieve the required wavelength and intensity.
- Ensuring protective measures like UV shields or filters are in place.

- Preparing ancillary items, such as eye protection for the patient (e.g., goggles for newborns).

Positioning the Patient
Proper positioning ensures maximum exposure to the therapeutic light while maintaining patient comfort:

- For neonatal jaundice, the infant is usually placed in an incubator or under a phototherapy lamp.
- For dermatological conditions, the affected skin areas should be fully exposed to the light source.
- For SAD, the patient should sit at a prescribed distance from the light box, typically at eye level.

Monitoring During Phototherapy
Observing Patient Response
Continuous monitoring is critical to ensure safety and efficacy. Nurses should:

- Check for signs of adverse reactions, such as skin rash, dehydration, or eye irritation.
- Record changes in the patient's condition, including bilirubin levels in neonates or skin improvement in dermatological cases.
- Monitor the psychological state of patients undergoing phototherapy for SAD.

Maintaining Safety Standards
Safety is paramount in phototherapy. Nurses must:

- Ensure that protective eye gear is worn throughout the session.
- Periodically inspect the skin for signs of burns or overexposure.

- Maintain appropriate hydration for infants undergoing phototherapy to prevent dehydration.

Adhering to Treatment Protocols

Each phototherapy session may vary in duration and frequency depending on the treatment plan. Nurses are responsible for:

- Adhering to prescribed session timings and intervals.
- Documenting each session's details, including start and end times and any observations.
- Adjusting the light intensity per the healthcare provider's instructions.

Post-Phototherapy Care

After a phototherapy session, nurses should provide appropriate aftercare to ensure the patient's well-being:

- Inspect the treated skin or area for any signs of irritation.
- Reassess and record bilirubin levels or other relevant metrics.
- Educate patients or caregivers about potential after-effects and follow-up care.

Challenges in Phototherapy

Nurses may encounter several challenges during phototherapy, including:

- Equipment Malfunctions: Regular maintenance and calibration are essential to avoid interruptions.
- Patient Non-Compliance: Especially in cases of SAD, patients may be reluctant to adhere to the recommended duration or frequency.
- Adverse Reactions: Quick identification and resolution of any side effects are vital.

Phototherapy is a powerful and versatile treatment method, and nurses play an indispensable role in its implementation and monitoring. By ensuring proper preparation, meticulous monitoring, and patient-centered care, nurses can maximize the benefits of phototherapy while minimizing risks, thereby contributing significantly to patient outcomes.

 Maintain optimal temperature of client

Nurses ensure the well-being of their clients, including maintaining an optimal body temperature to support recovery and overall health. This task involves vigilance, precision, and a keen understanding of medical protocols.

Temperature Monitoring and Assessment

The first step in maintaining an optimal temperature is to regularly monitor and assess the client's body temperature. Nurses use tools such as thermometers—oral, tympanic, rectal, or infrared—depending on the patient's condition and convenience. Regular temperature checks help detect anomalies such as fever or hypothermia early, allowing timely intervention.

Regulating Environmental Conditions

Nurses ensure that the client's immediate environment promotes thermal comfort. This involves:

- Adjusting room temperature using air conditioning or heating systems.
- Managing humidity levels to prevent discomfort due to dryness or excessive moisture.
- Providing adequate ventilation to maintain air circulation without causing drafts.

Use of Appropriate Clothing and Bedding

Clothing and bedding play a key role in temperature regulation. Nurses recommend or provide garments suited to the client's needs, ensuring breathability or insulation, as necessary. Bedding materials are chosen carefully, for instance:

- Light sheets and breathable blankets for clients with fever.

- Warm, insulated bedding for clients at risk of hypothermia.

Application for Medical Interventions

For clients experiencing extreme temperatures, medical interventions may be required:

- For fever: Nurses administer antipyretics, ensure hydration, and apply cooling techniques, such as using cold compresses or tepid sponging.
- For hypothermia: Nurses utilize warming devices such as heated blankets and bear-huggers and monitors for signs of improvement.

Education and Encouragement

Nurses educate clients and their families about the importance of maintaining an optimal temperature. They encourage practices such as adequate hydration, proper nutrition, and wearing appropriate clothing based on weather conditions.

Special Considerations

Certain clients may require tailored approaches due to age, medical conditions, or surgical recovery. For example:

- Newborns: Nurses ensure skin-to-skin contact, use incubators, and monitor closely for signs of cold stress.
- Elderly clients: Precaution against hypothermia is emphasized, as older adults are more susceptible to temperature-related complications.
- Post-operative care: Nurses closely monitor temperature spikes due to infections or surgical reactions.

Maintaining optimal temperature is an integral aspect of nursing care, requiring a blend of observation, environmental control, interventions, and education. By staying attentive to each client's needs, nurses ensure comfort and contribute significantly to the healing process.

Monitor and care for clients on a ventilator

Caring for clients on a ventilator is an advanced nursing responsibility that requires both technical expertise and a compassionate approach. Ventilators, life-saving devices, assist patients who are unable to breathe adequately on their own. Nurses play a critical role in monitoring, managing, and ensuring the well-being of ventilated clients while advocating for their recovery and comfort.

Understanding the Client's Needs

The initial step in ventilator care involves understanding the client's underlying condition that necessitated the use of mechanical ventilation. This could range from acute respiratory failure, chronic obstructive pulmonary disease (COPD), pneumonia, trauma, or conditions such as neuromuscular diseases. Nurses must collaborate with the healthcare team to establish the goals of ventilatory support—whether it is to stabilize the patient short-term or provide long-term assistance.

Regular Monitoring and Assessment

Observing Vital Signs

Monitoring vital signs is integral to assessing a client's response to ventilation. Nurses routinely check the following:

- Respiratory rate: Ensuring the ventilator settings align with the patient's actual breathing patterns.
- Oxygen saturation (SpO2): Using pulse oximetry to confirm that oxygen delivery meets physiological needs.
- Heart rate and blood pressure: Evaluating the cardiovascular response to ventilatory support.

Evaluating Ventilator Parameters

Nurses verify ventilator settings prescribed by the physician, such as tidal volume, respiratory rate, positive end-expiratory pressure (PEEP), and fraction of inspired oxygen (FiO2). They monitor alarms to detect issues such as high airway pressure or disconnecting. Adjustments, when necessary, are communicated to the respiratory therapist or physician.

Respiratory Assessment

Frequent assessment of the client's respiratory status includes observation:

- Breath sounds for indications of fluid accumulation or atelectasis.
- Chest rise symmetry to identify potential complications such as pneumothorax.
- Work of breathing to ensure the ventilator is adequately supporting the patient.

Preventing Complications

Being on a ventilator places clients at risk for several complications. Nurses implement preventive measures to minimize these risks.

Ventilator-Associated Pneumonia (VAP)

One of the most common complications is VAP. Nurses employ measures such as:

- Performing regular oral care with antiseptic solutions to reduce bacteria.
- Maintaining the head of the bed elevated to 30-45 degrees unless contraindicated.
- Implementing daily sedation vacations to assess readiness for weaning from the ventilator.

Pressure Injuries

The endotracheal tube can exert pressure on the lips and oral mucosa. Nurses reposition the tube periodically and use protective devices to prevent sores.

Barotrauma and Volutrauma
Close monitoring of airway pressures and tidal volumes helps prevent lung injury caused by excessive ventilatory pressures or volumes.

Psychological Well-being
Being on a ventilator can be a distressing experience. Nurses provide reassurance through effective communication, even with non-verbal clients, and may employ tools like picture boards or hand signals to facilitate interaction.

Maintaining Hygiene and Comfort

A ventilated client's hygiene and comfort are priorities in their care plan.

Oral and Airway Care
In addition to oral hygiene to prevent infections, nurses suction secretions from the airway to maintain patency and reduce the risk of aspiration.

Skin Integrity
Frequent repositioning and monitoring of pressure points help avoid pressure ulcers. Special attention is given to areas around the endotracheal or tracheostomy tube.

Nutrition and Hydration
Ventilated clients often require enteral feeding or intravenous fluids to meet their nutritional needs. Nurses collaborate with dietitians to ensure optimal caloric intake.

Weaning and Extubating

For clients showing improvement, nurses play a pivotal role in the weaning process. This involves:

- Gradually reducing ventilatory support as per the physician's plan.

- Monitoring the client's ability to breathe independently through spontaneous breathing trials.
- Preparing for extubating by ensuring the client's airway is clear and they have adequate strength to maintain breathing.

Post-extubating care includes monitoring for signs of respiratory distress and providing oxygen therapy if needed.

Collaborative Care and Documentation

Nurses work in tandem with respiratory therapists, physicians, and other healthcare professionals to deliver comprehensive care. Accurate documentation of ventilator settings, patient responses, and any interventions performed is essential for continuity of care.

Monitoring and caring for clients on a ventilator demand a blend of technical knowledge, vigilance, and empathy. Nurses are at the forefront of ensuring that ventilatory support enhances recovery while minimizing the risks associated with its use. Their role encompasses everything from meticulous monitoring to fostering patient-centered care that promotes comfort and dignity. Ultimately, their expertise and dedication are central to the success of ventilator therapy.

Monitor and maintain devices and equipment used for drainage

Nurses monitor and maintaining drainage devices and equipment used in patient care. Proper management of these devices is essential to prevent complications, ensure effective drainage, and promote healing. Below is an in-depth exploration of how nurses can monitor and maintain surgical wound drains, chest tube suction systems, and negative pressure wound therapy devices.

Surgical Wound Drains

<u>Types of Surgical Wound Drains</u>
Surgical wound drains are used to remove excess fluids, such as blood, pus, or serous fluid, from a wound site. Common types include:

- Jackson-Pratt (JP) Drains: Closed suction systems that use a bulb to create negative pressure.
- Hemovac Drains: Large volume closed suction systems are often used for orthopedic surgeries.
- Pigtail Drains: Coiled catheters designed for specific drainage needs.

<u>Monitoring Surgical Wound Drains</u>
Nurses assess surgical wound drains regularly to ensure functionality and prevent complications:

- Drain Output: Measure and record the volume, color, and consistency of the fluid at regular intervals.
- Drain Patency: Check for blockages or clots within the tubing that may impede drainage.
- Skin Integrity: Inspect the insertion site for redness, swelling, or signs of infection.
- Secure Placement: Ensure the drain is securely fastened to prevent accidental dislodgment.

<u>Maintaining Surgical Wound Drains</u>
To maintain wound drains effectively, nurses perform the following tasks:

- Emptying the Reservoir: Regularly empty the drainage reservoir when it becomes half-full to preserve suction efficacy.
- Flushing the Tubing: Use sterile saline when clots or blockages are observed to maintain patency, as prescribed by the physician.

- Changing Dressings: Replace dressings around the insertion site using aseptic techniques to prevent infection.
- Documentation: Record observations of output quantity, characteristics, and dressing changes accurately.

Chest Tube Suction Systems

Purpose and Components
Chest tubes are used to evacuate air, fluid, or pus from the pleural space to restore normal lung function. They include:

- Drainage Tubing: Flexible tubing connecting the chest cavity to a collection system.
- Collection Chamber: Where the drainage accumulates.
- Suction Control: Used to regulate the amount of suction applied.

Monitoring Chest Tube Systems
Nurses ensure chest tube systems function properly by:

- Inspecting Tubing: Look for kinks, loops, or obstructions that could compromise drainage.
- Assessing Output: Monitor the amount and type of drainage in the collection chamber, noting excessive or unexpected changes.
- Checking System Integrity: Ensure airtight connections to prevent air leaks.
- Observing Respiratory Status: Regularly assess the patient's respiratory rate, breath sounds, and oxygen saturation.

Maintaining Chest Tube Systems

Maintaining chest tube systems involves:

- Securing Equipment: Tape all connections and ensure the tube is anchored to prevent displacement.
- Managing Suction: Adjust suction levels as prescribed to maintain effective drainage without causing tissue damage.
- Changing Collection Chambers: Replace chambers when full or as indicated by the manufacturer's guidelines.
- Infection Prevention: Clean and inspect the insertion site regularly for signs of infection.

Negative Pressure Wound Therapy (NPWT)

Overview of NPWT

Negative pressure wound therapy involves the application of controlled negative pressure to a wound site to promote healing. Common components include:

- Foam Dressing: Covers the wound and provides a surface for suction.
- Adhesive Film: Creates an airtight seal over the dressing.
- Vacuum Pump: Generates negative pressure to remove fluids and promote granulation tissue formation.

Monitoring NPWT Systems

Effective monitoring of NPWT systems includes:

- Pressure Settings: Check that the vacuum pump is set to the prescribed pressure level.
- Seal Integrity: Ensure the adhesive film is intact and preventing air leaks.
- Fluid Collection: Assess the canister for fluid accumulation and replace when full.
- Wound Condition: Monitor wound edges and surrounding skin for signs of irritation or infection.

Maintaining NPWT Systems

Key maintenance tasks for NPWT systems include:

- Changing Dressings: Replace foam dressings and adhesive film every 48 to 72 hours or as needed.
- Cleaning Components: Clean reusable components like tubing and pumps as per manufacturer instructions.
- Addressing Leaks: Promptly reseal any air leaks to ensure effective therapy.
- Adhering to Protocols: Follow institutional guidelines and protocols for NPWT care.

Monitoring and maintaining drainage devices and equipment require vigilance, technical knowledge, and adherence to best practices. By ensuring these systems function properly, nurses contribute significantly to patient recovery and the prevention of complications. Whether managing surgical wound drains, chest tube suction systems, or NPWT devices, meticulous care and documentation are essential for delivering quality healthcare and optimizing patient outcomes.

Perform and manage care of client receiving peritoneal dialysis

Peritoneal dialysis is a form of renal replacement therapy that uses the peritoneal membrane as a filtration surface to remove waste products, excess fluid, and toxins from the body. Nurses play a crucial role in ensuring the safety, effectiveness, and comfort of clients undergoing peritoneal dialysis.

Preparation and Client Education

Initial Assessment

- Assess the client's medical history, renal function, and understanding of peritoneal dialysis.
- Evaluate the client's ability to perform self-care if home dialysis is planned.
- Identify potential contraindications such as abdominal scarring or infections.

Education and Training

- Explain the procedure, its purpose, and potential risks.
- Teach clients how to perform peritoneal dialysis, including aseptic technique to prevent infections.
- Highlight the importance of adherence to prescribed schedules and dietary restrictions.

Performing Peritoneal Dialysis

Preparation

- Gather necessary supplies: dialysate solution, tubing sets, masks, gloves, and antiseptic.
- Ensure the client has emptied their bladder and bowel, if required, for comfort during the procedure.
- Confirm the prescribed concentration and volume of the dialysate solution.

Catheter Site Management

- Inspect the catheter site for redness, swelling, or discharge and document findings.
- Clean the catheter site thoroughly using antiseptic solutions, following facility protocols.
- Secure the catheter to avoid accidental displacement.

Initiating Dialysis

- Connect the tubing system securely to the catheter using aseptic technique.
- Infuse the dialysate slowly into the peritoneal cavity, ensuring the client is comfortable.
- Monitor for any signs of discomfort, such as abdominal pain or bloating.

Drainage and Observation

- Allow the dialysate to dwell in the peritoneal cavity for the prescribed duration.
- Drain the dialysate into a collection bag, observing the fluid for cloudiness, blood, or unusual odor.
- Document the volume and characteristics of the effluent.

Ongoing Management

<u>Monitoring and Documentation</u>
- Regularly monitor the client's vital signs, weight, and fluid balance.
- Evaluate lab results, including serum electrolytes and creatinine levels, to assess treatment effectiveness.
- Record all observations, interventions, and client responses accurately.

<u>Preventing and Managing Complications</u>
- Educate the client on recognizing signs of infection, such as fever or abdominal tenderness, and reporting them promptly.
- Address peritonitis by following prescribed antibiotic protocols and adjusting dialysis schedules.
- Manage any mechanical complications, such as catheter obstruction or leakage.

<u>Psychosocial Support</u>
- Provide emotional support to help clients cope with the physical and psychological challenges of dialysis.
- Encourage open communication about their concerns and experiences.
- Connect clients with support groups and resources for additional help.

Coordination of Care

<u>Team Collaboration</u>
- Work closely with nephrologists, dietitians, and social workers to provide holistic care.
- Coordinate appointments and follow-ups to ensure continuity of care.

<u>Home Dialysis Support</u>
- Offer guidance for clients who perform dialysis at home, including troubleshooting common issues.
- Arrange periodic evaluations to monitor their technique and overall health.

The role of the nurse in managing care for clients receiving peritoneal dialysis is multifaceted, involving technical proficiency, patient education, and emotional support. By adhering to established protocols and maintaining a client-centered approach, nurses can help ensure the effectiveness of treatment and improve the quality of life for clients undergoing peritoneal dialysis.

Perform suctioning

Suctioning is a critical nursing procedure performed to clear the airway of mucus, secretions, or foreign materials, ensuring the patient can breathe effectively. Nurses are well-trained in this technique, adhering to protocols to minimize discomfort and prevent complications. Below is a comprehensive guide describing how nurses perform suctioning.

What is Suctioning?

Suctioning is a medical procedure utilized to remove obstructions from the airway of patients who cannot effectively clear them on their own. This can include mucus, blood, vomitus, or other secretions. Suctioning is typically required for patients with respiratory conditions, those on mechanical ventilators, or those recovering from surgery.

Types of Suctioning

There are several suctioning methods, depending on the patient's needs and the specific situation:

- Oral Suctioning: Removes secretions from the mouth and throat using a Yankauer suction catheter.
- Nasopharyngeal Suctioning: Clears the nasal passages and upper airway through a flexible catheter inserted into the nostril.
- Oropharyngeal Suctioning: Focuses on clearing the throat area using a catheter inserted through the mouth.
- Tracheal Suctioning: Targets secretions in the trachea, often performed on patients with tracheostomy tubes or those intubated with endotracheal tubes.

Preparation for Suctioning

Before beginning the suctioning procedure, nurses follow these preparatory steps to ensure safety and effectiveness:

Assess the Patient

The nurse reviews the patient's medical records, assesses respiratory status, and monitors signs of airway obstruction such as gurgling sounds, labored breathing, low oxygen saturation, or cyanosis.

Gather Necessary Equipment

The nurse collects all required supplies, which may include:

- Sterile suction catheter
- Suction machine and tubing
- Yankauer catheter (for oral suctioning)
- Personal protective equipment (PPE) such as gloves, gown, goggles, and mask
- Sterile saline solution
- Pulse oximeter
- Ambu bag (in case of emergencies)

Explain the Procedure

The nurse explains the suctioning process to the patient (if conscious) to reduce anxiety and ensure cooperation. For pediatric or elderly patients, additional reassurance may be provided.

Ensure a Safe Environment

The suctioning should be performed in a clean, well-lit area, with the suction machine properly connected to a power source and functioning correctly.

Steps in Performing Suctioning

Each step of the suctioning process is crucial for patient safety and procedural efficacy:

Position the Patient

The nurse positions the patient optimally based on the type of suctioning:

- For Oral/Nasopharyngeal Suctioning: Semi-Fowler's or Fowler's position is preferred.
- For Tracheal Suctioning: Position the patient supine, with the head slightly extended.

Proper positioning facilitates better access to the airway and improves secretion clearance.

Hand Hygiene and PPE

The nurse performs hand hygiene and dons appropriate PPE to maintain infection control and personal safety.

Prepare the Equipment

The suction catheter is attached to the suction tubing and machine. The nurse ensures the suction machine is set to the appropriate pressure:

- Adults: 100–150 mmHg
- Children: 100–120 mmHg
- Infants: 80–100 mmHg

A sterile saline solution is used to lubricate the catheter and test the suction function.

Insert the Catheter

The suction catheter is gently inserted into the patient's airway without applying suction during insertion to avoid tissue damage. The depth of insertion depends on the method:

- Oral/Nasopharyngeal: Insert until resistance is met or the patient coughs.
- Tracheal: Insert just beyond the tip of the tracheostomy or endotracheal tube.

Apply Suction

Suction is applied intermittently while withdrawing the catheter in a rotating motion. This technique minimizes mucosal damage and effectively clears secretions. Suctioning should not exceed 10–15 seconds in adults and less for children or infants.

Monitor the Patient

Throughout the procedure, the nurse monitors the patient's oxygen levels, heart rate, and overall response. If the patient shows signs of distress, the procedure is paused immediately, and oxygen is administered.

Post-Suction Care

After suctioning, the nurse flushes the catheter with sterile saline, removes PPE, and performs hand hygiene. The patient's comfort is reassessed, and oxygen therapy is adjusted if necessary.

Post-Procedure Documentation

Accurate documentation is crucial for continuity of care. The nurse records:

- The time and type of suctioning performed
- Patient's response and any complications
- Amount, consistency, and color of secretions

Complications and Safety Measures

While suctioning is generally safe, complications can occur if not performed correctly:

- Hypoxia
- Bradycardia due to vagus nerve stimulation
- Airway trauma
- Infection

To mitigate these risks, nurses adhere to established protocols, use sterile techniques, and conduct frequent patient assessments.

Suctioning is a vital procedure that ensures airway patency and improves respiratory function in patients unable to manage their secretions. By following precise techniques and prioritizing patient safety, nurses play a critical role in enhancing patient outcomes and comfort during this procedure.

Perform wound care and dressing change

Wound care and dressing changes are crucial components of nursing practice that ensure the healing and protection of injured tissue while preventing infections. Nurses follow meticulous protocols to deliver optimal care, tailored to the patient's specific needs.

Preparation for Wound Care

Gathering Supplies

Before starting the procedure, nurses ensure they have all the necessary supplies, which may include:

- Sterile gloves
- Clean and sterile dressing materials
- Antiseptic solution or wound cleanser
- Bandages or adhesive tapes
- Scissors and forceps (sterilized)
- Waste disposal bags

This preparation ensures efficiency during the process and minimizes the risk of contamination.

Patient Assessment

Nurses assess the patient's overall health and wound condition before proceeding. This includes evaluating:

- The location and size of the wound

- The type of wound (open, surgical, pressure ulcer, etc.)
- The presence of infection (redness, swelling, or drainage)
- Any allergies to dressing materials or wound care products

Ensuring Patient Comfort

Explaining the procedure to the patient is essential to alleviate anxiety. Nurses ensure the patient is in a comfortable position to facilitate access to the wound while minimizing discomfort during the procedure.

Steps to Perform Wound Care

Hand Hygiene

Proper hand hygiene is the first and most important step. Nurses thoroughly wash their hands with soap and water or use an alcohol-based sanitizer. This prevents the transfer of pathogens to the wound.

Applying Personal Protective Equipment (PPE)

Depending on the wound's condition, nurses wear PPE such as gloves, mask, and gown to protect both themselves and the patient.

Removing the Old Dressing

The old dressing is removed with care, ensuring minimal disruption to healing tissue. Nurses use sterile gloves and tools to avoid contaminating the wound. If the dressing adheres to the wound, saline or water may be used to moisten and gently loosen it.

Cleaning the Wound

The wound is cleansed using a prescribed solution to remove debris, dead tissue, and bacteria. Nurses work from the cleanest area to the dirtiest (typically from the center outward) to prevent contamination. Any drainage or exudate is carefully wiped away.

Inspecting the Wound

Post-cleaning, nurses inspect the wound for signs of healing or complications. They note:

- Changes in size, depth, or appearance of the wound
- Signs of infection (pus, odor, or worsening redness)
- The presence of granulation tissue indicating healing

Applying New Dressing

Choosing Appropriate Dressing

The choice of dressing depends on the wound type, its healing stage, and the patient's needs. Options include:

- Gauze dressings
- Hydrocolloid dressings
- Foam dressings
- Transparent film dressings
- Alginate dressings for wounds with heavy exudate

Placing the Dressing

Nurses apply the new dressing in a way that covers the wound completely and securely, ensuring it adheres well while allowing airflow if required for the healing process.

Securing the Dressing

The dressing is secured using adhesive tape, bandages, or other fastening methods as needed. Nurses ensure the dressing is snug but not too tight, avoiding pressure that could compromise circulation.

Documenting the Procedure

Afterward, nurses document the wound care process in the patient's medical record, including:

- The wound's condition and any changes observed
- The type of dressing applied
- Patient's response to the procedure

- Any recommendations or follow-up care

Considerations for Effective Wound Care

<u>Preventing Infection</u>

Nurses follow strict aseptic techniques to prevent contamination. They educate patients on the importance of hygiene and protecting the wound.

<u>Monitoring Progress</u>

Regular wound assessments are vital for tracking healing and identifying issues early. Nurses work closely with physicians to adjust treatment plans if necessary.

<u>Educating the Patient</u>

Patients are often advised on how to care for their wound at home, including:

- Steps for safe dressing changes
- Signs of infection to watch for
- Maintaining a balanced diet to promote healing

Wound care and dressing changes are fundamental responsibilities of nurses, requiring attention to detail, knowledge of medical practices, and compassion for the patient. By adhering to best practices, nurses help ensure optimal healing, minimize complications, and support the patient's recovery journey.

Provide ostomy care and education

Ostomy care and education are pivotal components of nursing practice for patients with tracheal or enteral ostomies. Nurses play a central role in ensuring patients and their families are equipped with the knowledge and skills to manage ostomies effectively, promoting better outcomes and enhancing quality of life.

Understanding Ostomy Types

Ostomies are surgically created openings in the body for the discharge of bodily waste or for accessing internal organs. Common types include:

- Tracheostomy: A surgical opening in the trachea to assist with breathing.
- Enterostomy: Includes gastrostomy and jejunostomy, which create access points for feeding tubes to deliver nutrition directly to the stomach or jejunum.

Each type of ostomy comes with its unique challenges and care requirements, necessitating individualized approaches to nursing care and education.

Providing Ostomy Care

Tracheal Ostomy Care

Nurses are responsible for the meticulous care of tracheostomies to prevent complications such as infection or obstruction. Key aspects include:

- Maintaining Airway Patency: Regular suctioning to remove secretions and prevent blockages.
- Cleaning the Stoma Site: Sterile techniques are utilized to clean the area around the stoma, minimizing the risk of infection.
- Managing Tracheostomy Tubes: Ensuring proper fit, securing ties, and periodically changing inner cannulas or tubes as needed.
- Monitoring for Complications: Observing for signs of infection, bleeding, or skin breakdown around the stoma.

Enteral Ostomy Care

Enteral ostomy management involves ensuring that feeding tubes function correctly while maintaining stoma health. Nurses focus on:

- Cleaning the Stoma: Daily cleansing with gentle techniques to prevent irritation or infection.
- Securing the Feeding Tube: Proper stabilization to avoid dislodgment or damage.
- Administering Nutritional Feeds: Ensuring proper protocols for safe and sterile administration of enteral nutrition.

- Preventing Complications: Monitoring for signs of leakage, infection, or tube obstruction.

Educational Support for Patients

<u>Initial Education Following Surgery</u>

After ostomy creation, nurses provide foundational education tailored to the patient's needs. Topics covered include:

- Understanding the Ostomy: Explaining the type of ostomy, its function, and the importance of care.
- Basic Hygiene: Demonstrating proper cleaning and maintenance of the stoma.
- Use of Devices: Training patients to use associated devices such as tracheostomy tubes, suction equipment, or enteral feeding systems.

<u>Long-term Education and Support</u>

Ongoing education is key to empowering patients to manage their ostomies with confidence. Nurses provide:

- Self-care Techniques: Teaching patients or caregivers how to independently handle daily care routines.
- Emergency Management: Guidance on handling situations such as tube dislodgment or bleeding.
- Lifestyle Adaptations: Counseling about physical activity, diet, and social interactions to accommodate the ostomy.
- Psychosocial Support: Addressing emotional challenges, such as body image concerns or anxiety, often associated with ostomies.

Collaborative Role

Nurses collaborate with other healthcare professionals, including physicians, dietitians, and occupational therapists, to ensure comprehensive care for patients with ostomies. This team approach allows for addressing both medical and emotional needs effectively.

Tools and Resources

Nurses often use visual aids, instructional pamphlets, and hands-on demonstrations to enhance patient comprehension. Additionally, they may refer patients to support groups or connect them with resources for ongoing assistance.

Monitoring and Follow-Up

Regular follow-up is essential for ensuring patients adapt well to their ostomies and to promptly identify and address complications. Nurses assess:

- Stoma condition and surrounding skin health.
- Functioning of tracheostomy or enteral devices.
- Adherence to care routines and nutritional protocols.

The role of nurses in providing ostomy care and education is indispensable. Through careful management, personalized education, and empathetic support, nurses empower patients to adapt to their ostomies, minimize complications, and lead fulfilling lives. By integrating medical expertise with compassionate care, nurses ensure that ostomy patients thrive both physically and emotionally.

Provide postoperative care

Postoperative care is a critical phase in a patient's recovery journey, and nurses play an indispensable role in ensuring the process is smooth and safe. Through a combination of clinical expertise, compassionate care, and meticulous monitoring, nurses address both the physical and emotional needs of patients after surgery.

Initial Assessment and Monitoring

Effective postoperative care begins immediately after the surgery when the patient is transferred to the recovery room or post-anesthesia care unit (PACU). During this stage, nurses focus on:

- Vital Sign Monitoring: Nurses assess the patient's heart rate, blood pressure, respiratory rate, temperature, and oxygen saturation at regular intervals to identify any signs of instability.
- Pain Management: They evaluate the patient's level of pain using standardized tools, such as the Numeric Pain Rating Scale, and administer prescribed pain medications or interventions.
- Consciousness and Neurological Status: Nurses monitor the patient's orientation, reflexes, and response to stimuli to ensure proper recovery from anesthesia.

Pain and Comfort Management

Pain control is a cornerstone of postoperative care. Nurses employ several strategies to manage pain effectively:

- Pharmacological Approaches: Administering prescribed analgesics, such as opioids, NSAIDs, or local anesthetics, while adhering to dosage and timing guidelines.
- Non-Pharmacological Techniques: Utilizing methods such as positioning, heat or cold therapy, relaxation techniques, and mindfulness exercises to alleviate discomfort.
- Patient Communication: Engaging with patients to understand their pain levels and adjusting care plans accordingly based on their feedback.

Wound Care and Infection Prevention

Postoperative wounds require careful attention to prevent complications such as infections or delayed healing:

- Inspecting Surgical Sites: Nurses regularly check the incision for signs of infection, such as redness, swelling, warmth, or discharge.
- Dressing Changes: They replace dressings according to the prescribed schedule, ensuring sterile techniques to minimize the risk of contamination.
- Education: Teaching patients and caregivers about proper wound care practices, including hygiene and recognizing warning signs of infection.

Postoperative Mobility and Rehabilitation

Encouraging movement and rehabilitation is essential to prevent complications such as blood clots, pneumonia, or muscle atrophy:

- Gradual Mobilization: Nurses assist patients in transitioning from bed rest to sitting, standing, and walking based on their readiness and surgical restrictions.
- Physical Therapy Coordination: Collaborating with physical therapists to implement exercises that promote strength, flexibility, and circulation.
- Prophylactic Measures: Utilizing tools like compression stockings or pneumatic devices to prevent deep vein thrombosis.

Nutrition and Hydration

Proper nutrition and hydration are vital for speeding up recovery and restoring energy:

- Monitoring Fluid Balance: Nurses track urine output and fluid intake to ensure patients remain adequately hydrated.
- Dietary Adjustments: Gradually reintroducing food based on the patient's tolerance, starting with liquids and soft foods before progressing to regular meals.
- Addressing Nausea: Administering antiemetics or suggesting dietary adjustments to manage nausea caused by anesthesia or medications.

Emotional and Psychological Support

Surgery can be an emotionally taxing experience, and nurses often provide psychological support alongside physical care:

- Listening and Encouragement: Offering empathy and reassurance to patients who may feel anxious, vulnerable, or overwhelmed.
- Patient Education: Ensuring patients understand their recovery process, including timelines and what to expect, to reduce uncertainty.

- Family Engagement: Including family members in discussions and providing them with guidance to support the patient effectively.

Preventing Postoperative Complications

Nurses remain vigilant to identify and address potential complications at the earliest:

- Managing Respiratory Issues: Encouraging deep breathing exercises or using incentive spirometry to prevent lung infections or atelectasis.
- Monitoring for Blood Clots: Observing for signs like swelling, tenderness, or discoloration in the extremities.
- Evaluating Gastrointestinal Function: Ensuring proper bowel function and preventing constipation through medications or dietary adjustments.

Patient Education and Discharge Planning

Preparing patients for discharge is a vital aspect of postoperative care aimed at empowering them to manage recovery at home:

- Care Instructions: Nurses provide detailed guidelines on medication schedules, wound care, mobility restrictions, and follow-up appointments.
- Warning Signs: Educating patients about symptoms that require immediate medical attention, such as fever, excessive pain, or unusual discharge.
- Support Resources: Offering contact information for healthcare teams and support services to ensure patients feel equipped to handle their recovery.

Postoperative care delivered by nurses is a delicate balance of clinical precision and compassionate support. Nurses serve as a bridge between surgery and recovery, ensuring that patients regain their health with minimal complications and maximum comfort. Their role extends beyond medical interventions, encompassing emotional reassurance and patient empowerment, making them integral to the healing process. Whether in the hospital or at home, the care provided by nurses truly makes a difference in every patient's recovery journey.

Manage the care of the client with a fluid and electrolyte imbalance

Fluid and electrolyte balance is an integral part of maintaining the physiological functions of the human body. Imbalances can lead to a variety of complications, ranging from mild discomfort to life-threatening conditions. Nurses play a pivotal role in identifying, managing, and educating clients about fluid and electrolyte imbalances. This document explores the strategies and responsibilities of nurses in managing care for clients experiencing these imbalances.

Understanding Fluid and Electrolyte Imbalances

Fluid and electrolyte imbalances occur when the levels of water and electrolytes such as sodium, potassium, calcium, magnesium, and chloride in the body are not within normal ranges. These imbalances may result from various causes, including dehydration, overhydration, chronic illnesses, medication usage, or acute medical conditions like vomiting, diarrhea, or kidney failure.

Common Signs and Symptoms

Clients with fluid and electrolyte imbalances may exhibit symptoms such as:

- Dehydration or edema (swelling)
- Fatigue or weakness
- Dizziness and confusion
- Muscle cramps or spasms
- Irregular heartbeat
- Changes in blood pressure

Diagnostic Tools and Procedures

Nurses work in collaboration with healthcare providers to identify the imbalance through:

- Blood tests to measure electrolyte levels
- Urine analysis to monitor kidney function
- Assessment of vital signs, including blood pressure and heart rate
- Evaluation of client history and symptoms

Nursing Interventions for Managing Fluid and Electrolyte Imbalances

Assessment and Monitoring

Nurses begin by conducting a thorough assessment of the client's condition. Monitoring includes:

- Measuring input and output of fluids
- Recording daily weight changes
- Observing signs of dehydration or overhydration
- Monitoring laboratory values for electrolyte levels

Regular monitoring allows nurses to detect changes early and prevent complications.

Rehydration Therapy

For dehydration, nurses may administer oral rehydration solutions, or intravenous (IV) fluids based on the severity of the imbalance. They ensure the correct type of IV fluid is prescribed and monitor the infusion rate to prevent fluid overload.

Electrolyte Replacement

Electrolyte imbalances, such as hypokalemia (low potassium) or hypernatremia (high sodium), require targeted interventions. Nurses may:

- Administer electrolyte supplements orally or intravenously
- Educate clients about dietary sources of electrolytes, such as bananas for potassium or dairy products for calcium

Medication Management

Nurses are responsible for administering medications prescribed to address specific imbalances, such as diuretics for managing fluid overload or potassium-sparing drugs. They monitor the side effects and effectiveness of the medications.

Preventive Care

Education is a cornerstone of nursing care. Nurses teach clients strategies to prevent fluid and electrolyte imbalances, including:

- Ensuring adequate fluid intake
- Balancing dietary intake with rich sources of electrolytes
- Recognizing early signs of imbalance
- Managing underlying conditions like diabetes or kidney disease

Special Considerations

Pediatric Clients

Children are especially vulnerable to dehydration and electrolyte imbalances due to their smaller body mass and higher metabolic rate. Nurses ensure careful fluid administration and educate parents about symptoms and prevention.

Older Adults

Aging affects the body's ability to regulate fluid and electrolytes. Nurses pay special attention to older adults, who may be more prone to dehydration or medication-induced imbalances. Coordination with caregivers is often vital.

<u>Clients with Chronic Conditions</u>

For clients with conditions such as heart failure or kidney disease, nurses collaborate with healthcare teams to tailor fluid and electrolyte management to their specific needs.

Collaborative Approach

Managing fluid and electrolyte imbalances often requires team effort. Nurses work alongside physicians, dietitians, and pharmacists to ensure comprehensive care. They act as advocates for the client, providing regular updates on progress and adjusting care plans, as necessary.

Nurses play an indispensable role in the management of fluid and electrolyte imbalances. Through diligent assessment, timely interventions, and education, they help clients achieve stability and prevent further complications. Their ability to blend technical expertise with compassionate care makes them a cornerstone of healthcare delivery in addressing this critical aspect of client well-being.

 Monitor and maintain arterial lines

Arterial lines (or art lines) are critical tools in healthcare settings, particularly for patients requiring continuous blood pressure monitoring or frequent blood sampling. Proper monitoring and maintenance of arterial lines by nurses are vital to ensure patient safety, minimize complications, and maintain accurate readings.

Monitoring Arterial Lines

<u>Ensuring Accurate Readings</u>

Nurses must frequently check the arterial line setup to ensure it is functioning correctly. Key steps include:

- Verifying the zeroing of the transducer to atmospheric pressure. This step is performed at the beginning of each shift or whenever the setup is adjusted.

- Positioning the transducer at the level of the patient's approximately the fourth intercostal space at the mid-axillary line.
- Inspecting waveform quality on the monitor to identify damping or artifact issues that could affect accuracy.

Monitoring for Complications
Nurses must also remain vigilant for signs of complications, including:

- Infection: Regularly observe the insertion site for redness, swelling, or discharge.
- Ischemia: Assess the distal circulation by checking skin color, temperature, and capillary refill.
- Bleeding: Ensure the arterial line is securely connected and inspect for any signs of leakage.

Maintaining Arterial Lines

Daily Care Practices
To maintain the arterial line:

- Change dressing around the insertion site according to hospital protocols, typically every 7 days or sooner if it becomes soiled or loose.
- Ensure the tubing and connections are tightly secured and free from kinks.
- Flush the arterial line with a small amount of heparinized saline solution using the pressure bag system to keep the line patent.

Preventing Infection
Proper aseptic techniques are essential:

- Always clean the insertion site with an appropriate antiseptic during dressing changes.

- Use sterile gloves and equipment when handling the arterial line or drawing samples.
- Minimize unnecessary manipulation of the line to reduce infection risk.

Responding to Alarms

Arterial line alarms may indicate disconnection, occlusion, or abnormal readings. Nurses should respond promptly by:

- Checking connections and tubing for leaks or blockages.
- Reassessing the transducer level and zeroing if necessary.
- Reevaluating the patient's clinical condition to determine whether changes in readings correlate with their status.

Documentation and Communication

Accurate documentation is crucial for arterial line management. Nurses should record:

- Insertion site assessments, including any signs of complications.
- Steps taken during maintenance, such as dressing changes or flushing procedures.
- Blood pressure readings and any abnormalities observed.

Effective communication with the healthcare team ensures that arterial line issues or changes in patient status are addressed promptly.

Monitoring and maintaining arterial lines require diligence, skill, and a thorough understanding of their function. By following best practices, nurses ensure the safety and comfort of their patients while optimizing the utility of this vital medical device.

Manage the care of a client with a pacing device

Caring for a client with a pacing device, such as a pacemaker or an implantable cardioverter-defibrillator (ICD), requires specialized knowledge, meticulous attention to detail, and empathetic communication. Nurses play a critical role in ensuring that the device functions properly while addressing the client's physical and emotional needs.

Pre-Procedure Care

Client Education
- Explain the purpose of the pacing device and how it works in simple terms.
- Discuss the procedure, potential risks, and expected outcomes to alleviate anxiety.
- Address lifestyle changes, including activity or device restrictions.

Preparation
- Ensure that informed consent has been obtained.
- Conduct a thorough pre-procedure assessment, including vital signs, medical history, and allergies.
- Confirm that diagnostic tests, such as electrocardiograms (ECG) or imaging, have been completed.
- Prepare the client for fasting if required.

Post-Procedure Care

Immediate Care
- Monitor vital signs and cardiac rhythm closely for any abnormalities.
- Inspect the insertion site for signs of infection, bleeding, or swelling.
- Ensure that the pacing device is functioning properly by checking telemetry or device interrogation.
- Administer pain medication and other prescribed drugs as needed.

Education on Device Use
- Teach the client how to recognize signs of device malfunction, such as dizziness, palpitations, or syncope.
- Advise on restrictions, such as avoiding heavy lifting or raising the affected arm above shoulder level during the healing period.
- Discuss the need to avoid proximity to strong electromagnetic fields (e.g., certain tools, MRI machines).
- Provide instructions on maintaining a log of symptoms and follow-up appointments.

Long-Term Management

Regular Monitoring
- Schedule routine follow-ups to assess the pacing device's performance and battery life.
- Collaborate with cardiologists or electrophysiologists to address any device adjustments.

Lifestyle Modifications
- Encourage adherence to a heart-healthy diet and exercise plan, as approved by the healthcare provider.
- Promote smoking cessation and stress management strategies to support overall cardiovascular health.

Psychosocial Support

- Address any feelings of fear, anxiety, or depression associated with the implantation of a pacing device.
- Provide reassurance about the safety and effectiveness of the device.
- Connect clients with support groups or counseling services as needed.

Emergency Management

- Educate the client and family on identifying and responding to device-related emergencies, such as failure to pace or defibrillate.
- Provide written instructions and emergency contact numbers.

Managing the care of a client with a pacing device requires a balance of technical skills, education, and emotional support. Nurses serve as vital advocates, empowering clients to live confidently and safely with their devices while promoting optimal health and well-being.

 ## Manage the care of a client on telemetry

Telemetry monitoring is a critical aspect of healthcare that allows nurses to oversee a patient's cardiovascular status through continuous electronic monitoring. Nurses play an essential role in ensuring the effective use of telemetry to optimize patient outcomes.

Understanding Telemetry Monitoring

Telemetry is a technology that tracks and records a patient's heart rhythm and rate. It involves sensors and electrodes placed on the patient's body, which transmit data to a central monitoring system. Nurses interpret these readings to detect abnormalities, assess the patient's condition, and guide clinical interventions.

Preparation and Patient Admission

Effective telemetry care begins with proper preparation and admission. The nurse ensures the following:

- Obtaining medical history: A thorough review of the patient's history, including previous cardiac events and medications, helps the nurse anticipate potential complications.
- Educating the patient: Nurses explain the purpose of telemetry monitoring to the patient, addressing their concerns and ensuring they understand the importance of staying connected to the monitor.
- Placement of equipment: The nurse carefully applies electrodes to appropriate areas of the patient's body to ensure accurate readings. Proper skin preparation minimizes interference and discomfort.

Monitoring the Patient

During telemetry care, nurses maintain vigilance in monitoring the patient's status:

- Continuous observation: Nurses review telemetry data in real-time, identifying arrhythmias or changes in heart rate.
- Interpreting results: Using training and clinical expertise, nurses discern normal patterns from concerning anomalies that may require intervention.
- Responding to alarms: Telemetry systems alert nurses to critical changes, such as tachycardia or bradycardia. Prompt action ensures adverse events are mitigated.

Communication and Collaboration

Telemetry management necessitates effective communication and teamwork:

- Reporting findings: Nurses convey telemetry results to physicians and other healthcare providers, ensuring timely decisions for the patient's treatment plan.
- Collaborating with multidisciplinary teams: Nurses work closely with cardiologists, technicians, and other specialists to support the patient's care.

Implementing Interventions

Nurses must be prepared to act when telemetry readings indicate instability:

- Administering medications: Based on telemetry data, nurses may provide antiarrhythmics, vasodilators, or other drugs as prescribed.
- Initiating emergency protocols: In cases of cardiac arrest or life-threatening arrhythmias, nurses initiate resuscitation efforts and call for advanced support.

- Adjusting care plans: Telemetry findings may lead to modifications in the patient's treatment, such as increased monitoring frequency or additional tests.

Ensuring Patient Comfort

While telemetry is lifesaving, it can be intrusive. Nurses prioritize patient comfort through:

- Skin care: Regularly checking electrode sites to prevent irritation and addressing any discomfort promptly.
- Mobility and independence: Assisting patients to move safely without disrupting electrodes or monitoring systems.
- Psychological support: Reassuring anxious patients and providing emotional care to reduce stress.

Documenting and Evaluating

Documentation is a critical part of telemetry care:

- Recording findings: Nurses meticulously document telemetry data and interventions to create a comprehensive record for ongoing care.
- Evaluating effectiveness: Periodic assessment of how telemetry contributes to patient outcomes ensures optimal use of resources.

Challenges and Solutions

Telemetry management comes with challenges, such as alarm fatigue, technical errors, and patient non-compliance. Nurses address these issues through:

- Training: Regular education on telemetry systems and protocols to enhance proficiency.
- Troubleshooting equipment: Quick identification and resolution of technical problems to maintain system reliability.
- Patient engagement: Encouraging patients to adhere to monitoring requirements and participate actively in their care.

Ethical and Legal Considerations

Telemetry nurses uphold ethical standards by ensuring privacy and informed consent. They also stay compliant with legal regulations to safeguard patient data and avoid malpractice.

Managing the care of a client on telemetry requires a blend of clinical expertise, technological proficiency, and compassionate care. Nurses act as the cornerstone of telemetry monitoring, ensuring the technology is harnessed effectively for the patient's benefit. As advancements in medical technology continue, the role of telemetry nurses will remain vital in delivering high-quality, responsive cardiac care.

Manage the care of a client receiving hemodialysis or continuous renal replacement therapy

Hemodialysis (HD) and Continuous Renal Replacement Therapy (CRRT) are life-saving treatments provided to clients with renal failure or other critical conditions affecting kidney function. Effective nursing care plays an essential role in ensuring client safety, comfort, and positive outcomes during these therapies.

Understanding Hemodialysis and Continuous Renal Replacement Therapy

Hemodialysis

Hemodialysis is a process that removes waste, toxins, and excess fluids from the blood when the kidneys are no longer able to perform these functions adequately. It is typically performed in outpatient clinics, hospitals, or sometimes at home under the supervision of healthcare professionals.

Continuous Renal Replacement Therapy

CRRT, on the other hand, is often used in critical care settings for clients with acute kidney injury or multiorgan failure. It provides continuous blood purification over an extended period (24 hours or more), making it gentler for hemodynamically unstable clients compared to traditional hemodialysis.

Nursing Responsibilities in Hemodialysis

Assessment and Preparation

Nurses begin by assessing the client's medical history, current condition, and lab results such as electrolyte levels, blood urea nitrogen (BUN), and creatinine. They ensure the client is physically and emotionally prepared for the procedure, addressing any anxiety or concerns they may have.

Key preparatory tasks include:

- Ensuring vascular access is functional (e.g., arteriovenous fistula, graft, or central venous catheter).
- Checking vital signs and weight pre-dialysis to track fluid removal requirements.
- Administering prescribed medications, such as anticoagulants, to prevent clotting during the procedure.

Monitoring During Hemodialysis

During hemodialysis, nurses closely monitor the client for any complications, such as:

- Hypotension: A drop in blood pressure due to fluid and electrolyte shifts.
- Muscle cramps: Commonly caused by rapid fluid removal.
- Nausea or vomiting: Often linked to shifts in electrolytes.
- Bleeding: Resulting from anticoagulation therapy or issues with vascular access.

Nurses also ensure that the dialysis machine is functioning correctly, adjust flow rates as needed, and communicate with the dialysis technician to address technical issues promptly.

Post-Dialysis Care

After hemodialysis, nurses evaluate the client's condition to ensure stability. Key post-dialysis tasks include:

- Monitoring vital signs and weight to assess fluid removal.
- Inspecting vascular access sites for signs of infection or bleeding.
- Educating the client about post-dialysis fatigue and advising on hydration and dietary restrictions.

Nursing Responsibilities in Continuous Renal Replacement Therapy

Initiation and Setup

CRRT requires meticulous preparation, as the therapy is continuous and often performed on critically ill clients. Nurses:

- Set up the CRRT system and prime the tubing to prevent air embolism.
- Ensure proper placement and function of vascular access devices.
- Verify prescribed settings, such as ultrafiltration rates and anticoagulation protocols.

Ongoing Monitoring

Given the continuous nature of CRRT, nurses maintain vigilant monitoring for complications and therapy effectiveness:

- Assessing hemodynamic stability, including blood pressure, heart rate, and temperature.
- Tracking lab values (e.g., electrolytes, acid-base balance) and adjusting therapy parameters accordingly.
- Checking for clotting in the circuit and ensuring adequate anticoagulation.

- Observing fluid balance to prevent overload or dehydration.

Infection Prevention

Nurses play a critical role in minimizing infection risks by maintaining sterility during catheter care, dressing changes, and tubing management. Regular inspection of vascular access sites is paramount.

Client Comfort and Family Support

Since CRRT is often performed on critically ill clients, nurses provide emotional support to both the client and their family. They educate family members on the purpose and process of CRRT, fostering understanding and reducing anxiety.

Education and Advocacy

In both hemodialysis and CRRT, nurses are educators and advocates. They guide clients and families to:

- Dietary and fluid restrictions to avoid further renal complications.
- Medication adherence for controlling comorbidities such as hypertension and diabetes.
- Recognizing signs of infection or complications related to vascular access.

Advocacy includes collaborating with the healthcare team to ensure the therapy aligns with the client's condition and goals of care.

Nursing care management for clients undergoing hemodialysis or CRRT involves a blend of technical expertise, vigilant monitoring, compassionate support, and client education. By maintaining high standards of care and fostering a collaborative environment, nurses play a vital role in improving outcomes and enhancing the quality of life for clients receiving renal replacement therapies.

Manage the care of a client with alteration in hemodynamics, tissue perfusion, and hemostasis

The management of clients with alterations in hemodynamics, tissue perfusion, and hemostasis requires a holistic, informed, and diligent approach by the nurse. These alterations may arise due to conditions such as shock, sepsis, trauma, or chronic illnesses, and they require careful monitoring and timely interventions to prevent complications.

Understanding the Clinical Context

Before initiating care, the nurse must understand the client's condition thoroughly, including the underlying cause of the hemodynamic imbalance, impaired tissue perfusion, or altered hemostasis. This involves reviewing the client's medical history, current symptoms, and laboratory results, such as blood pressure, cardiac output, oxygen saturation, platelet counts, coagulation profiles, and lactate levels.

Hemodynamics

Hemodynamics refers to the dynamics of blood flow, which is critical for maintaining sufficient oxygen and nutrient delivery to tissues. Alterations may occur due to conditions such as heart failure, hypovolemia, or sepsis.

Tissue Perfusion

Tissue perfusion involves the flow of blood through the capillaries to supply oxygen and remove waste products. Impaired perfusion can lead to cellular hypoxia and organ dysfunction.

Hemostasis

Hemostasis, the process of blood clotting and maintaining vascular integrity, is crucial for preventing excessive bleeding or thrombotic events. Disorders such as disseminated intravascular coagulation (DIC) or thrombocytopenia can disrupt hemostasis.

Nursing Interventions

Comprehensive Assessment
The nurse begins with a thorough assessment:

- Monitoring vital signs, including blood pressure, heart rate, respiratory rate, and temperature.
- Observing for signs of poor perfusion, such as cyanosis, cold extremities, delayed capillary refill, and altered mental status.
- Evaluating lab work, such as arterial blood gases (ABGs), coagulation studies, and lactate levels, to determine the severity of the alteration.

Hemodynamic Support
Depending on the client's hemodynamic status:

- Administering intravenous fluids to restore volume in cases of hypovolemia.
- Using vasopressors or inotropes like norepinephrine or dobutamine to enhance cardiac output and systemic vascular resistance in shock states.
- Monitoring central venous pressure (CVP), pulmonary artery pressure, or other invasive hemodynamic parameters as prescribed.

Enhancing Tissue Perfusion
To ensure adequate oxygen delivery and waste removal:

- Administering supplemental oxygen or mechanical ventilation as needed.
- Positioning the client to optimize circulation, such as elevating the legs in hypovolemic shock.

- Encouraging mobility (if appropriate) to prevent stasis and enhance peripheral circulation.

Managing Hemostasis

For clients with altered coagulation:

- Administering anticoagulants, such as heparin, to prevent thromboembolic events in hypercoagulable states.
- Providing blood products, such as platelets or fresh frozen plasma, in cases of active bleeding or coagulopathy.
- Monitoring for signs of bleeding or clot formation and intervening promptly.

Communication and Collaboration

The nurse works closely with the interdisciplinary team, including physicians, respiratory therapists, and pharmacists, to ensure coordinated care. Regular updates and discussions about the client's status and needs are critical.

Client Education and Support

Helping the client and their family understand the condition and treatment plan is an integral part of nursing care. This includes:

- Explaining the importance of prescribed treatments and medications.
- Teaching signs and symptoms that require immediate medical attention, such as worsening breathlessness, chest pain, or uncontrolled bleeding.
- Providing emotional support to alleviate stress and anxiety related to the illness.

Evaluation and Reassessment

Continuous monitoring and reassessment are essential to evaluate the effectiveness of interventions and adapt the care plan as needed. Improvements in vital signs, lab results, and client symptoms serve as positive indicators of recovery.

The nurse plays a pivotal role in the management of clients with alterations in hemodynamics, tissue perfusion, and hemostasis. By combining clinical knowledge, vigilant monitoring, timely interventions, and compassionate care, the nurse can significantly improve client outcomes and promote recovery.

Educate client regarding acute or chronic condition

Nurses educate clients dealing with acute or chronic conditions. Whether assisting clients in understanding a sudden, short-term illness or a long-term, ongoing health issue, nurses are crucial in empowering individuals to take charge of their health and make informed decisions regarding treatment and lifestyle adjustments. Education is not merely about providing information; it involves fostering understanding, promoting adherence to treatment plans, and enabling self-management of health conditions.

Understanding Acute and Chronic Conditions

Acute Conditions

Acute conditions are characterized by sudden onset and a relatively short duration. These may include illnesses such as infections, injuries, or other medical emergencies like appendicitis or pneumonia. Nurse education in acute situations often revolves around immediate care, recovery expectations, and the prevention of complications.

Chronic Conditions

Chronic conditions, on the other hand, are long-lasting and often require ongoing management. These may include diabetes, hypertension, heart disease, and arthritis. Client education in chronic care focuses on understanding the condition, managing symptoms, adhering to treatment plans, and maintaining quality of life over the long term.

Steps in Educating Clients

Assessing Client Knowledge and Needs

Before initiating education, nurses must assess the client's baseline knowledge regarding their condition. This can involve asking open-ended questions, conducting interviews, and evaluating the client's understanding of medical terminology, symptoms, and treatment options. The nurse must also identify specific needs, such as linguistic preferences, cultural considerations, or cognitive limitations.

Providing Tailored Information

Education must be customized to each client's condition, needs, and circumstances. For acute conditions, nurses may focus on the immediate steps required, such as medication instructions, wound care, or recognizing warning signs of complications. For chronic conditions, education may include detailed explanations of the disease process, dietary guidelines, exercise recommendations, and coping strategies.

Using Clear and Simple Language

Medical jargon can be overwhelming for clients, especially those new to managing health conditions. Nurses should use simple, clear language and provide analogies or visual aids where appropriate to enhance understanding. For example, when explaining blood sugar levels to a diabetic client, visual charts can be particularly useful.

Incorporating Visual and Practical Tools

Teaching methods should include visual aids, pamphlets, videos, and hands-on demonstrations. For example, clients with diabetes may benefit from live demonstrations on how to use blood glucose monitors. Similarly, wound care instructions can include step-by-step demonstrations.

Encouraging Questions and Interaction

Education should not be one-way communication. Nurses should encourage clients to ask questions, express concerns, and discuss their experiences. This approach helps identify misconceptions and ensures the client fully understands the material.

Setting Goals and Action Plans

For chronic conditions, nurses work collaboratively with clients to set achievable goals, such as maintaining blood pressure within a certain range or adhering to a weight management plan. Acute conditions may also involve short-term goals, such as completing a course of antibiotics or resting for a prescribed duration.

Monitoring and Following Up

Education does not end after the initial session. Nurses should follow up to monitor progress, reinforce learning, and address new concerns. Tracking adherence to treatment plans and assessing ongoing health outcomes are crucial components of effective education.

Strategies for Effective Education

Using Technology

Modern technology has enabled nurses to provide education through apps, online platforms, and telehealth services. Clients can access reliable resources, track symptoms, and stay connected with their healthcare providers.

Cultural Sensitivity

Cultural beliefs and values can significantly impact how clients perceive and respond to health education. Nurses must be culturally sensitive, adapting their approaches to respect the client's background and preferences.

Motivational Interviewing

This technique involves engaging clients in conversations that inspire behavior change. By exploring a client's goals and values, nurses can encourage adherence to treatment plans and lifestyle modifications.

Peer Support Programs

Connecting clients with peer support groups can foster a sense of community and provide emotional and practical guidance. Nurses often facilitate these connections, especially for chronic conditions where long-term support is beneficial.

Examples of Client Education

Acute Condition Example: Post-Surgical Care

Nurses educate clients about wound care, medication schedules, recognizing signs of infection, and physical activity restrictions. They might demonstrate how to change surgical dressings or provide written instructions to ensure clarity.

Chronic Condition Example: Diabetes Management

Nurses educate diabetic clients on monitoring blood sugar levels, administering insulin, maintaining a balanced diet, and recognizing symptoms of hypo- or hyperglycemia. Clients are also taught self-care techniques to manage stress and its impact on blood sugar.

Challenges in Client Education

Health Literacy

Limited health literacy can hinder a client's ability to understand medical instructions and make informed decisions. Nurses must identify these gaps and provide additional support.

Language Barriers

Clients who speak a different language may face difficulties in understanding educational materials. Nurses should leverage interpreters and translated resources to bridge this gap.

Time Constraints

In busy medical settings, nurses may struggle to allocate enough time for thorough education. Creative solutions, such as follow-up calls or group sessions, can help address this challenge.

Educating clients about acute and chronic conditions is a dynamic and essential aspect of nursing care. Through tailored information, clear communication, and ongoing support, nurses empower clients to take control of their health and navigate the complexities of their conditions. By fostering trust, understanding, and collaboration, nurses ensure that education becomes a cornerstone of effective treatment and improved quality of life.

Manage the care of a client with impaired ventilation/oxygenation

Impaired ventilation and oxygenation pose significant challenges for client care and can result from a variety of conditions such as respiratory diseases, cardiac issues, trauma, infections, or post-operative complications. Nurses play a critical role in the management of these clients by providing holistic and informed care that encompasses assessment, intervention, therapeutic communication, and collaboration with other healthcare professionals.

Assessment and Monitoring

Effective care begins with comprehensive and continuous assessment. Nurses gather vital information to monitor the client's respiratory status and identify changes that may require immediate intervention.

Initial Assessment

- Vital Signs: Monitoring respiratory rate, heart rate, blood pressure, and oxygen saturation using pulse oximetry. Hypoxemia or tachypnea may signal impaired oxygenation.
- Physical Examination: Observing for signs such as cyanosis, use of accessory muscles, nasal flaring, or abnormal breath sounds (e.g., wheezing, crackles).
- Subjective Data: Asking the client about symptoms such as dyspnea, chest pain, or fatigue to understand the severity and impact on their daily life.

Diagnostic Evaluations

Nurses collaborate with the medical team to ensure diagnostic tests are performed:

- Arterial Blood Gas (ABG): Analyzing oxygen (PaO2) and carbon dioxide (PaCO2) levels in the blood for hypoxemia or hypercapnia.
- Imaging Studies: Ensuring chest X-rays or CT scans are completed to identify conditions such as pneumonia, pleural effusion, or pulmonary embolism.
- Laboratory Tests: Monitoring hemoglobin levels, as they directly affect oxygen transport.

Interventions

Once an impaired ventilation or oxygenation issue is identified, nurses implement interventions tailored to the client's specific needs. These interventions can be categorized as immediate, supportive, and preventative.

Immediate Interventions

- Airway Management: Ensuring a patent airway by suctioning secretions, positioning the client (e.g., semi-Fowler's), or administering nebulized treatments.
- Oxygen Therapy: Administering supplemental oxygen via nasal cannula, simple mask, or high-flow systems based on severity.
- Pharmacologic Interventions: Administering prescribed bronchodilators, corticosteroids, or antibiotics for conditions like asthma or infections.

Supportive Interventions

- Mechanical Ventilation: Assisting clients who require invasive or non-invasive ventilation support, such as CPAP or BiPAP.
- Hydration:** Ensuring adequate fluid intake to maintain mucosal hydration and prevent thickened secretions.
- Psychological Support: Recognizing the anxiety and fear linked to respiratory distress and providing reassurance while fostering therapeutic communication.

Preventative Measures

- Infection Control: Implementing strict infection prevention techniques, including hand hygiene, personal protective equipment (PPE), and isolation protocols when necessary.
- Educational Support: Teaching clients breathing exercises (e.g., pursed-lip breathing) and how to use incentive spirometers to improve lung function.
- Lifestyle Modifications: Encouraging smoking cessation, balanced nutrition, and regular physical activity adapted to their respiratory capacity.

Collaboration with Multidisciplinary Teams

Nurses work closely with respiratory therapists, physicians, dietitians, and other healthcare professionals to optimize client outcomes.

- Respiratory Therapy: Consulting therapists for advanced interventions like nebulization and ventilator settings.
- Medication Management Collaborating with pharmacists to ensure appropriate dosing and timing of medications.
- Physical Therapy: Involving physiotherapists to aid in pulmonary rehabilitation and mobility.

Documentation and Evaluation

Documenting interventions, client responses, and progress is essential for effective care management. Nurses evaluate the effectiveness of interventions and modify care plans, as necessary.

Key Points for Documentation
- Oxygen saturation levels before and after therapy.
- Client's subjective feedback on breathing ease.
- Any adverse reactions to treatments or medications.

Criteria for Evaluation
- Improvement in ABG or other diagnostic parameters.
- Reduction in symptoms like dyspnea or cyanosis.
- Enhanced ability to perform daily activities without respiratory compromise.

Ethical and Cultural Considerations

Providing care for clients with impaired ventilation and oxygenation often involves sensitive ethical decisions, such as the use of advanced life support. Nurses must also respect cultural values and preferences regarding treatment.

Ethical Practices
- Advocating for the client's autonomy in decision-making.
- Ensuring informed consent for interventions like mechanical ventilation.
- Balancing aggressive treatment with palliative care when appropriate.

Cultural Competence
- Understanding cultural attitudes toward oxygen therapy and invasive procedures.
- Tailoring communication and education to align with the client's beliefs and language proficiency.

Managing care for clients with impaired ventilation or oxygenation is an intricate process requiring vigilance, technical knowledge, and compassion. Nurses are central to ensuring effective assessment, timely interventions, and the promotion of long-term respiratory health. By adopting a multidisciplinary and client-centered approach, they not only alleviate immediate distress but also empower clients to lead healthier lives despite their respiratory challenges.

Evaluate the effectiveness of the treatment plan for a client with an acute or chronic diagnosis

The role of a nurse in evaluating the effectiveness of treatment plans for clients with acute or chronic diagnoses is pivotal. Nurses act as the bridge between the medical team and the client, using their clinical expertise and a holistic approach to ensure the treatment plan achieves its intended outcomes. This process involves ongoing monitoring, communication, and adaptation to meet the client's needs.

Key Steps in Evaluation

Setting Measurable Goals

Effective evaluation begins at the planning stage. Nurses, in collaboration with healthcare teams, establish measurable and realistic goals for the client. Goals should be specific, achievable within a defined time frame, and tailored to the client's diagnosis. Examples of such goals include:

- Reducing pain levels from a score of 8 to 3 on a pain scale within 48 hours for acute conditions.
- Maintaining a stable blood glucose level between 70-130 mg/dL for clients with chronic diabetes over a period of weeks.

Setting clear goals provides a benchmark against which progress can be evaluated.

Monitoring Clinical Indicators

Nurses continuously monitor the client's clinical indicators to evaluate the effectiveness of the treatment plan. For clients with acute conditions, this may involve:

- Tracking vital signs such as heart rate, blood pressure, and oxygen saturation.
- Observing wound healing and signs of reduced inflammation or infection.

- Assessing pain levels and other symptomatic relief.

For chronic conditions, long-term monitoring might include:

- Reviewing lab results, such as HbA1c for diabetic patients or kidney function tests for those with renal disease.
- Monitoring medication adherence and its impact on the client's health.
- Evaluating physical and psychological well-being over time.

Conducting Patient Assessments

The nurse uses ongoing assessments to understand how the client responds to the treatment. This includes both objective and subjective evaluations:

- Objective Data: Measurements such as temperature, lab results, imaging studies, and physical exams.
- Subjective Data: Feedback from the client about symptoms, side effects, and overall well-being.

Regular assessments help nurses identify trends, improvements, or setbacks in the client's condition.

Collecting Client Feedback

Client involvement is central to evaluating treatment effectiveness. Nurses engage clients in discussions about their experiences, asking about improvements in symptoms, challenges faced, or changes in their quality of life. This feedback not only provides insight into the effectiveness of the treatment plan but also fosters a sense of empowerment and collaboration.

Reviewing Treatment Adherence

Treatment plans are only as effective as their implementation. Nurses assess whether clients are adhering to medications, dietary changes, exercise regimens, or other prescribed interventions. For clients with chronic conditions, adherence is often a critical factor, and non-compliance may necessitate adjustments to the plan or additional education.

Using Evidence-Based Tools

Nurses often employ evidence-based tools and scales to standardize the evaluation process. Common tools include:

- Pain Assessment Scales: Numeric Rating Scale (NRS), Visual Analog Scale (VAS), or Wong-Baker FACES Pain Scale.
- Functional Assessment Tools: Activities of Daily Living (ADL) scales, or tools like the Barthel Index.
- Quality of Life Measures: Questionnaires like the SF-36 or disease-specific tools for conditions like arthritis or asthma.

These tools enhance objectivity and provide a systematic approach to evaluation.

Collaborating with the Healthcare Team

Evaluation is a team effort. Nurses communicate their findings and observations with other members of the healthcare team, including physicians, physical therapists, dieticians, and social workers. This collaboration ensures a multi-disciplinary approach to refining the treatment plan based on the client's progress or challenges.

Adjusting the Treatment Plan

Identifying Barriers to Success

When a treatment plan fails to deliver the desired outcomes, nurses analyze potential barriers. These may include:

- Unanticipated side effects of medications.
- Lifestyle factors, such as stress, poor nutrition, or lack of family support.
- Economic or social determinants of health, such as difficulty affording medications or transportation to appointments.

Modifying Interventions

Based on the evaluation, nurses may recommend modifications to the treatment plan. This may involve:

- Changing medication dosages or prescribing alternative therapies.
- Suggesting additional interventions, such as counseling or physical therapy.
- Implementing educational strategies to improve client adherence.

The nurse ensures any changes are communicated effectively to the client and the healthcare team.

Evaluating Outcomes in Acute vs. Chronic Diagnoses

Acute Diagnoses

For acute conditions, such as post-surgical recovery or infections, evaluation focuses on short-term outcomes. Nurses prioritize indicators such as:

- Resolution of symptoms, such as fever or pain.
- Timely recovery, such as wound healing or mobility improvement.
- Prevention of complications, such as infections or adverse reactions.

Chronic Diagnoses

Chronic conditions, such as diabetes, hypertension, or arthritis, require a long-term approach. Evaluation focuses on sustainability and quality of life, with indicators such as:

- Stability of the condition, such as controlled blood pressure or glucose levels.
- Improved physical and psychological well-being.
- Reduced frequency of exacerbations or hospitalizations.

The nurse's role in evaluating the effectiveness of treatment plans is an ongoing and dynamic process. By combining clinical expertise, patient engagement, and evidence-based methods, nurses ensure that treatment plans are not only effective but also adaptable to the unique needs of each client. Whether addressing acute conditions or managing chronic illnesses, the ultimate goal is to empower clients to achieve the best possible health outcomes in a holistic and compassionate manner.

 ## Perform emergency care procedures

Nurses are integral to the healthcare system, particularly in emergency situations where quick thinking and effective action can make the difference between life and death. Their expertise spans multiple critical care techniques, ranging from stabilizing patients to administering life-saving medications.

Understanding Emergency Care

Emergency care refers to medical treatment provided in urgent scenarios, often characterized by severe injury, sudden illness, or life-threatening conditions. Nurses in emergency settings are trained to assess, prioritize, and address patients' needs rapidly while collaborating with other healthcare providers. These settings include hospital emergency rooms, ambulances, urgent care clinics, and disaster relief zones.

Key Responsibilities of Nurses in Emergency Care

Nurses play an essential role in emergency care, focusing on efficiency and precision. Their responsibilities include:

Rapid Assessment
Upon a patient's arrival, nurses perform a quick and thorough assessment of their condition. This process, termed triage, involves identifying the severity of the patient's symptoms, vital signs, and overall stability. Nurses classify patients into categories based on urgency, ensuring those in critical condition receive immediate attention.

Stabilization

Nurses are often tasked with stabilizing patients before further medical intervention. This includes managing airway obstructions, controlling severe bleeding, and addressing shock symptoms. Techniques such as cardiopulmonary resuscitation (CPR), defibrillation, and ventilatory support are commonly employed.

Administering Medications

In emergencies, nurses administer medications, including pain relievers, antiarrhythmics, and anticoagulants. They must calculate dosages accurately and monitor their effects on patients. Intravenous (IV) therapy is a frequent method employed to ensure rapid delivery of medication.

Monitoring Vital Signs

Continuous monitoring is critical in emergency care. Nurses track vital signs like heart rate, blood pressure, oxygen saturation, and respiratory rate, noting any changes that indicate improvement or deterioration.

Communication and Coordination

Effective communication is vital in emergencies. Nurses liaise between patients, families, and medical teams, ensuring all necessary information is conveyed. They often coordinate with physicians and specialists to execute care plans seamlessly.

Performing Critical Procedures

In emergencies, nurses may perform or assist with procedures such as wound suturing, catheterization, or inserting breathing tubes. They are trained to act swiftly and adhere to protocols to minimize risks and complications.

Emergency Care Procedures and Techniques

The procedures performed by nurses in emergency care vary depending on the situation. Here are some common techniques:

Cardiopulmonary Resuscitation (CPR)

When a patient experiences cardiac arrest, nurses initiate CPR to restore circulation and respiration. This involves chest compressions and rescue breaths delivered in a precise rhythm.

Defibrillation

Using automated external defibrillators (AEDs), nurses deliver controlled electric shocks to patients in life-threatening arrhythmias. AEDs guide nurses through the process, ensuring efficacy.

Managing Airway Obstructions

Nurses' clear airway blockages using suction equipment or manual techniques like the Heimlich maneuver. In severe cases, they may insert endotracheal tubes to secure breathing.

Controlling Hemorrhage

To stop severe bleeding, nurses apply direct pressure, dress wounds, or use tourniquets. Prompt action is essential to prevent blood loss and maintain circulation.

Treating Shock

Shock requires immediate attention, as it compromises blood flow to vital organs. Nurses manage symptoms by elevating the patient's legs, administering fluids, and monitoring complications.

Emergency Childbirth

In cases of sudden labor, nurses assist in delivering babies safely while ensuring the mother's and infant's health. They monitor vital signs and manage any complications that arise.

Handling Poisonings
Nurses treat poisonings by administering activated charcoal, inducing vomiting if appropriate, or coordinating antidote delivery. They also educate caregivers on preventive measures.

Essential Skills for Emergency Nurses

To excel in emergency care, nurses must possess a combination of technical knowledge, practical skills, and emotional resilience. Important qualities include:

- Critical Thinking: Nurses analyze situations quickly and make decisions under pressure.
- Technical Expertise: Familiarity with medical equipment and procedures is crucial.
- Communication: They must relay information clearly to patients, families, and teams.
- Compassion: Empathy helps nurses comfort patients and their loved ones during distressing times.
- Adaptability: Emergency settings are unpredictable, requiring flexibility and readiness.

Challenges Faced by Nurses in Emergency Care

Nurses encounter numerous challenges in emergency care, such as:

Stress and Burnout
The fast-paced environment and emotional toll can lead to fatigue and burnout. Nurses must prioritize self-care and seek support when needed.

Limited Resources
In disaster settings or understaffed facilities, nurses often work with limited supplies, making their roles even more demanding.

Communication Barriers

Language differences, patient confusion, or misinformation may hinder effective communication in emergencies.

Ethical Dilemmas

Nurses sometimes face ethical decisions, such as prioritizing care for patients when resources are scarce.

The Impact of Emergency Nurses

Emergency nurses are often the first point of contact in critical situations, making their role indispensable. Their ability to remain calm, act decisively, and provide expert care saves countless lives daily. They are the backbone of emergency healthcare, bridging the gap between initial intervention and specialized treatment.

Nurses in emergency care exemplify professionalism and courage, navigating high-stress environments to deliver life-saving treatment. Their compassion and expertise are fundamental to healthcare systems worldwide. As the demand for skilled emergency nurses grows, their contributions will continue to shape the future of patient care in moments that matter most.

Identify pathophysiology related to acute or chronic condition

Nurses play a vital role in the healthcare system, bridging the gap between medical science and patient care. One of their key responsibilities involves identifying the pathophysiology associated with acute and chronic conditions. This understanding allows nurses to provide more targeted and effective care, improve patient outcomes, and collaborate effectively with the broader medical team.

Understanding Pathophysiology

Pathophysiology refers to the functional changes within the body that result from disease or injury. It provides a detailed understanding of how normal physiological processes are altered in different health conditions. For nurses, grasping the pathophysiology of a condition involves understanding its causes, progression, and effects on the body, enabling them to interpret clinical symptoms and provide appropriate interventions.

Pathophysiology in Acute Conditions

Acute conditions are characterized by a sudden onset and a short duration. Examples include infections such as pneumonia, trauma-related injuries, or acute myocardial infarction. Identifying pathophysiology in these cases often requires quick assessment skills and the ability to recognize early warning signs.

Steps to Identify Pathophysiology in Acute Conditions:

- Patient History: Nurses gather detailed information about the patient's symptoms, medical background, and recent activities to identify triggers or contributing factors.
- Physical Assessment: A systematic examination, such as checking vital signs (e.g., fever, rapid breathing, or blood pressure fluctuations), helps detect abnormalities.
- Observation of Symptoms: Acute conditions often present specific symptoms such as pain, inflammation, or bleeding. Nurses correlate these symptoms with potential underlying pathophysiological changes.
- Collaboration with Diagnostics: Lab tests, imaging, or other diagnostic tools provide clarity on the condition. For example, elevated white blood cell counts may indicate an acute infection.
- Monitoring for Rapid Changes: Acute conditions can worsen quickly, so nurses must continuously observe and document any changes in the patient's condition.

Pathophysiology in Chronic Conditions

Chronic conditions, such as diabetes, hypertension, or chronic obstructive pulmonary disease (COPD), develop over time and are often long-lasting. Identifying pathophysiology in these cases involves an in-depth understanding of disease progression and its systemic impact.

Steps to Identify Pathophysiology in Chronic Conditions:
- Longitudinal Patient History: Nurses review the patient's health records to identify patterns or trends that suggest chronic disease development.
- Symptom Progression: Chronic conditions often involve gradual changes, such as persistent fatigue, swelling, or shortness of breath. Nurses note how symptoms evolve over time.
- Patient Education and Self-Reporting: Educating patients about their condition often leads to better self-monitoring and reporting, which can help nurses identify exacerbations or complications.
- Evaluation of Risk Factors: Factors such as lifestyle, genetics, and comorbidities are considered to understand their influence on disease's progression.
- Diagnostic Correlation: Routine lab results, like HbA1c levels in diabetic patients or lung function tests in COPD patients, are assessed to identify pathophysiological changes.

Key Skills for Nurses in Identifying Pathophysiology

- Critical Thinking: Nurses must analyze symptoms and lab results to connect them with underlying mechanisms.
- Clinical Observation: Acute and chronic conditions often present differently, requiring nurses to recognize subtle signs of deterioration or improvement.
- Interdisciplinary Collaboration: Working with physicians, specialists, and lab technicians ensures a comprehensive understanding of the condition.

- Effective Communication: Nurses must communicate findings clearly and concisely to ensure timely intervention.

Challenges in Identifying Pathophysiology

Despite their expertise, nurses may face challenges when identifying pathophysiology, including:

- Complex Symptoms: Some conditions present with overlapping or nonspecific symptoms, making diagnosis difficult.
- Time Constraints: In acute settings, nurses often have limited time to assess and intervene.
- Resource Limitations: Inadequate access to diagnostic tools or specialized care can hinder the identification process.

Identifying pathophysiology in acute and chronic conditions is a cornerstone of nursing practice. By leveraging their clinical expertise, observational skills, and knowledge of disease mechanisms, nurses play a crucial role in diagnosing and managing these conditions. Their ability to interpret changes in the body's function not only saves lives in acute settings but also enhances the quality of life for patients with chronic illnesses.

Recognize signs and symptoms of client complications and intervene

Nurses ensure the well-being of clients by identifying complications early and intervening appropriately. Their expertise in observation, assessment, and clinical decision-making enables them to act as frontline defenders in healthcare.

Identifying Signs and Symptoms

Observation and Monitoring

Nurses use their keen observational skills to monitor clients continuously. This involves keeping track of vital signs such as:

- Heart rate

- Blood pressure
- Respiratory rate
- Temperature

Beyond vital signs, nurses observe changes in physical appearance, behavior, and verbal communication that may indicate distress or complications.

Recognizing Early Warning Signs

Early signs of complications can vary depending on the condition being monitored. Common indicators include:

- Sudden pain or discomfort
- Unusual fatigue
- Changes in skin color (e.g., pallor or cyanosis)
- Shortness of breath
- Persistent nausea or vomiting
- Swelling or edema

Nurses are also trained to detect subtle changes that may not be immediately apparent, such as altered mental status or decreased urine output.

Using Clinical Tools and Technology

Modern healthcare provides nurses with advanced tools to aid in the recognition of complications. These include:

- Electronic health records (EHRs) for tracking patient history
- Diagnostic equipment like ECG machines and pulse oximeters
- Clinical scoring systems, such as the Glasgow Coma Scale or MEWS (Modified Early Warning Score)

Intervention Strategies

Immediate Response

When complications are identified, nurses prioritize immediate intervention. This may involve:

- Administering medications as prescribed
- Providing oxygen therapy
- Performing CPR or other emergency procedures
- Stopping treatments that may be causing adverse reactions

Collaborative Care

Nurses often work closely with multidisciplinary teams to address complications. This includes:

- Alerting physicians and specialists
- Coordinating diagnostic tests
- Implementing treatment plans
- Transferring clients to higher levels of care, such as ICU

Patient Education and Support

Intervention is not limited to clinical actions. Nurses educate clients and their families about managing conditions and recognizing potential complications at home. They provide reassurance, guidance, and emotional support during crises.

Documentation and Communication

Nurses meticulously document their observations, interventions, and outcomes. This ensures continuity of care and provides a record for future reference. Effective communication with other healthcare providers is essential for coordinated and efficient care.

The ability of nurses to recognize signs and symptoms of complications and intervene has a profound impact on client outcomes. By combining their clinical knowledge, observational skills, and compassionate care, nurses help ensure that complications are addressed promptly and effectively, safeguarding the health and lives of those they serve.

CHEAT SHEET 1

NORMAL LAB VALUES

Blood Chemistry

Sodium (Na+) - 135-145
Potassium (K+) - 3.5-5
Calcium (Ca2+) - 8.5-10.5
Magnesium (Mg2+) - 1.3-2.1
Chloride (Cl−) - 95-105

Complete Blood Count

Red blood cells count 4.2-6.1
Hemoglobin level
Adult male: 12-18
Hematocrit
Adult male: 37-52
White blood cell count
Adult: 5000-10,000
Child >2 yr: 5000-10,000, Newborn: 9000-30,000
Platelet count - 150,000-400,000

Urine Test

Chloride 110 to 250
Magnesium 7.3 to 12.2
Potassium 25 to 125
Protein 40 to 150
Sodium 40 to 220
Uric acid 250 to 750
pH 4.5 to 7.8
Specific gravity 1.016 to 1.022

Glucose Tolerance Test

Baseline, 70 to 110 mg/dL
30 minutes, 110 to 170 mg/dL
60 minutes, 120 to 170 mg/dL
90 minutes, 100 to 140 mg/dL
120 minutes, 70 to 120 mg/dL
Hemoglobin A1c (Hgb A1c): Fasting not required
4% to 5.9% (patient without diabetes)
Diabetic with good control, 7.5% or lower

Liver & Kidney Function Test

Liver
Albumin (g/dL) - 3.3 to 5
Bilirubin (mg/dL) - 0.3 to 1.0

Kidney
Blood urea nitrogen 10 to 20
Serum creatinine (mg/dL)
Females: 0.5-1.1
Males: 0.6-1.3

Thyroid
Thyroid-stimulating hormone (TSH) 0.2 to 5.4

Diabetic with fair control, 7.6% to 8.9% Diabetic with poor control, 9% or higher	
Lipid Profile	**Serum Enzymes and Cardiac Markers**
Total cholesterol - < 200 High-density lipoprotein cholesterol Males: > 45 Females: > 55 Low-density lipoprotein cholesterol < 130, Borderline high risk: 130-159, High risk: >159 Triglycerides Males: 40-160 Females: 35-135 Borderline high: 160-199 High: 200-499, Very high: >500	*Creatine kinase (CK)* Values: Creatine kinase, myocardial bound (CK-MB) is 0% to 5% of total *Troponins* Troponin I value lower than 0.6 and higher than 1.5 consistent with MI Troponin T value higher than 0.1 to 0.2 consistent with MI Therapeutic Medication Level Acetaminophen Tylenol; 10 to 20 Digoxin 0.5 to 2 Lithium 0.5 to 1.3 Phenytoin 10 to 20 Theophylline 10 to 20

CHEAT SHEET 2
Fluids and Electrolyte Imbalances

The treatment for fluid and electrolyte imbalances involves identifying the imbalance and identify the underlying cause, treat symptoms, and implementing corrective therapy through either replacement or restriction measures and monitor imbalances.

Fluids

The core principle of fluid balance is that the amount of water lost from the body must equal the amount of water taken in. Fluid imbalances occur when the body has too much or too little fluid, affecting homeostasis.

Distribution and Imbalances:

- Intracellular Fluid (ICF): ~60% of body water, inside cells.
- Extracellular Fluid (ECF): ~40% of body water, includes intravascular (plasma) and interstitial (between cells) fluid.
- Fluid Volume Deficit (Hypovolemia/Dehydration)
- Fluid Volume Excess (Hypervolemia)

Mnemonics to Remember

- **Hypovolemia - TACHY** (Tachycardia/Anxiety/Concentrated urine/ Hypotension/Yearning for water).
- **Hypervolemia - SWELL** (Swelling/edema, Weight gain, Elevated BP, Lung crackles, Lots of fluid).

Quick Assessment Tips about Fluid

- Daily Weights: Most accurate indicator of fluid status (1 kg = 1 L fluid).
- I/O Monitoring: Strict measurement of all fluids in and out.
- Skin Turgor: Pinch skin on hand or abdomen; poor turgor indicates dehydration.
- Edema: Assess pitting (1+ to 4+ scale) in dependent areas (ankles, sacrum).

Nursing Interventions (physician orders required)

Hypovolemia

Administer IV fluids (NaCl or Lactated Ringer's), Monitor VS, I&O, weight, Encourage oral rehydration if appropriate, Assess skin turgor, mucous membranes.

Hypovolemia

Administer IV fluids (NaCl or Lactated Ringer's), Monitor VS, I&O, weight, Encourage oral rehydration if appropriate, Assess skin turgor, mucous membranes.

Electrolytes

Electrolytes are minerals in the body fluids (blood, urine, etc.) that carry an electric charge. They're essential for:
- Nerve and muscle function
- Hydration
- pH balance
- Moving nutrients into cells
- Removing waste

Key Electrolytes
- Sodium (Na^+): Regulates fluid balance, nerve/muscle function (135–145 mEq/L).
- Potassium (K^+): Critical for cardiac/muscle function (3.5–5.0 mEq/L).
- Calcium (Ca^{2+}): Bone health, muscle contraction, nerve signaling (8.5–10.5 mg/dL).
- Magnesium (Mg^{2+}): Muscle/nerve function, enzyme activity (1.5–2.5 mEq/L).

Mnemonics to Remember
Ca^{2+} & Mg^{2+} = Calm muscles

Low = Twitchy

High = Floppy

"Potassium pumps the heart"

"Sodium sucks" (Sodium pulls water with it $\rightarrow$ fluid balance)

Quick Assessment Tips about Electrolytes
- Na^+ = Neuro" – Sodium imbalances often cause confusion or seizures.
- K^+ = Cardiac" – Potassium changes affect heart rhythm.
- Low Ca^{2+} = Spasms – Watch for Chvostek's and Trousseau's signs.
- Mg^{2+} affects muscles and reflexes – think tremors vs. flaccidity.

Nursing Intervention (physician orders required)

Electrolyte Imbalance	Interventions
Low Sodium Level	Administer IV normal saline, Fluid restrictions
Elevated Sodium Level	Fluid replacement, diuretics, restrict sodium intake
Low Potassium Level	Administer po or IV potassium and monitor EKG
Elevated Potassium Level	Administer Kayexalate, IV insulin + glucose, Calcium gluconate (protect heart), Dialysis (severe)
Low Calcium glucose	Administer Calcium gluconate IV and Vitamin Ds
Elevated Calcium	Administer Loop diuretics, IV fluids to promote excretion and monitor for arrhythmias

Low Magnesium	Administer Magnesium sulfate IV or PO, monitor Deep Tendon Reflexes (DTRs) and respiratory status
Elevated Calcium Administer Calcium gluconate (for cardiac protection), IV fluids + diuretic, Dialysis if severe	Administer Calcium gluconate (for cardiac protection), IV fluids + diuretic, Dialysis if severe

CHEAT SHEET 3

ARTERIAL BLOOD GAS ANALYSIS

Using the Tic-Tac-Toe Methods

Interpreting arterial blood gas (ABG) readings can seem daunting at first, but the tic-tac-toe method provides a straightforward and visual approach to breaking down the results. This method transforms complex analysis into a logical step-by-step process. Here's how it works:

What is the Tic-Tac-Toe Method?

The tic-tac-toe method utilizes a simple 3x3 grid, resembling a tic-tac-toe board. Each box of the grid is assigned specific values that correspond to the three main components of an ABG reading:

- pH: Indicates whether the blood is acidic (7.45).
- $PaCO_2$: Reflects the level of carbon dioxide in the blood and indicates respiratory status. Normal values are 35–45 mmHg. Higher values suggest acidosis, while lower values suggest alkalosis.
- HCO_3^-: Represents bicarbonate levels and indicates metabolic status. Normal values are 22–26 mEq/L. Lower values suggest acidosis, while higher values suggest alkalosis.

Setting Up the Grid

Draw a 3x3 tic-tac-toe grid. Label the three rows with "Acidic," "Normal," and "Alkaline," and assign columns for each parameter: pH, $PaCO_2$, and HCO_3^-. It should look like this:

	pH	$PaCO_2$	HCO_3^-
Acidic			
Normal			
Alkaline			

Step-by-Step Interpretation

Follow these steps for interpreting ABG results using the tic-tac-toe method:

Step 1: Determine the pH

Check whether the pH value is acidic, normal, or alkaline, and place it into the appropriate box under the "pH" column. For instance:

- If pH = 7.30, place it in the "Acidic" row under pH.
- If pH = 7.40, place it in the "Normal" row under pH.
- If pH = 7.50, place it in the "Alkaline" row under pH.

Step 2: Evaluate $PaCO_2$

Next, analyze the $PaCO_2$ value. Determine if it's in the acidic (>45 mmHg), normal (35–45 mmHg), or alkaline (<35 mmHg) range, and mark the corresponding box under the "$PaCO_2$" column.

Step 3: Examine HCO_3^-

Lastly, assess the bicarbonate (HCO_3^-) levels. Plot the value under "Acidic" (26 mEq/L).

Step 4: Analyze the Pattern

With all three parameters mapped out on the grid, observe their alignment. The pattern provides insight into the type of imbalance. Here are the key possibilities:

- Respiratory Acidosis: pH is acidic, $PaCO_2$ is acidic, and HCO_3^- may be normal or compensatory (alkaline).
- Metabolic Acidosis: pH is acidic, HCO_3^- is acidic, and $PaCO_2$ may be normal or compensatory (alkaline).
- Respiratory Alkalosis: pH is alkaline, $PaCO_2$ is alkaline, and HCO_3^- may be normal or compensatory (acidic).
- Metabolic Alkalosis: pH is alkaline, HCO_3^- is alkaline, and $PaCO_2$ may be normal or compensatory (acidic).
- Mixed Disorders: Both $PaCO_2$ and HCO_3^- align with the pH, indicating a combination of respiratory and metabolic causes.

Compensation Status

Compensation refers to how the body attempts to restore balance:

- Uncompensated: Only one value aligns with the pH, while the other remains normal.
- Partially Compensated: Both $PaCO_2$ and HCO_3^- are abnormal, but the pH is still outside the normal range.
- Fully Compensated: $PaCO_2$ and HCO_3^- are abnormal, but the pH has returned to normal.

Practice Example

Let's say you receive these ABG results:
pH: 7.32 (Acidic)
$PaCO_2$: 50 mmHg (Acidic)
HCO_3^-: 24 mEq/L (Normal)

Using the tic-tac-toe method:
- Plot "pH" in the "Acidic" row.
- Place "$PaCO_2$" in the "Acidic" row.
- Mark "HCO_3^-" in the "Normal" row.

Result: This pattern suggests Uncompensated Respiratory Acidosis.

The tic-tac-toe method is an intuitive and engaging tool for interpreting ABG readings. By visualizing imbalances and compensation patterns, healthcare professionals can quickly identify and address respiratory or metabolic abnormalities, ensuring better patient outcomes.

Interventions
Respiratory Acidosis: Improve ventilation (e.g., oxygen therapy, positioning, encourage deep breathing).
Respiratory Alkalosis: Treat cause (e.g., reduce anxiety, adjust ventilator settings).
Metabolic Acidosis: Administer bicarbonate (if ordered), treat underlying cause (e.g., DKA protocol).
Metabolic Alkalosis: Replace fluids/electrolytes, treat cause (e.g., stop NG suction).
Monitor for **hypoxemia** (low PaO_2): Administer oxygen, monitor SpO_2.

CHEAT SHEET 4

EKG INTERPRETATION

Understanding the Basics of EKG Strips

An EKG strip records the heart's electrical impulses as they move through its chambers and conduction system. These impulses are captured and displayed as a series of waves and intervals on graph paper. An EKG is made up of various waveforms and intervals, each representing different stages of cardiac electrical activity.

Here's what you need to know about the components of an EKG strip:

Component	Description
EKG Grid	EKG strips are printed on graph paper with a grid consisting of small and large squares. Each small square measures 1 mm by 1 mm, and each large square consists of 5 small squares.
P Wave	Represents atrial depolarization (the electrical activation of the atria).
QRS Complex	Represents ventricular depolarization (the electrical activation of the ventricles).
T Wave	Represents ventricular repolarization (the resetting of electrical potential in the ventricles).
R Interval	Measures the time from the onset of the P wave to the start of the QRS complex, reflecting the conduction time through the atria and AV node.
QRS	Represents ventricular depolarization
QT Interval	Measures the time from the start of the QRS complex to the end of the T wave, representing the total time for ventricular depolarization and repolarization.
ST Segment	The flat, isoelectric section between the end of the QRS complex and the start of the T wave, which is critical in identifying ischemia or myocardial infarction.

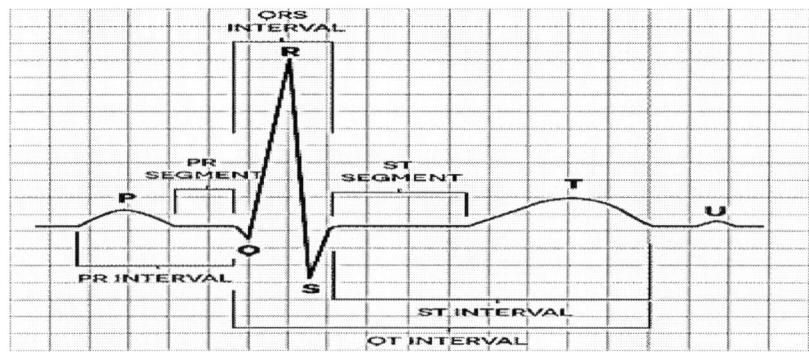

How to Interpret EKG Strips Step-by-Step

Electrocardiogram (EKG or ECG) strips are a vital tool in monitoring and diagnosing heart conditions. They provide a graphical representation of the heart's electrical activity, allowing healthcare professionals to assess heart rhythm, rate, and potential abnormalities. For beginners, interpreting EKG strips may seem daunting, but understanding the basics can lay a strong foundation for more advanced analysis.

Step	Details
Assess the Heart Rate	Count the number of R waves in a six-second strip and multiply by 10.
Evaluate the Rhythm	Regular: Distance between R waves is consistent. Irregular: R-R intervals vary, may indicate arrhythmias.
Analyze the P Wave	Check for P wave before each QRS complex. Verify uniform shape and size.
Measure the PR Interval	Normal: 0.12 to 0.20 seconds. Prolonged: May indicate first-degree AV block. Shortened: May suggest pre-excitation syndromes.
Inspect the QRS Complex	Normal duration: <0.12 seconds. Widened: Could indicate ventricular conduction delays.
Examine the ST Segment	It should be flat and on the isoelectric line. Elevation or depression may indicate myocardial ischemia or infarction.
Assess the T Wave	It should be upright in most leads, smooth, rounded shape. Inverted or peaked may indicate ischemia, hyperkalemia, etc.
Measure the QT Interval	Normal varies based on heart rate, generally <0.44 seconds. Prolonged may predispose to arrhythmias like Torsades de Pointes.

Normal Sinus Rhythm

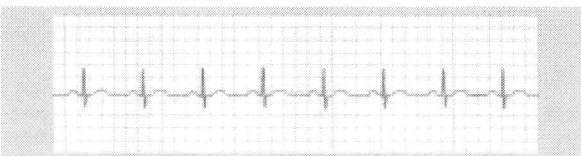

Normal sinus rhythm is the baseline rhythm for all EKGs. It's important for maintaining adequate blood flow and oxygenation.

Normal Sinus Rhythm Characteristics

- Rate: 60-100 beats per minute (BPM)
- Rhythm: Regular
- P Wave: Normal
- PR Interval: Normal
- QRS: Normal

Identify Common Abnormalities

Abnormality	Characteristics
Sinus Bradycardia	Heart rate below 60 beats per minute. Normal P waves, PR interval, and QRS complex.
Sinus Tachycardia	Heart rate above 100 beats per minute. Normal P waves, PR interval, and QRS complex.
Atrial Fibrillation	Irregularly irregular rhythm. Absence of distinct P waves. Variable ventricular rate.
Ventricular Tachycardia	Wide QRS complexes. Regular rhythm with a rapid ventricular rate. Absence of P waves.
Myocardial Infarction	ST segment elevation or depression. Pathological Q waves (wide and deep). T wave inversion.

Sinus Bradycardia

Bradycardia has a slower-than-normal heart rate. It can prevent the heart from pumping enough oxygen-rich blood.

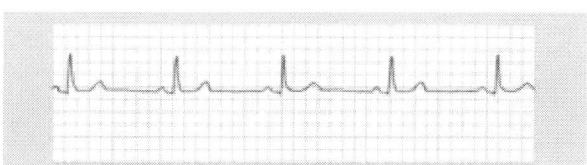

Bradycardia Characteristics

- Rate: Less than 60 BPM

- Rhythm: Regular
- P Wave: Normal
- PR Interval: Normal
- QRS: Normal

Potential causes of bradycardia include medications (beta-blockers) and the vagal maneuver (bearing down).

Atrial Fibrillation (A-Fib)

A-fib is a common arrhythmia that causes the heart to beat rapidly and irregularly. It occurs when the heart's electrical signals are disorganized, causing the atria (upper chambers) to quiver instead of contracting properly.

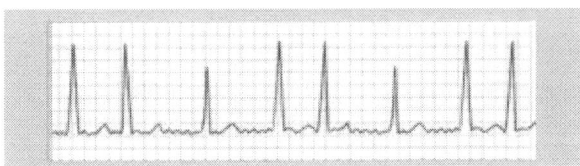

A-Fib Characteristics

- Rate: Usually over 100 BPM
- Rhythm: Irregular
- P Wave: None because the atria aren't contracting
- PR Interval: None because the atria aren't contracting
- QRS: Normal

Potential causes include alcohol (holiday heart), hyperthyroidism, open heart surgery, and pulmonary hypertension.

Ventricular Tachycardia (V-Tach)

V-tach is an extremely rapid heart rhythm originating from the ventricles when the sinoatrial (SA) node and the atrioventricular (AV) node fail to produce an impulse. In this scenario, the ventricles take over the responsibility of pacing the heart.

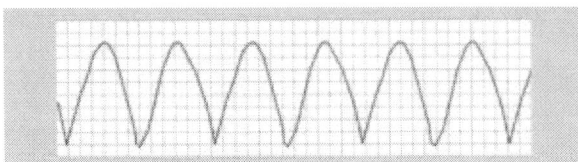

V-Tach Characteristics

- Rate: 100-250 BPM
- Rhythm: Regularly spaced and even like tombstones
- P Wave: None
- PR Interval: None

- QRS: Wide and even

Potential causes include cardiac injury (history of heart attack), electrolyte imbalances, medication toxicity, stimulants (caffeine, methamphetamines) or stress.

Ventricular Fibrillation (V-Fib)

V-fib is the deadliest rhythm. It's a chaotic pattern of electrical activity in the ventricles in which electrical impulses arise from many foci.

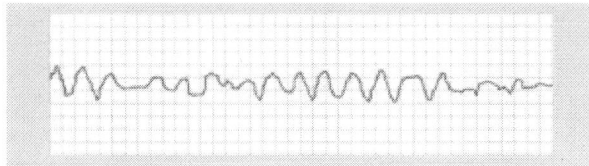

<u>V-Fib Characteristics</u>

- Rate: Unknown or indistinguishable
- Rhythm: Chaotic waveform and rhythm
- P Wave: None because the atria aren't contracting
- PR Interval: None because the atria aren't contracting
- QRS: None because the ventricles aren't fully contracting

V-fib can occur due to cardiac injury (heart attack, valvular disease), electrical imbalances (acid-base, electrolyte imbalances, electrical shock, unsuccessfully treated ventricular tachycardia), and medication toxicity.

Atrial Flutter (A-Flutter)

A-flutter is like A-fib. But the heart's electrical signals spread through the atria in a fast but regular rhythm instead of irregular.

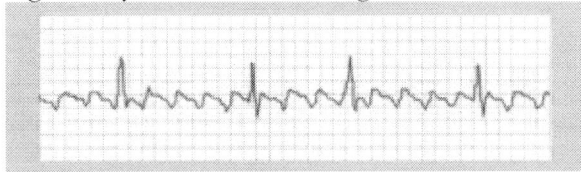

A-Flutter Characteristics

- Rate: 75-150 BPM
- Rhythm: Usually regular
- P Wave: No P wave
- PR Interval: None
- QRS: Usually normal
- Causes of A-flutter include heart disease, pulmonary embolism, or chronic obstructive pulmonary disease (COPD). Certain medications can also trigger it.

Asystole (Flatline)

Asystole is a cardiac arrest rhythm where the heart doesn't produce electrical activity. As a result, the heart stops beating, and the EKG monitor shows a total standstill.

Asystole Characteristics

- Rate: N/A
- Rhythm: N/A
- P Wave: N/A
- PR Interval: N/A
- QRS Duration: N/A
- Asystole Causes
- Causes of asystole include trauma or lethal cardiac rhythms like V-tach, V-fib, and ST-segment elevation myocardial infarction (STEMI).

Tips to improve EKG Interpretation

- Practice Regularly: Interpreting EKGs requires practice. Reviewing numerous strips will help you recognize patterns and abnormalities more quickly.
- Use a Systematic Approach: Follow the steps outlined above for every EKG to ensure that nothing is overlooked.
- Document Findings: Clearly note your observations, including rhythm, rate, intervals, and any abnormalities.

Interpreting EKG strips is an essential skill for healthcare professionals, and anyone involved in patient care. By understanding the basics of the heart's electrical activity, systematically analyzing each component of the EKG strip, and recognizing common abnormalities, you can effectively assess cardiac function and contribute to timely diagnosis and treatment. As with any skill, practice and continuous learning are key to mastering EKG interpretation.

CHEAT SHEET 5

MEDICATION CLASSIFICATIONS & NURSING
IMPLICATIONS

MEDICATIONS AND USE	NURSING IMPLICATIONS
ACE INHIBITOR (angiotensin converting enzyme inhibitors) Ending: -pril Example: captopril, lisinopril, ramipril. **Treat hypertension.**	Monitor blood pressure Teach patient to rise slowly Monitor potassium level Assess patient for renal impairment Assess patient for signs of angioedema
Angiotensin II receptor blockers (ARBs) Ending: -sartan Example: Losartan, valsartan, candesartan. **Treat hypertension.**	Monitor BP Monitor BUN, creatinine, electrolytes Check edema in feet and legs Assess angioedema
BETA BLOCKER Ending: -lol Example: atenolol, metoprolol, carvedilol. **Treat hypertension.**	Monitor blood pressure, heart rate, and rhythm Monitor signs of edema Monitor changes in labs (protein, BUN, and creatinine Monitor for hypoglycemia If HR less than 60 don't give
CALCIUM CHANNEL BLOCKERS Ending (not all): -pine Example: amlodipine, diltiazem, verapamil. **Treat hypertension.**	Monitor BP and pulse frequently Avoid grapefruit juice Do not open, crush, or chew sustained release capsule
ALPHA BLOCKERS Some end with: -sin Example: Terazosin **Treat hypertension**	Monitor BP and pulse Caution patient to change position slowly
CHOLESTEROL (lowering) Ending: -statin Example: Atorvastatin **Lower Cholesterol Levels**	Diet low in cholesterol and fat Monitor cholesterol and triglycerides levels
LOOP DIURETIC Ending (not all): -ide Example: Furosemide **Manage edema associated with heart failure**	Assess for tinnitus and hearing loss Monitor BP and pulse, daily weight, intake and output, lung sounds, skin turgor, and dehydration

ANTIANGINA Example: Nitroglycerin **Used to treat angina (chest pain)**	If signs of angina (chest pain) occur, do not wait until pain is severe, administer 1 tablet under the tongue every 5 minutes (limit is no more than 3 tablets in 15 minutes). Assess for headache, orthostatic hypotension, reflex tachycardia.

BRONCHODILATOR Example: Albuterol, epinephrine, theophylline **Treat reversible airway obstruction as result of asthma or chronic obstructive pulmonary disease (COPD).**	Drink adequate liquids Avoid smoking and other respiratory irritants. Administer around the clock as ordered to maintain therapeutic levels.
ANTIHISTAMINE Examples: Cetirizine, diphenhydramine, meclizine, promethazine **Treatment for allergy symptoms, motion sickness and insomnia**	Caution about drowsiness Do not administer antihistamines within 4 days of skin testing. Take with food Monitor intake and output
ANTIVIRALS Ending (not all): -vir Examples: Acyclovir, ritonavir **Treat AIDS, Herpetic lesions, shingles**	Administered around the clock as ordered. Assess for s/s of infection. Prevent the spread of infection.
ANTIFUNGAL AGENTS Ending (not all): -azole Examples: ketoconazole, and amphotericin B **Treatment for fungus infections**	Obtain a culture. Inspect infected areas of skin. Assess patient s/s of infection. Discontinue if skin irritation
ANTIINFLAMMATORY - CORTICOSTEROIDS Ending (not all): - sone & cort. Example: Prednisone, fludrocortisone, cortisone **Decrease inflammation, treatment for Addison disease.**	Decreased wound healing Osteoporosis Hyperglycemia
ANTIBIOTIC - AMINOGLYCOSIDE Ending: – cin & mycin Examples: Gentamicin, neomycin, tobramycin. **Kills bacteria**	Assess for s/s of nephrotoxicity. Notify HCP if diarrhea occurs.
ANTIBIOTIC – CEPHALOSPORINS Prefix – Ceph or Cef Example: Cefaclor, cefazolin, ceftriaxone. **Interfere with bacterial growth**	Assess for signs of nephrotoxicity. Notify the HCP if diarrhea occurs, it can promote the development of clostridium difficile infection.

ANTICOAGULANTS Ending: -arin Example: Heparin, enoxaparin, warfarin. **Treat clotting disorders and thin the blood.**	Enoxaparin sodium (Lovenox) is only administered subcutaneously. Protamine sulfate is the antidote for enoxaparin and heparin. Monitor partial thromboplastin time often for heparin (therapeutic levels are 1.5–2.0 times the control) and monitor PT & INR for warfarin. Monitor for signs of bleeding. Caution patients to not take aspirin. Vitamin K is antidote (warfarin).
THROMBOLYTICS Ending: -ase Examples: Alteplase, reteplase, streptokinase. **Treat myocardial infarction, pulmonary embolism, stroke, DVT, and arterial thrombosis**	Assess patient for bleeding every 15 minutes during the first hour of therapy. Monitor ECG continuously. Advice to avoid all unnecessary procedures such as shaving and vigorous tooth brushing.
IMMUNOSUPPRESSANTS Examples: Azathioprine, cyclosporine, fingolimod. Prevention of rejection and treatment of organ rejection.	• Assess for signs and symptoms of infection, anemia, and bleeding is critically important. • Assess liver function prior to administering this drug due to the risk for hepatotoxicity. • Assess for cardiovascular disorders as well as a history of GI and respiratory disorders. • Monitor white blood cell and platelet counts.
CHOLINERGIC AGENTS Examples: Bethanechol, muscarine, pilocarpine. **Treatment of urinary retention, treatment of glaucoma and myasthenia gravis.**	• Monitor blood pressure and pulse. • Instruct the patient to rise slowly from a supine or sitting position. Administer oral drug on empty stomach to decrease nausea and vomiting.
ANTICHOLINERGIC AGENTS Example: Oxybutynin, atropine. **Treat irritable bowel syndrome, urinary frequency, urgency, or urge incontinence. Reduce salivation and bronchial secretions prior to surgery.**	• Best given 30 minutes to 1 hour before meals and at bedtime. • Assist with oral hygiene and monitor stools & urine output. • Teach patient how to use saline eye drops if dry eyes are a problem. • Do not open or chew extended-release capsules.

HISTAMINE H2 ANTAGONISTS Ending : -tidine Examples: Cimetidine, famotidine, and nizatidine. **Treat gastroesophageal reflux disease (GERD), acid reflux, and gastric ulcers.**	• Administer with meals. • Advise to patient that smoking may decrease effectiveness. • Teach patient the signs of gastric bleeding and to notify the health care provider, if any occur.
ANTIDIARRHEALS Examples: loperamide, bismuth subsalicylate. **For the control and symptomatic relief of acute and chronic nonspecific diarrhea.**	• Assess bowel sounds for peristalsis. • Assess for abdominal pain and distention. • Do not give if bloody diarrhea is present or temperature is greater than 101° F. • Assess the frequency & consistency of stools. • Assess patient's fluid and electrolyte status and skin turgor for dehydration.
LAXATIVES Example: Psyllium, docusate salts, lactulose, magnesium citrate, senna, and bisacodyl **Facilitation of bowel movements with inactive colon or anorectal disorders.**	• Assess for abdominal distention, and presence of bowel sounds. • Assess color, consistency, and amount of stool produced. • Advise patient to increase fluid intake. • Advise patients, except those with spinal cord injuries, that laxatives should be used only for short-term therapy.
ANTIGOUT Examples: Allopurinol and probenecid. **Long-term treatment of gouty arthritis.**	• Do not administer medication during or within 2 to 3 weeks of an acute attack (probenecid). • Initially, symptoms may worsen until uric acid levels are decreased. • Encourage an increased intake of fluids to increase excretion of uric acid and to decrease concentration. • Teach patient to avoid smoked meats and high-protein diets.
BISPHOSPHONATE Examples: Alendronate, etidronate, ibandronate. **Treat and prevent osteoporosis in postmenopausal women, management of hypercalcemia.**	• Administer in the morning 30 minutes or more before the first food, beverage, or other medication of the day. • Orange juice, coffee, or food decreases effectiveness.

	• Patient should not lie down until after eating. • Monitor for signs of hypocalcemia.
NONSTEROIDAL ANTI-INFLAMMATOR DRUGS (NSAIDs) Examples: Aspirin, ibuprofen, and naproxen. **Treatment of fever, mild to moderate pain, osteoarthritis, rheumatoid arthritis, inflammation, and acute gout.**	• Administer with meals. • Advise to patient that smoking may decrease effectiveness. • Teach patient the signs of gastric bleeding and to notify the health care provider, if any occur.
SKELETAL MUSCLE RELAXANTS Examples: Baclofen, carisoprodol, diazepam. **Used for the relief of painful musculoskeletal conditions such as muscle spasms, often following injuries such as low back strain.**	• Avoid driving or activities requiring alertness until response to drug is known. • Avoid use of alcohol or other CNS depressants with these medications. • Assess patient for pain, muscle stiffness, and range of motion before and periodically throughout therapy.
OPIOID ANALGESICS Ending (not all): -one Example: Meperidine, methadone, morphine, hydromorphone, codeine, hydrocodone, and oxycodone **Alleviate moderate to severe pain.**	• Assess bowel function routinely. • Naloxone (Narcan) is an antidote in case of overdose. • Encourage patient to turn, cough, and breathe deeply every 2 hours to prevent atelectasis. • Advise to avoid driving or other activities requiring alertness until response to medication is known. • Caution patient to avoid use with CNS depressants.
BENZODIAZEPINES (ANTICONVULSANTS/ANTIANXIETY) Examples: Clonazepam, diazepam. **Treat insomnia, anxiety, and seizures.**	• Assess degree of anxiety and sedation level. • Monitor kidney and liver function. • Monitor respirations. • Encourage patient to take the medication immediately before going to bed and not participate in activities that require mental alertness after taking the medication.
ANTICONVULSANT/ANTIEPILEPTICS BISPHOSPHONATE Examples: Carbamazepine, gabapentin, valproic acid, phenobarbital, and phenytoin	• Periodic blood studies for therapeutic levels. • Teach patient to purchase a Medic-Alert bracelet.

457

Immediate treatment of seizures. Decrease the incidence and severity of seizures. Several anticonvulsants are used to treat neuropathic pain.	<ul><li>Teach patient to never abruptly discontinue medication.</li><li>With Dilantin, watch for gingival hyperplasia; encourage routine prophylactic dental care.</li><li>Do not give Tegretol (carbamazepine) with grapefruit juice.</li></ul>
PHENOTHIAZINES (ANTIPSYCHOTIC/ANTIEMETIC) Examples: Chlorpromazine, prochlorperazine, promethazine, hydroxyzine. **Treat psychosis in those clients with schizophrenia. Some phenothiazines, such as promethazine and prochlorperazine, are used to treat nausea & vomiting.**	<ul><li>Do not mix the liquid forms with any beverage containing caffeine, tannates, or pectin due to incompatibility.</li><li>Monitor liver enzymes and renal function.</li><li>Avoid overexposure to the sun. (Due to side effect of photosensitivity).</li><li>Monitor for anticholinergic effects.</li></ul>
TRICYCLIC ANTIDEPRESSANTS Ending (not all): -tyline Examples: Amitriptyline, nortriptyline, and doxepin **Treat depression, bipolar disorder, and fibromyalgia syndrome. Treat neuropathic pain, chronic insomnia, ADHD, and obsessive-compulsive disorder.**	<ul><li>Administer at bedtime to minimize problems with sedation.</li><li>Therapy usually continues for a minimum of 6 months; do not abruptly stop taking medication or a relapse may occur.</li><li>When depressed patient begins to feel better, the risk of suicide increases; monitor patient closely for mood changes or unusual changes in behavior.</li></ul>
MONOAMINE OXIDASE INHIBITORS (MAOIs) Example: Phenelzine and selegiline **Treat atypical depression, panic disorder, and obsessive-compulsive related disorders.**	<ul><li>Teach patient to avoid tyramine-rich foods that can lead to hypertensive crisis such as fermented meats [smoked sausage, pepperoni, salami], dried or cured fish, soy sauce, and ripe avocados.</li><li>Avoid chocolate and caffeinated beverages.</li><li>Avoid cold remedies, nasal decongestants, and asthma medications. Caution patient to avoid use with CNS depressants.</li></ul>

CHOLINESTERASE INHIBITORS Example: Donepezil and galantamine. **Manage Alzheimer's disease.**	• Assess patients for difficulty urinating. • Monitor for respiratory airway compromise and bradycardia. • Teach patient that the drug is not a cure but only slows progression of symptoms.
MAGNESIUM SULFATE **Treatment is to inhibit premature labor. Control seizure activity associated with preeclampsia or eclampsia.**	• Patellar reflex (knee jerk) should be tested before each parenteral dose of magnesium sulfate. • Monitor serum magnesium levels and renal function periodically throughout administration of parenteral magnesium sulfate. • Monitor newborn for hypotension, hyporeflexia, and respiratory depression. • Monitor pulse, BP, respirations, and ECG.
Rho (D) IMMUNE GLOBULINBISPHOSPHONATE **Used to prevent Rh immunization of the Rh-negative patient exposed to Rh-positive blood during termination of a pregnancy, or as the result of a delivery of a Rh-positive infant.**	• Using a separate sterile absorbent cotton or gauze pad for each eye, wash the unopened lids from the nose outward until free of blood, mucus, or meconium. • A new tube should be started for each infant. • Administer medication within 2 hours of birth. • Apply 1 cm ribbon of ointment to the lower conjunctival sac of each eye. It should be instilled from inner to outer canthus. • Assess eyes for drainage or crusting.
ERYTHROMYCIN OPHTHALMIC OINTMENT **Prevent ophthalmia neonatorum caused by N. gonorrhoeae and chlamydial ophthalmia caused by C. trachomatis.**	• Administer with meals. • Advise to patient that smoking may decrease effectiveness. • Teach patient the signs of gastric bleeding and to notify the health care provider, if any occur.

INSULIN	• Tell clients to admin SQ in the same general area for consistent rates of absorption: thigh (lowest), upper arm, abdomen (highest).
Short Duration: Rapid Acting (onset < than 30 min) Lispro, Aspart, Glulisine (duration 3-6 hrs) Short Duration: Slow Acting (onset 30-60 min) Regular Insulin (duration 6-10 hrs.) Intermediate Duration (onset 60-120 min) NPH Insulin (duration 16-24 hrs.) Long Duration: (onset 1.5-3 hrs.) Insulin Glargine (Lantus) (duration up to 24 hrs.) **Insulin is used to Treat Diabetes**	• Ensure proper storage: unopened stored in fridge, vials of premixed insulins can be stored for up to 3 months under refrigeration, premixed syringes can be kept in fridge for 1-2 weeks in vertical position with needles pointing up (gently move syringes back and forth before admin), store vial that is in use at room temp, avoid sunlight and intense heat and discard after 1 month. • Only NPH (Humulin) can be mixed with short-acting insulins. • Only short-acting insulins may be administered intravenously (IV). • Draw up clear before the cloudy insulin to prevent contaminating short-acting insulin with long-acting insulin.

CHEAT SHEET 6

COMMON MEDICAL DISORDERS

Pathophysiology, Signs/Symptoms, & Nursing Interventions

CARDIOVASCULAR	Pathophysiology	Signs and Symptoms	Nursing Interventions
Coronary Artery Disease (CAD)	Buildup of atheromatous plaques in coronary arteries, leading to reduced blood flow to myocardium	Chest pain or discomfort (angina), shortness of breath, palpitations, fatigue, myocardial infarction	Monitor vital signs and oxygen saturation, administer prescribed medications, educate on lifestyle modifications, encourage smoking cessation, prepare for procedures
Heart Failure	Heart's inability to pump blood effectively, leading to inadequate tissue perfusion	Dyspnea, edema, fatigue and weakness, jugular venous distension, weight gain	Monitor fluid balance and daily weights, administer diuretics and other medications, educate on dietary sodium restrictions, encourage physical activity, provide emotional support
Arrhythmias	Abnormalities in heart's electrical conduction system	Irregular or rapid heartbeat, dizziness, fatigue, shortness of breath, chest pain	Monitor ECG, administer antiarrhythmic medications, prepare for procedures, educate on avoiding stimulants, encourage adherence to anticoagulants
Valvular Heart Diseases	Dysfunction of one or more heart valves, leading to stenosis or regurgitation	Shortness of breath, fatigue, heart murmur, swelling in ankles or feet,	Monitor for signs of heart failure or embolic events, administer medications, educate on follow-up care, and valve replacement

		symptoms of heart failure	surgery, provide support for lifestyle changes
RESPIRATORY	**Pathophysiology**	**Signs and Symptoms**	**Nursing Interventions**
Asthma	Chronic inflammatory condition of the airways leading to hyperresponsiveness, swelling, and obstruction.	Wheezing, Shortness of breath, Chest tightness, Coughing	Monitor respiratory rate, oxygen saturation, and PEFR. Administer bronchodilators and corticosteroids. Education about trigger avoidance and inhaler use. Encourage hydration.
COPD	Progressive condition with persistent airflow limitation due to chronic bronchitis and emphysema.	Chronic productive cough, Dyspnea on exertion, Wheezing, Frequent respiratory infections, Barrel chest	Provide oxygen therapy, encourage pursed-lip breathing, assist with smoking cessation, promote physical activity, administer bronchodilators, anticholinergics, or corticosteroids.
Pneumonia	Infectious inflammation of lung parenchyma caused by bacteria, viruses, fungi, or aspiration.	Cough with purulent sputum, Fever and chills, Pleuritic chest pain, Dyspnea, Fatigue, Crackles, or rhonchi	Monitor vital signs, encourage deep breathing exercises, administer antibiotics or antivirals, promote hydration, offer small, frequent meals.
Tuberculosis (TB)	Caused by Mycobacterium tuberculosis, forming granulomas in the lungs leading to caseous necrosis if untreated.	Persistent cough, Hemoptysis, Night sweats, Weight loss, Low-grade fever, Fatigue	Place in airborne isolation, administer anti-tubercular medications, monitor for side effects, promote high-protein, high-calorie diet, educate about completing treatment.
ARDS	Severe inflammatory response to lung injury leading to	Tachypnea, Severe dyspnea, Cyanosis,	Provide mechanical ventilation with PEEP, monitor ABGs,

	pulmonary edema and reduced lung compliance.	Decreased oxygen saturation, Bilateral crackles, Confusion	position in prone, maintain fluid balance, address underlying cause.
RENAL	**Pathophysiology**	**Signs and Symptoms**	**Nursing Interventions**
Chronic Kidney Disease (CKD)	Gradual loss of kidney function, nephron damage, reduced GFR, accumulation of uremic toxins	Fatigue, weakness, anemia, swelling in extremities, altered mental status, hypertension	Monitor fluid intake/output, administer antihypertensive meds, educate on dietary restrictions, encourage dialysis compliance, provide psychological support
Acute Kidney Injury (AKI)	Sudden decline in kidney function, ischemia, nephrotoxic agents, obstruction, impaired filtration	Oliguria, anuria, edema, rapid weight gain, electrolyte imbalances, nausea, vomiting	Identify underlying cause, monitor vital signs/electrolytes, administer fluids, prevent infection, educate on worsening signs
Nephrotic Syndrome	Significant protein loss in urine, damage to glomerular basement membrane, hypoalbuminemia, hyperlipidemia, edema	Massive proteinuria, generalized edema, foamy urine, hyperlipidemia	Monitor serum albumin/lipids, administer diuretics, encourage low sodium/fat diet, watch for infection/thromboembolic events, provide emotional support
Polycystic Kidney Disease (PKD)	Genetic disorder, fluid-filled cysts in kidneys, decreased renal parenchyma, compromised filtration	Flank pain, hematuria, urinary tract infections, hypertension, progressive renal dysfunction	Educate on genetic counseling, monitor blood pressure, administer antihypertensive meds, advise on fluid intake, coordinate imaging, encourage adherence to meds/lifestyle changes
GASTROINTESTINAL	**Pathophysiology**	**Signs and Symptoms**	**Nursing Interventions**
GERD	LES fails to close, allowing acid reflux into esophagus	Heartburn, regurgitation,	Small frequent meals, elevate head of bed, avoid triggers,

		chronic cough, dysphagia	administer PPIs or H2 antagonists
PUD Peptic Ulcer Disease (PUD)	Erosion of stomach or duodenal lining, often due to H. pylori or NSAIDs	Epigastric pain, GI bleeding, nausea, vomiting	Monitor for GI bleeding, adhere to antibiotics, avoid NSAIDs and smoking, stress management
IBD Inflammatory Bowel Disease (IBD)	Chronic inflammation, Crohn's affects any GI part, UC affects colon and rectum	Chronic diarrhea, abdominal pain, weight loss, fatigue, joint pain	Administer anti-inflammatory meds, monitor nutrition, provide emotional support, and educate on flare-ups
IBS Irritable Bowel Syndrome (IBS)	Functional disorder with altered bowel habits and abdominal discomfort	Abdominal pain, diarrhea, constipation, bloating, urgency	High-fiber diet, relaxation techniques, food diary, administer antispasmodic or antidiarrheal meds
Hepatitis	Inflammation of the liver, often viral, alcohol, or autoimmune	Jaundice, fatigue, abdominal pain, dark urine, pale stool	Promote rest, low-fat high-protein diet, administer antivirals, educate on preventing transmission
Crohn's Disease	Chronic inflammatory bowel disease, dysregulated immune response, transmural inflammation	Persistent diarrhea, abdominal cramping and pain, weight loss, fatigue, fever, rectal bleeding	Administer anti-inflammatory and immunosuppressive medications, encourage low fiber diet during flare-ups, monitor for malnutrition, teach hydration, and stress management
Ulcerative Colitis	Continuous inflammation and ulceration of the mucosal layer of the colon and rectum	Bloody diarrhea, abdominal pain, and cramping, urgent need to defecate, fatigue, weight loss, fever during severe flares	Administer anti-inflammatory medications, encourage high protein and calorie diet, monitor dehydration, educate on avoiding trigger foods, provide emotional support
Gallstones	Hardened deposits of digestive fluid,	Severe pain in upper right	Administer pain relief medications, encourage

		abdomen, pain radiates to shoulder or back, nausea and vomiting, jaundice, fever, and chills	small low-fat meals, monitor for complications, prepare for surgical interventions, educate on dietary changes
	imbalance in bile substances leading to crystallization		
Diverticulitis	Inflamed or infected diverticula, often caused by blockage by stool or food particles	Lower left abdominal pain, fever, chills, constipation or diarrhea, nausea and vomiting, abdominal tenderness	Administer antibiotics, encourage clear liquid diet during acute episodes, reintroduce high-fiber diet, monitor for complications, educate on lifestyle changes
Pancreatitis	Inflammation of the pancreas, digestive enzymes activated within pancreas, autodigestion	Severe upper abdominal pain, nausea and vomiting, fever, increased heart rate, abdominal tenderness, signs of shock or organ failure	Administer pain relief and antiemetic medications, provide supportive care, encourage avoidance of alcohol, monitor for complications, educate.
NEUROLOGICAL	**Pathophysiology**	**Signs and Symptoms**	**Nursing Interventions**
Stroke (Cerebrovascular Accident)	Interruption of blood flow to the brain, causing oxygen deprivation and cell death	Weakness or numbness on one side, confusion, speech difficulties, visual disturbances, dizziness, severe headache	Monitor neurological status, administer medications, position to prevent aspiration, encourage mobility, educate about stroke signs
Parkinson's Disease	Loss of dopamine-producing neurons in the substantia nigra, affecting motor control	Resting tremors, bradykinesia, muscle rigidity, postural instability, non-motor symptoms like depression	Administer medications, provide physical therapy, encourage adaptive devices, monitor complications, offer emotional support

Multiple Sclerosis (MS)	Autoimmune attack on the myelin sheath, disrupting nerve signal transmission	Fatigue, muscle weakness, visual disturbances, numbness, coordination problems, cognitive changes	Promote energy conservation, encourage physical activity, administer therapies, support vision and balance, educate about relapses
Alzheimer's Disease	Accumulation of amyloid plaques and tau tangles, impairing neuronal communication	Memory loss, difficulty with tasks, disorientation, mood changes, cognitive decline	Maintain routine, provide a safe environment, use clear communication, support with memory aids, offer emotional support
Epilepsy	Abnormal electrical activity in the brain causing recurrent seizures	Seizures, loss of consciousness, postictal confusion, aura sensations	Ensure safety during seizures, administer medications, monitor seizure frequency, educate about lifestyle adjustments, provide emotional support
ONCOLOGY	**Pathophysiology**	**Signs and Symptoms**	**Nursing Interventions**
Lung Cancer	Exposure to tobacco smoke or toxins, mutations in KRAS and TP53	Persistent cough, hemoptysis, shortness of breath, weight loss, chest pain	Monitor respiratory status, teach breathing exercises, encourage smoking cessation
Breast Cancer	Hormonal influence, BRCA1/BRCA2 mutations, HER2 gene amplification	Painless lump, changes in breast shape or size, nipple discharge, skin changes	Assess for lymphedema, educate on self-breast exams, support during chemotherapy
Colorectal Cancer	Mutations in APC gene, microsatellite instability, chronic inflammation	Rectal bleeding, changes in bowel habits, abdominal pain, weight loss	Monitor for bowel obstruction, provide ostomy care education, encourage high-fiber diet
METABOLIC AND ENDOCRINE	**Pathophysiology**	**Signs and Symptoms**	**Nursing Interventions**

Diabetes Mellitus	Chronic hyperglycemia due to defects in insulin secretion, insulin action, or both	Increased thirst, Increased urination, Unexplained weight loss, Fatigue, Blurred vision, Slow healing of wounds	Monitor blood glucose levels, Promote dietary modifications, Administer prescribed medications, Educate patients about symptoms, Provide emotional support
Hyperthyroidism	Excessive production of thyroid hormones is often due to Graves' disease, thyroid nodules, or thyroiditis	Weight loss, Increased heart rate, Anxiety, Heat intolerance, Exophthalmos, Tremors	Monitor vital signs, Provide cool environment, Administer prescribed medications, Educate patients about treatment, Support patients undergoing therapy
Hypothyroidism	Insufficient levels of thyroid hormones leading to slowed metabolism	Fatigue, Weight gain, Cold intolerance, Dry skin and hair, Constipation, Depression	Monitor thyroid function tests, Administer hormone replacement therapy, Encourage balanced diet, Educate patients about medication adherence, Provide mental health support
Phenylketonuria (PKU)	Deficiency of enzyme phenylalanine hydroxylase leading to toxic effects on brain and nervous system	Intellectual disability, Seizures, Behavioral problems, Musty odor, Delayed developmental milestones	Ensure early screening, Educate caregivers about diet, Monitor growth and development, Provide emotional and dietary support
Metabolic Syndrome	Cluster of conditions increasing risk of cardiovascular diseases and diabetes	Abdominal obesity, Elevated blood pressure, Elevated fasting blood glucose, Abnormal cholesterol levels, Fatigue	Monitor blood pressure, blood glucose, and lipid profiles, Educate about lifestyle modifications, Encourage weight loss and smoking cessation, Administer prescribed medications, Provide

		counseling on stress management
Adrenal Insufficiency (Addison's Disease)	Chronic fatigue, muscle weakness, hyperpigmentation, low blood pressure, loss of appetite, salt cravings	Administer corticosteroid replacement, encourage sodium-rich diet, educate on stress management
Cushing's Syndrome	Weight gain, buffalo hump, muscle weakness, hypertension, skin bruising, high blood sugar	Assist with weight management, monitor for infection, provide emotional support

NGN NCLEX MANAGEMENT OF CARE QUESTIONS

Multiple Choice

1. A nurse manager schedules shift assignments. Which action demonstrates effective leadership?
A. Assigning only new graduates to night shifts
B. Avoiding conflict by letting staff choose freely
C. Assigning experienced staff to mentor new graduates
D. Rotating all nurses regardless of skillset

2. A staff nurse refuses to care for a violent patient. The manager's best response?
A. Fire the nurse for insubordination
B. Ask another nurse without explanation
C. Reassign based on staff competency and assess situation
D. Ignore the complaint

3. A nurse is consistently late. What's an appropriate manager action first?
A. Give a written warning immediately
B. Discuss reasons privately with the nurse
C. Dock pay without notice
D. Reassign the nurse permanently

4. Manager observes conflict between staff. What should the manager do first?
A. Ignore the situation to avoid escalation
B. Write up both staff members
C. Mediate discussion between both staff
D. Transfer one of the staff to a different unit

5. During budget cuts, which supplies should manager prioritize?
A. Non-sterile gloves and pillows
B. IV catheters and sterile gloves
C. Room decorations
D. Staff refreshments

6. Staff ask for vacation, but unit is short-staffed. Manager's best approach?
A. Deny request without discussion
B. Approve request and hope for float coverage
C. Explain staffing needs and offer alternate dates
D. Ignore the request

7. New research supports changing wound care. What should the manager do?
A. Tell nurses to continue current practices
B. Organize training based on the research
C. Ignore the new evidence
D. Assign change only to new nurses

8. Manager delegates ambulation of stable patient to NA. Is this appropriate?
A. Yes, with proper training and supervision
B. No, only RNs can ambulate patients
C. No, patient ambulation is high-risk
D. Yes, but only if a nurse is watching

9. Which task can be delegated to a nursing assistant?
A. Medication administration
B. Initial vital signs assessment
C. Assisting with meal tray delivery
D. Teaching insulin injection

10. Nurse must choose between staff meeting and giving patient report. What's the priority?
A. Attend the meeting for policy updates
B. Give patient report to ensure continuity of care
C. Skip both to manage workload
D. Delegate report to UAP

11. Manager schedules performance reviews. What metric should be included?
A. Accuracy of medication administration
B. Staff friendliness during patient interactions
C. Length of time spent on each task
D. Amount of overtime worked

12. A Staff nurse needs time off for a family emergency. What's the manager's best response?
A. Request open time-off, adjust schedule if possible
B. Deny the request and ask for a doctor's note
C. Assign an additional shift to the nurse
D. Allow time off without any conditions

13. A nurse is reporting errors frequently. What is the manager's first action?
A. Review unit protocols and provide refresher education
B. Issue a warning about the errors
C. Suspend the nurse for a probationary period

D. Ignore the errors and focus on other priorities

14. Manager planning for mass casualty. What is the first step?
A. Assign team leaders
B. Activate disaster preparedness plan
C. Secure extra staff for the unit
D. Begin screening patients for triage

15. A float nurse expresses anxiety about their assignment. What should the manager do?
A. Reassign the nurse to a different unit
B. Provide orientation and ensure adequate supervision
C. Ignore the anxiety and let the nurse adapt
D. Ask the nurse to leave for the day to avoid stress

16. Peer reviews reveal unprofessional behavior. What should the manager's first action be?
A. Immediately issue a formal warning
B. Meet privately with the nurse to discuss concerns
C. Ignore the review and focus on other tasks
D. Remove the nurse from the unit immediately

17. Which task can be delegated to UAP (Unlicensed Assistive Personnel)?
A. Administering a blood transfusion
B. Assessing wound healing
C. Assisting a patient with eating
D. Performing a respiratory assessment

18. A nurse is reporting to the manager about workplace issues. The manager should first:
A. Offer a solution without asking further questions
B. Listen attentively and assess the situation
C. Encourage the nurse to stop complaining
D. Immediately implement changes without evaluating need

19. What action should the nurse manager take when staff morale is low?
A. Implement team-building activities and express appreciation
B. Ignore the issue and continue as usual
C. Issue disciplinary action for poor morale
D. Increase work hours to address staffing shortages

20. Which statement demonstrates effective communication in management?
A. "I don't have time to listen to complaints right now."

B. "Let's discuss your concerns and find a way to improve the situation."

C. "If you don't like it, you can leave."

D. "This is the way it is. Just deal with it."

21. Multiple Response

Which actions demonstrate effective delegation? (Select all that apply.)

A. Assigning a nurse to administer medications to a critical patient

B. Delegating a stable patient's ambulation to a nursing assistant

C. Giving the UAP responsibility for wound care

D. Assigning a skilled RN to supervise a new graduate

E. Ensuring the nursing assistant understands the task and is appropriately trained

Case Scenario

22. A nurse manager is reviewing staffing for an upcoming shift. The unit is short-staffed, and one nurse calls in sick. The manager has two options:

Assign a UAP to help with routine tasks and have a nurse take on the more complex patients.

Call a float nurse who is unfamiliar with the unit and may need extra time for orientation.

What action should the manager take to maintain patient safety and staff well-being?

A. Assign the UAP to assist the nurses, focusing on patient safety and efficient delegation

B. Immediately call the float nurse to avoid overloading the current staff

C. Cancel elective procedures to free up more staff

D. Assign more patients to the existing nurses to avoid calling in extra help

23. Drag and Drop

Arrange the following steps in the correct order for managing a conflict between two staff members:

Steps:

Offer both staff members the opportunity to express their perspectives.

Mediate a discussion between the involved parties.

Review possible solutions and facilitate a compromise.

Document the outcome of the conversation.

Follow up with both staff members to ensure resolution.

24. Drop-Down

Select the most appropriate action for each scenario:

Scenario 1:

A nurse is concerned about the possibility of a needle-stick injury.

Scenario 2:

A patient's condition deteriorates suddenly and requires emergency intervention.

Scenario 3:

A nursing assistant reports that a patient is not following instructions and is becoming increasingly agitated.

Action: "Document the incident and notify the supervisor."

Action: "Activate the emergency response team and ensure the patient is stabilized."

Action: "Assess the situation and provide de-escalation techniques or notify the charge nurse."

25. Multiple Response

Which of the following actions are appropriate for managing staffing during a crisis? (Select all that apply.)

A. Offering overtime to available nurses

B. Relying on untrained staff to manage critical patients

C. Prioritizing the most urgent patients for care

D. Canceling non-urgent procedures to free up staff for critical care

E. Encouraging cross-training among team members

26. Case Scenario

A nurse manager notices that several staff members are complaining about long shifts and burnout. What should the manager do first to address this issue?

A. Immediately reduce the length of shifts for all staff

B. Hold a meeting to discuss the concerns and explore solutions

C. Ignore the complaints, assuming the staff will adjust over time

D. Issue a warning for unprofessional behavior regarding complaints

27. Drag and Drop

Order the following steps in the appropriate sequence for handling a medication error:

Steps:

Inform the healthcare provider and assess the patient's condition.

Notify the charge nurse and document the error.

Report the error to the appropriate regulatory body.

Review and analyze the situation to prevent future errors.

Complete an incident report.

28. Drop-Down

Choose the most appropriate response for each scenario involving delegation:

Scenario 1:

A nurse needs to delegate the task of taking vital signs for stable patients.

Scenario 2:

A nurse needs to delegate medication administration to another nurse.

Scenario 3:
A nurse needs to delegate wound care to a nursing assistant.
Response: "Delegate to UAP with appropriate training."
Response: "Delegate to a licensed nurse."
Response: "Delegate to a licensed nurse."

29. Case Scenario
A nurse is facing challenges in managing a high patient load during a busy shift. Which of the following actions is the most effective for prioritizing care?
A. Focusing on tasks that can be completed quickly
B. Delegating non-nursing tasks to other staff members
C. Performing tasks in the order they were assigned
D. Attending to the most critical patients first and delegating less urgent tasks

30. Multiple Response
Which of the following are appropriate strategies for preventing staff burnout? (Select all that apply.)
A. Encourage regular breaks and time off
B. Limit overtime and extra shifts
C. Promote a supportive and positive work environment
D. Assign the most challenging tasks to the same individuals regularly
E. Offer professional development opportunities

31. Multiple Response
Which of the following tasks are appropriate for a nurse manager to delegate to a licensed practical nurse (LPN)? (Select all that apply.)
A. Administering oral medications to stable patients
B. Assisting with patient admission assessments
C. Performing an initial assessment of a newly admitted patient
D. Educating patients on complex procedures
E. Monitoring stable patients for changes in condition

32. Case Scenario
A nurse manager is reviewing an incident where a nurse failed to complete patient documentation on time, which delayed medication administration. What is the most appropriate action for the manager to take?
A. Issue a verbal warning and provide counseling on time management
B. Fire the nurse immediately for negligence
C. Ignore the incident, as it was a minor issue
D. Send the nurse for additional training on documentation

33. Drag and Drop
Order the following steps in the correct sequence when a staff member reports feeling overwhelmed due to workload:
Steps:
Discuss workload issues with the staff member to understand concerns
Adjust workload distribution to prevent burnout
Provide emotional support and validation of concerns
Assess available resources and staffing needs
Follow up regularly to ensure workload remains manageable

34. Drop-Down
Choose the best action for the manager in each of the following scenarios:
Scenario 1:
A nurse has repeatedly missed scheduled breaks, and their performance is suffering as a result.
Scenario 2:
A nursing assistant is unsure how to assist with a specific patient care task.
Scenario 3:
A nurse is feeling stressed due to high patient load.
Action: "Have a one-on-one meeting to discuss the impact of missed breaks and support with time management."
Action: "Provide direct supervision and further training to ensure the task is done safely."
Action: "Offer emotional support, review workload priorities, and consider additional help if needed."

35. Multiple Response
Which of the following are effective strategies to enhance team communication in a healthcare setting? (Select all that apply.)
A. Establishing regular team huddles to discuss patient needs
B. Encouraging direct communication during handoff report
C. Ignoring interpersonal conflicts to avoid disruptions
D. Implementing a structured reporting system for critical information
E. Using email as the primary form of communication

36. Case Scenario
A nurse manager is reviewing patient outcomes after a new policy was implemented to decrease patient falls. The fall rate has not improved, and staff reports confusion about the policy. What should the nurse manager do next?
A. Reaffirm the policy without discussing the issues

B. Assess staff understanding of the policy and provide additional training if needed

C. Fire staff members who failed to implement the policy correctly

D. Remove the policy and try another intervention

37. Drag and Drop

Arrange the steps in the correct order for addressing a nurse's concerns about a lack of support from the team:

Steps:

Ask the nurse to provide specific examples of the issues.

Listen actively and acknowledge the nurse's feelings.

Discuss potential solutions and strategies to improve team dynamics.

Implement the agreed-upon changes and monitor the situation.

Follow up regularly to evaluate whether the issues have been resolved.

38. Drop-Down

Select the best management action for each scenario:

Scenario 1:

A nurse is struggling to manage the workload during a shift with many complex patients.

Scenario 2:

A staff member repeatedly asks for clarification on routine tasks.

Scenario 3:

A nurse expresses frustration with a new electronic health record (EHR) system.

Action: "Offer additional training sessions and support to ease the transition to the new system."

Action: "Reassign some patients to other nurses or staff to balance the workload."

Action: "Provide additional training or mentorship to address gaps in knowledge."

39. Case Scenario

A nurse manager is tasked with reducing the incidence of hospital-acquired infections (HAIs) on the unit. Which of the following strategies would be most effective in achieving this goal?

A. Provide staff with reminders about hand hygiene and infection control protocols

B. Focus only on patients with open wounds or surgical sites

C. Increase patient turnover to reduce the risk of infection

D. Ignore patient-related infection concerns and focus on administrative tasks

40. Multiple Response

Which of the following tasks can be delegated to a nursing assistant? (Select all that apply.)

A. Administering oral medications to patients

B. Assisting a patient with ambulation

C. Taking vital signs on a stable patient

D. Performing wound care on a complex wound

E. Assisting with meal trays and feeding

41. A nurse manager is reviewing the hospital's staffing plan for the next week. Which action will best address potential staffing shortages?

A. Increase the number of on-call staff and request volunteers for extra shifts

B. Cancel elective procedures to free up staff resources

C. Reassign patients to other units to balance the workload

D. Hire temporary staff from an agency without reviewing their qualifications

42. Which of the following is the best approach for a nurse manager to ensure patient safety during a period of high census and limited staffing?

A. Prioritize the most critical patients and delegate routine tasks to UAP

B. Assign nurses to additional patients beyond their usual workload to minimize delays

C. Delay discharge procedures to avoid the need for readmissions

D. Focus on non-urgent tasks and delay care for less critical patients

43. A nurse is working with a UAP who is struggling to perform vital signs accurately. What is the nurse's best action?

A. Send the UAP home for the day to avoid errors

B. Review the proper procedure for measuring vital signs and provide additional training

C. Document the UAP's failure and file a report with the supervisor

D. Ignore the mistake and allow the UAP to continue without further intervention

44. A nurse is preparing to delegate tasks to a UAP. Which task is most appropriate for delegation?

A. Administering a patient's prescribed IV pain medication

B. Monitoring a patient's respiratory status following surgery

C. Assisting a patient with activities of daily living, such as bathing

D. Assessing the patient's level of consciousness after a head injury

45. A nurse manager notices a decline in staff morale and productivity. Which action should the nurse manager take first?

A. Increase the staff's workload to motivate them to perform better

B. Provide staff with recognition and opportunities for feedback

C. Ignore the issue and focus on other management tasks

D. Send staff to a team-building retreat without addressing underlying concerns

46. Which of the following is a priority action for a nurse manager when dealing with a potential ethical dilemma in the workplace?

A. Ignore the dilemma and focus on other responsibilities

B. Investigate the issue thoroughly and involve the ethics committee if needed

C. Implement a policy that all nurses must follow without discussion

D. Address the situation only if it escalates into a formal complaint

47. Which of the following should a nurse manager prioritize when planning staff education programs?

A. Developing programs based on the most recent healthcare trends

B. Creating education sessions based on the staff's previous training experiences

C. Identifying knowledge gaps through staff feedback and performance evaluations

D. Implementing mandatory training sessions for all employees, regardless of their needs

48. Which of the following is the nurse manager's role in supporting a nursing staff member who is dealing with grief after a patient's death?

A. Ignore the situation, assuming the nurse will recover on their own

B. Offer emotional support, provide resources for counseling, and encourage time off if needed

C. Discuss the patient's death in detail with the nurse to help them process the situation

D. Tell the nurse to move on and focus on the next patient immediately

49. When managing a team of nurses, which of the following should the nurse manager focus on to improve patient care outcomes?

A. Increase the number of patients assigned to each nurse to maximize efficiency

B. Promote collaboration among team members and encourage a culture of safety

C. Avoid involving nurses in decision-making processes to prevent confusion

D. Limit communication with physicians to avoid misunderstandings

50. A nurse manager is assigning tasks during a busy shift. Which task should be delegated to the most experienced nurse on the unit?

A. Ambulating a patient who is recovering from minor surgery

B. Administering routine medications to stable patients

C. Assessing a newly admitted patient with multiple comorbidities

D. Assisting with a patient's meals in the dining room

51. A nurse manager observes that a staff nurse frequently uses disruptive behavior when addressing patient concerns. What should the manager do first?

A. Issue a formal written reprimand immediately

B. Monitor the nurse's behavior and provide feedback privately

C. Transfer the nurse to a different unit to prevent further disruptions

D. Ignore the behavior and hope it resolves on its own

52. When developing a plan of care for a patient, the nurse manager should prioritize which of the following?
A. Ensuring the plan of care is tailored to the patient's specific needs and preferences
B. Following standardized care protocols without considering the patient's unique situation
C. Focusing only on the physical health needs and ignoring emotional well-being
D. Assigning the same plan of care for all patients with similar diagnoses

53. During a staff meeting, a nurse expresses concern about unsafe staffing levels. What should the nurse manager's first response be?
A. Ignore the concern and focus on other issues
B. Acknowledge the concern and explore potential solutions, such as adjusting the staffing schedule
C. Tell the nurse to work through the concern, as staffing issues are a common problem
D. Assign more patients to other nurses to alleviate the shortage

54. Which of the following is an effective strategy for reducing patient readmissions?
A. Increasing the length of hospital stays for patients who are stable
B. Enhancing discharge planning and providing follow-up care instructions to patients
C. Avoiding communication with the patient's primary care provider
D. Encouraging patients to stay in the hospital for as long as possible to prevent readmissions

55. A nurse manager is reviewing the effectiveness of a newly implemented quality improvement initiative. Which of the following is the best way to evaluate its success?
A. Reviewing patient satisfaction surveys and feedback from staff
B. Waiting several months before evaluating the results
C. Ignoring patient complaints since they are usually not related to quality improvement efforts
D. Focusing only on quantitative data, such as the number of patients treated

56. Multiple Response
Which of the following are appropriate actions for a nurse manager when dealing with a staff conflict? (Select all that apply.)
A. Listen to both parties involved to understand the perspectives
B. Ignore the conflict to avoid disrupting the work environment
C. Mediate a resolution to address the underlying issues
D. Discipline one party based on hearsay without investigating
E. Encourage open and respectful communication between staff members

57. Case Scenario

A nurse manager is concerned that a new employee is not adhering to hospital policies regarding infection control. What is the best course of action?

A. Issue a written warning immediately for policy violations

B. Provide the new employee with a mentor to assist in learning proper policies

C. Ignore the behavior as the new employee will learn in time

D. Reassign the new employee to a different unit to avoid further policy violations

58. Drag and Drop

Order the following steps for dealing with a nurse's frequent tardiness:

Steps:

Discuss the tardiness issue with the nurse in a private setting

Document the conversation and outline expectations moving forward

Offer support to address any underlying issues affecting punctuality

Provide clear consequences if tardiness continues

Follow up to monitor the nurse's improvement

59. Drop-Down

Select the most appropriate action for each of the following situations:

Scenario 1:

A nurse is struggling to manage their workload during a particularly busy shift.

Scenario 2:

A nurse expresses that they are feeling emotionally exhausted after dealing with multiple critical patients.

Scenario 3:

A nurse manager observes a staff member consistently not following patient safety protocols.

Action: "Provide emotional support and consider offering time off or counseling resources."

Action: "Investigate the issue, provide corrective feedback, and offer additional training if needed."

Action: "Offer assistance, reassign patients if necessary, and ensure the nurse has the resources they need."

60. Multiple Choice

What is the primary goal when a nurse manager implements a staffing model based on patient acuity?

A. To ensure nurses are assigned the same number of patients each day

B. To ensure that more experienced nurses care for high-acuity patients

C. To promote equal distribution of work regardless of patient needs

D. To allow the nurse manager to reduce staff numbers during high-acuity shifts

61. Case Scenario

A nursing assistant has been observed taking longer than usual to complete routine tasks. The nurse manager is concerned. What should be the nurse manager's first step?

A. Assign the nursing assistant additional tasks to improve efficiency

B. Speak with the nursing assistant to understand the reason for the delay

C. Remove the nursing assistant from patient care duties immediately

D. Document the behavior and notify human resources

62. Multiple Response

Which of the following are key responsibilities of a nurse manager in ensuring quality patient care? (Select all that apply.)

A. Developing and enforcing patient care policies

B. Managing staff schedules and patient assignments

C. Providing direct patient care during high-acuity situations

D. Addressing staff concerns about workload and safety

E. Evaluating patient satisfaction through surveys and feedback

63. Multiple Response

Which of the following actions are appropriate for a nurse manager when dealing with staff conflict? (Select all that apply.)

A. Facilitate a private meeting between the conflicting parties to address the issue

B. Publicly reprimand one of the parties to set an example for the rest of the team

C. Actively listen to both sides of the conflict to understand the issue thoroughly

D. Encourage open communication and resolution strategies between staff members

E. Avoid intervening and allow the staff members to resolve the issue on their own

64. Multiple Choice

A nurse manager is dealing with a staff member who is frequently calling out sick. What is the most effective way to address the issue?

A. Ignore the absences and let the situation resolve itself

B. Have a private conversation with the staff member to understand the reason for frequent absences

C. Assign extra shifts to the staff member to compensate for missed work

D. Reprimand the staff member in front of their colleagues to address the issue

65. Case Scenario

A nurse is consistently arriving late for their shifts, which is affecting patient care. What should the nurse manager do first?

A. Issue a written warning immediately

B. Have a one-on-one discussion with the nurse to explore the reasons for the tardiness

C. Reassign the nurse to a different shift without further discussion

D. Ignore the issue as it is a minor problem

66. Multiple Choice
What is the first step for a nurse manager when initiating a quality improvement project aimed at reducing patient falls?
A. Implement the plan and monitor results
B. Identify the underlying causes of patient falls
C. Provide education to patients on fall prevention
D. Increase the nurse-to-patient ratio to improve supervision

67. Drag and Drop
Place the following actions in the correct order when a nurse manager is addressing a patient complaint about care:
Steps:
Acknowledge the patient's concerns and apologize for the experience
Investigate the issue thoroughly, gathering information from staff
Provide the patient with a clear resolution or action plan
Follow up with the patient to ensure satisfaction
Document the complaint and resolution

68. Multiple Response
Which of the following are effective strategies for preventing burnout in nursing staff? (Select all that apply.)
A. Providing regular breaks and rest periods during shifts
B. Encouraging open communication about workload concerns
C. Increasing patient load to improve efficiency
D. Offering counseling or support services for staff
E. Allowing nurses to rotate between departments for variety

69. Multiple Choice
A nurse manager is reviewing the effectiveness of a newly implemented patient education program. What data should they prioritize when evaluating the program's success?
A. Feedback from patients and families regarding the clarity of information
B. The total number of educational sessions provided
C. The amount of time spent on each session
D. The number of educational handouts distributed

70. Multiple Choice
A nurse manager is reviewing a staffing plan for the following week. Which of the following strategies should be used to address predicted staffing shortages?

A. Reduce the number of patients assigned to each nurse to balance the workload
B. Request volunteers to pick up extra shifts or offer to work overtime
C. Cancel elective procedures to reduce the number of patients in the unit
D. Reassign staff to other units without considering their experience or expertise

71. Case Scenario
A nurse notices that a newly hired nurse is struggling with patient assessment skills. What is the nurse manager's best course of action?
A. Ignore the issue, as the nurse will eventually improve on their own
B. Provide additional training and mentorship to help improve their skills
C. Assign the newly hired nurse to less complex patients to avoid errors
D. Send the nurse home for the day and ask them to return when they feel ready
Answer: B
Rationale: Providing additional training and mentorship will help the nurse improve their skills and ensure patient safety is not compromised.

72. Multiple Response
Which of the following are common causes of nurse burnout? (Select all that apply.)
A. Excessive overtime and mandatory extra shifts
B. A lack of support from management and colleagues
C. Consistently low patient satisfaction scores
D. High nurse-patient ratios leading to increased workload
E. Opportunities for professional development and career advancement

73. Drop-Down
Select the best action to address each of the following staff concerns:
Scenario 1:
A nurse reports feeling overwhelmed by their workload and not having enough time to complete essential tasks.
Scenario 2:
A nurse manager notices that a staff member has not been following infection control protocols.
Scenario 3:
A nurse complains about not receiving enough recognition for their hard work.
Action: "Acknowledge the nurse's contributions and consider implementing a formal recognition program."
Action: "Review the protocols with the staff member and provide further training if necessary."
Action: "Provide a temporary reduction in workload and assist with time management strategies."

74. Multiple Choice

A nurse manager is observing a staff nurse struggling to communicate effectively with patients from diverse cultural backgrounds. What should be the nurse manager's first step?

A. Offer immediate disciplinary action for failure to communicate properly

B. Arrange cultural competency training for the nurse and the entire team

C. Ignore the situation as it is a minor issue and hope it improves

D. Assign the nurse to work only with patients from the same background to avoid issues

75. Case Scenario

A nurse manager is evaluating the quality of care on a unit. Which of the following should be prioritized when gathering data for quality improvement initiatives?

A. Collecting feedback from patients and families regarding their care experience

B. Focusing only on incident reports of adverse events to evaluate care quality

C. Reviewing the unit's financial reports to assess resource usage

D. Relying only on staff self-assessments of their own performance

NGN NCLEX MANAGEMENT OF CARE ANSWERS

1. Answer: C
Rationale: Supports staff development and ensures safe patient care. Experienced staff mentoring new graduates improves team competence overall.

2. Answer: C
Rationale: This response considers both the nurse's safety and the patient's needs, balancing ethical concerns.

3. Answer: B
Rationale: A private discussion allows the manager to understand the reasons for tardiness and address the root cause of the issue.

4. Answer: C
Rationale: Early intervention through mediation promotes open communication and resolves conflict constructively.

5. Answer: B
Rationale: IV catheters and sterile gloves are critical for patient care and infection control, making them non-negotiable.

6. Answer: C
Rationale: Balances the needs of the unit and the well-being of the staff by offering flexibility.

7. Answer: B
Rationale: Encourages evidence-based practice, ensuring that all staff are updated with the latest clinical standards.

8. Answer: A
Rationale: It's appropriate to delegate stable tasks to a trained and competent nursing assistant under supervision.

9. Answer: C
Rationale: Assisting with meal tray delivery is non-invasive, routine, and within the scope of practice for nursing assistants.

10. D. Delegate report to UAP

Answer: B
Rationale: The safe handoff of patient care takes priority to ensure continuity and minimize risk.

11. Answer: A
Rationale: Medication administration is directly tied to patient safety, making it a critical performance metric.

12. Answer: A
Rationale: Flexible scheduling helps meet both the needs of the staff and the demands of the unit.

13. Answer: A
Rationale: Ensuring the nurse is well-trained and understands protocols helps prevent future errors.

14. Answer: B
Rationale: A coordinated response requires initiating the disaster preparedness plan to ensure readiness.

15. Answer: B
Rationale: Offering orientation and support reduces anxiety and ensures safe care.

16. Answer: B
Rationale: Addressing concerns privately promotes professional growth and resolution.

17. Answer: C
Rationale: Assisting with feeding is a non-invasive task appropriate for UAP.

18. Answer: B
Rationale: Listening to the nurse and understanding the issue fully is the first step in addressing workplace concerns.

19. Answer: A
Rationale: Addressing morale with team-building activities and recognition fosters a positive work environment.

20. Answer: B
Rationale: Open communication, especially when addressing concerns, encourages problem-solving and team collaboration.

21. Answer: B, D, E
Rationale: Proper delegation involves ensuring that tasks are assigned based on the skill level of staff and that they are trained appropriately.

22. Answer: A
Rationale: Assigning a UAP to routine tasks and allowing nurses to focus on more complex care supports patient safety while also being mindful of staffing needs.

23. Correct Order:
$1 \rightarrow 2 \rightarrow 3 \rightarrow 4 \rightarrow 5$
Rationale: The correct process involves giving both parties a chance to speak, mediating a constructive discussion, finding a solution, documenting, and following up to ensure the situation is resolved.

24. Answers:
Scenario 1: "Document the incident and notify the supervisor."
Scenario 2: "Activate the emergency response team and ensure the patient is stabilized."
Scenario 3: "Assess the situation and provide de-escalation techniques or notify the charge nurse."
Rationale: Each response is tailored to the severity of the situation, emphasizing safety and appropriate escalation when necessary.

25. Answer: A, C, D, E
Rationale: Effective management during a crisis involves prioritizing urgent care, offering overtime to available nurses, and cross-training staff to increase flexibility and care capacity.

26. Answer: B
Rationale: The manager should first listen to staff concerns, provide a forum for open discussion, and work together to find sustainable solutions to address burnout.

27. Correct Order:
$1 \rightarrow 2 \rightarrow 5 \rightarrow 3 \rightarrow 4$
Rationale: The proper sequence prioritizes patient safety, communication with relevant parties, documentation, and analyzing the incident for improvement.

28. Answers:
Scenario 1: "Delegate to UAP with appropriate training."
Scenario 2: "Delegate to a licensed nurse."
Scenario 3: "Delegate to a licensed nurse."
Rationale: Proper delegation requires ensuring that tasks are assigned based on the skill level and scope of practice of the individual being delegated to.

29. Answer: D
Rationale: Prioritizing care based on patient acuity ensures that critical patients receive the necessary attention while delegating less urgent tasks.

30. Answer: A, B, C, E
Rationale: Preventing burnout involves promoting work-life balance, providing support, and offering opportunities for growth.

31. Answer: A, E
Rationale: LPNs can administer medications to stable patients and monitor for changes in condition. However, they are not typically responsible for complex patient education or initial assessments.

32. Answer: A
Rationale: The manager should address the issue with counseling and time management training to prevent future occurrences, rather than resorting to punitive measures immediately.

33. Correct Order:
$1 \rightarrow 3 \rightarrow 4 \rightarrow 2 \rightarrow 5$
Rationale: Addressing concerns first, providing support, evaluating resources, adjusting workloads, and following up ensures that the staff member's concerns are appropriately addressed.

34. Answers:
Scenario 1: "Have a one-on-one meeting to discuss the impact of missed breaks and support with time management."
Scenario 2: "Provide direct supervision and further training to ensure the task is done safely."
Scenario 3: "Offer emotional support, review workload priorities, and consider additional help if needed."
Rationale: Each response ensures that the staff member receives appropriate support and training to help address their issue effectively.

35. Answer: A, B, D
Rationale: Regular team huddles, direct communication, and structured reporting systems help improve the clarity and efficiency of team communication, which enhances patient safety.

36. Answer: B
Rationale: The manager should first assess whether the staff fully understands the policy. Additional training or clarification may be needed to improve adherence.

37. Correct Order:
$1 \rightarrow 2 \rightarrow 3 \rightarrow 4 \rightarrow 5$
Rationale: Listening first, discussing solutions, and then following up ensures the problem is addressed and resolved effectively.

38. Answers:
Scenario 1: "Reassign some patients to other nurses or staff to balance the workload."
Scenario 2: "Provide additional training or mentorship to address gaps in knowledge."
Scenario 3: "Offer additional training sessions and support to ease the transition to the new system."
Rationale: Each action ensures the staff member receives support, training, or resources to address their specific needs.

39. Answer: A
Rationale: Regular reminders and adherence to infection control protocols are key strategies for preventing hospital-acquired infections.

40. Answer: B, C, E
Rationale: Nursing assistants can assist with routine tasks like ambulation, taking vital signs for stable patients, and feeding. They cannot perform tasks like administering medications or complex wound care.

41. Answer: A
Rationale: Increasing the number of on-call staff and requesting volunteers for extra shifts are effective strategies to manage staffing shortages and ensure patient care is not compromised.

42. Answer: A
Rationale: Prioritizing critical patients and delegating routine tasks to UAP ensures that patients receive the most urgent care while allowing for efficient use of available resources.

43. Answer: B
Rationale: It is important to address performance issues with additional training and guidance to ensure patient safety and improve skills.

44. Answer: C
Rationale: Assisting with activities of daily living (ADLs) is an appropriate task for delegation to UAP, as it falls within their scope of practice.

45. Answer: B
Rationale: Providing recognition and seeking staff feedback helps address morale issues, create a supportive work environment, and improve productivity.

46. Answer: B
Rationale: Ethical dilemmas require careful investigation, and involving the ethics committee ensures that the issue is handled in accordance with legal and professional guidelines.

47. Answer: C
Rationale: Prioritizing education based on identified knowledge gaps ensures that staff training is relevant, effective, and aligned with patient care needs.

48. Answer: B
Rationale: Providing emotional support and resources for counseling demonstrates the manager's role in supporting staff through difficult experiences.

49. Answer: B
Rationale: Promoting collaboration and a culture of safety among team members is essential for improving patient care outcomes and fostering a positive work environment.

50. Answer: C
Rationale: The most experienced nurse should assess the newly admitted patient with multiple comorbidities, as this requires advanced clinical judgment and critical thinking.

51. Answer: B
Rationale: Addressing disruptive behavior privately with feedback allows for a constructive conversation and provides an opportunity for improvement without immediate punitive measures.

52. Answer: A
Rationale: The plan of care should be individualized to meet the patient's specific needs, preferences, and circumstances to promote better outcomes.

53. Answer: B
Rationale: Acknowledging the concern and collaboratively finding solutions ensures that staffing levels are adequate for patient safety and staff well-being.

54. Answer: B
Rationale: Effective discharge planning and follow-up care are key strategies for preventing readmissions and ensuring that patients have the resources they need to manage their care post-discharge.

55. Answer: A
Rationale: Evaluating the effectiveness of a quality improvement initiative should involve both quantitative data and qualitative feedback from patients and staff to ensure a comprehensive assessment.

56. Answer: A, C, E
Rationale: It is important to listen to both parties, mediate a resolution, and encourage open communication to resolve conflicts effectively and maintain a positive work environment.

57. Answer: B
Rationale: The best course of action is to provide support through mentorship to ensure the employee fully understands and adheres to infection control policies.

58. Correct Order:
1 → 3 → 2 → 4 → 5
Rationale: Discussing the issue, offering support, documenting the conversation, and providing clear consequences ensures a fair and supportive approach to improving punctuality.

59. Answers:
Scenario 1: "Offer assistance, reassign patients if necessary, and ensure the nurse has the resources they need."
Scenario 2: "Provide emotional support and consider offering time off or counseling resources."
Scenario 3: "Investigate the issue, provide corrective feedback, and offer additional training if needed."
Rationale: These actions are designed to address both personal and professional concerns, ensuring both the nurse's well-being and patient safety are prioritized.

60. Answer: B
Rationale: The primary goal is to assign experienced nurses to high-acuity patients to ensure safe, effective care based on patient needs.

61. Answer: B
Rationale: The first step is to understand the reasons for the delay, as there could be underlying issues affecting the nursing assistant's performance.

62. Answer: A, B, D, E
Rationale: A nurse manager is responsible for policy development, managing staff, addressing staff concerns, and evaluating patient satisfaction to ensure quality care.

63. Answer: A, C, D
Rationale: Addressing conflict through private discussion, listening to both parties, and encouraging open communication fosters a resolution and maintains a positive work environment.

64. Answer: B
Rationale: A private conversation allows the nurse manager to understand the root cause of the absences and provide appropriate support or accommodations.

65. Answer: B
Rationale: The nurse manager should discuss the issue with the nurse to understand the reason for tardiness and provide solutions, if needed.

66. Answer: B
Rationale: Identifying the underlying causes of patient falls is the first step in creating an effective strategy to reduce falls.

67. Correct Order:
1 → 2 → 3 → 4 → 5
Rationale: Acknowledging, investigating, and providing a resolution ensures the patient feels heard, and follow-up ensures satisfaction.

68. Answer: A, B, D, E
Rationale: Regular breaks, open communication, support services, and departmental rotation help reduce stress and prevent burnout among nursing staff.

69. Answer: A
Rationale: Patient and family feedback provides the

70. Answer: B
Rationale: Requesting volunteers or offering overtime allows for flexibility in staffing without reducing the quality of care or affecting patient safety.

71. Answer: B
Rationale: Providing additional training and mentorship will help the nurse improve their skills and ensure patient safety is not compromised.

72. Answer: A, B, D
Rationale: Burnout is commonly caused by excessive work hours, lack of support, and high patient-to-nurse ratios, which increase stress and fatigue.

73. Answers:
Scenario 1: "Provide a temporary reduction in workload and assist with time management strategies."
Scenario 2: "Review the protocols with the staff member and provide further training if necessary."
Scenario 3: "Acknowledge the nurse's contributions and consider implementing a formal recognition program."
Rationale: Addressing workload concerns, reinforcing proper infection control practices, and recognizing staff contributions all contribute to a healthy, efficient work environment.

74. Answer: B
Rationale: Cultural competency training will help improve the nurse's communication skills and ability to provide high-quality care to a diverse patient population.

75. Answer: A
Rationale: Collecting feedback from patients and families provides valuable insight into the quality of care and can guide improvements in care delivery.

NGN NCLEX SAFETY AND INFECTION CONTROL QUESTIONS

Multiple Choice

1. Which of the following is the most effective way to prevent the spread of infection in a healthcare setting?
A) Using antibiotics as a precautionary measure
B) Performing hand hygiene regularly
C) Wearing gloves at all times
D) Restricting visitors to the hospital

2. Which of the following PPE items should be worn when caring for a patient in droplet isolation?
A) N95 respirator
B) Face shield and gloves
C) Surgical mask and gloves
D) Gown and surgical mask

3. What is the primary purpose of standard precautions in healthcare?
A) To prevent the spread of airborne pathogens
B) To ensure patients do not contract hospital-acquired infections
C) To prevent healthcare workers from acquiring bloodborne infections
D) To protect patients from invasive procedures

4. What is the most appropriate action to take if a nurse accidentally sticks themselves with a needle?
A) Report the incident to the supervisor and clean the wound
B) Ignore it if the needle was used on a patient with no known infections
C) Disinfect the needle and continue working
D) Immediately begin taking antibiotics

5. Which of the following is a critical component of a healthcare facility's infection control program?
A) Employee health screening
B) Restricting patient visitors
C) Providing patient education on nutrition
D) Monitoring patient satisfaction surveys

6.   Multiple Response Questions

Which of the following are common routes of transmission for healthcare-associated infections (HAIs)? (Select all that apply)

A) Contact transmission

B) Droplet transmission

C) Vector transmission

D) Airborne transmission

7.   When should healthcare workers wear gloves? (Select all that apply)

A) When performing a blood draw

B) When providing wound care

C) When feeding a patient

D) When handling soiled linen

Drag and Drop Question

8.   Match the type of isolation with the appropriate precautions.

Categories:

Airborne precautions

Droplet precautions

Contact precautions

Precautions:

Wear N95 respirator, place patient in an isolation room with negative airflow.

Wear a surgical mask and gloves when entering the patient's room.

Wear gloves and gown; use dedicated equipment.

Case Scenario Questions

9.   Case: A nurse is preparing to care for a patient who has been diagnosed with methicillin-resistant Staphylococcus aureus (MRSA). The nurse is in charge of ensuring proper infection control measures are taken. Which of the following actions should the nurse take?

A) Disinfecting the room after each patient visit

B) Wearing gloves and a gown when entering the room

C) Placing the patient in a private room and wearing only gloves

D) Administering antibiotics without consulting the doctor

10. Case: A patient is admitted with symptoms of pneumonia and is placed under droplet precautions. Which of the following interventions is most important in preventing the spread of infection?

A) Wearing a surgical mask when in the patient's room

B) Disinfecting the patient's belongings

C) Using a gown and gloves when handling the patient's linens

D) Limiting the number of visitors

Drop-Down Question
11. Select the correct PPE for each situation:
When caring for a patient with tuberculosis (TB):
Correct PPE:
N95 mask
Gloves
Gown

Multiple Choice Questions
12. What is the most effective method of disinfecting surfaces that may be contaminated with Clostridium difficile (C. difficile)?
A) Using a bleach-based solution
B) Using an alcohol-based hand sanitizer
C) Using a hydrogen peroxide solution
D) Using soap and water

Multiple Response Questions
13. Which of the following are components of a facility's emergency preparedness plan for infection control? (Select all that apply)
A) Stockpiling PPE
B) Staff training on infection control protocols
C) Screening for infectious diseases upon patient admission
D) Providing free vaccinations to all patients

Multiple Choice Questions
14. What is the most important action when caring for a patient with a central venous catheter (CVC) to reduce the risk of infection?
A) Changing the catheter site every 48 hours
B) Applying antimicrobial ointment at the insertion site
C) Using aseptic technique when handling the catheter and dressing
D) Keeping the catheter site open to the air

15. Which of the following is an example of a healthcare-associated infection (HAI)?
A) Influenza contracted from a family member
B) A surgical wound infection that develops after surgery
C) A cold contracted from a co-worker
D) Strep throat contracted at school

16. Which of the following is the primary goal of infection control in healthcare settings?
A) To ensure all patients receive antibiotics
B) To minimize the risk of infection for patients and healthcare workers
C) To prevent all forms of viral infections
D) To encourage the use of antibiotics to treat all infections

17. A nurse is caring for a patient with a confirmed diagnosis of Clostridium difficile. Which of the following precautions should the nurse implement?
A) Airborne precautions with an N95 mask
B) Droplet precautions with a surgical mask
C) Contact precautions with gloves and a gown
D) No special precautions are necessary

18. Multiple Response Questions
Which of the following actions should be performed before entering a room with a patient on contact precautions? (Select all that apply)
A) Wash hands with soap and water
B) Wear a gown
C) Wear a surgical mask
D) Wear gloves

19. Which of the following are potential sources of infection in the healthcare setting? (Select all that apply)
A) Contaminated equipment
B) Poor hand hygiene
C) Proper waste disposal
D) Direct patient contact

Drag and Drop Question
20. Match the type of infection with the appropriate precaution type.
Infection Types:
Tuberculosis (TB)
Influenza
Methicillin-resistant Staphylococcus aureus (MRSA)
Precautions:
Airborne precautions
Droplet precautions
Contact precautions

Case Scenario Questions

21. Case: A nurse is caring for a patient with a urinary tract infection (UTI) caused by Escherichia coli (E. coli). The nurse is preparing to assist the patient with a catheter change. Which of the following is the most important action to reduce the risk of infection?
A) Wash the catheter with soap and water
B) Use a sterile technique when changing the catheter
C) Apply an antiseptic solution to the catheter
D) Use gloves, but no other precautions are necessary

22. Case: A nurse is assigned to care for a patient on droplet precautions due to a suspected diagnosis of meningitis. Which of the following PPE items should the nurse wear when entering the patient's room?
A) Gloves and N95 mask
B) Surgical mask and gloves
C) Gown, gloves, and surgical mask
D) Gown, gloves, and N95 mask

Drop-Down Question

23. Select the appropriate PPE for a patient in isolation due to confirmed measles:
Correct PPE:
N95 respirator
Gloves
Gown

Multiple Choice Questions

24. Which of the following is a key element of proper hand hygiene?
A) Handwashing with soap and water for at least 15 seconds
B) Handwashing with soap and water for at least 20 seconds
C) Handwashing with alcohol-based sanitizer for at least 30 seconds
D) Using hand sanitizer only when hands are visibly clean

25. Which of the following actions is necessary when disinfecting a surface contaminated with blood or body fluids?
A) Using a disinfectant that is effective against HIV and hepatitis B
B) Using alcohol-based hand sanitizer
C) Wiping the surface with a dry cloth

D) Rinsing the area with water only

Multiple Response Questions

26. Which of the following are considered standard precautions in infection control? (Select all that apply)
A) Wearing gloves when in contact with a patient's blood or bodily fluids
B) Wearing a surgical mask when interacting with a patient
C) Using hand hygiene before and after patient contact
D) Avoiding direct patient contact if the patient has a cold

Multiple Choice Questions

27. Which of the following is a risk factor for developing healthcare-associated infections (HAIs)?
A) Receiving IV antibiotics
B) Not receiving a flu vaccine
C) Avoiding catheter use in hospitalized patients
D) Ensuring proper wound dressing changes

28. Which of the following PPE items is most appropriate for a nurse caring for a patient with a wound infection on contact precautions?
A) N95 respirator and gloves
B) Surgical mask and gown
C) Gown and gloves
D) Gloves and face shield

29. A nurse is preparing to give a bed bath to a patient in isolation for an influenza diagnosis. What type of precautions should the nurse follow?
A) Droplet precautions
B) Contact precautions
C) Airborne precautions
D) Standard precautions

30. Which of the following actions is most appropriate when preparing to remove gloves after patient contact in a contact isolation room?
A) Wash hands first, then remove gloves
B) Remove gloves without touching the outer surface
C) Disinfect gloves before removing them
D) Remove gloves after disinfecting the patient's room

Multiple Response Questions

31. Which of the following statements about infection control are true? (Select all that apply)

A) Infection control measures are only needed for patients who are symptomatic.

B) Routine environmental cleaning and disinfection help reduce the spread of infection.

C) All healthcare workers should receive the flu vaccine to protect themselves and their patients.

D) Visitors should never enter the rooms of patients on isolation precautions.

32. Which of the following are key components of a healthcare facility's infection prevention and control program? (Select all that apply)

A) Employee vaccination programs

B) Hand hygiene education

C) Restricting visitor access during outbreaks

D) Providing antibiotics for all admitted patients

Drag and Drop Question

33. Match the infection with the correct precaution category.

Infections:

Chickenpox (Varicella)

Influenza

Norovirus

Precautions:

Airborne precautions

Droplet precautions

Contact precautions

Case Scenario Questions

34. Case: A nurse is preparing to assist a patient in the ICU with a tracheostomy. The nurse is aware that the patient is at high risk for infections. What is the most important action to prevent infection?

A) Use sterile technique when handling the tracheostomy tube

B) Clean the tracheostomy site with soap and water

C) Administer antibiotics as a preventive measure

D) Ensure the patient remains on a ventilator at all times

35. Case: A patient who has been on antibiotic therapy for several days develops a fever and diarrhea. The healthcare provider suspects Clostridium difficile. Which of the following actions should the nurse implement?

A) Continue antibiotic therapy as prescribed

B) Place the patient in a private room on contact precautions

C) Administer an antidiarrheal medication

D) Perform a sputum culture to confirm the diagnosis

Drop-Down Question
36. Select the correct PPE for a patient with suspected tuberculosis (TB):
Correct PPE:
N95 respirator
Gloves
Gown

Multiple Choice Questions
37. When should a nurse wear gloves in a healthcare setting?
A) When taking a blood pressure reading
B) When administering oral medications
C) When handling patient wounds or bodily fluids
D) When entering a patient's room to talk to the patient

38. Which of the following is the best method to prevent the spread of multidrug-resistant organisms (MDROs) in a healthcare setting?
A) Administering more potent antibiotics to patients
B) Strict adherence to hand hygiene and isolation precautions
C) Reducing the number of patient admissions to the hospital
D) Wearing gloves and gowns without handwashing

Multiple Response Questions
39. Which of the following are standard precautions to prevent the spread of infections in healthcare settings? (Select all that apply)
A) Performing hand hygiene before and after patient contact
B) Wearing gloves when handling contaminated materials
C) Wearing a surgical mask for all patients
D) Using alcohol-based hand sanitizer when hands are visibly dirty

Drag and Drop Question
40. Match the infection with its most appropriate isolation precaution.
Infections:
Tuberculosis
Influenza
Hepatitis B
Precautions:
Airborne precautions
Droplet precautions
Contact precautions

Multiple Choice Questions

41. Which of the following is the primary purpose of contact precautions?
A) To prevent the spread of airborne pathogens
B) To prevent the spread of pathogens that are transmitted by direct or indirect contact
C) To protect against bloodborne infections
D) To reduce the risk of viral infections

42. Which of the following types of personal protective equipment (PPE) is essential when performing a procedure that involves potential exposure to blood?
A) N95 respirator and gloves
B) Gloves and a gown
C) Gown, gloves, and eye protection
D) Gloves only

43. Which of the following is the most appropriate method for disinfecting patient-care equipment after use?
A) Use a disinfectant effective against viruses, bacteria, and fungi
B) Use soap and water to clean the equipment
C) Wipe the equipment with a dry cloth to remove dust
D) Submerge the equipment in warm water for 15 minutes

44. What is the best way to prevent the spread of respiratory infections in healthcare settings?
A) Wearing gloves at all times
B) Using proper hand hygiene and wearing a surgical mask
C) Restricting patient visitors
D) Administering antibiotics to all patients

45. Which of the following is the correct order for donning personal protective equipment (PPE)?
A) Gloves, gown, mask, goggles
B) Mask, gown, gloves, goggles
C) Gown, gloves, goggles, mask
D) Gown, mask, goggles, gloves

Multiple Response Questions

46. Which of the following are actions that can help minimize the risk of surgical site infections? (Select all that apply)
A) Administering prophylactic antibiotics before surgery
B) Keeping the surgical area sterile during the procedure
C) Allowing the patient to leave the operating room immediately after surgery
D) Properly cleaning and dressing the surgical wound post-operation

47. Which of the following are common strategies for preventing the spread of Clostridium difficile (C. difficile) infections? (Select all that apply)
A) Use alcohol-based hand sanitizers to clean hands after patient contact
B) Use bleach-based disinfectants to clean surfaces
C) Place the patient in a private room
D) Administer antibiotics to prevent infection

Drag and Drop Question
48. Match the correct isolation precaution with the disease.
Diseases:
Influenza
Tuberculosis
MRSA (Methicillin-resistant Staphylococcus aureus)
Precautions:
Droplet precautions
Airborne precautions
Contact precautions

Case Scenario Questions
49. Case: A nurse is preparing to administer an injection to a patient. The patient has a history of Hepatitis B and is placed under isolation precautions. Which of the following is the most important action the nurse should take?
A) Wear gloves and a surgical mask
B) Wear gloves and a gown
C) Wear gloves, a gown, and a face shield
D) Wear gloves and a face shield

50. Case: A nurse notices that a patient's IV site has become red, swollen, and warm to the touch, and the patient has a fever. What action should the nurse take first?
A) Administer antibiotics as ordered
B) Remove the IV and clean the site with alcohol
C) Notify the healthcare provider and follow protocol for potential infection
D) Monitor the patient's vital signs and continue infusing fluids

Drop-Down Question
51. Select the appropriate PPE for caring for a patient with suspected measles:
Correct PPE:
N95 respirator
Gloves
Gown

Multiple Choice Questions

52. Which of the following methods is most effective for sterilizing surgical instruments?
A) Cleaning with soap and water
B) Using an autoclave
C) Wiping with a disinfectant
D) Using ultraviolet light

53. Which of the following is the most appropriate action to take when a healthcare worker is exposed to a needle stick injury?
A) Immediately report the injury to the supervisor and seek post-exposure prophylaxis
B) Clean the wound with water and continue working
C) Apply antibiotic ointment to the injury
D) Wait until the end of the shift and then report the injury

Multiple Response Questions

54. Which of the following measures are effective for preventing the transmission of MRSA in a healthcare setting? (Select all that apply)
A) Isolating patients with MRSA in private rooms
B) Performing hand hygiene before and after patient contact
C) Using contact precautions when caring for patients with MRSA
D) Administering antibiotics to all patients on admission

Drag and Drop Question

55. Match the infection type with the appropriate method of transmission.
Infections:
Hepatitis A
Tuberculosis
Norovirus
Methods of Transmission:
Fecal-oral transmission
Airborne transmission
Contact transmission

Multiple Choice Questions

56. Which of the following is the most effective method to prevent the spread of infection in the operating room?
A) Using a face mask and gloves
B) Performing a pre-surgical skin antiseptic on the patient
C) Administering antibiotics to the patient before surgery
D) Sterilizing all equipment before use

57. Which of the following is a correct use of personal protective equipment (PPE) when caring for a patient with a respiratory infection like pneumonia?
A) Use only gloves and gown
B) Use gloves, gown, and N95 respirator
C) Use gloves and a surgical mask
D) Use gloves, gown, surgical mask, and face shield

58. When should a nurse change gloves during patient care?
A) After touching any surface in the patient's room
B) After coming in contact with any patient fluids or broken skin
C) After washing the patient's hands
D) After interacting with family members in the room

59. Which of the following is the best way to prevent the spread of respiratory droplets when a patient with a contagious disease coughs or sneezes?
A) Asking the patient to cover their mouth with their hand
B) Asking the patient to wear a surgical mask
C) Providing a tissue for the patient to cover their mouth
D) Isolating the patient in a separate room with negative airflow

Multiple Response Questions
60. Which of the following actions are recommended for preventing the spread of infections in a healthcare setting? (Select all that apply)
A) Regularly disinfecting surfaces that come in contact with patients
B) Ensuring patients with suspected infections are placed in appropriate isolation
C) Allowing visitors to freely enter patient rooms
D) Wearing PPE according to the patient's infection risk level

61. Which of the following actions help prevent the spread of C. difficile infections in a hospital setting? (Select all that apply)
A) Using alcohol-based hand sanitizers after patient contact
B) Using soap and water to wash hands after patient contact
C) Isolating patients diagnosed with C. difficile
D) Administering antibiotics to all patients

Drag and Drop Question

62. Match the correct isolation precaution to the corresponding pathogen.

Pathogens:

Measles

Streptococcus pneumoniae

Norovirus

Precautions:

Airborne precautions

Droplet precautions

Contact precautions

Norovirus → Contact precautions

Case Scenario Questions

63. Case: A nurse is caring for a patient who is immunocompromised and has a central venous catheter (CVC) in place. What is the most important intervention to prevent infection?

A) Perform strict hand hygiene before and after handling the catheter

B) Use a regular antiseptic to clean the catheter insertion site

C) Change the CVC dressing weekly, even if it appears clean

D) Limit patient movement to reduce exposure

64. Case: A nurse is preparing to care for a patient with suspected tuberculosis (TB). What is the most important precaution the nurse should take?

A) Wear a surgical mask when entering the room

B) Wear an N95 respirator

C) Isolate the patient in a private room without negative airflow

D) Provide the patient with a face mask

Drop-Down Question

65. Select the appropriate PPE for a patient with suspected flu:

Correct PPE:

Surgical mask

Gloves

Gown

Multiple Choice Questions

66. When should a nurse remove their gloves when caring for a patient with a wound infection?

A) After touching any non-contaminated surface

B) After touching the patient's body
C) Before touching the patient's body but after touching contaminated surfaces
D) Immediately after touching the wound

67. Which of the following is the primary role of standard precautions in healthcare settings?
A) To prevent healthcare workers from contracting communicable diseases from patients
B) To ensure all patients are treated with the same infection control measures
C) To protect patients from being exposed to infectious agents
D) To limit patient contact with the healthcare environment

Multiple Response Questions
68. Which of the following are effective ways to prevent catheter-associated urinary tract infections (CAUTIs)? (Select all that apply)
A) Keep the catheter closed and secure
B) Perform hand hygiene before and after catheter care
C) Remove the catheter as soon as possible
D) Use antibiotics to prevent infection

Drag and Drop Question
69. Match the infection with the appropriate antibiotic class.
Infections:
MRSA
Streptococcus pneumoniae
Escherichia coli (E. coli)
Antibiotic Classes:
Penicillins
Cephalosporins
Vancomycin
Escherichia coli (E. coli) → Cephalosporins

Case Scenario Questions
70. Case: A nurse is preparing to administer a vaccination to a patient who has a history of an allergic reaction to eggs. What is the most appropriate action?
A) Administer the vaccine as ordered
B) Contact the healthcare provider to verify if the vaccine is safe
C) Administer an alternative vaccine that does not contain egg protein
D) Delay the vaccine until the patient has a reaction

Multiple Choice Questions
71. Which of the following actions is the most effective in reducing the risk of infection in a healthcare setting?

A) Restricting patient movement within the facility
B) Routinely disinfecting all surfaces and equipment
C) Administering antibiotics to all incoming patients
D) Restricting visitors to only immediate family members

72. A nurse is caring for a patient with a surgical wound. Which of the following is the most important intervention to reduce the risk of wound infection?
A) Administering prophylactic antibiotics before the wound is cleaned
B) Applying a dry, sterile dressing to the wound
C) Using antiseptic to cleanse the wound before dressing
D) Applying an adhesive bandage to keep the wound closed

73. Which of the following best describes the proper sequence for donning PPE when entering an isolation room?
A) Gloves, gown, mask, goggles
B) Gown, mask, gloves, goggles
C) Gown, mask, goggles, gloves
D) Mask, gown, gloves, goggles

Multiple Response Questions
74. Which of the following are considered standard precautions to prevent infection transmission in healthcare settings? (Select all that apply)
A) Using disposable gloves when handling blood or body fluids
B) Wearing a gown when caring for all patients
C) Using proper hand hygiene after patient contact
D) Wearing an N95 mask when caring for patients with respiratory infections

75. Which of the following are recommended actions for preventing the spread of infections during patient care? (Select all that apply)
A) Clean hands before and after patient contact
B) Wear gloves for all patient interactions
C) Ensure proper ventilation in patient rooms
D) Use alcohol-based hand sanitizers after patient care

NGN NCLEX SAFETY AND INFECTION CONTROL ANSWERS

1. Answer: B) Performing hand hygiene regularly
   Rationale: Hand hygiene is the most effective method for preventing the transmission of pathogens in healthcare settings.

2. Answer: C) Surgical mask and gloves
   Rationale: Droplet precautions require wearing a surgical mask and gloves to prevent transmission through respiratory droplets.

3. Answer: C) To prevent healthcare workers from acquiring bloodborne infections
   Rationale: Standard precautions are designed to protect healthcare workers from exposure to infectious materials, especially bloodborne pathogens.

4. Answer: A) Report the incident to the supervisor and clean the wound
   Rationale: An accidental needle stick requires immediate reporting for proper post-exposure protocols and wound cleaning to prevent infection.

5. Answer: A) Employee health screening
   Rationale: Employee health screening ensures that healthcare workers are free from communicable diseases that could be transmitted to patients.

6. Answer: A) Contact transmission, B) Droplet transmission, D) Airborne transmission
   Rationale: HAIs are commonly transmitted via contact, droplet, and airborne routes. Vector transmission (e.g., via insects) is less common in healthcare settings.

7. Answer: A) When performing a blood draw, B) When providing wound care, D) When handling soiled linen
   Rationale: Gloves should be worn when there is potential contact with bodily fluids or contaminated materials.

8. Answer:
Airborne precautions → Wear N95 respirator, place patient in an isolation room with negative airflow.
Droplet precautions → Wear a surgical mask and gloves when entering the patient's room.
Contact precautions → Wear gloves and gown; use dedicated equipment.
Rationale: Each isolation type has specific protocols to reduce the risk of transmission of different pathogens.

9. Answer: B) Wearing gloves and a gown when entering the room
    Rationale: MRSA is a contact-transmitted infection. Wearing gloves and gowns prevents the spread to other patients and staff.

10. Answer: A) Wearing a surgical mask when in the patient's room
    Rationale: Wearing a surgical mask helps prevent the spread of droplet-borne pathogens like pneumonia.

11. Correct PPE:
N95 mask
Gloves
Gown
Rationale: For TB, the patient is under airborne precautions, requiring an N95 mask and gloves. A gown may also be needed depending on the situation.

12. Answer: A) Using a bleach-based solution
    Rationale: Clostridium difficile spores are highly resistant, and bleach is effective in killing them.

13. Answer: A) Stockpiling PPE, B) Staff training on infection control protocols, C) Screening for infectious diseases upon patient admission
    Rationale: Emergency preparedness includes PPE, training, and screening to control infections during emergencies, but vaccinations for all patients may not be a facility-wide requirement.

14. Answer: C) Using aseptic technique when handling the catheter and dressing
    Rationale: Proper aseptic technique reduces the risk of infection at the catheter insertion site.

15. Answer: B) A surgical wound infection that develops after surgery
    Rationale: HAIs are infections that occur during the course of receiving healthcare, such as after surgery.

16. Answer: B) To minimize the risk of infection for patients and healthcare workers
    Rationale: Infection control aims to minimize the transmission of infections to protect both patients and healthcare workers.

17. Answer: C) Contact precautions with gloves and a gown
    Rationale: C. difficile is transmitted through contact with spores, requiring gloves and gown for protection.

18. Answer: A) Wash hands with soap and water, B) Wear a gown, D) Wear gloves
    Rationale: Contact precautions require hand hygiene, gloves, and a gown, but not a surgical mask unless respiratory issues are present.

19. Answer: A) Contaminated equipment, B) Poor hand hygiene, D) Direct patient contact
    Rationale: Contaminated equipment, poor hand hygiene, and direct patient contact are common sources of infection.

20. Answer:
Tuberculosis (TB) → Airborne precautions
Influenza → Droplet precautions
Methicillin-resistant Staphylococcus aureus (MRSA) → Contact precautions
Rationale: TB requires airborne precautions, influenza requires droplet precautions, and MRSA requires contact precautions due to its spread through direct contact.

21. Answer: B) Use a sterile technique when changing the catheter
    Rationale: A sterile technique must be used during catheter changes to prevent introducing pathogens into the urinary tract.

22. Answer: C) Gown, gloves, and surgical mask
    Rationale: Droplet precautions require a surgical mask, gloves, and gown, but not an N95 mask.

23. Correct PPE:
N95 respirator
Gloves
Gown
Rationale: Measles is transmitted through airborne droplets, requiring an N95 respirator and standard isolation precautions, including gloves and gowns.

24. Answer: B) Handwashing with soap and water for at least 20 seconds
    Rationale: Hand hygiene with soap and water for 20 seconds is the gold standard for removing pathogens from hands.

25. Answer: A) Using a disinfectant that is effective against HIV and hepatitis B
    Rationale: Bloodborne pathogens like HIV and hepatitis B require specific disinfectants to ensure proper decontamination.

26. Answer: A) Wearing gloves when in contact with a patient's blood or bodily fluids, C) Using hand hygiene before and after patient contact

Rationale: Standard precautions include gloves when handling bodily fluids and using hand hygiene regularly.

27. Answer: A) Receiving IV antibiotics
Rationale: IV antibiotics can disrupt normal flora, increasing the risk of developing healthcare-associated infections (HAIs), especially in immunocompromised patients.

28. Answer: C) Gown and gloves
    Rationale: Contact precautions require gown and gloves to prevent the spread of pathogens through contact with infected materials.

29. Answer: A) Droplet precautions
    Rationale: Influenza is transmitted through respiratory droplets, so droplet precautions are necessary when interacting with the patient.

30. Answer: B) Remove gloves without touching the outer surface
    Rationale: Gloves should be removed carefully to avoid touching the outer surface, which may be contaminated.

31. Answer: B) Routine environmental cleaning and disinfection help reduce the spread of infection, C) All healthcare workers should receive the flu vaccine to protect themselves and their patients
    Rationale: Infection control measures are necessary for all patients, symptomatic or not. Routine cleaning and vaccination are key practices, but visitors may enter rooms with isolation precautions if following proper PPE guidelines.

32. Answer: A) Employee vaccination programs, B) Hand hygiene education, C) Restricting visitor access during outbreaks
    Rationale: Employee vaccination, hand hygiene education, and visitor restrictions are integral to infection prevention in healthcare settings.

33. Answer:
Chickenpox (Varicella) → Airborne precautions
Influenza → Droplet precautions
Norovirus → Contact precautions
Rationale: Chickenpox requires airborne precautions, influenza requires droplet precautions, and norovirus requires contact precautions to prevent transmission.

34. Answer: A) Use sterile technique when handling the tracheostomy tube
    Rationale: Sterile technique is essential to prevent introducing pathogens during tracheostomy care.

35. Answer: B) Place the patient in a private room on contact precautions
Rationale: C. difficile is transmitted via contact with spores, so contact precautions are necessary to prevent its spread.

36. Correct PPE:
N95 respirator
Gloves
Gown
Rationale: TB is an airborne disease, so the N95 respirator is required along with gloves and a gown for patient care.

37. Answer: C) When handling patient wounds or bodily fluids
Rationale: Gloves should be worn whenever there is potential contact with bodily fluids or broken skin to reduce infection risk.

38. Answer: B) Strict adherence to hand hygiene and isolation precautions
Rationale: Preventing the spread of MDROs requires strict infection control measures, including hand hygiene and isolation precautions.

39. Answer: A) Performing hand hygiene before and after patient contact, B) Wearing gloves when handling contaminated materials
Rationale: Hand hygiene and wearing gloves are essential standard precautions. A surgical mask is not required for all patients, and alcohol-based hand sanitizers may not be effective when hands are visibly dirty.

40. Answer:
Tuberculosis → Airborne precautions
Influenza → Droplet precautions
Hepatitis B → Contact precautions
Rationale: Tuberculosis requires airborne precautions, influenza requires droplet precautions, and hepatitis B requires contact precautions due to its transmission through blood.

41. Answer: B) To prevent the spread of pathogens that are transmitted by direct or indirect contact
Rationale: Contact precautions are used to prevent the transmission of infections spread through direct or indirect contact with contaminated surfaces or patient secretions.

42. Answer: C) Gown, gloves, and eye protection
Rationale: When performing procedures with the potential for exposure to blood or

bodily fluids, gown, gloves, and eye protection are necessary to reduce the risk of transmission.

43. Answer: A) Use a disinfectant effective against viruses, bacteria, and fungi
Rationale: Disinfecting patient-care equipment with a broad-spectrum disinfectant ensures it is free of harmful pathogens.

44. Answer: B) Using proper hand hygiene and wearing a surgical mask
Rationale: Hand hygiene and wearing a surgical mask when interacting with patients are key to preventing the transmission of respiratory infections.

45. Answer: D) Gown, mask, goggles, gloves
Rationale: The proper sequence for donning PPE is gown first, followed by mask, goggles, and gloves.

46. Answer: A) Administering prophylactic antibiotics before surgery, B) Keeping the surgical area sterile during the procedure, D) Properly cleaning and dressing the surgical wound post-operation
Rationale: Administering antibiotics, maintaining sterile technique, and proper wound care all reduce the risk of surgical site infections.

47. Answer: B) Use bleach-based disinfectants to clean surfaces, C) Place the patient in a private room
Rationale: Alcohol hand sanitizers are ineffective against C. difficile spores. Bleach is a recommended disinfectant, and placing the patient in a private room helps prevent transmission.

48. Answer:
Influenza → Droplet precautions
Tuberculosis → Airborne precautions
MRSA → Contact precautions
Rationale: Influenza is transmitted through droplets, tuberculosis through airborne transmission, and MRSA requires contact precautions to prevent transmission via contaminated surfaces or direct contact.

49. Answer: B) Wear gloves and a gown
Rationale: Hepatitis B is transmitted through blood and bodily fluids, so gloves and a gown are necessary when dealing with the patient to prevent contamination.

50. Answer: C) Notify the healthcare provider and follow protocol for potential infection
    Rationale: The symptoms may indicate an infection at the IV site, and immediate action, including notifying the healthcare provider, is required.

51. Correct PPE:
N95 respirator
Gloves
Gown
Rationale: Measles is transmitted through airborne droplets, so an N95 respirator is required, along with gloves and a gown to protect against contact transmission.

52. Answer: B) Using an autoclave
    Rationale: An autoclave uses high-pressure steam to sterilize surgical instruments, making it the most effective method for preventing infection.

53. Answer: A) Immediately report the injury to the supervisor and seek post-exposure prophylaxis
    Rationale: Reporting the injury promptly and following post-exposure protocols is essential to reduce the risk of infection from needle stick injuries.

54. Answer: A) Isolating patients with MRSA in private rooms, B) Performing hand hygiene before and after patient contact, C) Using contact precautions when caring for patients with MRSA
    Rationale: Isolating patients, practicing proper hand hygiene, and using contact precautions are critical measures for preventing MRSA transmission.

55. Answer:
Hepatitis A → Fecal-oral transmission
Tuberculosis → Airborne transmission
Norovirus → Contact transmission
Rationale: Hepatitis A is spread through the fecal-oral route, tuberculosis through airborne droplets, and norovirus through direct contact with contaminated surfaces.

56. Answer: D) Sterilizing all equipment before use
    Rationale: Proper sterilization of surgical instruments is crucial in preventing the transmission of infections in the operating room.

57. Answer: B) Use gloves, gown, and N95 respirator
    Rationale: An N95 respirator is necessary for respiratory infections like pneumonia to protect against airborne transmission.

58. Answer: B) After coming in contact with any patient fluids or broken skin
    Rationale: Gloves should be changed immediately after exposure to patient fluids or broken skin to prevent cross-contamination.

59. Answer: B) Asking the patient to wear a surgical mask
    Rationale: A surgical mask is effective in preventing the spread of respiratory droplets when a patient with a contagious disease coughs or sneezes.

60. Answer: A) Regularly disinfecting surfaces that come in contact with patients, B) Ensuring patients with suspected infections are placed in appropriate isolation, D) Wearing PPE according to the patient's infection risk level
    Rationale: Regular surface disinfection, appropriate isolation, and proper PPE are key to preventing the spread of infections.

61. Answer: B) Using soap and water to wash hands after patient contact, C) Isolating patients diagnosed with C. difficile
    Rationale: Alcohol-based hand sanitizers do not effectively kill C. difficile spores; soap and water are necessary. Isolation also helps prevent transmission.

62. Answer:
Measles → Airborne precautions
Streptococcus pneumoniae → Droplet precautions
Norovirus → Contact precautions
Rationale: Measles requires airborne precautions, Streptococcus pneumoniae requires droplet precautions, and norovirus requires contact precautions.

63. Answer: A) Perform strict hand hygiene before and after handling the catheter
    Rationale: Hand hygiene is the most effective method to prevent the introduction of pathogens when handling CVCs.

64. Answer: B) Wear an N95 respirator
    Rationale: TB is transmitted through airborne droplets, so an N95 respirator is necessary to protect the nurse from inhaling the infectious particles.

65. Correct PPE:
Surgical mask
Gloves
Gown
Rationale: The flu is transmitted through droplets, so a surgical mask, gloves, and gown are necessary to prevent the spread of infection.

66. Answer: D) Immediately after touching the wound
    Rationale: Gloves should be removed immediately after contact with contaminated surfaces, such as a wound, to prevent the spread of infection.

67. Answer: B) To ensure all patients are treated with the same infection control measures
    Rationale: Standard precautions ensure uniform infection control practices, protecting both healthcare workers and patients.

68. Answer: A) Keep the catheter closed and secure, B) Perform hand hygiene before and after catheter care, C) Remove the catheter as soon as possible
    Rationale: Proper catheter care, including secure placement, hand hygiene, and early removal, helps prevent CAUTIs.

69. Answer:
MRSA → Vancomycin
Streptococcus pneumoniae → Penicillins
Escherichia coli (E. coli) → Cephalosporins
Rationale: Vancomycin is used to treat MRSA, penicillins for Streptococcus pneumoniae, and cephalosporins for E. coli.

70. Answer: B) Contact the healthcare provider to verify if the vaccine is safe
    Rationale: It is important to verify with the healthcare provider if a vaccine is safe for patients with egg allergies before administration.

71. Answer: B) Routinely disinfecting all surfaces and equipment
    Rationale: Regular disinfection of surfaces and equipment helps reduce the risk of cross-contamination and healthcare-associated infections.

72. Answer: C) Using antiseptic to cleanse the wound before dressing
    Rationale: Cleansing the wound with an antiseptic helps reduce the risk of infection before dressing it with sterile materials.

73. Answer: C) Gown, mask, goggles, gloves
    Rationale: The correct sequence for donning PPE is gown first, followed by mask, goggles, and gloves, ensuring the body is fully protected before touching anything.

74. Answer: A) Using disposable gloves when handling blood or body fluids, C) Using proper hand hygiene after patient contact
    Rationale: Standard precautions include wearing gloves and practicing proper hand

hygiene, but gowns and N95 masks are only necessary for specific types of patient isolation.

75. Answer: A) Clean hands before and after patient contact, C) Ensure proper ventilation in patient rooms
    Rationale: Hand hygiene and proper ventilation are key infection control measures, whereas gloves are not always necessary unless there is direct contact with bodily fluids.

NGN NCLEX HEALTH PROMOTION QUESTIONS

Multiple Choice Questions

1. Which of the following is the most effective method for promoting health in a community setting?
    A) Providing individual counseling for healthy lifestyle changes
    B) Organizing community health education programs
    C) Encouraging patients to read health-related pamphlets
    D) Distributing medications to individuals in need

2. A 40-year-old woman is scheduled for a mammogram. Which of the following should the nurse include in teaching the patient about the procedure?
    A) "It is a quick procedure with minimal discomfort."
    B) "You should avoid any food or drink before the test."
    C) "This procedure is recommended for women every two years after the age of 50."
    D) "You will need to stop taking any medications before the test."

Case Scenario

3. Case Scenario: A 65-year-old male with hypertension is visiting the clinic for a routine check-up. He reports feeling well and has no complaints. His blood pressure today is 152/94 mm Hg. Which of the following actions should the nurse take?
    A) Provide education about lifestyle modifications and schedule a follow-up in 3 months.
    B) Initiate antihypertensive medication and educate about the need for blood pressure monitoring at home.
    C) Suggest starting an exercise program immediately without medication.
    D) Recommend a low-sodium diet and wait for the next check-up in 6 months.

Multiple Response Questions

4. Which of the following are risk factors for developing Type 2 diabetes? (Select all that apply.)
    A) Sedentary lifestyle
    B) Family history of diabetes
    C) High-fat diet
    D) Age over 65
    E) Low BMI

Drop-Down Questions

5. The nurse is preparing to teach a patient with a recent diagnosis of asthma how to use a metered-dose inhaler (MDI). Which of the following should the nurse instruct the patient to do first?
   Drop-down Options: A) Exhale completely, B) Inhale deeply, C) Place the mouthpiece in the mouth, D) Press the inhaler

Drag-and-Drop Questions
6. Order the steps in the correct sequence for teaching a client about performing breast self-examination.
Steps:
   A) Stand in front of a mirror and look for any changes in breast appearance.
   B) Raise both arms above the head and look for changes in breast appearance.
   C) Lie down and use the pads of the fingers to palpate the entire breast tissue.
   D) Repeat the examination on the opposite breast.

7. Which of the following is the best source of vitamin C?
   A) Carrots
   B) Beef liver
   C) Oranges
   D) Eggs

8. A nurse is teaching a client with diabetes about carbohydrate counting. Which food item should the nurse recommend as a healthy carbohydrate choice for a diabetic meal plan?
   A) White bread
   B) Mashed potatoes
   C) Brown rice
   D) French fries

Exercise
9. Which of the following is a benefit of regular physical activity for elderly patients?
   A) Improved sleep patterns
   B) Increased joint pain
   C) Decreased circulation
   D) Reduced muscle strength

10. Which is an appropriate exercise for a patient recovering from hip surgery?
    A) Running
    B) Swimming

C) Weightlifting

D) Jumping rope

Vaccination

11. A 10-year-old child is due for a flu vaccine. Which vaccine should the nurse administer?

    A) Tdap

    B) MMR

    C) Inactivated Influenza Vaccine (IIV)

    D) HPV vaccine

12. A nurse is educating a pregnant woman about the safety of receiving vaccines. Which vaccine is recommended during pregnancy?

    A) Varicella

    B) Influenza (inactivated)

    C) Measles, Mumps, Rubella (MMR)

    D) Live Flu Vaccine (LAIV)

Screening Guidelines

13. At what age should a woman begin having mammograms according to current guidelines?

    A) 30

    B) 40

    C) 45

    D) 50

14. Which of the following is the recommended screening for colorectal cancer in asymptomatic adults aged 50 to 75?

    A) Colonoscopy every 10 years

    B) Stool DNA test every 3 years

    C) Flexible sigmoidoscopy every 5 years

    D) All of the above

Lifestyle Changes

15. A 55-year-old woman has been diagnosed with high blood pressure. Which of the following lifestyle changes should she adopt?

    A) Increase intake of salty foods to improve hydration

    B) Begin a low-fat, high-protein diet

    C) Increase physical activity, such as walking

D) Limit water intake to reduce fluid retention

16. A patient with a history of smoking asks for advice on quitting. Which of the following interventions should the nurse recommend?
    A) Gradually reduce the number of cigarettes smoked each day
    B) Use a nicotine patch without counseling
    C) Switch to e-cigarettes to reduce health risks
    D) Increase physical activity to distract from cravings

Chronic Disease Management

17. Which of the following actions is most important for a nurse to take when caring for a patient with chronic obstructive pulmonary disease (COPD)?
    A) Encourage the patient to stop all physical activity
    B) Teach the patient to monitor respiratory rate and oxygen saturation
    C) Recommend smoking cessation after symptoms have improved
    D) Decrease fluid intake to reduce edema

18. A patient with diabetes mellitus type 2 is experiencing frequent episodes of hypoglycemia. Which of the following is the most likely cause?
    A) Inconsistent timing of insulin injections
    B) Increased physical activity without adjustment of insulin
    C) Eating meals high in sugar
    D) Consuming high-protein snacks between meals

19. Cultural Competence in Health Promotion
When providing care for a Muslim patient, the nurse should be aware that which of the following might affect dietary choices?
    A) Preference for dairy products
    B) Avoidance of pork and alcohol
    C) Limited consumption of carbohydrates
    D) Preference for vegetarian meals

20. A nurse is caring for a Hispanic patient who is resistant to taking prescribed medications. The patient expresses a preference for herbal remedies. Which action should the nurse take?
    A) Insist that the patient follow the prescribed medication regimen
    B) Encourage the patient to only use the prescribed medications
    C) Discuss the use of herbal remedies in conjunction with prescribed medications
    D) Ignore the patient's preference for herbal remedies

Health Disparities

21. Which of the following groups is at greatest risk for health disparities related to access to healthcare?
    A) Middle-income urban residents
    B) Elderly residents in rural areas
    C) College-educated individuals
    D) Young professionals living in metropolitan areas

22. A nurse is teaching a patient with hypertension about lifestyle modifications. Which of the following strategies should the nurse include in the teaching plan?
    A) Limit salt intake to less than 3,000 mg per day
    B) Increase potassium intake through foods like bananas and potatoes
    C) Drink at least 3 cups of coffee a day to maintain alertness
    D) Limit exercise to once a week for 30 minutes

23. A 45-year-old woman with type 2 diabetes mellitus is being educated about foot care. Which of the following is the most important instruction for the nurse to provide?
    A) "Massage your feet daily to increase circulation."
    B) "Trim your toenails straight across to prevent ingrown toenails."
    C) "Wear tight-fitting shoes to help prevent blisters."
    D) "Avoid checking your feet for injuries to prevent self-diagnosis."

24. A patient with chronic kidney disease is on a restricted sodium diet. Which of the following should the nurse recommend for snacks?
    A) Potato chips
    B) Fresh fruit
    C) Processed meats
    D) Salted nuts

25. A nurse is caring for a patient from a Hindu background. The patient expresses the desire to avoid eating meat due to religious beliefs. Which of the following should the nurse do?
    A) Insist that the patient try to eat a balanced diet, including meat
    B) Explore plant-based protein alternatives to ensure adequate nutrition
    C) Encourage the patient to eat small portions of meat for health reasons
    D) Ignore the patient's dietary preferences as they are irrelevant to health

26. A nurse is teaching a Native American patient about the importance of regular physical activity. The patient expresses that physical activity is not valued in their culture. Which of the following actions should the nurse take?

A) Explain the benefits of physical activity in terms of modern medicine only
B) Suggest exercises that are aligned with the patient's cultural values
C) Advise the patient to ignore cultural values and follow the nurse's recommendation
D) Avoid discussing physical activity with the patient

27. Which of the following is the most effective strategy for promoting vaccination in a community?
A) Educating the community about the safety and efficacy of vaccines through outreach programs
B) Mandating vaccines for all residents in the community
C) Making vaccines available only in hospitals
D) Providing financial incentives for individuals who get vaccinated

28. Which of the following is a key component of a smoking cessation program?
A) Offering free nicotine replacement therapies to all patients
B) Providing education on the risks of smoking and offering emotional support
C) Encouraging the patient to quit without any professional support
D) Reducing smoking cessation-medication based on the patient's choice

29. At what age should men start getting screened for prostate cancer according to the American Cancer Society?
A) 35
B) 40
C) 45
D) 50

30. A 45-year-old woman is experiencing menopause. Which of the following should the nurse include in the teaching plan to promote bone health?
A) Avoid weight-bearing exercises
B) Increase intake of calcium and vitamin D
C) Limit physical activity to reduce injury risk
D) Avoid exposure to sunlight to prevent vitamin D toxicity

31. A nurse is counseling a patient on managing stress. Which of the following strategies should the nurse recommend to the patient?
A) Engage in activities that promote relaxation, such as yoga or meditation
B) Avoid socializing with friends and family to reduce stress
C) Increase caffeine intake to stay alert and energized
D) Focus solely on work to keep busy and distracted

32. Which of the following is the most appropriate recommendation for a patient with obesity who is attempting to lose weight?
    A) Focus on fad diets that promise rapid weight loss
    B) Aim for a gradual weight loss of 1 to 2 pounds per week
    C) Limit physical activity to reduce strain on joints
    D) Increase intake of high-calorie foods to boost metabolism

33. A patient with congestive heart failure is admitted to the hospital for worsening symptoms. Which of the following should the nurse prioritize in this patient's care plan?
    A) Encourage deep breathing exercises to increase oxygen intake
    B) Monitor for signs of fluid retention, such as edema or weight gain
    C) Encourage high-sodium snacks to increase fluid retention
    D) Monitor for signs of constipation related to the use of diuretics

34. A patient with asthma is experiencing increased shortness of breath. Which of the following should the nurse do first?
    A) Administer a prescribed bronchodilator
    B) Instruct the patient to sit up and rest
    C) Encourage the patient to increase fluid intake
    D) Call for a chest x-ray immediately

Case Scenario Questions

35. Case Scenario: A 70-year-old female patient is diagnosed with osteoporosis. The doctor prescribes calcium and vitamin D supplementation and recommends weight-bearing exercises. Which of the following is the nurse's most important role in educating the patient?
    A) To instruct the patient to avoid high-impact exercises, like running
    B) To encourage the patient to take calcium supplements with a glass of milk
    C) To explain the importance of regular, moderate weight-bearing activities like walking
    D) To advise the patient to use a cane to assist with balance during exercise

36. Case Scenario: A nurse is caring for a 55-year-old male with a family history of prostate cancer. The patient expresses concern about the possibility of developing the disease. Which of the following responses by the nurse is most appropriate?
    A) "Prostate cancer is rare, so there is nothing to worry about."

B) "Since you have a family history, you should consider starting prostate cancer screening at age 40."

C) "Prostate cancer screening is only necessary if you experience symptoms."

D) "It's important to start screening at age 45, given your family history."

Multiple Response Questions

37. Which of the following are risk factors for developing cardiovascular disease? (Select all that apply.)
    A) Smoking
    B) High-fat diet
    C) Regular physical activity
    D) Hypertension
    E) Advanced age

38. Which of the following lifestyle changes should be promoted to a patient who has been diagnosed with type 2 diabetes? (Select all that apply.)
    A) Adopting a low-sodium diet
    B) Engaging in 30 minutes of moderate exercise most days of the week
    C) Limiting carbohydrate intake to prevent spikes in blood sugar
    D) Increasing intake of fruits and vegetables for their fiber content
    E) Increasing daily sugar consumption to improve energy levels

Drop-Down Questions

39. The nurse is educating a client on how to use an inhaler. Which of the following steps should the nurse include in the instructions for the patient?
    Drop-down Options: A) Exhale completely, B) Inhale deeply, C) Hold your breath for 10 seconds, D) Repeat steps 1 to 3 for a second dose]

40. A nurse is teaching a patient with chronic obstructive pulmonary disease (COPD) how to manage their condition. Which of the following should be included in the teaching plan?
    Drop-down Options: A) Avoid all physical activity, B) Take medications as prescribed, C) Limit fluid intake to reduce coughing, D) Engage in high-impact exercise]

41. Drag-and-Drop Questions
    Place the following steps in the correct order for performing hand hygiene using soap and water.
    Steps:
    A) Wet hands with clean, running water
    B) Apply soap and lather hands
    C) Rub the front and back of hands for at least 20 seconds

D) Dry hands using a clean towel or air dry

42. Order the steps in the correct sequence for providing a patient with an intramuscular injection.
Steps:
A) Cleanse the injection site with an alcohol swab
B) Draw the prescribed amount of medication into the syringe
C) Insert the needle at a 90-degree angle into the muscle
D) Dispose of the needle in a proper sharps container

43. Drag and drop the following lifestyle changes in the correct sequence for promoting heart health in a patient with hypertension.
Lifestyle Changes:
A) Increase daily physical activity
B) Reduce sodium intake
C) Maintain a healthy weight
D) Limit alcohol consumption

Multiple Choice Questions
44. Which of the following is the most appropriate nursing intervention for a patient who is attempting to quit smoking?
A) Encourage the patient to avoid any triggers related to smoking, such as drinking alcohol or coffee.
B) Recommend the use of nicotine replacement therapy without any behavioral support.
C) Educate the patient about the health risks of smoking and provide resources for counseling and support groups.
D) Tell the patient to quit immediately without any additional support or follow-up.

45. A nurse is caring for a patient with diabetes who is experiencing frequent hypoglycemic episodes. Which of the following factors is most likely contributing to the patient's hypoglycemia?
A) Increased physical activity without adjusting insulin dosage
B) Increased carbohydrate intake
C) Consuming excessive protein
D) Not taking enough oral hypoglycemic medication

46. Which of the following is the primary benefit of implementing a heart-healthy diet in a patient with coronary artery disease (CAD)?
A) It helps lower cholesterol levels and reduces the risk of blood clot formation.

B) It increases blood pressure and reduces the effectiveness of medication.
C) It ensures that the patient gains weight to support healing after a heart attack.
D) It restricts the intake of fats and carbohydrates to improve the patient's metabolism.

Case Scenario Questions

47. Case Scenario: A 60-year-old woman with osteoarthritis is being taught about joint protection strategies. Which of the following should the nurse include in the teaching plan?
    A) Avoid all physical activity to reduce stress on the joints
    B) Use assistive devices like canes or walkers to help with walking and mobility
    C) Focus only on stretching exercises and avoid strengthening exercises
    D) Apply heat and cold packs to the joints only when there is visible swelling

48. Case Scenario: A 45-year-old male patient with a history of hypertension and smoking is admitted with shortness of breath and chest pain. Which of the following interventions is the priority?
    A) Administer oxygen as ordered
    B) Provide education on smoking cessation
    C) Assess for signs of congestive heart failure
    D) Encourage deep breathing exercises

Multiple Response Questions

49. Which of the following are common complications associated with uncontrolled diabetes? (Select all that apply.)
    A) Peripheral neuropathy
    B) Retinopathy
    C) Improved wound healing
    D) Increased risk for cardiovascular disease
    E) Chronic kidney disease

50. Which of the following lifestyle changes should be promoted to a patient with hypertension? (Select all that apply.)
    A) Limiting alcohol consumption
    B) Increasing salt intake to improve hydration
    C) Engaging in regular physical activity
    D) Losing weight if overweight or obese
    E) Reducing caffeine intake

Drop-Down Questions

51. A nurse is teaching a patient how to manage their newly prescribed inhaler for asthma. Which of the following should the nurse instruct the patient to do first?
Drop-down Options: A) Shake the inhaler well, B) Inhale deeply and hold for 10 seconds, C) Place the mouthpiece in the mouth, D) Exhale completely]

52. A nurse is teaching a patient with osteoarthritis how to properly use a heating pad. Which of the following is the most important instruction to include?
Drop-down Options: A) Use the heating pad for no more than 15-20 minutes at a time, B) Apply the heating pad directly to bare skin for the most effective heat, C) Use the heating pad continuously for an hour to achieve pain relief, D) Set the temperature to the highest setting for rapid pain relief

Drag-and-Drop Questions
53. Place the following steps in the correct order for performing a breast self-examination.
Steps:
A) Stand in front of a mirror and inspect both breasts
B) Raise arms above the head and inspect for changes
C) Lie down and palpate the breast tissue using the pads of the fingers
D) Repeat the examination on the opposite breast

54. Order the steps for performing CPR in the correct sequence.
Steps:
A) Call for emergency assistance (911)
B) Check for a pulse and breathing
C) Begin chest compressions if no pulse or breathing
D) Provide rescue breaths if trained

Multiple Choice Questions
55. A nurse is caring for a 40-year-old male who is overweight and has a family history of type 2 diabetes. Which of the following is the most important recommendation to prevent the development of diabetes?
A) Increase physical activity to at least 150 minutes per week
B) Start taking oral diabetes medications
C) Restrict carbohydrate intake severely
D) Focus on weight loss through intermittent fasting

56. Which of the following statements about hypertension is true?
A) Hypertension is a condition that only affects older adults.
B) Hypertension can lead to heart failure, stroke, and kidney disease if left untreated.

C) Individuals with hypertension should completely avoid exercise.

D) Blood pressure should be checked annually for individuals over the age of 60.

57. A 50-year-old woman is experiencing hot flashes and mood swings. She is seeking advice on menopause. Which of the following should the nurse recommend?

A) Start hormone replacement therapy (HRT) immediately to control symptoms

B) Consider lifestyle changes, including a balanced diet, exercise, and stress management

C) Avoid all physical activity to prevent further hormonal imbalances

D) Only focus on medication for symptom management

Case Scenario Questions

58. Case Scenario: A 25-year-old woman visits the clinic for a routine check-up. She mentions that she has been feeling very tired, experiencing weight gain, and has noticed her hair thinning. The nurse suspects hypothyroidism. Which of the following tests should the nurse anticipate to confirm the diagnosis?

A) Hemoglobin A1c test

B) Serum thyroid-stimulating hormone (TSH) test

C) Liver function tests

D) Blood glucose test

59. Case Scenario: A nurse is educating a 40-year-old male patient about preventive measures for prostate cancer. The patient asks about screening options. Which of the following should the nurse include in the teaching?

A) "Screening with a prostate-specific antigen (PSA) test is recommended annually for all men over 40."

B) "A digital rectal exam (DRE) should be performed annually for men over 40."

C) "Screening for prostate cancer should begin at age 50 for men with average risk."

D) "Prostate cancer screening is unnecessary unless symptoms appear."

Multiple Response Questions

60. Which of the following are health risks associated with smoking? (Select all that apply.)

A) Chronic obstructive pulmonary disease (COPD)

B) Increased risk of cancer
C) Improved cardiovascular health
D) Increased risk of stroke
E) Reduced fertility

61. Which of the following are common symptoms of depression in elderly patients? (Select all that apply.)
    A) Feelings of sadness and hopelessness
    B) Decreased appetite or overeating
    C) Increased energy and motivation
    D) Sleep disturbances (e.g., insomnia or excessive sleeping)
    E) Difficulty concentrating or making decisions

Drop-Down Questions

62. A nurse is providing dietary education to a patient with chronic kidney disease (CKD). Which of the following should the nurse instruct the patient to limit?
    Drop-down Options: A) Protein intake, B) Carbohydrate intake, C) Sodium intake, D) Fiber intake

63. A nurse is preparing to teach a patient how to use a blood pressure monitor at home. Which of the following should the nurse instruct the patient to do first?
    Drop-down Options: A) Sit in a comfortable chair with back support, B) Apply the cuff over the wrist, C) Record the measurement after the first reading, D) Inflate the cuff until a pulse is felt]

Drag-and-Drop Questions

64. Place the following steps in the correct order for preparing a patient for an abdominal assessment.
    Steps:
    A) Ask the patient to lie flat on the examination table
    B) Inspect the abdomen for any abnormal findings
    C) Palpate the abdomen to assess for tenderness
    D) Auscultate the abdomen for bowel sounds

65. Order the following steps for administering an intradermal injection.
    Steps:
    A) Cleanse the skin with an alcohol wipe
    B) Prepare the syringe with the medication

C) Insert the needle at a 10-15 degree angle

D) Withdraw the needle and apply pressure to the site

Multiple Choice Questions

66. A 45-year-old male with a family history of heart disease is visiting the clinic for a check-up. Which of the following should the nurse recommend as the most effective strategy for heart disease prevention?
    A) Begin taking daily aspirin
    B) Engage in moderate physical activity at least 150 minutes per week
    C) Start taking cholesterol-lowering medication
    D) Begin a low-fat diet without regard to other dietary factors

67. Which of the following should the nurse include in teaching about the benefits of the human papillomavirus (HPV) vaccine?
    A) The HPV vaccine is only recommended for males over the age of 50.
    B) The vaccine helps prevent cervical and other cancers caused by HPV.
    C) HPV vaccination is most effective in those already diagnosed with HPV.
    D) HPV vaccination is unnecessary once an individual becomes sexually active.

68. A nurse is teaching a patient with chronic liver disease about dietary changes. Which of the following foods should the nurse recommend the patient avoid?
    A) Lean meats, such as chicken and turkey
    B) High-sodium foods like processed snacks and canned soups
    C) Fresh vegetables and fruits
    D) Whole grains, like brown rice and quinoa

Case Scenario Questions

69. Case Scenario: A 60-year-old male with a history of hyperlipidemia is being treated for his condition. He asks the nurse about the benefits of a Mediterranean diet. Which of the following should the nurse respond?
    A) "The Mediterranean diet is low in fats and cholesterol, which will help reduce your lipid levels."
    B) "The Mediterranean diet emphasizes whole grains, fruits, vegetables, and healthy fats, which can help lower cholesterol and reduce heart disease risk."
    C) "The Mediterranean diet is rich in red meat and dairy, which will help improve your lipid profile."
    D) "This diet is not helpful for patients with hyperlipidemia, so you should avoid it."

70. Case Scenario: A 35-year-old woman presents with complaints of feeling fatigued, gaining weight, and having irregular menstrual cycles. The nurse suspects polycystic ovary syndrome (PCOS). Which of the following tests should the nurse anticipate to confirm this diagnosis?
    A) Thyroid function test
    B) Serum cortisol levels
    C) Pelvic ultrasound
    D) Serum liver enzymes

Multiple Response Questions
71. Which of the following lifestyle modifications are recommended for managing high blood pressure? (Select all that apply.)
    A) Limiting alcohol intake
    B) Increasing potassium and magnesium intake
    C) Reducing salt intake
    D) Avoiding caffeine altogether
    E) Engaging in regular aerobic exercise

72. Which of the following are common preventive measures for osteoporosis? (Select all that apply.)
    A) Adequate intake of calcium and vitamin D
    B) Regular weight-bearing exercise, such as walking or running
    C) Reducing alcohol and tobacco use
    D) Increasing caffeine intake to improve bone density
    E) Performing resistance training exercises

Drop-Down Questions
73. A nurse is preparing to teach a patient with chronic pain about non-pharmacological pain management techniques. Which of the following should the nurse suggest first? Drop-down Options: A) Deep breathing exercises, B) Acupuncture, C) Meditation, D) Use of ice and heat packs

74. A nurse is caring for a patient with gastroesophageal reflux disease (GERD). Which of the following interventions should the nurse recommend? Drop-down Options: A) Encourage the patient to eat large meals to prevent hunger pangs, B) Advise the patient to lie down immediately after eating to aid digestion, C) Recommend wearing tight clothing around the abdomen, D) Encourage the patient to avoid lying down after eating and eat smaller, more frequent meals]

Drag-and-Drop Questions

75. Place the following steps in the correct order for performing CPR on an adult patient.
    Steps:
    A) Check for responsiveness and call for help
    B) Begin chest compressions
    C) Check for breathing and pulse
    D) Open the airway

NGN NCLEX HEALTH PROMOTION ANSWERS

1. Answer: B) Organizing community health education programs
   Rationale: Community health education programs are most effective in promoting health by reaching a broad audience and providing information that can help individuals make informed decisions about their health.

2. Answer: A) "It is a quick procedure with minimal discomfort."
   Rationale: Mammograms are usually quick and cause minimal discomfort. They are typically recommended starting at age 40 for women, with a frequency of yearly or every two years, depending on the patient's individual health profile.

3. Answer: B) Initiate antihypertensive medication and educate about the need for blood pressure monitoring at home.
   Rationale: The patient's blood pressure is above the recommended level, and antihypertensive medications are typically started at this stage. Education on blood pressure monitoring is also important.

4. Answer: A) Sedentary lifestyle, B) Family history of diabetes, C) High-fat diet, D) Age over 65
   Rationale: Sedentary lifestyle, family history of diabetes, high-fat diet, and age are all established risk factors for Type 2 diabetes. Low BMI is not a risk factor.

5. Answer: A) Exhale completely
   Rationale: The first step in using a metered-dose inhaler is to exhale completely to allow for the maximum amount of inhaled medication.

6. Drag-and-Drop Questions
   Correct Order:
   > a. Stand in front of a mirror and look for any changes in breast appearance.
   > b. Raise both arms above the head and look for changes in breast appearance.
   > c. Lie down and use the pads of the fingers to palpate the entire breast tissue.
   > d. Repeat the examination on the opposite breast.

   Rationale: The steps are sequential: visually inspecting the breast, raising the arms to check for changes, palpating the breast tissue while lying down, and then repeating the process on the other breast.

7. Answer: C) Oranges

Rationale: Oranges are rich in vitamin C, an essential nutrient for the immune system and collagen production. While other foods may contain vitamin C, oranges are considered one of the best sources.

8. Answer: C) Brown rice
9. Rationale: Brown rice is a healthy carbohydrate choice because it is a whole grain and provides fiber, which helps in managing blood sugar levels. White bread and French fries are more processed and can cause rapid spikes in blood sugar.

10. Answer: A) Improved sleep patterns
Rationale: Regular physical activity helps improve sleep patterns, reduces anxiety, and can improve overall well-being, especially in elderly individuals. It also contributes to maintaining strength and circulation.

11. Answer: B) Swimming
Rationale: Swimming is a low-impact exercise that allows for full-body movement and helps improve strength without putting excess stress on the healing hip.

12. Answer: C) Inactivated Influenza Vaccine (IIV)
Rationale: The flu vaccine (IIV) is recommended annually for children over six months old. Tdap, MMR, and HPV vaccines are not specific to the flu se

13. Answer: B) Influenza (inactivated)
Rationale: Pregnant women are advised to receive the inactivated flu vaccine, as it protects both the mother and the fetus from complications related to influenza. Live vaccines, such as MMR or varicella, are not recommended during pregnancy.

14. Answer: B) 40
Rationale: Current guidelines recommend that women begin regular mammograms at age 40 and continue annually or biennially, depending on individual health conditions and risk factors.

15. Answer: D) All of the above
Rationale: Screening options for colorectal cancer include colonoscopy every 10 years, stool DNA testing every 3 years, and flexible sigmoidoscopy every 5 years. The choice depends on patient preference and healthcare provider recommendations.

16. Answer: C) Increase physical activity, such as walking
Rationale: Regular physical activity, such as walking, helps lower blood pressure, improves cardiovascular health, and aids in weight management, which can all help reduce hypertension.

17. Answer: A) Gradually reduce the number of cigarettes smoked each day
    Rationale: Gradually reducing cigarette consumption can help ease the transition to quitting. Combining nicotine replacement therapy (such as patches) with counseling has been shown to improve success rates.

18. Answer: B) Teach the patient to monitor respiratory rate and oxygen saturation
    Rationale: Monitoring respiratory rate and oxygen saturation is crucial in managing COPD. This helps in detecting early signs of respiratory distress and ensures timely intervention.

19. Answer: B) Increased physical activity without adjustment of insulin
    Rationale: Physical activity increases the body's demand for glucose. If insulin is not adjusted accordingly, it can lead to hypoglycemia due to the increased utilization of glucose during exercise.

20. Answer: B) Avoidance of pork and alcohol
    Rationale: Many Muslims avoid pork and alcohol due to religious beliefs. It is important for nurses to be aware of dietary restrictions based on a patient's cultural background when planning care.

21. Answer: C) Discuss the use of herbal remedies in conjunction with prescribed medications
    Rationale: It is important to respect a patient's cultural preferences while educating them about the potential interactions between herbal remedies and prescribed medications. Open discussion allows for informed decision-making.

22. Answer: B) Elderly residents in rural areas
    Rationale: Elderly individuals living in rural areas often face barriers to healthcare access, including long travel distances to providers and limited healthcare facilities, contributing to health disparities.

23. Answer: B) Increase potassium intake through foods like bananas and potatoes
    Rationale: Increasing potassium intake helps balance the effects of sodium and can assist in lowering blood pressure. Potassium-rich foods like bananas and potatoes are important for managing hypertension.

24. Answer: B) "Trim your toenails straight across to prevent ingrown toenails."

Rationale: Proper foot care is critical for diabetic patients to prevent complications like infections. Trimming toenails straight across helps prevent ingrown toenails, which can lead to injury and infection.

25. Answer: B) Fresh fruit
Rationale: Fresh fruits are naturally low in sodium and a good choice for patients with chronic kidney disease who must avoid excessive salt intake. Processed foods, such as chips and salted nuts, should be avoided.

26. Answer: B) Explore plant-based protein alternatives to ensure adequate nutrition
Rationale: Respecting cultural preferences is essential for providing holistic care. Exploring plant-based protein alternatives, such as legumes, tofu, and lentils, can ensure the patient meets their nutritional needs while respecting their beliefs.

27. Answer: B) Suggest exercises that are aligned with the patient's cultural values
Rationale: It is important for nurses to respect cultural values and work with the patient to find acceptable forms of physical activity. In some cultures, outdoor activities like walking or dancing may align better with traditional practices.

28. Answer: A) Educating the community about the safety and efficacy of vaccines through outreach programs
Rationale: Education is the most effective method for promoting vaccination, as it helps address concerns, correct misconceptions, and encourages informed decision-making within communities.

29. Answer: B) Providing education on the risks of smoking and offering emotional support
Rationale: A smoking cessation program should include both education on the health risks associated with smoking and emotional support to help the patient quit. Nicotine replacement therapies may also be offered, but education and support are key elements.

30. Answer: C) 45
Rationale: The American Cancer Society recommends that men start discussing prostate cancer screening with their healthcare provider at age 45, especially for those at high risk due to family history or ethnicity.

31. Answer: B) Increase intake of calcium and vitamin D
Rationale: Calcium and vitamin D are essential for bone health, especially in postmenopausal women who are at increased risk for osteoporosis. Weight-bearing exercises also promote bone strength and should be encouraged.

32. Answer: A) Engage in activities that promote relaxation, such as yoga or meditation

Rationale: Relaxation techniques like yoga and meditation are effective in managing stress and promoting overall well-being. Reducing social interaction or overworking may increase stress levels.

33. Answer: B) Aim for a gradual weight loss of 1 to 2 pounds per week
Rationale: Gradual weight loss of 1 to 2 pounds per week is considered safe and sustainable. Fad diets often lead to short-term results and potential nutritional deficiencies.

34. Answer: B) Monitor for signs of fluid retention, such as edema or weight gain
Rationale: Fluid retention is a key sign of worsening heart failure. Monitoring for edema, weight gain, and changes in fluid balance is critical in managing congestive heart failure.

35. Answer: A) Administer a prescribed bronchodilator
Rationale: Bronchodilators are the first-line treatment for acute asthma symptoms, as they help open the airways and relieve shortness of breath. Other interventions, like fluid intake or rest, are secondary to managing the immediate breathing difficulty.

36. Answer: C) To explain the importance of regular, moderate weight-bearing activities like walking
Rationale: Weight-bearing exercises, such as walking, are essential for strengthening bones and preventing fractures in individuals with osteoporosis. The nurse should focus on educating the patient on safe exercises that will support bone health.

37. Answer: D) "It's important to start screening at age 45, given your family history."
Rationale: The American Cancer Society recommends that men at high risk for prostate cancer, such as those with a family history, begin discussing screening with their healthcare provider at age 45. This approach allows for early detection and appropriate surveillance.

38. Answer: A) Smoking, B) High-fat diet, D) Hypertension, E) Advanced age
Rationale: Smoking, a high-fat diet, hypertension, and advanced age are known risk factors for cardiovascular disease. Regular physical activity is protective against cardiovascular disease, not a risk factor.

39. Answer: B) Engaging in 30 minutes of moderate exercise most days of the week, C) Limiting carbohydrate intake to prevent spikes in blood sugar, D) Increasing intake of fruits and vegetables for their fiber content
Rationale: Regular physical activity and a balanced diet with appropriate carbohydrate control are essential for managing blood sugar in type 2 diabetes. Increased intake of

fruits and vegetables helps with fiber, which stabilizes blood sugar. A low-sodium diet is generally recommended for overall health but not specific to diabetes management.

40. Answer: A) Exhale completely, B) Inhale deeply, C) Hold your breath for 10 seconds
Rationale: The correct sequence for using an inhaler is: exhale completely to empty the lungs, inhale deeply to draw the medication into the lungs, and hold the breath for 10 seconds to ensure that the medication reaches the lungs. If a second dose is needed, repeat the steps.

41. Answer: B) Take medications as prescribed
Rationale: It is essential for COPD patients to take their medications as prescribed to help manage symptoms and prevent exacerbations. Physical activity should be adjusted but not completely avoided, and fluid intake should not be restricted unless otherwise directed by a physician.

42.

Correct Order:
    a. Wet hands with clean, running water
    b. Apply soap and lather hands
    c. Rub the front and back of hands for at least 20 seconds
    d. Dry hands using a clean towel or air dry

Rationale: The proper steps for hand hygiene involve wetting hands with clean, running water, applying soap, lathering, and rubbing for at least 20 seconds, and drying with a clean towel or air drying. These steps reduce the transmission of germs and infections.

43. Correct Order:

B) Draw the prescribed amount of medication into the syringe
    a. Cleanse the injection site with an alcohol swab
    b. Insert the needle at a 90-degree angle into the muscle
    c. Dispose of the needle in a proper sharps container

Rationale: The first step is to draw the medication into the syringe, followed by cleaning the injection site to prevent infection. The needle is then inserted at a 90-degree angle, and proper disposal is the final step.

44. Correct Order:
    a. Reduce sodium intake
    b. Increase daily physical activity
    c. Maintain a healthy weight
    d. Limit alcohol consumption

Rationale: The recommended sequence for managing hypertension includes reducing sodium intake to lower blood pressure, followed by increasing physical activity, maintaining a healthy weight, and limiting alcohol consumption for overall cardiovascular health.

45. Answer: C) Educate the patient about the health risks of smoking and provide resources for counseling and support groups.
Rationale: Smoking cessation requires both behavioral support and medical interventions, such as nicotine replacement therapy. Providing education and access to support groups increases the likelihood of success.

46. Answer: A) Increased physical activity without adjusting insulin dosage
Rationale: Increased physical activity leads to greater glucose consumption by muscles, which may cause hypoglycemia if insulin dosages are not adjusted accordingly. It is important to monitor and adjust insulin levels when exercise levels increase.

47. Answer: A) It helps lower cholesterol levels and reduces the risk of blood clot formation.
Rationale: A heart-healthy diet focuses on reducing saturated fats, cholesterol, and sodium while increasing fiber, which can lower cholesterol levels and reduce the risk of blood clot formation, improving overall heart health.

48. Answer: B) Use assistive devices like canes or walkers to help with walking and mobility
Rationale: Assistive devices help alleviate joint stress, improve mobility, and reduce the risk of falls in patients with osteoarthritis. Physical activity, including stretching and strengthening exercises, should be encouraged within the patient's tolerance level.

49. Answer: A) Administer oxygen as ordered
Rationale: The priority intervention for a patient with chest pain and shortness of breath is to administer oxygen to ensure adequate oxygenation while further diagnostic assessments are performed. Other interventions, such as education, can follow once the patient is stabilized.

50. Answer: A) Peripheral neuropathy, B) Retinopathy, D) Increased risk for cardiovascular disease, E) Chronic kidney disease
Rationale: Uncontrolled diabetes can lead to complications such as peripheral neuropathy, retinopathy, cardiovascular disease, and chronic kidney disease. Diabetes does not improve wound healing; in fact, poor blood glucose control can impair healing.

51. Answer: A) Limiting alcohol consumption, C) Engaging in regular physical activity, D) Losing weight if overweight or obese, E) Reducing caffeine intake
Rationale: Lifestyle changes such as limiting alcohol, increasing physical activity, losing excess weight, and reducing caffeine intake are effective strategies for managing hypertension. Increased salt intake can exacerbate hypertension, so it should be avoided.

52. Answer: D) Exhale completely
    Rationale: The first step in using an inhaler is to exhale completely to empty the lungs, allowing for better inhalation of the medication.

53. Answer: A) Use the heating pad for no more than 15-20 minutes at a time
    Rationale: Heat therapy should be applied for no longer than 15-20 minutes at a time to avoid burns or skin damage. It should also be placed on top of a cloth or clothing to avoid direct skin contact, which could cause injury.

54. Correct Order:
    a. Stand in front of a mirror and inspect both breasts
    b. Raise arms above the head and inspect for changes
    c. Lie down and palpate the breast tissue using the pads of the fingers
    d. Repeat the examination on the opposite breast
    Rationale: The steps for performing a breast self-examination start with visual inspection in front of a mirror, followed by raising the arms to look for changes, then palpating the breast tissue while lying down, and finally repeating the process on the other breast.

55. Correct Order:
    a. Call for emergency assistance (911)
    b. Check for a pulse and breathing
    c. Begin chest compressions if no pulse or breathing
    d. Provide rescue breaths if trained
    Rationale: The first step in performing CPR is calling for emergency help. Next, the rescuer checks for a pulse and breathing, and if there is no pulse, chest compressions are started. Rescue breaths are provided if the rescuer is trained and able to do so.

56. Answer: A) Increase physical activity to at least 150 minutes per week
    Rationale: Physical activity is one of the most effective strategies for preventing the onset of type 2 diabetes, particularly in individuals with risk factors like obesity and a family history of the disease. The recommendation is to aim for at least 150 minutes of moderate exercise per week.

57. Answer: B) Hypertension can lead to heart failure, stroke, and kidney disease if left untreated.
    Rationale: Hypertension can cause serious complications, such as heart failure, stroke, and kidney disease, if not managed appropriately. It is important for individuals of all ages to regularly monitor their blood pressure, particularly if they have risk factors.

58. Answer: B) Consider lifestyle changes, including a balanced diet, exercise, and stress management
Rationale: Lifestyle changes, including a balanced diet, regular physical activity, and stress management, are important components of managing menopausal symptoms. Hormone replacement therapy (HRT) may be considered in some cases, but it is not the first-line recommendation for all women.

59. Answer: B) Serum thyroid-stimulating hormone (TSH) test
Rationale: The TSH test is the primary test used to evaluate thyroid function and is crucial in diagnosing hypothyroidism. The symptoms described by the patient (fatigue, weight gain, and hair thinning) are consistent with hypothyroidism.

60. Answer: C) "Screening for prostate cancer should begin at age 50 for men with average risk."
Rationale: Prostate cancer screening is typically recommended for men starting at age 50 if they are at average risk. Men at higher risk, such as those with a family history of prostate cancer, may need to begin screening earlier.

61. Answer: A) Chronic obstructive pulmonary disease (COPD), B) Increased risk of cancer, D) Increased risk of stroke, E) Reduced fertility
Rationale: Smoking is associated with numerous health risks, including COPD, various types of cancer, stroke, and reduced fertility. Smoking does not improve cardiovascular health but rather contributes to atherosclerosis and other cardiovascular issues.

62. Answer: A) Feelings of sadness and hopelessness, B) Decreased appetite or overeating, D) Sleep disturbances (e.g., insomnia or excessive sleeping), E) Difficulty concentrating or making decisions
Rationale: Depression in elderly individuals often presents as feelings of sadness, appetite changes, sleep disturbances, and difficulty with concentration. Increased energy and motivation are not typically symptoms of depression but may indicate improvement or another condition.

63. Answer: C) Sodium intake
Rationale: Patients with CKD need to limit their sodium intake to help control blood pressure and reduce the risk of fluid retention. Protein intake may need to be adjusted based on kidney function, but sodium restriction is more universally recommended.

64. Answer: A) Sit in a comfortable chair with back support
Rationale: Before taking a blood pressure reading, the patient should sit comfortably in a chair with back support and their arm at heart level. This ensures accurate readings and minimizes the risk of errors due to improper posture or positioning.

65. Correct Order:
    a. Ask the patient to lie flat on the examination table
    b. Inspect the abdomen for any abnormal findings
    c. Auscultate the abdomen for bowel sounds
    d. Palpate the abdomen to assess for tenderness

Rationale: The correct sequence for abdominal assessment is to first have the patient lie flat, followed by visual inspection, auscultation for bowel sounds, and then palpation to assess for tenderness, as palpation can alter bowel sounds.

66. Correct Order:
    a. Prepare the syringe with the medication
    b. Cleanse the skin with an alcohol wipe
    c. Insert the needle at a 10-15 degree angle
    d. Withdraw the needle and apply pressure to the site

Rationale: The correct order begins with preparing the syringe, followed by cleaning the skin, inserting the needle at a shallow angle, and then removing the needle while applying pressure to the site.

67. Answer: B) Engage in moderate physical activity at least 150 minutes per week
Rationale: Physical activity is a highly effective strategy for preventing heart disease, especially when combined with a healthy diet. Exercise helps reduce cholesterol, control weight, and lower blood pressure. Daily aspirin and medications may be considered based on individual risk, but lifestyle changes are key.

68. Answer: B) The vaccine helps prevent cervical and other cancers caused by HPV.
Rationale: The HPV vaccine is highly effective in preventing cancers related to HPV, such as cervical, anal, and throat cancers. It is recommended for individuals before they become sexually active, ideally between the ages of 11-12, but can be given to both males and females up to age 26.

69. Answer: B) High-sodium foods like processed snacks and canned soups
Rationale: Patients with liver disease often need to avoid high-sodium foods to prevent fluid retention and worsen symptoms of ascites. Lean meats, fresh vegetables, and whole grains are generally recommended in a liver-friendly diet.

70. Answer: B) "The Mediterranean diet emphasizes whole grains, fruits, vegetables, and healthy fats, which can help lower cholesterol and reduce heart disease risk."
Rationale: The Mediterranean diet is well-known for its heart-health benefits, emphasizing the consumption of healthy fats (like olive oil), whole grains, fruits, and vegetables. It helps lower cholesterol levels and reduce the risk of heart disease.

71. Answer: C) Pelvic ultrasound
    Rationale: A pelvic ultrasound is commonly used to diagnose PCOS, as it can detect ovarian cysts. PCOS is characterized by irregular menstrual cycles, excess androgen levels, and the presence of cysts in the ovaries.

72. Answer: A) Limiting alcohol intake, B) Increasing potassium and magnesium intake, C) Reducing salt intake, E) Engaging in regular aerobic exercise
    Rationale: Limiting alcohol, increasing potassium and magnesium, reducing salt intake, and regular aerobic exercise are all recommended lifestyle modifications to help manage high blood pressure. Caffeine may affect some individuals but is not universally restricted for managing hypertension.

73. Answer: A) Adequate intake of calcium and vitamin D, B) Regular weight-bearing exercise, such as walking or running, C) Reducing alcohol and tobacco use, E) Performing resistance training exercises
    Rationale: Preventive measures for osteoporosis include adequate intake of calcium and vitamin D, regular weight bearing and resistance exercises, and avoiding alcohol and tobacco. Increasing caffeine intake is not recommended for improving bone density.

74. Answer: A) Deep breathing exercises
    Rationale: Deep breathing exercises are one of the first-line non-pharmacological techniques for managing chronic pain. They help to relax the body, reduce muscle tension, and improve oxygenation, which can decrease the perception of pain.

75. Answer: D) Encourage the patient to avoid lying down after eating and eat smaller, more frequent meals
    Rationale: Lying down after eating can worsen GERD symptoms. Small, frequent meals help prevent the stomach from becoming too full, which can decrease the likelihood of reflux.

    Correct Order:
        a. Check for responsiveness and call for help
        b. Check for breathing and pulse
        c. Open the airway
        d. Begin chest compressions
    Rationale: The first step is checking for responsiveness and calling for help. Then, check for breathing and pulse. After opening the airway, begin chest compressions if there is no breathing or pulse.

NGN NCLEX PSYCHOSOCIAL INTEGRITY QUESTIONS

1. Multiple Choice
A nurse is caring for a client diagnosed with schizophrenia. The client exhibits disorganized speech and demonstrates delusions of grandeur. Which of the following interventions should the nurse implement first?
A) Encourage the client to engage in a group activity.
B) Administer prescribed antipsychotic medication.
C) Ensure a calm, quiet environment.
D) Provide education about the disorder to the client.

2. Case Scenario - Multiple Response
A nurse is providing care for a 16-year-old adolescent who is hospitalized for depression after expressing suicidal ideation. The nurse should assess for which of the following risk factors? (Select all that apply.)
A) Family history of depression
B) Recent loss of a close friend
C) Participation in an adolescent support group
D) Chronic physical illness
E) History of self-harm behavior

3. Drop-down
A nurse is providing education to a client about panic disorder. Which of the following strategies should the nurse include as a part of the client's treatment plan?
Use the drop-down menu to complete the sentence.

4. Multiple Choice
A nurse is assessing a client who has just been diagnosed with post-traumatic stress disorder (PTSD). Which of the following symptoms would the nurse most likely observe?
A) Flashbacks
B) Grandiosity
C) Hallucinations
D) Euphoria

5. Case Scenario - Multiple Response
A nurse is caring for a client with bipolar disorder during a manic episode. The client is displaying impulsive behaviors such as spending large amounts of money. The nurse should prioritize which of the following interventions? (Select all that apply.)
A) Administer prescribed mood stabilizers.
B) Set limits on the client's behavior in a firm, consistent manner.

C) Encourage the client to engage in social activities.
D) Ensure the client's environment is safe and free from stimuli that may escalate behaviors.
E) Provide frequent rest periods to prevent exhaustion.

6. Drag-and-Drop
Place the following interventions in the correct order of priority when caring for a client diagnosed with anxiety.
Offer a safe and quiet environment
Assess the severity of the anxiety.
Encourage deep breathing exercises.
Administer prescribed anti-anxiety medication.

7. Multiple Choice
A nurse is working with a client who has a history of borderline personality disorder. Which of the following is the most appropriate intervention for this client when they exhibit splitting behavior?
A) Set strict, non-negotiable limits.
B) Offer the client positive reinforcement for appropriate behaviors.
C) Ignore the behavior to reduce its impact.
D) Provide frequent phone calls for reassurance.

8. Multiple Choice
A nurse is caring for a client who has been diagnosed with obsessive-compulsive disorder (OCD). Which of the following is the most appropriate therapeutic approach?
A) Encouraging the client to ignore the compulsions.
B) Providing positive reinforcement for performing rituals.
C) Exploring the meaning of the compulsions in therapy.
D) Allowing the client to engage in rituals without interruption.

9. Case Scenario - Multiple Response
A nurse is caring for a client with major depressive disorder who has been prescribed an antidepressant. The nurse should teach the client about which of the following side effects of the medication? (Select all that apply.)
A) Weight gain
B) Sexual dysfunction
C) Drowsiness
D) Hypertension
E) Tremors

10. Multiple Choice

A nurse is caring for a client diagnosed with a personality disorder. The client is frequently angry, impulsive, and has difficulty maintaining stable relationships. The nurse understands that which of the following is the most likely diagnosis for this client?
A) Borderline personality disorder
B) Narcissistic personality disorder
C) Antisocial personality disorder
D) Histrionic personality disorder

11. Multiple Choice
A nurse is teaching a group of students about generalized anxiety disorder (GAD). Which of the following statements should the nurse include in the teaching?
A) GAD is characterized by excessive worry lasting at least 6 months.
B) Clients with GAD rarely experience physical symptoms.
C) GAD symptoms typically resolve without treatment.
D) Clients with GAD only experience anxiety during stressful situations.

12. Case Scenario - Multiple Response
A nurse is caring for a client diagnosed with a neurocognitive disorder. The client demonstrates short-term memory loss, difficulty performing familiar tasks, and confusion. Which of the following interventions should the nurse implement? (Select all that apply.)
A) Encourage the client to participate in activities that stimulate cognitive function.
B) Create a structured daily routine for the client.
C) Provide the client with memory aids, such as a calendar or a clock.
D) Limit the client's social interactions to avoid overstimulation.
E) Provide a quiet and isolated environment to reduce confusion.

13. Drop-down
A nurse is teaching a client with depression about the importance of medication adherence. The nurse should explain that antidepressants can take up to ___ weeks to show full therapeutic effects.
Use the drop-down menu to complete the sentence.

14. Multiple Choice
A nurse is caring for a client with an eating disorder who has been prescribed a selective serotonin reuptake inhibitor (SSRI). The client states, "I feel much better now, and I can stop taking the medication, right?" What is the nurse's best response?
A) "Yes, you can stop the medication once you feel better."
B) "It is important to continue taking the medication as prescribed to maintain the improvement."

C) "You should reduce the medication gradually to avoid withdrawal symptoms."
D) "You should switch to a different medication if you are feeling better."

15. Case Scenario - Multiple Response
A nurse is caring for a client diagnosed with a substance use disorder. The client expresses a desire to quit using alcohol but feels unable to do so. The nurse should encourage which of the following interventions? (Select all that apply.)
A) Motivational interviewing
B) Referral to a substance abuse counselor
C) Encouraging self-help group participation, such as AA
D) Confronting the client about their behavior to motivate change
E) Offering immediate discharge if the client does not express willingness to change

16. Drag-and-Drop
Arrange the following steps in the correct order for providing care to a client who is experiencing a panic attack.
Provide reassurance and a calm presence.
Encourage slow, deep breathing.
Assess the client's physical condition to rule out medical causes.
Ensure a quiet, low-stimulation environment.

17. Multiple Choice
A nurse is caring for a client with a diagnosis of post-traumatic stress disorder (PTSD) who has a history of childhood abuse. The client is demonstrating avoidance behaviors and is reluctant to talk about the trauma. Which of the following actions is most appropriate for the nurse to take?
A) Encourage the client to discuss the trauma immediately.
B) Respect the client's wishes to avoid discussing the trauma.
C) Use confrontation to make the client address the trauma.
D) Recommend that the client avoid thinking about the trauma to prevent distress.

18. Case Scenario - Multiple Response
A nurse is providing care for a client with anorexia nervosa. The nurse should include which of the following in the client's plan of care? (Select all that apply.)
Develop a healthy eating plan.
B) Monitor the client's weight and vital signs regularly.
C) Encourage the client to avoid group therapy to prevent stress.
D) Educate the client about the physical effects of malnutrition.
E) Offer non-judgmental support and encouragement.

19. Multiple Choice

A nurse is caring for a client diagnosed with a personality disorder who frequently seeks attention and becomes excessively emotional. The nurse should recognize this behavior as characteristic of which of the following disorders?

A) Antisocial personality disorder
B) Narcissistic personality disorder
C) Histrionic personality disorder
D) Avoidant personality disorder

20. Multiple Choice

A nurse is teaching a client with obsessive-compulsive disorder (OCD) about the purpose of cognitive-behavioral therapy (CBT). Which of the following statements should the nurse include in the teaching?

A) "CBT will help you eliminate all compulsive behaviors."
B) "CBT will teach you how to ignore distressing thoughts."
C) "CBT will help you identify and change negative thought patterns."
D) "CBT will focus on medication management to reduce your anxiety."

21. Multiple Choice

A nurse is providing care to a client with a diagnosis of major depressive disorder. The nurse recognizes that the client is at risk for suicide when the client states:

A) "I don't have the energy to do anything anymore."
B) "I'm just so tired of feeling like this."
C) "I will get better when the weather changes."
D) "It's hard to get out of bed, but I try every day."

22. Case Scenario - Multiple Response

A nurse is caring for a client diagnosed with panic disorder who has requested help in managing episodes of anxiety. Which interventions should the nurse prioritize for this client? (Select all that apply.)

A) Teach the client deep breathing techniques.
B) Encourage the client to avoid all stressful situations.
C) Provide reassurance and a calm presence during an anxiety attack.
D) Help the client identify triggers that contribute to anxiety.
E) Administer anti-anxiety medication as prescribed.

23. Drop-down

A nurse is educating a client diagnosed with schizophrenia about antipsychotic medications. The nurse should inform the client that it may take up to ____ weeks for the medication to be

effective.
Use the drop-down menu to complete the sentence.

24. Multiple Choice
A nurse is assessing a client who has been diagnosed with bulimia nervosa. The nurse should recognize that which of the following behaviors is characteristic of bulimia nervosa?
A) Self-induced vomiting after eating large amounts of food
B) Eating in small, frequent meals throughout the day
C) Restricting food intake to less than 500 calories per day
D) Exercising excessively after eating to prevent weight gain

25. Case Scenario - Multiple Response
A nurse is caring for a client who has been diagnosed with antisocial personality disorder. The client is exhibiting manipulative behaviors and violates the rights of others. Which interventions should the nurse implement? (Select all that apply.)
A) Set clear, consistent boundaries for behavior.
B) Use confrontation to address manipulative behaviors.
C) Provide opportunities for the client to participate in group therapy.
D) Remain firm and non-judgmental in interactions with the client.
E) Ignore minor violations of rules to avoid escalation.

26. Drag-and-Drop
Place the following nursing interventions for a client with severe anxiety in the correct order.
Ensure a calm, quiet environment.
Encourage slow, deep breathing.
Assess the client's level of anxiety.
Provide reassurance and comfort.

27. Multiple Choice
A nurse is caring for a client diagnosed with major depressive disorder who expresses feelings of worthlessness. The nurse should recognize that this symptom is associated with which of the following characteristics of depression?
A) Decreased energy
B) Altered mood
C) Cognitive distortions
D) Insomnia

28. Case Scenario - Multiple Response

A nurse is working with a client diagnosed with generalized anxiety disorder (GAD). The nurse is providing education about anxiety management techniques. Which of the following techniques should the nurse teach the client? (Select all that apply.)

A) Cognitive Behavioral Therapy (CBT)
B) Deep breathing exercises
C) Progressive muscle relaxation
D) Avoidance of anxiety-provoking situations
E) Regular physical exercise

29. Multiple Choice

A nurse is assessing a client with dissociative identity disorder (DID). The nurse should recognize which of the following behaviors as characteristic of DID?

A) A sudden inability to remember important personal information
B) The presence of two or more distinct personality states
C) A persistent fear of being judged or criticized by others
D) The experience of extreme mood swings that are not related to external events

30. Multiple Choice

A nurse is caring for a client who is receiving therapy for borderline personality disorder (BPD). The client exhibits a fear of abandonment and frequently engages in self-harm. The nurse should prioritize which intervention?

A) Encourage the client to explore past trauma during therapy sessions.
B) Set clear and consistent boundaries for behavior.
C) Provide praise and positive reinforcement for every small improvement.
D) Offer constant supervision to prevent self-harm.

31. Multiple Choice

A nurse is caring for a client with post-traumatic stress disorder (PTSD) who has been avoiding any discussions or reminders of the trauma. Which of the following interventions should the nurse prioritize?

A) Encourage the client to confront the traumatic memory in therapy.
B) Validate the client's feelings of fear and avoidance.
C) Teach the client to suppress any thoughts or memories related to the trauma.
D) Encourage the client to forget the trauma by focusing on positive thoughts.

32. Case Scenario - Multiple Response

A nurse is working with a client diagnosed with an eating disorder. The client is participating in therapy and is beginning to recognize maladaptive behaviors. Which of the following actions would indicate progress in therapy? (Select all that apply.)
A) The client is willing to express feelings about body image.
B) The client agrees to a higher caloric intake despite initial resistance.
C) The client exhibits less concern about food and weight.
D) The client continues to engage in purging behaviors.
E) The client reports feeling more in control of their emotions.

33. Multiple Choice
A nurse is educating a client about the side effects of an SSRI (selective serotonin reuptake inhibitor). Which of the following side effects should the nurse emphasize?
A) Sedation
B) Weight loss
C) Increased libido
D) Sexual dysfunction

34. Case Scenario - Multiple Response
A nurse is providing care to a client who has been diagnosed with a major depressive episode. Which of the following interventions should the nurse implement to help the client manage symptoms of depression? (Select all that apply.)
A) Encourage regular exercise.
B) Recommend an increase in social activities.
C) Assist the client in identifying and challenging negative thoughts.
D) Suggest that the client isolate from others to rest.
E) Administer prescribed antidepressants.

35. Drop-down
A nurse is working with a client who has generalized anxiety disorder (GAD). The nurse should instruct the client to practice _____ to help reduce anxiety.

36. Multiple Choice
A nurse is teaching a client diagnosed with bipolar disorder about the potential side effects of lithium therapy. Which of the following should the nurse include in the teaching?
A) Lithium is safe with no potential for toxicity.
B) Dehydration can increase the risk for lithium toxicity.
C) Lithium has no effect on renal function.
D) Lithium therapy requires no ongoing monitoring.

37. Case Scenario - Multiple Response

A nurse is caring for a client with schizophrenia who is exhibiting symptoms of paranoia and is suspicious of the nursing staff. Which interventions should the nurse implement? (Select all that apply.)
A) Establish trust by being consistent and honest with the client.
B) Avoid challenging the client's delusions directly.
C) Reassure the client that the staff is trustworthy and friendly.
D) Encourage the client to confront their suspicions in group therapy.
E) Provide clear and simple explanations of procedures.

38. Multiple Choice
A nurse is caring for a client diagnosed with narcissistic personality disorder. Which of the following characteristics is most commonly associated with this disorder?
A) Excessive concern for the feelings of others
B) A need for admiration and a lack of empathy
C) An intense fear of abandonment
D) A pattern of unstable and intense interpersonal relationships

39. Case Scenario - Multiple Response
A nurse is caring for a client diagnosed with obsessive-compulsive disorder (OCD). The client reports engaging in compulsive hand-washing rituals that last for more than 30 minutes per day. The nurse should focus on which of the following interventions? (Select all that apply.)
A) Set limits on the amount of time spent on hand-washing rituals.
B) Encourage the client to complete the rituals to reduce anxiety.
C) Provide a calm environment to minimize anxiety triggers.
D) Teach relaxation techniques to reduce the need for rituals.
E) Focus on modifying maladaptive behaviors with exposure and response prevention.

40. Multiple Choice
A nurse is teaching a client diagnosed with bipolar disorder about managing symptoms during a manic episode. Which of the following strategies should the nurse include in the teaching?
A) Engage in stimulating activities to release energy.
B) Use relaxation techniques to manage increased energy levels.
C) Avoid setting limits on impulsive behaviors to prevent conflict.
D) Encourage the client to make important decisions during the manic episode.

41. Multiple Choice

A nurse is caring for a client with a diagnosis of antisocial personality disorder. The client frequently manipulates other clients and the nursing staff. Which of the following strategies should the nurse implement to manage these behaviors?

A) Confront the client about their manipulative behavior.
B) Establish clear, firm, and consistent boundaries.
C) Allow the client to manipulate the environment to reduce tension.
D) Ignore manipulative behaviors to avoid conflict.

42. Case Scenario - Multiple Response

A nurse is working with a client diagnosed with anorexia nervosa. The client is resistant to increasing caloric intake. Which interventions should the nurse prioritize? (Select all that apply.)

A) Monitor the client's weight and vital signs daily.
B) Set a target weight and focus on reaching it as quickly as possible.
C) Provide a structured meal plan with small, frequent meals.
D) Offer praise for any attempts to eat, regardless of the quantity.
E) Encourage family involvement in the treatment process.

43. Multiple Choice

A nurse is caring for a client diagnosed with major depressive disorder who is showing signs of psychomotor retardation. Which of the following interventions should the nurse prioritize?

A) Provide frequent physical activity opportunities to improve energy.
B) Offer the client choices to encourage decision-making.
C) Engage in frequent conversations to stimulate interaction.
D) Set realistic goals for small, achievable tasks.

44. Case Scenario - Multiple Response

A nurse is caring for a client diagnosed with schizophrenia who is displaying hallucinations. Which of the following interventions should the nurse implement? (Select all that apply.)

A) Maintain a calm and non-threatening demeanor.
B) Encourage the client to challenge the hallucinations.
C) Provide distraction through activities to help redirect the client's focus.
D) Acknowledge the client's hallucinations and discuss them in detail.
E) Establish a routine to provide structure and reduce confusion.

45. Drop-down

A nurse is educating a client about the use of selective serotonin reuptake inhibitors (SSRIs) for treating depression. The nurse should explain that the full therapeutic effects of SSRIs typically take _____ weeks to be felt.

46. Multiple Choice
A nurse is caring for a client who is diagnosed with bipolar disorder. The client is currently experiencing a manic episode and is engaging in risky behaviors. Which of the following interventions is most appropriate?
A) Allow the client to express their thoughts and ideas without interruption.
B) Set firm limits on risky behaviors while maintaining a calm demeanor.
C) Encourage the client to plan for the future and set long-term goals.
D) Offer frequent reassurances that the client's feelings are normal.

47. Case Scenario - Multiple Response
A nurse is assessing a client diagnosed with generalized anxiety disorder (GAD). The client reports feeling excessively worried about various aspects of life, including work, relationships, and health. Which of the following interventions should the nurse implement? (Select all that apply.)
A) Teach the client relaxation techniques, such as deep breathing.
B) Encourage the client to avoid stressful situations as much as possible.
C) Provide the client with information about the symptoms of anxiety.
D) Recommend cognitive-behavioral therapy (CBT) to address negative thought patterns.
E) Focus on positive reinforcement of adaptive coping strategies.

48. Multiple Choice
A nurse is working with a client diagnosed with borderline personality disorder who is displaying impulsivity and engaging in self-destructive behaviors. Which of the following interventions should the nurse prioritize?
A) Establish a consistent and structured routine for the client.
B) Encourage the client to express emotions in a healthy, non-destructive way.
C) Set clear and firm boundaries to prevent manipulation.
D) Help the client identify the triggers for self-destructive behaviors.

49. Case Scenario - Multiple Response
A nurse is caring for a client who has been diagnosed with a substance use disorder and is in a rehabilitation program. The client expresses a desire to quit using alcohol but feels overwhelmed by the process. Which interventions should the nurse implement? (Select all that apply.)
A) Discuss the steps involved in recovery and help set realistic short-term goals.
B) Provide information about the effects of alcohol on the body to reinforce the importance of quitting.
C) Encourage participation in support groups, such as Alcoholics Anonymous (AA).

D) Push the client to stop drinking immediately to prevent relapse.

E) Offer emotional support and express confidence in the client's ability to succeed.

---

50. Multiple Choice

A nurse is caring for a client with schizophrenia who is receiving antipsychotic medication. The nurse should monitor the client for which of the following side effects?

A) Insomnia

B) Hyperactivity

C) Tardive dyskinesia

D) Increased appetite

51. Multiple Choice

A nurse is caring for a client diagnosed with schizophrenia who is experiencing auditory hallucinations. Which of the following interventions should the nurse implement?

A) Encourage the client to argue with the voices to gain control.

B) Distract the client with activities to redirect their focus.

C) Validate the content of the hallucinations to help the client feel understood.

D) Discontinue the client's antipsychotic medication.

52. Case Scenario - Multiple Response

A nurse is caring for a client with a history of bipolar disorder who is currently experiencing a depressive episode. Which interventions should the nurse implement to help manage this client's symptoms? (Select all that apply.)

A) Encourage the client to participate in activities they enjoy.

B) Set small, achievable goals for the client.

C) Offer frequent emotional support and validation.

D) Suggest the client avoid making major life decisions until they feel better.

E) Encourage the client to increase their sleep duration to reduce fatigue.

53. Multiple Choice

A nurse is working with a client diagnosed with obsessive-compulsive disorder (OCD). The client engages in compulsive hand-washing rituals. Which of the following is the nurse's best initial intervention?

A) Encourage the client to stop the hand-washing behavior immediately.

B) Set a time limit for the hand-washing ritual and gradually reduce it.

C) Allow the client to engage in the hand-washing ritual for as long as needed.

D) Ignore the behavior to prevent power struggles.

---

54. Case Scenario - Multiple Response

A nurse is working with a client diagnosed with a personality disorder who is exhibiting impulsivity and intense emotional responses. Which interventions should the nurse implement? (Select all that apply.)
A) Set clear, consistent boundaries for behavior.
B) Use confrontation to challenge the client's emotional responses.
C) Validate the client's feelings and help them express emotions in healthy ways.
D) Offer immediate rewards for desirable behavior.
E) Encourage the client to avoid situations that trigger emotional responses.

55. Drop-down
A nurse is teaching a client about the use of lithium for managing bipolar disorder. The nurse should instruct the client to monitor for signs of _____ while taking lithium.

56. Multiple Choice
A nurse is working with a client diagnosed with generalized anxiety disorder (GAD). Which of the following is the most appropriate goal for the nurse to set with this client?
A) The client will stop worrying about daily events completely.
B) The client will identify triggers of anxiety and use coping strategies.
C) The client will avoid stressful situations to prevent anxiety.
D) The client will achieve total relaxation at all times.

57. Case Scenario - Multiple Response
A nurse is caring for a client diagnosed with major depressive disorder who is at risk for suicide. Which of the following interventions should the nurse prioritize? (Select all that apply.)
A) Establish a supportive and trusting relationship with the client.
B) Involve the client in group therapy sessions.
C) Remove any potentially harmful objects from the client's environment.
D) Encourage the client to verbalize thoughts about suicide.
E) Limit the client's social interactions to prevent emotional overload.

58. Multiple Choice
A nurse is assessing a client diagnosed with a dissociative disorder who reports experiencing periods of "losing time" or feeling detached from their body. Which of the following conditions does this description suggest?
A) Dissociative identity disorder
B) Depersonalization-derealization disorder
C) Post-traumatic stress disorder
D) Somatic symptom disorder

59. Case Scenario - Multiple Response

A nurse is caring for a client diagnosed with alcohol use disorder. The client has expressed a desire to quit drinking but is experiencing withdrawal symptoms. Which interventions should the nurse implement? (Select all that apply.)
A) Administer prescribed medications, such as benzodiazepines, to manage withdrawal symptoms.
B) Provide frequent monitoring of vital signs to detect complications.
C) Offer reassurance that withdrawal symptoms will subside on their own.
D) Educate the client about the importance of continued sobriety after withdrawal.
E) Encourage the client to increase physical activity to alleviate withdrawal symptoms.

60. Multiple Choice
A nurse is caring for a client who is diagnosed with a major depressive episode and is receiving an antidepressant. The client reports feeling more energized but still experiencing sadness and hopelessness. Which of the following should the nurse be concerned about?
A) The client may be improving and should be encouraged to continue medication.
B) The client is at an increased risk for suicide due to higher energy levels.
C) The client is experiencing a normal response to antidepressant medication.
D) The client is no longer depressed and should be encouraged to stop medication.

61. Multiple Choice
A nurse is providing care for a client diagnosed with post-traumatic stress disorder (PTSD). The client frequently has flashbacks to a traumatic event. Which of the following interventions is most appropriate for the nurse to implement during a flashback?
A) Encourage the client to relive the trauma to gain control over it.
B) Provide reassurance and offer grounding techniques to help the client reconnect to the present.
C) Ask the client to describe the flashback in detail to process the trauma.
D) Avoid discussing the flashback with the client to reduce distress.

62. Case Scenario - Multiple Response
A nurse is caring for a client diagnosed with a personality disorder who demonstrates chronic feelings of emptiness and difficulty with self-identity. Which interventions should the nurse prioritize? (Select all that apply.)
A) Set clear, consistent boundaries for behavior.
B) Focus on increasing the client's self-esteem.
C) Encourage the client to engage in therapy that addresses identity issues.

D) Provide frequent reassurance to help stabilize the client's emotions.

E) Encourage the client to take responsibility for their behaviors.

63. Multiple Choice

A nurse is providing education to a client diagnosed with generalized anxiety disorder (GAD). Which of the following statements indicates that the client understands the teaching about managing anxiety?

A) "I should try to avoid all stressful situations to keep my anxiety under control."

B) "I can use deep breathing exercises when I feel anxious."

C) "I should ignore my worries and hope they go away."

D) "Taking medication will eliminate my anxiety completely."

64. Case Scenario - Multiple Response

A nurse is caring for a client diagnosed with anorexia nervosa. The client has expressed a desire to begin treatment. Which interventions should the nurse implement to support the client? (Select all that apply.)

A) Offer frequent snacks and small, frequent meals.

B) Establish a structured eating plan to ensure nutritional intake.

C) Avoid discussing food and weight to prevent triggering anxiety.

D) Encourage the client to take control of meal planning and decisions.

E) Monitor the client's weight regularly and ensure that they are meeting targets.

65. Multiple Choice

A nurse is caring for a client diagnosed with bipolar disorder during a manic episode. The client is engaging in reckless spending and making impulsive decisions. Which intervention should the nurse prioritize?

A) Encourage the client to make decisions with input from family members.

B) Offer a calming environment to reduce the client's level of stimulation.

C) Set firm limits on the client's behavior and offer redirection when needed.

D) Allow the client to express their feelings freely without interruption.

66. Case Scenario - Multiple Response

A nurse is caring for a client diagnosed with major depressive disorder who is beginning antidepressant therapy. The client expresses concern about potential side effects. Which of the following side effects should the nurse discuss with the client? (Select all that apply.)
A) Nausea and gastrointestinal upset
B) Sedation and drowsiness
C) Sexual dysfunction
D) Increased energy and hyperactivity
E) Weight loss

67. Multiple Choice
A nurse is working with a client diagnosed with a substance use disorder who has been abstinent for 3 weeks. The client expresses a desire to return to drinking "socially." Which response by the nurse is most appropriate?
A) "It is possible to drink in moderation if you have been sober for a few weeks."
B) "Drinking socially is not safe for someone with your history of alcohol use."
C) "You should never drink again to avoid relapse."
D) "Have you considered joining a support group to help with your desire to drink?"

68. Case Scenario - Multiple Response
A nurse is caring for a client diagnosed with obsessive-compulsive disorder (OCD). The client is engaging in repetitive hand-washing rituals. Which interventions should the nurse prioritize? (Select all that apply.)
A) Encourage the client to stop the hand-washing behavior immediately.
B) Set a time limit for the hand-washing ritual and gradually reduce it.
C) Provide a calm and structured environment to reduce anxiety.
D) Use cognitive-behavioral therapy (CBT) to help the client challenge obsessive thoughts.
E) Allow the client to complete the hand-washing ritual to avoid anxiety.

69. Multiple Choice
A nurse is caring for a client diagnosed with borderline personality disorder. The client frequently tests the boundaries of the nurse-client relationship by displaying manipulative behavior. Which intervention should the nurse prioritize?
A) Encourage the client to express their feelings in a safe and non-destructive manner.
B) Set clear, firm boundaries for behavior and maintain consistency.
C) Focus on improving the client's self-esteem through positive reinforcement.
D) Avoid discussing feelings of manipulation with the client to reduce conflict.

70. Case Scenario - Multiple Response

A nurse is caring for a client diagnosed with schizophrenia. The client is refusing to take prescribed medication due to a belief that the medication is part of a conspiracy. Which of the following interventions should the nurse implement? (Select all that apply.)
A) Respect the client's refusal to take medication and provide support.
B) Explain the purpose of the medication and its benefits in simple terms.
C) Offer medication in a non-coercive, respectful manner.
D) Encourage the client to speak with their family about medication.
E) Acknowledge the client's feelings and provide education about the disorder.

71. Multiple Choice
A nurse is providing care for a client diagnosed with depression who has been prescribed a selective serotonin reuptake inhibitor (SSRI). The nurse is educating the client about potential side effects. Which of the following side effects should the nurse include in the teaching?
A) Insomnia
B) Hypertension
C) Weight loss
D) Sexual dysfunction

72. Case Scenario - Multiple Response
A nurse is caring for a client diagnosed with borderline personality disorder who is frequently engaging in self-harm behaviors. Which interventions should the nurse prioritize? (Select all that apply.)
A) Set clear, consistent boundaries with the client.
B) Encourage the client to talk about the self-harm behavior.
C) Validate the client's emotional experience.
D) Promote the development of healthy coping mechanisms.
E) Avoid confrontation regarding self-harm behaviors.

73. Multiple Choice
A nurse is assessing a client diagnosed with post-traumatic stress disorder (PTSD). The nurse notes that the client is avoiding reminders of the traumatic event and frequently experiences hyperarousal. Which of the following interventions is most appropriate?
A) Encourage the client to confront the trauma immediately.
B) Teach the client coping strategies such as relaxation techniques.
C) Suggest that the client avoid any discussion of the trauma to prevent distress.
D) Recommend that the client return to the situation where the trauma occurred.

74. Case Scenario - Multiple Response

A nurse is caring for a client diagnosed with schizophrenia. The client is exhibiting delusional thinking and disorganized speech. Which of the following interventions should the nurse implement? (Select all that apply.)

A) Offer reassurance that the delusions are not real.

B) Maintain a calm and non-threatening approach.

C) Focus on the client's reality rather than engaging in delusions.

D) Encourage the client to discuss their delusions in detail.

E) Provide a structured, predictable environment to reduce confusion.

75. Multiple Choice

A nurse is caring for a client with obsessive-compulsive disorder (OCD) who is engaging in repetitive checking behaviors. The nurse should prioritize which of the following interventions?

A) Allow the client to complete the checking behavior to prevent anxiety.

B) Encourage the client to stop the checking behavior immediately.

C) Set limits on the checking behavior and gradually reduce the time spent on it.

D) Ignore the behavior and allow the client to manage it independently.

NGN NCLEX PSYCHOSOCIAL INTEGRITY ANSWERS

1. Answer: C) Ensure a calm, quiet environment.
Rationale: The first priority in the care of a client with schizophrenia exhibiting disorganized speech and delusions is to ensure a calm and quiet environment. This will reduce stimulation, which can exacerbate the client's symptoms.

2. Answer: A) Family history of depression, B) Recent loss of a close friend, D) Chronic physical illness, E) History of self-harm behavior
Rationale: Risk factors for suicide in adolescents include a family history of depression, a recent loss, chronic physical illness, and a history of self-harm behavior. Participation in a support group is generally protective and does not increase risk.

3. Answer: Cognitive Behavioral Therapy (CBT)
Rationale: Cognitive Behavioral Therapy (CBT) is an evidence-based treatment for panic disorder, helping clients recognize and change thought patterns that contribute to anxiety.

4. Answer: A) Flashbacks
Rationale: Flashbacks are a hallmark symptom of PTSD, where clients relive traumatic events. Grandiosity, hallucinations, and euphoria are more commonly associated with other psychiatric conditions.

5. Answer: A) Administer prescribed mood stabilizers, B) Set limits on the client's behavior in a firm, consistent manner, D) Ensure the client's environment is safe and free from stimuli that may escalate behaviors
Rationale: During a manic episode, it is crucial to administer mood stabilizers as prescribed, set firm limits to control impulsivity, and provide a safe environment. Encouraging social activities is inappropriate during this phase, and while rest is important, safety is the priority.

6. Answer:
Assess the severity of the anxiety.
Encourage deep breathing exercises.
Offer a safe and quiet environment.
Administer prescribed anti-anxiety medication.
Rationale: The first step is to assess the severity of anxiety, then provide calming interventions like deep breathing, followed by creating a calm environment, and medication administration if needed.

7. Answer: A) Set strict, non-negotiable limits.

Rationale: Clients with borderline personality disorder often engage in splitting, where they view others as all good or all bad. Setting strict, clear limits helps to manage this behavior and maintain a stable therapeutic relationship.

8. Answer: C) Exploring the meaning of the compulsions in therapy.
Rationale: Cognitive-behavioral therapy (CBT) is effective for OCD, which often involves exploring and challenging the meaning of compulsive behaviors. Ignoring compulsions or providing reinforcement for rituals is not effective in treatment.

9. Answer: A) Weight gain, B) Sexual dysfunction, C) Drowsiness
Rationale: Common side effects of antidepressants include weight gain, sexual dysfunction, and drowsiness. Hypertension and tremors are not typically associated with antidepressant medications.

10. Answer: A) Borderline personality disorder
Rationale: Clients with borderline personality disorder often experience intense emotions, impulsivity, and difficulty with relationships. The traits described in the question align with borderline personality disorder.

11. Answer: A) GAD is characterized by excessive worry lasting at least 6 months.
Rationale: Generalized anxiety disorder is characterized by excessive, uncontrollable worry lasting for at least 6 months, often accompanied by physical symptoms such as restlessness, fatigue, and muscle tension.

12. Answer: A) Encourage the client to participate in activities that stimulate cognitive function, B) Create a structured daily routine for the client, C) Provide the client with memory aids, such as a calendar or a clock
Rationale: For clients with neurocognitive disorders, promoting cognitive stimulation, providing structure, and using memory aids are effective strategies. Limiting social interactions and isolating the client may contribute to further cognitive decline.

13. Answer: 4 to 6 weeks
Rationale: Antidepressants typically take 4 to 6 weeks to show full therapeutic effects, and clients should be informed about the importance of continuing the medication even if they do not notice immediate improvement.

14. Answer: B) "It is important to continue taking the medication as prescribed to maintain the improvement."
Rationale: It is important for clients to continue taking antidepressants as prescribed even after they feel better, as premature discontinuation can lead to a relapse of symptoms.

15. Answer: A) Motivational interviewing, B) Referral to a substance abuse counselor, C) Encouraging self-help group participation, such as AA

Rationale: Motivational interviewing helps clients explore and resolve ambivalence about behavior change. Referring to a counselor and encouraging self-help groups like Alcoholics Anonymous (AA) provide ongoing support. Confrontation is not typically helpful for individuals with substance use disorders, and immediate discharge is not appropriate.

16. Answer:

Provide reassurance and a calm presence.

Ensure a quiet, low-stimulation environment.

Encourage slow, deep breathing.

Assess the client's physical condition to rule out medical causes.

Rationale: The first priority during a panic attack is providing reassurance and creating a calm environment. Breathing exercises can help manage symptoms, and a physical assessment is necessary if the symptoms could be related to a medical issue.

17. Answer: B) Respect the client's wishes to avoid discussing the trauma.

Rationale: In PTSD, it is important to respect the client's boundaries. Pushing them to discuss trauma prematurely can cause further harm. Trauma-focused therapy may be appropriate at a later stage, after establishing a therapeutic relationship.

18. Answer: A) Develop a healthy eating plan, B) Monitor the client's weight and vital signs regularly, D) Educate the client about the physical effects of malnutrition, E) Offer non-judgmental support and encouragement

Rationale: A healthy eating plan, regular monitoring, and education about the effects of malnutrition are important components of care for anorexia nervosa. Group therapy is often beneficial, so avoiding it would not be appropriate.

19. Answer: C) Histrionic personality disorder

Rationale: Histrionic personality disorder is characterized by excessive emotionality and attention-seeking behavior. Individuals with this disorder often use dramatic gestures to gain attention.

20. Answer: C) "CBT will help you identify and change negative thought patterns."

Rationale: Cognitive-behavioral therapy (CBT) helps clients identify and change negative thought patterns and behaviors, which is especially useful for managing symptoms of OCD.

21. Answer: B) "I'm just so tired of feeling like this."

Rationale: This statement suggests a sense of hopelessness and emotional exhaustion, which is a key warning sign of suicidal ideation. The other statements do not indicate an immediate risk for suicide.

22. Answer: A) Teach the client deep breathing techniques, C) Provide reassurance and a calm presence during an anxiety attack, D) Help the client identify triggers that contribute to anxiety, E) Administer anti-anxiety medication as prescribed
Rationale: Deep breathing techniques, providing reassurance, and helping identify triggers are all important interventions for managing panic attacks. Avoiding stressful situations entirely is not practical, and medication may be needed but should not be the only approach.

23. Answer: 4 to 6 weeks
Rationale: Antipsychotic medications can take 4 to 6 weeks to achieve therapeutic effects. It is important for clients to adhere to the medication regimen even if they do not feel immediate improvement.

24. Answer: A) Self-induced vomiting after eating large amounts of food
Rationale: A hallmark behavior of bulimia nervosa is binge eating followed by compensatory behaviors such as self-induced vomiting. The other behaviors listed are more characteristic of anorexia nervosa or are not specific to bulimia nervosa.

25. Answer: A) Set clear, consistent boundaries for behavior, D) Remain firm and non-judgmental in interactions with the client
Rationale: Clients with antisocial personality disorder need clear and consistent boundaries. Being firm and non-judgmental is essential to maintaining a therapeutic relationship. Confrontation may escalate conflict, and ignoring violations would undermine the therapeutic process.

26. Answer:
Ensure a calm, quiet environment.
Assess the client's level of anxiety.
Encourage slow, deep breathing.
Provide reassurance and comfort.
Rationale: First, create a calm environment, then assess the client's level of anxiety. Breathing exercises help manage anxiety, and reassurance can be offered once the client is calmer.

27. Answer: C) Cognitive distortions

Rationale: Feelings of worthlessness are a form of cognitive distortion that can occur in depression. This distortion causes the individual to have negative thoughts about themselves.

28. Answer: A) Cognitive Behavioral Therapy (CBT), B) Deep breathing exercises, C) Progressive muscle relaxation, E) Regular physical exercise
Rationale: Cognitive Behavioral Therapy (CBT), deep breathing, progressive muscle relaxation, and regular exercise are all effective techniques for managing anxiety. Avoiding anxiety-provoking situations can contribute to avoidance behavior, which is counterproductive.

29. Answer: B) The presence of two or more distinct personality states
Rationale: Dissociative identity disorder is characterized by the presence of two or more distinct personality states. Memory loss (dissociation) is also a key feature, but the primary defining characteristic is the existence of multiple identities.

30. Answer: B) Set clear and consistent boundaries for behavior.
Rationale: Setting clear and consistent boundaries is essential in managing BPD because clients with this disorder often test limits and may engage in manipulative behaviors. While praise and supervision are important, boundaries are critical to the therapeutic relationship.

31. Answer: B) Validate the client's feelings of fear and avoidance.
Rationale: It is important to validate the client's feelings and provide a safe space for them. Confronting traumatic memories should gradually be done in therapy under the guidance of a professional. Suppression or encouragement to forget can cause further distress.

32. Answer: A) The client is willing to express feelings about body image, B) The client agrees to a higher caloric intake despite initial resistance, C) The client exhibits less concern about food and weight, E) The client reports feeling more in control of their emotions
Rationale: Progress in therapy for eating disorders includes the client acknowledging body image concerns, accepting higher caloric intake, and showing less preoccupation with food and weight. Continuing purging behaviors reflects a lack of progress.

33. Answer: D) Sexual dysfunction
Rationale: Sexual dysfunction is a common side effect of SSRIs. Sedation may occur but is less common, and weight loss or increased libido are not typical side effects of SSRIs.

34. Answer: A) Encourage regular exercise, B) Recommend an increase in social activities, C) Assist the client in identifying and challenging negative thoughts, E) Administer prescribed antidepressants

Rationale: Encouraging exercise, social interaction, cognitive-behavioral therapy (CBT), and antidepressant medication are all effective strategies for managing depression. Isolation is not recommended, as it can worsen symptoms.

35. Answer: relaxation techniques
Rationale: Relaxation techniques, such as deep breathing and progressive muscle relaxation, are effective methods to reduce anxiety in clients with GAD.

36. Answer: B) Dehydration can increase the risk for lithium toxicity.
Rationale: Dehydration can lead to lithium toxicity because it affects the kidneys' ability to excrete lithium. Ongoing monitoring of renal function and lithium levels is necessary to ensure safety.

37. Answer: A) Establish trust by being consistent and honest with the client, B) Avoid challenging the client's delusions directly, E) Provide clear and simple explanations of procedures
Rationale: Establishing trust, avoiding direct confrontation with delusions, and offering clear explanations are essential when working with clients with paranoia. Reassurance should be offered cautiously, as it may increase suspicion, and confronting delusions in therapy may not be effective.

38. Answer: B) A need for admiration and a lack of empathy
Rationale: Clients with narcissistic personality disorder often exhibit a grandiose sense of self-importance, a need for excessive admiration, and a lack of empathy for others.

39. Answer: A) Set limits on the amount of time spent on hand-washing rituals, C) Provide a calm environment to minimize anxiety triggers, D) Teach relaxation techniques to reduce the need for rituals, E) Focus on modifying maladaptive behaviors with exposure and response prevention
Rationale: Setting limits, minimizing anxiety triggers, teaching relaxation techniques, and using cognitive-behavioral therapy (CBT) such as exposure and response prevention are appropriate interventions for OCD. Encouraging the client to complete rituals is not helpful and may reinforce the behavior.

40. Answer: B) Use relaxation techniques to manage increased energy levels.
Rationale: During a manic episode, relaxation techniques are helpful in managing excess energy. Stimulating activities can exacerbate mania, and it is essential to set limits and avoid making decisions during this time to prevent risky behaviors.

41. Answer: B) Establish clear, firm, and consistent boundaries.

Rationale: Clients with antisocial personality disorder often engage in manipulative behaviors. Establishing clear and consistent boundaries is essential to maintaining a therapeutic relationship and reducing manipulation.

42. Answer: A) Monitor the client's weight and vital signs daily, C) Provide a structured meal plan with small, frequent meals, D) Offer praise for any attempts to eat, regardless of the quantity, E) Encourage family involvement in the treatment process
Rationale: Monitoring the client's weight and vital signs daily is important to track physical progress. Providing a structured meal plan, offering praise for small successes, and involving family in treatment are all helpful strategies for clients with anorexia nervosa.

43. Answer: D) Set realistic goals for small, achievable tasks.
Rationale: Clients with psychomotor retardation often experience slowed movements and difficulty completing tasks. Setting small, achievable goals helps the client feel successful and promotes engagement in their care.

44. Answer: A) Maintain a calm and non-threatening demeanor, C) Provide distraction through activities to help redirect the client's focus, E) Establish a routine to provide structure and reduce confusion
Rationale: Clients with hallucinations benefit from a calm demeanor, distractions, and structured routines. Encouraging the client to challenge hallucinations may lead to further distress, and discussing hallucinations in detail could reinforce them.

45. Answer: 4 to 6 weeks
Rationale: SSRIs can take 4 to 6 weeks to achieve full therapeutic effects, so it is important for clients to continue their medication as prescribed even if they do not experience immediate improvement.

46. Answer: B) Set firm limits on risky behaviors while maintaining a calm demeanor.
Rationale: During a manic episode, it is essential to set firm limits on risky behaviors to protect the client from harm. Maintaining a calm demeanor helps reduce agitation and prevent escalation.

47. Answer: A) Teach the client relaxation techniques, such as deep breathing, C) Provide the client with information about the symptoms of anxiety, D) Recommend cognitive-behavioral therapy (CBT) to address negative thought patterns, E) Focus on positive reinforcement of adaptive coping strategies
Rationale: Teaching relaxation techniques, providing psychoeducation, recommending CBT, and reinforcing adaptive coping strategies are all effective ways to help manage generalized

anxiety disorder. Avoiding stressful situations may not be practical and could reinforce avoidance behavior.

48. Answer: C) Set clear and firm boundaries to prevent manipulation.
Rationale: Setting clear and firm boundaries is essential when working with clients who have borderline personality disorder to prevent manipulation and provide structure. While other interventions are also important, boundary setting is the priority.

49. Answer: A) Discuss the steps involved in recovery and help set realistic short-term goals, B) Provide information about the effects of alcohol on the body to reinforce the importance of quitting, C) Encourage participation in support groups, such as Alcoholics Anonymous (AA), E) Offer emotional support and express confidence in the client's ability to succeed
Rationale: Discussing recovery steps, providing education, encouraging support group participation, and offering emotional support are all critical components of care for clients in rehabilitation for substance use disorder. Pushing the client to quit immediately can increase stress and resistance.

50. Answer: C) Tardive dyskinesia
Rationale: Tardive dyskinesia is a potential side effect of long-term antipsychotic medication use. It is characterized by involuntary movements, typically of the face or extremities. Monitoring for this side effect is crucial in clients receiving antipsychotic therapy.

51. Answer: B) Distract the client with activities to redirect their focus.
Rationale: Clients experiencing auditory hallucinations may benefit from redirection to activities that engage their attention and help distract them from the voices. Arguing with the voices or validating them can reinforce the hallucinations, and discontinuing medication could lead to a relapse.

52. Answer: B) Set small, achievable goals for the client, C) Offer frequent emotional support and validation, D) Suggest the client avoid making major life decisions until they feel better
Rationale: Setting small goals, offering emotional support, and avoiding major life decisions during a depressive episode help manage symptoms. While encouraging the client to engage in enjoyable activities is important, it should be done gradually and when the client is ready.

53. Answer: B) Set a time limit for the hand-washing ritual and gradually reduce it.
Rationale: Setting a time limit for compulsive behaviors and gradually reducing the time spent on them is an effective approach to managing OCD. Encouraging the client to stop the behavior abruptly can lead to increased anxiety and resistance.

54. Answer: A) Set clear, consistent boundaries for behavior, C) Validate the client's feelings and help them express emotions in healthy ways
Rationale: Setting clear boundaries and validating the client's emotions while helping them express themselves in healthy ways are essential for managing impulsive behaviors. Confrontation may escalate emotions, and avoiding triggers is not a practical long-term solution.

55. Answer: lithium toxicity
Rationale: Lithium toxicity is a serious side effect, and clients should be educated about the signs, such as tremors, confusion, and gastrointestinal distress. Regular monitoring of blood levels is important to avoid toxicity.

56. Answer: B) The client will identify triggers of anxiety and use coping strategies.
Rationale: The goal for clients with GAD is to help them identify anxiety triggers and develop coping strategies to manage their anxiety. Completely eliminating worry or avoiding stressors is unrealistic and not helpful.

57. Answer: A) Establish a supportive and trusting relationship with the client, C) Remove any potentially harmful objects from the client's environment, D) Encourage the client to verbalize thoughts about suicide
Rationale: Establishing trust, ensuring safety by removing harmful objects, and encouraging the client to discuss suicidal thoughts are essential interventions. Involvement in group therapy may not be appropriate during a crisis, and limiting social interactions may lead to further isolation.

58. Answer: B) Depersonalization-derealization disorder
Rationale: Depersonalization-derealization disorder is characterized by periods of feeling detached from one's body or experiences, often described as "losing time" or feeling unreal. This is distinct from dissociative identity disorder, PTSD, and somatic symptom disorder.

59. Answer: A) Administer prescribed medications, such as benzodiazepines, to manage withdrawal symptoms, B) Provide frequent monitoring of vital signs to detect complications, D) Educate the client about the importance of continued sobriety after withdrawal
Rationale: Medications such as benzodiazepines are commonly prescribed to manage alcohol withdrawal symptoms, and frequent monitoring of vital signs is necessary to detect complications like seizures. Education about long-term sobriety is important, but reassurance alone is insufficient for managing withdrawal.

60. Answer: B) The client is at an increased risk for suicide due to higher energy levels.

Rationale: Clients who begin to feel more energized but still experience sadness and hopelessness may be at an increased risk for suicide. The increase in energy may allow them to act on suicidal thoughts. Close monitoring is needed during this time.

61. Answer: B) Provide reassurance and offer grounding techniques to help the client reconnect to the present.
Rationale: During a flashback, it is important to offer reassurance and grounding techniques to help the client reconnect to the present moment. Encouraging the client to relive the trauma or asking them to describe it in detail can increase distress.

62. Answer: A) Set clear, consistent boundaries for behavior, C) Encourage the client to engage in therapy that addresses identity issues, E) Encourage the client to take responsibility for their behaviors
Rationale: Clients with personality disorders often benefit from clear boundaries, therapy that focuses on self-identity, and encouragement to take responsibility for their behaviors. Focusing too much on reassurance can reinforce emotional instability, and self-esteem issues should be addressed through therapeutic interventions.

63. Answer: B) "I can use deep breathing exercises when I feel anxious."
Rationale: Deep breathing exercises are a helpful technique for managing anxiety. Avoiding stress entirely is unrealistic and ignoring worries or expecting medication to completely eliminate anxiety are not effective approaches to managing GAD.

64. Answer: A) Offer frequent snacks and small, frequent meals, B) Establish a structured eating plan to ensure nutritional intake, E) Monitor the client's weight regularly and ensure that they are meeting targets
Rationale: Frequent snacks and a structured eating plan are essential for addressing nutritional needs. Monitoring weight is important for tracking progress. Avoiding discussions about food and weight may reinforce the disorder, and giving the client too much control over meal planning is not appropriate during treatment.

65. Answer: C) Set firm limits on the client's behavior and offer redirection when needed.
Rationale: Setting firm limits and offering redirection are essential during a manic episode to manage impulsivity and prevent harmful behaviors. A calming environment and decision-making input can help, but firm boundaries are critical to ensuring safety.

66. Answer: A) Nausea and gastrointestinal upset, B) Sedation and drowsiness, C) Sexual dysfunction

Rationale: Common side effects of antidepressants include gastrointestinal upset, sedation, and sexual dysfunction. Increased energy and hyperactivity are typically not associated with antidepressants, and weight loss is not a common side effect.

67. Answer: B) "Drinking socially is not safe for someone with your history of alcohol use."
Rationale: For clients with a substance use disorder, drinking socially is risky and could lead to relapse. The nurse should provide education about the risks of returning to alcohol use and emphasize the importance of continued sobriety.

68. Answer: B) Set a time limit for the hand-washing ritual and gradually reduce it, C) Provide a calm and structured environment to reduce anxiety, D) Use cognitive-behavioral therapy (CBT) to help the client challenge obsessive thoughts
Rationale: Setting time limits and gradually reducing rituals, providing a calm environment, and using CBT are evidence-based interventions for managing OCD. Allowing the client to continue the rituals can reinforce the behavior and increase anxiety.

69. Answer: B) Set clear, firm boundaries for behavior and maintain consistency.
Rationale: Clients with borderline personality disorder benefit from clear, consistent boundaries to manage manipulative behaviors and establish a stable therapeutic relationship. Encouraging healthy expression of feelings is important, but boundary setting is the priority.

70. Answer: B) Explain the purpose of the medication and its benefits in simple terms, C) Offer medication in a non-coercive, respectful manner, E) Acknowledge the client's feelings and provide education about the disorder
Rationale: The nurse should provide education about the medication and its benefits, offer it in a respectful manner, and acknowledge the client's feelings. Coercion or dismissing the client's beliefs may damage trust and hinder engagement in treatment.

71. Answer: D) Sexual dysfunction
Rationale: Sexual dysfunction is a common side effect of SSRIs. Insomnia, hypertension, and weight loss are not typically associated with SSRIs.

72. Answer: A) Set clear, consistent boundaries with the client, C) Validate the client's emotional experience, D) Promote the development of healthy coping mechanisms
Rationale: Setting clear boundaries, validating emotions, and encouraging healthy coping mechanisms are key interventions for clients with borderline personality disorder. Confrontation should be avoided, and discussing self-harm in a non-judgmental way is appropriate to promote safety.

73. Answer: B) Teach the client coping strategies such as relaxation techniques.
Rationale: Teaching coping strategies like relaxation techniques is an appropriate intervention for managing hyperarousal and avoidance behaviors in clients with PTSD. Confronting trauma too soon or encouraging avoidance can worsen symptoms.

74. Answer: B) Maintain a calm and non-threatening approach, C) Focus on the client's reality rather than engaging in delusions, E) Provide a structured, predictable environment to reduce confusion
Rationale: Maintaining a calm approach and focusing on the client's reality are essential in managing delusions and disorganized speech. Providing structure and predictability helps reduce confusion. Engaging in delusions or offering reassurance that they are not real can escalate the situation.

75. Answer: C) Set limits on the checking behavior and gradually reduce the time spent on it.
Rationale: Gradually reducing the time spent on compulsive behaviors and setting clear limits are key interventions for managing OCD. Allowing the behavior to continue or encouraging the client to stop abruptly may increase anxiety and resistance.

NGN NCLEX BASIC CARE AND COMFORT QUESTIONS

Multiple Choice
1. A nurse is assisting a client with low vision to navigate their home safely. Which intervention is most appropriate?
   A. Recommend rearranging furniture to create clear pathways.
   B. Suggest using a walker for balance.
   C. Provide a hearing aid to enhance environmental awareness.
   D. Teach the client to use a blood glucose monitor.

Multiple Response
2. A nurse is developing a care plan for a client with a physical impairment due to paralysis. Which interventions should the nurse include? (Select all that apply.)
   A. Collaborate with a physical therapist for passive range-of-motion exercises.
   B. Teach the client to use a wheelchair for mobility.
   C. Recommend installing grab bars in the bathroom.
   D. Administer a hearing aid fitting.
   E. Provide counseling to address emotional well-being.

Case Scenario
3. Scenario: A 45-year-old client with diabetic neuropathy reports difficulty feeling their feet, increasing their fall risk. The nurse performs a sensory assessment.
   Question: Which tool or method should the nurse prioritize to assess sensory deficits?
   A. Blood pressure monitoring
   B. Monofilament testing
   C. Reflex hammer testing
   D. Pulse oximetry

Drop Down
4. A nurse is teaching a client with hearing impairment to communicate effectively. Select the most appropriate strategy from the drop-down menu:
   Provide a magnifying glass
   Coordinate with a sign language interpreter
   Recommend a screen reader
   Teach tactile navigation

Drop Down

5. A nurse is educating a client with a recent amputation on using a prosthetic limb. Drag and drop the steps in the correct order for safe prosthetic use:
   A. Check the prosthetic for proper fit.
   B. Assess the residual limb for skin integrity.
   C. Demonstrate how to don the prosthetic.
   D. Teach the client to navigate stairs with the prosthetic.

Multiple Choice
6. Which action best promotes emotional well-being for a client with a sensory impairment?
   A. Restrict family visits to reduce stress.
   B. Encourage participation in a support group.
   C. Limit the use of assistive devices.
   D. Avoid discussing the impairment.

Multiple Response
7. A nurse is advocating for a client with a physical impairment. Which resources should the nurse help the client access? (Select all that apply.)
   A. Vocational training programs
   B. Accessible housing services
   C. High-protein diet plans
   D. Legal protection services
   E. Advanced surgical consultations

Case Scenario
8. Scenario: A client with blindness is learning to use a white cane for mobility. Question: What is the nurse's priority when teaching this client?
   A. Ensure the cane is the correct length for the client's height.
   B. Teach the client to read braille.
   C. Recommend a hearing test.
   D. Provide a wheelchair for backup mobility.

Drop Down
9. A client with a spinal cord injury requires mobility assistance. Select the most appropriate assistive device from the drop-down menu:
   Hearing aid
   Wheelchair
   Magnifier
   Blood glucose monitor

Multiple Choice

10. What is the primary goal of environmental modifications for a client with a physical impairment?
    A. Improve aesthetic appeal of the home
    B. Reduce fall risks and promote independence
    C. Enhance auditory stimulation
    D. Increase medication adherence

Multiple Choice
11. A nurse is assessing a client for alterations in bowel elimination. Which finding indicates a need for further evaluation?
    A. Regular bowel movements every 2 days
    B. Hard, dry stools with straining
    C. Clear urine output of 1500 mL/day
    D. High-fiber diet intake

Multiple Response
12. A nurse is collecting a health history for a client with urinary incontinence. Which factors should be included in the assessment? (Select all that apply.)
    A. Frequency of urine output
    B. Use of diuretics
    C. Recent weight changes
    D. History of urinary tract infections
    E. Favorite hobbies

Case Scenario
13. Scenario: A 60-year-old client reports frequent diarrhea after starting a new medication.
    Question: What should the nurse do first?
    A. Administer an antidiarrheal medication.
    B. Collaborate with the physician to review the medication.
    C. Recommend a low-fiber diet.
    D. Perform a bladder scan.

Drop Down
14. A client with constipation is prescribed a laxative. Select the most appropriate nursing action from the drop-down menu:

Encourage reduced fluid intake
Increase dietary fiber intake
Administer an antidiarrheal agent
Restrict physical activity

Drag and Drop
15. A nurse is planning care for a client with urinary retention. Drag and drop the interventions in the correct order of priority:
A. Administer a prescribed bladder relaxant.
B. Perform a bladder scan to assess residual urine.
C. Encourage adequate hydration.
D. Insert a catheter if necessary.

Multiple Choice
16. Which diagnostic test is most appropriate for evaluating bowel elimination issues?
A. Urinalysis
B. Stool test for occult blood
C. Blood glucose test
D. Electrocardiogram

Multiple Response
17. A nurse is promoting healthy habits for a client with bowel elimination issues. Which recommendations should be included? (Select all that apply.)
A. Increase dietary fiber intake
B. Encourage adequate hydration
C. Restrict physical activity
D. Use laxatives daily
E. Incorporate regular exercise

Case Scenario
18. Scenario: A client with an ostomy reports skin irritation around the site.
Question: What is the nurse's best action?
A. Apply a moisturizer to the irritated area.
B. Clean the area with a pH-balanced cleanser.
C. Restrict fluid intake to reduce output.
D. Change the ostomy bag less frequently.

Drop Down

19. A client with urinary incontinence is starting a bladder training program. Select the primary goal from the drop-down menu:
Increase urine output
Establish regular elimination patterns
Reduce dietary fiber intake
Limit mobility.

Multiple Choice
20. What is the nurse's role in managing a client with an ostomy?
    A. Restrict all dietary changes
    B. Provide education on ostomy care
    C. Avoid skin assessments
    D. Limit family involvement

Multiple Choice
21. A nurse is preparing to perform bladder irrigation. What is the priority action?
    A. Use warm water for the irrigation solution.
    B. Maintain aseptic technique.
    C. Administer the solution rapidly.
    D. Avoid documenting the procedure.

Multiple Response
22. Which supplies are necessary for performing ear irrigation? (Select all that apply.)
    A. Warm saline solution
    B. Kidney-shaped basin
    C. Sterile gloves
    D. Cold water
    E. Bulb syringe

Case Scenario
23. Scenario: A client requires eye irrigation after a chemical splash.
    Question: How should the nurse direct the irrigation solution?
    A. From the outer corner to the inner corner of the eye
    B. From the inner corner to the outer corner of the eye
    C. Directly into the pupil
    D. Across both eyes simultaneously

Drop Down
24. During bladder irrigation, the nurse observes the outflow. Select the finding that requires immediate action from the drop-down menu:
Clear outflow

Presence of blood clots
Mild patient discomfort
Consistent flow rate

Drag and Drop

25. A nurse is performing ear irrigation. Drag and drop the steps in the correct order:
    A. Dry the ear with a clean towel.
    B. Direct warm saline into the ear canal.
    C. Position the client upright with a towel over the shoulder.
    D. Place a kidney-shaped basin to catch fluid.

Multiple Choice

26. What is the purpose of warming the irrigation solution to body temperature for ear irrigation?
    A. To enhance wax removal
    B. To prevent dizziness or discomfort
    C. To sterilize the solution
    D. To increase solution viscosity

Multiple Response

27. Which actions should a nurse take after completing bladder irrigation? (Select all that apply.)
    A. Document the procedure and findings.
    B. Monitor for patient discomfort.
    C. Discard the irrigation solution.
    D. Restrict fluid intake.
    E. Assess the outflow for clarity.

Case Scenario

28. Scenario: A client undergoing eye irrigation reports persistent irritation after the procedure.
    Question: What should the nurse do next?
    A. Apply a cold compress to the eye.
    B. Assess the eye for signs of injury.
    C. Administer an oral analgesic.
    D. Restrict the client's vision temporarily.

Drop Down

29. A nurse is preparing for bladder irrigation. Select the most appropriate solution from the drop-down menu:

Tap water
Sterile saline
Warm saline
Glucose solution

30. Multiple Choice
    What is the nurse's priority when performing any irrigation procedure?
    A. Complete the procedure quickly
    B. Ensure patient comfort and safety
    C. Use non-sterile equipment
    D. Limit patient communication

Multiple Choice
31. A nurse is performing a skin assessment. Which finding indicates a risk for pressure injury?
    A. Smooth, hydrated skin
    B. Redness over bony prominences
    C. Normal skin temperature
    D. Elastic skin turgor

Multiple Response
32. Which interventions should a nurse implement to maintain skin integrity for a bedridden client? (Select all that apply.)
    A. Reposition the client every 2 hours.
    B. Use harsh soaps for hygiene.
    C. Apply moisturizers to dry skin.
    D. Use pressure-relieving mattresses.
    E. Restrict fluid intake.

Case Scenario
33. Scenario: A client with limited mobility develops a stage 1 pressure injury.
    Question: What is the nurse's priority intervention?
    A. Apply a hydrocolloid dressing.
    B. Increase repositioning frequency.
    C. Administer an antibiotic cream.
    D. Restrict the client's movement.

Drop Down
34. A nurse is assessing a client's skin. Select the tool most appropriate for evaluating pressure ulcer risk from the drop-down menu:

Blood glucose monitor
Braden Scale
Pulse oximeter
Reflex hammer

Drag and Drop
35. A nurse is caring for a client with dry skin. Drag and drop the interventions in the correct order of priority:
    A. Apply a moisturizer.
    B. Assess skin for cracking.
    C. Clean the skin with a pH-balanced cleanser.
    D. Educate the client on hydration.

Multiple Choice
36. What is the purpose of using pH-balanced cleansers for skin hygiene?
    A. To enhance skin color
    B. To prevent stripping natural oils
    C. To increase skin temperature
    D. To reduce skin elasticity

Multiple Response
37. Which signs should a nurse document during a skin assessment? (Select all that apply.)
    A. Skin discoloration
    B. Presence of wounds
    C. Normal heart rate
    D. Dry, cracked skin
    E. Edema

Case Scenario
38. Scenario: A client with diabetes has dry, cracked skin on their feet.
    Question: What should the nurse teach the client to prevent complications?
    A. Soak feet in hot water daily.
    B. Apply moisturizer regularly.
    C. Wear tight-fitting shoes.
    D. Avoid self-inspection of feet.

Drop Down
39. A client is at risk for skin breakdown. Select the most effective preventive measure from the drop-down menu:

Restrict fluid intake
Use pressure-relieving cushions
Apply alcohol-based cleansers
Limit repositioning

Multiple Choice
40. Why is nutritional support important for maintaining skin integrity?
    A. It enhances skin color.
    B. It promotes skin repair and resilience.
    C. It reduces skin temperature.
    D. It limits skin hydration.

Multiple Choice
41. A nurse is applying a cast to a client's arm. What is the priority assessment before application?
    A. Check for skin integrity.
    B. Measure blood pressure.
    C. Assess respiratory rate.
    D. Evaluate hearing ability.

Multiple Response
42. Which actions should a nurse take when maintaining a client's brace? (Select all that apply.)
    A. Check for signs of wear.
    B. Clean the brace regularly.
    C. Restrict patient mobility.
    D. Inspect skin for irritation.
    E. Adjust the brace without physician approval.

43. Case Scenario
    Scenario: A client with a leg cast reports numbness in their toes.
    Question: What is the nurse's priority action?
    A. Elevate the leg further.
    B. Assess for neurovascular compromise.

C. Apply a warm compress.

D. Encourage ambulation.

Drop Down

44. A nurse is removing a splint. Select the most appropriate action from the drop-down menu:

Cut the splint with a cast cutter

Unfasten straps gently

Apply pressure to the limb

Use warm water to loosen the splint

Drag and Drop

45. A nurse is applying a traction system. Drag and drop the steps in the correct order:

A. Verify physician orders.

B. Assess the affected area for swelling.

C. Secure the traction weights.

D. Check alignment of the limb.

Multiple Choice

46. What should a nurse teach a client about caring for a removable brace?

A. Wear it only at night.

B. Clean it regularly to maintain hygiene.

C. Tighten it daily to ensure fit.

D. Avoid checking for skin irritation.

Multiple Response

47. Which findings during cast maintenance require immediate reporting? (Select all that apply.)

A. Normal skin temperature

B. Tingling in the affected limb

C. Discoloration of toes

D. Stable alignment of the cast

E. Swelling around the cast

Case Scenario

48. Scenario: A client with a new knee brace reports discomfort during ambulation.

Question: What should the nurse do first?

A. Remove the brace immediately.

B. Assess the fit of the brace.

C. Administer an analgesic.

D. Restrict all ambulation.

Drop Down

49. A nurse is preparing to apply a splint. Select the most important step from the drop-down menu:

Apply without padding

Ensure proper alignment

Use non-sterile materials

Restrict blood flow

Multiple Choice

50. What is the nurse's role after removing an orthopedic device?

A. Restrict all physical therapy.

B. Assess the area for skin irritation.

C. Avoid documenting the procedure.

D. Limit patient education.

Multiple Choice

51. A nurse is promoting circulation for a bedridden client. Which intervention is most effective?

A. Restrict fluid intake.

B. Perform passive range-of-motion exercises.

C. Apply cold compresses to limbs.

D. Limit repositioning.

Multiple Response

52. Which interventions promote circulation in a post-operative client? (Select all that apply.)

A. Encourage early ambulation.

B. Use sequential compression devices.

C. Restrict fluid intake.

D. Elevate the legs slightly.

E. Apply warm compresses.

Case Scenario

53. Scenario: A client recovering from hip surgery is at risk for deep vein thrombosis. Question: What is the nurse's priority intervention?

A. Administer a diuretic.

B. Encourage early ambulation.

C. Restrict leg elevation.

D. Apply a cold pack.

Drop Down

54. A nurse is using a mechanical device to promote circulation. Select the most appropriate device from the drop-down menu:

Hearing aid

Sequential compression device

Wheelchair

Magnifier

55. Drag and Drop

A nurse is assisting a client with limited mobility to promote circulation. Drag and drop the interventions in the correct order of priority:

A. Perform passive range-of-motion exercises.

B. Apply pneumatic compression stockings.

C. Reposition the client every 2 hours.

D. Encourage fluid intake.

56. Multiple Choice

Why is leg elevation used to promote circulation?

A. To reduce venous return

B. To increase swelling

C. To improve venous return

D. To restrict blood flow

57. Multiple Response

Which actions should a nurse take to promote circulation in a client with limited mobility? (Select all that apply.)

A. Perform active range-of-motion exercises.

B. Use compression garments.

C. Restrict fluid intake.

D. Encourage bedside exercises.

E. Monitor skin for complications.

Case Scenario

58. Scenario: A client with a history of venous insufficiency reports leg swelling.

Question: What should the nurse recommend?

A. Restrict all physical activity.

B. Elevate the legs slightly.

C. Apply a hot compress.

D. Limit hydration.

Drop Down

59. A nurse is promoting circulation for a client. Select the most appropriate nutritional advice from the drop-down menu:

Restrict all nutrients

Advise a diet rich in vascular health nutrients

Avoid protein intake

Limit vitamin intake

Multiple Choice

60. What is the primary benefit of sequential compression devices?

A. Enhance auditory stimulation

B. Promote blood flow

C. Reduce skin hydration

D. Limit joint mobility

Multiple Choice

61. A nurse is assessing a client's pain. Which question best evaluates the quality of pain?

A. "When did the pain begin?"

B. "Can you describe what the pain feels like?"

C. "How long does the pain last?"

D. "Where is the pain located?"

Multiple Response

62. Which non-verbal indicators should a nurse observe for pain in a non-verbal client? (Select all that apply.)

A. Facial grimacing

B. Normal heart rate

C. Guarding behavior

D. Restlessness

E. Stable blood pressure

Case Scenario

63. Scenario: A client rates their pain as 8/10 after surgery.

Question: What is the nurse's priority intervention?

A. Encourage distraction with music.

B. Administer a prescribed opioid.

C. Apply a cold pack without assessment.

D. Restrict all pain interventions.

Drop Down

64. A nurse is selecting a pain scale for a 5-year-old child. Select the most appropriate scale from the drop-down menu:

Numeric Pain Scale

Visual Analog Scale

Faces Pain Scale

Pittsburgh Sleep Quality Index

Drag and Drop

65. A nurse is managing a client's chronic pain. Drag and drop the interventions in the correct order of priority:

A. Administer prescribed non-opioid medication.

B. Teach relaxation techniques.

C. Assess pain intensity and quality.

D. Consult with a physical therapist.

Multiple Choice

66. What is the purpose of teaching relaxation techniques for pain management?

A. To increase pain intensity

B. To reduce stress and discomfort

C. To restrict mobility

D. To limit medication use entirely

Multiple Response

67. Which actions should a nurse take when managing pain collaboratively? (Select all that apply.)

A. Consult with a physician for medication adjustments.

B. Restrict patient education.

C. Collaborate with a physical therapist.

D. Engage a counselor for emotional support.

E. Avoid reassessing pain levels.

Case Scenario
68. Scenario: A client with neuropathic pain is prescribed an adjuvant medication.
Question: For what should the nurse monitor?
A. Improved hearing
B. Side effects like drowsiness
C. Increased blood glucose
D. Reduced skin integrity

69. Drop Down
A client reports mild pain (3/10). Select the most appropriate intervention from the drop-down menu:
Administer an opioid
Apply heat therapy
Restrict all activity
Administer an antibiotic

70. Multiple Choice
Why is ongoing pain reassessment important?
A. To limit medication use
B. To ensure interventions remain effective
C. To restrict patient mobility
D. To avoid documentation

71. Multiple Choice
A nurse is discussing aromatherapy with a client. What is a potential benefit?
A. Cure chronic illnesses
B. Promote relaxation and reduce stress
C. Replace all medications
D. Enhance visual acuity

Multiple Response
72. Which complementary therapies should a nurse consider for a client with chronic pain? (Select all that apply.)
A. Aromatherapy
B. Acupressure
C. Dietary supplements
D. High-dose antibiotics
E. Meditation

Case Scenario

73. Scenario: A client with asthma is interested in aromatherapy.

Question: For what should the nurse assess?

A. Potential hearing loss

B. Allergic reactions to essential oils

C. Increased blood pressure

D. Improved skin integrity

Drop Down

74. A client is considering dietary supplements. Select the most important nursing action from the drop-down menu:

Encourage high doses without consultation

Assess for medication interactions

Restrict all supplement use

Avoid patient education

Drag and Drop

75. A nurse is integrating acupressure into a client's care plan. Drag and drop the steps in the correct order:

A. Assess the client's medical history.

B. Identify appropriate pressure points.

C. Apply pressure to relieve tension.

D. Monitor for adverse effects.

NGN NCLEX BASIC CARE AND COMFORT ANSWERS

1. Answer: A
    Rationale: Rearranging furniture to create clear pathways reduces fall risks and enhances safety for clients with visual impairments, as outlined in the document under environmental modifications.

2. Answers: A, B, C, E
    Rationale: The document highlights passive range-of-motion exercises, wheelchair use, environmental modifications like grab bars, and counseling as key interventions for clients with physical impairments. A hearing aid is irrelevant for paralysis.

3. Answer: B
    Rationale: Monofilament testing is a standard method to assess sensory deficits in clients with neuropathy, as it evaluates touch sensation, aligning with the document's emphasis on sensory assessments.

4. Answer: Coordinate with a sign language interpreter
    Rationale: The document specifies that nurses facilitate communication for hearing-impaired clients by coordinating with sign language interpreters, making this the most appropriate strategy.

5. Answer: B, A, C, D
    Rationale: The document emphasizes assessing skin integrity first to prevent complications, checking the prosthetic fit, demonstrating its use, and then teaching advanced skills like stair navigation.

6. Answer: B
    Rationale: The document notes that connecting clients to support groups fosters resilience and emotional well-being by allowing them to share experiences.

7. Answers: A, B, D
    Rationale: The document highlights advocacy roles, including securing vocational training, accessible housing, and legal protections. Diet plans and surgical consultations are not mentioned in this context.

8. Answer: A
    Rationale: The document emphasizes training clients to use white canes effectively, which includes ensuring proper fit for safe mobility.

9. Answer: Wheelchair
   Rationale: A wheelchair is the most appropriate device for a client with a spinal cord injury to enhance mobility, as per the document.

10. Answer: B
    Rationale: The document states that environmental modifications, such as grab bars and ramps, aim to reduce fall risks, and promote independence.

11. Answer: B
    Rationale: Hard, dry stools with straining suggest constipation, requiring further evaluation, as per the document's assessment criteria.

12. Answers: A, B, D
    Rationale: The document emphasizes assessing frequency, medication use (e.g., diuretics), and history of conditions like urinary tract infections for elimination issues.

13. Answer: B
    Rationale: The document prioritizes addressing underlying causes, such as medication side effects, by collaborating with the healthcare team.

14. Answer: Increase dietary fiber intake
    Rationale: The document recommends increasing dietary fiber to ease constipation, complementing laxative use.

15. Answer: B, C, A, D
    Rationale: The document prioritizes assessing residual urine volume (bladder scan), encouraging hydration, administering medications, and then using a catheter if needed.

16. Answer: B
    Rationale: The document lists stool tests to detect blood, infection, or parasites as appropriate for bowel elimination issues.

17. Answers: A, B, E
    Rationale: The document recommends fiber, hydration, and exercise to promote bowel motility, while daily laxative use is not advised unless prescribed.

18. Answer: B
    Rationale: The document emphasizes using pH-balanced cleansers for skin hygiene to prevent irritation around ostomy sites.

19. Answer: Establish regular elimination patterns
    Rationale: The document states that bladder training aims to manage incontinence by establishing regular elimination patterns.

20. Answer: B
    Rationale: The document highlights educating clients and caregivers on ostomy care as a key nursing responsibility.

21. Answer: B
    Rationale: The document emphasizes maintaining aseptic technique to prevent infection during bladder irrigation.

22. Answers: A, B, E
    Rationale: The document lists warm saline, a kidney-shaped basin, and a bulb syringe as necessary for ear irrigation. Cold water and sterile gloves are not required.

23. Answer: B
    Rationale: The document specifies flushing the solution from the inner to the outer corner to prevent contaminants from affecting the unaffected eye.

24. Answer: Presence of blood clots
    Rationale: The document notes that blood clots in the outflow indicate a need for further assessment and intervention.

25. Answer: C, D, B, A
    Rationale: The document outlines positioning the client, placing the basin, directing the solution, and drying the ear as the correct sequence.

26. Answer: B
    Rationale: The document states that warming the solution prevents dizziness or discomfort during ear irrigation.

27. Answers: A, B, E
    Rationale: The document emphasizes documenting the procedure, monitoring for discomfort, and assessing outflow clarity. Discarding solution and restricting fluids are not mentioned.

28. Answer: B
    Rationale: The document highlights assessing for persistent irritation or injury post-irrigation to determine further care needs.

29. Answer: Sterile saline

Rationale: The document specifies using sterile saline or a prescribed solution for bladder irrigation to maintain safety.

30. Answer: B

Rationale: The document emphasizes precision, care, and patient-centered approaches to ensure comfort and safety during irrigations.

31. Answer: B

Rationale: The document lists redness over bony prominences as a sign of potential pressure injury.

32. Answers: A, C, D

Rationale: The document recommends repositioning, moisturizing, and using pressure-relieving devices. Harsh soaps and fluid restriction are not advised.

33. Answer: B

Rationale: The document prioritizes increasing repositioning to relieve pressure and prevent worsening of stage 1 pressure injuries.

34. Answer: Braden Scale

Rationale: The document specifies the Braden Scale for assessing pressure ulcer risk.

35. Answer: B, C, A, D

Rationale: The document prioritizes assessing skin condition, cleaning with appropriate cleansers, applying moisturizers, and educating on hydration.

36. Answer: B

Rationale: The document states that pH-balanced cleansers prevent stripping natural oils, maintaining skin integrity.

37. Answers: A, B, D, E

Rationale: The document lists skin discoloration, wounds, dry/cracked skin, and edema as key findings to document.

38. Answer: B

Rationale: The document recommends applying moisturizers to prevent cracking and reduce infection risk.

39. Answer: Use pressure-relieving cushions
    Rationale: The document highlights pressure-relieving devices as effective for preventing skin breakdown.

40. Answer: B
    Rationale: The document emphasizes nutrition's role in promoting skin repair and resilience.

41. Answer: A
    Rationale: The document emphasizes assessing skin integrity before applying orthopedic devices to prevent complications.

42. Answers: A, B, D
    Rationale: The document recommends checking for wear, cleaning, and inspecting skin for irritation. Restricting mobility and unapproved adjustments are not advised.

43. Answer: B
    Rationale: The document highlights monitoring for neurovascular compromise, such as numbness, as a priority during cast maintenance.

44. Answer: Unfasten straps gently
    Rationale: The document specifies unfastening straps for splint removal to avoid injury.

45. Answer: A, B, D, C
    Rationale: The document outlines verifying orders, assessing the area, checking alignment, and securing weights as the correct sequence.

46. Answer: B
    Rationale: The document emphasizes cleaning removable braces to maintain hygiene.

47. Answers: B, C, E
    Rationale: The document lists tingling, discoloration, and swelling as signs of neurovascular compromise requiring immediate attention.

48. Answer: B
    Rationale: The document prioritizes assessing the fit of orthopedic devices to ensure comfort and functionality.

49. Answer: Ensure proper alignment
    Rationale: The document emphasizes proper alignment to ensure device effectiveness and prevent complications.

50. Answer: B
    Rationale: The document highlights assessing for skin irritation post-removal to ensure proper care.

51. Answer: B
    Rationale: The document emphasizes passive range-of-motion exercises to improve circulation in immobile clients.

52. Answers: A, B, D
    Rationale: The document lists early ambulation, sequential compression devices, and leg
    elevation as effective for circulation. Warm compresses and fluid restriction are not mentioned.

53. Answer: B
    Rationale: The document highlights early ambulation to reduce the risk of deep vein thrombosis post-surgery.

54. Answer: Sequential compression device
    Rationale: The document specifies sequential compression devices as effective for promoting circulation.

55. Answer: C, A, B, D
    Rationale: The document prioritizes repositioning, followed by range-of-motion exercises, compression devices, and hydration.

56. Answer: C
    Rationale: The document states that elevating legs improves venous return to enhance circulation.

57. Answers: A, B, D, E
    Rationale: The document lists active range-of-motion, compression garments, bedside exercises, and skin monitoring as circulation-promoting actions.

58. Answer: B
    Rationale: The document recommends leg elevation to reduce swelling and improve circulation in venous insufficiency.

59. Answer: Advise a diet rich in vascular health nutrients
    Rationale: The document emphasizes nutrition supporting vascular health to promote circulation.

60. Answer: B
    Rationale: The document states that sequential compression devices promote blood flow by mimicking movement.

61. Answer: B
    Rationale: The document specifies that asking about the pain's description (e.g., sharp, dull) evaluates its quality.

62. Answers: A, C, D
    Rationale: The document lists facial grimacing, guarding, and restlessness as non-verbal pain indicators.

63. Answer: B
    Rationale: The document prioritizes pharmacological interventions like opioids for severe pain (8/10).

64. Answer: Faces Pain Scale
    Rationale: The document recommends the Faces Pain Scale for children due to its use of facial expressions.

65. Answer: C, A, B, D
    Rationale: The document prioritizes pain assessment, followed by pharmacological intervention, non-pharmacological techniques, and consultation.

66. Answer: B
    Rationale: The document states that relaxation techniques reduce stress and alleviate pain.

67. Answers: A, C, D
    Rationale: The document emphasizes interdisciplinary collaboration with physicians, therapists, and counselors, while reassessment and education are key.

68. Answer: B
    Rationale: The document notes that adjuvant medications (e.g., antidepressants) require monitoring for side effects like drowsiness.

69. Answer: Apply heat therapy
    Rationale: The document recommends non-pharmacological interventions like heat therapy for mild pain.

70. Answer: B
    Rationale: The document emphasizes reassessing pain to ensure interventions are effective and to adjust care plans.

71. Answer: B
    Rationale: The document lists promoting relaxation and reducing stress as benefits of aromatherapy.

72. Answers: A, B, C, E
    Rationale: The document includes aromatherapy, acupressure, dietary supplements, and relaxation techniques like meditation as complementary therapies.

73. Answer: B
    Rationale: The document notes that aromatherapy may trigger allergies or asthma, requiring assessment for allergic reactions.

74. Answer: Assess for medication interactions
    Rationale: The document emphasizes assessing for drug interactions with supplements to ensure safety.

75. Answer: A, B, C, D
    Rationale: The document prioritizes assessing medical history, identifying pressure points, applying acupressure, and monitoring for effects.

NGN NCLEX PHARMACOLOGY &
PARENTERAL THEARAPY QUESTIONS

Multiple Choice
1. What is the primary action of beta-blockers in the management of hypertension?
A) Vasodilation
B) Decrease heart rate
C) Increase renal perfusion
D) Increase blood pressure

Multiple Response
2. Which of the following medications are commonly used to treat Type 2 Diabetes? (Select all that apply)
A) Insulin
B) Metformin
C) Sulfonylureas
D) Lisinopril

Case Scenario
3. A 45-year-old patient with chronic heart failure is prescribed furosemide. The nurse should monitor for which of the following potential side effects?
A) Hypokalemia
B) Hyperkalemia
C) Hyperglycemia
D) Hypoglycemia

Drop-down
4. Select the correct medication class that includes amlodipine.
Amlodipine → [Select: Calcium Channel Blocker | Beta-blocker | ACE Inhibitor | Diuretic]

Drag and Drop
5. Match the medication with its appropriate side effect.
Methotrexate → [Select: Nausea | Nephrotoxicity | Bone Marrow Suppression]
Lithium → [Select: Tremors | Blurred Vision | Hyperkalemia]
Prednisone → [Select: Weight Loss | Hypertension | Hypotension]

Multiple Choice

6. Which of the following medications is most likely to cause anaphylactic reactions?
Penicillin
B) Metformin
C) Furosemide
D) Omeprazole

Multiple Choice
7. A nurse is caring for a patient receiving IV potassium chloride. The nurse should be most concerned if which of the following occurs?
A) The IV rate is set to 10 mEq/hr.
B) The patient reports burning at the IV site.
C) The patient reports mild leg cramping.
D) The patient has a potassium level of 4.0 mEq/L.

Multiple Response
8. Which of the following are common side effects of opioids? (Select all that apply)
A) Constipation
B) Diarrhea
C) Respiratory depression
D) Hypertension

Case Scenario
9. A patient is prescribed warfarin (Coumadin) for the prevention of blood clots. What should the nurse prioritize in monitoring for this patient?
A) Platelet count
B) International Normalized Ratio (INR)
C) Blood pressure
D) Urine output

Multiple Choice
10. Which of the following medications is most commonly used as a first-line treatment for hypertension?
A) Losartan
B) Furosemide
C) Amlodipine
D) Lisinopril

Drag and Drop
11. Match the type of insulin to its typical onset time.
Rapid-acting insulin → [Select: 15-30 minutes | 30-60 minutes | 1-2 hours]
Short-acting insulin → [Select: 15-30 minutes | 30-60 minutes | 1-2 hours]

Intermediate-acting insulin → [Select: 4-6 hours | 1-2 hours | 2-4 hours]
Long-acting insulin → [Select: 12-24 hours | 30-60 minutes | 4-6 hours]

Multiple Choice
12. Which of the following should be a priority consideration when administering an opioid analgesic to a post-operative patient?
A) Vital signs, especially respiratory rate
B) Blood glucose levels
C) Renal function
D) Hemoglobin levels

Multiple Choice
13. A patient who has been prescribed methotrexate for rheumatoid arthritis is most at risk for which of the following?
A) Hypercalcemia
B) Hepatotoxicity
C) Hyperglycemia
D) Hypokalemia

Case Scenario
14. A nurse is administering intravenous morphine for pain relief. The patient develops slow, shallow respirations. What is the nurse's priority action?
A) Administer naloxone
B) Increase the morphine dose
C) Assess the patient's pain level
D) Apply oxygen therapy

Multiple Choice
15. Which laboratory test should be monitored for a patient taking digoxin?
A) Serum potassium levels
B) Liver function tests
C) B-type natriuretic peptide (BNP)
D) Serum creatinine levels

Multiple Response
16. Which of the following are common side effects of corticosteroids? (Select all that apply)
A) Weight gain
B) Increased risk of infection
C) Hypoglycemia
D) Osteoporosis

Multiple Choice
17. A nurse is caring for a patient receiving an opioid analgesic. Which assessment finding would most concern the nurse?
A) Constipation
B) Urinary retention
C) Sedation
D) Respiratory rate of 8 breaths per minute

Multiple Choice
18. Which of the following medications should be avoided in a patient with a known allergy to sulfonamides?
A) Hydrochlorothiazide
B) Metformin
C) Atenolol
D) Lorazepam

Case Scenario
19. A patient on warfarin has a PT/INR of 5.0. What is the nurse's first action?
A) Administer Vitamin K
B) Increase the warfarin dose
C) Notify the healthcare provider
D) Reduce the warfarin dose

Multiple Choice
20. Which of the following medications is used as a first-line treatment for chronic asthma?
A) Albuterol
B) Beclomethasone
C) Ipratropium
D) Montelukast

Multiple Choice
21. What is the most important nursing action before administering a blood transfusion?
A) Ensure the patient is receiving the correct blood type.
B) Check for allergic reactions from previous transfusions.
C) Administer a pre-transfusion dose of antihistamine.
D) Confirm that the patient has been NPO for 8 hours.

Case Scenario
22. A patient is receiving a blood transfusion and begins to experience chills, fever, and back pain. What is the nurse's first action?

A) Continue the transfusion at a slower rate.
B) Stop the transfusion and assess the patient's vital signs.
C) Administer acetaminophen for the fever.
D) Notify the healthcare provider immediately.

Multiple Choice
23. Which of the following is the most important nursing consideration when caring for a patient with a central venous line (CVL)?
A) Ensure the CVL is placed in the correct anatomical location.
B) Change the CVL dressing every 72 hours.
C) Check for patency by aspirating the line.
D) Administer only peripheral IV medications through the CVL.

Multiple Response
24. Which of the following are signs of a central venous line-related infection? (Select all that apply)
A) Redness and swelling at the insertion site
B) Fever
C) Increased white blood cell count
D) Decreased blood pressure

Multiple Choice
25. Which of the following is most important to include in patient education for a new prescription of warfarin (Coumadin)?
A) Avoid eating foods high in vitamin K.
B) Discontinue all other medications when starting warfarin.
C) Increase fluid intake to 3 liters per day.
D) Take the medication only when you experience symptoms of a clot.

Case Scenario
26. A patient is prescribed a new medication regimen after discharge. What should be the nurse's priority when providing patient education?
A) Explain the potential side effects of the medications.
B) Discuss the purpose of the medications in simple terms.
C) Provide a written schedule for when and how to take each medication.
D) Instruct the patient to contact the pharmacy if they have any concerns.

Multiple Choice
27. Which of the following is a common side effect of opioid analgesics that requires monitoring?

A) Hypertension
B) Diarrhea
C) Sedation
D) Hyperglycemia

Multiple Response
28. Which of the following interventions are appropriate when managing a patient's pain with an opioid? (Select all that apply)
A) Monitor respiratory rate
B) Administer the medication on a fixed schedule
C) Encourage fluid intake to prevent constipation
D) Provide a non-opioid analgesic for breakthrough pain

Multiple Choice
29. Which of the following is the priority nursing assessment for a patient receiving parenteral nutrition (PN)?
A) Bowel sounds
B) Blood glucose levels
C) Serum electrolyte levels
D) Temperature

Case Scenario
30. A patient receiving parenteral nutrition has developed signs of infection at the catheter insertion site. What should be the nurse's priority action?
A) Administer antibiotics as ordered.
B) Remove the catheter and notify the healthcare provider.
C) Increase the flow rate of the parenteral nutrition.
D) Change the dressing around the catheter.

Multiple Choice
31. Which of the following is the most common complication associated with IV therapy?
A) Hyperglycemia
B) Phlebitis
C) Hypertension
D) Diarrhea

Multiple Response
32. Which of the following are signs of infiltration at an IV site? (Select all that apply)
A) Swelling at the insertion site
B) Coolness of the skin around the IV site

C) Redness at the insertion site
D) Pain and tenderness at the site

Multiple Choice
33. What is the primary nursing responsibility when administering a controlled substance?
A) Ensure the patient understands the risk of addiction.
B) Document the administration in the patient's chart.
C) Double-check the medication dose and patient identity.
D) Withhold the medication if the patient requests a higher dose.

Question 34: Multiple Choice
34. A nurse is administering a Schedule II controlled substance. Which of the following actions must the nurse take?
A) Complete a controlled substance log and have another nurse witness the waste of any unused medication.
B) Administer the medication and document the dose after the patient leaves the unit.
C) Verify the patient's identity only once before administration.
D) Store the medication in a standard medication drawer, separate from other drugs.

Multiple Choice
35. Which of the following is an essential step in ensuring medication safety when administering to a patient?
A) Administer medications as quickly as possible to minimize errors.
B) Confirm the patient's identity using two identifiers.
C) Ask the patient to review their medication orders before administration.
D) Encourage the patient to take medications on their own without supervision.

Case Scenario
36. A nurse is preparing to administer a medication and notices the patient's chart indicates a potential drug interaction with another prescribed medication. What is the nurse's next action?
A) Administer the medication and monitor the patient for side effects.
B) Hold the medication and notify the healthcare provider about the potential interaction.
C) Adjust the dosage based on the patient's history.
D) Ask the patient if they have noticed any issues with their current medications.

Multiple Choice
37. What is the most common adverse reaction associated with blood transfusions?
A) Hemolytic reaction
B) Allergic reaction

C) Febrile non-hemolytic reaction
D) Sepsis

Multiple Choice
38. When administering blood products, how often should the nurse monitor the patient's vital signs?
A) Every 15 minutes for the first hour, then every 30 minutes
B) Every 30 minutes for the entire transfusion
C) Once before and once after the transfusion
D) Every hour, if no symptoms of reaction occur

Multiple Response
39. Which of the following are potential complications of a central venous line? (Select all that apply)
A) Air embolism
B) Thrombosis
C) Sepsis
D) Diarrhea

Multiple Choice
40. A nurse is preparing to remove a central venous line. What is the correct procedure for removal?
A) Place the patient in a sitting position and apply pressure to the insertion site after removal.
B) Place the patient in a Trendelenburg position and apply pressure after removal.
C) Ask the patient to perform the Valsalva maneuver while the line is removed.
D) Remove the line quickly and apply a sterile dressing immediately.

Multiple Choice
41. A patient is prescribed a new inhaler for asthma. Which of the following should the nurse emphasize during patient education?
A) Shake the inhaler before each use.
B) Use the inhaler only when experiencing an asthma attack.
C) Hold your breath for 10 seconds after inhaling the medication.
D) Discard the inhaler after 30 days of use.

Multiple Choice
42. Which of the following is the most appropriate action for a nurse when providing medication education to an elderly patient who has hearing impairment?
A) Use written instructions and clear verbal communication.
B) Speak louder and faster to ensure they hear you.

C) Provide verbal instructions only, as they may not be able to read.

D) Avoid providing education if the patient has difficulty hearing.

Multiple Choice

43. Which of the following is a non-pharmacological method of pain relief that a nurse might use for a patient with chronic pain?

A) Acupuncture

B) Morphine sulfate

C) Ibuprofen

D) Codeine

Case Scenario

44. A patient is receiving an epidural opioid for pain control after surgery. What is the nurse's priority concern?

A) Monitoring for respiratory depression

B) Ensuring the patient is mobile every 2 hours

C) Administering laxatives to prevent constipation

D) Encouraging the patient to eat a high-protein diet

Multiple Choice

45. What is the most common complication of parenteral nutrition (PN)?

A) Hyperglycemia

B) Electrolyte imbalance

C) Infection

D) Vitamin deficiency

Multiple Choice

46. A patient on parenteral nutrition is being transitioned to oral nutrition. What should the nurse ensure before discontinuing the parenteral nutrition?

A) The patient is able to tolerate at least 75% of their daily caloric needs by mouth.

B) The patient's bowel movements have returned to normal.

C) The patient has gained weight within the last 24 hours.

D) The patient is no longer receiving any IV fluids.

Multiple Response

47. What are common signs of phlebitis at an IV site? (Select all that apply)

A) Redness and warmth at the site

B) Swelling at the site

C) Pain and tenderness around the site

D) Pallor at the insertion site

Multiple Choice

48. Which of the following is the most appropriate action when an IV infusion site shows signs of infection?
A) Continue the infusion at a slower rate.
B) Remove the IV catheter and apply a sterile dressing.
C) Increase the infusion rate to flush the catheter.
D) Switch to a different vein and continue the same IV fluid.

Multiple Choice

49. Which of the following is true about administering controlled substances in a hospital setting?
A) Nurses can administer controlled substances without a second witness for documentation.
B) A second nurse must verify the dosage and patient before administering any controlled substance.
C) The nurse can delegate the administration of controlled substances to unlicensed personnel.
D) Documentation of controlled substances is only required at the end of the shift.

Multiple Choice

50. What is the most important safety consideration when handling controlled substances?
A) Ensure medications are stored securely in the patient's room.
B) Double-check the patient's identity before administering any controlled substance.
C) Dispose of unused medications in a regular trash container.
D) Administer controlled substances only to patients who request them.

Multiple Choice

51. If a physician orders 500 mL of a solution to be infused over 4 hours, what is the rate in mL/hr?
A) 50 mL/hr
B) 100 mL/hr
C) 125 mL/hr
D) 150 mL/hr

Multiple Choice

52. A medication order reads: "Administer 250 mg of medication every 6 hours." If the available dosage is 500 mg per tablet, how many tablets should the nurse administer?
A) 1 tablet
B) 1.5 tablets
C) 2 tablets
D) 0.5 tablets

Multiple Choice

53. If a patient is prescribed 0.5 grams of a medication, and the available concentration is 250 mg per 5 mL, how many mL should the nurse administer?
A) 5 mL
B) 10 mL
C) 15 mL
D) 20 mL

Multiple Choice

54. What is the nurse's priority action if a patient begins showing signs of a transfusion reaction, such as fever, chills, and back pain?
A) Increase the transfusion rate to finish quickly.
B) Stop the transfusion immediately and notify the healthcare provider.
C) Administer acetaminophen to reduce the fever.
D) Continue the transfusion, as the symptoms are common and not serious.

Multiple Choice

55. Which of the following is essential in preventing bacterial contamination during blood transfusion?
A) Warm the blood before transfusion.
B) Only use fresh blood from a reputable source.
C) Maintain aseptic technique during blood handling and administration.
D) Use a blood filter that is not required for red blood cell transfusions.

Multiple Choice

56. What is the correct position for a patient when inserting a central venous catheter?
A) Supine with the head slightly elevated
B) Prone with the head turned to one side
C) Trendelenburg with the head lower than the feet
D) Sitting upright with the head at a 45-degree angle

Multiple Response

57. Which of the following are signs of a pneumothorax after central venous catheter insertion? (Select all that apply)
A) Decreased breath sounds on one side
B) Increased heart rate
C) Jugular vein distension
D) Shortness of breath

Multiple Choice

58. A nurse is educating a patient about using a metered-dose inhaler (MDI). Which instruction should the nurse include?
A) Inhale rapidly to ensure deep penetration of the medication.
B) Hold your breath for at least 10 seconds after inhalation.
C) Use the inhaler only when experiencing an asthma attack.
D) Take a deep breath in before activating the inhaler.

Multiple Choice
59. Which of the following is an important point to emphasize during education for a patient newly prescribed a transdermal nicotine patch?
A) Apply the patch to the area of the body with the most hair.
B) Place the patch on the same area every day for consistent nicotine absorption.
C) Rotate the application site daily to avoid skin irritation.
D) Keep the patch on continuously, even while bathing or swimming.

Multiple Response
60. Which of the following are signs that a patient may be experiencing opioid toxicity? (Select all that apply)
A) Bradycardia
B) Respiratory depression
C) Hypothermia
D) Nausea and vomiting

Multiple Choice
61. A nurse is caring for a patient who has been prescribed long-term opioid therapy for chronic pain. Which of the following is a potential side effect that should be monitored closely?
A) Insomnia
B) Weight loss
C) Hyperglycemia
D) Constipation

Multiple Choice
62. A nurse is caring for a patient receiving parenteral nutrition (PN) and notices that the patient's blood glucose level has increased. What is the best action for the nurse to take?
A) Increase the insulin dose according to protocol.
B) Decrease the rate of the PN infusion.
C) Administer oral glucose to treat the hypoglycemia.
D) Assess the patient for signs of infection.

Multiple Choice

63. What is the best method for preventing complications associated with long-term parenteral nutrition?
A) Limit the duration of parenteral nutrition to 48 hours.
B) Ensure that the PN solution is administered via a central venous catheter.
C) Administer parenteral nutrition through peripheral IV lines.
D) Rotate the infusion site every 12 hours.

Multiple Choice
64. What is the most appropriate action when an IV catheter becomes dislodged or is no longer patent?
A) Increase the infusion rate to force the medication through the catheter.
B) Remove the catheter and insert a new one at a different site.
C) Flush the catheter with saline to restore patency.
D) Apply heat to the site and wait for the catheter to regain patency.

Multiple Choice
65. A nurse is preparing to start an IV infusion. Which of the following is the most important action to reduce the risk of infection?
A) Use a large-bore needle for easy insertion.
B) Prepare the site with alcohol or antiseptic solution and let it dry.
C) Ensure that the infusion is started at a very slow rate.
D) Use a glass IV container for all infusions.

Multiple Choice
66. What is the correct procedure for disposing of unused controlled substances?
A) Flush them down the toilet.
B) Discard them in the regular trash after crushing them.
C) Return them to the pharmacy for disposal.
D) Dispose of them in a secure, authorized disposal container with a witness.

Multiple Choice
67. What is the nurse's primary responsibility when administering a Schedule II controlled substance?
A) Ensure that the medication is stored securely in the patient's room.
B) Verify the medication with a second nurse before administration.
C) Ensure that the medication is administered exactly as prescribed without any alterations.
D) Allow the patient to store their own medication for convenience.

Multiple Choice

68. A patient is prescribed 1.5 mg of lorazepam (Ativan) IV push. The available concentration is 4 mg/2 mL. How many mL will the nurse administer?
A) 0.75 mL
B) 1 mL
C) 1.5 mL
D) 2 mL

Multiple Choice
69. The physician orders 500 mL of D5W to be infused at 75 mL/hr. How many hours will it take to administer the entire volume?
A) 4 hours
B) 5 hours
C) 6 hours
D) 7 hours

Multiple Choice
70. If a doctor orders 600 mg of a medication and the available concentration is 200 mg/5 mL, how many mL should the nurse administer?
A) 10 mL
B) 15 mL
C) 20 mL
D) 25 mL

Multiple Choice
71. Which of the following is an early sign of a hemolytic transfusion reaction?
A) Fever and chills
B) Chest pain and shortness of breath
C) Nausea and vomiting
D) Itching and rash

Multiple Response
72. Which of the following actions should a nurse take when a blood transfusion reaction occurs? (Select all that apply)
A) Stop the transfusion immediately
B) Infuse saline through the same IV line
C) Obtain a urine sample for analysis
D) Notify the healthcare provider

Multiple Choice
73. When assessing a patient with a central venous line, what is an early sign of a central line-associated bloodstream infection (CLABSI)?

A) Pain at the catheter insertion site
B) A warm and red catheter insertion site
C) Fever and chills
D) Decreased blood pressure

Multiple Choice
74. What is the primary concern when a patient with a central venous catheter develops swelling in the neck or face?
A) Air embolism
B) Pneumothorax
C) Catheter-related thrombosis
D) Septicemia

Multiple Choice
75. Which of the following statements by a patient indicates that they need further education regarding their new prescription for atorvastatin (Lipitor)?
A) "I will take this medication every day, even if I feel fine."
B) "I can eat grapefruit while taking this medication to help with my cholesterol."
C) "I should have regular liver function tests while on this medication."
D) "I will inform my doctor if I have unexplained muscle pain."

NGN NCLEX PHARMACOLOGY AND PARENTERAL THEARAPY ANSWERS

1.   Answer: B) Decrease heart rate
Rationale: Beta-blockers primarily work by blocking beta-adrenergic receptors, which decreases heart rate and myocardial contractility, reducing cardiac output, and lowering blood pressure.

2.   Answer: B) Metformin, C) Sulfonylureas
Rationale: Metformin and Sulfonylureas are commonly used in Type 2 Diabetes management. Insulin is typically used for Type 1 Diabetes or in later stages of Type 2. Lisinopril is an ACE inhibitor, used for blood pressure control, not specifically for diabetes.

3.   Answer: A) Hypokalemia
Rationale: Furosemide is a loop diuretic that can lead to electrolyte imbalances, including hypokalemia, because it promotes potassium excretion through the kidneys.

4.   Answer: Calcium Channel Blocker
Rationale: Amlodipine is a calcium channel blocker that works by relaxing blood vessels and improving blood flow, which helps lower blood pressure.

5.   Answer:
Methotrexate → Bone Marrow Suppression
Lithium → Tremors
Prednisone → Hypertension
Rationale: Methotrexate can cause bone marrow suppression. Lithium can cause tremors as a common side effect. Prednisone, a corticosteroid, is known to cause hypertension.

6.   Answer: A) Penicillin
Rationale: Penicillin is a common cause of anaphylaxis, an acute allergic reaction. Other options do not commonly cause this severe reaction.

7.   Answer: B) The patient reports burning at the IV site.
Rationale: Potassium chloride can be irritating to veins and can cause burning or discomfort at the IV site, which requires careful monitoring. Rapid infusion or improper dilution can also lead to serious complications like hyperkalemia.

8.   Answer: A) Constipation, C) Respiratory depression
Rationale: Opioids frequently cause constipation and respiratory depression as common side effects. Diarrhea and hypertension are less commonly associated with opioid use.

9. Answer: B) International Normalized Ratio (INR)
Rationale: Warfarin is an anticoagulant, and the effectiveness of the medication is monitored by the INR. The INR ensures that the blood's clotting ability is within a therapeutic range.

10. Answer: D) Lisinopril
Rationale: Lisinopril is an ACE inhibitor, commonly used as a first-line treatment for hypertension due to its ability to block the RAAS system, which regulates blood pressure.

11. Answer:
Rapid-acting insulin → 15-30 minutes
Short-acting insulin → 30-60 minutes
Intermediate-acting insulin → 1-2 hours
Long-acting insulin → 12-24 hours
Rationale: The onset times of insulin vary by type, with rapid-acting insulin starting the quickest and long-acting insulin having a more gradual onset.

12. Answer: A) Vital signs, especially respiratory rate
Rationale: Opioids can depress the respiratory system, leading to respiratory depression, so monitoring vital signs, especially respiratory rate, is critical in opioid administration.

13. Answer: B) Hepatotoxicity
Rationale: Methotrexate is known to be hepatotoxic, and patients receiving this medication require regular liver function tests.

14. Answer: A) Administer naloxone
Rationale: Naloxone is an opioid antagonist that reverses opioid-induced respiratory depression, making it the priority action in this scenario.

15. Answer: A) Serum potassium levels
Rationale: Digoxin toxicity is more likely to occur when potassium levels are low, so monitoring potassium levels is critical for patients taking this medication.

16. Answer: A) Weight gain, B) Increased risk of infection, D) Osteoporosis
Rationale: Corticosteroids can cause weight gain, increase the risk of infection, and lead to osteoporosis due to long-term use, while hypoglycemia is not a typical side effect.

17. Answer: D) Respiratory rate of 8 breaths per minute
Rationale: A respiratory rate of 8 breaths per minute indicates respiratory depression, a serious side effect of opioid use. Immediate intervention is required.

18. Answer: A) Hydrochlorothiazide
Rationale: Hydrochlorothiazide is a thiazide diuretic, and it contains a sulfonamide group, so it should be avoided in patients with sulfonamide allergies.

19. Answer: C) Notify the healthcare provider
Rationale: An INR of 5.0 is elevated, putting the patient at risk for bleeding. The healthcare provider should be notified immediately to determine the appropriate intervention.

20. Answer: B) Beclomethasone
Rationale: Beclomethasone is an inhaled corticosteroid used as a first-line treatment for chronic asthma. Albuterol is a short-acting bronchodilator used for acute relief, and Montelukast is a leukotriene receptor antagonist used as an adjunctive treatment.

21. Answer: A) Ensure the patient is receiving the correct blood type.
Rationale: The most important step before administering blood is ensuring the correct blood type is matched between the donor and the recipient to prevent life-threatening reactions.

22. Answer: B) Stop the transfusion and assess the patient's vital signs.
Rationale: These symptoms suggest a possible transfusion reaction. The first action should be to stop the transfusion immediately and assess the patient's vital signs before further action is taken.

23. Answer: A) Ensure the CVL is placed in the correct anatomical location.
Rationale: Proper placement of the central venous line is critical to prevent complications such as air embolism or thrombosis. Regular monitoring and maintaining the CVL is important, but placement accuracy is the top priority.

24. Answer: A) Redness and swelling at the insertion site, B) Fever, C) Increased white blood cell count
Rationale: Signs of infection related to a central venous line include redness, swelling, fever, and an elevated white blood cell count. Decreased blood pressure may occur in severe infections or sepsis but is not the earliest sign.

25. Answer: A) Avoid eating foods high in vitamin K.
Rationale: Warfarin is an anticoagulant that works by inhibiting vitamin K-dependent clotting factors. Educating the patient about avoiding large fluctuations in vitamin K intake (found in foods like spinach, kale, and broccoli) helps maintain stable anticoagulation levels.

26. Answer: C) Provide a written schedule for when and how to take each medication.

Rationale: Providing a clear, written schedule helps patients understand how to properly administer their medications and prevents errors. It's important to provide clear instructions about the schedule and administration times.

27. Answer: C) Sedation
Rationale: Opioids commonly cause sedation, which can lead to respiratory depression and increase the risk of falls. Monitoring the patient's sedation level is important, especially in the early stages of opioid administration.

28. Answer: A) Monitor respiratory rate, B) Administer the medication on a fixed schedule, C) Encourage fluid intake to prevent constipation
Rationale: Monitoring respiratory rate is critical to prevent respiratory depression, and fluid intake helps reduce constipation, a common opioid side effect. Administering opioids on a schedule ensures effective pain management, while non-opioid analgesics should be considered for breakthrough pain.

29. Answer: B) Blood glucose levels
Rationale: Parenteral nutrition can significantly impact blood glucose levels, as the solution is high in glucose. Regular monitoring of blood glucose is necessary to prevent hyperglycemia.

30. Answer: B) Remove the catheter and notify the healthcare provider.
Rationale: Signs of infection at the catheter insertion site require removal of the catheter and urgent evaluation by the healthcare provider to prevent sepsis or other complications.

31. Answer: B) Phlebitis
Rationale: Phlebitis, or inflammation of the vein, is the most common complication associated with IV therapy. It can result from irritation by the IV catheter or the infusion solution.

32. Answer: A) Swelling at the insertion site, B) Coolness of the skin around the IV site
Rationale: Infiltration occurs when IV fluids leak into the surrounding tissue, leading to swelling and coolness around the IV site. Redness and warmth are more indicative of infection or phlebitis.

33. Answer: C) Double-check the medication dose and patient identity.
Rationale: Ensuring the correct medication and dose are administered is the nurse's primary responsibility when administering controlled substances. Additionally, appropriate documentation and patient education are important.

34. Answer: A) Complete a controlled substance log and have another nurse witness the waste of any unused medication.
Rationale: Controlled substances must be documented carefully, and the waste of any unused portions requires another nurse to witness it. Proper documentation and security measures are necessary to comply with legal and institutional policies.

35. Answer: B) Confirm the patient's identity using two identifiers.
Rationale: Using two identifiers (e.g., name and birthdate) is a critical step in preventing medication errors. This ensures that the right patient receives the right medication.

36. Answer: B) Hold the medication and notify the healthcare provider about the potential interaction.
Rationale: Identifying a potential drug interaction is critical, and the nurse should withhold the medication and notify the healthcare provider for further assessment and adjustment of the medication regimen.
37.
Answer: C) Febrile non-hemolytic reaction
Rationale: Febrile non-hemolytic reactions are the most common and are usually caused by antibodies against white blood cells in the transfused blood. Symptoms include fever and chills, but they are generally not life-threatening.

38. Answer: A) Every 15 minutes for the first hour, then every 30 minutes
Rationale: Vital signs should be monitored closely, especially during the first hour of transfusion, to detect any early signs of transfusion reactions. Frequent monitoring helps catch any complications quickly.

39. Answer: A) Air embolism, B) Thrombosis, C) Sepsis
Rationale: Central venous lines are associated with serious complications such as air embolism, thrombosis (clot formation), and infection (sepsis). Diarrhea is not directly associated with central venous line use.

40. Answer: B) Place the patient in a Trendelenburg position and apply pressure after removal.
Rationale: Placing the patient in a Trendelenburg position reduces the risk of air embolism during central venous line removal. Applying pressure helps control any bleeding at the insertion site.

41. Answer: A) Shake the inhaler before each use.

Rationale: Shaking the inhaler ensures the medication is evenly distributed. The patient should also be instructed to use the inhaler regularly, even when symptoms are not present, to manage asthma effectively.

42. Answer: A) Use written instructions and clear verbal communication.
Rationale: Written instructions and clear, slow verbal communication are effective ways to educate patients with hearing impairment, ensuring they fully understand their treatment plan.

43. Answer: A) Acupuncture
Rationale: Acupuncture is a non-pharmacological method of pain relief commonly used for chronic pain management. The other options are pharmacological pain relief methods.

44. Answer: A) Monitoring for respiratory depression
Rationale: Epidural opioids are potent and can lead to significant respiratory depression, which requires close monitoring. This is the most critical concern after administering this form of pain management.

45. Answer: C) Infection
Rationale: The most common and serious complication of parenteral nutrition is infection, particularly due to the use of central venous catheters. Proper aseptic technique and regular monitoring for signs of infection are critical.

46. Answer: A) The patient is able to tolerate at least 75% of their daily caloric needs by mouth.
Rationale: Transitioning from parenteral to oral nutrition requires that the patient can consume enough calories and nutrients orally to maintain nutritional status. Bowel movements and weight gain are not immediate indicators for discontinuing PN.

47. Answer: A) Redness and warmth at the site, B) Swelling at the site, C) Pain and tenderness
around the site
Rationale: Phlebitis is inflammation of the vein, typically presenting with redness, warmth, swelling, and pain at the insertion site. Pallor is more indicative of infiltration or improper placement of the IV.

48. Answer: B) Remove the IV catheter and apply a sterile dressing.

Rationale: If infection is suspected at the IV site, the IV catheter should be removed, and a sterile dressing should be applied to the site. The nurse should also notify the healthcare provider for further management.

49. Answer: B) A second nurse must verify the dosage and patient before administering any controlled substance.
Rationale: Controlled substances require careful documentation and a second nurse verification before administration to prevent errors and misuse.

50. Answer: B) Double-check the patient's identity before administering any controlled substance.
Rationale: Proper patient identification is crucial when administering controlled substances to prevent errors, ensuring that the correct patient receives the prescribed medication.

51. Answer: B) 100 mL/hr
Rationale: To calculate the infusion rate, divide the total volume by the total time. 500 mL ÷ 4 hours = 100 mL/hr.

52. Answer: A) 1 tablet
Rationale: The available dosage is 500 mg per tablet, and the order calls for 250 mg. Therefore, the nurse would administer 1 tablet (500 mg ÷ 2 = 250 mg).

53. Answer: B) 10 mL
Rationale: First, convert 0.5 grams to milligrams: 0.5 g = 500 mg. Next, divide the desired dose (500 mg) by the concentration (250 mg per 5 mL). 500 mg ÷ 250 mg/5 mL = 10 mL.

54. Answer: B) Stop the transfusion immediately and notify the healthcare provider.
Rationale: The most important step is to stop the transfusion immediately and notify the healthcare provider. The patient could be experiencing an allergic or hemolytic reaction, which requires prompt intervention.

55. Answer: C) Maintain aseptic technique during blood handling and administration.
Rationale: Aseptic technique is crucial to prevent bacterial contamination of blood products. Blood should always be handled and administered under sterile conditions.

56. Answer: C) Trendelenburg with the head lower than the feet
Rationale: The Trendelenburg position helps increase venous return to the heart, making the insertion of a central venous catheter easier and reducing the risk of air embolism.

57. Answer: A) Decreased breath sounds on one side, B) Increased heart rate, D) Shortness of

breath
Rationale: A pneumothorax (air in the pleural space) can result in decreased breath sounds, increased heart rate due to hypoxia, and shortness of breath. Jugular vein distension may be related to other issues like heart failure or fluid overload.

58. Answer: B) Hold your breath for at least 10 seconds after inhalation.
Rationale: Holding the breath for 10 seconds helps to ensure that the medication is fully absorbed into the lungs. Rapid inhalation can cause the medication to be less effective.

59. Answer: C) Rotate the application site daily to avoid skin irritation.
Rationale: Rotating the site reduces the risk of skin irritation and ensures optimal absorption. The patch should not be placed on the same spot each time.

60. Pain Management (Continued)
Answer: B) Respiratory depression, C) Hypothermia, D) Nausea and vomiting
Rationale: Respiratory depression, hypothermia, and nausea are common signs of opioid toxicity. Bradycardia is not typically associated with opioid toxicity but may be seen in severe cases of overdose.

61. Answer: D) Constipation
Rationale: Constipation is a common and significant side effect of long-term opioid use. Patients on opioid therapy should be closely monitored, and laxatives may be recommended to prevent severe constipation.

62. Answer: A) Increase the insulin dose according to protocol.
Rationale: PN is high in glucose, which can lead to hyperglycemia. The nurse should follow institutional protocol to adjust insulin doses to maintain normal blood glucose levels.

63. Answer: B) Ensure that the PN solution is administered via a central venous catheter.
Rationale: Parenteral nutrition solutions are hypertonic and require central venous access to prevent vein irritation. Peripheral lines are not recommended for long-term PN.

64. Answer: B) Remove the catheter and insert a new one at a different site.
Rationale: If the catheter becomes dislodged or is not patent, it must be removed and replaced at a new site to avoid complications like infiltration or infection.

65. Answer: B) Prepare the site with alcohol or antiseptic solution and let it dry.
Rationale: Proper antiseptic technique before IV insertion helps to reduce the risk of infection. Allowing the antiseptic to dry ensures effective disinfection.

66. Answer: D) Dispose of them in a secure, authorized disposal container with a witness.

Rationale: Controlled substances must be disposed of according to institutional policy, typically requiring a witness to ensure proper disposal in a secure container designed for controlled substance waste.

67. Answer: B) Verify the medication with a second nurse before administration.
Rationale: A second nurse must verify all controlled substances before administration to prevent errors, ensure patient safety, and comply with regulations.

68. Answer: A) 0.75 mL
Rationale: To calculate the volume to administer, use the formula: (Desired dose ÷ Available dose) × Volume = mL to administer. (1.5 mg ÷ 4 mg) × 2 mL = 0.75 mL.

69. Answer: B) 5 hours
Rationale: To calculate the infusion time, divide the total volume by the infusion rate: 500 mL ÷ 75 mL/hr = 6.67 hours, which rounds to 5 hours for practical purposes.

70. Answer: B) 15 mL
Rationale: To calculate the mL required, use the formula: (Desired dose ÷ Available concentration) × Volume. (600 mg ÷ 200 mg) × 5 mL = 15 mL.

71. Answer: B) Chest pain and shortness of breath
Rationale: A hemolytic transfusion reaction occurs when the immune system attacks the transfused blood cells, often presenting with symptoms like chest pain, shortness of breath, and back pain.

72. Answer: A) Stop the transfusion immediately, B) Infuse saline through the same IV line, D) Notify the healthcare provider
Rationale: The first step is to stop the transfusion immediately, infuse saline to maintain IV access, and notify the healthcare provider to assess the patient and manage the reaction. Obtaining a urine sample may be necessary if hemolysis is suspected.

73. Answer: C) Fever and chills
Rationale: Fever and chills are the earliest signs of a central line-associated bloodstream infection. If left untreated, this can lead to more severe complications like sepsis.

74. Answer: C) Catheter-related thrombosis
Rationale: Swelling in the neck or face may indicate a thrombus (clot) formation in the central venous catheter or vein, which can obstruct blood flow and cause venous congestion.

75. Answer: B) "I can eat grapefruit while taking this medication to help with my cholesterol."

Rationale: Grapefruit can interfere with the metabolism of atorvastatin, increasing the risk of side effects. Patients should avoid grapefruit while on statins.

NGN NCLEX RISK POTENTIAL QUESTIONS

1. Multiple Choice Questions
   What is the primary purpose of monitoring vital signs in a patient?
   A. To diagnose specific diseases
   B. To provide insights into physiological status and detect changes
   C. To replace diagnostic testing
   D. To assess the patient's emotional state

2. Which vital sign is critical for evaluating respiratory and circulatory systems?
   A. Temperature
   B. Pulse
   C. Oxygen Saturation
   D. Blood Pressure

3. What should a nurse do first when a patient's oxygen saturation drops below 95%?
   A. Administer antipyretics
   B. Initiate oxygen therapy
   C. Reposition the patient to improve circulation
   D. Contact the physician immediately

4. Which step is essential before performing an ECG?
   A. Administering a sedative
   B. Confirming the physician's order
   C. Flushing the electrodes
   D. Checking the patient's temperature

5. What is the purpose of flushing a percutaneous feeding tube before and after feedings?
   A. To administer medications
   B. To prevent blockages
   C. To assess tube placement
   D. To increase nutrient absorption

6. When applying anti-embolic stockings, what should the nurse assess first?
   A. The patient's pain level
   B. The patient's skin condition and circulation
   C. The patient's respiratory rate
   D. The patient's dietary preferences

7. What is a key precaution to prevent healthcare-associated infections (HAIs)?
   A. Administering prophylactic antibiotics
   B. Maintaining sterile fields during procedures
   C. Limiting patient mobility
   D. Reducing documentation

8. What is the first step in a focused pain assessment?
   A. Administering analgesics
   B. Using a pain scale to quantify intensity
   C. Checking the patient's vital signs
   D. Reviewing the patient's medical history

9. What should a nurse do to prepare a patient for moderate sedation?
   A. Encourage eating a light meal
   B. Review the patient's medical history
   C. Administer a high dose of analgesics
   D. Avoid discussing the procedure

10. What is a key postoperative instruction for patients recovering from surgery?
    A. Resume heavy lifting immediately
    B. Monitor for signs of infection at the surgical site
    C. Avoid follow-up appointments
    D. Ignore dietary recommendations

Case Scenario
A 65-year-old patient is admitted to the medical-surgical unit with suspected pneumonia. The nurse notes the following vital signs: temperature 38.5°C, pulse 110 bpm, respiration rate 24 breaths/min, blood pressure 140/90 mmHg, and oxygen saturation 92%.
Multiple Choice

11. What should the nurse prioritize based on these vital signs?
    A. Administering antipyretics for fever
    B. Initiating oxygen therapy
    C. Checking the patient's blood glucose
    D. Encouraging deep breathing exercises

Multiple Response

12. Select all the actions the nurse should take based on the vital signs.
    A. Administer prescribed antipyretics
    B. Notify the physician of the oxygen saturation level
    C. Reposition the patient to improve breathing

D. Administer antihypertensive medication immediately

E. Document the vital signs

Drop-Down

13. Select the most likely cause of the patient's low oxygen saturation.

Infection

Arrhythmia

Hypoxemia

Hypertension

Case Scenario

A nurse is preparing to perform an ECG on a 55-year-old patient with chest pain. The physician has ordered the test to rule out cardiac abnormalities.

Multiple Choice

14. What is the first step the nurse should take?

A. Attach the leads to the electrodes

B. Confirm the physician's order

C. Calibrate the ECG machine

D. Clean the electrode sites

Drag-and-Drop

15. Arrange the steps of performing an ECG in the correct order.

Attach leads to electrodes

Confirm physician's order

Apply electrodes to chest, arms, and legs

Monitor and save results

Clean electrode sites

Multiple Response

16. Select all the areas where electrodes should be placed for an ECG.

A. Chest

B. Abdomen

C. Arms

D. Legs

E. Back

17. Case Scenario

A nurse is preparing to obtain a blood specimen from a 70-year-old patient with diabetes for routine lab work.

Multiple Choice

18. Which vein is commonly used for venipuncture?
    A. Femoral vein
    B. Median cubital vein
    C. Jugular vein
    D. Popliteal vein

Drop-Down
19. Select the correct angle for needle insertion during venipuncture.
 5-10 degrees
 15-30 degrees
 45-60 degrees
 90 degrees

Multiple Response
20. Select all the equipment needed for blood specimen collection.
    A. Thermometer
    B. Vacutainer tubes
    C. Tourniquet
    D. Alcohol swabs
    E. Pulse oximeter

Case Scenario
A 45-year-old patient is undergoing a colonoscopy with moderate sedation. The nurse is responsible for managing the patient during and after the procedure.
    Multiple Choice
21. What is a key goal of moderate sedation?
    A. Complete unconsciousness
    B. Reduction of anxiety and discomfort
    C. Elimination of respiratory function
    D. Increased heart rate

    Multiple Response
22. Select all the monitoring tasks the nurse should perform during moderate sedation.
    A. Track heart rate
    B. Observe level of sedation
    C. Monitor respiratory rate
    D. Administer antipyretics
    E. Check oxygen saturation

Drop-Down
23. Select the appropriate action if the patient shows signs of respiratory distress during moderate sedation.
 Administer analgesics
 Deliver supplemental oxygen
 Increase sedation dosage
 Reposition the patient to a prone position

Multiple Choice
24. What should a nurse do after collecting a urine specimen via clean-catch midstream?
    A. Store it at room temperature
    B. Label it with patient identifiers
    C. Discard it immediately
    D. Mix it with saline

25. What is the purpose of auscultating air injection sounds during gastrointestinal tube insertion?
    A. To confirm tube placement
    B. To measure tube length
    C. To prevent infection
    D. To assess patient comfort

26. What should a nurse do if a percutaneous feeding tube becomes blocked?
    A. Force the blockage with a syringe
    B. Flush with warm sterile water
    C. Replace the tube immediately
    D. Stop all feedings permanently

27. What is a key step in preventing complications with sequential compression devices (SCDs)?
    A. Applying them loosely
    B. Monitoring for proper inflation cycles
    C. Using them only at night
    D. Avoiding patient education

28. What is a primary nursing action to prevent falls in postoperative patients?
    A. Keeping beds at a high level
    B. Ensuring call bells are within reach

C. Encouraging rapid ambulation

D. Limiting patient monitoring

29. What should a nurse include in preoperative education for a patient?
    A. Encouraging a heavy meal before surgery
    B. Explaining fasting guidelines
    C. Avoiding discussion of risks
    D. Discouraging questions

30. What is a key component of a focused neurological assessment?
    A. Measuring blood glucose levels
    B. Evaluating pupil response
    C. Checking bowel sounds
    D. Assessing skin temperature

31. What is the purpose of the "teach-back" method in patient education?
    A. To reduce documentation
    B. To verify patient understanding
    C. To limit patient questions
    D. To replace written materials

Case Scenario

32. A nurse is preparing to insert a nasogastric tube for a patient requiring enteral feeding. What position should the patient be in during insertion?
    A. Prone position
    B. High Fowler's position
    C. Supine position
    D. Trendelenburg position

Drag-and-Drop

33. Arrange the steps for nasogastric tube insertion in the correct order.
    Secure the tube with adhesive tape
    Measure tube length
    Confirm placement with pH testing
    Insert tube through nostril
    Lubricate tube end

Multiple Response

34. Select all methods to confirm nasogastric tube placement.
    A. Auscultating air injection sounds

B. Checking pH of aspirated contents
C. Measuring blood pressure
D. Ordering an X-ray
E. Monitoring respiratory rate

Case Scenario
A patient has just undergone abdominal surgery and is in the recovery room. The nurse is providing postoperative education.
Multiple Choice
35. What should the nurse prioritize in postoperative education?
    A. Encouraging immediate heavy lifting
    B. Teaching wound care techniques
    C. Advising against follow-up appointments
    D. Ignoring pain management

Multiple Response
36. Select all postoperative instructions the nurse should provide.
    A. Monitor for signs of infection
    B. Resume normal diet immediately
    C. Avoid heavy lifting
    D. Recognize signs of complications
    E. Ignore follow-up appointments

Drop-Down
    37. Select the appropriate action if the patient reports severe pain at the surgical site.
        Ignore the pain as normal
        Assess pain using a pain scale
        Encourage heavy lifting
        Avoid notifying the physician

    Multiple Choice
    38. What should a nurse do after removing a nasogastric tube?
        A. Reuse the tube for another patient
        B. Dispose of it in a sharps container
        C. Flush it with saline
        D. Leave it at the bedside

    39. What is a common complication of a percutaneous feeding tube?
        A. Increased appetite

B. Tube dislodgement
C. Improved skin integrity
D. Reduced nutritional needs

40. What should a nurse assess before applying sequential compression devices (SCDs)?
    A. Patient's temperature
    B. Skin integrity and circulation
    C. Blood glucose levels
    D. Dietary preferences

41. What is a key component of safe medication administration?
    A. Ignoring the "Five Rights"
    B. Administering without checking prescriptions
    C. Verifying the right patient
    D. Avoiding documentation

42. What should a nurse do if a patient shows signs of infection at a feeding tube site?
    A. Ignore the symptoms
    B. Consult the healthcare team
    C. Remove the tube immediately
    D. Apply non-sterile dressing

43. What is a key step in collecting a sputum specimen?
    A. Using a non-sterile container
    B. Instructing the patient to cough deeply
    C. Mixing the sample with saline
    D. Collecting from the upper airway

44. What is the purpose of preoperative fasting guidelines?
    A. To increase patient comfort
    B. To prevent aspiration during anesthesia
    C. To reduce surgical time
    D. To improve wound healing

45. What should a nurse monitor during a procedure with moderate sedation?
    A. Blood glucose levels
    B. Level of sedation
    C. Dietary intake
    D. Skin temperature

46. What is a key postoperative monitoring task after moderate sedation?
    A. Encouraging immediate ambulation
    B. Evaluating level of consciousness
    C. Administering sedatives
    D. Ignoring vital signs

47. What is a key step in obtaining a clean-catch midstream urine specimen?
    A. Collecting the first stream of urine
    B. Stopping urination midstream
    C. Using a non-sterile container
    D. Mixing the sample with saline

48. What should a nurse do before inserting a nasogastric tube?
    A. Encourage the patient to eat a meal
    B. Verify the physician's order
    C. Avoid explaining the procedure
    D. Place the patient in a prone position

49. What is a key aspect of patient education for percutaneous feeding tubes?
    A. Encouraging irregular flushing
    B. Teaching daily cleaning routines
    C. Ignoring signs of infection
    D. Avoiding caregiver involvement

50. What should a nurse do if a patient's vital signs indicate an irregular pulse?
    A. Administer oxygen therapy
    B. Notify the physician
    C. Encourage rapid ambulation
    D. Ignore the finding

What is a key step in performing a focused respiratory assessment?
    A. Measuring blood glucose
    B. Listening to lung sounds
    C. Checking pupil response
    D. Assessing bowel sounds

51. What is a key benefit of preoperative education?
    A. Increased patient anxicty
    B. Reduced risk of complications

C. Elimination of follow-up care
D. Decreased patient adherence

52. What should a nurse do after obtaining a blood specimen?
    A. Reuse the needle
    B. Label the specimen accurately
    C. Store it at room temperature
    D. Discard it immediately

53. What is a key consideration for obtaining blood specimens from elderly patients?
    A. Using larger needles
    B. Applying a gentle approach
    C. Avoiding site selection
    D. Ignoring patient comfort

54. What is a key step in maintaining anti-embolic stockings?
    A. Washing them with harsh chemicals
    B. Inspecting for skin irritation
    C. Applying them loosely
    D. Avoiding replacement

55. What is a key nursing action to prevent medication errors?
    A. Ignoring the "Five Rights"
    B. Double-checking prescriptions
    C. Administering without verification
    D. Avoiding patient education

56. What should a nurse do if a patient shows signs of respiratory distress post-surgery?
    A. Encourage deep breathing exercises
    B. Ignore the symptoms
    C. Increase sedation
    D. Avoid notifying the physician

57. What is a key component of a focused cardiovascular assessment?
    A. Checking bowel sounds
    B. Assessing for edema
    C. Measuring skin temperature
    D. Evaluating pupil response

58. What is a key postoperative instruction for pain management?
    A. Avoiding pain medications
    B. Using prescribed analgesics
    C. Ignoring pain scales
    D. Encouraging heavy lifting

59. What should a nurse do to confirm understanding during patient education?
    A. Avoid asking questions
    B. Use the teach-back method
    C. Limit written resources
    D. Ignore patient feedback

60. What is a key step in collecting a stool specimen?
    A. Using a non-sterile container
    B. Providing a sterile collection kit
    C. Mixing the sample with saline
    D. Collecting from the bladder

61. What is a key monitoring task after moderate sedation?
    A. Encouraging immediate exercise
    B. Checking for airway obstruction
    C. Administering additional sedatives
    D. Ignoring vital signs

62. What should a nurse do before performing a glucose monitoring test?
    A. Avoid hand hygiene
    B. Gather necessary supplies
    C. Ignore the physician's order
    D. Skip patient education

63. What is a key step in preventing complications during venipuncture?
    A. Using a non-sterile needle
    B. Cleaning the skin with an antiseptic
    C. Ignoring patient positioning
    D. Avoiding tourniquet use

64. What is a key postoperative care task for patients with a nasogastric tube?
    A. Avoiding tube flushing
    B. Monitoring for abdominal discomfort

C. Encouraging immediate eating

D. Ignoring tube placement

65. What is a key component of a focused gastrointestinal assessment?

    A. Checking pupil response

    B. Assessing bowel sounds

    C. Measuring blood glucose

    D. Evaluating respiratory rate

66. What is a key step in applying sequential compression devices (SCDs)?

    A. Applying them loosely

    B. Ensuring a snug fit

    C. Avoiding pump connection

    D. Ignoring physician's orders

67. What should a nurse do if a patient's blood pressure is elevated during monitoring?

    A. Administer oxygen therapy

    B. Notify the physician

    C. Encourage rapid ambulation

    D. Ignore the finding

68. What is a key postoperative instruction for wound care?

    A. Keeping the wound wet

    B. Recognizing signs of infection

    C. Avoiding dressing changes

    D. Ignoring pain at the site

69. What is a key step in managing a patient during moderate sedation?

    A. Avoiding monitoring

    B. Observing for airway obstruction

    C. Administering high doses of sedatives

    D. Ignoring patient communication

70. What is a key step in collecting a nasopharyngeal swab?

    A. Using a non-sterile swab

    B. Inserting the swab gently into the nasopharynx

    C. Collecting from the throat

    D. Mixing the sample with saline

71. What should a nurse do to prepare a patient for a surgical procedure?
    A. Encourage eating a heavy meal
    B. Review the patient's medical history
    C. Avoid obtaining consent
    D. Skip hygiene instructions

72. What is a key component of a focused neurological assessment for a stroke patient?
    A. Measuring blood glucose
    B. Checking speech difficulties
    C. Assessing bowel sounds
    D. Evaluating skin temperature

73. What is a key step in maintaining a percutaneous feeding tube?
    A. Avoiding daily cleaning
    B. Inspecting the insertion site for infection
    C. Using non-sterile water for flushing
    D. Ignoring patient symptoms

74. What is a key nursing action to prevent falls in elderly patients?
    A. Raising bed height
    B. Providing non-slip footwear
    C. Encouraging rapid ambulation
    D. Limiting call bell access

75. What is a key step in performing a focused pain assessment?
    A. Ignoring patient feedback
    B. Inquiring about pain location
    C. Avoiding pain scales
    D. Skipping documentation

NGN NCLEX RISK POTENTIAL ANSWERS

1. Answer: B. To provide insights into physiological status and detect changes
   Rationale: The document states that vital signs are fundamental indicators of a person's physiological state, revealing trends that can signal underlying conditions or acute changes when monitored regularly.

2. Answer: C. Oxygen Saturation
   Rationale: The document specifies that oxygen saturation measures the percentage of oxygen in the blood, essential for evaluating respiratory and circulatory systems.

3. Answer: B. Initiate oxygen therapy
   Rationale: The document indicates that oxygen levels below 95% suggest hypoxemia, requiring urgent attention, such as initiating oxygen therapy.

4. Answer: B. Confirming the physician's order
   Rationale: The document lists confirming the physician's order as the first step in preparing for an ECG to ensure the procedure is authorized.

5. Answer: B. To prevent blockages
   Rationale: The document explains that flushing the feeding tube with sterile water or saline before and after feedings prevents blockages caused by formula residue or medication.

6. Answer: B. The patient's skin condition and circulation
   Rationale: The document emphasizes assessing the patient's skin condition and circulation before applying anti-embolic stockings to ensure proper fit and prevent complications.

7. Answer: B. Maintaining sterile fields during procedures
   Rationale: The document highlights maintaining sterile fields as a strategy to prevent infections during procedures like catheter insertion or wound dressing.

8. Answer: B. Using a pain scale to quantify intensity
   Rationale: The document states that nurses use pain scales, such as the Numeric Rating Scale, to quantify pain intensity during a focused pain assessment.

9. Answer: B. Review the patient's medical history
   Rationale: The document specifies that a pre-procedure assessment for moderate

sedation includes reviewing the client's medical history to identify risks and contraindications.

10. Answer: B. Monitor for signs of infection at the surgical site
Rationale: The document emphasizes educating patients on recognizing signs of infection, such as redness or swelling, to prevent postoperative complications.

11. Answer: B. Initiating oxygen therapy
Rationale: The document states that oxygen saturation below 95% suggests hypoxemia, requiring urgent attention such as initiating oxygen therapy.

12. Answers: A, B, C, E
Rationale: The document outlines immediate actions for abnormal vital signs, including administering antipyretics for fever, notifying the physician for low oxygen saturation, repositioning to improve breathing, and documenting findings. Administering antihypertensive medication requires a physician's order and further assessment.

13. Answer: Hypoxemia
Rationale: The document indicates that oxygen levels below 95% often suggest hypoxemia, which aligns with the patient's suspected pneumonia.

14. Answer: B. Confirm the physician's order
Rationale: The document lists confirming the physician's order as the first step in preparing for an ECG.

15. Answer:
Confirm physician's order
Clean electrode sites
Apply electrodes to chest, arms, and legs
Attach leads to electrodes
Monitor and save results
Rationale: The document outlines the ECG procedure steps in this order to ensure accuracy and patient safety.

16. Answers: A, C, D
Rationale: The document specifies that electrodes are applied to the chest, arms, and legs for an ECG.

17. Answer: B. Median cubital vein
Rationale: The document lists the median cubital vein as a common site for venipuncture.

18. Answer: 15-30 degrees
    Rationale: The document specifies inserting the needle at a 15-30 degree angle for venipuncture.

19. Answers: B, C, D
    Rationale: The document lists Vacutainer tubes, tourniquet, and alcohol swabs as necessary equipment for blood specimen collection.

20. Answer: B. Reduction of anxiety and discomfort
    Rationale: The document states that moderate sedation reduces anxiety and discomfort while maintaining responsiveness.

21. Answers: A, B, C, E
    Rationale: The document emphasizes monitoring heart rate, respiratory rate, oxygen saturation, and the level of sedation during moderate sedation.

22. Answer: Deliver supplemental oxygen
    Rationale: The document specifies delivering supplemental oxygen to manage respiratory distress during moderate sedation.

23. Answer: B. Label it with patient identifiers
    Rationale: The document emphasizes properly labeling specimens with patient identifiers to ensure accuracy and safety.

24. Answer: A. To confirm tube placement
    Rationale: The document lists auscultating air injection sounds as a method to confirm gastrointestinal tube placement.

25. Answer: B. Flush with warm sterile water
    Rationale: The document advises flushing with warm sterile water to manage a blocked feeding tube without damaging it.

26. Answer: B. Monitoring for proper inflation cycles
    Rationale: The document highlights monitoring for proper inflation and deflation cycles to ensure SCD functionality.

27. Answer: B. Ensuring call bells are within reach
    Rationale: The document lists ensuring call bells are within reach as a fall prevention measure.

28. Answer: B. Explaining fasting guidelines
    Rationale: The document emphasizes explaining fasting guidelines to prevent complications like aspiration during surgery.

29. Answer: B. Evaluating pupil response
    Rationale: The document includes evaluating pupil response as part of a focused neurological assessment.

30. Answer: B. To verify patient understanding
    Rationale: The document describes the teach-back method as a way to assess whether the client has understood the information provided.

31. Answer: B. High Fowler's position
    Rationale: The document specifies placing the patient in a high Fowler's position to reduce aspiration risk during nasogastric tube insertion.

32. Answer:
Measure tube length
Lubricate tube end
Insert tube through nostril
Confirm placement with pH testing
Secure the tube with adhesive tape
Rationale: The document outlines these steps in this order for safe nasogastric tube insertion.

33. Answers: A, B, D
    Rationale: The document lists auscultating air injection sounds, checking pH of aspirated contents, and ordering an X-ray as methods to confirm tube placement.

34. Answer: B. Teaching wound care techniques
    Rationale: The document emphasizes teaching wound care to prevent infections and promote healing.

35. Answers: A, C, D
    Rationale: The document highlights monitoring for infection, avoiding heavy lifting, and recognizing complications as key postoperative instructions.

36. Answer: Assess pain using a pain scale
    Rationale: The document specifies using pain scales to assess pain intensity and plan interventions.

37. Answer: B. Dispose of it in a sharps container
Rationale: The document states that the tube should be disposed of according to biohazard guidelines.

38. Answer: B. Tube dislodgement
Rationale: The document identifies tube dislodgement as a common complication that nurses should monitor for.

39. Answer: B. Skin integrity and circulation
Rationale: The document emphasizes assessing skin integrity and circulation to ensure safe SCD application.

40. Answer: C. Verifying the right patient
Rationale: The document lists the "Five Rights" of medication administration, including verifying the right patient.

41.
Answer: B. Consult the healthcare team
Rationale: The document advises consulting the healthcare team if signs of infection appear at the feeding tube site.

42. Answer: B. Instructing the patient to cough deeply
Rationale: The document specifies instructing the patient to cough deeply to obtain sputum from the lower respiratory tract.

43. Answer: B. To prevent aspiration during anesthesia
Rationale: The document states that fasting guidelines are followed to prevent aspiration during surgery.

44. Answer: B. Level of sedation
Rationale: The document emphasizes monitoring the level of sedation to ensure patient safety during moderate sedation.

45. Answer: B. Evaluating level of consciousness
Rationale: The document highlights evaluating the level of consciousness as a key post-sedation monitoring task.

46. Answer: B. Stopping urination midstream
Rationale: The document describes stopping urination midstream to minimize contamination during clean-catch collection.

47. Answer: B. Verify the physician's order
    Rationale: The document lists verifying the physician's order as a preparation step for nasogastric tube insertion.

48. Answer: B. Teaching daily cleaning routines
    Rationale: The document emphasizes teaching daily cleaning to prevent complications with feeding tubes.

49. Answer: B. Notify the physician
    Rationale: The document states that an irregular pulse may suggest arrhythmia or shock, requiring physician notification.

50. Answer: B. Listening to lung sounds
    Rationale: The document includes listening to lung sounds with a stethoscope as part of a focused respiratory assessment.

51. Answer: B. Reduced risk of complications
    Rationale: The document states that preoperative education reduces the risk of complications by ensuring patient compliance.

52. Answer: B. Label the specimen accurately
    Rationale: The document emphasizes labeling specimens with patient information, date, and time of collection.

53. Answer: B. Applying a gentle approach
    Rationale: The document notes that elderly patients have fragile veins, requiring a gentle approach.

54. Answer: B. Inspecting for skin irritation
    Rationale: The document emphasizes daily inspection for skin irritation under anti-embolic stockings.

55. Answer: B. Double-checking prescriptions
    Rationale: The document highlights double-checking prescriptions as part of safe medication administration.

56. Answer: A. Encourage deep breathing exercises
    Rationale: The document suggests repositioning or encouraging breathing exercises to improve respiratory function.

57. Answer: B. Assessing for edema
Rationale: The document includes assessing for edema as part of a focused cardiovascular assessment.

58. Answer: B. Using prescribed analgesics
Rationale: The document emphasizes educating patients about prescribed pain medications for postoperative pain management.

59. Answer: B. Use the teach-back method
Rationale: The document describes the teach-back method as a way to verify patient understanding.

60. Answer: B. Providing a sterile collection kit
Rationale: The document specifies providing sterile collection kits for stool specimen collection.

61. Answer: B. Checking for airway obstruction
Rationale: The document emphasizes ensuring the airway remains unobstructed post-sedation.

62. Answer: B. Gather necessary supplies
Rationale: The document lists gathering supplies as a preparation step for glucose monitoring.

63. Answer: B. Cleaning the skin with an antiseptic
Rationale: The document specifies cleaning the skin with an antiseptic solution to prevent infection during venipuncture.

64. Answer: B. Monitoring for abdominal discomfort
Rationale: The document emphasizes monitoring for abdominal discomfort to detect complications with nasogastric tubes.

65. Answer: B. Assessing bowel sounds
Rationale: The document includes checking bowel sounds as part of a focused gastrointestinal assessment.

66. Answer: B. Ensuring a snug fit
Rationale: The document specifies ensuring a snug but not tight fit for SCD application.

67. Answer: B. Notify the physician
    Rationale: The document states that elevated blood pressure may signal stress or chronic conditions, requiring physician notification.

68. Answer: B. Recognizing signs of infection
    Rationale: The document emphasizes teaching patients to recognize signs of infection for proper wound care.

69. Answer: B. Observing for airway obstruction
    Rationale: The document highlights observing for signs of airway obstruction during moderate sedation.

70. Answer: B. Inserting the swab gently into the nasopharynx
    Rationale: The document specifies gently inserting a swab into the nasopharynx for respiratory virus testing.

71. Answer: B. Review the patient's medical history
    Rationale: The document emphasizes reviewing medical history as part of preoperative assessment.

72. Answer: B. Checking speech difficulties
    Rationale: The document includes checking speech difficulties as part of a focused neurological assessment.

73. Answer: B. Inspecting the insertion site for infection
    Rationale: The document emphasizes inspecting the insertion site for signs of infection.

74. Answer: B. Providing non-slip footwear
    Rationale: The document lists providing non-slip footwear as a fall prevention measure.

75. Answer: B. Inquiring about pain location
    Rationale: The document specifies inquiring about the location, nature, and duration of pain during a focused pain assessment.

NGN NCLEX PHYSIOLOGICAL ADAPTATION QUESTIONS

1. Multiple Choice
   A nurse is preparing a patient for central line placement. Which position is most appropriate to facilitate the procedure?
   A. Supine
   B. Fowler's
   C. Trendelenburg
   D. Prone

2. Case Scenario
   A 45-year-old patient is scheduled for a thoracentesis to remove pleural fluid. The nurse is preparing the patient. What is the most appropriate position for the patient during the procedure?
   A. Supine with head elevated
   B. Seated upright with arms resting on a table
   C. Left lateral recumbent
   D. Prone with head turned to the side

3. Multiple Response
   During the thoracentesis, the nurse monitors the patient's vital signs. Which of the following should the nurse monitor during the procedure? (Select all that apply.)
   A. Blood pressure
   B. Oxygen saturation
   C. Heart rate
   D. Temperature
   E. Pain level

4. Drop-Down
   A nurse is assisting with a bronchoscopy. Select the most appropriate pre-procedural medication to administer as ordered by the physician.
   Bronchodilator
   Sedative
   Antibiotic
   Analgesic

5. Drag and Drop
   Place the steps for assisting with central line placement in the correct order.

A. Secure the central line and apply a sterile dressing.
B. Verify the physician's order and confirm patient identity.
C. Monitor the patient's vital signs during the procedure.
D. Prepare the sterile field with necessary instruments.

6. Multiple Choice
   After a bronchoscopy, what is a priority nursing action to monitor for complications?
   A. Encourage deep breathing exercises
   B. Observe for hypoxia or bronchospasm
   C. Administer a bronchodilator
   D. Check the patient's blood glucose

7. Multiple Response
   Which of the following are post-procedural tasks for a nurse after central line placement? (Select all that apply.)
   A. Educate the patient about the procedure.
   B. Secure the central line and apply a sterile dressing.
   C. Monitor for immediate complications like pneumothorax.
   D. Administer sedatives as needed.
   E. Document the procedure details.

8. Drop-Down
   During a thoracentesis, the nurse notices the patient's oxygen saturation dropping. The most appropriate immediate action is to:
   Stop the procedure and notify the physician.
   Increase the suction pressure.
   Reposition the patient to supine.
   Continue monitoring without intervention.

9. Multiple Choice
   What is the primary purpose of maintaining sterility during central line placement?
   A. To reduce patient discomfort
   B. To ensure accurate catheter placement
   C. To prevent infection
   D. To facilitate faster recovery

10. Multiple Choice
    Post-thoracentesis, the nurse is preparing to send collected fluid to the lab. Which complication should the nurse monitor for immediately after the procedure?
    A. Hyperglycemia

B. Pneumothorax

C. Urinary retention

D. Seizure activity

11. Multiple Choice

What is the primary purpose of phototherapy for neonatal jaundice?

A. To reduce skin inflammation

B. To break down excess bilirubin

C. To promote wound healing

D. To alleviate depressive symptoms

12. Multiple Response

A 2-day-old newborn is prescribed phototherapy for jaundice. Which pre-procedural tasks should the nurse perform? (Select all that apply.)

A. Review the infant's medical history for photosensitivity disorders.

B. Administer a sedative to the infant.

C. Ensure protective eye gear is in place.

D. Calibrate the light source for correct wavelength.

E. Educate the caregiver about the procedure.

13. Drop-Down

During phototherapy for psoriasis, the nurse observes a skin rash. The most appropriate action is to:

Continue the session and document the rash.

Stop the session and notify the healthcare provider.

Increase the light intensity.

Apply a moisturizer to the rash.

14. Drag and Drop

Arrange the steps for implementing phototherapy for neonatal jaundice in the correct order.

A. Position the infant under the phototherapy lamp.

B. Assess the infant's medical history.

C. Ensure protective eye gear is worn.

D. Monitor bilirubin levels during therapy.

15. Multiple Choice

Which condition is treated with bright light therapy mimicking sunlight?

A. Neonatal jaundice

B. Psoriasis

C. Seasonal Affective Disorder (SAD)

D. Eczema

16. Multiple Response

Which safety measures should the nurse prioritize during phototherapy? (Select all that apply.)

A. Ensure protective eye gear is worn.

B. Monitor for signs of dehydration.

C. Adjust light intensity without physician orders.

D. Inspect the skin for burns.

E. Maintain appropriate hydration.

17. Multiple Choice

The newborn undergoing phototherapy shows signs of dehydration. What is the most appropriate nursing action?

A. Increase the light intensity to speed up treatment.

B. Provide supplemental fluids as prescribed.

C. Discontinue phototherapy permanently.

D. Reposition the infant closer to the light source.

18. Drop-Down

For a patient with Seasonal Affective Disorder receiving phototherapy, the nurse should position the light box:

At eye level.

Above the patient's head.

Below the patient's waist.

Behind the patient's back.

19. Multiple Choice

What is a common challenge in phototherapy for Seasonal Affective Disorder?

A. Equipment malfunctions

B. Patient non-compliance

C. Risk of infection

D. Excessive bleeding

20. Multiple Choice

Post-phototherapy, the nurse reassesses the newborn's bilirubin levels. What should the nurse document after the session?

A. The infant's weight only

B. Bil782. Bilirubin levels and skin condition

C. The light intensity settings
D. The room temperature

21. Multiple Choice (MC)
    A nurse is monitoring a client with fever. Which intervention is most appropriate?
    A. Apply a heated blanket
    B. Use cold compresses
    C. Increase room humidity
    D. Restrict fluid intake

22. Multiple Response
    A 70-year-old client is hypothermic after exposure to cold weather. Which interventions should the nurse implement? (Select all that apply.)
    A. Apply a warming blanket
    B. Administer antipyretics
    C. Monitor for signs of improvement
    D. Provide warm fluids
    E. Use cold compresses

23. Drop-Down
    For a newborn at risk of cold stress, the nurse should prioritize:
    Skin-to-skin contact.
    Cold compresses.
    Light clothing.
    High room humidity.

24. Drag and Drop (DND)
    Arrange the steps for managing a client's hypothermia in the correct order.
    A. Monitor for signs of improvement.
    B. Apply a warming blanket.
    C. Assess body temperature.
    D. Provide warm fluids.

25. Multiple Choice (MC)
    Which thermometer is most appropriate for an elderly client with hypothermia?
    A. Oral
    B. Tympanic
    C. Rectal
    D. Infrared

26. Multiple Response (MR)
    Which environmental adjustments should the nurse make to maintain a client's optimal temperature? (Select all that apply.)
    A. Adjust room temperature
    B. Provide adequate ventilation
    C. Use heavy blankets for fever
    D. Manage humidity levels
    E. Ensure proper lighting

27. Multiple Choice
    The hypothermic client's temperature is improving. What should the nurse do next?
    A. Discontinue warming measures immediately
    B. Continue monitoring temperature
    C. Administer antipyretics
    D. Restrict fluid intake

28. Drop-Down
    For a client with fever, the nurse should select bedding that is:
    Heavy and insulated.
    Light and breathable.
    Synthetic and non-breathable.
    Wet and cooling.

29. Multiple Choice
    What is a key consideration for maintaining optimal temperature in post-operative clients?
    A. Monitor for temperature spikes due to infection
    B. Encourage heavy clothing
    C. Restrict ventilation
    D. Avoid hydration

30. Multiple Choice
    The elderly client is now normothermic. What education should the nurse provide to prevent future hypothermia?
    A. Avoid all fluids
    B. Wear appropriate clothing for weather conditions

C. Keep windows closed at all times

D. Use cooling devices regularly

31. Multiple Choice

What is a primary nursing responsibility for a client on a ventilator?

A. Adjusting ventilator settings independently

B. Monitoring vital signs continuously

C. Administering sedatives without orders

D. Repositioning the client every 8 hours

32. Multiple Response

A client with acute respiratory failure is on a ventilator. Which parameters should the nurse monitor? (Select all that apply.)

A. Tidal volume

B. Respiratory rate

C. Blood glucose

D. Positive end-expiratory pressure (PEEP)

E. Fraction of inspired oxygen (FiO2)

33. Drop-Down

The ventilator alarm indicates high airway pressure. The nurse should first:

Check for tubing obstructions.

Increase the tidal volume.

Administer a bronchodilator.

Reposition the client to prone.

34. Drag and Drop

Place the steps for preventing ventilator-associated pneumonia (VAP) in the correct order of priority.

A. Perform regular oral care with antiseptic solutions.

B. Maintain head of bed at 30-45 degrees.

C. Assess readiness for weaning.

D. Implement daily sedation vacations.

35. Multiple Choice

What is a potential complication of ventilator therapy?

A. Hyperglycemia

B. Barotrauma

C. Urinary retention

D. Seizure activity

36. Multiple Response
Which actions promote psychological well-being for a ventilated client? (Select all that apply.)
A. Use picture boards for communication
B. Provide reassurance
C. Restrict family visits
D. Use hand signals
E. Administer sedatives routinely

37. Multiple Choice
The client shows signs of respiratory distress during a spontaneous breathing trial. What should the nurse do?
A. Continue the trial for 30 minutes
B. Resume full ventilatory support
C. Administer a sedative
D. Increase the oxygen flow

38. Drop-Down
To prevent pressure injuries from an endotracheal tube, the nurse should:
Reposition the tube periodically.
Apply adhesive tape tightly.
Use non-sterile gloves.
Restrict oral care.

39. Multiple Choice
What is the purpose of daily sedation vacations in ventilator care?
A. To reduce medication costs
B. To assess readiness for weaning
C. To prevent oral infections
D. To improve blood pressure

40. Multiple Choice
The client is successfully extubated. What should the nurse monitor post-extubation?
A. Blood glucose levels
B. Signs of respiratory distress
C. Urinary output
D. Skin turgor

41. Multiple Choice

What is the purpose of a Jackson-Pratt drain?
A. To administer fluids
B. To remove excess wound fluids
C. To measure blood pressure
D. To deliver oxygen

42. Multiple Response
A client has a chest tube for pleural effusion. Which monitoring tasks should the nurse perform? (Select all that apply.)
A. Inspect tubing for kinks
B. Assess respiratory status
C. Check for air leaks
D. Monitor blood glucose
E. Record drainage output

43. Drop-Down
The nurse notices reduced drainage in a Hemovac drain. The most appropriate action is to:
Flush the tubing with sterile saline.
Increase suction pressure.
Remove the drain immediately.
Reposition the client to prone.
Answer: Flush the tubing with sterile saline.
Rationale: The document recommends flushing the tubing with sterile saline to maintain patency if drainage is reduced due to clots or blockages.

44. Drag and Drop
Arrange the steps for maintaining a chest tube system in the correct order.
A. Secure all connections.
B. Inspect tubing for obstructions.
C. Adjust suction levels as prescribed.
D. Clean the insertion site.

45. Multiple Choice
What is a key component of negative pressure wound therapy (NPWT)?
A. Oxygen delivery system
B. Vacuum pump

C. Intravenous fluid pump
D. Blood pressure monitor

46. Multiple Response
Which tasks are involved in maintaining NPWT systems? (Select all that apply.)
A. Change foam dressings every 48-72 hours
B. Clean reusable components
C. Increase pressure without orders
D. Reseal air leaks promptly
E. Monitor wound condition

47. Multiple Choice
The chest tube collection chamber is full. What should the nurse do?
A. Increase suction pressure
B. Replace the collection chamber
C. Flush the tubing with saline
D. Disconnect the system

48. Drop-Down
The nurse notices an air leak in an NPWT system. The most appropriate action is to:
Continue therapy and document the leak.
Reseal the adhesive film.
Remove the foam dressing.
Increase the vacuum pressure.

49. Multiple Choice
What is a priority when monitoring a surgical wound drain?
A. Check for blockages
B. Adjust suction without orders
C. Restrict patient movement
D. Apply non-sterile dressings

50. Multiple Choice
The client's surgical wound drain output is bloody. What should the nurse document?
A. The client's blood pressure only
B. The volume and color of the drainage
C. The room temperature
D. The client's pain level only

Multiple Choice

51. What is the primary purpose of peritoneal dialysis?
    A. To deliver oxygen to tissues
    B. To remove waste products and toxins
    C. To administer medications
    D. To measure blood pressure

52. Multiple Response
    A client is preparing for peritoneal dialysis at home. Which pre-procedural tasks should the nurse perform? (Select all that apply.)
    A. Assess the client's ability to perform self-care
    B. Administer a sedative
    C. Inspect the catheter site
    D. Educate the client on aseptic technique
    E. Check blood glucose levels

53. Drop-Down
    The peritoneal dialysis effluent appears cloudy. The most appropriate action is to:
    Continue the dialysis session.
    Notify the healthcare provider.
    Increase the dialysate volume.
    Reposition the client to supine.

54. Drag and Drop
    Arrange the steps for performing peritoneal dialysis in the correct order.
    A. Connect tubing to the catheter.
    B. Inspect the catheter site.
    C. Infuse the dialysate solution.
    D. Drain the dialysate into a collection bag.

55. Multiple Choice
    What is a potential complication of peritoneal dialysis?
    A. Hypoglycemia
    B. Peritonitis
    C. Seizure activity
    D. Skin rash

56. Multiple Response
    Which actions promote client comfort during peritoneal dialysis? (Select all that apply.)
    A. Infuse dialysate slowly

B. Monitor for abdominal pain
C. Restrict fluid intake
D. Secure the catheter
E. Provide emotional support

57. Multiple Choice
The client reports abdominal tenderness during peritoneal dialysis. What should the nurse do?
A. Continue the dialysis session
B. Stop the procedure and notify the provider
C. Increase the dialysate concentration
D. Reposition the client to prone

58. Drop-Down
The nurse is educating a client on home peritoneal dialysis. The most important topic is:
Dietary restrictions.
Exercise routines.
Blood pressure monitoring.
Pain management.

59. Multiple Choice
What should the nurse monitor to assess the effectiveness of peritoneal dialysis?
A. Blood glucose levels
B. Serum electrolyte levels
C. Skin turgor
D. Respiratory rate

60. Multiple Choice
The client's peritoneal dialysis is complete, and the effluent is clear. What should the nurse document?
A. The client's pain level only
B. The volume and characteristics of the effluent
C. The room temperature
D. The client's blood pressure only

61. Multiple Choice
What is the purpose of suctioning?
A. To administer medications
B. To clear airway obstructions
C. To measure oxygen levels
D. To deliver nutrition

62. Multiple Response

A client with a tracheostomy requires suctioning. Which equipment should the nurse gather? (Select all that apply.)

A. Sterile suction catheter

B. Pulse oximeter

C. Blood glucose monitor

D. Sterile saline solution

E. Personal protective equipment

63. Drop-Down

During tracheal suctioning, the client shows signs of distress. The nurse should:

Continue suctioning for 30 seconds.

Pause the procedure and administer oxygen.

Increase suction pressure.

Reposition the catheter deeper.

64. Drag and Drop

Arrange the steps for performing nasopharyngeal suctioning in the correct order.

A. Insert the catheter without suction.

B. Position the client in semi-Fowler's.

C. Apply intermittent suction while withdrawing.

D. Prepare the suction equipment.

65. Multiple Choice

What is a potential complication of suctioning?

A. Hyperglycemia

B. Hypoxia

C. Skin rash

D. Constipation

66. Multiple Response

Which actions ensure safe suctioning? (Select all that apply.)

A. Use sterile techniques

B. Monitor oxygen levels

C. Apply continuous suction

D. Limit suctioning to 10-15 seconds

E. Perform hand hygiene

Case Scenario

The suction catheter becomes clogged during the procedure.

67. Multiple Choice

What should the nurse do?

A. Increase suction pressure

B. Flush the catheter with sterile saline

C. Replace the catheter with a larger one

D. Continue suctioning with the clogged catheter

68. Drop-Down

The appropriate suction pressure for an adult client is:

50–80 mmHg

80–100 mmHg

100–150 mmHg

150–200 mmHg

69. Multiple Choice

What should the nurse document after suctioning?

A. The client's blood pressure only

B. The amount and color of secretions

C. The room humidity level

D. The client's dietary intake

70. Multiple Choice

The client's oxygen saturation improves post-suctioning. What is the next nursing action?

A. Discontinue oxygen therapy

B. Reassess the client's comfort

C. Increase suction frequency

D. Restrict fluid intake

71. Multiple Choice

What is the purpose of cleaning a wound from the center outward?

A. To reduce pain

B. To prevent contamination

C. To promote blood flow

D. To apply medication

72. Multiple Response

A client has a surgical wound requiring a dressing change. Which supplies should the nurse gather? (Select all that apply.)

A. Sterile gloves

B. Antiseptic solution

C. Blood pressure cuff

D. Sterile dressing materials

E. Adhesive tape

73. Drop-Down

The old dressing adheres to the wound. The nurse should:

Pull it off quickly.

Moisten it with saline.

Apply antiseptic directly.

Leave it in place.

74. Drag and Drop

Arrange the steps for performing a wound dressing change in the correct order.

A. Clean the wound with prescribed solution.

B. Remove the old dressing.

C. Apply the new dressing.

D. Perform hand hygiene.

75. Multiple Choice

Which dressing is appropriate for a wound with heavy exudate?

A. Gauze dressing

B. Hydrocolloid dressing

C. Alginate dressing

D. Transparent film dressing

NGN NCLEX PHYSIOLOGICAL ADAPTATION ANSWERS

1. Answer: C. Trendelenburg
   Rationale: The document states that the Trendelenburg position is used to facilitate central line insertion by promoting venous filling and reducing the risk of air embolism.

2. Answer: B. Seated upright with arms resting on a table
   Rationale: The document specifies that the patient is typically seated upright with arms resting on a table during thoracentesis to allow access to the pleural space and ensure patient comfort.

3. Answers: A, B, C, E
   Rationale: The document highlights monitoring vital signs (blood pressure, heart rate) and oxygen saturation during thoracentesis. Pain level is also relevant to assess patient comfort and detect complications.

4. Answer: Sedative
   Rationale: The document notes that nurses administer pre-procedural medications, such as sedatives, to prepare patients for bronchoscopy, ensuring comfort and reducing anxiety.

5. Answer: B, D, C, A
   Rationale: The document outlines the sequence: verify the order and patient identity (pre-procedural), prepare the sterile field (pre-procedural), monitor vital signs (intra-procedural), and secure the line with a dressing (post-procedural).

6. Answer: B. Observe for hypoxia or bronchospasm
   Rationale: The document emphasizes observing for complications like hypoxia or bronchospasm post-bronchoscopy to ensure patient safety.

7. Answers: B, C, E
   Rationale: The document lists securing the central line, monitoring for complications like pneumothorax, and documenting the procedure as post-procedural tasks. Education occurs pre-procedurally, and sedatives are not mentioned post-procedure.

8. Answer: Stop the procedure and notify the physician.
   Rationale: A drop in oxygen saturation indicates a potential complication, such as pneumothorax, requiring immediate cessation of the procedure and physician notification, as implied by the document's emphasis on monitoring for complications.

9. Answer: C. To prevent infection
   Rationale: The document stresses maintaining sterility to adhere to aseptic techniques, which primarily prevents infection during invasive procedures like central line placement.

10. Answer: B. Pneumothorax
    Rationale: The document identifies pneumothorax as a key complication to monitor post-thoracentesis due to the risk of lung injury during the procedure.

11. Answer: B. To break down excess bilirubin
    Rationale: The document states that phototherapy for neonatal jaundice uses blue or white light to break down excess bilirubin in newborns.

12. Answers: A, C, D, E
    Rationale: The document lists reviewing medical history, ensuring eye protection, calibrating the light source, and educating caregivers as pre-procedural tasks. Sedatives are not mentioned for neonatal phototherapy.

13. Answer: Stop the session and notify the healthcare provider.
    Rationale: The document emphasizes checking for adverse reactions like skin rash during phototherapy and taking appropriate action, such as stopping the session and notifying the provider.

14. Answer: B, C, A, D
    Rationale: The document outlines assessing medical history first, ensuring eye protection, positioning the infant, and then monitoring bilirubin levels during therapy.

15. Answer: C. Seasonal Affective Disorder (SAD)
    Rationale: The document specifies that bright light therapy is used for Seasonal Affective Disorder to alleviate depressive symptoms by mimicking sunlight.

16. Answers: A, B, D, E
    Rationale: The document emphasizes ensuring eye protection, monitoring for dehydration and burns, and maintaining hydration. Adjusting light intensity requires physician orders.

17. Answer: B. Provide supplemental fluids as prescribed.
    Rationale: The document highlights maintaining hydration to prevent dehydration, a potential complication of phototherapy, by providing fluids as prescribed.

18. Answer: At eye level.
    Rationale: The document specifies positioning the light box at eye level for patients with SAD to ensure effective light exposure.

19. Answer: B. Patient non-compliance
    Rationale: The document identifies patient non-compliance as a challenge in phototherapy for SAD, as patients may resist adhering to session schedules.

20. Answer: B. Bilirubin levels and skin condition
    Rationale: The document emphasizes documenting bilirubin levels and skin condition post-phototherapy to assess treatment effectiveness and detect complications.

21. Answer: B. Use cold compresses
    Rationale: The document recommends cooling techniques, such as cold compresses, for clients with fever to help reduce body temperature.

22. Answers: A, C, D
    Rationale: The document lists warming blankets, monitoring for improvement, and warm fluids as interventions for hypothermia. Antipyretics and cold compresses are used for fever, not hypothermia.

23. Answer: Skin-to-skin contact.
    Rationale: The document highlights skin-to-skin contact as a key intervention for newborns to prevent cold stress and maintain optimal temperature.

24. Answer: C, B, D, A
    Rationale: The document implies assessing temperature first, applying warming devices, providing warm fluids, and then monitoring for improvement.

25. Answer: C. Rectal
    Rationale: The document mentions rectal thermometers as an option for accurate temperature measurement, especially in hypothermia cases where precision is critical.

26. Answers: A, B, D
    Rationale: The document lists adjusting room temperature, providing ventilation, and managing humidity as environmental controls. Heavy blankets are inappropriate for fever, and lighting is not mentioned.

27. Answer: B. Continue monitoring temperature
    Rationale: The document emphasizes continuous temperature monitoring to ensure improvement and prevent recurrence of hypothermia.

28. Answer: Light and breathable.
    Rationale: The document recommends light, breathable bedding for clients with fever to promote cooling and comfort.

29. Answer: A. Monitor for temperature spikes due to infection
    Rationale: The document highlights monitoring for temperature spikes in post-operative clients due to potential infections or surgical reactions.

30. Answer: B. Wear appropriate clothing for weather conditions
    Rationale: The document emphasizes educating clients about wearing appropriate clothing to maintain optimal temperature and prevent hypothermia.

31. Answer: B. Monitoring vital signs continuously
    Rationale: The document stresses continuous monitoring of vital signs to assess the client's response to ventilatory support.

32. Answers: A, B, D, E
    Rationale: The document lists tidal volume, respiratory rate, PEEP, and FiO2 as ventilator parameters to monitor. Blood glucose is not relevant to ventilator care.

33. Answer: Check for tubing obstructions.
    Rationale: The document mentions monitoring alarms for issues like high airway pressure, which may indicate obstructions requiring immediate checking.

34. Answer: B, A, D, C
    Rationale: The document prioritizes elevating the head of the bed to prevent aspiration, followed by oral care, sedation vacations, and weaning assessment.

35. Answer: B. Barotrauma
    Rationale: The document identifies barotrauma as a complication due to excessive ventilatory pressures or volumes.

36. Answers: A, B, D
    Rationale: The document mentions using picture boards, providing reassurance, and using hand signals to support communication and comfort. Restricting visits and routine sedatives are not recommended.

37. Answer: B. Resume full ventilatory support
Rationale: The document implies that signs of distress during weaning trials require resuming ventilatory support to ensure patient safety.

38. Answer: Reposition the tube periodically.
Rationale: The document recommends repositioning the endotracheal tube to prevent pressure injuries to the lips and oral mucosa.

39. Answer: B. To assess readiness for weaning
Rationale: The document states that daily sedation vacations are used to assess the client's readiness to wean from the ventilator.

40. Answer: B. Signs of respiratory distress
Rationale: The document emphasizes monitoring for respiratory distress post-extubation to ensure airway stability.

41. Answer: B. To remove excess wound fluids
Rationale: The document describes Jackson-Pratt drains as closed suction systems used to remove blood, pus, or serous fluid from a wound site.

42. Answers: A, B, C, E
Rationale: The document lists inspecting tubing, assessing respiratory status, checking for air leaks, and recording drainage output as key monitoring tasks for chest tubes.

43. Answer: Flush the tubing with sterile saline.
Rationale: The document recommends flushing the tubing with sterile saline to maintain patency if drainage is reduced due to clots or blockages.

44. Answer: B, A, C, D
Rationale: The document suggests first inspecting tubing for obstructions, securing connections, adjusting suction, and then cleaning the insertion site.

45. Answer: B. Vacuum pump
Rationale: The document describes the vacuum pump as a key component of NPWT, generating negative pressure to promote wound healing.

46. Answers: A, B, D, E
Rationale: The document lists changing dressings, cleaning components, resealing leaks,

and monitoring wound condition as NPWT maintenance tasks. Increasing pressure requires orders.

47. Answer: B. Replace the collection chamber
Rationale: The document states that full collection chambers should be replaced according to manufacturer guidelines.

48. Answer: Reseal the adhesive film.
Rationale: The document emphasizes promptly resealing air leaks to ensure effective NPWT.

49. Answer: A. Check for blockages
Rationale: The document highlights checking for blockages to ensure drain patency and prevent complications.

50. Answer: B. The volume and color of the drainage
Rationale: The document emphasizes documenting the volume, color, and consistency of drain output to monitor for complications.

51. Answer: B. To remove waste products and toxins
Rationale: The document states that peritoneal dialysis uses the peritoneal membrane to remove waste, excess fluid, and toxins.

52. Answers: A, C, D
Rationale: The document lists assessing self-care ability, inspecting the catheter site, and educating on aseptic technique as pre-procedural tasks. Sedatives and blood glucose checks are not mentioned.

53. Answer: Notify the healthcare provider.
Rationale: The document notes that cloudy effluent may indicate peritonitis, requiring immediate notification of the provider.

54. Answer: B, A, C, D
Rationale: The document outlines inspecting the catheter site, connecting tubing, infusing dialysate, and draining the effluent in that order.

55. Answer: B. Peritonitis
Rationale: The document identifies peritonitis as a key complication due to the risk of infection at the catheter site.

56. Answers: A, B, D, E
    Rationale: The document mentions slow infusion, monitoring for pain, securing the catheter, and providing emotional support to ensure comfort. Fluid restriction is not mentioned.

57. Answer: B. Stop the procedure and notify the provider
    Rationale: The document states that abdominal tenderness may indicate infection, requiring immediate cessation and provider notification.

58. Answer: Dietary restrictions.
    Rationale: The document emphasizes educating clients on dietary restrictions to support the effectiveness of peritoneal dialysis.

59. Answer: B. Serum electrolyte levels
    Rationale: The document highlights monitoring serum electrolytes and creatinine levels to evaluate dialysis effectiveness.

60. Answer: B. The volume and characteristics of the effluent
    Rationale: The document emphasizes documenting the volume and characteristics of the effluent to monitor for complications and treatment effectiveness.

61. Answer: B. To clear airway obstructions
    Rationale: The document defines suctioning as a procedure to remove mucus, blood, or other secretions from the airway.

62. Answers: A, B, D, E
    Rationale: The document lists sterile suction catheters, pulse oximeters, sterile saline, and PPE as necessary for suctioning. Blood glucose monitors are not relevant.

63. Answer: Pause the procedure and administer oxygen.
    Rationale: The document states that suctioning should be paused if the client shows distress, with oxygen administered as needed.

64. Answer: B, D, A, C
    Rationale: The document outlines positioning the client, preparing equipment, inserting the catheter, and applying suction in that order.

65. Answer: B. Hypoxia
    Rationale: The document identifies hypoxia as a potential complication of suctioning if not performed correctly.

66. Answers: A, B, D, E
Rationale: The document emphasizes sterile techniques, monitoring oxygen levels, limiting suction time, and hand hygiene. Continuous suction is avoided to prevent tissue damage.

67. Answer: B. Flush the catheter with sterile saline
Rationale: The document recommends flushing the catheter with sterile saline to clear blockages.

68. Answer: 100–150 mmHg
Rationale: The document specifies 100–150 mmHg as the appropriate suction pressure for adults.

69. Answer: B. The amount and color of secretions
Rationale: The document emphasizes documenting the amount, consistency, and color of secretions post-suctioning.

70. Answer: B. Reassess the client's comfort
Rationale: The document highlights reassessing the client's comfort post-suctioning to ensure their well-being.

71. Answer: B. To prevent contamination
Rationale: The document states that cleaning from the cleanest area (center) outward prevents contamination of the wound.

72. Answers: A, B, D, E
Rationale: The document lists sterile gloves, antiseptic solution, sterile dressing materials, and adhesive tape as necessary supplies. A blood pressure cuff is not relevant.

73. Answer: Moisten it with saline.
Rationale: The document recommends moistening an adherent dressing with saline to gently loosen it and avoid tissue damage.

74. Answer: D, B, A, C
Rationale: The document outlines hand hygiene first, followed by removing the old dressing, cleaning the wound, and applying the new dressing.

75. Answer: C. Alginate dressing

Rationale: The document specifies alginate dressings for wounds with heavy exudate due to their absorbent properties.

COMPREHENSIVE 1 NGN NCLEX QUESTIONS

Multiple Choice
1. A nurse is prioritizing care for four clients. Which client should the nurse assess first?
   A. A client with a blood pressure of 120/80 mmHg, reporting mild headache.
   B. A client with a respiratory rate of 28 breaths/min and oxygen saturation of 92%.
   C. A client with a temperature of 100.4°F and stable vital signs.
   D. A client scheduled for discharge in 2 hours.

Multiple Choice
2. A nurse is preparing to administer a medication via intramuscular injection. Which action best ensures client safety?
   A. Using a 25-gauge needle for the injection.
   B. Aspirating before injecting the medication.
   C. Injecting the medication rapidly.
   D. Administering the injection in the arm.

Multiple Choice
3. A nurse is teaching a client about breast self-examination (BSE). When is the best time to perform BSE?
   A. The day after menstruation ends.
   B. During menstruation.
   C. Two weeks before menstruation.
   D. Any time during the month.

Multiple Choice
4. A client with depression expresses feelings of hopelessness. Which response by the nurse is most therapeutic?
   A. "You have so much to live for."
   B. "I understand how you feel; let's talk about what's been going on."
   C. "Things will get better soon."
   D. "Why do you feel this way?"

Multiple Choice
5. A nurse is assisting a client with mobility issues to reposition in bed. Which action should the nurse take to prevent injury?
   A. Pull the client up using the bed sheets.
   B. Use a draw sheet and assistance from another nurse.
   C. Lift the client by holding their arms.
   D. Encourage the client to move independently.

Multiple Choice

6. A nurse is administering heparin 5,000 units subcutaneously. What is the most appropriate injection site?
   A. Deltoid muscle.
   B. Ventrogluteal site.
   C. Abdomen, 2 inches from the umbilicus.
   D. Upper thigh.

Multiple Choice

7. A client is receiving a blood transfusion. Which symptom should the nurse report immediately as a potential transfusion reaction?
   A. Heart rate of 80 beats/min.
   B. Temperature increase of 1°C.
   C. Mild itching at the infusion site.
   D. Urine output of 50 mL/hr.

Multiple Choice

8. A client with heart failure is experiencing dyspnea. Which position should the nurse place the client in to improve breathing?
   A. Supine with legs elevated.
   B. Prone with head turned to the side.
   C. Fowler's position.
   D. Trendelenburg position.

Case Scenario: Questions 9-14

Scenario: A nurse is managing care for a 65-year-old client admitted with pneumonia. The client has a history of COPD, is receiving oxygen at 2 L/min via nasal cannula, and has an IV of normal saline at 100 mL/hr. Vital signs: BP 140/90 mmHg, HR 88 bpm, RR 24 breaths/min, SpO2 94%, Temp 99.8°F. The client reports chest pain on inspiration

Multiple Choice

9. Which assessment finding should the nurse prioritize?
   A. Blood pressure of 140/90 mmHg.
   B. Chest pain on inspiration.
   C. Temperature of 99.8°F.
   D. Heart rate of 88 bpm.

Multiple Response

10. Select all interventions the nurse should implement for this client.
    A. Administer oxygen at 4 L/min.
    B. Encourage deep breathing and coughing.

C. Notify the healthcare provider of chest pain.
D. Administer acetaminophen for fever.
E. Increase IV fluids to 150 mL/hr.

Drop-Down
11. Select the most appropriate nursing diagnosis for this client.
Impaired Gas Exchange
Acute Pain
Risk for Infection
Ineffective Airway Clearance

Drag and Drop
12. Place the following steps for administering oxygen therapy in the correct order.
Verify the provider's order.
Adjust the flow rate to 2 L/min.
Assess the client's oxygen saturation.
Apply the nasal cannula.

Multiple Choice
13. The client's oxygen saturation drops to 88%. What is the nurse's priority action?
    A. Increase oxygen to 4 L/min.
    B. Notify the healthcare provider.
    C. Place the client in a supine position.
    D. Administer a bronchodilator.

Multiple Response
14. Select all factors that may contribute to the client's chest pain.
    A. Pneumonia-related inflammation.
    B. COPD exacerbation.
    C. Recent surgery.
    D. Pleural effusion.
    E. Anxiety.

Multiple Choice
15. A nurse is caring for a client with MRSA in a private room. Which precaution is most appropriate?
    A. Droplet precautions.
    B. Contact precautions.
    C. Airborne precautions.
    D. Standard precautions only.

Multiple Response

16. A nurse is educating a community group on preventing cardiovascular disease. Which recommendations should the nurse include? (Select all that apply.)
    A. Maintain a BMI below 25.
    B. Exercise for 30 minutes most days of the week.
    C. Consume a diet high in saturated fats.
    D. Monitor blood pressure regularly.
    E. Avoid smoking.

Drop-Down

17. A client with anxiety is hyperventilating. Select the most therapeutic nursing intervention.
Encourage slow, deep breathing.
Administer a sedative.
Place the client in a supine position.
Instruct the client to leave the room.

18. Place the steps for performing a sterile dressing change in the correct order.
Apply sterile gloves.
Remove the old dressing.
Clean the wound with sterile saline.
Open the sterile dressing kit.

Multiple Choice

19. A client is prescribed digoxin 0.25 mg daily. The nurse notes a heart rate of 58 bpm. What is the nurse's best action?
    A. Administer the dose as prescribed.
    B. Hold the dose and notify the provider.
    C. Administer half the dose.
    D. Recheck the heart rate in 1 hour.

Multiple Choice

20. A client is scheduled for a colonoscopy. Which instruction should the nurse include to reduce the risk of complications?
    A. Avoid drinking clear liquids on the day of the procedure.
    B. Take all prescribed medications the morning of the procedure.
    C. Follow the bowel prep instructions exactly.
    D. Drive home after the procedure.

Multiple Response)

21. A client with diabetic ketoacidosis (DKA) is receiving IV insulin. Which findings indicate the client's condition is improving? (Select all that apply.)
    A. Blood glucose of 180 mg/dL.
    B. Serum potassium of 4.0 mEq/L.
    C. pH of 7.35.
    D. Bicarbonate of 10 mEq/L.
    E. Respiratory rate of 16 breaths/min.

Infection Control (Questions 22-27)

Scenario: A nurse is caring for a 45-year-old client with a surgical wound infection. The client is on contact precautions, receiving vancomycin IV, and has a wound culture positive for Staphylococcus aureus. Vital signs: BP 130/80 mmHg, HR 92 bpm, RR 18 breaths/min, Temp 101.2°F.

Multiple Choice

22. Which personal protective equipment (PPE) should the nurse wear when entering the client's room?
    A. Mask and gloves.
    B. Gown and gloves.
    C. Gown, gloves, and face shield.
    D. Mask, gown, and gloves.

Multiple Response

23. Select all actions the nurse should take to prevent the spread of infection.
    A. Wash hands before and after client contact.
    B. Use sterile gloves for wound care.
    C. Dispose of PPE in a biohazard container.
    D. Allow visitors without PPE.
    E. Clean reusable equipment after use.

Drop-Down

24. Select the most appropriate nursing action for the client's fever.
Administer acetaminophen as prescribed.
Apply a cooling blanket.
Increase IV fluids.
Administer an antibiotic.

Drag and Drop

25. Place the steps for administering IV vancomycin in the correct order.
Verify the medication order.
Assess the IV site for patency.
Administer the medication over 60 minutes.

Document the administration.

Multiple Choice

26. The client reports itching after receiving vancomycin. What is the nurse's priority action?
    A. Stop the infusion and notify the provider.
    B. Slow the infusion rate.
    C. Administer diphenhydramine.
    D. Monitor the client for 30 minutes.

Multiple Response

27. Select all potential complications of a surgical wound infection.
    A. Sepsis.
    B. Delayed wound healing.
    C. Hypoglycemia.
    D. Abscess formation.
    E. Dehydration.

Multiple Choice

28. A nurse is counseling a pregnant client about nutrition. Which food should the nurse recommend as a good source of iron?
    A. White bread.
    B. Spinach.
    C. Bananas.
    D. Milk.

Multiple Choice

29. A client with a terminal illness expresses fear of dying. Which nursing action is most appropriate?
    A. Reassure the client that death is a natural process.
    B. Encourage the client to focus on positive memories.
    C. Listen actively and explore the client's fears.
    D. Refer the client to a spiritual counselor immediately.

Multiple Response

30. A nurse is assisting a client with chronic pain. Which non-pharmacological interventions should the nurse suggest? (Select all that apply.)
    A. Guided imagery.
    B. Cold therapy.
    C. Increased bed rest.
    D. Progressive muscle relaxation.
    E. Limiting fluid intake.

Multiple Choice
31. A client is prescribed furosemide 40 mg IV. Select the most important assessment before administration.
Blood pressure.
Blood glucose.
Respiratory rate.
Temperature.

Multiple Choice
32. A client with a history of seizures is prescribed phenytoin. Which laboratory value should the nurse monitor?
    A. Hemoglobin.
    B. Serum creatinine.
    C. Liver function tests.
    D. Blood glucose.

Multiple Choice
33. A client with hypovolemic shock is receiving IV fluids. Which finding indicates the client's condition is improving?
    A. Blood pressure of 90/60 mmHg.
    B. Urine output of 40 mL/hr.
    C. Heart rate of 120 bpm.
    D. Respiratory rate of 28 breaths/min.

Case Scenario Questions 34-39
Scenario: A 30-year-old client is admitted with suicidal ideation and a history of bipolar disorder. The client is placed on suicide precautions and prescribed lithium. Vital signs are stable, but the client appears withdrawn and refuses to eat.
Multiple Choice
34. What is the nurse's priority action for this client?
    A. Administer lithium as prescribed.
    B. Encourage the client to eat a full meal.
    C. Perform a suicide risk assessment.
    D. Contact the client's family.

Multiple Response
35. Select all interventions to ensure the client's safety on suicide precautions.
    A. Remove sharp objects from the room.
    B. Allow the client to keep a belt.
    C. Check on the client every 15 minutes.

D. Provide plastic utensils for meals.
E. Keep the bathroom door open.

Drop-Down
36. Select the most appropriate nursing diagnosis for this client.
Risk for Self-Harm
Imbalanced Nutrition: Less Than Body Requirements
Social Isolation
Ineffective Coping

Drag and Drop
37. Place the steps for administering lithium in the correct order.
Check the client's serum lithium level.
Verify the medication order.
Administer the medication with food.
Educate the client about side effects.

Multiple Choice
38. The client's serum lithium level is 1.8 mEq/L. What is the nurse's best action?
    A. Administer the next dose as scheduled.
    B. Hold the dose and notify the provider.
    C. Administer half the dose.
    D. Recheck the level in 4 hours.

Multiple Response
39. Select all signs of lithium toxicity the nurse should monitor for.
    A. Tremors.
    B. Nausea.
    C. Increased appetite.
    D. Confusion.
    E. Polyuria.

Multiple Choice
40. A nurse is delegating tasks to an unlicensed assistive personnel (UAP). Which task is appropriate to delegate?
    A. Administering oral medications.
    B. Assisting with ambulation.
    C. Assessing a client's pain level.
    D. Developing a care plan.

Multiple Response

41. A nurse is preparing a sterile field. Which actions maintain sterility? (Select all that apply.)
    A. Opening the sterile package away from the body.
    B. Touching only the outer 1-inch border of the field.
    C. Adding supplies by dropping them onto the field.
    D. Reaching over the sterile field to adjust equipment.
    E. Using sterile gloves to handle supplies.

Multiple Choice
42. A nurse is teaching a client about colorectal cancer screening. At what age should routine screening begin for average-risk individuals?
    A. 40 years.
    B. 45 years.
    C. 50 years.
    D. 55 years.

Multiple Choice
43. A client with schizophrenia is experiencing auditory hallucinations. Which nursing response is most appropriate?
    A. "I don't hear the voices you're hearing."
    B. "Tell the voices to stop talking."
    C. "Why are you hearing voices?"
    D. "Ignore the voices and they'll go away."

Drop-Down
44. A client with constipation is prescribed a high-fiber diet. Select the best food to recommend.
White rice.
Broccoli.
Ice cream.
Chicken breast.

Multiple Choice
45. A client is receiving morphine for pain. Which side effect should the nurse monitor for?
    A. Hypertension.
    B. Respiratory depression.
    C. Hyperglycemia.
    D. Increased urine output.

Multiple Response
46. A client is preparing for surgery. Which preoperative interventions reduce the risk of complications? (Select all that apply.)

A. Verify informed consent.
B. Administer antibiotics as prescribed.
C. Encourage smoking cessation.
D. Allow the client to eat a light meal.
E. Remove nail polish.

Multiple Choice
47. A client with chronic kidney disease is experiencing hyperkalemia. Which food should the nurse instruct the client to avoid?
A. Apples.
B. Bananas.
C. Green beans.
D. Rice.

Case Scenario Questions 48-53
Scenario: A 55-year-old client with atrial fibrillation is prescribed warfarin 5 mg daily. The client's INR is 2.5, and they report bruising on their arms. Vital signs are stable.
48. What is the nurse's best action regarding the bruising?
A. Apply ice to the bruises.
B. Hold the next dose of warfarin.
C. Assess for additional bleeding.
D. Administer vitamin K.

Multiple Response
49. Select all teaching points for a client on warfarin.
A. Avoid green leafy vegetables.
B. Report signs of bleeding.
C. Take the medication at the same time daily.
D. Increase intake of vitamin K-rich foods.
E. Monitor INR regularly.

Drop-Down
50. Select the therapeutic INR range for a client with atrial fibrillation.
1.5-2.0
2.0-3.0
3.0-4.0
4.0-5.0

Drag and Drop
51. Place the steps for administering warfarin in the correct order.
Verify the medication order.

Check the client's INR.
Administer the medication.
Document the administration.

Multiple Choice

52. The client's INR increases to 4.2. What is the nurse's priority action?
    A. Administer the next dose as prescribed.
    B. Hold the dose and notify the provider.
    C. Administer vitamin K.
    D. Recheck the INR in 4 hours.

Multiple Response

53. Select all signs of warfarin overdose the nurse should monitor for.
    A. Blood in the urine.
    B. Increased appetite.
    C. Nosebleeds.
    D. Confusion.
    E. Bruising.

Multiple Choice

54. A nurse is coordinating discharge for a client with heart failure. Which teaching point is most important?
    A. Limit physical activity to avoid fatigue.
    B. Weigh daily and report a gain of 2-3 pounds in 24 hours.
    C. Increase sodium intake to prevent hyponatremia.
    D. Take diuretics in the evening.

Multiple Choice

55. A nurse is caring for a client with a central venous catheter. Which action prevents catheter-related infections?
    A. Change the dressing weekly.
    B. Use sterile technique for dressing changes.
    C. Flush the catheter with saline only.
    D. Avoid using an occlusive dressing.

Multiple Response

56. A nurse is teaching a client about diabetes management. Which instructions should the nurse include? (Select all that apply.)
    A. Check blood glucose levels regularly.
    B. Follow a consistent meal plan.
    C. Avoid all carbohydrates.

D. Inspect feet daily.

E. Exercise regularly.

Multiple Choice

57. A client with substance use disorder is reluctant to attend a support group. Which response by the nurse is most therapeutic?

A. "You'll feel better if you go."

B. "What concerns do you have about attending?"

C. "Everyone benefits from support groups."

D. "You don't have to go if you don't want to."

Drag and Drop

58. Place the steps for assisting a client with a bedpan in the correct order.

Place the client on the bedpan.

Raise the head of the bed.

Provide privacy.

Wash hands and don gloves.

Multiple Choice

59. A client is prescribed albuterol via inhaler. Which instruction should the nurse provide?

A. Inhale quickly and shallowly.

B. Hold breath for 10 seconds after inhaling.

C. Use the inhaler every 2 hours.

D. Rinse the mouth after each use.

Multiple Choice

60. A client is at risk for falls. Which intervention should the nurse implement?

A. Keep the bed in the highest position.

B. Ensure the call light is within reach.

C. Leave the room dimly lit.

D. Allow the client to ambulate without assistance.

Multiple Response

61. A client with acute pancreatitis is admitted. Which laboratory findings should the nurse expect? (Select all that apply.)

A. Elevated amylase.

B. Decreased lipase.

C. Elevated white blood cell count.

D. Decreased calcium.

E. Elevated glucose.

Questions 62-67

Scenario: A 70-year-old client with a hip fracture is postoperative day 1 after a total hip replacement. The client is receiving heparin for DVT prophylaxis and has a sequential compression device (SCD) in place. Vital signs: BP 110/70 mmHg, HR 90 bpm, RR 16 breaths/min, Temp 98.6°F.

Multiple Choice

62. Which assessment finding indicates a potential complication?

    A. Pain at the surgical site.
    B. Swelling and warmth in the calf.
    C. Heart rate of 90 bpm.
    D. Clear lung sounds.

Multiple Response

63. Select all interventions to prevent postoperative complications.

    A. Encourage early ambulation.
    B. Apply SCDs continuously.
    C. Administer heparin as prescribed.
    D. Encourage a high-fat diet.
    E. Monitor for signs of infection.

Drop-Down

64. Select the most appropriate nursing diagnosis for this client.

Risk for Infection

Impaired Physical Mobility

Acute Pain

Risk for Bleeding

Drag and Drop

65. Place the steps for applying SCDs in the correct order.

Wrap the sleeves around the client's legs.

Connect the sleeves to the pump.

Turn on the pump.

Ensure proper fit and alignment.

Multiple Choice

66. The client reports shortness of breath. What is the nurse's priority action?

    A. Increase the oxygen flow rate.
    B. Notify the healthcare provider.
    C. Remove the SCDs.
    D. Administer a pain medication.

Multiple Response
67. Select all signs of a pulmonary embolism the nurse should monitor for.
A. Chest pain.
B. Tachypnea.
C. Hypoxemia.
D. Bradycardia.
E. Fever.

Multiple Choice
68. A nurse is leading a team caring for multiple clients. Which task should the nurse perform rather than delegate?
A. Taking vital signs.
B. Evaluating a client's response to treatment.
C. Assisting with hygiene care.
D. Ambulating a client.

Multiple Response
69. A nurse is caring for a client with tuberculosis. Which precautions should the nurse implement? (Select all that apply.)
A. Wear an N95 respirator.
B. Place the client in a negative pressure room.
C. Use gloves for all client contact.
D. Allow visitors without masks.
E. Dispose of waste in a biohazard container.

Multiple Choice
70. A nurse is teaching a client about smoking cessation. Which strategy is most effective?
A. Gradually reducing cigarette use.
B. Using nicotine replacement therapy.
C. Avoiding all social situations.
D. Relying on willpower alone.

Drop-Down
71. A client with post-traumatic stress disorder (PTSD) is experiencing a flashback. Select the most appropriate nursing action.
Administer an anxiolytic.
Provide a quiet, safe environment.
Encourage the client to discuss the trauma.
Distract the client with a task.

Multiple Choice

72. A client with arthritis reports difficulty dressing. Which assistive device should the nurse recommend?

A. Walker.

B. Button hook.

C. Bedside commode.

D. Incentive spirometer.

Multiple Response

73. A client is receiving IV fluids. Which complications should the nurse monitor for? (Select all that apply.)

A. Fluid overload.

B. Infiltration.

C. Hyperglycemia.

D. Phlebitis.

E. Air embolism.

Multiple Choice

74. A client is receiving chemotherapy. Which laboratory value should the nurse monitor closely?

A. White blood cell count.

B. Blood urea nitrogen.

C. Serum sodium.

D. Hemoglobin A1c.

Multiple Choice

75. A client with a spinal cord injury is at risk for autonomic dysreflexia. Which symptom should the nurse monitor for?

A. Hypotension.

B. Severe headache.

C. Tachypnea.

D. Hypothermia.

COMPREHENSIVE 1 NGN NCLEX ANSWERS

1. Answer: B
Rationale: The client with a respiratory rate of 28 breaths/min and oxygen saturation of 92% indicates potential respiratory distress, which is a priority due to its impact on airway and breathing. The other clients have stable or less urgent conditions.

2. Answer: B
Rationale: Aspirating before injecting ensures the needle is not in a blood vessel, preventing inadvertent intravenous administration. A 25-gauge needle is too small for IM injections, rapid injection can cause discomfort, and the arm may not always be the appropriate site.

3. Answer: A
Rationale: The best time to perform BSE is a few days after menstruation ends (around day 5-7 of the cycle) when breast tissue is least affected by hormonal changes, reducing discomfort and improving accuracy.

4. Answer: B
Rationale: This response validates the client's feelings and encourages open communication, which is therapeutic. Options A and C are dismissive, and D may seem confrontational.

5. Answer: B
Rationale: Using a draw sheet with assistance ensures proper body mechanics and prevents injury to both the client and nurse. Pulling sheets or lifting by arms risks injury, and independent movement may not be safe for a client with mobility issues.

6. Answer: C
Rationale: Subcutaneous heparin is best administered in the abdomen, at least 2 inches from the umbilicus, to ensure adequate absorption and minimize bruising. The deltoid and ventrogluteal sites are used for intramuscular injections, and the thigh is less optimal.

7. Answer: B
Rationale: A temperature increase of 1°C during a transfusion may indicate a febrile non-hemolytic reaction, requiring immediate reporting. Mild itching could be monitored, and the other options are within normal limits.

8. Answer: C
Rationale: Fowler's position (semi-upright) promotes lung expansion and eases breathing

in clients with heart failure. Supine and Trendelenburg positions may worsen dyspnea, and prone is not ideal for respiratory distress.

9. Answer: B
    Rationale: Chest pain on inspiration may indicate a serious complication, such as pleuritis or pneumothorax, and requires immediate assessment. The other findings are less urgent.

10. Answers: B, C, D
    Rationale: Encouraging deep breathing and coughing promotes lung expansion, notifying the provider addresses the chest pain, and acetaminophen manages the low-grade fever. Increasing oxygen or IV fluids requires a provider's order.

11. Answer: Acute Pain
    Rationale: The client's chest pain on inspiration is the priority symptom, making Acute Pain the most appropriate nursing diagnosis at this time.

12. Answer: 1, 3, 4, 2
    Rationale: The nurse must verify the order, assess the client's oxygen needs, apply the device, and then adjust the flow rate to ensure safe and effective administration.

13. Answer: B
    Rationale: An oxygen saturation of 88% is critical for a client with COPD and pneumonia, requiring immediate notification of the provider for further orders. The other actions require a prescription or are inappropriate.

14.
Answers: A, D, E
Rationale: Pneumonia can cause pleural inflammation, pleural effusion is a common complication, and anxiety may exacerbate perceived pain. COPD exacerbation is less directly linked to inspiratory pain, and there is no surgical history.

15. Answer: B
    Rationale: MRSA requires contact precautions, including gloves and gown, to prevent transmission. Droplet and airborne precautions are not indicated, and standard precautions alone are insufficient.

16. Answers: A, B, D, E
    Rationale: Maintaining a healthy BMI, regular exercise, monitoring blood pressure, and avoiding smoking reduce cardiovascular risk. A diet high in saturated fats increases risk.

17. Answer: Encourage slow, deep breathing.
    Rationale: Slow, deep breathing helps reduce hyperventilation and promotes relaxation.

Sedatives require a prescription, supine positioning may not help, and leaving the room is not therapeutic.

18. Answer: 4, 2, 1, 3
Rationale: The nurse opens the sterile kit to maintain a sterile field, removes the old dressing, applies sterile gloves, and then cleans the wound to prevent contamination.

19. Answer: B
Rationale: A heart rate below 60 bpm is a contraindication for digoxin due to the risk of toxicity. The nurse should hold the dose and notify the provider.

20. Answer: C
Rationale: Following bowel prep instructions ensures a clear colon, reducing the risk of complications during the colonoscopy. Clear liquids are allowed, some medications may be held, and driving is unsafe post-procedure.

21. Answers: A, B, C, E
Rationale: A blood glucose of 180 mg/dL, normal potassium, normal pH, and normal respiratory rate indicate resolution of DKA. A bicarbonate of 10 mEq/L is still low, suggesting persistent acidosis.

22. Answer: B
Rationale: Contact precautions for a surgical wound infection require a gown and gloves. A face shield or mask is not needed unless there is a risk of splashing.

23. Answers: A, C, E
Rationale: Hand hygiene, proper PPE disposal, and cleaning equipment prevent infection spread. Sterile gloves are used for wound care but not for all contact, and visitors must wear PPE.

24. Answer: Administer acetaminophen as prescribed.
Rationale: Acetaminophen is the first-line treatment for fever. Cooling blankets and increased fluids require a provider's order, and antibiotics are already being administered.

25. Answer: 1, 2, 3, 4
Rationale: The nurse verifies the order, checks the IV site, administers the medication safely, and documents the administration.

26. Answer: A
Rationale: Itching may indicate an allergic reaction, requiring the infusion to be stopped

and the provider notified. Slowing the rate or administering diphenhydramine requires a prescription, and monitoring alone is insufficient.

27. Answers: A, B, D

    Rationale: Sepsis, delayed healing, and abscess formation are complications of wound infections. Hypoglycemia and dehydration are unrelated.

28. Answer: B

    Rationale: Spinach is a rich source of iron, essential for preventing anemia during pregnancy. The other options are not significant sources of iron.

29. Answer: C

    Rationale: Active listening and exploring fears validate the client's emotions and promote coping. Reassurance and focusing on positives may dismiss feelings, and referral may be premature.

30. Answers: A, B, D

    Rationale: Guided imagery, cold therapy, and progressive muscle relaxation are effective for pain management. Increased bed rest may worsen pain, and limiting fluids is unrelated.

31. Answer: Blood pressure.

    Rationale: Furosemide can cause hypotension, making blood pressure the most critical assessment before administration.

32. Answer: C

    Rationale: Phenytoin can cause hepatotoxicity, so liver function tests should be monitored. The other values are not directly affected.

33. Answer: B

    Rationale: A urine output of 40 mL/hr indicates improved renal perfusion, a sign of resolving hypovolemic shock. The other findings suggest ongoing instability.

34. Answer: C

    Rationale: Suicide precautions require ongoing risk assessment to ensure client safety. The other actions are secondary to immediate safety concerns.

35. Answers: A, C, D, E

    Rationale: Removing sharp objects, frequent checks, plastic utensils, and keeping the bathroom door open reduce suicide risk. A belt is a ligature risk.

36. Answer: Risk for Self-Harm
   Rationale: Suicidal ideation makes Risk for Self-Harm the priority nursing diagnosis.

37. Answer: 2, 1, 3, 4
   Rationale: The nurse verifies the order, checks the lithium level to ensure safety, administers with food to reduce GI upset, and educates about side effects.

38. Answer: B
   Rationale: A lithium level of 1.8 mEq/L is toxic (therapeutic range: 0.6-1.2 mEq/L). The nurse should hold the dose and notify the provider.

39. Answers: A, B, D, E
   Rationale: Tremors, nausea, confusion, and polyuria are signs of lithium toxicity. Increased appetite is not associated.

40. Answer: B
   Rationale: Assisting with ambulation is within the UAP's scope of practice. Administering medications, assessing pain, and developing care plans require nursing judgment.

41. Answers: A, C, E
   Rationale: Opening packages away from the body, dropping supplies, and using sterile gloves maintain sterility. The outer 1-inch border is considered non-sterile, and reaching over the field risks contamination.

42. Answer: B
   Rationale: The American Cancer Society recommends colorectal cancer screening for average-risk individuals starting at age 45.

43. Answer: A
   Rationale: Acknowledging that the nurse does not hear the voices validates the client's experience while grounding them in reality. The other responses are dismissive or inappropriate.

44. Answer: Broccoli.
   Rationale: Broccoli is high in fiber, promoting bowel regularity. The other options are low in fiber.

45. Answer: B
   Rationale: Morphine, an opioid, can cause respiratory depression, a life-threatening side effect requiring close monitoring.

46. Answers: A, B, C, E
    Rationale: Verifying consent, administering antibiotics, encouraging smoking cessation, and removing nail polish (for pulse oximetry accuracy) reduce risks. Eating before surgery increases aspiration risk.

47. Answer: B
    Rationale: Bananas are high in potassium, which should be avoided in hyperkalemia. The other foods are low in potassium.

48. Answer: C
    Rationale: Bruising may indicate bleeding, a side effect of warfarin. Assessing for other signs of bleeding is the priority. Ice may help but is not the priority, and holding the dose or administering vitamin K requires a provider's order.

49. Answers: A, B, C, E
    Rationale: Green leafy vegetables (high in vitamin K) should be limited, bleeding signs reported, medication taken consistently, and INR monitored. Increasing vitamin K intake counteracts warfarin.

50. Answer: 2.0-3.0
    Rationale: The therapeutic INR range for atrial fibrillation is 2.0-3.0 to balance anticoagulation and bleeding risk.

51. Answer: 1, 2, 3, 4
    Rationale: The nurse verifies the order, checks the INR for safety, administers the medication, and documents the administration.

52. Answer: B
    Rationale: An INR of 4.2 is above the therapeutic range, indicating a bleeding risk. The nurse should hold the dose and notify the provider.

53. Answers: A, C, E
    Rationale: Blood in the urine, nosebleeds, and bruising are signs of warfarin overdose due to excessive anticoagulation. Increased appetite and confusion are not directly related.

54. Answer: B
    Rationale: Daily weighing and reporting significant weight gain indicate fluid retention, a key heart failure management strategy. Limiting activity, increasing sodium, or evening diuretics are incorrect.

55. Answer: B

    Rationale: Sterile technique during dressing changes prevents infection. Dressings may need more frequent changes, flushing includes heparin in some cases, and occlusive dressings are required.

56. Answers: A, B, D, E

    Rationale: Regular glucose monitoring, consistent meals, daily foot inspections, and exercise are key to diabetes management. Avoiding all carbohydrates is unnecessary and harmful.

57. Answer: B

    Rationale: Exploring the client's concerns encourages open communication and addresses barriers to treatment. The other responses are dismissive or non-therapeutic.

58.

Answer: 4, 3, 2, 1

Rationale: The nurse washes hands and dons gloves, provides privacy, raises the bed for comfort, and places the bedpan to assist the client safely.

59. Answer: B

    Rationale: Holding the breath for 10 seconds allows the medication to reach deep into the lungs. Quick inhalation is incorrect, usage frequency depends on the prescription, and rinsing is for steroid inhalers.

60. Answer: B

    Rationale: Keeping the call light within reach ensures the client can request help, reducing fall risk. The bed should be low, the room well-lit, and assistance provided for ambulation.

61. Answers: A, C, D, E

    Rationale: Acute pancreatitis causes elevated amylase, white blood cell count, and glucose, and decreased calcium due to fat necrosis. Lipase is typically elevated, not decreased.

62. Answer: B

    Rationale: Swelling and warmth in the calf may indicate a deep vein thrombosis (DVT), a serious complication. Surgical pain is expected, and the other findings are normal.

63. Answers: A, B, C, E
    Rationale: Early ambulation, SCDs, heparin, and infection monitoring prevent complications like DVT and infection. A high-fat diet is not indicated.

64. Answer: Impaired Physical Mobility
    Rationale: A hip fracture and recent surgery make Impaired Physical Mobility the priority diagnosis, affecting recovery and complication risk.

65. Answer: 1, 4, 2, 3
    Rationale: The nurse wraps the sleeves, ensures proper fit, connects to the pump, and turns it on to ensure effective DVT prophylaxis.

66. Answer: B
    Rationale: Shortness of breath may indicate a pulmonary embolism, a life-threatening complication. The provider should be notified immediately.

67. Answers: A, B, C
    Rationale: Chest pain, tachypnea, and hypoxemia are classic signs of pulmonary embolism. Bradycardia and fever are not typically associated.

68. Answer: B
    Rationale: Evaluating a client's response to treatment requires nursing judgment and cannot be delegated. The other tasks are within the scope of unlicensed personnel.

69. Answers: A, B, E
    Rationale: Tuberculosis requires airborne precautions, including an N95 respirator, negative pressure room, and proper waste disposal. Gloves are not required for all contact, and visitors need masks.

70. Answer: B
    Rationale: Nicotine replacement therapy is evidence-based and effective for smoking cessation. Gradual reduction, avoiding social situations, or willpower alone are less effective.

71. Answer: Provide a quiet, safe environment.
    Rationale: A quiet, safe environment helps ground the client during a flashback. Medications require a prescription, discussing trauma may escalate symptoms, and distraction may not be effective.

72. Answer: B
    Rationale: A button hook assists with dressing, addressing fine motor difficulties caused by arthritis. The other devices are unrelated to dressing.

73. Answers: A, B, D, E
    Rationale: Fluid overload, infiltration, phlebitis, and air embolism are complications of IV therapy. Hyperglycemia is not directly related unless dextrose is used.

74. Answer: A
    Rationale: Chemotherapy can cause bone marrow suppression, leading to a decreased white blood cell count and increased infection risk.

75. Answer: B
    Rationale: Autonomic dysreflexia causes severe headache due to sudden hypertension. Hypotension, tachypnea, and hypothermia are not typical symptoms.

COMPREHENSIVE 2 NGN NCLEX QUESTIONS

Case Scenario Questions 76-80
   Scenario: A 50-year-old client with chronic obstructive pulmonary disease (COPD) is admitted with an acute exacerbation. The client is receiving albuterol via nebulizer and oxygen at 2 L/min. Vital signs: BP 150/90 mmHg, HR 100 bpm, RR 26 breaths/min, SpO_2 90%.
   Multiple Choice
1. Which finding indicates the client's condition is worsening?
   A. Respiratory rate of 26 breaths/min.
   B. Oxygen saturation of 88%.
   C. Heart rate of 100 bpm.
   D. Blood pressure of 150/90 mmHg.

2. Multiple Response
   Select all interventions the nurse should implement.
   A. Administer albuterol as prescribed.
   B. Increase oxygen to 4 L/min.
   C. Monitor arterial blood gases.
   D. Position the client in Fowler's position.
   E. Encourage fluid restriction.

3. Drop-Down
   Select the most appropriate nursing diagnosis for this client.
   Ineffective Breathing Pattern
   Impaired Gas Exchange
   Activity Intolerance
   Risk for Infection

4. Drag and Drop
   Place the steps for administering a nebulizer treatment in the correct order.
   Verify the medication order.
   Instruct the client to breathe deeply.
   Add the medication to the nebulizer.
   Turn on the nebulizer.

   Multiple Response
5. Select all potential complications of a COPD exacerbation.
   A. Respiratory failure.
   B. Pneumothorax.

C. Hypoglycemia.
D. Cor pulmonale.
E. Sepsis.

Drag and Drop Question
6. Match the type of isolation precaution with the correct infection.
Infections:
Influenza
Tuberculosis (TB)
Norovirus
Precautions:
Airborne precautions
Droplet precautions
Contact precautions

Case Scenario Question
7. Case: A nurse is caring for a patient who has been placed on contact precautions due to a wound infection. The nurse is preparing to change the patient's dressing. Which of the following actions should the nurse take first?
    A) Don gloves and gown
    B) Clean the wound with antiseptic solution
    C) Administer pain medication to the patient
    D) Prepare sterile dressings and materials

8. Drop-Down Question
Select the most appropriate personal protective equipment (PPE) for a patient with suspected tuberculosis (TB):
Correct PPE:
N95 respirator
Gloves
Gown

Multiple Choice Question
9. Which of the following is the most important action in preventing the transmission of Clostridium difficile (C. difficile) in a healthcare setting?
    A) Use alcohol-based hand sanitizers after patient contact
    B) Isolate patients with C. difficile in a private room
    C) Disinfect all patient care equipment with alcohol-based wipes
    D) Wear gloves and a surgical mask when caring for patients

Multiple Response Question

10. Which of the following are appropriate actions to take when a nurse is exposed to blood during a needle stick injury? (Select all that apply)

A) Clean the wound with soap and water immediately
B) Report the injury to a supervisor
C) Wait for the shift to end before reporting the injury
D) Follow post-exposure protocols for potential infection

Case Scenario Question

11. Case: A nurse is caring for a patient with suspected viral meningitis, which is transmitted by respiratory droplets. The patient is placed on droplet precautions. Which of the following PPE should the nurse wear when entering the patient's room?

A) Gloves and gown
B) N95 respirator and gloves
C) Surgical mask and gloves
D) Gloves, gown, and surgical mask

Multiple Choice Question

12. Which of the following is the most effective strategy for preventing hospital-acquired infections (HAIs) related to the urinary catheter?

A) Administering antibiotics to prevent infection
B) Using aseptic technique during catheter insertion and care
C) Changing the catheter every 48 hours
D) Keeping the catheter disconnected from the drainage bag

Multiple Response Question

13. Which of the following actions should be taken to reduce the risk of infection when handling contaminated linen? (Select all that apply)

A) Wear gloves when handling soiled linen
B) Avoid shaking the linen to prevent airborne particles
C) Discard contaminated linen in the regular trash
D) Place contaminated linen in a designated, closed container or bag

14. Place the following steps for administering an insulin injection in the correct order. Steps:

A) Wash hands thoroughly
B) Cleanse the injection site with an alcohol swab
C) Prepare the syringe with the appropriate dose of insulin
D) Insert the needle at a 90-degree angle into the subcutaneous tissue

Multiple Choice Questions

15. Which of the following is the primary purpose of prenatal vitamins during pregnancy?
A) To prevent gestational diabetes
B) To ensure the baby receives all the nutrients it needs for growth
C) To treat nausea and vomiting in early pregnancy
D) To increase maternal weight gain

16. A 32-week pregnant woman is diagnosed with gestational diabetes. Which of the following actions is the most appropriate for managing her condition?
A) Immediate induction of labor
B) A low-carb diet and regular blood glucose monitoring
C) Strict bed rest to prevent complications
D) Administering insulin only if blood glucose levels exceed 200 mg/dL

17. A nurse is assessing a pregnant woman who is 12 weeks into her pregnancy. Which of the following signs would be an early indicator of a normal pregnancy?
A) Quickening (feeling the baby move)
B) Positive pregnancy test result
C) Fetal heart rate audible by Doppler
D) The uterus is palpable above the symphysis pubis

18. Which of the following is the most appropriate nursing action for a woman in active labor with ruptured membranes?
A) Encourage the woman to walk around to facilitate labor progress
B) Monitor for signs of infection and assess fetal heart rate regularly
C) Administer antibiotics immediately to prevent infection
D) Instruct the woman to refrain from pushing until fully dilated

Case Scenario Questions

19. Case Scenario: A 25-year-old woman at 30 weeks' gestation presents to the clinic complaining of severe headaches, visual disturbances, and swelling in her hands and face. Which of the following conditions is the nurse most concerned about?
A) Preeclampsia
B) Hyperemesis gravidarum
C) Placental abruption
D) Pregnancy-induced hypertension

20. Case Scenario: A 40-year-old woman in labor has a history of a previous cesarean section. She is now attempting a vaginal birth after cesarean (VBAC). Which of the following is the priority nursing intervention during labor?
A) Administering oxytocin to stimulate contractions
B) Continuous fetal heart rate monitoring

C) Encouraging deep breathing and relaxation techniques
D) Restricting fluid intake to prevent complications

Multiple Response Questions

21. Which of the following are common complications of preterm labor? (Select all that apply.)
A) Respiratory distress syndrome (RDS)
B) Intraventricular hemorrhage (IVH)
C) Low birth weight (LBW)
D) Hypertension
E) Necrotizing enterocolitis (NEC)

22. Which of the following are signs of postpartum depression? (Select all that apply.)
A) Feeling hopeless and overwhelmed
B) Difficulty bonding with the baby
C) Excessive happiness and euphoria
D) Sleep disturbances
E) Persistent sadness or crying

Drop-Down Questions

23. A nurse is educating a pregnant woman about the importance of folic acid supplementation. The nurse should instruct the patient to take folic acid daily to reduce the risk of:
Drop-down Options: A) Preterm labor, B) Neural tube defects, C) Placenta previa, D) Ectopic pregnancy]

24. A nurse is teaching a pregnant woman about the signs of labor. Which of the following should the nurse include in the teaching?
Drop-down Options: A) Severe abdominal pain, B) Regular contractions that get closer together, C) Blurred vision, D) Increase in appetite

25. Drag-and-Drop Questions
Order the following steps for performing a physical examination during a routine prenatal visit.
Steps:
    A) Check the patient's weight and blood pressure
    B) Measure the fundal height
    C) Auscultate fetal heart tones
    D) Review lab results and previous medical history

26. Place the following steps in the correct order for preparing a pregnant woman for a cesarean section.
   Steps:
E) Place an intravenous (IV) line
F) Administer preoperative medications as ordered
G) Perform the surgical scrub and prepare the sterile field
H) Assist the patient to the operating room

Case Scenario - Multiple Response

27. A nurse is caring for a client diagnosed with a substance use disorder who has been abstinent for 6 months. The client expresses a desire to attend a social event where alcohol will be present. Which interventions should the nurse prioritize? (Select all that apply.)
A) Encourage the client to attend the social event and practice moderation.
B) Discuss alternative activities that do not involve alcohol.
C) Encourage the client to attend a support group meeting prior to the event.
D) Help the client develop a plan for coping with potential triggers at the event.
E) Reassure the client that their abstinence is secure and that they are in control.

Multiple Choice

28. A nurse is caring for a client diagnosed with major depressive disorder who is prescribed an antidepressant. The client expresses frustration with the medication, stating, "I've been taking the medication for a few weeks and still feel the same." What is the nurse's most appropriate response?
A) "You should stop the medication if you don't notice any improvement."
B) "It may take 4 to 6 weeks for the medication to show its full effects."
C) "You should increase the dose of the medication to see results faster."
D) "Perhaps the medication is not the right choice for you, and we should consider a different treatment."

Case Scenario - Multiple Response

29. A nurse is providing education to a client diagnosed with bipolar disorder during a depressive episode. Which of the following interventions should the nurse include in the education plan? (Select all that apply.)
A) Encourage regular sleep patterns and good nutrition.
B) Set small, achievable goals to avoid feelings of being overwhelmed.
C) Suggest that the client avoid any social interactions to reduce stress.
D) Discuss the importance of continuing medication even during a depressive phase.
E) Recommend that the client avoid any strenuous physical activity until they feel better.

Multiple Choice

30. A nurse is caring for a client diagnosed with a neurocognitive disorder (NCD). The client exhibits forgetfulness and difficulty managing activities of daily living. Which of the following interventions should the nurse implement?
A) Provide the client with a calendar and memory aids to help with orientation.
B) Encourage the client to perform all tasks independently to build self-esteem.
C) Discuss the possibility of using restraints to prevent wandering behaviors.
D) Limit the client's social interactions to avoid overstimulation.

Case Scenario - Multiple Response
31. A nurse is caring for a client diagnosed with major depressive disorder who is experiencing feelings of worthlessness. Which of the following interventions should the nurse prioritize? (Select all that apply.)
A) Offer positive reinforcement for any small achievement.
B) Encourage the client to engage in activities they used to enjoy.
C) Provide education on the importance of medication adherence.
D) Discuss the client's feelings of worthlessness in detail.
E) Set realistic, achievable goals for the client to accomplish.

Multiple Choice
32. Why should a nurse consult evidence-based research for complementary therapies?
    A. To limit their use entirely
    B. To determine efficacy and safety
    C. To avoid patient education
    D. To restrict interdisciplinary collaboration

Multiple Response
33. Which factors should a nurse consider when evaluating contraindications for complementary therapies? (Select all that apply.)
    A. Patient's medical history
    B. Current medications
    C. Room temperature
    D. Pregnancy status
    E. Favorite hobby

Case Scenario
34. Scenario: A client taking antidepressants wants to use St. John's Wort.
    What should the nurse advise?
    A. Start the supplement immediately.
    B. Consult with a physician due to potential interactions.

C. Increase the antidepressant dose.

D. Avoid all complementary therapies.

Drop Down

35. A client is using aromatherapy for stress relief. Select the most appropriate essential oil from the drop-down menu:

Peppermint

Lavender

Lemon

Eucalyptus

Multiple Choice

36. What is the nurse's role in integrating complementary therapies?

A. Discourage their use entirely

B. Ensure alignment with the treatment plan

C. Avoid monitoring for effectiveness

D. Limit patient communication

Multiple Choice

37. Which of the following is the most important instruction when teaching a patient to use a nasal spray decongestant?

A) Use the spray for more than three consecutive days to ensure effectiveness.

B) Tilt the head back while spraying the medication.

C) Hold the nasal spray upright while administering the dose.

D) Do not blow your nose immediately after using the spray.

Multiple Choice

38. Which of the following is an appropriate non-pharmacological intervention for a patient experiencing acute pain?

A) Provide a quiet, dark room for rest.

B) Encourage physical activity to increase circulation.

C) Offer a large meal to maintain energy levels.

D) Suggest the use of hot packs to reduce swelling in acute injuries.

Multiple Response

39. Which of the following are signs of opioid overdose? (Select all that apply)

A) Pinpoint pupils

B) Shallow, slow breathing

C) Confusion or drowsiness

D) Increased heart rate

Multiple Choice
40. A patient on parenteral nutrition (PN) is being transitioned to oral feeding. When is it most appropriate to stop PN?
A) Once the patient is able to tolerate half of their daily caloric needs orally.
B) When the patient has tolerated 75% of their caloric needs orally for 48 hours.
C) When the patient's weight has stabilized for 72 hours.
D) Once bowel function returns to normal.

Multiple Choice
41. Which of the following is a potential complication of parenteral nutrition (PN)?
A) Respiratory distress
B) Hyperglycemia
C) Renal failure
D) Dehydration

Multiple Choice
42. What is the correct action if a nurse notices redness and warmth at the IV insertion site?
A) Increase the infusion rate to improve circulation.
B) Apply a warm compress to the site.
C) Discontinue the IV and notify the healthcare provider.
D) Increase the flow rate to prevent clot formation.

Multiple Choice
43. Which of the following is the most common site for peripheral IV catheter placement?
A) Dorsum of the hand
B) Antecubital fossa
C) Radial artery
D) Jugular vein

Multiple Choice
44. What should be the nurse's action if a patient requests an early refill of a Schedule II controlled substance?
A) Fill the prescription as requested and document the request.
B) Refuse to fill the prescription and explain the reasons to the patient.
C) Fill the prescription as requested and notify the healthcare provider after the fact.
D) Inform the pharmacy to fill the prescription immediately.

Multiple Choice
45. Which of the following is a key principle for ensuring the safe administration of controlled substances in a hospital?

A) Administer the drug as soon as it is available from the pharmacy.
B) Double-check the medication and dosage with another nurse before administration.
C) Allow patients to take their own medications while in the hospital.
D) Store controlled substances in the patient's room for ease of access.

Multiple Choice
46. The physician orders 0.5 mg of lorazepam (Ativan) IV push. The available concentration is 1 mg/2 mL. How many mL should the nurse administer?
A) 0.5 mL
B) 1 mL
C) 2 mL
D) 0.25 mL

Multiple Choice
47. A patient is prescribed 200 mg of a medication. The available concentration is 100 mg/5 mL. How many mL should the nurse administer?
A) 5 mL
B) 10 mL
C) 15 mL
D) 20 mL

Multiple Choice
48. If the physician orders 1 liter of saline to be infused over 8 hours, what is the infusion rate in mL/hr?
A) 100 mL/hr
B) 125 mL/hr
C) 150 mL/hr
D) 200 mL/hr

49. What is a key postoperative instruction for patients with moderate sedation?
A. Encouraging immediate driving
B. Monitoring for difficulty breathing
C. Avoiding follow-up appointments
D. Ignoring medication instructions

50. What is a key step in collecting a 24-hour urine specimen?
A. Using a non-sterile container
B. Providing guidance on storage
C. Collecting only morning urine
D. Mixing with saline

51. What should a nurse do if a patient's nasogastric tube becomes dislodged?
    A. Reuse the tube
    B. Notify the healthcare team
    C. Ignore the issue
    D. Flush with saline

52. What is a key component of preoperative emotional support?
    A. Ignoring patient concerns
    B. Reassuring patients about the surgical team
    C. Avoiding communication
    D. Discouraging questions

53. What is a key step in post-procedure care after moderate sedation?
    A. Encouraging immediate exercise
    B. Monitoring for nausea
    C. Administering additional sedatives
    D. Ignoring vital signs

Multiple Response
54. Which observations indicate wound healing? (Select all that apply.)
    A. Presence of granulation tissue
    B. Increased redness and swelling
    C. Decreased wound size
    D. Presence of pus
    E. Improved skin integrity

Multiple Choice
55. The wound shows signs of infection. What should the nurse do?
    A. Continue the current dressing schedule
    B. Notify the healthcare provider
    C. Apply a heavier dressing
    D. Restrict wound cleaning

Drop-Down
56. The nurse is selecting a dressing for a dry wound. The most appropriate choice is:
 Alginate dressing.
 Hydrocolloid dressing.
 Foam dressing.
 Gauze dressing.

Multiple Choice

57. What should the nurse document after a dressing change?
    A. The client's dietary intake
    B. The wound's condition and changes
    C. The room lighting conditions
    D. The client's blood pressure only

Multiple Choice
58. The client's wound is healing well. What education should the nurse provide?
    A. Restrict all physical activity
    B. Recognize signs of infection
    C. Avoid all wound cleaning
    D. Increase dressing changes

Drag and Drop Question
59. Match the type of isolation precaution with the correct infection.
Infections:
Influenza
Tuberculosis (TB)
Norovirus
Precautions:
Airborne precautions
Droplet precautions
Contact precautions

Case Scenario Question
60. Case: A nurse is caring for a patient who has been placed on contact precautions due to a wound infection. The nurse is preparing to change the patient's dressing. Which of the following actions should the nurse take first?
A) Don gloves and gown
B) Clean the wound with antiseptic solution
C) Administer pain medication to the patient
D) Prepare sterile dressings and materials

Drop-Down Question
61. Select the most appropriate personal protective equipment (PPE) for a patient with suspected tuberculosis (TB):
Correct PPE:
N95 respirator
Gloves
Gown

Multiple Choice Question

62. Which of the following is the most important action in preventing the transmission of Clostridium difficile (C. difficile) in a healthcare setting?

A) Use alcohol-based hand sanitizers after patient contact
B) Isolate patients with C. difficile in a private room
C) Disinfect all patient care equipment with alcohol-based wipes
D) Wear gloves and a surgical mask when caring for patients

Multiple Response Question

63. Which of the following are appropriate actions to take when a nurse is exposed to blood during a needle stick injury? (Select all that apply)

A) Clean the wound with soap and water immediately
B) Report the injury to a supervisor
C) Wait for the shift to end before reporting the injury
D) Follow post-exposure protocols for potential infection

Case Scenario Question

64. Case: A nurse is caring for a patient with suspected viral meningitis, which is transmitted by respiratory droplets. The patient is placed on droplet precautions. Which of the following PPE should the nurse wear when entering the patient's room?

A) Gloves and gown
B) N95 respirator and gloves
C) Surgical mask and gloves
D) Gloves, gown, and surgical mask

Multiple Choice Question

65. Which of the following is the most effective strategy for preventing hospital-acquired infections (HAIs) related to the urinary catheter?

A) Administering antibiotics to prevent infection
B) Using aseptic technique during catheter insertion and care
C) Changing the catheter every 48 hours
D) Keeping the catheter disconnected from the drainage bag

Multiple Response Question

66. Which of the following actions should be taken to reduce the risk of infection when handling contaminated linen? (Select all that apply)

A) Wear gloves when handling soiled linen
B) Avoid shaking the linen to prevent airborne particles
C) Discard contaminated linen in the regular trash
D) Place contaminated linen in a designated, closed container or bag

Drag and Drop

67. Place the following steps in the correct order when a nurse is preparing a care plan for a newly admitted patient:

Steps:

Gather data from the patient, family, and health records

Set measurable goals for patient care

Develop interventions and nursing actions to meet the goals

Evaluate and modify the care plan as needed

Analyze and interpret data to identify patient problems

Multiple Choice

68. A nurse manager is creating a staff development program. What is the most important consideration when designing the program?

A. Developing a program that addresses the most recent healthcare trends

B. Ensuring that the program aligns with the hospital's goals and mission

C. Focusing on individual staff preferences for the types of training offered

D. Offering only mandatory training to reduce staff burden

Case Scenario

69. A nurse manager is concerned about the high turnover rate in the department. Which of the following actions should be prioritized to improve retention?

A. Increase staff working hours to reduce the need for hiring new staff

B. Provide more professional development opportunities and mentorship programs

C. Decrease the number of support staff to reduce costs

D. Implement stricter performance measures without offering support or feedback

Multiple Response

70. Which of the following are appropriate strategies for managing a diverse healthcare team? (Select all that apply.)

A. Fostering an inclusive work environment that values diverse perspectives

B. Assigning work based solely on seniority rather than expertise

C. Offering cultural sensitivity training to enhance communication among staff

D. Encouraging staff to learn from one another's unique experiences

E. Discouraging team-building activities to maintain professional boundaries

Multiple Choice

71. A nurse is creating a care plan for a client admitted with pneumonia. Which action demonstrates the nurse's adherence to the principle of integrating advanced directives into the client's plan of care?

A. Assessing the client's current pain level and administering analgesics as prescribed.

B. Educating the client and family about their rights regarding resuscitation and end-of-life decisions.
C. Delegating the administration of oral antibiotics to a Licensed Practical Nurse.
D. Prioritizing the client's ambulation schedule based on their current mobility status.

72. A Registered Nurse is planning to delegate tasks to a Licensed Practical Nurse (LPN) and Unlicensed Assistive Personnel (UAP). Which task is appropriate for the RN to delegate to an LPN?
A. Administering oral medications to a stable client and monitoring for expected outcomes.
B. Providing initial patient education on a newly diagnosed chronic illness.
C. Performing the initial admission assessment of a new client with an unstable cardiac condition.
D. Developing a complete comprehensive care plan for a client with multiple comorbidities.

73. A nurse is organizing their workload for the shift. Which strategy aligns with effective time management and workload organization for a Registered Nurse?
    A. Relying solely on memory to manage all patient care tasks without a checklist.
    B. Completing all documentation at the end of the shift to avoid interruptions.
    C. Taking frequent unscheduled breaks to mitigate the effects of burnout.
    D. Prioritizing patient needs based on acuity and complexity to allocate time efficiently.

74. A nurse is advocating cost-effective care. Which action is the most appropriate demonstration of practicing cost-effective care?
    A. Educating clients on self-care and healthy lifestyles to reduce hospital readmissions.
    B. Ordering extra medical supplies to ensure availability for potential emergencies.
    C. Administering antibiotics for viral infections to prevent secondary bacterial infections.
    D. Limiting necessary diagnostic tests to reduce overall healthcare expenses.

75. A Registered Nurse is initiating a client's plan of care. What is the initial step a nurse should take when initiating a plan of care?
    A. Formulating nursing diagnoses based on identified problem patterns.
    B. Conducting a comprehensive assessment to gather essential patient data.
    C. Coordinating with interdisciplinary team members for discharge planning.
    D. Setting priorities for patient interventions and expected outcomes.

COMPREHENSIVE 2 NGN NCLEX ANSWERS

1. Answer: B
    Rationale: An oxygen saturation of 88% indicates worsening hypoxemia, a critical concern in COPD exacerbation. The other findings are concerning but less acute.

2. Answers: A, C, D
    Rationale: Albuterol, monitoring ABGs, and Fowler's position address the exacerbation. Increasing oxygen requires a provider's order, and fluid restriction is not indicated.

3. Answer: Impaired Gas Exchange
    Rationale: The client's low oxygen saturation and respiratory distress indicate Impaired Gas Exchange as the priority diagnosis.

4. Answer: 1, 3, 4, 2
    Rationale: The nurse verifies the order, adds the medication, turns on the nebulizer, and instructs the client to breathe deeply for effective treatment.

5. Answers: A, B, D
    Rationale: Respiratory failure, pneumothorax, and cor pulmonale are complications of COPD exacerbation. Hypoglycemia and sepsis are not directly related.

6. Answer:
    Influenza → Droplet precautions
    Tuberculosis (TB) → Airborne precautions
    Norovirus → Contact precautions
    Rationale: Influenza requires droplet precautions, TB requires airborne precautions, and norovirus requires contact precautions.

7. Answer: A) Don gloves and gown
    Rationale: Proper PPE (gloves and gown) must be donned before handling the wound to prevent contamination and the spread of infection.

8. Correct PPE:
    N95 respirator
    Gloves
    Gown
    Rationale: Tuberculosis is an airborne infection, so an N95 respirator, gloves, and gown are required for proper protection.

9. Answer: B) Isolate patients with C. difficile in a private room
    Rationale: Isolation in a private room prevents the spread of C. difficile to other patients and healthcare workers.

10. Answer: A) Clean the wound with soap and water immediately, B) Report the injury to a supervisor, D) Follow post-exposure protocols for potential infection
Rationale: Immediate wound cleaning, reporting the injury, and following post-exposure protocols are critical in minimizing the risk of infection.

11. Answer: D) Gloves, gown, and surgical mask
Rationale: Droplet precautions require wearing gloves, a gown, and a surgical mask to prevent the spread of respiratory droplets.

12. Answer: B) Using aseptic technique during catheter insertion and care
Rationale: Aseptic technique is the best prevention against urinary tract infections (UTIs) related to catheter use.

13. Answer: A) Wear gloves when handling soiled linen, B) Avoid shaking the linen to prevent airborne particles, D) Place contaminated linen in a designated, closed container or bag
Rationale: Wearing gloves, avoiding shaking soiled linen, and placing it in a sealed container are key practices in preventing the spread of infections.

14. Correct Order:
A) Wash hands thoroughly
B) Cleanse the injection site with an alcohol swab
C) Prepare the syringe with the appropriate dose of insulin
D) Insert the needle at a 90-degree angle into the subcutaneous tissue
Rationale: The first step is washing hands, followed by cleansing the injection site with an alcohol swab, preparing the syringe, and then administering the insulin at the correct site.

15. Correct Order:
A) Wash hands thoroughly
B) Cleanse the injection site with an alcohol swab
C) Prepare the syringe with the appropriate dose of insulin
D) Insert the needle at a 90-degree angle into the subcutaneous tissue
Rationale: The first step is washing hands, followed by cleansing the injection site with an alcohol swab, preparing the syringe, and then administering the insulin at the correct site.

16. Answer: B) To ensure the baby receives all the nutrients it needs for growth
Rationale: Prenatal vitamins are specifically formulated to support fetal development and ensure that the mother is getting adequate levels of essential nutrients, such as folic acid, iron, and calcium, which are crucial during pregnancy.

17. Answer: B) A low-carb diet and regular blood glucose monitoring
Rationale: Gestational diabetes is typically managed with lifestyle modifications such as a low-carb diet, blood glucose monitoring, and, in some cases, insulin therapy. Immediate induction is not indicated unless there are additional complications, and bed rest is not a standard recommendation for gestational diabetes.

18. Answer: B) Positive pregnancy test result
Rationale: A positive pregnancy test result is one of the earliest indicators of pregnancy, confirming that hCG (human chorionic gonadotropin) is present in the urine. Quickening, fetal heart tones, and the palpable uterus occur later in the pregnancy.

19. Answer: B) Monitor for signs of infection and assess fetal heart rate regularly
Rationale: When membranes rupture, the risk of infection increases, so it is important to monitor for signs of infection, assess fetal heart rate regularly, and observe for any signs of fetal distress.

20. Answer: A) Preeclampsia
Rationale: Preeclampsia is a hypertensive disorder that typically occurs after 20 weeks of gestation and can present with symptoms such as severe headaches, visual disturbances, and swelling in the hands and face. Immediate medical intervention is necessary to manage this condition and prevent complications such as eclampsia.

21. Answer: B) Continuous fetal heart rate monitoring
Rationale: Continuous fetal heart rate monitoring is critical for women attempting a VBAC to detect early signs of uterine rupture, which is a potential complication of attempting a vaginal delivery after a cesarean section.

22. Answer: A) Respiratory distress syndrome (RDS), B) Intraventricular hemorrhage (IVH), C) Low birth weight (LBW), E) Necrotizing enterocolitis (NEC)
Rationale: Preterm labor can lead to various complications due to premature organ development, such as respiratory distress syndrome, intraventricular hemorrhage, low birth weight, and necrotizing enterocolitis. Hypertension is more commonly associated with preeclampsia rather than preterm labor itself.

23. Answer: A) Feeling hopeless and overwhelmed, B) Difficulty bonding with the baby, D) Sleep disturbances, E) Persistent sadness or crying
Rationale: Postpartum depression is characterized by feelings of sadness, hopelessness, difficulty bonding with the baby, sleep disturbances, and persistent crying. Excessive happiness and euphoria are not typical signs of postpartum depression.

24. Answer: B) Neural tube defects

Rationale: Folic acid supplementation is essential in the early stages of pregnancy to reduce the risk of neural tube defects, such as spina bifida. It is recommended that women take folic acid before conception and during early pregnancy.

25. Answer: B) Regular contractions that get closer together
Rationale: Regular contractions that become more frequent and intense are a key sign of labor. Severe abdominal pain, blurred vision, and increased appetite are not typical signs of labor and could indicate other complications.

26. Correct Order:
D) Review lab results and previous medical history
A) Check the patient's weight and blood pressure
B) Measure the fundal height
C) Auscultate fetal heart tones
Rationale: The first step is reviewing lab results and medical history to guide the physical exam. Then, assess the patient's weight and blood pressure, measure fundal height, and finally auscultate fetal heart tones to assess fetal well-being.

27. Correct Order:
A) Place an intravenous (IV) line
B) Administer preoperative medications as ordered
C) Perform the surgical scrub and prepare the sterile field
D) Assist the patient to the operating room
Rationale: The IV line is placed first for medication administration, followed by giving preoperative medications, preparing the sterile field, and then assisting the patient to the operating room.

28. Answer: B) Discuss alternative activities that do not involve alcohol, C) Encourage the client to attend a support group meeting prior to the event, D) Help the client develop a plan for coping with potential triggers at the event
Rationale: Discussing alternatives, preparing the client with coping strategies, and encouraging participation in support groups are essential to managing triggers and maintaining sobriety. Encouraging the client to attend an event with alcohol could lead to relapse, and reassurance alone is not enough to prevent a setback.

29. Answer: B) "It may take 4 to 6 weeks for the medication to show its full effects."
Rationale: It typically takes 4 to 6 weeks for antidepressants to show full therapeutic effects. Clients should be informed about this timeline to reduce frustration and encourage adherence to the treatment regimen.

30. Answer: A) Encourage regular sleep patterns and good nutrition, B) Set small, achievable goals to avoid feelings of being overwhelmed, D) Discuss the importance of continuing medication even during a depressive phase

Rationale: Encouraging regular sleep and nutrition, setting small goals, and emphasizing medication adherence are important for managing depressive episodes in bipolar disorder. Social isolation and avoiding physical activity are not typically helpful for managing depression and can contribute to worsening symptoms.

31. Answer: A) Provide the client with a calendar and memory aids to help with orientation.
Rationale: Using memory aids, such as a calendar, is helpful in managing symptoms of neurocognitive disorders and promoting independence. Encouraging complete independence or using restraints is inappropriate, and limiting social interaction can worsen isolation and depression.

32. Answer: A) Offer positive reinforcement for any small achievement,
B) Encourage the client to engage in activities they used to enjoy, C) Provide education on the importance of medication adherence, E) Set realistic, achievable goals for the client to accomplish
Rationale: Offering positive reinforcement, encouraging engagement in enjoyable activities, providing education about medication, and setting achievable goals help the client manage feelings of worthlessness and engage in treatment. Discussing feelings of worthlessness in detail can sometimes reinforce negative thinking patterns.

33. Answer: B
Rationale: The document emphasizes consulting research to ensure the efficacy and safety of complementary therapies.

34. Answers: A, B, D
Rationale: The document lists medical history, medications, and pregnancy as key factors for assessing contraindications.

35. Answer: B
Rationale: The document highlights the risk of interactions between St. John's Wort and antidepressants, requiring physician consultation.

36. Answer: Lavender
Rationale: The document recommends lavender oil for promoting relaxation and reducing stress.

37. Answer: B

Rationale: The document emphasizes integrating therapies safely by aligning them with the overall treatment plan.

Answer: C) Hold the nasal spray upright while administering the dose.

Rationale: Holding the nasal spray upright ensures the correct dosage is delivered to the nasal passages. Using the spray for more than 3 consecutive days can lead to rebound congestion.

38. Answer: A) Provide a quiet, dark room for rest.

Rationale: Resting in a quiet, dark environment can help reduce sensory stimulation and manage acute pain. Hot packs can worsen inflammation in acute injuries, and physical activity and large meals can exacerbate pain.

39. Answer: A) Pinpoint pupils, B) Shallow, slow breathing, C) Confusion or drowsiness

Rationale: Opioid overdose can result in pinpoint pupils, shallow and slow breathing, confusion, and drowsiness. An increased heart rate is not typically a sign of overdose; in fact, it may indicate an impending emergency due to respiratory distress.

40. Answer: B) When the patient has tolerated 75% of their caloric needs orally for 48 hours.

Rationale: PN should be gradually decreased once the patient can tolerate 75% of their nutritional needs orally for 48 hours to ensure the patient continues to receive adequate nutrition.

41. Answer: B) Hyperglycemia

Rationale: PN solutions are high in glucose, which can lead to hyperglycemia. Monitoring blood glucose levels is essential to prevent this complication. Respiratory distress, renal failure, and dehydration are not common complications associated with PN.

42. Answer: C) Discontinue the IV and notify the healthcare provider.

Rationale: Redness and warmth at the IV site suggest potential phlebitis, and the IV should be discontinued to prevent further complications. The healthcare provider should be notified for further management.

43. Answer: A) Dorsum of the hand

Rationale: The dorsum of the hand is the most common site for peripheral IV catheter placement due to its accessibility and ease of insertion.

44. Answer: B) Refuse to fill the prescription and explain the reasons to the patient.

Rationale: Controlled substances, especially Schedule II drugs, should not be refilled early. The nurse should refuse the request and explain the legal and safety implications. The healthcare provider should be notified for further guidance.

45. Answer: B) Double-check the medication and dosage with another nurse before administration.
Rationale: A second nurse verification is a key principle to ensure the correct medication, dose, and patient identity are confirmed before administering controlled substances.

46. Answer: B) 1 mL
Rationale: To calculate the volume to administer: (Desired dose ÷ Available dose) × Volume = mL to administer. (0.5 mg ÷ 1 mg) × 2 mL = 1 mL.

47. Answer: B) 10 mL
Rationale: To calculate the volume to administer, use the formula: (Desired dose ÷ Available concentration) × Volume = mL to administer. (200 mg ÷ 100 mg) × 5 mL = 10 mL.

48. Answer: B) 125 mL/hr
Rationale: To calculate the infusion rate, divide the total volume by the time in hours. 1000 mL ÷ 8 hours = 125 mL/hr.

49. Answer: B. Monitoring for difficulty breathing
Rationale: The document emphasizes educating patients to monitor for symptoms like difficulty breathing post-sedation.

50. Answer: B. Providing guidance on storage
Rationale: The document specifies providing guidance on proper storage for 24-hour urine collection.

51. Answer: B. Notify the healthcare team
Rationale: The document advises communicating complications like tube dislodgement to the healthcare team.

52. Answer: B. Reassuring patients about the surgical team
Rationale: The document emphasizes reassuring patients about the surgical team's competence to reduce anxiety.

53. Answer: B. Monitoring for nausea
Rationale: The document lists monitoring for adverse effects like nausea as a post-sedation care task.

54. Answers: A, C, E
Rationale: The document identifies granulation tissue, decreased wound size, and improved skin integrity as signs of healing. Redness, swelling, and pus indicate infection.

55. Answer: B. Notify the healthcare provider
Rationale: The document emphasizes notifying the provider if signs of infection, such as pus or worsening redness, are observed.

56. Answer: Hydrocolloid dressing.
Rationale: The document suggests hydrocolloid dressings for wounds with minimal exudate to maintain moisture and promote healing.

57. Answer: B. The wound's condition and changes
Rationale: The document emphasizes documenting the wound's condition and any changes observed during dressing changes.

58. Answer: B. Recognize signs of infection
Rationale: The document highlights educating clients about recognizing signs of infection to ensure proper wound care at home.

59. Answer:
Influenza → Droplet precautions
Tuberculosis (TB) → Airborne precautions
Norovirus → Contact precautions
Rationale: Influenza requires droplet precautions, TB requires airborne precautions, and norovirus requires contact precautions.

60. Answer: A) Don gloves and gown
Rationale: Proper PPE (gloves and gown) must be donned before handling the wound to prevent contamination and the spread of infection.

61. Correct PPE:
N95 respirator
Gloves
Gown
Rationale: Tuberculosis is an airborne infection, so an N95 respirator, gloves, and gown are required for proper protection.

62. Answer: B) Isolate patients with C. difficile in a private room
Rationale: Isolation in a private room prevents the spread of C. difficile to other patients and healthcare workers.

63. Answer: A) Clean the wound with soap and water immediately, B) Report the injury to a supervisor, D) Follow post-exposure protocols for potential infection

Rationale: Immediate wound cleaning, reporting the injury, and following post-exposure protocols are critical in minimizing the risk of infection.

64. Answer: D) Gloves, gown, and surgical mask
Rationale: Droplet precautions require wearing gloves, a gown, and a surgical mask to prevent the spread of respiratory droplets.

65. Answer: B) Using aseptic technique during catheter insertion and care
Rationale: Aseptic technique is the best prevention against urinary tract infections (UTIs) related to catheter use.

66. Answer: A) Wear gloves when handling soiled linen, B) Avoid shaking the linen to prevent airborne particles, D) Place contaminated linen in a designated, closed container or bag
Rationale: Wearing gloves, avoiding shaking soiled linen, and placing it in a sealed container are key practices in preventing the spread of infections.

67. Correct Order:
1 → 5 → 2 → 3 → 4
Rationale: Data collection is the first step in creating an effective care plan, followed by analyzing the information, setting goals, and developing interventions. Evaluation ensures the plan is effective.

68. Answer: B
Rationale: The staff development program should align with the hospital's overall goals and mission to ensure it supports both staff growth and the institution's needs.

69. Answer: B
Rationale: Providing opportunities for professional development and mentorship helps improve job satisfaction and retention rates by supporting staff in their career growth.

70. Answer: A, C, D
Rationale: Fostering inclusivity, offering cultural sensitivity training, and encouraging learning from one another promote a harmonious and productive team environment.

71. Answer: (B) Educating the client and family about their rights regarding resuscitation and end-of-life decisions.
Rationale: Integrating advanced directives involves discussing the client's wishes for future care, such as a living will, durable power of attorney, or health care proxy. This aligns with educating the client about their rights regarding resuscitation and end-of-life decisions.

72. Answer: (A) Administering oral medications to a stable client and monitoring for expected outcomes.
Rationale: LPNs can administer most medications and perform assessments on stable clients, but initial assessments, care plan development, and initial patient education are generally within the scope of practice for a Registered Nurse.

73. Answer: (D) Prioritizing patient needs based on acuity and complexity to allocate time efficiently.
Rationale: Prioritizing patient care based on acuity and complexity is a key strategy for effective workload management. This ensures that critical tasks receive immediate attention and resources are allocated efficiently.

74. Answer: (A) Educating clients on self-care and healthy lifestyles to reduce hospital readmissions.
Rationale: Patient education on self-care and healthy lifestyles is a strategy for cost-effective care because it can minimize hospital readmissions, thereby reducing unnecessary expenses and optimizing resource use.

75. Answer: (B) Conducting a comprehensive assessment to gather essential patient data.
Rationale: The initial step in initiating a client's plan of care is to conduct a comprehensive assessment. This assessment gathers the necessary physical, psychological, environmental, cultural, and spiritual data to inform subsequent steps like nursing diagnoses and planning.

62627640R00400